Recent Social Trends in the United States 1960-1990

Series Comparative Charting of Social Change
Series Editor: Simon Langlois
Volume Editor: Howard M. Bahr

Theodore Caplow, Howard M. Bahr,
John Modell and Bruce A. Chadwick

Recent Social Trends in the United States 1960-1990

Campus Verlag · Frankfurt am Main
McGill-Queen's University Press
Montreal & Kingston · London · Buffalo

Canadian Cataloguing in Publication Data

Main entry under title:
Recent Social Trends in the United States :
1960-1990
(Comparative charting of social change,
ISSN 1183-1952)
«Prepared for the International Research Group for
the Comparative Charting of Social Change.»
Includes bibliographical references and index.
ISBN 0-7735-0872-4

1. United States—Social conditions—1960-1990.
2. United States—Social conditions—1980.
I. Caplow, Theodore II. International Research
Group for the Comparative Charting of Social Change
III. Series.

HN59.2.R33 1991   973.92   C91-090103-1

CIP-Titelaufnahme der Deutschen Bibliothek

Recent social trends in the United States : 1960 – 1990 /
Theodore Caplow ... – Frankfurt am Main : Campus Verlag;
Montreal ; Kingston ; London ; Buffalo : McGill-Queen's
Univ. Press, 1991
   (Comparative charting of social change)
   ISBN 3-593-34403-3 (Campus)
   ISBN 0-7735-0872-4 (McGill-Queen's Univ. Press)
NE: Caplow, Theodore

Copyright © 1991 by Campus Verlag GmbH, Frankfurt/Main
Published simultaneously in Canada and the United States
by McGill-Queen's University Press
Legal deposit 2nd quarter 1991
Bibliothèque nationale du Québec
Printed in Germany

RECENT SOCIAL TRENDS

IN THE UNITED STATES

1960-1990

CONTENTS

The Comparative Charting of Social Change

Recent Social Trends in the United States, 1960-1990, is the first volume of a series. Similar volumes describing recent social trends in France, West Germany, and Quebec, will be published later this year, and other countries, beginning with Spain, will be covered in subsequent years.

These national profiles of social change all have the same format. Each consists of 78 trend reports grouped under 17 main topics, and the sequence of reports--from 0.1 Demographic Trends to 17.5 Trends in National Identity--is identical for every profile.

The object of this exercise is to provide appropriate data bases for the cross-national comparison of recent social trends. That work is well under way. A collection of papers comparing trends in the family, in the workplace, in social movements, in conflict resolution, and in value systems, will be published in the same series in 1991.

The collective author of the series goes by the mellifluous name of the International Research Group on the Comparative Charting of Social Change in Advanced Industrial Societies, or more shortly as the Comparative Charting Group. It is an entirely voluntary organization that evolved out of an informal collaborative relationship established in the 1970s between an investigation of social change in French communities called the Observation de Changement Social and a concurrent American effort known as the Middletown III project. A little later, Henri Mendras formed the working group on social trends that developed the original version of our present trend list and applied it to France. They published their results under the group pseudonym of Louis Dirn. Caplow, the principal investigator of the Middletown III project, came to Paris to participate in the deliberations of the Louis Dirn group for several months in 1983. A little later, Louis Dirn began to exchange visits and data with Wolfgang Glatzer and his colleagues at Frankfurt, who were analyzing social trends in the Federal Republic. In 1987 Mendras accepted a visiting appointment at the University of Virginia during which a close relationship was established with researchers who were studying social trends in Quebec under the leadership of Simon Langlois at Laval University.

The first work session of the Comparative Charting Group convened in Paris in May 1987. Subsequent work sessions were held at Bad Homburg in May 1988, Quebec in December 1988, Charlottesville in May 1989 and Nice in December 1989. The scholarly yield of the project has increased with each session.

The Comparative Charting Group is divided into national teams. The roster as of January 1990 is shown in Appendix A. It includes historians, political scientists and economists, although the majority are sociologists. The team coordinators are Henri Mendras for France, Wolfgang Glatzer and Karl Otto Hondrich for West Germany, Simon Langlois for Quebec, Theodore Caplow for the United States, and Sebastian del Campo for Spain. Applications from several other national teams are pending. For the purposes of this project, Quebec is treated as a national society.

The participation of individual scholars in the national teams, and of the national teams in the international group, is entirely voluntary. Simon Langlois and the Institut Quebecois pour Recherche sur la Culture provide the project with a highly efficient secretariat but there is no executive authority at all. Each national team is responsible for its own funding and internal operations. Work is assigned and deadlines are set by consensus at the semi-annual work sessions. This loose organization has worked so exceedingly well that we are tempted to propose it as a model for other international projects of social research.

The general purposes of this collective effort are: (1) to prepare a comprehensive, numerically-grounded description of recent social trends in advanced, industrial societies; (2) to identify similarities and differences among these national societies with respect to ongoing social trends; (3) to subject these similarities and differences to comparative analysis; (4) to develop a non-traditional model of social change to accommodate these data; (6) to establish benchmarks for future tracking of social trends.

The data module of this project is a trend report. It covers one of the 78 numbered topics in the List of Trends and Indicators developed by the Comparative Charting Group by revising the classification originally proposed by Louis Dirn. The Table of Contents of this volume is an abbreviated version of that list. The fuller version is shown in Appendix B. The numbered topics and subtopics provide a common outline for the national profiles.

Most trend reports present and interpret multiple trends related to the designated topic. A trend report has four sections: an abstract of findings, an explanatory text, a collection of statistical tables or charts, and a bibliography of the sources drawn upon.

The trends described in these reports are empirical and quantitative. They are based on time-series of good quality, quality being measured by explicit criteria. To be used in a trend report, a series must consist of empirical enumerations or measurements, must refer to an entire national society or to a representative sample of it, must cover a period of at least ten years and end no earlier than 1983, must include data for three or more points or intervals of time recorded contemporaneously, must be amenable to independent verification and must be replicable in the same national society and replicable also in other national societies.

The factual emphasis is fundamental. No trend is included that is not known with practical certainty, and no directionality is asserted without empirical data. Often, we have located studies of these tendencies by other scholars and used them to challenge or buttress our own interpretations. At all times, these empirical predilections keep alive the happy possibility that what we find may surprise us. And indeed it often has.

Our preference for relatively hard data restricts most of the trend reports to recent decades, since many interesting statistical series do not go back very far or lose reliability as they recede to earlier years. There are some happy exceptions; in demography and macro-economics, for example, we have an abundance of good data from the nineteenth century and some from the eighteenth. But with the progress of the work, it has become increasingly clear that a sharp focus on the period 1960-1990 is appropriate as well as expedient. For reasons that may vary somewhat from country to country, an astonishing number of social trends show a point of inflection close to 1960 and the thirty year period following 1960 has seemed to exhibit exceptional coherence.

It should be emphasized that the tendencies documented in these national profiles are not merely interpretations of the quantitative series. They reflect an underlying sense of social theory and of social reality that goes far beyond the raw data. The themes we have chosen, our methods of examining the available indicators, our decisions about selective emphasis among the evidence at hand, and our estimation of the significance or insignificance of observed trends, constitute an intellectual structure derived from diverse national and disciplinary perspectives. This structure is described with exemplary clarity in the Introduction by John Modell and Yannick Lemel which follows.

The present volume is intended primarily as a reference manual. It is meant to be consulted on particular points. Few readers will want to read it straight through, although it can be done and has been found enjoyable. What we present here is source material for the analysis and understanding of recent social change in one country, gathered for our own purpose of cross-national comparison but potentially useful for many other purposes. Unless specifically noted otherwise, the trends discussed and tables presented apply to the U.S. as a whole.

The publication of this volume marks the beginning rather than the end of the intellectual enterprise for which the Comparative Charting Group was formed. Our aim is to construct a better model of social change in the modern world than has heretofore been available.

When we met in Paris in 1987 to establish permanent connections among the ongoing investigations of social change that had occupied us in our respective countries during the previous decade, we were aware that although our separate studies had attracted a fair amount of scholarly and popular attention, they had not advanced our understanding of contemporary industrial societies as much as they should have, for want of a comparative perspective. Without systematic international comparisons, it is impossible to determine whether the trends we discover in a particular national society are local accidents or features of a larger system.

We were specifically interested in the late twentieth century, the major industrial· countries, and the social structure and institutional patterns that characterize the behavior of large populations, especially those associated with the family, work, leisure, religion, education, government, politics and voluntary associations. As we compared our separate bodies of work, we had the impression of being surrounded by the bits and pieces of a new theoretical model waiting to be assembled, a model that does not require social change to resemble scientific-technical progress, that takes the future to be open rather than ordained, and that acknowledges the mixture of objective and subjective elements in social reality.

The construction of national profiles in comparable form was a preliminary task that had to be done in order to prepare for the construction of such a model. But in preparing these trend reports, we learned a great deal we had not previously known about the American condition in the late twentieth century. We trust that our readers will find them equally instructive.

Acknowledgements

Like other national teams in the International Research Group on the Comparative Charting of Social Change in Advanced Industrial Societies, the U.S. team, which presently includes John Modell of Carnegie Mellon University, Howard M. Bahr and Bruce A. Chadwick of Brigham Young University, and Theodore Caplow of the University of Virginia, is responsible for its own funding and internal operations. We gratefully acknowledge the support and assistance of many others.

Special thanks are due to the Council for European Studies which provided the grant that made possible the U.S. team's participation in the Comparative Charting Group from 1987 to 1989; to its director Ioannis Sinanoglou, who facilitated our work in every possible way; to Richard Rockwell of the Social Science Research Council, who aided and encouraged us at an early stage; to the Werner Reimers Stiftung for subsidizing the U.S. team's travel to the May 1988 meeting at Bad Homburg, and to the Institute Quebecois pour Recherche sur la Culture who partially subsidized our travel to the 1988 meeting at Quebec.

Our three universities have all drawn on their limited free resources for our benefit. We are especially grateful to Dexter Whitehead and Paul R. Gross, directors in succession of the Center for Advanced Study at Virginia, and to Stan L. Albrecht and Donovan E. Fleming, deans of the College of Family, Home, and Social Sciences at Brigham Young. We acknowledge the generous support of that institution's David M. Kennedy Center of International Studies, and that of the Faculty Development Fund of Carnegie Mellon University.

Achsah Carrier was a productive member of the U.S. team from December 1988 to July 1989. Louis Hicks and Joan Snapp at Virginia, were extraordinarily helpful in the preparation of this volume.

We are all under great obligation to the two leading members of the Canadian team, Simon Langlois and Gary Caldwell, for providing the efficient bi-lingual secretariat that keeps the international project going and to Simon Langlois for his service as General Editor of this series.

We owe a large debt to Norene C. Petersen, who heroically managed--and remanaged-- the copyediting and final preparation of the manuscript, and to Brigham Young University's Center for Studies of the Family, for making her available to us.

The book is put forward as a collective work, but readers who want to communicate with the writers of particular trend reports will find those attributions in Appendix B. Readers who discover errors of fact and mistakes of judgement in the following pages are urged to complain to the most accessible author.

Theodore Caplow
Charlottesville, Va.
January, 1990

by Yannick Lemel (France) and John Modell (USA)

The long-term goals of the International Research Group on the Comparative Charting of Social Change are quite ambitious, at least challenging. We aim eventually to produce studies that can be said to discern and compare across nations the nature of change within social systems.

The volume offered here is considerably more modest, being one of four parallel volumes depicting selected aspects of social change within single nations, constructed according to agreed-upon principles and incorporating certain shared assumptions. Despite this modesty, because it is designed to contribute to the eventual construction of a truly sociological account, it differs considerably from the kind of "social reports" that both governmental and non-governmental agencies in many nations commonly issue.

While we intend and expect that the volume in hand will have value in and of itself, but, by our own research process, it must also be understood clearly as an intermediate product. In this light, the ambition of the volume is essentially descriptive. Even so the material is in a highly-organized and -processed form, put together in such a way as to further the International Research Group's continuing research into the nature of systemic social change within modern nations. Accordingly, the shared assumptions and operating principles underlying the larger project deserve explication here.

A good place to begin is to contrast the project's orientation with that of another approach to the comparative study of social change that was common not so long ago: the so-called "modernization" approach. If the "social report" typically presents summary accounts of more-or-less disconnected social trends, "modernization" studies move to the opposite extreme, and seek to summarize as many observed trends as possible under a single master trend, often called modernization and often ascribed virtually causal influence over its individual components, at least rhetorically.

By contrast to modernization studies, the underlying assumptions of the International Research Group are less heroic. We do not begin with a view of "social change" in its totality, afterward trying to discern its manifestations in one aspect of society after another. Rather, through the careful examination of multiple indicators wherever possible, we seek to discern tendencies that show clear-cut directionality in the 45-years period under study, and thereby to build up toward an account of systemic social change from the examination of observed tendencies with similar directionality and timing, each seen as context to one another.

The tendencies documented here, and in the three companion volumes, then, are not simply the quantitative series commonly found in social reports. They differ in reflecting an underlying sense of social reality and of social theory that is far more divorced from the data series that, like social reports, we include, and from the statistics systems that organize the "raw" data in the first place. The tendencies that form the subjects of our accounts, are therefore much more than simply statistical reports with no pretence to special sociological relevance. The themes that we have chosen, our methods of examining the available indicators, our decisions about selective emphasis among the evidence at hand, and our estimation of trends from the information at our disposal (for such inferences must be made in comparing successive states) are the reasons we characterize the tendencies presented here as "sociologically driven empirical categories." They are, once again, neither social reports nor yet sociological analyses. But they owe much to our intention of moving toward the latter.

Two points about the tendencies that we investigate deserve emphasis. First, they are all closely underlain by empirical measurement. While available data for some tendencies is quite full and covers in a satisfyingly quantitative way many related phenomena, this is not always the case. What is well documented in one nation may be poorly documented in another.

Nevertheless, no tendency is included that is not known with a reasonable degree of empirical certainty. We asserted directionality for no tendency for which we had not at minimum located a number of well-comparable observations, which included at least one for a point in the 1980s. Further, we have located where possible studies of these tendencies or aspects of them by other scholars, and used these to challenge or buttress our empirical understanding of change. At all times, our empirical predilections keep alive the happy possibility that what we find will surprise us. Having said this, however, we reemphasize that one can never know social reality directly, but only through the prism of a theory. Without theory, reflection is disoriented, and, so, too, is observation.

Perhaps the most substantial decision that we made at the outset of our work was to focus upon sociological categories. This means we have little to say about several whole realms of phenomena that often are emphasized in accounts of change in the twentieth century, (including accounts in the "modernization" vein) notably the economic, the political, and the psychological. (Of course, distinctions among realms is not airtight, and we choose to include documentation here of change in the realm of technology, often subsumed under the "economic," of electoral participation, clearly itself an important element of politics, and of attitudes, often understood as "psychological").

Over the past century, the discipline of sociology has developed around a core observation: that individuals choose their behaviors in the light of their relations to others, relations that if not material are nonetheless facts, structured by shared perspectives upon past practice. Sociological accounts treat individual behavior under the aspect of social roles, argue that the functioning of groups gives comprehensible form to social conflict and social negotiation, indicates that inequality may be understood as the outcome of the interaction of large social groupings. These shared sociological perspectives themselves form a system of sorts. Note that in the preceding sentence, the "system" being claimed is not a system of discrete interrelationships among individuals, a kind of map, but rather a system of modes governing individuals' other-regarding behavior. That is what we mean when we emphasize that the tendencies documented in this volume are theoretical and sociological.

For a number of reasons, it is probably fair to say that sociological accounts are less common than accounts emphasizing many other aspects of change, and perhaps less self-evident to our contemporaries. For this reason, we expect that the tendencies that we document here, and the connections that we will eventually be able to discern and analyze, will provide some useful surprises.

Although the present volumes present substantial textual expositions of tendencies, expositions that are not merely verbal restatements of underlying time series, they offer no literally causal explanations. The formal apparatus required to construct causal accounts does not form a part of the research reflected in these pages. Rather, we seek to offer a kind of explanation that is more often found in interpretive social science than in the kind of positivistic accounts often associated with the presentation of time series of quantitative data: explanation through context. Strictly speaking, our accounts are descriptive, however dense and suggestive, however fleshed out with interpretation. Essentially, our procedure involves embedding the exposition of one particular indicator series with those of related series, to suggest the induction of a common underlying tendency, the examination of tendencies in the context of one another to induce realms of change within which observed covariation "makes sense", and so forth. The process is one according to which we do not and will not pretend exact knowledge of causal mechanisms. It rather is designed to bring to light regularities for which causal explanation may then be sought.

The pioneering kernel within the International Research Group is French, an adventurous group of interdisciplinary scholars and amateurs who for six years have met almost weekly. Apart from constituting the French "team", this group supplied to the current research the particular "theory" that provided most of the list of tendencies upon which all national teams thereupon gathered empirical data. The goal of the French group was to discern and document the inner systemic connections among aspects of social change in France. From their years of work, in which large quantities of empirical data were gathered, indicators constructed, modified, and rejected, and tendencies "recognized" among the welter (with the aid of broadly agreed-upon theoretical commonalties within the group), a large list of discernible tendencies emerged. At three international meetings since that date, members of the four national "teams" refined the initial list of tendencies, reflecting both modest theoretical differences and larger differences in the statistical systems of the four nations. It is, then, a consensually-derived and not highly abstract French theory, modified consensually in international debate, upon which all four volumes are based. But it is still a French theory. And the predictably imperfect fit of this non-native theory to the emerging pictures in the other three nations provided many of the surprises that we hoped to find. We will undoubtedly find additional and more various frustrations as we undertake systematic comparison. Despite the certainty of some frustration, the International Research Group is comfortable with the decision to adopt the French schema. It is, we believe, empirical enough to allow comparison without suggesting that all non-French tendencies represent deficiencies rather than differences.

Additionally, the model developed by the French group was not necessarily followed by the three other groups. By comparing the four volumes, the reader can see that the national styles range from the theoretical view point of the French to the precised empirical results of the Quebec group or the Germans. Finally, each team was able to follow or to adapt the specified general scheme within the context of the collaboration to its own particular culture or national institutions.

As we move to the next stage of our group research, the comparison of change in national social systems over historical time, we anticipate developing two kinds of hypotheses. The first have to do with interconnections among clusters of tendencies. The second relate to possible underlying variations that conceivably might reflect the essence of what distinguishes the French from the Germans, or the people of Quebec from citizens of the United States. Such hypotheses, however based on empirical materials such as those laid out in this volume, will not be based on explicit causal reasoning or methodologies designed to support them, but will be offered as interpretation and hypothesis only, subject to subsequent testing.

Systematic students of social change, including those employing other kinds of analytic approaches, are thus among the audiences for whom these researches are intended. But we hope that their usefulness will not be limited to this professional audience. Rather, we anticipate that each of these four national volumes will serve as a compendium of carefully-selected and well-explicated social trends for reference by persons with a wide variety of purposes. We can hardly expect many casual readers, but we hope too that the work will be of interest to both natives and others seeking to acquaint themselves in a systematic way with important realms of change in any of these evolving national societies. Finally, we hope that the occasional reader will share with the International Research Group the challenge of comparison, or bringing together the sometimes surprisingly different tendencies in these four dynamic, democratic societies, seen in systemic comparison, to make sense for themselves--whether formally or informally--of the grand subject of change.

TOPIC 0: CONTEXT

0.1 DEMOGRAPHIC TRENDS

Since the end of World War II, the United States has experienced rapidly changing population dynamics. The pattern of change was the most abrupt in fertility trends. A "baby boom" of more than a decade was followed by an even longer period of decline. Fertility decline was only slightly offset by a trend toward increased longevity, and by increased immigration, both legal and illegal.

The exceptionally rapid rate of population growth long characteristic of the United States began to fade in the latter half of the nineteenth century, and, after massive European immigration was enjoined in the 1920s, the continuing secular decline of fertility dominated the picture (Table 1). Fertility turned up for two decades following the mid-1930s, and this is reflected in population increases that were greater for the 1940s and 1950s than for several previous decades. But after the "baby boom" was over, overall population growth continued to falter, amounting to only slightly greater than 1% per year in the 1970s. By the 1980s, annual growth was often less than one percent, very low by American standards, although considerably higher than in many contemporaneous western societies. The continuing decline has occurred despite increased immigration. (Perhaps measurement difficulties--undocumented immigrants, particuarly from Latin American nations--have contributed to undercounts of the population, but not of an order that would materially change the slow rates of population growth reported.

There are definite signs that a very modest upturn in fertility (particularly among women in their 30's) has reversed a long and very substantial downswing that began in the late 1950s. At that date, an unexpected upward movement of fertility--the "baby boom"--dating in a tentative way from before World War II and in a highly visible way from about 1950--had seemingly reversed a marked secular downward trend in fertility of over a century's standing. It is common nowadays to understand the "baby boom" as an aberration, and the long downward secular trend as having resumed thereafter. The recent upturn is so slight that it hardly challenges this interpretation. The Gross Reproduction Rate and the age-specific birth rate indicate that this phase peaked in the late 1950s, at a level that implied about one and three-quarters daughters per woman, an increase of over one-half a daughter since the end of the war. Fertility, having grown gradually, declined gradually thereafter, the rate of decline being at its most rapid through the latter 1960s and into the early 1970s. Much the same rise and decline that white women experienced was also experienced by nonwhite women.

The age-specific sources of the baby boom can be found among mothers of modal ages--most especially their 20's. The post-baby boom decline, however, while participated in by women of all ages, was especially prominent in the fertility record of older women, until the rapid downturn at the end of the 1960s. By contrast, the most recent period of dramatic decline was most evident among women 18-24 (presumably because of the rising median age at marriage), although there continued to be a retreat from fertility among the oldest mothers as well. The recent reversal is so modest that we cannot with any security locate it in any particular part of the age spectrum.

Overall, the crude death rate in the United States declined by about one-fifth between 1945 and 1982. It has done so, essentially in two brief periods of marked reduction--1945 to about 1955, and about 1970 to about 1979--surrounded by plateaus. In contrast to earlier periods of fertility decline, when most of the reduction has taken place at very young ages (with very substantial impact on population size, for very many years, roughly comparable in demographic effect to a like increase in fertility), the recent mortality decline took place substantially at the older ages, the result, perhaps, of heroic medical triumphs over fatal diseases. The welfare impact of mortality reduction at this end of the age distribution is quite different from that at the other end, especially in that it comes on top of a (demographically far more significant) decline in fertility. That "aging" has become a very vital topic in the United States in this period is a product not just of the change in the age distribution, but because of the material costs and subsequent lifetime impact of the way in which many survivors have been brought through medical crises (Table 2).

The postwar decline in crude mortality (deaths per person alive per year) has taken place despite a sharp decline in fertility, producing a population with relatively many older persons with presumably higher probabilities of dying in any given year. An age-adjusted measure indicates that inherent morality rates declined by about 20% from 1945 to 1955 and by about 18% from 1970 to 1979--and by about 42% over the entire postwar period to 1982.

In the United States, there are sharp differentials in mortality according to both sex and race. The age-standardized decline in non-white mortality over the postwar period was 47%, slightly greater than the 42% registered for whites. But even so, as of 1982, the age-standardized mortality of nonwhites exceeded that of whites by 32%.

Women have been even more advantaged in age-standardized mortality relative to men than whites are to nonwhites: women's mortality rate in 1982 was only 56% that of men's, compared to 72% in 1945. A consequence of these differentials is that there are many more widows than widowers.

The age structure of the American population has changed considerably since World War II (Table 3). Initially aging at its older end, the product of the prior long-term trend of fertility decline, by 1950 the proportion of the population that was quite young was also somewhat larger than that in the previous decade because of the upturn in fertility that began in mid-Depression, was postponed by the war, and was succeeded by a sharp baby boom in the immediate postwar. These two trends both continued through the decade of the 1950s: thus, in 1960, the proportion of the population that was 65 years old or older was 9.2%, as compared with 8.5% a decade earlier--this in spite of a vast increase in the proportion in the population who were quite young, owing to the revival and continuation of the baby boom throughout the decade. Some 40% of the whole American population was under 20 years of age in 1960, a figure that far exceeded the 33% in 1950.

After 1960 the baby boom receded, but it continues to impact U. S. society as its crest moves up the age distribution. As all this happens, the proportion at the oldest end of the population pyramid becomes greater and greater--especially among women, who are less prone to death in their 60s and 70s. The proportion of the population 65 and older, 9.2% in 1950, rose gradually to 11.9% in 1985. The proportion over 75 (considered now to be a more appropriate indicator to suggest severe welfare needs owing to the far greater likelihood of chronic illness and to widowhood) has increased even more dramatically. With the aging of the population and the increasing advantage of women over men in survivorship, the sex ratio has consistently declined, starting at the older ages.

The most acute indicators of the extent of population mobility, of course, are those that refer to the briefest interval: in the United States, such counts were taken with a year's interval annually from 1947 to 1970, and then again in the 1980s. These data indicate a substantial tendency to move over the entire period, with a modest downward trend from the early-1960s on, that probably reflects as much as anything else a change in the age structure of the population, older persons being less likely to move than those in the earlier stages of family formation. Up through the 1950s, almost one in five Americans would typically move in a given year, a proportion reduced by the mid-1980s to about one in six. Mobility that involved a relatively short move, within the same county, often reflecting a change in residence without implying a change in job, was responsible for most of this decline in mobility. Longer-distance mobility, on the other hand, accounting intially for about one-third of all mobility, declined not at all.

The proportion of the American population that is rural declined modestly in the 1940s, rapidly in the 1950s and 1960s, and quite modestly once again in the 1970s (Table 4). At the same time, the urban population was essentially redistributing itself into smaller-size cities--typically suburbs, or, even more precisely, smaller population nodes within a gradually-redefined "daily urban system" that is itself more nearly continuous in form than once and in which its various nodes (including residential) are decreasingly concentrated in space and decreasingly congregated. Indeed, a portion of the absolute growth in rural places during the decade of the 1970s can be attributed to continuities of politically unincorporated rural places within "daily urban systems." Because of clearly- recognized and probably widely-shared residential preferences, and time-economies subserved thereby, the size of "city" under which the great bulk of redistributive growth has taken place is under 250,000, and especially below (but in the vicinity of) 50,000. A datum visible in the table that many observers find particularly symbolic of change is the absolute decline after 1970 in the population of large cities.

The composition of the American population in the postwar period (Table 5) has remained approximately four-fifths native-born white. The foreign-born white population, which was most characteristic of and perhaps responsible for the distinctive flavor of American society through the century preceding World War II, however, has declined markedly through the period under study here. So, presumably, has the proportion of the population composed of "second-generation" Americans: the American-born children of immigrants. The nonwhite portion of the American population, on the other hand, has increased substantially since the war, in part through increased immigration of persons of color.

References

U.S. Bureau of the Census. 1960 Census of Population. Detailed Characteristics, U.S. Summary. Washington, D.C.: USGPO, 1963.

U.S. Bureau of the Census. 1970 Census of Population, General Social and Economic Characteristics, U.S. Summary. Washington, D.C: USGPO, 1972.

U.S. Bureau of the Census. 1980 Census of Population. Detailed Population Characteristics, Volume D Part 1, U. S. Summary. Washington, D.C., USGPO, 1984.

U.S. Bureau of the Census. Historical Statistics of the United States. Washington, D.C.: USGPO, 1975.

------. Statistical Abstract of the United States, 1989. Washington, D. C., 1989.   Annual. Previous years as cited.

U.S. National Center for Health Statistics. Vital Statistics of the United States, II-Mortality. Washington, D. C.: USPGO, various years.

Table 1.   POPULATION SIZE AND SOURCES OF POPULATION CHANGE, BY
           FIVE-YEAR PERIODS, 1945-1987 (Annual Averages)

	Initial Population (1,000s)	Rate per 1,000 Midyear Population				
		Net Growth	Births	Deaths	Natural Increase	Immi-gration
1945-49	139,767	15.7	24.1	10.1	14.0	1.6
1950-54	151,135	17.1	24.8	9.5	15.2	1.8
1955-59	164,588	17.2	24.8	9.4	15.4	1.8
1960-64	179,386	14.9	22.6	9.4	13.2	1.9
1965-69	193,223	10.7	18.3	9.5	8.7	2.1
1970-74	203,849	10.6	16.1	9.3	6.8	1.7
1975-79	214,931	10.4	14.9	8.7	6.3	2.0
1980-84	226,451	10.1	15.7	8.6	7.1	2.9
1985-87	238,207	9.5	15.6	8.7	6.9	2.6

Note: Includes overseas admissions into, less discharges from,
Armed Forces, and "errors of closure."

SOURCE: Based on <u>Statistical Abstract 1989</u>, p. 9.

Table 2.   AVERAGE YEARS OF LIFE REMAINING AT BEGINNING OF AGE
            INTERVAL, 1960-1981

Year	Years of Life Remaining	
	Males	Females
At birth:		
1960	66.6	73.1
1970	67.1	74.8
1981	70.4	77.9
At age 20:		
1960	49.6	55.5
1970	49.6	56.7
1981	52.1	59.2
At age 50:		
1960	22.8	27.6
1970	23.2	28.9
1981	26.2	30.9
At age 75:		
1960	7.9	9.4
1970	8.4	10.5
1981	9.0	11.6

SOURCE: Based on U.S. National Center for Health Statistics,
     various years.

Table 3. AGE STRUCTURE OF THE POPULATION, 1950-1987

			Age			
Year	Under 5	5-17	18-24	25-44	45-64	65+
1950	11%	19%	12%	30%	20%	8%
1960	11	24	10	26	20	9
1970	8	26	12	24	20	10
1980	7	21	13	28	20	11
1987	8	18	11	32	19	12

SOURCES: Based on U.S. Bureau of the Census, 1963, p. 358;
Statistical Abstract 1989, p. 13.

Table 4.   PERCENTAGE OF POPULATION LIVING IN CITIES OF DIFFERENT
            SIZE, AND IN RURAL PLACES, 1950-1980

| | City Population | | | | | |
Year	All Urban	1,000,000 +	250,000- 999,000	50,000- 249,000	Under 50,000	Rural
1950	64%	11%	11%	12%	29%	36%
1960	70	10	12	14	34	30
1970	73	9	11	15	38	27
1980	74	8	10	16	40	26

SOURCE: Based on <u>Statistical Abstract 1985</u>, p. 22; <u>1979</u>, p. 23.

Table 5. RACE AND NATIVITY OF THE POPULATION, 1940-1980

Year	White Native	White Foreign-born	Nonwhite
1940	81%	9%	10%
1950	82	7	11
1960	83	5	11
1970	83	4	12
1980	79	4	17

SOURCE: Based on U.S. Bureau of the Census, 1972, p. 361;
   <u>Statistical Abstract 1984</u>, p. 7.

These trends are singularly mixed. On the one hand, the U.S. continues to have the largest and strongest national economy, and an economic expansion of unprecedented length has followed the brief recession of 1982-83. On the other hand, the extraordinary accumulation of public and private debt in recent years has retarded capital growth and changed the United States from the leading international creditor to the leading debtor.

In 1985, the United States had the second highest GNP per capita, (exceeded only by the United Arab Emirates) but its GNP per capita growth rate from 1973 to 1985 was exceeded by 43 other countries. The stage was set for a rapid decline in GNP per capita rank, and according to newspaper reports, Japan, Switzerland and Iceland--among others--may have passed the U.S. in 1987.

The U.S. net international investment position, which had been positive since World War I, declined precipitously from +$136 billion in 1982 to -$368 billion in 1987. During that same brief period, U.S. assets abroad increased slightly but foreign assets in the U.S. more than doubled from $688 billion to $1,536 billion (Table 1).

In constant dollars, the gross stock of fixed private capital in the U.S. increased by a respectable but not impressive 44% between 1975 and 1987 (Table 2). Personal saving increased from $124.8 billion in 1975 to a peak of $251.6 billion in 1984, then declined abruptly to $128.9 billion in 1987 (Table 3). Fixed nonresidential private capital--in constant dollars--increased by 49% from 1975 to 1987 but this was insufficient to accomplish any significant modernization of plant and equipment, whose age remained unchanged at around 15 years for plant and 7.5 years for equipment throughout the period (Table 4).

Public debt increased spectacularly during the same interval, rising from $764 billion in 1975 to $2.7 trillion in 1986; it is expected to reach $3 trillion in 1988 (Table 5).

The merchandise trade balance with other countries, which had been moderately positive in the 1960s and moderately negative in the early 1970s, moved to an unprecedented negative level, -$29 billion, in 1977, and by 1987 had reached the spectacular figure of -$152 billion; only about a third of this deficit was attributable to oil imports (Table 6).

The per capita consumption of energy in the U.S., measured in kilograms of coal equivalents, declined slightly from 10,386 in 1980 to 9,489 in 1986 but remained much higher than in other advanced countries. This is a primary measure of economic activity in modern societies but an ambiguous one because technological progress tends to lower the energy requirements of many devices and processes (Table 7).

Table 8 shows per capita GNP, disposable personal income and personal consumption expenditures from 1950 to 1987 in constant dollars. There was some improvement in living standards during the period 1975 to 1987 but it was very modest compared to the spectacular increases in real income that occurred between 1950 and 1975. The proportion of population below the poverty level, which had been decreasing sharply prior to 1970, leveled off at that time and rose slightly in the 1980s (Table 9).

There were other signs of stress attributable to the spendthrift tendencies in the U.S. economy. The rate of business failures, which was approximately level from 1960 to 1980, increased sharply in 1981-1986, as did the outstanding liabilities of businesses that failed (Table 10). The delinquency rate of nonresidential mortgages showed a similar trend as did both business and personal bankruptcies (Table 11).

References

U.S. Bureau of the Census. Statistical Abstract of the United States, 1989. Washington, D.C., 1989. Annual. Previous years as cited.

Context

Table 1.   INTERNATIONAL INVESTMENT POSITION OF THE U.S., 1982-1987

Year	Foreign Assets in the U.S. (billions)	Net International Investment Position (billions)
1982	$ 688	$ 137
1983	785	89
1984	893	4
1985	1061	-111
1986	1341	-269
1987	1536	-368

SOURCE: Based on <u>Statistical Abstract 1989</u>, p. 776.

Table 2.   VALUE OF U.S. PRODUCTIVE AND RESIDENTIAL CAPITAL, 1975-
1987

Year	1982 Dollars (billions)
1975	$8,313
1980	9,813
1983	10,570
1984	10,887
1985	11,254
1986	11,602
1987	11,945

SOURCE: Based on <u>Statistical Abstract 1989</u>, p. 532; <u>1987</u>, p. 515.

Table 3. NET SAVINGS OF HOUSEHOLDS, 1970-1987

Year	Current Dollars (billions)
1970	$ 60
1975	125
1980	162
1982	235
1983	191
1984	252
1985	174
1986	168
1987	129

SOURCE: Based on <u>Statistical Abstract 1989</u>, p. 435.

Table 4a.   VALUE OF PRODUCTIVE CAPITAL, 1970-1986

Year	1982 Dollars (billions)
1970	$3,738
1975	4,513
1980	5,420
1984	6,128
1985	6,340
1986	6,530

Table 4b.   AVERAGE AGE OF PRODUCTION EQUIPMENT AND STRUCTURES, 1970-1986

Year	Equipment (Years)	Structures (Years)
1970	7.5	15.1
1975	7.5	14.8
1978	7.5	15.0
1979	7.4	15.0
1980	7.4	14.9
1981	7.4	14.9
1982	7.6	14.9
1983	7.6	15.0
1984	7.6	15.0
1985	7.6	15.1
1986	7.6	15.2

SOURCE: Based on <u>Statistical Abstract 1988</u>, pp. 508-509; <u>1987</u>, p. 514.

Table 5.   PUBLIC DEBTS, ALL LEVELS OF GOVERNMENT, 1960-1986

Year	Current Dollars (billions)
1960	$356
1965	417
1970	514
1975	764
1980	1,250
1981	1,368
1982	1,552
1983	1,836
1984	2,082
1985	2,396
1986	2,788

SOURCE: Based on <u>Statistical Abstract 1989</u>, p. 267; <u>1987</u>, p. 249.

Table 6. NATIONAL MERCHANDISE TRADE BALANCE, 1960-1987

Year	Current Dollars (billions)
1960	$5
1965	5
1966	4
1967	4
1968	1
1969	1
1970	3
1971	-2
1972	-6
1973	1
1974	-5
1975	9
1976	-8
1977	-29
1978	-31
1979	-28
1980	-24
1981	-27
1982	-32
1983	-58
1984	-108
1985	-132
1986	-153
1987	-152

SOURCE: Based on <u>Statistical Abstract 1989</u>, p. 786.

Table 7a. ENERGY CONSUMPTION PER CAPITA, 1980-1986

Year	Energy Consumption (kilograms of coal equivalents)
1980	10,386
1984	9,577
1986	9,489

Table 7b. PER CAPITA ENERGY CONSUMPTION IN ADVANCED INDUSTRIAL
COUNTRIES, 1986

Country	Energy Consumption (kilograms of coal equivalents)
U.S.	9,489
Canada	9,694
France	3,881
Italy	3,211
Japan	3,625
Sweden	4,893
United Kingdom	5,363
West Germany	5,672

SOURCE: Based on Statistical Abstract 1989, p. 833-834; 1987, p.
833.

Table 8. PER CAPITA GNP, INCOME, AND PERSONAL CONSUMPTION
EXPENDITURES, 1950-1987 (constant 1982 dollars)

Year	GNP	Income	Personal Consumption Expenditure
1950	$ 7,935	$ 5,220	$4,834
1955	9,045	5,714	5,287
1960	9,213	6,036	5,561
1965	10,741	7,027	6,362
1970	11,781	8,134	7,275
1971	11,964	8,322	7,409
1972	12,426	8,562	7,726
1973	12,948	9,042	7,972
1974	12,760	8,867	7,826
1975	12,478	8,944	7,926
1976	12,961	9,175	8,272
1977	13,431	9,381	8,551
1978	13,993	9,735	8,808
1979	14,182	9,829	8,904
1980	13,994	9,722	8,783
1981	14,114	9,769	8,794
1982	13,614	9,725	8,818
1983	13,964	9,930	9,139
1984	14,771	10,419	9,489
1985	15,121	10,625	9,840
1986	15,401	10,929	10,160
1987	15,770	11,012	10,334

SOURCE: Based on <u>Statistical Abstract 1989</u>, p. 424.

Table 9.   PERCENTAGE OF POPULATION BELOW POVERTY LINE, 1960-1987

Year	Below Poverty Line
1960	22%
1966	15
1969	12
1970	13
1975	12
1976	12
1977	12
1978	11
1979	12
1980	13
1981	14
1982	15
1983	15
1984	14
1985	14
1986	14
1987	14

SOURCE: Based on <u>Statistical Abstract 1989</u>, p. 452.

Table 10. BUSINESS FAILURES, 1970-1987

Year	Failures (per 10,000 firms)	Current Liabilities (millions)
1970	44	$ 1,888
1975	43	4,380
1980	42	4,635
1981	61	6,955
1982	88	15,611
1983	110	16,073
1984	107	29,269
1985	115	36,937
1986	120	44,724
1987*	102	36,337

*Preliminary

SOURCE: Based on <u>Statistical Abstract 1989</u>, p. 525.

Table 11. BANKRUPTCIES, 1950-1987

Year	Bankruptcies (1,000s)
1950	33
1955	59
1960	110
1965	180
1970	194
1975	254
1980	278
1981	360
1982	368
1983	375
1984	344
1985	365
1986	478
1987	561

SOURCE: Based on Statistical Abstract 1989, p. 527.

0.3 MACRO-TECHNOLOGICAL TRENDS

There is evidence both for and against a general decline in American technology in the past two decades. On the one hand, the GNP has continued to grow without an increase in petroleum consumption and the U.S. continues to dominate such fields as artificial intelligence, genetic engineering, and space travel. On the other hand, since the early 1970's, the number of doctorates in mathematics and science awarded by American universities has declined, industrial horsepower has remained steady, and overall competitive ability appears to have declined. Studies prior to 1983 paint an especially gloomy portrait; recent figures indicate a partial turnaround.

The recent inability of the U.S. to compete effectively with Japan and other industrialized countries in a number of important industries has convinced some observers that American technology is declining--perhaps irreversibly.

There is some evidence to the contrary. The major U.S. technological achievement of the past two decades has been the steady growth of the gross national product without significant growth in energy consumption (Table 1).

In the three fields that Dyson (1987) identifies as central to technological development in the next century--artificial intelligence, genetic engineering, and space travel --research and development has been concentrated in the U.S., although many innovative applications have been made in other countries. Even in space travel, where the practical capacities of the Soviet program may be equal in some respects, American technology has an unmistakable lead.

On the other hand, there are disquieting indications about both the progress of science and the application of scientific discoveries to production in this country. As Table 2 shows, the number of doctorates in mathematics and the sciences conferred by American universities declined substantially from 1971 to 1986. And it is clear from Table 4 that industrial horsepower has remained approximately level since the early 1970s. Baumol and McLennon in a 1985 study of U.S. productivity performance remark that

> For more than one and a half decades before 1983, there was a pervasive and very substantial decline in productivity growth rates throughout most sectors of the U.S. economy. Moreover, for at least that same length of time, productivity grew far less rapidly in the United States than it did in the countries that are now our main economic rivals. The recovery years 1983 and 1984 have brought an upturn in U.S. productivity growth, as is typical of this stage of the business cycle (p.3).

An earlier (1980) but much more detailed study directed by John Ullman examined the relation of technology and productivity separately by industries and found trends ranging from rapid growth to rapid decline but an overall loss of competitiveness for the system as a whole. Ullman ascribes the problem to lowered rates of innovation and excessive reliance on economies of scale. Other observers blame demographic changes in the labor force, insufficient saving and investment, insufficient research and development, the cost of complying with anti-pollution and safety regulations, union restraints on managerial initiative, managerial emphasis on short-term profits, cheating by workers, excessive defense spending, excessive wage levels, the bureaucratization of management, economically irrational mergers, the trade practices of foreign governments, distorted exchange rates, and the inadequacies of public education. It is likely that each of these factors played some part; the precise mix is not ascertainable.

More recently, under the pressure of the trade deficit and a rapidly rising foreign debt, there have been some signs of a turnaround. Table 5 shows impressive increases in industrial research and development between 1980 and 1985. That trend has continued.

References

Beniger, James R. The Control Revolution: Technological and Economic Origins of the Information Society. Cambridge, MA: MIT Press, 1986.

Baulol, William J. and Kenneth McLennan, eds. Productivity Growth and U.S. Competitiveness. New York: Oxford University Press, 1985.

Colton, Joel and Stuart Bruchey, eds. Technology, the Economy and Society: The American Experience. New York: Columbia University Press, 1987.

Dyson, Freeman J. Infinite in All Directions. New York: Harper and Row, 1988.

Mensch, Gerhard. Stalemate in Technology: Innovations Overcame the Depression. Cambridge, MA: Ballinger, 1979.

Ullman, John E. (ed.). The Improvement of Productivity: Myths and Realities. New York: Praeger, 1980.

U.S. Bureau of the Census. Statistical Abstract of the United States, 1989. Washington, D.C., 1989. Annual. Previous years as cited.

Table 1. GROSS NATIONAL PRODUCT AND ENERGY CONSUMPTION, 1970–
1987

Year	GNP (billions of constant 1982 dollars)	Energy Consumption (quadrillion BTUs)
1970	$ 2,416	66.4
1975	2,695	70.6
1980	3,187	76.0
1981	3,249	74.0
1982	3,166	70.8
1983	3,279	70.5
1984	3,501	74.1
1985	3,619	73.9
1986	3,722	74.3
1987	3,847	76.0*

*Preliminary

SOURCE: Based on <u>Statistical Abstract, 1989</u>, pp. 421 and 555; <u>1988</u>, p. 407.

Table 2.   EARNED DOCTORATES IN PHYSICAL SCIENCES AND MATHEMATICS,
           1971-1986

Year	Physical Science Doctorates Awarded	Mathematics Doctorates Awarded
1971	4,390	1,199
1975	3,626	975
1980	3,089	724
1981	3,141	728
1982	3,286	681
1983	3,269	698
1984	3,306	695
1985	3,403	699
1986	3,551	742

SOURCE: Based on Statistical Abstract, 1989, p. 157.

Table 3.   GRADUATE DEGREES CONFERRED ON NONRESIDENT ALIENS, 1984

Field	Masters % of total	Doctorates % of total
Engineering	28	44
Mathematics	24	36
Physical Sciences	19	20

SOURCE: Based on Statistical Abstract, 1989, p. 158.

Table 4.   PRIME MOVERS, 1950-1987

Year	Total Horsepower of All Prime Movers (millions)	Percent of Total Horsepower that Is Automotive
1950	4,868	90%
1955	7,158	93
1960	11,008	94
1965	15,096	95
1970	20,408	95
1975	25,100	95
1980	28,922	95
1985	32,529	95
1987	33,266	95

SOURCE: Based on <u>Statistical Abstract, 1989</u>, p. 554.

Table 5.   RESEARCH AND DEVELOPMENT, 1975-1986

	R & D Funds (billions)	R & D as Percent of Net Sales
1975	$ 24	3%
1980	45	3
1985	78	4
1986	81	5

SOURCE: Based on <u>Statistical Abstract 1989</u>, p. 579.

1.1 YOUTH

Various external forces have combined to modify greatly the experience of youth since World War II. Schooling has become far more extended; housing has become far more available, even for young persons living alone; more young people are employed while in school; and the schools seem more willing to permit or even encourage sharing non-familial authority over children with employers of child labor. As age at marriage has increased, other arrangements, like non- or pre-marital cohabitation, have become widely accepted.

The duration of the schooling of American youth increased in linear fashion from the end of World War II through the 1960s. This linear upward trend was a continuation of a growth pattern that had lasted the better part of a century (Grant and Snyder, 1986, Tables 6 and 9). Schooling for children 5 to 13 years of age was virtually universal before 1945; by the early 1960s, it had become nearly universal for children aged 14 to 17. Only in the early 1970s was the long upward trend in the typical duration of education temporarily reversed.

The reversal--during which the proportion enrolled in school at ages 18 and 19 dropped from a peak of 50% (in 1968) to a low point of 43% (in 1974)--can be attributed in part to uncertainties about the return to college education in a changing job market, and to the loss of a substantial incentive to continue formal education with the reduction of the Vietnam draft call and then the phasing out of the military draft altogether. The reversal also occurred, in slightly more muted form, among young people in their early twenties.

After the mid-1970s, the typical amount of formal education young people attained once again increased, although not rapidly. Hidden within the general upward trend is a powerful difference by gender. At the end of World War II, young women were less likely than young men to continue education beyond high school. Since that time, however, their enrollment in higher education has been converging upon that of males. Over the past two decades, average men's duration of education has declined slightly in contrast to women's extension of their schooling.

In the late 1940s, substantial proportions of enrolled students would drop out before each of the four grades of high school; by the early 1960s, entry to high school and then passage into its second year became almost universal (some would say pro forma). The proportion attaining a high school diploma peaked around 1970, didn't increase further until the late 1980s.

A correlative of these trends has been the growing tendency of educational institutions to promote pupils at a rate that depended more exclusively upon their chronological age, and less upon school achievement. At age 15, for instance, the proportion among those currently in school at the modal school grade (tenth grade) increased from 35% in 1950 to 50% in 1970, before decreasing slightly to 47% in 1980 (U. S. Bureau of the Census, Census of Population, various years). In 1950, 9% of those age 15 had been a year or more younger than their classmates, a proportion that declined steadily to 2% in 1980. Even more radical was the decline from 14% in 1950 to 2% in 1980 of 15-year-olds who had been "left back" so often that their typical classmate was three or more years older than they.

"Denesting" on the part of American youth has, on the whole, moved only somewhat earlier in the life course (U. S. Bureau of the Census, Census of Population, various years). According to the 1950 Census, 42% of young men at 20-24 years of age and 28% of young women of that age were living as "children" in the household of one or both of their parents. By 1960, these proportions had declined (as youthful marriage increased) to 33% and 21%, respectively. By 1980, the proportion had moved back up toward the 1950 reading, to 37% and 27%, once again primarily because youthful marriage was much less common. The trend toward increased living with parents among 20-24-year-olds continued in the 1980s (U. S. Bureau of the Census, Current Population Survey, Series P-20, annual numbers on "Marital Status and Living Arrangements").

In the first decades after World War II, earlier denesting was partly a product of higher numbers of young adults living in residential groups, primarily in connection with higher education. More recently, some offset to the extended coresidence with parents that might be expected to accompany later age at marriage has come from an increasing tendency for young people to move into their own dwelling units, commonly alone, or in same-sex groups, or, in a smaller but rapidly-growing number of cases, in mixed-sex unmarried groups, typically couples. This aspect of "denesting" is not unique to the period of youth, but also has occurred among widowed or divorced people of all ages (Kobrin, 1976; Michael, Fuchs, and Scott, 1980).

In the past forty years, irregular, occasional, or seasonal employment has become increasingly commingled with school enrollment as the modal experience of late adolescence. This trend is even more markedly characteristic of girls than of boys (U. S. Bureau of the Census, Census of Population, various years). (Males are still somewhat more likely to be employed than are females, whether in school or not, at any given age, although only marginally so for most categories.) Over this same period, hours of employment for young people in school have also increased, more for males than for females. Full-time employment combined with school is still very rare in the high-school ages, and rather rare at college ages. However, there is much more part-time employment than formerly. Only rarely are young people reported to be engaged in part-time work rather than full time "for economic reasons--because of slack work, job changing during the week, material shortages, inability to find full-time work, etc." Apart from this kind of electively irregular employment, and also excluding seasonal employment, young workers have come to be particularly prone to unemployment, the vulnerable ages coming to extend into the early 20s. On the whole, the younger the person, the higher the unemployment rate. The secular growth trend in youthful unemployment has been considerably overlaid by business-cycle variation. Both young males and young females have experienced roughly the same patterns. Unemployment rates among black youth are much higher than among white youth.

Youth unemployment can most precisely be understood as an aspect of "irregular employment" when it pertains to young people enrolled in school. Perversely, perhaps, the unemployment rate for young people in school has long been, and, in absolute terms, has increasingly been, considerably lower than that for like young people who have finished their schooling. The far higher and markedly accelerating rate of unemployment among those not enrolled in school has been identified as a major social problem: the difficulty of entering into a dependable worklife without schooling credentials is seen as a deteriorating aspect of the American labor market, and is associated strongly with a "secondary labor market" that is in part racially defined.

The timing of first marriage has followed a curvilinear pattern since World War II, with current median ages at first marriage higher than at any time in the past century. A marriage boom followed the demobilization after World War II, and the resulting early marriage rates lasted for several years. In the mid-1950s, a new marriage boom, this time no product of war disruption, lowered median ages at marriage yet again.

This boom, however, was short-lived, especially for women, whose median age at marriage turned upward definitively by 1960. Men shortly followed suit, although the change in women's timing somewhat exceeded that of men's: first marriages of brides to grooms, as a result, are of people whose ages are somewhat more nearly alike than previously, i.e., age homogamy has increased. The dominant fact is that median age at first marriage has continued to rise.

There is some question whether (because median age at first marriage is commonly estimated from proportions married at single years of age) this trend is partly a statistical byproduct of the lifetime abandonment of marriage by some Americans. It is for this reason important to note that the median and mean ages at marriage as shown in marriage registrations are also increasing, and almost as markedly as the census-based measure. Furthermore, we should note that the proportion of the population never marrying has not increased much. Marriage seems to have been postponed rather than replaced by the increase in unmarried heterosexual cohoabitation.

References

Grant, H. Vance and Thomas D. Snyder. <u>Digest of Education Statistics 1985-86</u>. Washington, D. C., 1986.

Kobrin, Frances E. "The Primary Individual and the Family: Changes in Living Arrangements in the United States Since 1940." <u>Journal of Marriage and the Family</u> 38 (1976): 233-239.

Michael, Robert T., Victor R. Fuchs, and Sharon R. Scott. "Changes in the Propensity to Live Alone: 1950-1976." <u>Demography</u> 17 (1980): 39-53.

U. S. Bureau of the Census. <u>Census of Population. Social and Economic Characteristics of the Population, United States Summary</u>, various years.

------. <u>Current Population Survey</u>, Series P-20, "Marital Status and Living Arrangements." Annual.

As the American population has "aged" in the last few decades, the problems of old persons have been more commonly decried. Nevertheless, the evidence suggests that the material circumstances of old people have on average improved considerably. Longevity has increased, and at least some acute diseases affecting the old have been challenged medically. Chronic conditions, however, are still as prominent as in earlier decades. Older people have higher incomes and are less prone to poverty.

Since the end of World War II old people in the United States have in numerous ways experienced a period of unusual gain in well-being (Siegel and Davidson, 1984). At the same time, and perhaps for this very reason, the imperfections of their circumstances--particularly the loneliness of many and their relatively reduced prestige following retirement--have led to a widespread perception of a crisis among the American elderly. As the population has aged, older people have acquired more political power.

The life expectancy of older Americans has been extended considerably, although not at an even pace nor to the same extent for men and women. Table 1 summarizes average life expectancies at ages 60, 70, and 80, at dates extending from 1940 to 1981. The table shows not a single reversal. The 1950s and the first half of the 1960s were a period of very slow increase of life expectancy for men, and more rapid increase for women. Men's situations improved somewhat by the early 1970s, and there were more dramatic increases for them in the latter half of the decade. Older women's lives were lengthening even more rapidly in this period. While there are modest variations from time to time, the figures in the table suggest that the medical and perhaps environmental improvements that lengthened life were operating on all age groups, and thus each decade of life, at these ages, was healthier than before.

Understanding men's patterns of retirement from work is far easier than understanding those of women. Trends in men's retirement can easily be described from their proportions in the labor force by age, as shown in Table 2. Here we see that shortly after World War II, when annual data of this sort first begin, about half of all men 65 and older were still in the labor force. This proportion had declined to well under one in five by 1981, although a part of this is a function of the increasing average age among people aged 65 and over. At ages 55-64, the same pattern of essentially linear, steady movement into retirement age can also be seen. In 1947, only one in ten men in this age group had left the labor force; by 1981 three in ten had. And there are some signs of earlier labor-force departure even among men aged 45-54. By interpolation we can infer that if the median age at retirement from the labor force for men (voluntary or otherwise) was around 65 at the end of the war, it was close to 60 by 1981.

Part-time employment has become increasingly characteristic of older workers. For men aged 65+, the percentage in the labor force employed part-time increased 30% in 1960 to 45% in 1984.

Unemployment rates have not risen for men of retirement age. Although most older men do not suffer from unemployment, when they do, they often take this as a cue to retire altogether.

Seen from the perspective of the worklife, men have been rapidly gaining years in retirement, simultaneously from a reduction of the age at which retirement typically takes place and from an extension of expectation of life. From 1950 to 1979-80, the average inactive (non-working) years for men from age 20 on doubled, from 7.5 to 15.0, and the proportion of the adult lifespan spent out of the labor force increased from 15% to 29%.

Women, on the other hand, have seen their average years outside of gainful employment decline just about as much as those of men have increased. Part-time employment for women is more common than for men, and has increased since the 1960s. Because the maximum proportion of women in the labor force at any given age does not--as does men's--approach unity, we cannot simply infer the pace of retirement from the changing proportions in the labor force at successive ages. From the cross-sectional period data available, it appears that while the proportions of women in the labor force at age 55-64 increased through the period under study, just as did the proportions of women at work at every lower age, the proportions of women working at age 65 or over did not increase at all. Women's retirement was expected by this age, much as it was for most men. Beyond this, there are indications of women's retirement trends by examining changes in the relative proportions of women in the labor force at successive age groups. The proportions of women "retiring" between age 45-54 and 55-64 declined between the war and the late 1960s, and increased thereafter.

Limited data covering 1964 to 1977 (Siegel and Davidson, 1984) indicate that the number of residents in segregated old-age facilities has risen somewhat, although it hardly can be said to have become a modal experience, or even a very common locus of retirement, except perhaps at the very end of life for those with somewhat exceptional life-spans. In 1977, for instance, only 26% of aged women of 85 years and older live in nursing and personal-care homes, and only 15% of men of that age.

Good trend data on the health of older people is hard to find. The trends that are identifiable do not all seem to point toward improvements, especially in chronic conditions (Erhart and Berlin, 1974). Data from the National Center for Health Statistics for 1958 to 1967 on acute conditions point to improvements, amounting to substantial gains over the decade, for older men and especially older women. On the other hand, chronic conditions monitored over this same period by the NCHS suggest a modest deterioration, again for both men and women (National Center for Health Statistics, 1973, 1981). The NCHS report comments that a part of the apparent deterioration is probably due to improvements in reporting (previous underreporting of chronic conditions). The subsequent NCHS surveys indicate that among those 65 years or older, limitation of mobility due to chronic conditions afflicted 49% of men and 44% of women in 1979, up from 47% and 40%, respectively, seven years earlier. NCHS data from 1982, not reported separately for sex, indicate a reduction between 1969-70 and 1982 in proportions of persons over 65 with activity limitations and especially with major activity limitations (U.S. Bureau of the Census, 1986: 114). Bed-disability days reported for persons over 65 increased between 1975 and 1982, after having declined between 1970 and 1975. The observed modest deterioration of health obviously might in part be a function of increasing intolerance of activity limitation, and in part an extension of the life expectancy of old people, especially those with chronic diseases.

Rates of hypertension, a condition subject to precise monitoring, and measured by examinations rather than personal reports, probably have declined. Men and women at age 65-74 show a reduction in proportions with this condition from 76 per 100 to 70 per 100 between 1960-62 and 1976-80. Taken together with the very favorable mortality trends, the data on this condition suggest that health care has been so widely and effectively extended that many whose elder years might once have been cut short by death have instead lingered on. Such persons are responsible, in part, for the increase in very aged residents in segregated facilities for the elderly.

Relative to the population as a whole, old people are disadvantaged in terms of their current incomes, but relatively advantaged in asset ownership. Reasons for the disadvantage, most obviously, relate to the labor-force status of most old people, but, as well, to their relative lack of education. Be this as it may, and despite the increased tendency for older people to be retired, Table 3 suggests that over the decades of the 1960s and 1970s the relative income of older people improved markedly. The improvement was especially notable for married couples, but it also shows up in the entire population of older persons living in families.

The income streams of older people have greatly extended and expanded over the past decades. Since 1941-42, the proportion with income from assets--interest and stock dividends most commonly--has almost doubled, and income from pensions (aside from Social Security) has more than doubled (Yeas and Grad, 1987; U.S. Bureau of the Census, 1987). The proportion of persons aged 65 or older receiving Social Security income was less than one in ten in 1945, rose to four in ten in 1955, three in four in 1965, and by 1983 was over nine in ten (Yeas and Grad, 1987). The median net worth of both married and non-married, male and female, older persons increased six- to twenty-fold in constant dollars between 1942 and 1982. Much, but by no means all of this increase in assets was a product of the approximate doubling in the proportion of older people who owned their own homes.

References

Erhardt, Carl L. and Joyce E. Berlin, eds. Mortality and Morbidity in the United States. Cambridge: Harvard University Press, 1974.

National Center for Health Statistics. Current Estimates from the Health Interview Survey. United States--1972 ("Vital and Health Statistics, Series 10, Number 85"). Rockville, MD: NCHS, 1973.

------. Current Estimates from the Health Interview Survey. United States--1979 ("Vital and Health Statistics, Series 10, Number 136"). Rockville, MD: NCHS, 1981.

Siegel, Jacob S. and Maria Davidson. Demographic and Socioeconomic Aspects of Aging in the United States (U.S. Bureau of the Census, Current Population Survey, Series P-23, No. 138). Washington, D.C.: USGPO, 1984.

U.S. Bureau of the Census. Current Population Survey. Series P-70 No. 7. Washington, D.C.: USGPO, 1987.

------. Statistical Abstract of the United States, 1986. Washington, D.C., 1986.

Ycas, Martynas A. and Susan Grad. "Income of Retirement-Aged Persons in the United States." Social Security Bulletin 50 (July, 1987).

Table 1. EXPECTATION OF LIFE AT SELECTED AGES, BY SEX, 1939-41
          TO 1981

Age	1939-41	1949-51	1959-61	1965	1970	1975	1981
			Males				
60	15.0	15.7	15.9	15.9	16.1	16.8	17.8
70	9.5	10.1	10.3	10.4	10.6	10.9	11.5
80	5.4	5.9	6.0	6.2	6.6	6.8	6.9
			Females				
60	16.9	18.5	19.5	20.0	20.8	21.8	22.5
70	10.6	11.7	12.4	12.8	13.6	14.4	15.1
80	6.0	6.7	6.7	7.0	8.0	8.7	9.0

SOURCE: Based on U.S. National Center for Health Statistics,
     Vital Statistics of the United States 1965, Volume II,
     Mortality, Part A, Table 5-5; 1975, Table 5-4; 1981, Table
     5-4.

Table 2. CIVILIAN LABOR FORCE PARTICIPATION RATES FOR OLDER
          PERSONS, 1950-1987

Year	Males Age		Females Age	
	55-64	65+	55-64	65+
1950	87.9%	39.6%	32.5%	10.6%
1960	86.8%	33.1%	37.2%	10.8%
1965	84.6%	27.9%	41.1%	10.0%
1970	83.0%	26.8%	43.0%	9.7%
1975	75.6%	21.6%	40.9%	8.2%
1980	72.1%	19.0%	41.3%	8.1%
1985	67.9%	15.8%	42.0%	7.3%
1987	67.6%	16.3%	42.7%	7.4%

SOURCE: Based on Education and Training Report of the President
1982, Table A-5; Statistical Abstract 1989, p. 376.

Table 3. MEDIAN FAMILY INCOMES OF PERSONS 65+, AS PERCENTAGE OF
          INCOMES OF ALL PERSONS OF SIMILAR MARITAL STATUS, 1960-
          1980

	All families		Married-Head Families		Unrelated Persons	
Year	Whole	Per Capita	Whole	Per Capita	Male	Female
1960	49%	--	48%	73%	53%	70%
1970	48	77	47	75	50	76
1975	54	84	52	80	56	81
1980	56	86	58	82	52	74

SOURCE: Based on U.S. Bureau of the Census. <u>Current Population
       Reports</u>, Series P-60, various numbers.

TOPIC 2: MICROSOCIAL

2.1 SELF-IDENTIFICATION

On the whole, there is little evidence that in the U.S. individuals have been transferring their loyalties to more particularistic entities, even though declines in (for example) stated confidence in a wide variety of society-wide institutions suggest that American society at large may suffer from an affiliative deficit. Class awareness is relatively modest, and shows little trend in intensity. The salience of racial identity seems to be declining; attachment to neighborhood has inclined and declined, and ties to religion seem to have attenuated slightly (see chapters 9.2 and 11.5). Perhaps Americans continue their fascination with the nuclear family (Campbell, Converse, and Rogers, 1976; Veroff, Douvan, and Kulka, 1981), seeking to satisfy there the microsocial needs that others may direct to class, race, religion, or locality.

Numerous surveys have asked Americans what social class, if any, they belonged to, generally presenting response categories such as "upper," "middle," "working," and "lower" (Converse et al., 1980, p. 22; Smith, 1980, pp. 23-24; Davis and Smith, 1986, p. 218). When they are presented such lists, most Americans agree to answer. The numbers refusing to select a class identification are usually 1% or less. The proportions identifying themselves with the upper class has ranged from 2% to 4%. Comparable figures for "lower class" are 4% and 7%, neither of these showing any trend whatsoever. Most people consider themselves "middle" or "working class." Identification has changed gradually over the period, with the last 25 years being a period of growing identification with the middle class and a declining working class.

The early postwar period--one of remarkable growth in the inclusiveness of the economic rewards of American prosperity--was a time when increasing proportions of Americans identified with the working class, instead of the middle class. One must suspect that there is a powerfully ideological element here. In any case, by the mid-1950s the percentage of Americans identifying with the working class was twice as large as that self-identifying with the middle class. But then there was a reversal, and there began a slow upward drift, approaching and then surpassing the point where half the American population identified itself as middle class.

How to interpret this trend with respect to identification with class as such isn't entirely clear. While the downward leg probably reflects ideological commitment to the American ideology of refusing to consider oneself "better" than others--rejection of a microsocial identification--it is not certain whether the subsequent, long-lasting upward leg represents merely a more-or-less realistic assessment of a general shift away from blue-collar toward white-collar jobs, and thus arguably a rise in microsocial attachment of a real sort, or rather a loss of commitment to a national ideology without its being replaced by anything more than a thoroughly amorphous middle-class identification.

Research by Jackman and Jackman (1983), based on data from 1975, indicates that it is the self-identified poor and working class who identify most strongly with their own classes, especially, but not exclusively, among blacks. The upper class is minute but rather strongly identified, too. The middle class by contrast is far less intense in its commitment to class; this is almost as true for those who identify as "upper-middle" as for those whose "middle" is unmodified. This finding is consistent with the speculation that the increasing identification with the middle class is consistent with a generally declining microsocial commitment to class.

That there should be a substantial and persistent gender differential, with women regularly about 5% more likely than men to identify themselves as middle class, suggests once again the amorphousness of class identification in the U.S. Data from the General Social Survey (GSS) on the disparity between wives' and husbands' assessments of social class indicate that in recent years there has been a major shift in the basis of class assessment among employed married women: there has been a marked heightening of the impact of women's own educational levels and the income derived from their own jobs, and a corresponding decline in the impact of their husbands' occupations (Davis and Robinson, 1988). On this evidence, it is difficult to find added microsocial indentification over time in Americans' class identification, inasmuch as an increasingly individualistic basis of subjective class assessment would suggest that class is less rather than more congruent with other important personal ties.

The relationship of self-designated social class to achieved education (Converse et al., 1978) is fascinating, suggesting that essentially, as the distribution of education has shifted upward over the years, the distribution of perceived class has also shifted upward precisely because within categories of perceived education, there has been no change in the distribution of self-perceived class. In 1952, about 25% of those who had had only grade school education thought themselves "upper" or "middle" class; in 1978, about 26% of persons at that education level said they were "upper" or "middle" class. Over that 26 year period, the percentage of the population with only grade school education had declined from 40% to 12%. At the other end of the educational scale, 74% of the college-educated in 1952 and 70% in 1978 considered themselves "upper" or "middle" class, and the proportion having some college education had increased from 15% to 36%. Presumably, the level of education one attains is closely linked with one's social class in the not-very incisive American ideology of class. In any case, these data do not argue for an increase in close identification with one's class.

Detailed tabulation indicates a very marked trend in the difference between the self-identification of whites and blacks, in the form of a convergence of blacks upon whites (Converse et al., 1980). In 1952, for instance, the proportion of blacks who identified themselves with the middle class was only 11% (10% identified themselves with the "lower" class in that survey); in 1978, 25% said that they were of the middle class. The last figure represented about half of the proportion of self-identified middle class whites. But the convergence is as notable as the disparity, because in 1952, the ratio of self-identified middle class members among blacks as compared to whites was only about one-fourth. We shall below see evidence that racial identification has markedly declined over the period in question; the reduced correlation between race and social class is a component in this decline.

It is a commonplace that for American blacks, race is a category of very powerful moment, an important source of social identity and political orientation. At least historically, it is probably meaningful to understand race in the United States as a category of caste, rather than of social class. In this interpretation, nothing is more important than the question of intermarriage. A variety of survey data from 1972 to 1983 (Schuman, Steeh, and Bobo, 1985) indicates that somewhat over three quarters of American blacks favor intermarriage, at least in principle. Whites, on the other hand, are much less likely to favor intermarriage. When they were first asked this question, in 1958, only 4% said they favored intermarriage. The proportion favoring intermarriage has since risen enormously, reaching 40% in 1983, although blacks still are far more favorable to the idea. It is apparent that on this indicator, consciousness of race, as a microsocial unit, has declined for whites (although it is still quite present), and has remained about constant for blacks. Whites (but not blacks) were also asked whether they favored or opposed legislation prohibiting the intermarriage of whites and blacks (such legislation being on the books in several states at the time the question was first asked). Fewer than four in ten whites rejected the idea of such legislation, when they were first asked about it in 1963, but after that date a regularly rising tide of disapproval of antimiscegenation legislation began, slightly cresting, however, in 1977, after which it receded. As of 1982, two-thirds rejected the idea of such a law. But by 1985, the proportion rejecting was 72%.

These data argue, if anything, for an irregular secular decline in microsocial identifcation on the basis of race. It is unfortunate that the far milder, far more benign, far more politically acceptable microsocial identification with ethnic identities based on national origin rather than race have left little trace in the survey trends literature. Many say that this form of identification has risen in the past several decades, but is probably so amorphous as to have slight meaning. This might be less true for identification with groups like the various categories of Hispanics and Asians who have recently immigrated.

Regional identity, perhaps meaningful when one's nation contains a Quebec or a Brittany, hardly seems so when one is thinking about Texas or Vermont. In fact, the once-distinctive South definitely has become less so since World War II. The same is probably true of Northern New England, although we have been unable to locate trend data to document this point.

The GSS (Smith, 1980; Davis and Smith, 1986) regularly asks a pair of questions about "How often you do the following things: . . . "spend a social evening with friends who live outside the neighborhood" and "spend a social evening with someone who lives in your neighborhood." The comparison of the trends may suggest something about neighborhood, surely in the American context a favored source of microsocial commitment. We here tabulate the proportion that spends at least several times a month with friends outside the neighborhood, and with someone from the neighborhood. The indication certainly suggests no trend toward, and perhaps a small trend away from a relative social (and by extension identificational) orientation to immediate neighborhood. Between 1964 and 1983 the proportions spending social evenings in the neighborhood declined from 41% to 34%, while socializing outside the neighborhood increased from 36% to 43%; but then, by 1986, the mix of activities moved back in a more neighborly direction, to 39% and 40%, respectively.

Although there is some evidence suggesting that American religiosity has not greatly declined, and considerable evidence that in a long-run perspective it is relatively high (by comparison with most nations in Western Europe), the most obvious population-based data series (Table 1) point to a decline over the postwar period, perhaps leveling off or even reversing in very recent years.

References

Campbell,Angus, Philip E. Converse, and W. L. Rodgers. The Quality of American Life. New York: Russell Sage Foundation, 1976.

Converse, Philip E., Jean D. Dotson, Wendy J. Hoag, and William H. McGee III. American Social Attitudes Data Sourcebook 1947-1978. Cambridge: Harvard Unversity Press, 1980.

Davis, James Allan and Tom W. Smith. General Social Surveys, 1972-1986: Cumulative Codebook. Chicago: National Opinion Research Center, 1986.

Davis, Nancy J. and Robert V. Robinson. "Class Identification of Men and Women in the 1970's and 1980's." American Sociological Review 53 (1988): 103-112.

Jackman, Mary R. and Robert W. Jackman. Class Awareness in the United States. Berkeley: University of California Press, 1983.

Schuman, Howard, Charlotte Steeh, and Lawrence Bobo. Racial Attitudes in America: Trends and Intepretations. Cambridge: Harvard University Press, 1985.

Smith, Tom W. A Compendium of Trends on General Social Survey Questions. NORC Report No. 129. Chicago: National Opinion Research Center, 1980.

Veroff, Joseph, Elizabeth Douvan, and Richard A. Kulka. The Inner American: A Self-Portrait from 1957 to 1976. New York: Basic Books, 1981.

Effective kin support is facilitated by proximate residence or living in the same household. Despite a modest reversal in the 1980s, the long-term trend is toward less co-residence and more independent living. An associated trend is a consistent increase in living alone or in non-family households. This increase in non-family living, combined with declining fertility, means a general decline in the experience of day-to-day child-rearing, and associated changes in the nature of kin-support activities. Adult children live somewhat farther from their parents than formerly, but the frequency of contact with parents or other relatives has not changed appreciably since good national data on the topic became available in the early 1970s. Patterns of intergenerational aid and exchange are likewise stable.

There is no standard definition of what constitutes a kinship network; it may include only those relatives with whom one exchanges goods and services, or all the kindred one would recognize on the street. Our discussion considers three kinds of networks: relatives known to a person, relatives with whom one interacts more or less frequently; and members of one's household.

Size of Kinship Networks

Studies of "helper networks"--persons with whom one exchanges visits, goods and services and to whom one can turn in times of need--have found that such networks include both kin and nonkin. The most important extended family tie is between adult children and their parents. The essential element in the solidarity of kin networks is the socioemotional distance between kin. Frequency of contact parallels that distance, and the important bonds as indicated by frequency of contact are parent-child, then sibling-sibling, and then other bonds. Stated differently, family of orientation ties are primary; where they are absent, other relatives and fictive kin are substituted ("Where there are no children, siblings and other relatives, the so-called extended kin, often take the place of children in helping old people remain integrated within the society") (Shanas, 1973, pp. 506-510).

There is little national trend data on the total number of "kin acquaintances". Relevant local studies show wide variation in size of kin networks. In the 1963 benchmark study of urban kinship by Bert Adams (1968, p. 20), white adults married for 20 years or less reported an average of 27.6 kin acquaintances. Fourteen years later in another middle-sized city, the Middletown researchers found an average of 18.1 kin acquaintances per adult respondent, including 4.8 "close kin" (members of one's families of orientation or procreation). At about the same time, Fischer's study of social networks in northern California turned up operative networks (consisting of those that one would actually ask to help out or visit in various circumstances) that averaged 18.5 persons, including 7.7 relatives (4.3 close kin) (Fischer, 1982, pp. 37-39).

Fisher's definition of networks of "active involvement" is perhaps a better definition than "kin acquaintance" because the literature suggests that distance attenuates kinship ties. Shanas (1973, p. 507) argues that it is not enough for an older person just to "have" relatives: "For them to function as social supports for the old person they must be physically close to him and see him often." This point is disputed by Fischer (1982, p. 354), who cites several studies showing the "persistence of kinship interaction and mutual support in spite of considerable geographic separation," and, in particular, Klatzky's (1971) 1965 national survey showing that although fewer than half of respondents' fathers lived in the same city as their sons, yet "support is forthcoming even when contact is sporadic, and it is especially forthcoming in situations of crisis that demand considerable sacrifice from the help-giver." Fischer also cites Adams' (1968) finding that only close kinship ties survive the attenuation of distance. Contact with and support of distant kin is mostly limited to parents and children. Brothers and sisters, cousins, and other relatives living far away are not very significant in people's lives.

Fertility trends are relevant to the size of kinship networks, because the most important kinship ties are to parents, siblings, and one's own children. As number of children per family decreases, so does the number of potential "close kin." If families become progressively smaller, than each cohort of adults has fewer siblings, and each set of aging parents has fewer children.

Whether one has a large or small set of kin acquaintances, the critical variables for active kin involvement seem to be household structure (co-residence) and proximity of residence, i.e., whether close kin live in or near one's household. Lee (1980, p. 924-925) makes this point in his decade review of research on kinship:

> The extent to which non-nuclear kin combine to form household or domestic units is a critical dimension of kinship structures and the very low frequency of such behavior in the United States is most often explained by reference to Goode's (1963) theory. . . [While the rate of co-residence has been decreasing] the rate of proximate residence between elderly parents and their adult children has been increasing; thus, residential separation of the generations does not mean social isolation.

Household and Family Size

Since 1950, the number of households in the U.S. has doubled, from 43.6 million to 91.1 million in 1988. Over the same period, mean household size declined from 3.37 to 2.64, a drop of 20 percent. Most of that decline occurred between 1965 and 1980, but U.S. households continued to shrink during the 1980s (Table 1).

The modal U.S. household continues to be a two-person household, and that modal situation is slightly more common than it used to be. In 1987, two-person households accounted for 32 percent of all households, compared to 29 percent in 1950. Much of the decline in household size is due to an increase in one-person households, which rose from 11 percent of all households in 1950 to 24 percent in 1987. At the same time, there has been a decline in large households (five or more persons) from 20 percent of all households in 1950 to 11 percent in 1987 (Statistical Abstract 1989, p. 46; 1979, p. 46). These changes reflect a general trend toward "independent living" in which young people left the parental nest and set up their own households, retirees opted to maintain separate households rather than moving in with kin, and the divorced, separated, or never-married likewise chose to keep or set up separate households. "One type of independent living is now virtually universal--newly married couples immediately setting up their own households rather than living for a time in a parental household, which was still not uncommon in 1950" (Thornton and Freedman, 1985, p. 35).

This trend toward independent living also shows up in the last three rows Table 1, which show dramatic declines between 1950 and 1980 in the percentage of families residing with a related subfamily and in the percentage of married couples who do not maintain separate households. In the 1980s the trend was reversed, and by 1988, 3.7 percent of families lived with a related subfamily, a rate almost twice that of 1980. Most of the increase was due to an unprecedented increase in the number of single-parent, mother-child subfamilies "doubling up" with other families.

The long-term decline in the percentage of families living with related subfamilies is paralleled by another trend that does not show a reversal in the 1980s, namely a consistent decline in the percentage of the population living in families. In 1955, 6.1 percent of the population lived alone or with non-relatives; by 1988, the figure stood at 13.6 percent (Table 2).

While the size of households declined, American families increased in size between 1950 and 1965, peaking at an average of 3.70 persons. Since 1965, families have grown progressively smaller, shrinking to an average of 3.17 persons by 1988. That decline reflects decreased fertility, manifested in more childlessness and fewer children in families that do have children. By 1985, the typical American family had no children under age 18, and the large family was increasingly rare. In 1965, 11 percent of families had four or more children under age 18; by 1987, fewer than three percent did (Table 3).

The combination of more non-family households, more childless families, and fewer children in families having children, has produced a general decline in the experience of day-to-day child-rearing as part of American life. By the mid-1980s, the typical family did not include minor children, and almost two-thirds of all households had no children present (see also Helmick and Zimmerman, 1984, pp.403-404).

Spatial Distribution and Kinship Interaction

Proximity to kindred can be conceptualized in several ways: as distance or as time, and from the standpoint of the parent or that of the children. Few national kinship studies have included items on proximity. Most relevant studies are small-scale and limited to a single city or community. Some studies of older people have produced data on how far away is the child who lives closest or how often an aged parent sees the child seen most often. Such an approach produces higher proximity rates than those obtained by asking grown children how far away their parents live, thereby producing figures which represent all children, not merely those living closest to parents (cf. Moss et al., 1985).

Findings from three national studies of older people conducted between 1957 and 1975, combined with data on older people from the General Social Survey of 1986, suggest a growing spatial separation of adult children and their parents over the three decades (Table 4). One relevant change is the decline in the probability that older people and their grown children live together in the same household. Between 1957 and 1975, the percentage of older people who shared households with their children dropped by half, from 36 to 18 percent, and then stabilized at the lower rate. Adult children and their parents are less likely to live in the same household, and if they do live separately, the children's homes are farther away than they used to be. In 1957, 85 percent of older parents lived within a 30-minute trip of their nearest child; by the mid-1980s, only about 60 percent had a child living that near.

Data on adult children's proximity to parents from seven studies over the period 1963-1986 are summarized in Table 5. Four are local studies of unknown generalizability, three are national samples. Taken together, these data suggest considerable stability in the proximity of parents to grown children. For the period represented (1963-1986), between one-third and one-half of respondents having parents said that they and their parents lived in the same community, and between two-thirds and three-fourths had parents within two-to-three hours travel. The only exception is Phoenix, where much of the population had migrated in within two decades, and even in Phoenix half of the adults said their parents' homes were within two hours' drive.

Kinship Contacts and Family Rituals

We have been unable to locate published national data on trends in family rituals. There are a few community surveys of unknown generalizability (cf. Williamson, 1962, 1963; Caplow, 1982), but we have been unable to locate trend data even for individual communities.

As for the frequency of visits between parents and children, or between adults and their relatives, there are many local studies, but types of respondents vary (sometimes older people, sometimes young adults, sometimes all adults, often whites only) and so do definitions of "family" or "kindred" (parents may be considered separately, combined with "close" or "near" kindred, or simply included in a composite "family and relatives" category). Such differences would make it difficult to establish trends even if it were possible to dismiss the regional differences. Examples of good local studies which are problematic for trend construction due to problems in comparability of respondents or differences in categories used in analysis are Farber, 1981; Adams, 1968; Rosenberg and Anspach, 1973; Winch and Greer, 1968; Petrowsky, 1976; Kutner, et al., 1956; Kohen, 1983; Streib, 1965; Reiss, 1962; and Fischer, 1982.

In view of these problems, we decided not to try to construct "pseudo-national" data or to string together community studies but to limit discussion to the relatively few items for which national data are available. These data support the position that there has been little change in frequency of kinship interaction. For the period 1974-88, between 35 and 38 percent of adults said they spent a social evening with relatives at least once a week, and about 70 percent reported such occasions at least monthly (Table 6). The same lack of trend appears in reports of interaction with parents. Over the period 1969-88, about 30 percent of adult children with living parents spent a social evening with their parents at least weekly, and there is no evidence that such visits are either more or less frequent than they were two decades ago (Table 7).

Reports from aged parents on visits with at least one of their children reveal even higher rates of parent-child contact. Four out of five parents aged 65 and over questioned in national surveys in 1957, 1962, and 1975 reported having seen one of their children in the past seven days (Shanas, 1979, p.7).

Network support. Since about 1950 kinship studies have repeatedly demonstrated that contemporary American families are embedded in a network of kindred, that patterns of mutual aid between generations are the rule rather than the exception, and that the "isolated nuclear family" and elderly parents alienated and ignored by their children are more mythological than typical (Shanas, 1979). The body of research documenting the patterns of mutual aid between the generations consists mostly of local, small-scale studies, and there has not been much direct replication. Rather than focusing directly on temporal change in flow of aid between generations, researchers have more often worked to identify correlates of family network exchange, e.g., is the kin network of the middle class more or less extensive than in the working class, or are blacks more likely than whites to be embedded in a healthy exchange network (Lee, 1979, pp. 48-50; Taylor, 1985; Chatters et al., 1985). Most research has been cross-sectional.

Findings from five national studies of parent-adult child mutual aid are summarized in Table 8. The only clear trend in evidence is stability: both the forms of mutual aid and their incidence in the population seem to have changed little between 1957 or 1962 and 1989. Some analysts, noting the increase in the "all forms . . ." category of help from parents to children between 1962 and 1975, offer this conclusion:

> These data clearly suggest that older persons have become more integrated into their families over time. While 60 percent of the 1962 aged sample assisted their children, by 1975 this figure had increased to over 70 percent. An even greater increase is noted with help to grandchildren. The kinds of help given by older people to their children most frequently consist of gifts (69%), help with grandchildren (36%), and housekeeping (28%). . . . During this same period of time, however, virtually no change in the overall receipt of assistance by older persons is noted, and reports of financial assistance to the elderly have substantially declined . . . (Bengtson et al., 1985, pp. 322-323).

More data are needed to document that conclusion firmly, but the evidence in Table 8 does suggest, at the very least, that there has been no apparent decline in mutual assistance between generations. The summary of a 1989 Gallup survey on kinship ties in America provides some recent corroboration for this point:

> Challenging those who believe the American family is in decline, a recent Gallup Poll shows family ties still bind across the nation. Changing lifestyles, distance, divorce and the demands of life in the '80s do not prevent most Americans from staying connected to their extended families--parents and grandparents, brothers and sisters, uncles and aunts (Hugick, 1989, p. 27).

Throughout the period for which there are published data, between one-half and two-thirds of parents have provided grown children with help during illnesses, financial aid, child care, and advice. Aid from grown children to their parents is less frequent, with gifts and help during illnesses the most common forms of aid.

Data on intergenerational aid and exchange are available in other recent studies whose published findings do not lend themselves to ready inclusion in the statistical trends considered above (cf. Morgan, 1983; Lee, 1982; Moon, 1983; Taylor, 1985).

Microsocial 51

References

Adams, Bert N. Kinship in an Urban Setting. Chicago: Markham, 1968.

Bengtson, Vern L., Neal E. Cutler, David J. Mangen and Victor W. Marshall. "Generations, Cohorts, and Relations Between Age Groups." In Handbook of Aging and the Social Sciences, 2nd ed., edited by Robert H. Binstock and Ethel Shanas, pp. 304-338. New York: Van Nostrand Reinhold. 1985.

Caplow, Theodore. "Christmas Gifts and Kin Networks." American Sociological Review 47 (1982): 383-392.

Caplow, Theodore, Howard M. Bahr, Bruce A. Chadwick, Reuben Hill, and Margaret Holmes Williamson. Middletown Families: Fifty Years of Change and Continuity. Minneapolis: University of Minnesota Press, 1982.

Chatters, Linda M., Robert J. Taylor, and James Jackson. "Size and Composition of the Informal Helper Networks of Elderly Blacks." Journal of Gerontology 40 (1985): 605-614.

Davis, James. General Social Surveys, 1972-1988: Cumulative Codebook. Chicago: National Opinion Research Center, 1980.

Davis, James A. and Tom W. Smith. General Social Surveys, 1972-1988: Cumulative Codebook. Chicago: National Opinion Research Center, 1988. Annual. Previous editions as cited.

Farber, Bernard. Conceptions of Kinship. New York: Elsevier, 1981.

Fischer, Claude S. "The Dispersion of Kinship Ties in Modern Society: Contemporary Data and Historical Speculation." Journal of Family History 7 (1982): 353-375.

Goode, William J. World Revolution and Family Patterns. New York: Free Press, 1963.

Harris, Louis, and Associates. The Myth and Reality of Aging in America. Washington, D.C.: National Council on the Aging, 1975.

Helmick, Sandra A. and Judith D. Zimmerman. "Trends in the Distribution of Children Among Households and Families." Child Welfare 63 (1984): 401-409.

Hugick, Larry. "Women Play the Leading Role in Keeping Modern Families Close." Gallup Report 286 (1989): 27-35.

Klatzky, Sheila. Patterns of Contact with Relatives. Washington, D.C.: American Sociological Assoc., 1971.

Kohen, Janet A. "Old But Not Alone: Informal Social Supports Among the Elderly by Marital Status and Sex." Gerontologist 23 (1983): 57-63.

Kutner, Bernard, et al. Five Hundred Over Sixty: A Community Survey on Aging. New York: Russell Sage Foundation, 1956.

Lee, Gary R. "Kinship in the Seventies: A Decade Review of Research and Theory." Journal of Marriage and the Family 42 (1980): 923-934.

------. "Effects of Social Networks on the Family." In Contemporary Theories About the Family: Research Based Theories, Volume I, edited by Wesley R. Burr, Reuben Hill, F. Ivan Nye and Ira L. Reiss, pp. 27-56. New York: Free Press, 1979.

------. "Intergenerational Exchange and Subjective Well-being Among the Elderly." Journal of Marriage and the Family 44 (1982): 217-224.

Moon, Marilyn. "The Role of the Family in the Economic Well-Being of the Elderly." Gerontologist 23 (1983): 45-50.

Morgan, James N. "The Redistribution of Income by Families and Institutions and Emergency Help Patterns." In Five Thousand American Families--Patterns of Economic Progress, Vol. X, Analyses of the First Thirteen Years of the Panel Study of Income Dynamics, by Greg J. Duncan and James N. Morgan, pp. 1-59. Ann Arbor: University of Michigan, Survey Research Center, 1983.

Moss, Miriam S., Sidney Z. Moss, and Elizabeth L. Moles. "The Quality of Relationships Between Elderly Parents and Their Out-of-Town Children." Gerontologist 25 (1985): 134-140.

Petrowsky, Marc. "Marital Status, Sex, and the Social Networks of the Elderly." Journal of Marriage and the Family 38 (1976): 749-756.

Reiss, Paul J. "The Extended Kinship System: Correlates of and Attitudes on Frequency of Interaction." Marriage and Family Living 24 (1962): 333-339.

Rosenberg, George and Donald F. Anspach. Working Class Kinship. Lexington, Mass.: Lexington Books, D. C. Heath, 1973.

Shanas, Ethel. "Family-kin Networks and Aging in Cross-cultural Perspective." Journal of Marriage and the Family 35 (1973): 505-511.

------. The Health of Older People, 1957 (printed codebook). ICPSR ed. Ann Arbor, Mich.: Inter-university Consortium for Political and Social Research, 1985a.

------. The Health of Older People: A Social Survey. Cambridge, MA: Harvard University Press, 1962.

------. National Survey of the Aged, 1975 (printed codebook). ICPSR ed. Ann Arbor, Mich.: Inter-university Consortium for Political and Social Research, 1982.

------. National Survey of the Aged, [United States], 1962 (printed codebook). 1st ICPSR ed. Ann Arbor, Mich.: Inter-university Consortium for Political and Social Research, 1985b.

------. "Social Myth as Hypothesis: The Case of the Family Relations of Old People." Gerontologist 19 (1979): 3-9.

Stehouwer, Jan. "The Household and Family Relations of Old People." In Old People in Three Industrial Societies by Ethel Shanas, et al., pp. 177-226. New York: Atherton Press, 1968.

Streib, Gordon F. "Intergenerational Relations: Perspectives of the Two Generations on the Older Parent." Journal of Marriage and the Family 27 (1965): 469-476.

Taylor, Robert J. "The Extended Family as a Source of Support to Elderly Blacks." Gerontologist 25 (1985): 488-495.

Thornton, Arland and Deborah Freedman. "The Changing American Family: Living Arrangements and Relationships with Kin." Economic Outlook USA (Second Quarter, 1985): 34-38.

U.S. Bureau of the Census. Statistical Abstract of the United States, 1989. Washington, D.C., 1989. Annual. Previous years as cited.

Williamson, Margaret Holmes. "Family Symbolism in Festivals." In Middletown Families: Fifty Years of Change and Continuity, by Theodore Caplow, et al., pp. 225-245. Minneapolis: University of Minnesota Press, 1982.

------. "Middletown Rituals, 1942-1980." In All Faithful People: Change and Continuity in Middletown's Religion, by Theodore Caplow, et al., pp. 128-145. Minneapolis: University of Minnesota Press, 1983.

Winch, Robert F. and Scott A. Greer. "Urbanism, Ethnicity, and Extended Familism." Journal of Marriage and the Family 30 (1968): 40-45.

Table 1.   FAMILY AND HOUSEHOLD SIZE, AND PRESENCE OF RELATED
           SUBFAMILIES, 1950-1988

Characteristic	1950	1955	1960	1965	1970	1975	1980	1985	1988
Mean h'hold size	3.37	3.33	3.33	3.29	3.14	2.94	2.76	2.69	2.64
Mean family size	3.54	3.59	3.67	3.70	3.58	3.42	3.29	3.23	3.17
Percent of all families residing with related subfamilies									
Total	6%	5%	3%	3%	2%	2%	2%	4%	4%
Mother-child subfamilies	2	4	2	2	1	1	1	2	2
Percent of all married couples without own household	6	4	2	2	1	1	1	2	2

SOURCE: Based on <u>Statistical Abstract 1989</u>, p. 45; <u>1979</u>, p. 44.

Table 2. NUMBER OF OWN CHILDREN UNDER AGE 18, 1950-1987

Percent of Families Having	1950	1955	1960	1965	1970	1975	1980	1985	1987
No children	48%	45%	43%	43%	44%	46%	48%	50%	51%
1 child	21	19	18	18	18	20	21	21	21
2 children	17	19	18	17	17	18	19	19	18
3 children	8	10	11	11	11	9	8	7	7
4+ children	6	8	9	11	10	7	4	3	3

SOURCE: Based on <u>Statistical Abstract 1989</u>, p. 51; <u>1979</u>, p. 47.

Table 3. POPULATION LIVING IN FAMILIES, AS PERCENTAGE OF TOTAL POPULATION, 1950-1988

Year	Population in Families
1950	94%
1955	94
1960	93
1965	92
1970	91
1975	91
1980	88
1985	87
1988	86

SOURCE: Based on <u>Statistical Abstract 1989</u>, pp. 7, 45; <u>1979</u>, p. 50; <u>1974</u>, pp. 5, 40.

Table 4.   LOCATION OF NEAREST CHILD OF ALL PERSONS AGED 65 AND
           OVER HAVING CHILDREN, 1957-1975

Proximity of Nearest Child	1957	1962	1975	1986* Son	Dau
Same household	36%	28%	18%	21%	14%
10 minutes journey or less (walking distance)	23	33	34	21	23
11-30 minutes journey (short ride away)	25	16	23	13	18
More than 30 minutes	15	23	25	45	44
TOTAL	99%	100%	100%	100%	99%

* Includes all adults having children aged 18 and over; the
first column refers to sons, the second to daughters; "nearest
child" in the 1986 data refers to son or daughter "you have the
most contact with," and the second and third categories of
proximity are defined "less than 15 minutes" and "between 15 and 30
minutes."

SOURCE: The 1957-75 figures are from three nationwide probability
        surveys of non-institutionalized persons aged 65 and over. See
        Shanas, 1979, p. 6; Stehouwer, 1968, p. 193; and Shanas, 1962,
        p. 98. The 1986 figures are computed from Davis and Smith,
        1987, pp. 397-399.

Table 5. PERCENTAGE OF RESPONDENTS RESIDING IN OR NEAR THE SAME
COMMUNITY AS THEIR PARENTS, ADULTS WITH LIVING PARENTS,
VARIOUS STUDIES, 1963-1986

Date	Citation*	Site	Parents in Community	Residing within 100 mi.	Total
1963-64	1	Greensboro, N. C.	35%	25%	60%
1965	2	United States	46[a]	25[a]	71[a]
1969	3	United States	50[b]	25[b]	75[b]
1977	4	Middletown	43	28	71
1977-78	5	No. California	--[c]	--[c]	74[c]
1978	6	Phoenix, Ariz.	--[d]	--[d]	54[d]
1986	7	United States	33[e]	33[e]	66[e]
1986	7	United States	36[f]	34[f]	70[f]

[a] Refers to fathers only, and to 150 miles rather than 100.

[b] "In community" includes the categories "live with," "neighbor,"
and "2-10" miles distant; the outer boundary is 150 miles rather
than 100.

[c] Considered within the 100-mile limit were the categories "< 5
minutes drive," "5 to 60 minutes drive," and "> 1 hour drive";
considered outside the limit was "outside North. Calif."

[d] Applies to parents in the entire state, which the author defines
as within two-hours' drive, "because the major populations centers
in the state are within a two-hour drive from Phoenix; the population in the remaining areas is sparse" (Farber, 1981, p. 163).
Furthermore, the author recognizes that there are fewer kin
(presumably including parents) living nearby in Phoenix than in
much of the rest of the nation: "Because most people in the
Phoenix area have immigrated from other sections of the United
States since 1950, only a small minority of uncles, aunts, and
cousins reside locally . . . (p. 179)." This percentage is for
mothers living in Arizona; Farber presents results for mothers and
fathers separately rather than "parents", and the percentage of
mothers living in Arizona is slightly higher than that of fathers
(49%).

Table 5. PERCENTAGE OF RESPONDENTS RESIDING IN OR NEAR THE SAME
          COMMUNITY AS THEIR PARENTS, ADULTS WITH LIVING PARENTS,
          VARIOUS STUDIES, 1963-1986 (continued)

---

[e] Refers to fathers only; "In community" includes the categories
"lives in the same household," and "less than 15 minutes" usual
"door-to-door" time from respondent's to father's home. Considered
within the 100-mile limit were usual "door-to-door" times of 15
minutes to 2 hours.

[f] Refers to mothers only; see note e above.

* 1: Adams, 1968, p. 38. Respondents were white, once-married,
married for 20 years or less.
  2: Klatzky, 1971, p. 8. Analysis was limited to data on married
men collected from the men or their wives.
  3: Moss et al., 1985, p. 136. Respondents were adults aged 65 and
over.
  4: Caplow et al., 1982, p. 379. Respondents were adults.
  5: Fischer, 1982, p. 363. Respondents were adult heads of
households and their spouses.
  6: Farber, 1981, p. 164. Respondents were ever-married adults
aged 18-45.
  7: Davis and Smith, 1987, pp. 391-393. Respondents were adults.

SOURCE: Based on sources cited above.

Table 6.   FREQUENCY THAT ADULTS "SPEND A SOCIAL EVENING WITH
           RELATIVES," 1974-1988

Frequency	1974	1975	1977	1978	1982	1983	1986	1988
Almost every day	9%	7%	8%	7%	8%	6%	10%	10%
Once or twice a week	29	32	29	29	27	26	27	27
Several times a month	19	17	18	19	18	20	15	18
About once a month	16	17	17	14	17	16	17	15
Several times a year	16	16	16	19	18	19	18	18
Once a year, or less	11	11	11	12	12	13	13	12
Total	100	100	99	100	100	100	100	100
Total (N)**	(1482)	(1488)	(1526)	(1526)	(1497)	(1594)	(1464)	(984)

* The question read, "How often [do] you . . . spend a social
evening with relatives."
** Totals do not include "don't know" or "no answer" responses.

SOURCE: Based on Davis and Smith, 1988, p. 208; 1987, p. 204; 1985,
        p. 187; and Davis, 1980, p. 122.

Table 7. FREQUENCY THAT ADULT CHILDREN HAVING PARENTS "SPEND A
          SOCIAL EVENING WITH YOUR PARENTS," 1969-1984

Frequency	1969*	1978	1982	1983	1985	1986	1988
Almost every day	25%	5%	11%	8%	9%	10%	10%
Once or twice a week	8	22	21	22	16	22	18
Several times a month, or once a month	28	29	29	29	34	26	26
Several times a year	22	21	16	18	18	20	18
Once a year, or less	17	23	23	22	23	23	28
Total	100%	100%	100%	99%	100%	101%	100%
Total (N)**	(7864)*	(975)	(1036)	(1100)	(1057)	(1018)	(730)

* Respondents were 3,996 elderly parents in the National Senior
Citizens Survey of 1969; the number of cases above is the number of
children whose frequency of interaction with parents was reported
by the parents. Category headings are those of the NORC General
Social Survey for the years 1978-1988; in the 1969 survey the
corresponding headings were, respectively, daily, 2-3 times a week,
2-4 times a month, 2-3 times a year, and once a year or never. The
apparent reversal in the frequencies in the first two categories
between 1969 and 1978 is due to differences in item wording. The
1969 item asked how frequently respondents saw each child, rather
than the "spend a social evening" question of the 1978-88 surveys.
** Total N's for 1978-1988 reflect the deletion of "not appropriate
(no such relatives)" responses along with the "don't know" and "no
answer" responses.

SOURCE: Based on Davis and Smith, 1988, p. 210; 1987, p. 206; 1985,
     p. 189; 1980, p. 124; and Moss, et al., 1985, p. 136.

Table 8. EXCHANGE OF GOODS AND SERVICES BETWEEN PARENTS
AND THEIR ADULT CHILDREN, 1957-1989

Help from Children to Parents	1 1957	2 1962*	3 1974**	4 1975*	5 1989**
All forms, or unspecif.	67%	68%	--%	68%	--%
Help during illness	5	2	--	8	--
Financial help	40	36	--	15	30
Advice	3	--	--	--	65
Gifts, unspecified	--	21	--	19	94
Household tasks, errands, etc.	20	13	--	14	76
Transportation	8	15	--	23	--
Help from Parents to Children					
All forms, or unspecif.	58	60	--	68	--
Help during illness	4	2	68	3	--
Financial help	39	--	45	14	40
Care of children	18	12	54	15	30
Advice	3	--	39	--	65
Gifts, unspecified	--	14	90	16	83
Household tasks, errands, etc.	20	15	34	13	42

* Except for the "all forms . . ." row, figures for specific kinds
of help refer to the past month.
** Figures for specific kinds of help refer to the past year.

SOURCE: Based on material in the following:
   1. Shanas, 1985a, pp. 251-255, national sample of persons aged
60+, respondents having children or other close younger relatives,
N=c.1936, items "Do you help your children or close relatives in
any way? . . . How do (would) you help them?" and
"Do your children or close relatives help you in any way . . . How
would you say they (would) help you?"
   2. Shanas, 1985b, pp. 122-128, national sample of persons aged
65+, respondents having children, N=c.2003, items "Are you able to
do anything to help your children, even small things? . . . During
the last month what sort of things did you do. . . ?" and "Do your
children or relatives help you in any way, even with small things?
. . . During the last month what sort of things did your children
do . . .?"
   3. Harris, 1975, p. 74; national sample of adults,
supplemented by additional sample of persons 65+, respondents
aged 65+ having children, N=c.2294, item "Do you ever help your
children/grandchildren in any of the following ways?"

Table 8.   EXCHANGE OF GOODS AND SERVICES BETWEEN PARENTS
           AND THEIR ADULT CHILDREN, 1957-1989 (continued)

---

   4. Shanas, 1982, pp.155-172, national sample of adults aged
65+, respondents having children, N=c.1673, items "Are you able to
do anything to help your child(ren) in any way--even small things?
. . . How about during the last month--are there any things you did
to help your child(ren)?" and "Do your children help you in any
way, even with small things? . . . During the last month, what
sorts of things did your children do to help you?"
   5. Hugick, 1989, p. 30, national sample of adults, respondents
with at least one parent living, N=816, items "I want to ask about
the kinds of things your parent(s) may have done for you during the
past year. Have they . . . ?" and "And how about the kinds of
things you may have done for your parent(s) during the past year?"

Since World War II there has been a reversal of a long-established trend in the United States toward the more-than-proportional development of relatively more populous local jurisdictions of an "urban" sort. At the same time, the near stasis in number of "rural" jurisdictions has continued.

The United States never had a "primate" city that dominated the great majority of urban functions, as Paris did in France. Rather, a sturdy regionalism maintained an urban hierarchy the relationships among the levels of which changed only slightly (in the direction of concentration toward the top) until the middle of the present century. Since that date, improved personal transportation and communication, and a preference for amenities more easily found in less-congested places have led to a reversal of the trend toward concentration. Large cities have found themselves increasingly unable to extend their geographical boundaries as voters have expressed a preference for relative local autonomy, and service-oriented special districts and fee-for-service arrangements have substituted for extensive local governments in providing public services.

However, many cities experiencing rapid growth since World War II have annexed surrounding small local governments. At least through 1970, the population annexed to central cities constituted much the largest part of the period's increase of center-city population.

The pointed research note of Lichter, Fuguitt, and Heaton (1985) develops quite precisely the "rurbanization" trends in the United States between 1950 and 1980 (Table 1). Their argument is, essentially, that since 1950, there has been a degree of decentralization of population, a net redistribution of population concentration from higher-order jurisdictions to lower-order ones, and especially to places that are outside the ambit of cities. They are particularly concerned to establish that this movement has taken place in two stages, the second commencing sometime after the 1970 census. " . . .'Nonmetropolitan' and 'rural' are not simply interchangeable concepts; nor is the revival of rural growth simply an artifact of growth rates computed on small population bases. Rather, the new pattern of growth in nonmetropolitan America is largely a result of the repopulation of rural areas" (p. 97).

Their data, largely aggregate census data, show that in the 1950-60 and 1960-70 decades, nine-tenths of U.S. population growth occurred in metropolitan areas (as of 1974 definitions, based on the presence of a city of 50,000 within the county or of substantial proportions of workers commuting from the county to such a city in a nearby county, or otherwise economically integrated with the central city, or if primarily nonagricultural and substantially urbanized), but in the 1970's, over one-third of all growth occurred in nonmetropolitan counties. Furthermore, throughout the whole period, the largest part of the growth within metropolitan areas occurred in very small places, under 2500 population. Much of this movement was the "filling in" of suburban areas, however "rural" in appearance, as urban-oriented people responded to the fresh land made more accessible by the spread of excellent roads. In the 1970-80 decade, however, the growth pole outside of metropolitan places shifted decisively to places under 2,500, that can only be called rural, but definitely not farm-related.

The postwar period was one of rapid construction of single-family, suburban houses. As a result, by 1960, the proportion of single-family houses was unusually high, amounting to over three in four (Table 2). Changes after this date in the economics of the construction business, in fertility trends (delay of parenthood), in mortgage interest rates, and in costs of fuel for commuting promoted a relative increase in multiple-family dwellings, despite a continuing population drift outward from central cities. Between 1980 and 1985, however, single-family dwellings recorded a slightly more than proportionate increase, after a two-decade decline. The proportion of housing units that were owned by their occupants rather than rented increased through the period, to nearly two in three.

Single-family dwellings continued their numerical dominance in new building even as they declined proportionately. The next largest number of new units created during the relative slump in single-family building was in quite large buildings, of five units or more. But the most rapid growth upon a small base was that of mobile homes and trailers, which the census reports distinguish from single-family houses. The number of second homes increased from 1.8 million at the 1970 census to 2.8 million in 1980, a rise of from 2.6% to 3.2% of all housing units (Roseman, 1985).

References

Lichter, Daniel T., Glenn V. Fuguitt, and Tim B. Heaton. "Components of Nonmetropolitan Population Change: The Contributions of Rural Areas." Rural Sociology 50 (1985): 88-98.

Roseman, Curtis C. "Living in More than One Place: Second Homes in the United States - 1970 and 1980." Sociology and Social Research (1985): 63-64.

U.S. Bureau of the Census. Statistical Abstract of the United States, 1989. Washington, D. C., 1989. Annual. Previous years as cited.

Table 1. PERCENTAGE CHANGE AND DISTRIBUTION OF ABSOLUTE GROWTH
          BY SIZE OF PLACE AND METROPOLITAN/NONMETROPOLITAN
          STATUS, 1950-1980

Population	Percentage Change			Distribution of Growth		
	1950 to 1960	1960 to 1970	1970 to 1980	1950 to 1960	1960 to 1970	1970 to 1980
Metropolitan:						
Over 500,000	0%	0%	-5%	0%	0%	-7%
200,000-499,000	16	12	-0	6	7	-0
50,000-199,000	17	10	6	10	9	7
25,000-49,000	29	23	7	6	8	3
10,000-24,000	46	29	16	10	11	7
2,500-9,000	55	37	21	11	12	8
Under 2,500	48	27	21	51	44	46
Nonmetropolitan:						
Over 25,000	10	4	7	1	1	1
10,000-24,000	16	7	8	3	2	2
2,500-9,000	14	8	10	4	3	4
Under 2,500	-2	3	20	-2	4	30

SOURCE: Based on Lichter, Fuguitt, and Heaton, 1985, pp. 92, 94.

Table 2.   SELECTED CHARACTERISTICS OF HOUSING, 1960-1985

Characteristic	1960	1970	1980	1983	1985
Seasonal and Migratory	3%	1%	2%	2%	3%
Owner-occupied	62	63	64	60	61
Single-unit structures	77	69	66	66	65

SOURCE: Based on Statistical Abstract 1989, p. 705; 1986, p. 729.

Americans recognize intuitively that in their federal system, power is more national than local, and more so than at earlier times in our history. And there is considerable sentiment against further centralization of governmental functions at the national level, and, as much as possible, to return jurisdictional and budgetary control to the presumably more responsive local level. Inspection of trend data, however, indicates that it has been local government whose growth since the end of World War II has been the more prominent, but that such growth has been achieved without corresponding increases in citizen control.

Taken all together, governmental employment has grown very rapidly as a portion of the total U.S. labor force since the end of World War II. Whereas in 1946, 13.5% of the civilian nonagricultural labor force was employed in government at one level or another, by 1962 the figure was up to 16.6%, and by 1986 was up slightly more, to 16.8%. The pace of growth in governmental employment at every level was the most rapid during the first twenty or so postwar years, and has declined considerably since. But growth has by no means happened to the same extent at the several levels of government. As is seen from Table 1, the growth in employment by the Federal Government--representing the unit of government whose growth in significance has probably been the most visible to most Americans, has been extremely modest, well below that of the entire labor force. On the other hand, state government employment (states in the U.S. are the nonnational units of government that are regionally more extensive than localities) grew by more than four times between 1946 and 1982, and local government employment more than trebled over the same period. Roughly half of state and local governmental employment is in education (public education below the college level in the U.S. being a local function), and such employment increased almost fivefold during this period.

Despite the marked growth in the postwar period in overall employment in local government, the number of elected local officials has declined somewhat. The figures cover the period 1957 to 1977, and point to a redistribution within the general category of local elected officials of the kind of official that is most prominent. Especially marked has been the rapid decline of elected school-board officials--presumably as greater reliance has been placed upon professional expertise on the part of superintendents of schools--and the corresponding (if not so rapid) increase in the proportion of elected officials who are identified with the most stereotypical general-political leadership in localities: the mayors of municipalities, and, to a lesser extent, the county commissioners and other county-level officials. The trends overall suggest something of steady state in the quantity of electoral control over local affairs, and a focusing within local elected officialdom on the more obviously "political" realms. There is a counter-trend, however, in the growth of numbers of elected officials in "special districts": "units of government . . . formed usually to perform a single function, such as fire protection, drainage, or irrigation, although some are permitted to and do perform multiple functions (Statistical Abstract 1989, p. 293)."

Relevant to the patterns of growth of local government have been two major shifts in their locus. The first of these is the great decline in the number of local school districts, as reflected in Table 2. Even as the numbers of local employees grew markedly, the number of localized units to which they reported declined no less markedly. School districts have consolidated throughout the period--often amidst considerable local controversy--in order to take advantage of economies of scale and to provide more varied services. At the same time, "special districts" have more than doubled in number, providing a wide variety of services with varying numbers of employees per district. Such districts often incorporate large number of localities, and often cross-cut them. Accordingly, they represent "locality" only in a very special sense: most commonly, the lines that they follow have meaning, if to anyone not employed directly by them, only to the most assiduous of their particular customers. As they have often enough assumed functions formerly vested in "historical "local governments (for reasons akin to those of consolidated school districts), the rapid growth of employment by them would perhaps seem to indicate the growth of public authority but not local authority.

Local government budgets (the figures exclude those for states, as well as for the Federal government) have grown enormously since the end of World War II, from less than $10 billion in 1946 to $315 billion in 1981-82. For a time, expenditures of localities outran revenue. But the enlargement of intergovernmental transfer payments--particularly from the mid-1960's onward, has overcome the implied local budget deficits of the decade and a half preceding. Local debt service, accordingly, has not risen as a proportion of all local expenditures. The enlargment of intergovernmental transfers has allowed localities to expand services without running heavily into debt, as the Federal government increasingly elected to have services delivered locally.

There has been no master trend in the long-term growth in local provision. Certain infrastructure expenditures--notably highways, which after the early 1950's were to a considerable extent Federally funded--have declined in the proportion that they constitute of total local government expenditure, while others--notably sewerage and housing and community services--have increased somewhat, although not with a perfect linear trend. It is commonplace that major cities face an infrastructure crisis, but, presumably, even the older suburbs are in considerably better shape than the central cities.

Public welfare expenditures follow the business cycle to a degree, of course. Police provision varies a bit from time to time, but is essentially stable. Economies, evidently, have been achieved in fire protection, perhaps stemming from housing stock being built that is less prone to destruction by fire. Health and hospital expenditures, on the other hand, have grown sharply, and will continue to do so in view of the continuing aging of the population and its apparently limitless taste for medical provision.

The largest single category of local expenditure, by far, is education, and what we have seen since World War II here is a curvilinear trend, probably superimposed on an essentially linear upward one. On the whole, costs of primary and secondary schooling per pupil have risen over the period. But the number of pupils as a proportion of the population has fluctuated widely, not because enrollment rates have varied, but because of changes in the age composition. In the 1980s, with fewer additional children to fit into schools, there is far less demand for new school buildings. And with fewer young couples in the voting population, there are fewer in the electorate who will support new bond issues for schools.

References

U.S. Bureau of the Census. <u>1982 Census of Governments, Volume 6, Number 4, Topical Studies: Historical Statistics on Governmental Finances and Employment</u>. Washington, D.C.: USGPO, 1985.

------. <u>Statistical Abstract of the United States, 1989</u>. Washington, D.C., 1989. Annual. Previous years as cited.

Table 1.   PUBLIC EMPLOYEES (CIVILIAN ONLY), BY LEVEL OF
           EMPLOYMENT

Year	Employees (1000s)			
	Federal	State	Local	Total
1946	2434	804	2762	6000
1952	2583	1060	3461	7104
1957	2439	1300	4307	8046
1962	2539	1680	5169	9388
1967	2993	2335	6539	11867
1972	2795	2957	8007	13759
1977	2848	3491	9120	15459
1982	2848	3744	9249	15861
1987	3019	4068	9846	16933

SOURCE: Based on <u>1982 Census of Governments</u>, 1985, p. 1;
    <u>Statistical Abstract 1989</u>, p. 293.

Table 2. NUMBERS OF LOCAL GOVERNMENTAL UNITS, BY TYPE

Year	County	Municipal	Township	School District	Special District
1952	3052	16807	17202	67355	12340
1957	3050	17215	17198	50454	14424
1962	3043	18000	17142	34678	18323
1967	3049	18048	17105	21782	21264
1972	3044	18517	16991	15781	23885
1977	3042	18862	16822	15174	25962
1982	3041	19076	16734	14851	28588
1987	3042	19200	16691	14721	29532

SOURCE: Based on <u>1982 Census of Governments</u>, 1985, p. 1;
    <u>Statistical Abstract 1989</u>, p. 293.

There are many more voluntary associations than there used to be. In 1987 there were almost 21,000 nationally-oriented nonprofit associations, and more than twice that many regional and local associations. About 70% of Americans belong to one or more voluntary associations, and one adult in four has at least three memberships. There is no evidence of change in overall membership rates since 1974, when good national data became available. However, there is some evidence that affiliation rates rose slightly between the 1950s and the 1970s. The modal voluntary association is the trade-commercial organization; in 1987, one-fifth of all organizations were trade-commercial, down from one-fourth 20 years earlier. The percent of the population belonging to fraternal associations, veterans' organizations, and labor unions has declined slightly since 1974; membership rates in other types of organizations have remained stable.

Number, Size and Type

Summary statistics on local and regional associations are not available, although they might be compiled from individual entries published in various directories and encyclopedias of associations. A recent encyclopedia of regional, state, and local organizations (Martin, 1988) contains almost 50,000 entries. Over the period 1961-1987 the number of national associations tripled, from 7,403 to 20,884. The rate of increase in number of associations was more than twice the rate of population growth.

Trends in the number and type of national non-profit organizations are summarized in Table 1. Of the 16 types of association described in the table, the trade/commercial organization is most common, accounting for one of every five voluntary associations in 1987. Although there are more trade/commercial organizations than any other type, the percent of all national associations devoted to trade and business has consistently declined, from 28% in 1968 to 19% in 1987.

Other types of associations manifesting substantial declines in their proportionate representation among all national associations since 1968 are organizations devoted to fraternal, foreign interest, and ethnic concerns, religious associations, labor unions, and Greek letter societies. Types of organizations that have consistently increased their relative position over this period include associations devoted to public affairs (from 4% to 11% of all associations), social welfare (from 4% to 8%), and to hobbies and avocational pursuits (from 4% to 7%). The percent of national associations devoted to educational and cultural matters rose sharply during the 1970s but in the 1980s declined until by 1986 it had returned to the 13% level of the late 1960s.

In absolute numbers, only two of the 16 types of organizations showed a decline over the two decades (1968-87): labor unions (from 237 to 233) and fraternal/foreign interest/ethnic associations (from 640 to 539). Among the impressive absolute gains are the more than four-fold increases in the number of public affairs associations (from 446 to 2,217) and social welfare organizations (from 389 to 1,641) (Statistical Abstract 1989, p. 57; 1970, p. 40).

Participation and Leadership

A standard definition of "voluntary associations" or "formal associations" refers to "all formally organized groups . . . except economic concerns (stores, corporations), governmental agencies, and schools." All non-profit organizations that are not part of some level of government are included (Bell and Force, 1956, p. 26). Typically, memberships in religious denominations, per se, are not counted, but "church-related" associations are.

Most U.S. adults belong to one or more associations. The first national studies of membership in voluntary associations (Wright and Hyman, 1958; Hyman and Wright, 1971) reported that voluntary association membership was not characteristic of a majority of Americans in the 1950s and 1960s, but those findings have been challenged on the grounds that the questions pertained only to local organizations, that labor unions were not included, and that there were not sufficient probes to help respondents remember all their affiliations (Babchuk and Booth, 1969, pp. 32-33).

Subsequent national surveys, summarized in Table 2, found that in the 1970s and 1980s about two-thirds of Americans belonged to voluntary associations. Apparently membership in associations became slightly more common in the late 1960s or early 1970s than it had been in previous decades (see Table 2, as well as Hyman and Wright, 1971). However, over the period for which there are directly comparable trend data (1974-1987), about 30 percent of adults claim to have no memberships of any kind and among other respondents there is no discernible trend either upward or downward in number of memberships.

Trends in membership rates for specific kinds of organizations are shown in Table 3. There are modest, fairly consistent declines across the 14-year period in affiliation with fraternal groups, veterans groups, and labor unions. The other types of association manifest relative stability or variation with no apparent trend.

Changes in Objectives and Activities

We have been unable to locate national trend data on changes in the objectives and activities of voluntary associations. Presumably the tendency toward rational management and bureaucratization in business organizations is paralleled in voluntary associations, but we cannot demonstrate that fact. There are case studies, such as Sills' (1957) classic demonstration of goal displacement in the National Foundation for the March of Dimes, or Walsh and Warland's (1983) depiction of mobilization processes following a nuclear accident, but the organizations studied represent such a small part of the 21,000 national associations that it is impossible to generalize from them. On the other hand, there are studies of trends in business organizations, such as Fligstein's (1985) account of the spread of the multidivisional form among large firms, that may also apply to voluntary associations.

References

Babchuk, Nicholas and Alan Booth. "Voluntary Association Membership: A Longitudinal Analysis." American Sociological Review 34 (1969): 31-45.

Bell, Wendell and Maryanne T. Force. "Urban Neighborhood Types and Participation in Formal Associations." American Sociological Review 21 (1956): 25-34.

Curtis, James. "Voluntary Association Joining: A Cross-National Comparative Note." American Sociological Review 36 (1971): 872-880.

Davis, James Allan. General Social Surveys, 1972-1980: Cumulative Codebook. Chicago: National Opinion Research Center, 1980.

Davis, James Allan and Tom W. Smith. General Social Surveys, 1972-1987: Cumulative Codebook. Chicago: National Opinion Research Center, 1987. Annual. Previous years as cited.

Fischer, Claude S. To Dwell Among Friends: Personal Networks in Town and City. Chicago: University of Chicago Press, 1982.

Fligstein, Neil. "The Spread of the Multidivisional Form Among Large Firms, 1919-1979," American Sociological Review 50 (1985): 377-391.

Hyman, Herbert H. and Charles R. Wright. "Trends in Voluntary Association Memberships of American Adults: Replication Based on Secondary Analysis of National Sample Surveys." American Sociological Review 36 (1971): 191-206.

Martin, Susan B., ed. Encyclopedia of Associations: Regional State, and Local Organizations, 1988-89. 1st ed. Detroit, Mich.: Gale Research Inc., 1988.

Sills, David L. The Volunteers. Glencoe, Ill.: Free Press, 1957.

U.S. Bureau of the Census. Statistical Abstract of the United States, 1988. Washington, D.C., 1987. Annual. Previous years as cited.

Walsh, Edward J. and Rex H. Warland. "Social Movement Involvement in the Wake of a Nuclear Accident: Activists and Free Riders in the TMI Area." American Sociological Review 48 (1983): 764-780.

Wright, Charles R. and Herbert H. Hyman. "Voluntary Association Memberships of American Adults: Evidence from National Surveys." American Sociological Review 23 (1958): 284-294.

Table 1. NUMBER OF NATIONAL NON-PROFIT ASSOCIATIONS, BY TYPE,
          1968-1987

Type	1968	1969	1970	1972	1973	1975	1977
Trade, business, commercial	28%	27%	27%	24%	23%	22%	22%
Agriculture	5	5	5	5	5	5	5
Legal, governmental, public admin., military	3	3	3	3	3	4	4
Scientific, engineering, tech.	5	5	5	6	6	7	7
Educ., cultural	12	13	13	16	16	17	16
Social welfare	4	4	4	6	6	6	6
Health, medical	8	8	8	8	9	9	9
Public affairs	4	5	5	6	6	6	7
Fraternal, foreign interest, nationality, ethnic	6	6	6	4	4	4	3
Religious	8	7	7	6	6	6	6
Veteran, hereditary, patriotic	2	2	2	2	2	2	2
Hobby, avocational	4	4	4	5	5	5	5
Athletic, sports	3	3	3	3	3	3	3
Labor unions	2	2	2	2	2	2	2
Chambers of Commerce	1	1	1	1	1	1	1
Greek letter soc.'s	3	3	3	3	3	2	2
Other	2	2	2	--	--	--	--
Total	100	100	100	100	100	101	100
Total (N)	10299	10933	10734	11919	12628	12866	13273
Trade, business, commercial	22%	21%	20%	20%	19%	19%	19%
Agriculture	5	5	5	5	5	4	4
Legal, governmental, public admin., military	3	4	4	4	3	3	3
Scientific, engineering, tech.	7	7	7	6	7	6	7
Educ., cultural	16	16	16	15	15	13	14
Social welfare	6	7	7	7	8	9	8
Health, medical	9	10	10	10	10	10	10
Public affairs	7	7	9	10	10	11	11
Fraternal, foreign interest, nationality, ethnic	3	3	3	3	3	3	3

Table 1.   NUMBER OF NATIONAL NON-PROFIT ASSOCIATIONS, BY TYPE,
           1968-1987 (continued)

Type	1978	1980	1982	1984	1985	1986	1987
Religious	6	5	5	5	5	5	5
Veteran, heredi- tary, patriotic	2	1	1	1	1	2	2
Hobby, avocational	6	6	7	7	7	7	6
Athletic, sports	3	3	4	4	4	4	4
Labor unions	2	2	1	1	1	1	1
Chambers of Commerce	1	1	1	1	1	1	1
Greek letter soc.'s	2	2	2	2	2	2	2
Other	--	--	--	--	--	--	1*
Total	100	100	102	101	101	100	101
Total (N)	13589	14726	16518	18170	19121	20076	20884

* Fan clubs.

SOURCE: Computed from Statistical Abstract 1989, p. 57; 1988, p.
   55; 1986, p. 52; 1985, p. 53; 1984, p. 59; 1979, p. 56;
   1978, p. 55; 1975, p. 48; 1973, p. 44; 1970, p. 40.

Table 2. NUMBER OF MEMBERSHIPS IN VOLUNTARY ASSOCIATIONS,
          UNITED STATES ADULTS, 1953-1987

Year	None	One	Two	Three	Four	Five+	Total	Total (N)
1953	47%	31%	12%	5%	4%	--	99%	2,809
1958	38	32	16	7	8	--	101	2,691
1960	43	25	14	18	--	--	100	970
1974	25	26	19	12	8	10	100	1,484
1975	28	29	18	11	7	8	101	1,490
1977	28	28	16	11	7	10	100	1,530
1978	28	27	18	13	7	7	100	1,532
1980	34	25	17	11	6	7	100	1,468
1983	27	26	19	11	7	10	100	1,599
1984	32	24	18	11	6	9	100	1,473
1986	28	25	18	11	9	10	101	1,470
1987	32	27	17	9	6	9	100	1,466
1988	29	26	19	10	7	9	100	997

NOTE: For the General Social Surveys (1974-1987), the item read,
"Here is a list of various organizations. Could you tell me whether
or not you are a member of each type?" The total number of
memberships is computed by summing the number of "yes" responses,
and thus technically is a total of types of membership rather than
number of organizations. The item in the NORC surveys of 1953 and
1958 referred explicitly to member- ships of the respondent and/or
other family members. It read: "Does anyone in the family belong to
a labor union? What other organizations--like clubs, fraternal
orders, professional associations, or civic groups--with ten or
more people in them, do adults in the family belong to?". All
things considered, this question is preferable to the other used in
national surveys by NORC during the same period, which limited
responses to local organizations ("Do you happen to belong to any
groups or organizations in the community here? Which ones? Any
others?"). The 1960 figures are from the Almond-Verba five-nation
study; the item read: "I shall list a number of organizations.
Please tell me whether you are a member. . . ."

SOURCE: Computed from Davis and Smith, 1988, p. 346; 1987, p. 342;
    Davis, 1980, p. 129; Curtis, 1971, p. 874; Hyman and Wright,
    1971, p. 196.

Table 3. MEMBERSHIP IN VOLUNTARY ASSOCIATIONS, BY TYPE OF
          ASSOCIATION, UNITED STATES, 1974-1987

Type of Organization	1974	1975	1977	1978	1980	1983	1984	1986	1987	1988
Fraternal	14%	11%	10%	10%	11%	10%	9%	9%	9%	9%
Service clubs	9	8	11	8	9	10	11	11	9	11
Veterans	9	8	8	7	7	7	7	6	6	9
Political clubs	5	4	5	3	3	5	4	4	4	4
Labor unions	16	16	17	15	13	14	14	11	13	13
Sports groups	18	19	19	20	17	21	21	21	19	20
Youth groups	10	10	10	9	8	11	10	11	9	11
School service	18	14	13	14	10	14	12	14	12	13
Hobby, garden	10	9	9	9	9	10	9	9	9	10
Fraternities, sororities	5	4	4	4	4	5	6	5	5	4
Nationality	4	3	3	3	3	4	3	5	2	2
Farm	4	4	4	4	4	4	4	4	4	3
Literary, art, disc./study	9	9	9	9	9	10	9	9	7	9
Professional, academic	13	12	13	13	13	16	16	15	15	14
Church-affil.	42	40	39	36	30	38	34	40	30	36
Other	10	9	10	10	10	10	9	12	12	11

NOTE: The item read, "Here is a list of various organizations.
Could you tell me whether or not you are a member of each type?"
The base for these percentages excludes don't know and no answer
responses.

SOURCE: Computed from Davis and Smith, 1988, pp. 342-346; 1987, pp.
    338-342; Davis, 1980, pp. 125-129.

National trend data on sociability date from the early 1970s. Between 25 and 30 percent of Americans socialize with their neighbors weekly, and about the same percentage never do. Two-thirds socialize with friends at least monthly; about half patronize bars or taverns. Socializing with neighbors shows a slight downward trend, 1974-1988, but there is no change in socializing with friends or rates of tavern sociability. Another kind of sociability, volunteerism, seems to have increased since the mid-1970s.

The best available data on national trends in sociability are the annual General Social Surveys, which provide figures on frequency of interaction with neighbors and friends beginning in 1974. However, items on friends' characteristics were not included until the mid-1980s. In 1986 respondents were asked where their best friend lived, and how many of their close friends were also neighbors. Results suggest that friendship is highly local: 46 percent of best friends lived within 15 minutes of the respondent, and 84 percent lived within a one-hour trip. On the other hand, while close friends are readily accessible, they generally are not immediate neighbors: only 18 percent of all close friends were identified as neighbors in the 1986 survey (Davis and Smith, 1987, pp. 407-408).

Studies of friendship using local or regional samples suggest that urban dwellers have more friends than rural or small town residents and that the number of one's close friends is positively related to income and other types of resources (Fischer, 1982, pp. 57, 116-117; see also Laumann, 1973, and Verbrugge, 1977). We have been unable to locate published data which chart changes in the correlates of friendship over time.

Table 1 presents trends in the frequency of interaction with neighbors and friends, and of tavern-going, 1974-1988. There is no evidence of change in the frequency of spending a "social evening" with friends outside the neighborhood: about 20 percent have such a gathering at least weekly, and another 40 percent, at least monthly. Similarly, there are no signs of change in rates of tavern-sociability: about one-eighth of all respondents report going to a bar or tavern at least weekly, and just over half say they never do. There is a slight decline in socializing with neighbors: in 1974-1977 between 55% and 61% said they spent at least one evening per month socializing with neighbors; for 1985-88 the corresponding range is 51%-54%.

Network Support

In the mid-1980s items on social network and support from friends, kindred, and others were added to the General Social Survey. Responses to the 1985 GSS network items are the first survey network data of national scope. The questions referred to persons with whom a respondent "discusses important matters," and the data allow identification of "core discussion networks" of American adults. The exact definition of the "important matters" was not ascertained, but it is argued that this form of questioning reflects "moderately intense content that represents a middle ground between between acquaintanceship and kinship" (Marsden, 1987, p. 123). Researchers discovered that the discussion networks were small (the mean number of alters was three, and only about five percent of respondents had networks of six or more alters), centered on kin, relatively dense (most of the alters were personally close to one another), and homogeneous with regard to race and, to a lesser degree, age and education. One respondent in four had "inadequate" or "marginal" networks of size zero or one (Marsden, 1987, pp. 124-126).

The 1986 GSS contained questions about help that one might request from friends, neighbors, kindred, or others. The responses demonstrate the dominant position of kindred in the support network and the minimal support expected from neighbors. Friends fall in between, more important than neighbors but far less likely than relatives to be seen as a first or second option when help is needed. Incidentally, the situations in which friends are most likely to be called upon are those representing a breakdown of some sort in marriage/kin relations ("a problem with your husband, wife or partner"), and even then relatives are 1.5 times as likely as friends to be defined as the appropriate helping persons (Davis and Smith, 1986, pp. 411-422).

Also relevant are items on participation in volunteerism included in five Gallup polls between 1977 and 1987. The percent of respondents claiming involvement in "charity or social service activities, such as helping the poor, the sick or the elderly" rose consistently and without exception, from 27% in 1977 to 39% in 1987 (Gallup Report, 1987, p. 33).

References

Davis, James Allan. General Social Surveys, 1972-1980: Cumulative Codebook. Chicago: National Opinion Research Center, 1980.

Davis, James Allan and Tom W. Smith. General Social Surveys, 1972-1988: Cumulative Codebook. Chicago: National Opinion Research Center, 1988. Annual. Previous years as cited.

Fischer, Claude S. To Dwell Among Friends: Personal Networks in Town and City. Chicago: University of Chicago Press, 1982.

Gallup Report 262: (1987): 33.

Laumann, Edward O. Bonds of Pluralism: The Form and Substance of Urban Social Networks. New York: John Wiley & Sons, 1973.

Marsden, Peter V. "Core Discussion Networks of Americans." American Sociological Review 52 (1987): 122-131.

Verbrugge, L. M. "The Structure of Adult Friendship Choices." Social Forces 56 (1977): 576-597.

Table 1. TRENDS IN SOCIABILITY: FREQUENCY OF INTERACTION WITH
          NEIGHBORS AND FRIENDS, AND TAVERN-GOING, 1974-1987

		Frequency				
Item and Year	(N)*	At least weekly	At least monthly, not weekly	At least yearly-not monthly	Never	Total
Spends social evenings with neighbors						
1974	(1476)	31%	30%	18%	22%	101%
1975	(1485)	28	28	20	24	100
1977	(1524)	27	28	21	24	100
1978	(1522)	30	23	22	25	100
1982	(1499)	25	29	24	22	100
1983	(1592)	26	27	22	26	101
1985	(1527)	24	27	24	26	101
1986	(1467)	28	26	20	26	100
1988	(984)	25	26	20	28	99
Spends social evenings with friends						
1974	(1478)	22	40	26	11	99
1975	(1485)	21	40	26	13	100
1977	(1523)	22	42	26	10	100
1978	(1526)	21	37	30	12	100
1982	(1497)	22	43	26	9	100
1983	(1594)	21	43	24	11	99
1985	(1529)	22	41	27	10	100
1986	(1465)	22	41	25	12	100
1988	(986)	21	44	25	10	100
Goes to bar or tavern						
1974	(1462)	12	15	20	53	100
1975	(1476)	9	16	19	56	100
1977	(1525)	12	18	20	50	100
1978	(1528)	11	16	22	51	100
1982	(1495)	12	16	23	50	101
1983	(1593)	11	17	22	50	100
1985	(1529)	10	19	22	49	100
1986	(1463)	9	16	22	53	100
1988	(983)	9	16	23	51	99

* N's do not include Don't Know and No Answer responses.
NOTE: The items read "... how often [do] you ... Spend a social
evening with someone who lives in your neighborhood? ... Spend a
social evening with friends who live outside the neighborhood?...
Go to a bar or tavern?"

SOURCE: Based on Davis and Smith, 1988, p. 209; 1987, p. 205;
        Davis, 1980, p. 123.

3.1 FEMALE ROLES

Mothering occupies a relatively smaller part of women's activities than heretofore, while employment has become more important. Child care is increasingly in group centers away from home. Women devote less time than formerly to housework and child care but still do most of both. They have achieved near parity with men in educational attainment, but occupational segregation by sex remains high, though declining. Earnings differentials by sex have changed little; employed women earn about two-thirds as much as employed men. Despite gains in economic and political power and growing representation in high status occupations, women remain disadvantaged. Unrealistic standards of beauty and feminity complicate women's role enactment, and certain over-adaptation pathologies are more common than before. Public opinion is increasingly favorable to women's rights and gender equality. The 1980s woman is more likely than her predecessors to perceive sexism in employment or economic life and less likely to define it as legitimate.

Maternal Roles and Child Care

Family size and composition. American women, and American families generally, are less involved in parenting than they used to be. The demographic basis for this decline is apparent in trends in household and family size, a topic treated in Chapter 2.2 (Kinship). Among the patterns noted there are declines in family size and in parenting, as represented both by fewer households having any children under 18, and fewer children per household in those households having children.

Further evidence of the decline in mothering is the substantial increase after 1960 in the percent of women who had no children living with them. As may be seen in Table 1, among married couples in 1960, over 61% had children at home; for a clear majority of women, day-to-day life included mothering. Since then, the number of families with underage children has declined consistently, and in the early 1980s the childless family--the family without a child under age 18--became the rule rather than the exception among U.S. families.

Among families headed by female householders the trend has been in the other direction. In the 1950s, women headed about one-tenth of all families, and such families were less likely than others to include children. After 1960, the percentage of households headed by women increased rapidly--by 1986 they amounted to one-sixth of all families--and since 1975 families headed by women have been more likely than other families to include children. Even so, in 1987 there were five times as many married women as female heads of household, and therefore, for women generally, mothering was increasingly atypical. Of all women with families, including married women and female heads of household, fewer than half had minor children in their families (Statistical Abstract 1989, p. 48).

Attitudes about parenting and child care. Several studies of change in attitudes about sex roles and traditional family values have included items on mothering, child care, and women's participation in the labor market. While there are relatively few items that have been asked repeatedly over a 15+ year period in national samples, there are numerous comparisons over shorter periods, and these may be combined to document the trend toward less traditional attitudes about parenting and child care, including preferences for smaller families, acceptance of simultaneous mothering and labor force participation for mothers, and growing repudiation of the traditional notion that only wife- and motherhood are truly fulfilling for a woman (Table 2).

Child care. Only since about 1960 has public opinion supported day care as a legitimate and non-deviant family practice (Seaver and Cartwright, 1986, p. 12). Analysis of trends in child care for 1958-1985 (Table 3) reveals a marked decline of in-home care for pre-school children whose mothers work full-time. In 1958, more than half of these mothers used in-home care; by 1985, less than one-fourth did. There were corresponding increases in the use of caregivers in other homes, and in group care centers. In 1985, own-home care was the third most frequent choice, after the use of others' homes (42%) and group care centers (28%). Among mothers employed part-time, there was much less change, and own-home care remained the arrangement of choice for more than 40% of the mothers, but by 1985 there had been significant increases in use of group care facilities by these mothers also. Moreover, there is little evidence that the trend toward more out-of-home care, and especially out-of-home group care, has reached its limit. The authors of a recent analysis of day-care trends conclude:

> The remarkable increase in the number of children cared for in day care centers over the last decade has shown that parents are willing to use formal group care arrangements for their pre-school children and, increasingly, for their infants and toddlers as well. There is no indication that this trend will slow anytime soon. An increasing proportion of younger school-age children are also cared for in centers after school. . . . In addition, the proportion of children in female-headed and small families, which are more likely to use group care in centers, has not declined, but rather has inceased, supporting our conclusion that the demand for formal child care programs will continue to grow over the next ten years (Hofferth and Phillips, 1987: 567-568).

Housework

Changes in time devoted to housework are considered in detail in Chapter 13.4 (Time Use). Time devoted to housework ("family care" or "household work") varies considerably by age as well as sex. For married housewives, family care time declined between 1965 and 1975 by about 10%, from 50 to 45 hours per week. For married women employed outside the home, there was a comparable decline, from 29 to 25 hours per week. Married men devoted about one-fifth as much time to household work as unemployed housewives, and one-fourth as much as wives who worked: their weekly hours increased slightly, from nine to ten, over the same period. That general pattern--modest decline in housework time for women, and a very slight increase for men--holds for the entire 1965-81 period for which good time-use data are available.

The decline in time devoted to housework and family care by married women is partly due to a change in lifestyle whereby families eat fewer meals at home, and when they do eat at home they are more likely to eat "instant," pre-prepared and pre-packaged meals. Between 1950 and 1980, the fraction of family food expenditures spent on meals away from home doubled, rising to 33% (Brown, 1987, p. 34; see also Robey and Russell, 1983, p. 19). In terms of women's roles, an apparent consequence of this trend is that the aspects of the wife/mother role associated with home cooking and food preparation have become less important over the past four decades. According to the U.S. Bureau of Labor Statistics (Robey and Russell, 1983: 18), the trend also reflects "the increased proportion of single-person consumer units, the greater number of working wives, the prevalence of school lunch programs, and the spread of fast-food chains."

Another way to look at trends in housework is to consider the availability of "labor-saving" appliances in U.S. homes. While refrigerators, vacuum cleaners, washers, electric irons, and toasters were used in most households in 1953, only 3% of households had dishwashers, 4% had clothes dryers, 12% had freezers, and 30% had an electric mixer. By the 1980s, electric mixers became so common the government stopped publishing statistics about them, and by 1984 over one-third of households had dishwashers, freezers, and microwave ovens, and almost two-thirds owned a clothes dryer (Statistical Abstract 1989, p. 709; 1982-83, p. 758; 1967, p. 729). An essential part of the contemporary "housekeeper" or "housewife" role is skill in operating dozens of technological aids to cooking, cleaning, and comfort, from the humidifier and the air conditioner to the frost-free refrigerator and the microwave oven.

Educational Differentials

Historically the average American woman has been a little better educated than her male counterpart, but men have dominated the upper levels of educational attainment. Despite the fact that men have consistently been about 1.5 times as likely as women to complete four or more years of higher education, it was not until 1970 that median educational attainment of men equaled that of women. As may be seen in Table 4, the absolute changes in educational attainment have been substantial: between 1940 and 1987 median years of schooling increased from 8.6 to 12.7 for men and from 8.7 to 12.6 for women. Over the same period, the percentage of the white population completing at least four years of higher education rose from 6% to 24% for men, and from 4% to 17% for women.

The trend toward higher education quadrupled the percent of the population completing college, but did not greatly change sex differentials in educational attainment. In 1940, when less than 5% of the white population had college degrees, men were 1.5 times as likely as women to have graduated from college. As higher education become more universal, the male advantage actually increased: in 1970, with 11% of white population college-educated, men were 1.7 times as likely as women to be in that group. By 1987, 24% of men and 17% of women had college degrees, putting women's relative disadvantage back to the 1940 level (Table 4).

Recent changes in sex differentials in education are more apparent if one considers the sex composition of successive cohorts of college graduates. That is, what percentage of all who complete a course of higher education in a given year are women, and how has that percentage changed? Table 5 traces trends in the number and sex distribution of degrees in higher education for the period 1950-85. The progress of women to near parity in bachelors and masters degrees is notable. They show significant gains even in doctorates awarded: In 1950, one degree-recipient in four was female; in 1985, half were. In the 1980s, women received one-third of all doctorates, compared to less than one-tenth in the 1950s.

Another indicator of educational attainment is performance on standardized achievement tests. With two exceptions--a brief, early (1967-70) advantage on the verbal ability portion of the Scholastic Aptitute Test (SAT), and the entire run of English specialty scores on the American College Testing Program (ACT)--the average scores for men are uniformly higher than those for women. Moreover, there is no evidence of convergence or divergence. The male advantage in SAT verbal and mathematics scores, and in the ACT composite, math, social studies and natural science scores, was about the same in 1987 as in the early 1970s (Statistical Abstract 1989, p. 144). Further documentation of sex-differences in educational attainment and possible explanations for these differentials appear in Lipman-Blumen and Tickamyer's (1975) review article on "sex roles in transition."

Occupational Differentials

The increased representation of women in the labor force over the past 40 years--a truly dramatic change (see Chapter 3.4, Women's Employment)--has not been accompanied by much change in the kinds of jobs women have. Among the descriptions of continuity in occupational differentiation by sex during this period are Gross (1968), Treiman and Terrell (1975), and Taeuber and Valdisera (1986). While there have been modest increases in women's representation in many occupations formerly all or predominantly male, the occupational structure remains sharply segregated by sex. With the exception of private household work, which accounted for 10% of women's jobs in the 1950s but less than 2% by 1982, the typical occupations of working women in the 1980s are much the same as the "women's occupations" of the 1950s. Across the entire 38-year span, the two categories of clerical workers and service workers (including private household work) account for about half of women's jobs, compared to one-eighth for men.

The study of occupational differentials by sex across the entire period is complicated by the fact that in the early 1980s the Census Bureau changed its occupational classification system, and the new system is not directly comparable to the old. As a result, two tables are needed to trace changes in the occupational distribution of American women: Table 6 covers the period 1950-1982, using the old occupational categories, and Table 7 covers 1982-1988, using the new category system. Trends apparent include a growing percentage of women workers in professional occupations; a sharper increase in their representation in managerial jobs (from 10% in 1956 to 18% in 1982, and a corresponding increase between 1982 and 1988); a decline in their employment as operatives, from 20% in 1950 to 6% in 1988; the decline of private household work noted above; and an increase in their representation among service workers until 1975, followed by stabilization near the 1975 level. Some of these changes parallel changes in men's work as well. For example, the growing representation of women in professional jobs represents a structural change in the nature of American employment more than a reduction in sex differentiation in these jobs.

To highlight sex differences in occupation, we computed ratios showing the degree to which women were under- (ratios under 1.00) or over-represented in a given occupational category (Tables 7 and 8). The ratio is directly interpretable: a value of 2.0 means that there are twice as many women in a category as would appear if women's representation in that category were the same as men's, a value of .5 means that there are half as many, and a value of 1.0 means that men and women are equally represented in the category.

The most striking thing about the ratios in Tables 7 and 8 is the lack of trend apparent over the 38-year period in most occupations. Over the entire period, women are slightly over-represented in the professions and among technicians and sales workers; greatly underrepresented among craft workers, laborers, and farmers (but not farm laborers, until the 1980s); slightly underrepresented among operatives; and greatly over-represented among service workers, clerical workers, and private household workers. Counterbalancing the declining differentiation in private household work (from 100-to-one in the 1950s to 17-to-one in 1988) is an increase in women's over-representation in clerical work, at least until 1982, when the female/male ratio stood at 5.5, compared to 4.3 in 1950.

Paula England's systematic assessment of research on sex segregation in occupation between 1900 and 1976 supports the finding of little change. She concludes that:
> The 1920s and the 1950s brought small increases in segregation. The 1970s brought negligible change. Other decades brought small amounts of decrease, with the largest decline in the 1940s (England, 1981, p. 288).

As of 1976, she contends, the women's movement had not had much effect on occupational sex segregation.
> . . . it is telling that the combined forces of changing sex roles, the women's movement, and affirmative action should have less impact on segregation during the 1970s than a war did in the 1940s (England, 1981, p. 287; see also Jones and Rosenfeld, 1989).

Studies of the impacts of various supply and demand factors upon women's access to employment opportunities in large U.S. metropolitan areas for the period 1950-80 (Jones and Rosenfeld, 1989) suggest that male unemployment, increased representation of government jobs in the local economy, higher educational achievement among women, and growth in the manufacturing sector of the economy are factors associated with increased women's access to better occupations. Persisting differentials in the desirability of sex-typed jobs reflect popular opinion on whether the jobs are "female" or "male." In local labor markets, women thus seem to compete with men more successfully over time for access to predominantly male white collar occupations, but men do not seem to compete with women for access to female white collar jobs, especially lower-level ones (Jones and Rosenfeld, 1989, p. 687).

Earnings and Power Differences

Earnings differences. Women's earnings are consistently lower than men's. The ratio of women's to men's earnings over the three decades 1955-1987 runs at about .60, showing virtually no change until the late 1970s when a small but continuing annual increase begins. By the mid-1980s, employed women's median incomes had risen to between 64% (annual) and 70% (weekly) of men's incomes, a significant increase over their level in prior decades (see Table 9). Inspection of the ratios of women's to men's earnings within occupational categories (Statistical Abstract 1988, p. 395) reveals remarkably little variation across occupations. With the exceptions of sales occupations, where women do worse (.48) and farming, forestry, and fishing occupations, where they do a little better (.75), women in 1987 earned between 60% and 69% of what men earned, regardless of type of occupation.

Reasons for the differences between men's and women's earnings are not fully understood. Much of the difference is attributable to the fact that women are concentrated in jobs that pay less than the jobs most men hold. Sexual discrimination in the labor market, differing experience and educational skills, and lower commitment or work attachment among women are cited as contributory factors (Taeuber and Valdisera, 1986, pp. 31-33). There is evidence that even when women enter high status managerial and professional occupations, "they tend to be contained within those specialties which pay most poorly, are least prestigious, and are for various reasons considered 'feminine' or compatible with feminine skills" (Lipman-Blumen and Tickamyer, 1975, pp. 307-308). There is a sizable research literature on attempts to identify variables that contribute to the persistence of earnings inequality by sex and to measure their individual and combined effects (see, for example, Taylor, Gwartney-Gibbs, and Farley, 1986; Sokoloff, 1988). Some of the slight decrease in earnings inequality since the mid-1970s may be attributable to very modest declines in occupational sex segregation over the same period (Bianchi and Rytina, 1986; England, 1981; Beller, 1984).

Selected power differences. The indicators of power we shall consider include wife's economic dependency on her husband, possession of wealth, employment in selected high-status occupations, membership in labor unions, and represention among elected officials. Four of these five yield trends showing consistent, though gradual, increases in women's power. The exception is the representation of women among top wealthholders, where the trend seems to be relative stability rather than growing female power.

One measure of women's subordination is the extent to which a wife's share of family income depends upon economic transfer from her husband. As economic dependency is often conceptualized, if he has an income and she does not, she is totally dependent upon him; if her income supports the family, and he has none, he is totally dependent upon her. This way of looking at family economics ignores any contribution either spouse may make to family income via household work. Estimates of the degree of economic dependency among U.S. couples for the period 1940-80 (Sorensen and McLanahan, 1987, p. 669) reveal, both for whites and nonwhites, declining dependency among wives. Over the 40-year period, the percentage of totally dependent wives drops from 84% to 31% among white couples and from 68% to 27% among nonwhites. The percentage of couples where husband and wife contribute fairly equally to the family income---where they are economically independent--also increases, rising from 3% to 12% among nonwhites and from 3% to 8% among whites.

Women's power is also reflected in the wealth they control. Table 10 traces trends in the representation of women among the nation's top wealthholders, 1953-1982. The percentage of women among wealthy Americans increased slightly over these three decades, but there were substantial reversals. The percentage of women among the top wealthholders varies from 33% to 39%, with "peaks" of 39% in 1972 and 1982, and lows of 33% and 34% in 1953 and 1976, respectively. No consistent trend appears.

Women's social power is reflected in their growing representation in high status occupations (see, for example, Sokoloff, 1988). Among the "male" professions traditionally defined as inappropriate for women are engineering, mathematics, and other "hard" sciences. U.S. government statistics on the number and characteristics of scientists and engineers in the labor force reveal steady growth in the proportion of women among them, from about 9% in 1974 to over 15% in 1986 (see column two of Table 11). Most of the increase is among scientists rather than engineers: in 1974, 18% of workers classified as scientists were women; by 1986, 28% were. Women are much less likely to be engineers, but there too their representation has gradually increased (from 0.5% in 1974 to 4% in 1986).

Another high-status occupation from which American women were once excluded is the law. In 1951, 2.5% of the nation's 200,000 lawyers were women, and that percentage held constant for the next 20 years. Then, between 1970 and 1985, women entered the profession in unprecedented numbers. Their absolute gains were remarkable: in the decade of the 1970s, the number of female lawyers increased five times, from 9,000 to 45,000, and between 1980 and 1985 their number doubled, to 85,542. That amounted to 13% of all lawyers in the nation, hardly parity, but still a noteworthy increase in women's power over a brief span (see Table 11, column three).

The activities of labor unions have helped to raise wages and improve benefits for American workers. Although the power of organized labor relative to management seems less in the 1980s than in earlier decades (see Chapter 9.1, Labor Unions), increased involvement of women in labor unions should magnify their influence upon their own working conditions and practices. Rates of union membership by women since 1956 are given in column one of Table 11. Their representation increases each decade, most substantially in the 1980s. By 1987, 35% of union members were women, up from 18% three decades before.

The proportion of women among elected officials is an indicator of women's political power. Columns four and five of Table 11 summarize the representation of women in state legislatures and the U.S. Congress. Although women continue to be underrepresented in both contexts, it is noteworthy that their participation in state legislatures doubled between 1975 and 1987, rising from 8% to 16%, and that their representation in Congress was consistently higher in the 1980s than in previous decades.

Differentiating Attitudes, Practices, & Consumption Styles

While women enact their various roles they are expected to conform, as far as possible, to accepted standards of beauty and grooming. Further, in developed societies like the U.S., the mass media impose fairly uniform standards of women's beauty and fashion, and international commercial conglomerates dictate frequent changes in fashion (Mazur, 1986, pp. 282-282). It is possible to estimate the direction of change in such standards by noting variations in the personifications of beauty and feminine excellence officially rewarded by agencies of society. One official recognition of these attributes is the annual Miss America contest, and the body measurements of Miss America contestants may be seen as approximations to the national ideal of the feminine form. A charting of changes in contestants' average height, weight, and waist, bust, and hip size reveals a trend toward slimmer, taller women, especially since the mid-1960s (Mazur, 1986, p. 291). In the 1970s and 1980s, some women responded to the ideal that slim was beautiful by the pathological overadaptations of anorexia nervosa and bulimia. Others sought cosmetic surgery. Mazur (1986, p. 300) documents both trends, showing a rapid rise in the incidence of breast augmentation operations between 1962 and 1979 and a corresponding growth in the medical literature on anorexia nervosa.

Some market research suggests that in consumer behavior employed women differ markedly from fulltime housewives, and that the interests and values of these two categories of women are becoming more distinctive (Bartos, 1982). Between 1971 and 1983, the percentage of working women who said they viewed their work as a career rather than "just a job" increased from 29% to 49%. At the same time, the percentage of the nonemployed housewives who said they planned to stay at home also increased slightly (Wattenberg, 1984, p. 20).

Changes relevant to the definitions and enactment of women's roles also appear in reports of satisfaction with marriage. Survey data for 1972-86 reveal a sizable decline in the association between being married and reporting feelings of happiness, with married women showing a larger decline in happiness than married men. In 1986 married persons were still more apt than the never-married to declare themselves "very happy," but the relative advantage among married women had declined in less than 15 years from 37% to 13% (Glenn, 1987, p. 352). Other evidence for a decline in the perceived favorability of the married state shows up in a 1976 replication of a 1957 national survey. In 1957, 43% said that one's life was improved by being married; two decades later, only 30% agreed. There was a corresponding decline in disapproval of people who do not marry (Table 12).

Popular support for the changes in women's roles and for their heightened political and economic power is widespread and growing. For instance, the percent of adults agreeing that women should "leave running the country to men" declined by one-third, from 36% to 24%, between 1977 and 1988; there was a similar decline in disapproval of women working outside the home when they didn't have to (Table 12). By 1985, three-fourths of the population said they favored efforts "to strengthen and change women's status in society," and by 1987 the former preference among both sexes for male bosses or supervisors had yielded to a majority position of no preference for either sex. In the 1980s, women were more likely than they had been to assert that their job opportunities were inferior to men's, more likely to express discontent about male-female differentials in power and opportunity, and less likely to define those differentials as natural or legitimate (Table 13).

References

Bartos, Rena. The Moving Target: What Every Marketer Should Know About Women. New York: Free Press, 1982.

Beller, Andrea H. "Trends in Occupational Segregation by Sex and Race, 1960-1981." In Sex Segregation in the Workplace: Trends, Explanations, Remedies, edited by Barbara F. Reskin, pp. 11-25. Washington, D.C.: National Academy Press, 1984.

Bianchi, Suzanne M. and Nancy Rytina. "The Decline in Occupational Sex Segregation during the 1970s: Census and CPS Comparisons." Demography 23 (1986): 79-86.

Brown, Clair. "Consumption Norms, Work Roles, and Economic Growth, 1918-1980." In Gender in the Workplace, edited by Clair Brown and Joseph A. Pechman, pp. 13-58. Washington, D.C.: Brookings Institution, 1987.

Davis, James Allan and Tom W. Smith. General Social Surveys, 1972-1988: Cumulative Codebook. Chicago: National Opinion Research Center, 1988. Annual. Previous years as cited.

Employment and Earnings. Washington, D.C.: U.S. Bureau of Labor Statistics, 1989. Monthly. Previous years as cited.

England, Paula. "Assessing Trends in Occupational Sex Segregation, 1900-1976." In Sociological Perspectives on Labor Markets, edited by Ivar Berg, pp. 273-295. New York: Academic Press, 1981.

Freeman, Richard and Jonathan S. Leonard. "Union Maids: Unions and the Female Work Force." In Gender in the Workplace, edited by Clair Brown and Joseph A. Pechman, pp. 189-216. Washington, D.C.: Brookings Institution, 1987.

Gallup Report 256-257 (1987): 18.

Glenn, Norval D. "Continuity Versus Change, Sanguineness Versus Concern: Views of the American Family in the Late 1980s." Journal of Family Issues 8 (1987): 348-354.

------. "Social Trends in the United States: Evidence from Sample Surveys." Public Opinion Quarterly 51 (1987): S109-S126.

Gurin, Patricia. "Women's Gender Consciousness." Public Opinion Quarterly 49 (1985): 143-163.

Hofferth, Sandra L. and Deborah A. Phillips. "Child Care in the United States, 1970 to 1995." Journal of Marriage and the Family 49 (1987): 559-571.

Jones, Jo Ann and Rachel A. Rosenfeld. "Women's Occupations and Local Labor Markets: 1950 to 1980." Social Forces 67 (1989): 66-692.

Koziara, Karen Shallcross, Michael H. Moskow, and Lucretia Dewey Tanner. Working Women: Past, Present, Future. Washington, D.C.: Bureau of National Affairs, 1987.

Lipman-Blumen, Jean and Ann. R. Tickamyer. "Sex Roles in Transition: A Ten-Year Perspective." Annual Review of Sociology 1 (1975): 297-337.

Mazur, Allan. "U.S. Trends in Feminine Beauty and Overadaptation." Journal of Sex Research 22 (1986): 281-303.

"Opinion Roundup." Public Opinion (August/September 1984): 36.

Robey, Bryant Robey and Cheryl Russell. "How Consumers Spend." American Demographics 5 (1983): 17-21.

Seaver, Judith W. and Carol A. Cartwright. Child Care Administration. Belmont, CA: Wadsworth, 1986.

Select Committee on Children, Youth, and Families, U.S. House of Representatives, 100th Congress. U.S. Children and Their Families: Current Conditions and Recent Trends, 1987. Washington, D.C.: USGPO, 1987.

Sokoloff, Natalie J. "Evaluating Gains and Losses by Black and White Women and Men in the Professions, 1960-1980." Social Problems 35 (1988): 36-53.

Sorensen, Annemette and Sara McLanahan. "Married Women's Economic Dependency, 1940-1980." American Journal of Sociology 93 (1987): 659-687.

Taeuber, Cynthia M. and Victor Valdisera. Women in the American Economy. U.S. Bureau of the Census, Current Population Reports, Series P-23, No. 146. Washington, D.C.: USGPO, 1986.

Taylor, Patricia A., Patricia A. Gwartney-Gibbs, and Reynolds Farley. "Changes in the Structure of Earnings Inequality by Race, Sex, and Industrial Sector, 1960-1980." In Research in Social Stratification and Mobility: A Research Annual, Vol. 5, 1986 edited by Robert V. Robinson, pp. 105-138. Greenwich, Conn.: JAI Press, 1986.

Thornton, Arland and Deborah Freedman. "Changes in the Sex Role Attitudes of Women, 1962-1977: Evidence from a Panel Study." American Sociological Review 44 (1979): 831-842.

------. "Changing Attitudes Toward Marriage and Single Life." Family Planning Perspectives 14 (1982): 297-303.

Treiman, Donald and K. Terrell. "Women, Work, and Wages--Trends in the Female Occupational Structure Since 1940." In Social Indicator Models, edited by Kenneth Land and Seymour Spilerman, pp. 157-199. New York: Russell Sage Foundation, 1975.

U.S. Bureau of the Census. Statistical Abstract of the United States, 1989. Washington, D.C., 1989. Annual. Previous years as cited.

Wattenberg. Ben J. "Madison Avenue's Audience: Interview with Rena Bartos." Public Opinion (August/September, 1984): 19-20, 59.

Wilkins, Shirley and Thomas A. W. Miller. "Working Women: How It's Working Out." Public Opinion (October/November, 1985): 448.

Table 1. THE DECLINE IN MOTHERING: PERCENTAGES OF MARRIED
          COUPLES AND FEMALE HOUSEHOLDERS HAVING NO CHILDREN
          OF THEIR OWN UNDER AGE 18 PRESENT IN THE HOUSEHOLD,
          1951-1986 (1000s, except percent)

Year	Total Families (N)	% with no child	Married Couples (N)	% with no child	Female Householders (N)	% with no child
1951	39822	43%	34556	41%	4040	46%
1955	41934	41	36395	40	4225	44
1960	45062	40	39335	39	4494	43
1965	47836	41	41648	40	5006	42
1970	51237	44	44436	43	5580	48
1975	55712	46	46971	46	7242	39
1980	58426	48	48180	49	8540	38
1984	61997	50	50090	51	9878	40
1986	63558	50	50933	52	10211	40
1987	64491	50	51537	52	10445	40

SOURCE: Statistical Abstract 1989, p. 50; 1988, p. 48; 1986, p.
    44; 1981, p. 47; 1976, p. 43; 1971, p. 39; 1966, p. 37;
    1961, p. 39; 1956, p. 48; 1952, p. 46.

Table 2.   CHILD CARE ARRANGEMENTS FOR CHILDREN UNDER FIVE
             WHO HAVE EMPLOYED MOTHERS, 1958-1985

Usual Weekly Child-Care Arrangement	1958	1965	1977	1982	1985
Mother employed full-time					
Care in child's home	57%	47%	29%	27%	24%
By father	15	10	11	11	11
Other	42	37	18	16	13
Care in another home	27	37	47	46	42
By relative	14	18	21	21	15
Other	13	20	27	25	27
Group care center	4	8	15	20	28
Other arrangements	12	7	9	7	5
Mother employed part-time					
Care in child's home	--	47	43	41	42
By father	--	23	23	21	24
Other	--	24	20	20	18
Care in another home	--	17	29	36	28
By relative	--	9	13	16	15
Other	--	8	16	19	14
Group care center	--	3	9	8	15
Other arrangements	--	33	19	15	15

SOURCE: Based on Select Committee on Children, Youth, and
    Families, 1987; <u>Statistical Abstract 1989</u>, p. 370.

Table 3. PERCENTAGE OF RESPONDENTS AGREEING WITH SELECTED
          STATEMENTS ABOUT MOTHERING AND CHILD-REARING,
          1962-1986

Item	1962	1972	1974	1977	1980	1983	1985
1. The ideal number of children for a family is three or more	--	50%	44%	42%	--	39%	36%
2. The most satisfying and interesting life [comes from] combining marriage, career, & children	--	--	52	--	--	--	63
3. If free to do either, would prefer to stay home and take care of house and family	--	--	63	--	53%	48	--
4. By nature women are happiest when they are making a home & caring for children (Strongly <u>disagreed</u>)	--	12	--	--	--	26	--
5. It's perfectly all right for women to be very active in clubs, politics, & other outside activities before the children are grown up	42%	--	--	60	--	--	--

SOURCE: Based on the following:
   1.   Glenn, 1987, p. S120, respondents are all adults.
   2.   Wilkins and Miller, 1985, p. 45, respondents are women.
   3.   Opinion Roundup, 1984, p. 36, respondents are women.
   4.   Gurin, 1985, p. 155, respondents are women.
   5.   Thornton and Freedman, 1979, p. 833, respondents are
        newly married women and mothers, Detroit metropolitan
        area.

Table 4.   YEARS OF SCHOOL COMPLETED, BY SEX, FOR WHITES AGE 25
           AND OVER, 1940-1960

| Year and Sex | Years of School Completed | | | | | | | Total | Median |
| | Elementary | | | High school | | College | | | |
	0-4	5-7	8	1-3	4+	1-3	4+		
1940									
Men	12%	18%	31%	15%	13%	5%	6%	100%	8.7
Women	10	17	29	16	18	6	4	100	8.8
1950									
Men	9	16	22	17	19	7	8	99	9.3
Women	8	14	21	18	25	8	5	99	10.1
1960									
Men	7	14	19	19	22	9	10	100	10.7
Women	6	12	18	20	29	9	6	100	11.2
1970									
Men	5	10	13	18	29	11	14	100	12.1
Women	4	9	13	19	36	11	8	100	12.1
1980									
Men	3	6	8	14	32	16	21	100	12.5
Women	2	6	8	16	39	16	13	100	12.6
1987									
Men	2	4	6	11	36	17	24	100	12.8
Women	2	4	6	11	43	17	17	100	12.6

SOURCE: Based on <u>Statistical Abstract 1989</u>, p. 131; <u>1988</u>, p.
          125; <u>1967</u>, p. 114.

Table 5.   EARNED DEGREES CONFERRED, BY LEVEL OF DEGREE AND SEX OF
           RECIPIENT, 1950-1986 (1000s, except percent)

Year	Total No.%	Male	Bachelor's No.%	Male	Master's No.%	Male	Doctorates No.%	Male
1950	499	76%	434	76%	58	71%	7	91%
1955	354	65	288	64	58	67	9	91
1960	479	66	395	65	75	68	10	90
1965	668	62	539	59	112	68	16	89
1970	1073	60	833	58	209	60	30	87
1975	1316	57	988	56	294	55	34	79
1980	1330	53	999	53	298	51	33	70
1985	1374	51	1055	51	286	50	33	66
1986	1384	51	1062	50	289	50	34	65

SOURCE: Based on <u>Statistical Abstract 1989</u>, p. 156; <u>1988</u>, p. 149.

Table 6. EMPLOYED CIVILIANS BY OCCUPATION AND SEX, 1950-1982

Occupation	1950	1956	1960	1965	1970	1975	1980	1982
Professional, technical	13%	11%	12%	13%	15%	16%	17%	18%
Managers & admin's	4	5	5	4	4	5	7	7
Sales workers	9	7	8	7	7	7	7	7
Clerical workers	28	30	30	31	35	35	35	34
Craft & kindred workers	1	1	1	1	1	2	2	2
Operatives, exc. transport	20	18	15	15	14	11	10	9
Transport equip. operatives	--*	--*	--*	--*	--*	1	1	1
Nonfarm laborers	1	--*	--*	--*	1	1	1	1
Private household workers	9	10	10	9	5	3	2	2
Other service workers	12	13	15	15	16	18	17	17
Farmers & farm mgrs.	1	1	1	1	--*	--*	--*	--*
Farm laborers & supervisors	3	4	4	3	2	1	1	1
Total	100	100	101	99	100	100	100	99
Total (N)**	15437	20272	22196	25145	29667	33553	41283	43256

* Included in the above operatives category.
** 1000s; the total for 1950 does not include persons in the "occupation not reported" category.

NOTE: 1950 figures are from the U.S. census of population; the 1956 figures are for April; the others are all annual averages.

SOURCE: Based on <u>Statistical Abstract 1956</u>, p. 208; <u>Employment and Earnings</u>, 1961, p. xv; 1966, p. 77; 1971, p. 127; 1976, p. 147; 1982, p. 164; 1983, p. 157.

Table 7. EMPLOYED CIVILIANS BY OCCUPATION (NEW CATEGORIES)
          AND SEX, AND FEMALE/MALE RATIOS*, 1982-1988

				Female/Male Ratios*		
Occupation	1982	1985	1988	1982	1985	1988
Executive, administrative						
& managerial	7%	9%	11%	.6	.7	.8
Professional						
speciality	14	14	14	1.2	1.2	1.2
Technicians &						
related support	3	3	3	1.1	1.1	1.1
Sales						
occupations	12	13	13	1.1	1.2	1.2
Administrative support						
including clerical	31	29	28	5.3	5.2	5.0
Private						
household	2	2	2	23.0	20.0	17.0
Protective						
service	--	1	1	.2	.2	.2
Service, exc. private						
hshld. & protective	16	16	16	2.4	2.3	2.3
Precision production,						
craft, & repair	2	2	2	.1	.1	.1
Machine operators,						
assemblers, inspectors	8	7	6	.9	.9	.8
Transportation &						
material moving	1	1	1	.1	.1	.1
Handlers, cleaners,						
helpers & laborers	2	2	2	.3	.3	.3
Farming, forestry,						
& fishing	1	1	1	.3	.2	.2
Total	100	100	100	--	--	--
Total (N)	43256	47259	51696	--	--	--

* Computed by dividing the percentage of employed females in each
category by the percentage of employed males in that category.

SOURCE: Based on <u>Employment and Earnings</u>, 1984, p. 177; 1986, p.
        174; 1989, p. 182.

Table 8. RATIOS OF PERCENTAGE EMPLOYED FEMALES TO PERCENTAGE
          EMPLOYED MALES IN OCCUPATIONAL CATEGORIES, EMPLOYED
          CIVILIANS, 1950-1982

Occupation	1950	1956	1960	1965	1970	1975	1980	1982
Professional, technical	1.7	1.2	1.1	1.1	1.0	1.1	1.1	1.1
Managers & admin's	.4	.4	.4	.3	.3	.4	.5	.5
Sales workers	1.3	1.3	1.2	1.2	1.2	1.1	1.1	1.1
Clerical workers	4.3	4.4	4.2	4.5	4.9	5.4	5.5	5.5
Craft & kindred workers	.1	.1	.1	.1	.1	.1	.1	.1
Operatives, exc. transport	1.0	.8	.8	1.0	.7	.9	.9	.9
Transport equip. operatives	--	--	--	.0	.1	.1	.1	.1
Nonfarm laborers	.1	.1	.0	.1	.1	.1	.2	.2
Private household workers	43.0	104.0	98.0	87.0	51.0	34.0	25.0	23.0
Other service workers	2.1	2.1	2.3	2.2	2.5	2.1	2.0	1.9
Farmers & farm mgrs.	.1	.1	.1	.1	.1	.1	.2	.2
Farm laborers & supervisors	.6	1.2	1.0	.9	.8	.6	.5	.4
Total (N)**	15437	20272	22196	25145	29667	33553	41283	43256

NOTE: The female/male ratios above are comparisons of the
percentage of all female workers in a given occupation with the
percentage of all male workers in that same occupation. They do not
reflect the sex composition of the workforce in a given occupation
in any way, but rather the degree to which men are women are under-
(ratios below 1.0) or over-represented in the ocupations.

SOURCE: Based on Statistical Abstract 1956, p. 208; Employment and
    Earnings, 1961, p. xv; 1966, p. 77; 1971, p. 127; 1976, p.
    147; 1982, p. 164; 1983, p. 157.

Table 9. MEDIAN ANNUAL AND USUAL WEEKLY EARNINGS OF FULL-TIME
          WOMEN WORKERS AS PERCENT OF MEN'S EARNINGS, 1955-1987

| | Percent of Median for Male Workers | |
Year	Women's Annual Earnings*	Women's Weekly Earnings**
1955	64%	--%
1960	61	--
1965	60	--
1970	59	62
1973	--	62
1975	59	62
1976	60	62
1977	59	62
1978	60	61
1979	60	62
1980	60	63
1981	59	65
1982	62	65
1983	64	67
1984	64	68
1985	--	68
1986	--	69
1987	--	70

* Year-round, full-time workers only.

** Includes all full-time workers, regardless of weeks worked; excludes income from self-employment.

SOURCE: Based on Koziara and Tanner, 1987, p. 43; Statistical Abstract 1989, p. 406; 1979, p. 420.

Table 10. WOMEN'S REPRESENTATION AMONG TOP WEALTHHOLDERS, 1953–
1982 (1000s, except percent)

Year	Top Wealthholders*		Percent Women
	Total	Women	
1953	1979	648	33%
1958	3009	1073	36
1962	4132	1594	39
1969	9013	3370	37
1972	12815	5006	39
1976	8695	2913	34
1982	4378	1719	39

* Gross assets of $60,000 or more, 1953-1972; over $120,000, 1976; and $300,000 or more, 1982.

SOURCE: Based on <u>Statistical Abstract 1988</u>, p. 438; <u>1984</u>, p. 479.

Table 11. SELECTED INDICATORS OF WOMEN'S SOCIAL AND POLITICAL
POWER: REPRESENTATION IN LABOR UNIONS AND AMONG
SCIENTISTS AND ENGINEERS, LAWYERS, AND IN STATE
LEGISLATURES AND THE U.S. CONGRESS, 1951-1987

	Representation of Women (percent) among:			Legislators	
Year	Members of Labor Unions	Scientists & Engineers	Lawyers	State	National
1951			2%		
1954			2		
1956	18%		--		
1957	--		3		3%
1960	18		3		--
1961	--		--		3
1963	--		3		--
1966	19		3		--
1967	--		--		2
1968	19		--		--
1969	--		--		2
1970	21		3		--
1971	--		--		2
1972	22		--		--
1973	24		--		3
1974	--	9%	--	--	--
1975	--	--	--	8%	4
1976	--	9	--	--	--
1977	--	--	--	9	3
1978	--	--	--	--	--
1979	--	--	--	10	3
1980	31	12	8	10	--
1981	--	--	--	12	4
1982	--	--	--	12	--
1983	35	--	--	13	4
1984	36	13	--	13	--
1985	--	--	13	15	5
1986	--	15	--	15	--
1987	35	--	--	16	5

SOURCE: Based on Freeman and Leonard, 1987, p. 191; Statistical
Abstract 1989, p.416; 1988, pp. 170, 244, 248, 562; 1980, p.
628; 1979, pp. 509, 513; 1974, pp. 365, 433; 1967, p. 160.

Table 12. ATTITUDES ABOUT MARRIAGE, WORK, AND WOMEN'S ROLES, 1957-1988

Attitude	1957	1972	1976/77*	1982	1985	1988
Negative toward a person who does not want to marry**	53%	--	34%	--	--	--
Affirm that marriage makes one's life better**	43	--	30	--	--	--
Agree that women should take care of running their homes and leave running the the country to men	--	--	38	27%	26%	20%
Disapprove of married woman earning money in business or industry if she has a husband who can support her	--	35%	34	25	14	19

* 1976 for the first two items above, 1977 for the last two.

** The items read, "Suppose all you knew about a man [male respondents]/woman [female respondents] was that he/she did not want to get married. What would you guess he/she was like?" and "Thinking about a man's [male respondents]/woman's [female respondents] life, how is a man's/woman's life changed by being married? Responses could be positive, negative, or neutral.

SOURCE: Based on Thornton and Freedman, 1982, p. 299; Glenn, 1987, p. 46; and Davis and Smith, 1988, p. 230.

Table 13. ATTITUDES ABOUT WOMEN'S WORK STATUS AND SOCIAL
          OPPORTUNITIES, BY SEX, 1970-1987

Attitude	1970	1972	1975	1980	1983	1985	1987
Favor efforts to raise women's status							
Men	44%	49%	--%	64%	--%	69%	--%
Women	40	48	--	64	--	73	--
Strongly agree that many qualified women can't get good jobs							
Women	--	41	--	--	52	--	--
Said women have too little power relative to men							
Women	--	--	45*	--	57	--	--
Reject the "natural endowments" explanation of men's social dominance							
Women	--	36	--	--	55	--	--
Agreed women have equal job opportunities							
Men	--	--	46	--	--	--	48
Women	--	--	49	--	--	--	35
Agreed women have equal chance for executive opportunities							
Men	--	--	43	--	--	--	50
Women	--	--	37	--	--	--	46
Have no preference for either sex as a boss							
Men	--	--	32	--	--	--	57
Women	--	--	27	--	--	--	39
Would prefer to work for a man							
Men	--	--	63	--	--	--	29
Women	--	--	60	--	--	--	37

* 1976

SOURCE: Based on <u>Gallup Report</u>, 1987, p. 18; Wilkins and Miller, 1985, p. 45; Gurin, 1985, p. 155.

There are definite signs that a modest upturn in fertility (particularly at older ages) has reversed a long and very substantial downswing that began in the late 1950s. At that date, a surprising upward movement of fertility--the "baby boom"--dating from before World War II and, more prominently, from about 1950--had seemingly overcome a marked secular downward trend in fertility of over a century's standing. Nowadays, the "baby boom" is commonly seen as a temporary deviation from a longterm trend toward lessened fertility, a trend that may be seen as having resumed thereafter. Alternatively, at least the post-1960s portion of the fertility decline is sometimes seen as a turning away from "traditional" and toward "new" or "elective" family forms, an interpretation to which the relative increase in nonmarital fertility gives credence. Nonmarital fertility, however, increasingly characterizes the nonwhite population, rather than becoming a generally practiced arrangement.

Two measures among the many available suffice to describe these trends in fertility, the Gross Reproduction Rate and the Age-Specific birth rate (Tables 1 and 2), both period rates rather than cohort rates. The Gross Reproduction Rate combines current age-specfic birth rates to estimate the average number of daughters who would be born to a woman who survived her entire fertile period. This measure peaked in 1957, at a level that implied about one and three-quarters daughters per woman, an increase of over one-half a daughter since the end of the war. This rate, having increased gradually, declined gradually thereafter, the rate of decline being its most rapid through the latter 1960s and into the early 1970s. Much the same rise and decline that white women experienced was also experienced by nonwhite women.

The age-specific sources of the baby boom can be found among mothers of modal ages--most especially their 20s. The post-baby boom decline, however, while participated in by women of all ages, was especially prominent in the fertility record of older women, until the rapid downturn at the end of the 1960s, when most decline was the product of behaviors of women 18-24 (presumably because of the upward movement of the median age at marriage), although there continued to be a retreat from fertility among the oldest mothers as well. The recent reversal is so modest that we cannot with much security locate it in any particular part of the age spectrum, although scattered evidence indicates that the age-specific fertility schedule has shifted later in the fertile years.

The baby boom was accomplished without any substantial increase in the numbers of completed families larger than four children. Rather, childlessness was nearly banished, becoming almost as rare as it had been in the nineteenth century. The modal number of children shifted upward toward three from two.

Completed fertility of women still in the fertile ages cannot, of course, be measured, and so discussion of post-baby-boom family-size trends must be extrapolated from period-based counts of births by birth order. We find, in examining data of this sort, that the trend away from large families continued quite markedly and consistently, with parity-specific birth rates declining quite generally as the baby boom faded, except for first children. In the first phase of the post-baby-boom retreat from parenthood, fertility rates were marginally the most reduced at the parities that had been the most associated with the universal, medium-size families of the baby boom. In the sharp, brief "baby bust" of the early 1970s, all parities shared in the trend.

Thereafter, very large families became even more rare, although most of modest increase in 1970s fertility was explained by first and second births.

Part of the significance of out-of-wedlock fertility derives from the proportion of all births in a given year that it provides, and part from its absolute incidence among unmarried women. Because both age-specific proportions married and age-specific marital fertility have varied greatly since World War II, illegitimacy as a phenomenon is tricky to interpret.

Overall illegitimacy rates per unmarried woman increased sharply from the end of the war to the mid-1960s, when the rate of increase declined, leveling off after 1970, until the end of the decade, after which it began to rise once again (Table 3). (Improved fertility-control mechanisms, including abortion, rather than a reduction in premarital sexual exposure was probably the reason for the temporary decline.) Because, however, the marital fertility rate declined quite sharply after the late 1950s, the proportion of all births that were illegitimate (Table 4) continued to increase throughout this entire period, and quite dramatically (Vinovskis 1988).

Moreover, both the rate of out-of-wedlock fertility and the ratio of such births to all births were considerably higher and growing more quickly among the black population than among the whites. In part, black illegitimacy ratios rose rapidly because the decline in marital fertilty was sharpest among black women. Furthermore, because most unmarried women are young, because illegitimacy rates among the sexually active unmarried are higher among the young, and because rates of premarital sexual activity were increasing, at least toward the end of this period (and especially among young black women), the whole set came to be seen by many observers as syndromatically related to the "tangle of pathology" of the ghetto black family.

Particularly striking from the standpoint of the argument that maintains that the black trends indicate the formation of a distinctive and self-reproducing family system are figures on subsequent legitimation by marriage. It is apparent from the data compiled by O'Connell and Moore (1980) that in fact young women became rapidly more unlikely, both absolutely and especially relative to opportunities, to legitimate premaritally-born children. In the early postwar period, perhaps two in five black women aged 20-24 who became pregnant before marriage and eventually bore the children, legitimated them by marriage, as did about two in three white women at that age and in the same situation. By the end of the 1970s, however, a majority of premaritally pregnant white women aged 20-24 who eventually gave birth did so as married women, while this proportion declined to fewer than one in four among black women. This racial disparity is part of the evidence offered in support of the notion that there are now at least two widely-held and divergent ideologies concerning the relationship of childbirth and marriage in the United States.

References

O'Connell, Martin and Maurice J. Moore. "The Legitimacy Status of First Births to U.S. Women Aged 15-24, 1939-1978." Family Planning Perspectives 12 (January/February 1980): 18-19.

U.S. Bureau of the Census. Historical Statistics of the United States, I. Washington, D.C.: USGPO, 1975.

U.S. National Center for Health Statistics, Vital Statistics of the United States 1986, Volume I--Natality. Rockville, MD, 1986.

Vinovskis, Maris. An "Epidemic" of Adolescent Pregnancy. Historical and Policy Considerations. New York: Oxford University Press, 1988.

Table 1.   GROSS REPRODUCTION RATE*, U.S. WOMEN, 1945-1986

Year	All	White	Nonwhite
1945	1212	1175	1493
1950	1505	1446	1940
1955	1745	1675	2255
1960	1783	1720	2241
1965	1428	1357	1919
1970	1207	1158	1509
1975	864	819	1120
1980	896	850	1143
1981	885	839	1120
1982	892	848	1112
1983	879	835	1095
1984	880	836	1093
1985	898	853	1112
1986	895	848	1118

*The gross reproduction rate represents the number of daughters that a hypothetical cohort of women born on the same date would bear if they all survived from birth through the childbearing period and they all experienced the age-specific fertility rate current in the year given in the left stub. The figures for 1945-55 represent births adjusted for underregistration.

SOURCE: Based on National Center for Health Statistics, 1988, p. 4.

Table 2. AGE-SPECIFIC BIRTH RATES FOR WOMEN AGED 15-44, 1945-1986

Year	15-19	20-24	25-29	30-34	35-39	40-44
1945	51.1	138.9	132.2	100.2	56.9	16.6
1950	81.6	196.8	166.1	103.7	52.9	15.1
1955	90.3	241.6	190.2	116.0	58.6	16.1
1960	89.1	258.1	197.4	112.7	56.2	15.5
1965	70.5	195.3	161.6	94.4	46.2	12.8
1970	68.3	167.8	145.1	73.3	31.7	8.1
1975	55.6	110.3	106.3	53.6	19.5	4.6
1980	53.0	115.1	112.9	61.9	19.8	3.9
1981	52.7	111.8	112.0	61.4	20.0	3.8
1982	52.9	111.3	111.0	64.2	21.1	3.9
1983	51.7	108.3	108.7	64.6	22.1	3.8
1984	50.9	107.3	108.3	66.5	22.8	3.9
1985	51.3	108.9	110.5	68.5	23.9	4.0
1986	50.6	108.2	109.2	69.3	24.3	4.1

SOURCE: Based on National Center for Health Statistics, 1988, p. 6.

Table 3.   BIRTH RATES FOR UNMARRIED WOMEN AGED 15-44, BY RACE,
           1950-1986

Year	All	White	Nonwhite	Black
1950	14.1	6.1	71.2	--
1955	19.3	7.9	87.2	--
1960	21.6	9.2	98.3	--
1965	23.4	11.6	97.4	--
1970	26.4	13.9	89.9	95.5
1975	24.5	12.4	79.0	84.2
1980	29.4	17.6	77.2	82.9
1981	29.6	18.2	75.4	81.4
1982	30.0	18.8	73.9	79.6
1983	30.4	19.3	72.3	77.7
1984	31.0	20.1	71.4	76.8
1985	32.0	21.8	73.2	78.8
1986	34.3	23.2	74.8	80.9

NOTE: Rates for 1950-1979 are estimated.

SOURCE: Based on National Center for Health Statistics, 1988, p.
        54-55.

Table 4. RATES OF OUT-OF-WEDLOCK BIRTHS, BY RACE, 1945-1986

	Births to Unmarried Women, per 1000 Total Births		
Year	All Births	Births to White Women	Births to Black Women
1945	42.9	23.6	--
1950	39.8	17.5	--
1955	45.3	18.6	--
1960	52.7	22.9	--
1965	77.4	39.5	--
1970	106.9	56.6	375.8
1975	152.5	73.0	487.9
1980	184.3	110.4	552.5
1981	189.2	115.9	559.5
1982	194.3	120.7	566.8
1983	202.8	127.7	582.0
1984	210.0	134.1	592.3
1985	220.2	144.7	601.3
1986	233.7	157.1	612.1

NOTE: Rates for 1945-1979 are estimated.

SOURCE: Based on National Center for Health Statistics, 1988, p. 53.

American society has long shown a very strong commitment to marriage. Nearly universal and relatively early marriage have long characterized the population. During the period under study, age at marriage declined, then advanced. There is mixed evidence suggesting that if marriage is not being questioned as a valued institution, it is being supplemented by nonmarital cohabitation, even as a context for childbearing. The marital institution has been modified substantially in one regard: in the incorporation of divorce as a normatively-acceptable mode of transition from one marriage to another.

Most Americans eventually marry. Lifelong singleness has been relatively infrequent, even during periods like the 1930s when patterns of lifelong childlessness became fairly common (Cherlin, 1981; Modell, 1985). Even though marriage has come to be considerably postponed, Americans have continued to marry sooner or later. As late as 1987, only about one in 20 American men and women, age 65 or older, had never married.

In fact, the propensity to marry at some time has increased over the past four decades. For example, among persons 55-64 years of age, the proportion of the male population never married dropped from 8.4% to 4.2% between 1950 and 1983, and there was a similar decline among females (from 7.9% to 4.4%) (U.S. Bureau of the Census, Current Population Survey, Series P-20).

However, the fact that persons now aged 55 and over are somewhat more likely to have married than their predecessors does not necessarily mean that the same high proportion of today's young adults will eventually marry. Since 1970, there has been a marked increase in single living. Between 1970 and 1987, the percentage of never-married men aged 25-29 more than doubled, rising from 19% to 42%; among women, it tripled, from 10% to 29%. The next older cohort experienced a similar reduction in proportion married (Table 1). While some of the change is due to postponement of marriage, some undoubtedly reflects a decreasing propensity to marry at all, and it appears that the proportion of the U.S. population who live their entire lives without marrying is likely to double, rising from the historical 5-6% to 10-12% or more.

The shift to increased proportions of single persons in the adult population is even more pronounced among blacks. Between 1970 and 1987 the proportion of the total adult population never-married increased from 16% to 22%, but among blacks, it increased from 21% to 32% (Statistical Abstract 1989, pp. 42-43).

Average age at first marriage remained fairly stable between 1950 and 1965, at about age 23 for men and 20 for women. After 1965, women's age at marriage began to increase, and for the next 20 years it continued to rise. The increase for men began a little later, in 1970, and has likewise continued ever since. However, higher age at marriage does not necessarily mean that Americans have backed away from marriage in any definitive sense; delaying marriage does not mean avoiding it. The marriage rate has increased almost every year since the late 1950s, with the exception of the mid-1970s: number of marriages per 1,000 population reached a peak in 1972, declined until 1977 (when it was still considerably higher than at the end of the 1950s), and then began to rise again.

There have been substantial changes in the social significance of marriage. Increasingly, the population has included people particularly prone to marriage because they were themselves recently divorced (Table 3). Thus we find that at the same time that overall marriage rates were, by and large, increasing, the likelihood of first marriages occurring to unmarried women of the ages usually defined as the most marriageable was rapidly declining--doing so, in fact, every year from 1969 to 1983. In 1983, the rate of marriage to unmarried women 15-44 years of age was only five-eighths as high as at the postwar peak (even excepting the immediate marriage bulge shortly after the war) of 1956.

In 1970, 57% of marriages contracted were by women marrying for the first time, compared to about 75% in 1960. By 1983 the proportion of all marriages that were first marriages had dropped slightly below half. The women most rapidly withdrawing from (or avoiding) marriage were younger women, and included both the previously unmarried and the divorced. In the older ages, far less affected by the reduction in marriage propensities, divorced women were increasingly represented among the unmarried. By the early 1980s marriage was making a modest recovery, and that recovery was located mainly among women age 25 and over rather than the younger women.

The trend in the American divorce rate since World War II has included two components. The first of these is a strong underlying tendency toward increased divorce; this trend can be found since the middle of the nineteenth century (Preston and McDonald, 1979; Cherlin, 1981). Overlying this tendency, however, have been shorter-term tendencies, responding to economically-induced stress, the difficulties of maintaining marriages during war and other disturbing external events, and, it seems, attitudinal currents regarding the morality of divorce itself. Thus, the spike of extremely high divorce rates with which our period opens (1945) was within five years succeeded by gradually declining divorce rates, and it was not until the mid-1960s that the divorce rate turned upward again. When it did so, it did so sharply, continuing until the late 1970s, when it leveled off and declined slightly (Table 4).

In view of the sizable annual fluctuations around the century-long upward secular trend in divorce, it may make sense to examine instead divorce probabilities by date of marriage, a proposal made by Preston and McDonald (1979). Such a procedure smooths out the fluctuations, and makes the upward trend more easily describable. Marriages contracted in the 1950s are found to have been more durable than might be expected from the rising divorce trend, and marriages contracted from the mid-1960s on are found to have been somewhat more fragile than expected. Remarriages seem to have been approximately as subject to divorce as initial marriages.

There appears to have been little change in the point of marriage at which divorces occur (Plateris, 1981). Since the end of World War II, the median duration of marriages broken by divorce has varied between 5.8 and 7.5 years, with maximum durations occurring in the low-divorce 1950s and again in recent years.

On the whole, the statistical evidence suggests a finding of no change in the duration of marriages ending in divorce, even though the secular increase in divorce points to an increasing willingness to dissolve marriages. On the whole, the increasing divorce rates suggest a relatively unproblematic incorporation of divorce and divorced people within the marriage system, as first marriages are increasingly seen as temporary.

One indication of this is the increased percentage of marriages with children that end in divorce, despite the also increasing proportion of all marriages that are childless. Another indication is the high rate of remarriage. Even more directly to the point is the growing proportion of divorced persons who marry single, never-married persons in their second or subsequent unions. In the 1950s and 1960s divorce carried a heavy stigma; it hardly does any longer.

Good national trend data on the frequency of concubinage, or even on extramarital sex relations is unavailable (cf. Chapter 13.7, Forms of Erotic Expression). However, there are data on people's definitions of how acceptable such behavior is. The General Social Survey began in 1973 to include the following question: "What is your opinion about a married person having sexual relations with someone other than the marriage partner? Is it always wrong, almost always wrong, wrong only sometimes, or not wrong at all?" The distribution of responses shows no change, 1973-1988: Between 70% and 75% say extramarital sex is "always wrong" and an additional 15% say it is "almost always wrong" (Smith, 1980; Davis and Smith, 1988).

Two time series, based on large and carefully drawn samples of young people, indicate that sometime around the mid-1970s affirmation of cohabitation as a value reached a peak and declined thereafter, having fallen short of becoming normative. In the first, assent to an item asking college freshmen for their response to cohabitation as an experimental period, posed positively toward the notion that a couple should live together for some time before deciding to get married, peaked at 43% for girls in 1976 and 55% for boys in 1977, and then declined (Bayer, 1981). The second time series is based on an annual survey of high school seniors (Herzog and Bachman, 1982). The first question posed cohabitation as a prior supplement to marriage ("it is usually a good idea"), while the second posed it as an arrangement rightly precluded by marriage ("fuller and happier lives" were based on legal marriage "rather than staying single or just living with someone"). Between 1976 and 1980, male students gradually withdrew their assent to cohabitation as a supplement to marriage, and female students were increasingly likely to agree that marriage ought to preclude prior cohabitation. The survey also offered an item that hypothetically rejected monogamy, because "having a close intimate relationship is too restrictive for the average person." Fewer than a quarter of the students accepted this notion. In other words, monogamy was not at issue among a majority of young people in the mid-1970s. Still, nonmarital cohabitation has increased considerably. Between 1970 and 1987, the number of unmarried couples living together increased fourfold. By 1987 there were 2.5 million such households, or 2.6% of all households (Table 5).

Although marriage continues to be a dominant and vital institution, there are also signs of what Kingsley Davis (1985) calls "declining marital output"--for instance, the reduced relationship of marriage and child-bearing and child-rearing.

Between 1970 and 1985, the proportion of family households with a child under 18 that were headed by both husband and wife declined sharply, from 89% to 78%. That is, the proportion of all families with children that deviated from the two-parent norm in existence, at least, in 1970, had more than doubled. Demographically, the whole explanation is the simultaneous increase in childbirth outside of marriage and of divorce among couples with children.

Tabulations based on longitudinal data gathered from a fairly large, representative national survey of households (Table 6) permit us to estimate the proportion of their lifetimes that children from successive birth cohorts spent in households (families) of various types. White children born in 1950-54 spent on average 92% of their years with both parents, as compared to 82% of the white children born a decade later. This proportion is projected to decline far more sharply, based on experience to date, for white children born later. Black children, less likely than white children to live with both parents even in the 1950-54 birth cohort, experienced a more rapidly declining probability of life in two-parent households. Among those born 1965-69, who had not completed childhood at the time of the study, only slightly over half of childhood had been spent in a two-parent situation. When we limit the calculation to the experience of successive cohorts of children born into two-parent, first-married families, there is a similar downward trajectory--children spending less time in two-parent families--but a lower rate of decline such that the change between the 1950-54 and the 1961-69 cohort is only 7% (13% for blacks). It is these "modal" two-parent, first marriage families that best resisted the downward trend in two-parent experience for their children.

References

Bayer, Alan E. and Gerald W. McDonald. "Cohabitation Among Youth: Correlates of Support for a New American Ethic," unpublished paper, 1981.

Cherlin, Andrew J. Marriage, Divorce, Remarriage. Cambridge: Harvard University Press, 1981.

Davis, Kingsley. "The Future of Marriage". In Contemporary Marriage, edited by Kingsley Davis, pp. 25-52. New York: Russell Sage Foundation, 1985.

Davis, James Allan and Tom W. Smith. General Social Surveys, 1972-1988: Cumulative Codebook. Chicago: National Opinion Research Center, 1988. Annual. Previous years as cited.

Herzog, A. Regula and Jerald S. Bachman. Sex Role Attitudes Among High School Seniors. Research Report Series. Ann Arbor: Survey Research Center, University of Michigan, 1982.

Hofferth, Sandra L. "Updating Children's Life Course." Journal of Marriage and the Family 47 (1985): 93-115.

Modell, John. "Historical Reflections on American Marriage." In Contemporary Marriage, edited by Kingsley Davis, pp. 181-186. New York: Russell Sage Foundation, 1985.

Plateris, Alexander A. Duration of Marriage in the United States. National Center for Health Statistics, Vital and Health Statistics, Series 21, No. 38, 1981.

Preston, Samuel H. and John McDonald. "The Incidence of Divorce within Cohorts of American Marriages Contracted Since the Civil War." Demography 16 (1979): 1-25.

Smith, Tom W. A Compendium of Trends on General Social Survey Questions. Chicago: National Opinion Research Center, 1980.

Thornton, Arland W. "Cohabitation and Marriage in the 1980s". Demography 25 (1988): 497-508.

U. S. Bureau of the Census. Current Population Survey. Series P-20, 1988.

------. Statistical Abstract of the United States, 1989. Washington, D.C.: 1989. Annual. Previous years as cited.

U. S. National Center for Health Statistics, Vital Statistics of the United States 1975, Volume III--Marriage and Divorce. Rockville, MD, 1979.

Table 1. SINGLE (NEVER MARRIED) PERSONS, BY AGE AND SEX, 1970-
1987

Sex and Age	1970	1975	1980	1985	1987
Males, Age					
18-19	93%	93%	94%	97%	97%
20-24	55	60	69	76	78
25-29	19	22	33	39	42
30-34	9	11	16	21	23
35-39	7	9	8	10	12
40-44	6	7	7	9	7
45-54	7	6	6	6	6
55-64	8	6	5	6	6
65 and over	7	5	5	5	4
Total	19	21	24	25	25
Females, Age					
18-19	76	78	83	87	90
20-24	36	40	50	58	61
25-29	10	14	21	26	29
30-34	6	7	9	13	15
35-39	5	5	6	8	8
40-44	5	5	5	5	6
45-54	5	5	5	5	4
55-64	7	5	4	4	4
65 and over	8	6	6	5	5
Total	14	15	17	18	19

SOURCE: Based on Statistical Abstract 1989, p. 43.

Table 2. MEDIAN AGE AT FIRST MARRIAGE, 1950-1986

Year	Males	Females
1950	22.8	20.3
1955	22.6	20.2
1960	22.8	20.3
1965	22.8	20.6
1970	22.5	20.6
1975	22.7	20.8
1980	23.6	21.8
1983	24.4	22.5
1985	24.8	23.0
1986	25.7	23.1

SOURCE: Based on <u>Current Population Survey</u>, Series P-20, 1988, p. 6; <u>Statistical Abstract 1989</u>, p. 86, <u>1974</u>, p. 66.

Table 3. AGE-SPECIFIC FIRST MARRIAGE AND REMARRIAGE RATES OF
DIVORCEES

Year	First marriages Per 1000 Single Women of Age			Remarriages per 1000 Divorced Women of Age	
	18-19	20-24	25-44	14-24	25-44
1960	208.4	263.9	--	--	--
1965	166.9	237.3	96.4	512.3	176.3
1970	151.4	220.1	82.5	413.4	179.6
1975	115.0	143.8	81.7	319.6	158.6
1980	87.3	119.8	74.9	236.4	122.8
1981	80.7	110.0	79.3	282.2	129.1
1982	78.5	111.9	80.7	263.6	129.6
1983	72.6	106.9	79.2	250.1	126.0
1984	72.1	104.4	80.5	244.3	120.8

SOURCE: Based on <u>Statistical Abstract 1988</u>, p. 83; <u>1985</u>, p. 80.

Table 4. DIVORCE RATES, 1945-1985

	Divorces	
Year	Per 1000 Population	Per 1000 Married Women Age 15+
1945	3.5	14.4
1950	2.6	10.3
1955	2.3	9.3
1960	2.2	9.2
1965	2.5	10.6
1970	3.5	14.9
1975	4.8	20.3
1976	4.9	21.3
1977	5.0	21.1
1978	5.1	21.9
1979	5.3	22.8
1980	5.2	22.6
1981	5.3	22.6
1982	5.0	21.7
1983	4.9	21.3
1984	5.0	21.5
1985	5.0	21.7

SOURCE: Based on National Center for Health Statistics, 1976, pp. 2-5; Statistical Abstract 1989, p. 85; 1988, p. 83; 1987, p. 80.

Table 5.   UNMARRIED-COUPLE HOUSEHOLDS

Year	Unmarried Couple Households* (1000s)
1970	523
1977	957
1978	1137
1980	1589
1981	1808
1982	1863
1983	1891
1984	1988
1985	1983
1986	2220
1987	2334

*"Unmarried couples" are two unrelated adults of the opposite sex sharing the same household.

SOURCE: Based on Thornton, 1988, p. 501; <u>Statistical Abstract 1989</u>, p. 44; <u>1988</u>, p. 42; <u>1984</u>, p. 47; <u>1985</u>, p. 40.

Table 6. PROPORTION OF THEIR FIRST 18 YEARS CHILDREN SPENT WITH
          TWO PARENTS IN THE HOUSEHOLD, FOR ALL CHILDREN AND FOR
          CHILDREN BORN INTO FIRST-MARRIAGE HUSBAND-WIFE
          FAMILIES, BY BIRTH COHORT, 1950-1954 to 1965-1969,

| Children's | Birth Cohort | | | |
Characteristics	1950-54	1955-59	1960-64	1965-69
	Percent of Childhood in Two-Parent Households			
All children				
White	92%	89%	82%	81%
Black	78	71	61	56
Children of first marriage, husband-wife couples				
White	94	92	86	87
Black	90	84	76	77

SOURCE: Based on Hofferth, 1985, p. 107.

American women are increasingly employed outside the home; their labor force participation rates have more than doubled since 1940. The most striking increases are among marr:.:d women, especially those with young children. Most employed women work full-time. Their employment as unpaid workers in family enterprises has declined dramatically.

Labor Force Participation

The growing participation of women in the labor force has been called "perhaps the most important labor market development of the century" (Marshall and Paulin, 1987, p. 1). In fact, most of their movement into the labor force has occurred in the past half-century. In 1900, one woman in five was employed, and over the next 40 years, the percentage of women in the labor force increased only six percent, or less than two percent per decade (Marshall and Paulin, 1987, p. 8).

In 1940 just over one-fourth of U.S. women participated in the labor force. They made more dramatic gains in the next decade. During World War II over one-third of adult women were employed outside the home, and after the war many did not leave the workforce. By 1950, 31% were in the labor force, and by 1960, 35%. In the 1960s there was striking growth, almost one percent per year, such that by 1970, 43% of women were in the labor force. The trend since 1970 has been consistent annual increase at a lower rate. By 1980 the labor force participation rate of U.S. women stood at 51%, and in 1988 it was 56% (Table 1).

With respect to marital status, it has always been the single women who were most likely to work. In 1950, half of all single women were in the labor force; by 1986, two-thirds were. Until the late 1960s, divorced and widowed women participated more in the labor force than the married women, but in 1966 the rate for married women surpassed that of the widowed and divorced, and since then labor force participation of married women has continued to increase faster than that for the widowed and divorced. The percentage of all married women in the labor force increased to 41% in 1970, 51% in 1980, and 57% in 1988. The corresponding rates for widowed and divorced women were 36%, 41%, and 43%. Thus, while both single women and the widowed and divorced have also increased their labor force participation, the sharpest gains have been among married women, whose participation rates rose from 25% in 1950 to 57% in 1988 (Table 1).

In 1940, most working women were single, divorced, or widowed; by 1950, a majority were married women. Since the mid-1950s, the marital-status composition of the female labor force has stabilized. In other words, while labor force participation has almost doubled over the past 35 years, the relative "mix" of married, single, and divorced or separated women in the labor force has remained remarkably stable: in 1955, 59% of female labor force were married women, 25% were single, and 16% were divorced or widowed. In 1988, the percentages were once again 59, 25, and 16, respectively. In the interim, the proportion of married women in the female labor force had gradually risen to a peak of 64% in 1969, and over the next decade declined and stabilized at about 60% (Statistical Abstract 1989, p. 385; 1979, p. 400).

Black women have higher labor force participation rates than white women, but the differences are declining and convergence seems imminent. In 1955, 46% of black and 34% of white women were in the labor force. Over the next three decades labor force participation increased among both, but the rates of increase were higher for whites. By 1987, 58% of black women were in the labor force, but their advantage over white women had shrunk to only 2% (Table 2).

The most dramatic change in the composition of the female labor force is the increased participation in paid work by married women with young children. In 1950, only 12% of married women with children under age six were in the labor force. Between one-fourth and one-third of married women without preschool children worked, but the great majority of women with small children did not (see Table 3). Over the next 28 years, mothers of young children joined the labor force in record numbers. Their labor force participation rate doubled between 1950 and 1965, and doubled again between 1965 and 1985. By 1988, mothers with children under age six had a labor force participation rate of over 57%, a rate higher than that for American women generally. Some observers see the increased employment of mothers of young children as a key indicator of the extent to which women have been incorporated into the economy. Ben Wattenberg (1985, p. 183), for instance, argues that their striking gain in labor force participation "reveals the across-the-board nature of the march of women into the labor force. Today, clearly, the working woman is omnipresent in every demographic pigeonhole."

Work at Home, Paid and Unpaid

Attention to increased labor force participation captures only part of the change in women's work roles. Traditionally, much of women's work has been unpaid family work and work, paid or unpaid, done at home rather than in other settings. Brown and Pechman (1987, p. 1) argue that the dramatic shift in women's work roles is the change "from primarily unpaid work at home to a combination of paid market work and traditional unpaid work."

The U.S. government has only recently begun to collect data on work at home, but there are good data on changes in the number of unpaid family workers, wherever they happen to work. Table 4 traces the changes in the number and percentage of unpaid family workers among employed women generally for the period 1962-1988. The same consistent, substantial trend appears in the agricultural and nonagricultural industries: a long-term decline in the number of women who are unpaid family workers.

In the quarter-century summarized in Table 4, the number of unpaid family workers among women in the nonagricultural labor force dropped by more than half at a time when the labor force was expanding. As a percentage of employed women, the 26-year decline goes from 2.4% to .4%, with no sign of stabilizing. Among agricultural workers the shift away from unpaid family work for women is even more striking. In 1962, over half of all women working in agriculture were unpaid family workers. Over the years--again in the context of an expanding female work force--the absolute number of such women declined from over half a million to 99,000, and their percentage of all women working in agriculture dropped from 56% to 15%. By 1988, less than one-sixth of the women working in agriculture were unpaid.

We have no trend data on work at home. The first national data on the topic were collected in a cross-sectional survey by the U.S. Census Bureau in 1985. It revealed that about

10% of employed Americans do some of their work at home, and 2.2 million workers do all of their work at home. Two-thirds of those who work entirely at home are women (Statistical Abstract 1987, p. 370; Horvath, 1986; see also Chapter 13.6, Household Production).

Part- and Full-time Employment

Figures on part- and full-time employment among U.S. women are available in the General Social Surveys for the period 1972-1988 (Table 5). Over this 16-year period the percentage of women in the labor force rose from 37% to 56%, with most of the increase in full-time rather than part-time work. In the early and mid-1970s, 25-30% of all women were employed full-time, compared to 35-40% in the 1980s. The percentage of women working part-time rose only slightly, from 10-12% in the 1970s to 12-14% in the 1980s. Two clear trends among women not in the labor force show up in Table 5: The percentage of retired women more than doubles over the 16-year period, increasing from about 5% to 12% of all women, and the percentage who list their primary activity as "keeping house" declines consistently and markedly, from 53% in 1972 to 27% in 1988. In fact, the contrast between that trend and the increasing percentage of women working full-time highlights the change in women's activities over this period: until the late 1970s, the dominant activity of American women was "keeping house." By the mid-1980s, a majority had paying jobs, full-time employment was the most typical situation, and fewer than one-third of adult women were full-time homemakers.

Among women who work, the percentage who work full-time has increased slightly. As may be seen by comparing the percentages for full- and part-time in Table 5, in the 1980s about 70% of women in the labor force worked full-time. In the early 1970s the percentage full-time had been about five points lower.

Finally, analysis of reports of the number of hours per week worked by women who classify themselves as full-time or part-time workers reveals two trends: "full-time" work for women increasingly means at least 35 hours per week, and part-time workers are working more hours than formerly (Table 6). In 1988, 84% of full-time women workers reported work weeks of 40 or more hours, compared to 66% in 1973. The trend to more hours by women employed part-time is not entirely consistent in the data presented in Table 6, but its direction is apparent. In the 1970s, the odds that a part-time woman employee was working at least 30 hours per week run at about one in six; in the 1980s, they increase to about one in four. Thus, not only are more women working, but it seems that those who work are working more hours.

References

Brown, Clair and Joseph A. Pechman, eds. Gender in the Workplace. Washington, D.C.: The Brookings Institution, 1987.

Davis, James Allan and Tom W. Smith. General Social Surveys, 1972-1988: Cumulative Codebook. Chicago: National Opinion Research Center, 1988.

------. General Social Surveys, 1972-1988 [machine-readable data file], NORC ed. Chicago: National Opinion Research Center, producer, 1988; Storrs, CT: Roper Public Opinion Research Center, University of Connecticut, distributor.

Horvath, Francis W. "Work at Home: New Findings from the Current Population Survey." Monthly Labor Review 109 (1986): 31-35.

Marshall, Ray and Beth Paulin. "Employment and Earnings of Women: Historical Perspective." In Working Women: Past, Present, Future, edited by Karen Shallcross Koziara, Michael H. Moskow and Lucretia Dewey Tanner, pp. 1-36. Washington, D.C.: Bureau of National Affairs, Inc., 1987.

U.S. Bureau of Labor Statistics. Employment and Earnings. Monthly.

U.S. Bureau of the Census. Statistical Abstract of the United States, 1989. Washington, D.C., 1989. Annual. Previous years as cited.

Wattenberg, Ben J. The Good News Is the Bad News Is Wrong. New York: Simon & Schuster, 1985 (Touchstone edition).

Table 1. MARITAL STATUS AND WOMEN'S PARTICIPATION IN THE LABOR
FORCE, 1940-1988

	Female Labor Force as Percent of Female Population*			
Year	Total	Single	Married	Widowed or Divorced
1940	27%	48%	17%	32%
1944	35	59	25	36
1947	30	51	21	35
1950	31	50	25	36
1955	34	46	29	36
1960	35	44	32	37
1965	37	40	36	36
1970	43	53	41	36
1975	46	57	45	38
1980	51	62	51	41
1985	54	65	55	43
1987	55	65	56	43
1988	56	65	57	43

* Women 14 years old and over through 1965; 16 years old and over thereafter.

SOURCE: Based on Statistical Abstract 1989, p. 385; 1987, p. 373.

Table 2. WOMEN'S PARTICIPATION IN THE CIVILIAN LABOR FORCE, BY
          RACE, 1955-1987

| Year | Female Civilian Labor Force as Percent of Female Population* | |
	White	Black**
1955	34%	46%
1960	36	48
1965	38	49
1970	43	50
1975	46	49
1980	51	53
1985	54	56
1987	56	58

* Women 16 years old and over; percentage base is the total
noninstitutional population.
** For 1970 and before, includes other nonwhite races.

SOURCE: Based on <u>Statistical Abstract 1989</u>, p. 376; <u>1979</u>, p. 394;
       <u>1974</u>, p. 336.

Table 3. LABOR FORCE PARTICIPATION RATES* FOR WIVES, HUSBAND
PRESENT, BY PRESENCE AND AGE OF CHILDREN, 1950-1988

| | Presence and Age of Children | | |
| | None | Age 6-17 | Under |
Year	under 18	only	age 6
1950	30%	28%	12
1955	33	35	16
1960	35	39	19
1965	38	43	23
1970	42	49	30
1975	44	52	37
1980	46	62	45
1985	48	68	53
1987	48	71	57
1988	49	72	57

* Married women in the labor force as percent of married women in
the population.

SOURCE: Based on <u>Statistical Abstract 1989</u>, p. 386; <u>1979</u>, p.401.

Table 4.   UNPAID FAMILY WORKERS (UFWs) AMONG EMPLOYED WOMEN AGE
           16 AND OVER, BY CLASS OF INDUSTRY, ANNUAL AVERAGES,
           1962-1988

Year	Nonagricultural Industries			Agricultural Industries		
	Total Workers*	UFWs*	Percent UFWs	Total Workers*	UFWs*	Percent UFWs
1962	22,031	532	2	924	517	56
1963	22,554	506	2	925	489	53
1964	23,341	517	2	878	480	55
1965	24,289	540	2	856	470	55
1966	25,652	511	2	774	411	53
1967	26,214	454	2	682	358	52
1968	27,146	439	2	660	373	56
1969	28,441	462	2	644	367	57
1970	29,067	449	2	601	339	56
1971	29,278	459	2	598	316	53
1972	30,439	461	2	633	314	50
1973	31,828	477	2	619	283	46
1974	32,825	434	1	591	251	42
1975	32,974	424	1	580	239	41
1976	34,512	407	1	582	227	39
1977	36,081	437	1	605	236	39
1978	38,221	429	1	661	225	34
1979	39,793	412	1	652	206	32
1980	40,636	349	1	646	197	30
1981	41,488	335	1	658	176	27
1982	42,591	348	1	665	166	25
1983	43,367	325	1	680	156	23
1984	45,262	283	1	652	148	23
1985	46,615	251	1	644	125	19
1986	48,054	219	--	652	115	18
1987	49,668	221	--	666	95	14
1988	51,019	220	--	676	99	15

* Numbers in 1000s; total workers includes wage and salary workers,
self-employed workers, and unpaid family workers.

SOURCE: Computed from U.S. Bureau of Labor Statistics, *Employment
        and Earnings*, monthly. The tables on "employed civilians by
        age, sex, and class of worker" (household data, annual
        averages) that are the basis for these figures are published
        each January.

Table 5. DETAILS OF WOMEN'S LABOR FORCE STATUS, 1972-1988

	In Labor Force			Not	in	Labor	Force	
	Works	Works	Unempl. or temp.					
	full	part	not at	Re-	In	Keeps		
Year	time	time	work	tired	school	house	Other	Total
1972	25%	10%	3%	6%	2%	53%	2%	101%
1973	26	13	2	4	3	52	1	101
1974	27	10	5	3	2	52	1	100
1975	29	12	2	5	3	48	1	100
1976	27	10	3	7	2	51	--	100
1977	38	9	3	5	2	42	1	100
1978	31	13	3	7	2	42	2	100
1980	33	11	4	6	3	42	1	100
1982	37	13	4	7	2	36	2	101
1983	35	12	4	7	2	37	2	99
1984	39	13	3	8	3	33	1	100
1985	36	13	4	11	3	32	1	100
1986	34	12	4	11	3	35	1	100
1987	41	13	3	11	4	27	2	101
1988	39	14	3	12	4	27	1	100

NOTE: The percentage bases (N's) for the above figures are women in the respective General Social Surveys, excluding missing data, namely 1972, 806; 1973, 803; 1974, 793; 1976, 820; 1977, 837; 1978, 889; 1980, 827; 1982, 867; 1983, 909; 1984, 875; 1985, 846; 1986, 849; 1987, 825; and 1988, 843.

SOURCE: Davis and Smith, 1988 [machine-readable data file].

Table 6.   DISTRIBUTION OF EMPLOYED WOMEN BY HOURS WORKED AT   ALL
JOBS, WEEK PRECEDING INTERVIEW, 1973-1988

	Hours Worked Preceding Week						
Year	1-9	10-19	20-29	30-34	35-39	40+	Total
Women Employed "Full Time"							
1973	1%	1%	4%	8%	21%	65%	100%
1974	--	2	1	6	13	78	100
1975	--	--	3	9	14	74	100
1976	--	--	4	8	16	71	99
1977	--	1	3	6	14	76	100
1978	--	--	--	4	21	75	100
1980	--	--	2	3	15	80	100
1982	--	1	3	7	18	71	100
1983	--	--	1	6	18	74	100
1984	--	--	2	4	13	80	99
1985	--	--	--	2	15	83	100
1986	--	--	2	3	12	82	99
1987	--	1	1	3	15	79	99
1988	--	1	2	4	9	84	100
Women Employed "Part Time"							
1973	9	37	43	6	1	4	100
1974	5	42	35	13	4	1	100
1975	11	37	39	8	4	2	101
1976	9	38	28	17	4	4	100
1977	10	34	44	11	1	--	100
1978	16	29	36	13	3	3	100
1980	10	37	37	10	2	4	100
1982	15	29	30	20	2	4	100
1983	13	25	36	21	3	3	101
1984	10	25	46	13	4	3	101
1985	20	21	38	15	5	2	101
1986	14	24	29	19	8	6	100
1987	10	29	41	10	4	6	100
1988	13	25	32	17	7	6	100

NOTE: Percentage bases (N's) for the above figures are women in the
respective surveys working full or part time at the time of the
survey. Listing "full time" and then "part time" workers for each
year, the N's are 1973: 206, 102; 1974: 216, 78; 1975: 232, 101;
1976: 224, 81; 1977: 318, 71; 1978: 272, 112; 1980: 274, 90; 1982:
317, 112; 1983: 319, 111; 1984: 341, 114; 1985: 309, 112; 1986:
286, 96; 1987: 335, 107; and 1988: 326, 117.

SOURCE: Davis and Smith, 1988 [machine-readable data file].

Contraceptive practice was becoming near-universal in the years immediately following World War II, so that by the mid-1960s those not practicing contraception (and not desiring conception) did so either inadvertently or in ignorance or carelessness. Within marriage, favor shifted rapidly toward, and then to an extent away from, the pill and the IUD, "foolproof" methods depending upon women. When these methods proved to have certain health liabilities, sterilization became popular. Trend data are lacking on contraceptive methods among the unmarried, but cross-sectional surveys indicate that these were both more casual and more female-dependent than among married couples, with abortion widely practiced as a backup measure.

Unfortunately, almost all the extensive American trend data on contraceptive use is based on married women, for until recently, posing the question to unmarried women was thought inappropriate or unlikely to result in reliable responses. There are data from a careful national survey in 1982 on current contraceptive use among never-married women. Among the findings: at age 15-17 years, 83% did not use contraception, and at ages 20-44 years, 48% did not (Bachrach and Mosher 1984). Of these figures, 70% of the adolescent women, and 23% of the mature women had never had intercourse. That is, of the adolescent women, 13% (less than half of those who had ever had coitus) did not use contraception, while of single women aged 20-44, 25% (or about one in three who had ever had coitus) did not employ contraception. In other words, by 1982, a majority of sexually active unmarried women, of whatever age, were contraceptors. (The results say nothing, of course, about the proportion of their intercourse that was protected by their perhaps occasional contraceptive use). Much of this rather broad contraceptive use among the single was a product of "the pill." Other data indicate that it has indeed been the pill that facilitated a great expansion of sexual activity by young, single people in the 1970s.

A sense of trends in contraception among married women is derived from a cohort tabulation of series of representative national surveys of women in the fertile ages, conducted at five-year intervals from the mid-1950s (Table 1). Looking down the column reflecting contraceptive practice, we find that as recently as the mid-1950s, contraception was unknown to as many as one-third of women less than five years into their marriages, a proportion that declined sharply to only five percent by the early 1970s. Throughout, the adoption of contraception was partly a product of the exigencies of marriage itself, most commonly the attainment of a desired number of children. But this pattern was clearly on the decline, and by the early 1970s, virtually all married couples practiced contraception at least sometimes, virtually from the start of their marriages.

Table 2 summarizes trends in the contraceptive status of currently married white and black women 15 to 44 years of age, from 1965 through 1982, based on excellent national surveys. The overall proportion who currently employed contraception was already almost as high in 1965 as it was to become by 1976 or 1982. The racial differences in contraceptive practice are so large as to compel notice--although the overall point is that by the 1960s, both blacks and whites typically contracepted within marriage, and with something like the same likelihood, in sharp contrast to unmarried women, among whom blacks were substantially more likely to risk pregnancy by omitting contraception. Particularly notable among blacks is the far smaller proportions than among whites who contracepted by "male" methods: condom or male sterilization. There are several patterns that differ sharply from whites to blacks. Female sterilization, for instance, is common to both--more common initially among blacks, subsequently more popular among whites--but male sterilization is an option scarcely ever exercised among black men, while it had become quite common among white men by 1982. Condoms, likewise, were far less widely adopted by blacks than whites. "Male" methods, then, have been much less attractive to blacks than to whites. Likewise, periodic abstinance--typically the "rhythm method" prescribed for Catholics--held relatively slight attraction for blacks (few of whom are Catholics) even when relatively many white couples practiced this method.

Other patterns were common to whites and blacks. Withdrawal was hardly ever practiced as the method of choice. Shortly-before-intercourse applications, like the diaphragm and the condom, were declining in popularity as the period under examination began, but won a reprieve when use of the pill and the IUD, which had grown rapidly in popularity into the mid-70s, dropped off as women began fearing health consequences. By the early 1980s, sterilization-- generally of the wife--had become the most popular method among married couples, practiced by 40% of white couples and 23% of black couples.

References

Bachrach, Christine A. and William D. Mosher. "Use of Contraception in the United States, 1982." National Center for Health Statistics Advance Data, Number 102 (December 4, 1984).

U.S. Bureau of the Census. Statistical Abstract of the United States, 1989. Washington, D.C., 1989.

U.S. National Center for Health Statistics. Patterns of Aggregate and Individual Changes in Contraceptive Practice, United States, 1965-1975 (Vital and Health Statistics, Series 3, No. 17, 1979).

Table 1. PERCENTAGE OF WOMEN WHO HAVE NEVER USED CONTRACEPTION,
BY DURATION OF MARRIAGE AND MARRIAGE COHORT: CURRENTLY
MARRIED WHITE WOMEN AT TIME OF SURVEY AND AGED 18-39,
BOTH SPOUSES MARRIED ONCE: MARRIAGE COHORTS OF 1946-50
TO 1971-75

Marriage Cohort 1941-45	Duration of Marriage in Years				
	<5	5-9	10-14	15-19	20-24
1941-45	--	--	23%	20%	19%
1946-50	--	--	21	18	13
1951-55	32%	14%	11	15	9
1956-60	24	12	10	5	--
1961-65	15	8	5	--	--
1966-70	10	2	--	--	--
1971-75	5	--	--	--	--

SOURCE: Based on U.S. National Center for Health Statistics 1979,
Table 5. The data are from surveys of 1955, 1960, 1965,
1970, and 1975.

Table 2.   CURRENT CONTRACEPTIVE PRACTICE REPORTED BY MARRIED
           WOMEN AGED 15-44, BY RACE, 1965-1982

	1965	1973	1976	1982
Whites:				
Sterilized wife	4%	16%	19%	28%
Sterilized husband	3	8	10	11
Pill	15	25	23	13
IUD	0	7	6	5
Diaphragm	7	2	3	5
Condom	14	10	7	10
Foam	2	3	3	2
Periodic abstinance	7	3	3	3
Withdrawal	--	2	2	1
All other	10	2	2	1
Blacks:				
Sterilized wife	9	14	11	21
Sterilized husband	0	1	2	2
Pill	12	26	22	16
IUD	2	8	6	6
Diaphragm	3	1	2	3
Condom	10	3	5	4
Foam	3	3	4	2
Periodic abstinance	2	1	1	2
Withdrawal	--	0	2	0
All other	16	3	4	3

SOURCES: Based on U.S. Bureau of the Census, 1989, p. 69;
    Bachrach and Mosher, 1984, Table 2.

Topic 4: Labor Market

4.1 UNEMPLOYMENT

Unemployment, being a function of the business cycle, cannot be expected to show a long-term secular trend. The rate oscillates continuously in response to business conditions. Differentials in unemployment, such as those associated with education, gender, age, and ethnicity, are relatively stable from year to year and some of them do exhibit long-term trends.

Unemployment is a cyclical phenomenon. The general unemployment rate fluctuated within a limited range from 1948 to 1975, exceeding 6.0 only in 1958 and 1961, and dipping below 1.3 only in 1953. Since 1975, it has fluctuated at a higher level, dipping below 6.0 only in 1979 and 1989 and reaching 9.7 in 1982 (BLS Bulletin 2217, June 1985, and current press reports).

Unemployment rates for women workers were consistently somewhat higher than for men until 1981; since then they have been consistently somewhat lower (Table 1).

The unemployment rate for nonwhite workers parallels the general unemployment rate, but runs nearly twice as high. There has been no appreciable change in the differential since 1950 (Table 1).

Unemployment rates are strongly influenced by education, being 4.8 times as high for non-graduates of high schools as for college graduates in 1985. It was 5.5 in 1975, and 6.3 in 1985, suggesting a weak trend, but the more important consideration is that the unemployment rate among college graduates ranged only between 1.3 and 3.6 between 1965 and 1985, while for non-graduates of high schools, it ranged from 5.6 to 21.4 (Table 2). A more detailed set of trend figures covering the years 1965, 1974, 1978 and 1985 shows no change at all in the education differential over that period (Summers, 1986).

Marriage, like education, confers advantages with respect to unemployment. Married men are the least susceptible to unemployment, followed by married women, divorced, separated or widowed women, divorced, separated or widowed men, and single men. This order did not change between 1965 and 1985 but the relative advantage of married men diminished (Table 2).

The unemployment rate for youths aged 16 to 19 parallels the general unemployment rate but runs more than twice as high (Table 3). There has been no appreciable change in the differential since 1948. However, unemployment figures for youths are somewhat unreliable because large numbers of them are not counted in the civilian labor force, although out of school. A better measure for youths not in school is joblessness, estimated at 63.9% for blacks, and 37.5% for whites in 1985 (Table 3, and Rees, 1986). Some analysts perceive a relative increase in the black-white differential since 1950, but the trend data are inconclusive.

References

Rees, A. "An Essay on Youth Joblessness." Journal of Economic Literature, 24 (1986): 613-628.

Summers, L. H. "Why Is the Unemployment Rate So Very High near Full Employment?" Brookings Papers on Economic Activity 2 (1986): 339-383.

U.S. Bureau of the Census. Statistical Abstract of the United States, 1989. Washington, D.C., 1989.

U.S. Department of Labor. Handbook of Labor Statistics. Washington, D.C., Bureau of Labor Statistics, 1985, Bulletin 2217.

Table 1. UNEMPLOYMENT RATES, 1950-1983

Year	All Civilian Workers	Men, 20 yrs and Older	Women, 20 yrs and Older	Nonwhites
1950	5.3	4.7	5.1	9.0
1960	5.5	4.7	5.1	10.2
1970	4.9	3.5	4.8	8.2
1980	7.1	5.9	6.4	13.1
1983	9.6	8.9	8.1	17.8

SOURCE: Based on Handbook of Labor Statistics, 1985, p. 64.

Table 2. UNEMPLOYMENT RATES BY MARITAL STATUS AND EDUCATION, 1965-1985

Marital Status/Education	1965	1985
Marital Status:		
Single Men	10.1	12.7
Married Men	2.4	4.3
Divorced, separated, or widowed men	7.2	9.2
Single women	8.2	10.7
Married women	4.5	5.6
Divorced, separated, or widowed men	5.4	8.3
Education:		
Less than five years	7.1	11.3
Five to eight years	5.6	13.0
One to three years of high school	7.4	15.9
Four years of high school	4.1	8.0
One to three years of college	3.3	5.1
Four or more years of college	1.4	2.6

SOURCE: Summers, 1986, p. 350.

The most influential work in this field (Braverman 1974) discussed the degradation of work in the twentieth century under monopoly capitalism, and this position continues to be taken by Marxist scholars (Gordon, Edwards and Reich, 1982; Crompton and Jones, 1984). It postulates deskilling as a general tendency, attributable to the machinations of capitalist managers. The empirical research stimulated by this argument has developed mixed findings, but the weight of the evidence seems to contradict the deskilling hypothesis (Spenner, 1979; Rumberger, 1981; Penn, 1986; Form, 1987; DiPrete, 1988).

The gross profiles of the U.S. occupational distribution from 1950 to 1987 (Table 1) suggest a process of skilling rather than deskilling: each of the conspicuously skilled categories--professionals, managers, and craftsmen--increased, each of the conspicuously unskilled categories--laborers, farm laborers and domestic servants--decreased sharply. The proportion of operatives also declined. The category that increased most sharply--clerical workers--is too heterogeneous for easy interpretation.

Table 2 shows trends in the absolute numbers of craft workers in the U.S. labor force for the same period. The only conspicuous decline occurred among compositors and typesetters, largely displaced by automation.

A more plausible variant of the deskilling argument is the hypothesis of increasing overeducation in the labor force (Rumberger, 1981), based on the perception that the skill level of blue collar and lower white collar occupations has not risen to match the rising educational levels of entrants to these occupations (Table 3). Jaques (1986) conceives this mismatch in another way, noting that in nearly all bureaucratic employment systems, the abilities of the work force are greater, on average, than the abilities called for by the job classifications, so that many workers are underutilized.

The concept of skill is probably too ambiguous for the precise delineation of trends. Skill includes such varied elements as dexterity and work speed; mastery of tools, materials and processes; the duration and quality of training; the ability to cope with emergencies; autonomy and self-direction; the time-horizon of tasks; versatility and improvisation; and weight of responsibility. It overlaps inextricably with such elements of occupational reward as pay, authority, tenure, and immunity from inspection. All skilled occupations display a mix of these elements. No two display the same mix. The skills of an airline pilot, a concert pianist, and a master plumber cannot be arrayed on a common scale.

Spenner (1983) proposes the reduction of the dimensions of skill to two--substantive complexity and autonomy-control--but this simplification creates more problems than it solves.

The concept of overeducation is ambiguous in a different way. It seems to imply either that no worker should be educated beyond the minimum level required to perform the most skilled job he is likely to hold or else that all workers with the same level of education should be assigned equally skilled work. Neither of these positions is entirely persuasive.

Form's review of research on skill degradation summarizes matters admirably:

"Skill degradation theory found most support in early case studies of dying crafts. Later historical research into a wider set of occupations demonstrated that these early findings could not be generalized. Still later studies of all occupations in the labor force pointed to little or no aggregate skill change" (1987, page 44).

References

Braverman, H. Labour and Monopoly Capitalism. New York: Monthly Review Press, 1974.

Clogg, Clifford and James W. Schokley. "Mismatch Between Occupation and Schooling: A Prevalence Measure, Recent Trends and Demographic Analysis." Demography 21 (1984): 235-257.

Crompton, Rosemary and Gareth Jones. White Collar Proletariat: Deskilling and Gender in Clerical Work. New York: Macmillan, 1984.

DiPrete, Thomas A. "The Upgrading and Downgrading of Occupations: Status Redefinition vs. Deskilling as Alternative Theories of Change." Social Forces 66 (1988): 725-746.

Form, William. "On the Degradation of Skills." Annual Review of Sociology 13 (1987): 29-47.

Gordon, David W., Richard Edwards and Michael Reich. Segmented Work, Divided Workers: The Historical Transformation of Labor in the United States. New York: Cambridge University Press, 1982.

Jaques, Elliot. Personal communication, 1985.

Penn, Roger. "Where Have All the Craftsmen Gone?: Trends in Skilled Labor in the United States of America Since 1940." British Journal of Sociology 37 (1986): 569-580.

Rodriguez, Orlando. "Occupational Shifts and Educational Upgrading in the American Labor Force Between 1950 and 1970." Sociology of Education 51 (1978): 55-67.

Rumberger, Russell W. "The Changing Skill Requirements of Jobs in the U.S. Economy." Industrial and Labor Relations Review 34 (1981): 578-590.

Smith, Herbert L. "Overeducation and Underemployment: An Agnostic Review." Sociology of Education 59 (1986): 85-99.

Spenner, Kenneth I. "Temporal Change in the Skill Level of Work." American Sociological Review 48 (1979): 824-837.

Table 1.   EMPLOYED PERSONS BY MAJOR OCCUPATION GROUP, 1950-1987

Occupation	1950	1960	1970	1980	1986*
Professional & technical	8%	11%	14%	16%	16%
Managers & administrators	11	11	11	11	12
Sales workers	6	6	6	6	12
Clerical workers	13	15	17	19	16
Craft & kindred workers	13	13	13	13	12
Operatives, incl. transport	20	18	18	14	11
Laborers, except farm	6	5	5	5	4
Service workers	11	12	12	13	13
Farmers and farm workers	12	8	4	3	3
Total	100	99	100	100	99

* These percentages are not exactly comparable to the previous columns due to the Census Bureau's reclassification of occupational categories. Combinations of either the new or the old categories do not exactly match the other system. The sudden doubling of the number of sales workers in 1986 is due to changes in classification schemes. The present rough attempt to fit the 1986 figures to the previous system was accomplished as follows: Professional & technical = professional specialty + technicians & related support; Managers & administrators = executive, administrative, & managerial; Sales workers = sales occupations; Clerical workers = administrative support, including clerical; Craft & kindred workers = precision production, craft, & repair; Operatives = machine operators, assemblers, & inspectors + transportation and material moving occupations; Laborers = handlers, equipment cleaners, helpers, & laborers; Service workers = service occupations; Farmers and farm workers = Farming, forestry, & fishing.

SOURCE: Statistical Abstract 1988, p. 376; 1984, p. 417; 1974, p. 350

Table 2. WORKERS IN TRADITIONAL CRAFT OCCUPATIONS, 1950-1980

| | Workers (1000s) | | | |
Occupation	1950	1960	1970	1980
Carpenters	985	924	922	1,305
Painters	431	416	359	422
Machinists	534	516	390	511
MIllwrights	60	68	81	134
Toolmakers	157	187	207	194
Electricians	324	356	483	626
Plumbers and				
pipefitters	296	331	398	502
Welders	276	387	566	791
Compositors and				
typesetters	179	183	162	71
Mechanics and				
repairmen	1768	2301	2503	3983

SOURCE: Based on Penn, 1986, p. 573.

Table 3. PROPORTION OF U.S. WORKERS "OVER-EDUCATED" FOR CURRENT
          JOBS, BY GENDER AND RACE, 1970 AND 1980

Sex-Color Group	Completed Years of Schooling	"Over-educated" 1970	1980	Absolute Increase
Nonblack males	13-15	21%	33%	12%
	16	49	54	5
	17+	40	47	7
Nonblack females	13-15	18	21	3
	16	23	36	13
	17+	32	41	9
Black males	13-15	39	42	3
	16	35	56	21
	17+	40	46	6
Black females	13-15	23	33	9
	16	18	42	24
	17+	46	49	3

SOURCE: Based on Clogg, Clifford, and Schokley, 1984, p. 246.

Since 1960, there has been a slow steady rise in the proportion of male workers holding part-time jobs, but the much larger segment of the female labor force employed part-time has not changed in relative size. U.S. workers have no general right to job security or to due process in dismissal, but such rights have been established for many specific job categories by contract, custom or statute. The employment of non-unionized blue collar workers, however, remains extremely precarious and no trend toward improved job security is discernible.

Table 1 shows the numbers of employed full-time and part-time workers in the U.S. by gender and age from 1968 to 1985, part-time work being defined as less than 35 hours per week. There are some difficulties with these data because the category "part-time" includes both voluntary and involuntary part-time employment. Thus people who seek out part-time employment are lumped together with those who are forced into it by economic circumstances. There is evidence, however (Nardone, 1986, p. 14), that the majority of those who work part-time do so voluntarily.

During the period covered by the table, the percentage of male workers employed part-time rose significantly; the much greater percentage of female workers employed part-time remained unchanged. In shorter time intervals, part-time employment tends to rise when unemployment rises.

It is surprisingly difficult to separate precarious employment from steady employment in U.S. labor market data, which record employment, unemployment and length of unemployment, but not length of employment. Information on the precariously employed is itself precarious, for workers in this category tend to evade bureaucratic procedures. The scarcity of data largely accounts for the neglect of precarious employment in the ongoing debate on the structured labor market, a concept that implies the division of the labor market into two sectors: one with high wages, job security and opportunity for promotion, and the other with low wages, high turnover and poor working conditions (Wilkinson, 1981).

The sparse available evidence suggests that U.S. workers change jobs rather frequently. The median American male worker will holds approximately eleven jobs in the course of his working life (Hashimoto and Raisian, 1985, p. 725). But job mobility decreases sharply with age (see Hall, 1982).

The right to continued employment is not generally acknowledged in the United States, although many specific occupations enjoy tenure rights established by contract, custom, or statute. Rodgers and Steiber (1985, p. 35) note that, "termination of non-unionized employees has been subject to the 'employment-at-will' doctrine--that is, employers have the right to discharge 'at will'. Only employees covered by collective bargaining agreements are generally protected against unjust discharge by grievance and arbitration procedures." Despite much academic and union criticism of this doctrine, it has remained in place, except as modified by civil rights legislation which inhibits the selective discharge of workers according to ethnicity, gender, age, or handicapped status. Excepting issues of discrimination, most non-unionized workers in the private sector are, from a legal standpoint, precariously employed.

When plants are closed in the U.S., the employer is not ordinarily obligated to provide notice, severance pay, or alternative opportunities for the displaced personnel. Although states and localities have considered imposing such requirements, very few have done so (Aboud and Schram, 1987). The only federal legislation so far is a 1988 statute requiring large employers to give a few weeks' notice of plant closings.

By and large, the courts have sustained the employer's right to hire and fire at will, and have been reluctant to grant tenure rights or even the right to due process in dismissal where there is no civil rights issue. According to Aaron (1985, p. 65):

the private-sector employment relation in the United States differs quite remarkably from that in other industrialized countries in the world, almost all of which have statutory protection against unjust dismissal for all employees whether or not they are represented by unions.

Nevertheless, many occupations do have extensive tenure rights based on contract, as in the case of unionized workers, custom, as in the familiar case of college professors, or statute, as in the case of nearly all government employees. Moreover, many white collar workers enjoy an informal right to continued employment which is unenforceable but seldom breached.

The sparse data available do not show any strong recent trends in the precariousness of employment. Table 2 shows the annual discharge rate in manufacturing industry (those fired rather than "laid off") from 1960 to 1982.

Precarious jobs seem to fall into three categories: employment in depressed or failing industries, seasonal employment, and the marginal low-paid jobs available to illegal immigrants, the mentally retarded, and other vulnerable persons.

Insofar as trends can be discerned, there has been a high rate of displacement from manufacturing industries from 1975 to the present as the industrial component of the labor force has shrunk (as discussed in Chapter 4.4, Sectors of the Labor Force). Between 1981 and 1986, more than 2.5 million workers lost their jobs because of industrial plant closings (Monthly Labor Review, June 1987) and the displacement was generally permanent. The number of illegal immigrants, by definition uncountable, also increased rapidly from 1975 to 1987, principally from Mexico, and the number of ex-mental patients on the job market increased by perhaps half a million during that interval because of deinstitutionalization programs that transferred most of the inmate population of mental institutions back into the community. Seasonal employment shows no particular trend since 1975 (Statistical Abstract 1989, p. 381).

References

Aaron, Benjamin. "The Ownership of Jobs: Observations on the American Experience." In Job Equity and Other Studies in Industrial Relations, edited by Walter Fogel, pp. 50-98. Los Angeles: University of California, Institute of Industrial Relations, 1982.

Aboud, Antone and Sanford F. Schram. "Overview of Legislation." In Deindustrialization and Plant Closure, edited by Paul D. Staudohar and Holly E. Brown. Lexington, MA: Lexington Books, 1987.

Hall, Robert E. "The Importance of Lifetime Jobs in the U.S. Economy." American Economic Review 72 (1982): 716-724.

Hashimoto, Masanori and John Raisian. "Employment Tenure and Earnings Profiles in Japan and the United States." American Economic Review 75 (1985): 721-735.

Nardone, Thomas J. "Part-time Workers, Who Are They?" Monthly Labor Review 109 (February, 1986): 13-19.

Rodgers, R.C. and Jack Steiber. "Employee Discharge in the 20th Century: A Review of the Literature." Monthly Labor Review 109 (September 1986): 34-40.

Wilkinson, Frank. The Dynamics of Labour Market Segmentation. London: Academic Press, 1981.

Table 1.   PROPORTIONS OF MALE AND FEMALE LABOR FORCE EMPLOYED
           PART-TIME, 1968-1985

Year	Percent of Labor Force Part-Time	
	Male	Female
1968	5%	22%
1970	5	23
1980	6	23
1985	7	24

SOURCE: Based on Nardone, 1986, pp. 13-19.

Table 2.   ANNUAL DISCHARGE RATES PER 100 EMPLOYEES, MANUFACTURING
           INDUSTRIES, 1960-1982

Year	Discharge Rate
1960	3%
1965	4
1970	5
1975	3
1982	5

SOURCE: Based on Rodgers, 1986, p. 37.

Employment in the service-producing sectors of the U.S. labor force has been growing much faster than employment in the goods-producing sector for the past three decades. There has been no absolute decline in the goods-producing sector to support the hypothesis of deindustrialization, but the relative contribution of services, and especially of intangible commodities, to the gross national product has grown by leaps and bounds.

The categories of primary (agriculture and mining), secondary (manufacturing and other goods production) and tertiary (service) sectors are not commonly used in the compilation or analysis of U.S. labor statistics, but the Bureau of Labor Statistics does distinguish between goods-producing industries (mining, construction and manufacturing) and service-producing industries (transportation, public utilities, wholesale and retail trade, finance, insurance, real estate etc.). Agriculture is sometimes included in the goods-producing sector and sometimes reported separately. The goods-producing sector has seen little growth since World War II, while the service-producing sector has grown considerably, so much so that it has been suggested with some alarm that the U.S. is undergoing "deindustrialization" (Bluestone and Harrison, 1982; Reich, 1982; Harper's Magazine, 1985). Kutscher and Personick (1986) argue, however, that the fear of deindustrialization is overblown, saying that the service sector has not grown at the expense of the goods-producing sector, but in addition to it.

The part of the labor force in the service-producing sector has grown substantially since 1959 (Table 1) while the number of goods-producing employees has risen only slightly. Consequently the relative importance of goods-producing and service-producing sectors have changed. In 1959 the goods-producing sector accounted for 40% of employment and the service-producing sector 60%. By 1984 the goods-producing sector accounted for 28% and the service-producing sector for 72%. The important fact to note, however, is that the increase in services did not mean a decline in goods-producing employment. Of all the goods-producing industries, only agriculture saw a real decline in employment over this period, from 8% of the labor force down to 3%. The goods-producing sector as a whole continued to grow in this period, adding 2.5 million jobs, though the service-producing sector far outdistanced it, with 36.5 million new jobs. According to Urquhart (1984) most of the growth in service-producing sector jobs was attributable to the increase in women's participation in the labor force.

Although their measures of service output are questionable, Kutscher and Personick calculate that the output of the service-producing sector increased from 45% to 53% of the total between 1959 and 1984 while the output of the goods-producing sector declined from 55% to 47%.

Among the fastest growing industries of the service-producing sector are those that produce intangible commodities. The providers of intangible commodities overlap with the industries loosely and confusingly called "services" in the federal statistics, a category that includes hotels and lodging, personal and domestic services, advertising, employment agencies, computer and data processing, auto repair, motion pictures, amusements, legal services, health services, educational services, social services and more. Those providing financial and insurance services, another major set of intangible commodities, are reported separately, as "finance, insurance and real estate."

Employment in the industries producing intangible commodities grew by an impressive 200% between 1970 and 1986, and many providers of intangible commodities grew even faster (Statistical Abstract 1988, p. 380). Between 1970 and 1986 health services employment increased by 215%, business services by 285%, and legal services by 317%.

There is no single explanation for the spectacular recent growth of the service-producing sector, but the various explanations that have been offered involve elements of both push and pull. Recent technological innovations have introduced entire new families of intangible commodities (most obviously in the fields of medicine, information technology, and communication) with high levels of consumer demand. In other areas (legal, accounting and educational services, for example) the increasing complexity of legislation and social regulation has compelled consumers to obtain more and more professional services.

References

Bluestone, Barry, Benjamin Friedman, Bennett Harrison, Robert Z. Lawrence, and Charles L. Schultze. "Do We Need an Industrial Policy?" Harper's 270 (February, 1985): 35-48.

Bluestone, Barry. The Deindustrialization of America. New York: Basic Books, 1982.

Kutscher, R. and J.A. Mark. "The Service-producing Sector: Some Common Perceptions." Monthly Labor Review 106 (1983): 21-24.

Reich, Robert B. "Industrial Policy." New Republic (March 31, 1982): 28-30.

Urquhart, M. "The Employment Shift to Services: Where Did it Come From?" Monthly Labor Review 107 (1984): 15-22.

U.S. Bureau of the Census. Statistical Abstract of the United States, 1988. Washington, D.C., 1988.

Table 1. EMPLOYMENT BY MAJOR SECTOR, 1959-84

Sector	1959	1969	1979	1984
Goods-producing				
Agriculture	8%	4%	3%	3%
Mining	1	1	1	1
Construction	6	5	6	6
Manufacturing	25	25	21	18
Durable	14	15	13	11
Non-durable	11	10	8	7
Total goods-producing	40	35	31	28
Service-producing				
Government	12	15	16	15
Private	48	50	53	57
Total service-producing	60	65	69	72
Total labor force	100	100	100	100

SOURCE: Kutscher and Personick (1986), p. 5.

4.5 COMPUTERIZATION OF WORK

The trends in this area are complex and fast-moving, marked by qualitative changes in the technology and its uses as well as large quantitative changes over short periods of time.

The first electronic digital computer COLOSSUS was built in Britain in 1943, to decipher the German Enigma code. The first U.S. computer ENIAC went into operation at the University of Pennsylvania in 1946; it weighed 30 tons. The first commercial computer UNIVAC I was installed at General Electric in 1954. About 15,000 mainframes of that type were built in the following decade. Planar transistors were developed in 1959, integrated circuits soon after, the microprocessor chip in 1971. Chip capacity has increased rapidly from year to year with a corresponding decline in the cost per bit of memory. New materials like gallium arsenide and new methods like optical transmission promise to continue and probably accelerate these trends. Progressive miniaturization permitted the introduction of minicomputers in the 1960s and of personal computers in the 1970s. Current developments include supercomputers of unprecedented power and extremely tiny microcomputers, as well as the acquisition by computers of new abilities. For example, some advanced graphics programs can generate motion pictures showing real people in action sequences that are entirely simulated.

The major trend lines of what may fairly be called the Electronic Revolution can be traced by counting people and money. The number of computer specialists in the labor force rose from 167,000 in 1974 to 576,000 in 1986--an increase of 345% in 12 years. The number of academic degrees awarded in computer and information sciences from 1971 to 1986 is shown in Table 1. The number of doctorates more than doubled during that interval, while the number of master's degrees increased by 508% and of bachelor's degrees by 1754%!

The trend in the value of computer equipment shipped by U.S. manufacturers has been equally spectacular (Table 2). Combining the three computer categories--electronic computers, peripheral equipment for electronic computing systems, and parts and attachments for the same-- the value of shipments went from $7.5 billion in 1975 to $49.8 billion in 1987, with a substantial increase in every intervening year. Other sources quote higher dollar amounts but show the same steep trend. Growth in personal computers was even more rapid (Table 3).

The numerous sociological and psychological effects ascribed to the introduction of computers (e.g., Turkle, 1984) await confirmation by empirical data.

References

Brod, Craig. Techno Stress: The Human Cost of the Computer Revolution. Reading, MA: Addison-Wesley, 1984.

Caporael, Linda R. "Computers, Prophecy, and Experience: A Historical Perspective." Journal of Social Issues 40 (1984): 15-30.

Dertouzos, Michael L. and Joel Moses, eds. The Computer Age: A Twenty-Year View. Cambridge, MA: The MIT Press, 1979.

Dutton, William H., Everett M. Rogers and Suk-Ho Jun. "Diffusion and Social Impacts of Personal Computers." Communication Research 14 (1987): 219-250.

Forester, Tom. High-Tech Society. Cambridge, MA: The MIT Press, 1987.

Inmon, William. Technomics: The Economics and Technology of the Computer Industry. Homewood, IL: Dow-Jones-Irwin, 1986.

Roszak, Theodore. The Cult of Information. New York: Pantheon Books, 1986.

Siegel, Lenny and John Markoff. The Dark Side of the Chip: The High Cost of High Tech. New York: Harper and Row, 1985.

Simons, Geoff. Silicon Shock: The Menace of the Computer Invasion. Oxford: Basil Blackwell, 1985.

Shallis, Michael. The Silicon Idol: The Micro Revolution and its Social Implications. Oxford: Oxford University Press, 1984.

Turkle, Sherry. The Second Self: Computers and the Human Spirit. New York: Simon and Schuster, 1984.

U.S. Bureau of the Census. Statistical Abstract of the United States, 1989. Washington, D.C., 1989.

Table 1.   COMPUTER AND INFORMATION SCIENCES DEGREES CONFERRED,
           1971-1986

Year	Bachelor's	Master's	Doctorates
1971	2,388	1,588	128
1975	5,033	2,299	213
1981	15,121	4,218	252
1986	41,889	8,070	344

SOURCE: Based on <u>Statistical Abstract 1989</u>, p. 157.

Table 2.   VALUE OF U.S. SHIPMENTS OF COMPUTERS, PERIPHERALS
           AND PARTS, 1975-1987

Year	Dollar Value (billions)
1975	$ 7.5
1980	24.3
1985	46.7
1987	49.8

SOURCE: Based on <u>Statistical Abstract 1989</u>, p. 742.

Table 3.   DOMESTIC PERSONAL COMPUTERS IN USE

Year	Computers (millions)
1981	2.1
1982	5.5
1983	12.2
1984	19.2
1985	25.3
1986	31.2
1987	37.8

SOURCE: Based on <u>Statistical Abstract 1989</u>, p. 743.

Topic 5: Labor and Management

5.1 STRUCTURING OF JOBS

In the past generation, U.S. industrial management has largely abandoned time-and-motion engineering, with its mechanistic treatment of workers, and turned to an emphasis on worker-management communication, participatory management, job-sharing and enrichment, and flexible scheduling. But none of these arrangements have become universal or have changed workplace conditions dramatically. Technological innovation remains the most important element in the reorganization of work, somewhat retarded by the relatively slow growth of research and development expenditures since 1960.

The concept of "scientific management" seems largely to have disappeared from business literature in the United States. Taylorism, with its technique of time-and-motion study, is viewed as an historical episode, and there is no apparent interest in reviving it. The currently fashionable management strategies seem to revolve around quality-of-workplace programs and worker-management cooperation in the improvement of productivity and product quality, rather than the classic strategies of managerial manipulation. However, Merkel (1980) contends that the scientific management movement left a profound cultural legacy in which management and administration are visualized abstractly rather than situationally.

The current managerial literature is much concerned with allowing workers some degree of participation in management (and thereby encouraging them to work harder and make their firms more profitable). Programs of this type seem to have multiplied since 1975, although it is difficult to find numerical evidence.

The cooperative movement (Gunn, 1984, Whyte and Blasi, 1984, pp. 129-30) represents an older form of worker self-management which has been feebly active in the United States for most of this century without ever generating much momentum. Rosen, Klein and Young (1986, p. 17) estimate that there are about 800 worker cooperatives operating in the U.S., though most of them are very small and they are often "alternative" businesses such as book stores and health food stores. One reason may be that cooperatives lack the tax advantages required by large enterprises.

Federal legislation does provide tax advantages for groups of employees who buy out their employers and establish firms that are wholly self-managed. Whyte and Blasi (1984) wrote that there had been a "striking expansion" in the number of employee-owned firms in the 1970s, so that by 1981 the Internal Revenue Service had records of at least 5,000 companies that had shared ownership with their employees. According to Rosen, Klein and Young (1986) there were about 7,000 employee stock ownership programs then operating in the United States, in about 10-15% of which employees owned a controlling interest.

The interest in self-management is also reflected by the recent growth of "worker participation" and "quality of worklife" schemes that concede some degree of worker participation in decision-making. Programs of this kind, some ostensibly modeled on Japanese industrial practices, have proliferated in the 1980s. For example, as of 1983 more than 11,000

Ford Motor Company workers were said to be involved in "voluntary problem-solving groups or more extensive decision-making roles" (Kornbluh, 1984, p. 90). Unfortunately, statistics on these programs are rare. Kochan, Katz and Mower (1984, p. 7) report, however, that

> according to one set of estimates, in early 1982 approximately 1,000 companies had Quality Circles under way, 100 companies had more advanced forms of work reorganization experiments involving autonomous work groups and another 500 or so companies were engaged in Scanlon Plan type (productivity gains sharing) projects.

Although union officials were initially suspicious of such programs, they have come to view them more favorably. Some unions, including the United Auto Workers, the United Steelworkers and the Communications Workers, have negotiated contracts that mandate union-management participation experiments. A white paper issued by the AFL-CIO Executive Council in 1985 recommended that organized labor actively encourage the establishment of quality of worklife programs (Raskin, 1986, p. 26), but this interest does not appear to have been sustained.

Job sharing, as the term is used in the United States, has little resemblance to the elaborate job enrichment schemes common in European industry. It refers to a procedure whereby employees accept a reduced work week as an alternative to being laid off. The details of such arrangements vary among the ten states that approve short-term compensation; such approval is required because unemployment benefits are managed by the states rather than by the federal government (Nemirow, 1984, p. 34; Schiff, 1986, p. 28).

The first job-sharing schemes were set up during the Depression. They were generally unpopular because they involved merely a reduction of hours, usually imposed by the employer, without any financial assistance (Nemirow, 1984, p. 35). The idea was revived in the recession of the 1970s, however, and a number of companies tried it temporarily, some until recovery (Pan Am) and some until bankruptcy (the Washington Star) (Nemirow, 1984, p. 36). Surveys indicated that these programs were well received by the workers involved, although they were not widely copied.

Job enrichment, like self-management, is a tactic for improving the quality of workplace life, as part of a management effort to improve productivity, reduce absenteeism and maintain employee morale. Herzberg's influential 1968 paper on job enrichment spoke of it as enhancing "achievement, recognition for achievement, the work itself, responsibility, and growth or advancement." The paper was very well received by the business and business school communities: according to the Harvard Business Review's editors (in Herzberg, 1987, p. 109) it had sold more than 1.2 million reprints by September 1987, 300,000 more than any other HBR article. Many companies have experimented with job enrichment programs, and many of these experiments have been described in published reports, some of which show highly favorable results and some of which do not. However, it is not possible to determine how many firms have attempted job enrichment, and it is often unclear exactly what goes on under that name.

A much more widespread form of job restructuring has been flexible scheduling or "flextime." The practice was virtually unknown prior to 1970 but grew rapidly thereafter (Staines and Pleck, 1983). Mellor (1986), summarizing the results of a question on work schedules included in the Census Bureau's Current Population Survey of 1985, noted that in May, 1985 about 9.1 million full-time American workers had flexible work schedules. Flexible scheduling was least common for teenagers, and highest for the 35-44 and 65 and over age groups. Men were more likely than women to have flexible schedules, and whites more likely than blacks and hispanics. Flexibility also varied with occupation, being as low as 4% for machine operators and as high as 30% for computer scientists. Flexible scheduling was slightly more common in the private sector (12.6%) than in the public sector (11.3%). Within the public sector, however, 20% of federal government employees had flexible schedules, as authorized by The Federal Employees Flexible and Compressed Work Schedules Act of 1978.

Another form of job structuring arises from the application of research and development to production processes. The private industrial sector is responsible for about half of the research and development activity in the United States (National Science Board, 1986). Table 1 shows the trend since 1960. Measured in constant dollars, outlays have barely kept up with GNP, a fact to which some observers attribute the decline of American industrial competitiveness.

References

Gunn, Christopher Eaton. Worker Self-Management in the United States. Ithaca: Cornell University Press, 1984.

Herzberg, Frederick. "One More Time: How Do You Motivate Employees?" Harvard Business Review 65 (September-October 1987: 109-120; originally published 1968.

Kochan, Thomas A., Harry C. Katz and Nancy R. Mower. Worker Participation and American Unions: Threat or Opportunity. Cambridge, MA: The W.E. Upjohn Institute for Employment Research, 1984.

Kornbluh, Hy. "Work Place Democracy and Quality of Work Life: Problems and Prospects." The Annals of the American Academy of Political and Social Science 473 (1984): 88-95.

Mellor, Earl F. "Shift Work and Flexitime: How Prevalent are They?" Monthly Labor Review 109 (1986): 14-22.

Merkle, Judith. Management and Ideology: The Legacy of the International Scientific Management Movement. Berkeley: University of California Press, 1980.

National Science Board. Science Indicators, The 1985 Report. Washington, D.C.: USGPO, 1985.

Nemirow, Martin. "Work-sharing Approaches: Past and Present." Monthly Labor Review 107 (1984): 34-39.

Raskin, A.H. "Labor: A Movement in Search of a Mission." In Unions in Transition: Entering the Second Century, edited by Seymour Martin Lipset, pp. 3-38. San Francisco: Institute for Contemporary Studies, 1986.

Rosen, Corey M., Katherine J. Klein and Karen M. Young. Employee Ownership in America: The Equity Solution. Lexington, MA: Lexington Books, 1986.

Schiff, Frank W. "Short-time Compensation: Assessing the Issues." Monthly Labor Review 109
    (1986): 28-30.

Staines, Graham L. and Joseph H. Pleck. The Impact of Work Schedules on the Family. Ann
    Arbor, Michigan: University of Michigan, Survey Research Center, Institute for Social
    Research, 1983.

U.S. Bureau of the Census. Statistical Abstract of the United States, 1989. Washington, D.C.,
    1989.

Whyte, William Foote and Joseph R. Blasi. "Employee Ownership and the Future of Unions."
    The Annals of the American Academy of Political and Social Science 473 (1984): 128-40.

Table 1.   RESEARCH AND DEVELOPMENT EXPENDITURES, 1960-1987

Year	1982 Dollars (billions)	Percent of GNP
1960	$43.6	3%
1965	59.4	3
1970	62.4	3
1975	59.9	2
1980	73.2	2
1987	100.1	3

SOURCE: Based on <u>Statistical Abstract 1989</u>, p. 576.

During the past twenty years, personnel administration in American employment systems has changed its name and its function. Now known as human resource management (HRM), it has become a kind of mediator between the management of an employment system and the numerous government agencies that regulate the recruitment, hiring, training, placement, treatment, promotion and dismissal of employees in all sizeable employment systems. (I use the term employment system to denote any enterprise or agency, public, private or mixed, in which personnel actions are managed bureaucratically. Jaques (1986) estimates that more than 90% of full-time workers in the U.S. labor force are employees of such systems).

As a result of the Civil Rights Act of 1964 and hundreds of other statutes, court decisions, and administrative rulings, employment systems in the U.S. have come under increasingly strict public mandates to provide designated minorities (Blacks, Hispanics, Asians, Native Americans) with at least equal access to jobs and promotions; to remove gender specifications from job and promotion openings; to provide job and promotion opportunities to physically and mentally handicapped persons; to provide evidence of nondiscrimination in hiring and promotion with respect to age, sexual preference, marital status, pregnancy, and certain illnesses; to provide equal pay for equal work to all these categories of employees; and to modify requirements for hiring or promotion that have the effect of discriminating against any of them. Additionally, they are required: to refrain from hiring illegal aliens; to abolish mandatory retirement; to prevent sexual harassment in the workplace; to advertise job openings; to provide advance notice of layoffs; to justify individual dismissals; to provide health insurance to employees in some jurisdictions; to provide maternity and paternity leaves and child care in some jurisdictions; to fund pension plans adequately; and to maintain adequate grievance procedures. These multiple new requirements--the foregoing list is not exhaustive--are monitored by human resource managers.

HRM responsibilities have also been enlarged by the growth of fringe benefits and costs in U.S. employment systems. As Table 1 shows, the aggregate cost of fringe benefits paid by American employers increased by almost 3000% from 1950 to 1979 and the rate of increase was approximately the same for public and private fringe benefit programs. Further increases have occurred since 1979. HRM departments are responsible for monitoring these programs, calculating entitlements, maintaining records, and keeping the accounts.

The tables cover only those fringe benefits that have a precise dollar relationship to wages and salaries. There are many other types of fringe benefit, however, some old, like paid holidays and vacations and employee discounts, others quite new, like prepaid legal services and subsidized commuting. All of them have participated in the rapid expansion of cost and coverage characteristic of fringe benefits in general. These programs too come under the jurisdiction of HRM departments.

Some new fringe benefits are conferred voluntarily by employers, others are attributable to collective bargaining; the greater number result from governmental pressure exerted through statutes, regulations, or the threat of litigation. The welfare state developed later in the United States than in other advanced industrial nations. The entitlements provided through employment systems have developed in an uncoordinated way in response to diverse public and private initiatives and the procedures associated with them are complex and difficult to administer. Administrative errors can be very costly for an enterprise that is found to be in violation of statutes or regulations or to have failed in any of its innumerable obligations towards job applicants, employees, or former employees.

It is understandable therefore that HRM has changed in a few years from a relatively minor service activity--limited to hiring, job classification, and personnel records--to a principal management activity. This trend has been marked not only by the adoption of a more glamorous designation but also by a sharp upgrading in the pay, prestige and influence of human resource managers (Heidrick and Struggles, 1984).

References

Bell, D. and W. Marclay. "Trends in Retirement Eligibility and Pension Benefits, 1974-83." Monthly Labor Review 110 (1987): 18-25.

Heidrick and Struggles. Human Resources: Function in Transition. Chicago: Heidrick and Struggles, 1984.

Jaques, Elliot. Personal communication, 1985.

U.S. Department of Labor. Employee Benefits in Medium and Large Firms, 1981. Bulletin 2140. Washington, D.C.: USGPO, 1982.

------. Employee Benefits in Medium and Large Firms, 1986. Bulletin 2281. Washington, D.C.: USGPO, 1987.

Yung-Ping Chen. "The Growth of Fringe Benefits: Implications for Social Security." Monthly Labor Review 104 (1981): 3-10.

Table 1.   EMPLOYER-PAID FRINGE BENEFITS, 1950-1979

Year	Cost of Benefits (billions)
1950	$ 7.8
1960	23.0
1970	63.2
1979	225.0

SOURCE: Based on Yung-Ping, 1981.

The number of U.S. business firms has grown steadily since 1960. The labor force is almost evenly divided among small, medium, large, and giant firms. Both the formation and the failures of business firms increased during the 1980s. The proportion of women-owned business has increased dramatically since 1970; minority businesses have done rather poorly despite strong official encouragement. Employee stock ownership has expanded greatly since 1974. Outright ownership and management by employees under the ESOP legislation, although much publicized, remains relatively rare.

The total number of United States firms increased dramatically from 2.7 million in 1960 to 5.0 million in 1985 (Table 1). The number of people employed rose correspondingly--from 48 million to 81 million. The vast majority of U.S. firms employ less than 20 people; the percentage decreased very slightly from 91% in 1965 to 88% in 1985. The employed labor force is distributed almost evenly among firms with 1-19, 20-99, 100-499 and more than 500 employees (Table 2).

The business failure rate, which oscillated without a clear trend from 1960 to 1980, rose sharply in the 1980s. In 1978 the bankruptcy laws were changed to allow firms to file for bankruptcy even though they remained financially operational, but these so-called Chapter 11 bankruptcies account for only a fraction of business bankruptcies, which increased steadily from 278,000 in 1980 to 561,000 in 1987 (Statistical Abstract 1989, p. 527). Many small businesses, of course, disappear without the formality of a bankruptcy. Generally speaking, older businesses are less susceptible to failure.

In 1972 there were 402,000 women-owned firms in the U.S., 4.6% of the total number. This rose to 702,000 firms in 1977 and then to 2.9 million or 23% of the total in 1982 (Bureau of the Census, Surveys of Women-Owned Businesses, 1974, 1979, 1985). More recent figures do not seem to be available. Most women-owned businesses are individual proprietorships and until 1982 the Census Bureau identified the gender of owners of these firms using the name of the first person listed in the appropriate section of the individual tax returns. But since on most tax returns filed by married couples, the husband's name is listed first, the bureau counted these firms as owned by men, and women owners were grossly under-represented. The 1982 Survey of Women-Owned Business corrected this error. However, the correction makes it appear as though the number of women proprietors had increased very dramatically. There is no way to judge the truth of the matter until another census of women-owned businesses is made (see Russell, 1987).

In 1972 there were 195,000 black-owned firms, 2.3% of the total. By 1977 there were 231,000 and by 1982, 339,000 or 2.8% of the total. Thus, although the number of black-owned firms nearly doubled, their percentage hardly changed at all (Bureau of the Census, Surveys of Minority-owned Business Enterprise, 1972, 1977, 1982). Most of the increase in black proprietorships occurred in sole proprietorships with receipts under $5,000, rather than in the larger and more profitable firms. Indeed, aggregate sales receipts for black-owned firms declined 9.6% between 1977 and 1982, after adjustment for inflation (O'Hare and Suggs, 1986). Despite strong encouragement at all levels of government, subsidized loans, and mandatory set-asides in government procurement, the progress of this sector has been discouraging. In 1987, minority business firms, including numerous firms owned by "other nonwhites" garnered only 2.7% of the dollar volume of all federal contracts awarded (Statistical Abstract 1989, p. 529).

The most significant change in the internal organization of American firms in recent years has been the increase in the number of employee-owned firms. This change followed from the introduction, beginning in 1974, of new legislation that used tax incentives and other means to encourage the formation of Employee Stock Ownership Programs (ESOPs) in which companies gave shares of stock to their employees or sold them at a significant discount. These programs served two distinct purposes: to provide productivity incentives, and to prevent plant closings by allowing workers to take over the management of failing establishments. These worker takeovers have aroused wide interest, but they account for only about 2% of all ESOP programs. Rosen, Klein and Young (1986) identified 65 employee takeovers of this kind, of which 90% were still in business at the time of their study, and some had been conspicuously successful.

In 1974, when the facilitating legislation was first introduced, there were about 300 ESOPs in the United States. Rosen, Klein and Young (1986, pp. 16-17) estimate that by 1984 there were about 7,000, involving more than 10 million employee shareholders. According to the same authors,

the average ESOP firm is larger than the average U.S. company, since few ESOP firms have under 10-15 employees (due to high ESOP legal costs); 10-20% of ESOPs appear to be in very large firms and typically transfer only small amounts of stock to employees; the rest average about 15-40% of stock owned by the ESOP. In a typical ESOP employees receive an amount equivalent to 5-15% of their payroll in stock [each year] . . . . Employees vote their stock on all issues in 25-30% of all ESOPs; in most of the remainder they vote only on certain limited issues required by law (Rosen, Klein and Young, 1986, pp. 16-17).

References

O'Hare, William and Robert Suggs. "Embattled Black Businesses." American Demographics 8
(April, 1986): 26-31.

Rosen, Corey M., Katherine J. Klein, and Karen M. Young. Employee Ownership in America.
Lexington, MA: Lexington Books, 1986.

Russell, Cheryl. "What a Difference a Way Makes." American Demographics 7 (October, 1987):
7.

U.S. Bureau of the Census. County Business Patterns, 1985. U.S. Summary. Washington, D.C.:
USGPO, 1987. Previous years as cited.

------. Historical Statistics of the United States, Colonial Times to 1970 (Bicentennial edition).
Washington, D.C., USGPO, 1975.

------. Survey of Minority-Owned Business Enterprise, 1982. Washington, D.C., USGPO, 1982.
Previous years as cited.

------. Survey of Women-Owned Businesses, 1982. Washington, D.C.: USGPO, 1985. Previous
years as cited.

------. Statistical Abstract of the United States, 1989. Washington, D.C., 1989. Annual. Previous
years as cited.

Table 1.   U.S. FIRMS, 1960-1985

Year	Total Concerns in Business (1000s)	Index of Net Business Formation (1967=100)	Business Failures (1000s)
1960	2,708	95	15
1965	2,527	100	14
1970	2,442	109	11
1975	2,679	110	11
1980	2,780	130	12
1985	4,990*	121	57
1987**	6,004	121	61

*Base change in 1983--data not directly comparable to preceding years.
**Preliminary

SOURCE: Based on Statistical Abstract 1989, p. 525; 1987, p. 509.

Table 2.   DISTRIBUTION OF EMPLOYMENT BY EMPLOYMENT-SIZE CLASS OF REPORTING UNITS, 1965-1985

Number of Employees in Firm	Proportion of Labor Force		
	1965	1975	1985
1-19	27%	27%	27%
20-99	24	27	29
100-499	23	23	24
500+	26	23	20

SOURCE: Based on U.S. Bureau of the Census, County Business Patterns,1965, p. 1-20; 1975, p. xix; 1985.

6.1 OCCUPATIONAL STATUS

The U.S. labor force has grown faster than the population; by 1987, 66% of adults were in the labor force. Higher proportions of women and young adults are working, and fewer middle-aged and older men. Analysts are divided about whether changes in the occupational structure represent class convergence or continuity of existing patterns of inequality. Although there has been an upgrading of the occupational structure as a whole, over half of employed men still work in blue-collar occupations. There is no evidence of recent proletarianization of the U.S. work force; instead, there has been a steady rise in the percentage of workers employed in professional, managerial, and technical occupations. Shifts in the industrial location of employment include substantial declines in agriculture and manufacturing, increases in service and financial sectors, and until 1975, in government employment. Self-employment has declined to less than 9% of all workers, and unpaid family work has virtually disappeared.

Between 1950 and 1987 the U.S. labor force doubled, rising from 63 million to 122 million workers. Most of the increase came from national population growth, but part of it reflected higher rates of participation in the labor force. Between 1950 and 1987 the proportion of the adult population in the labor force increased from 60% to 66% (Table 1), and this increase reflected, among other things, a combination of declining labor force participation by men and increasing participation by women. Other subtrends masked in general expansion of labor force participation included higher rates of employment among young adults, earlier retirement by older men, and convergence of the labor force participation rates of black and white women (Table 2).

The labor force is increasingly dominated by young workers. In 1960, 40% of the labor force consisted of workers aged 45 and over, compared to only 28% in 1987. In other words, by the late 1980s, almost three-fourths of the American labor force was under age 45, and half was under age 35 (see Table 3). The increasingly youthful composition of the labor force is not merely a reflection of change in the age composition of the society as a whole. It is also a consequence of real declines in the labor force participation rates of middle-aged and older men. Between 1960 and 1988, labor force participation among married men age 65 and over dropped from 37% to 17%, and among married men aged 45-64, from 93% to 82%. Over the same period, labor force participation for married women of the same ages increased (Statistical Abstract 1989, p. 385).

There are two dominant, opposing interpretations about what has happened to the U.S. occupational structure over the past half century. They are variously labelled the "mainstream" and "conflict" perspectives, or the "convergence" and "stability" approaches. Class convergence theory builds on America's ideological heritage of classlessness and on the economic abundance that followed World War II. It recognizes sharp differences between the upper and lower strata of American society in earlier times, but argues that, over time, these differences have become smaller and that Americans are much more a classless society now than they used to be. At base, the argument is that the poor have begun to "catch up," and that the economic affluence of recent decades has moved many of the poor into the middle classes. According to one summary,

> The basic premise of convergence theory is that a combination of economic, social, and political forces in the postwar world has increased the affluence of huge sectors of the population, reduced poverty, diffused education, homogenized life styles, and expanded citizenship and has thus substantially reduced the importance of social class in American society. Convergence theorists anticipated a continuation of these trends which would lead both to further reductions of class differences and to a corresponding decline in the power of social-class analysis to explain contemporary social life (Blumberg, 1980, p. 17).

Specifically, the convergence theorists argue that in the postwar period the absolute income of the American people has increased, thereby raising the standard of living for almost everyone. They maintain that there has been a real decrease in material scarcity, that the "standard package" of the goods and services an affluent society can provide its citizens is, or at least until recently has been, ever more widely distributed.

The convergence theorists point to the changes in the occupational structure and the nature of work, such that fewer workers are engaged in producing goods and more in providing services; to the replacement of much unskilled labor by automation; to near universal literacy and public education; to widely available higher education; and to a growing cultural standardization fostered by the mass media. They claim that working class and middle class people are increasingly alike in income, education, and life style and that, as a result, the old gap between the working class and higher strata has been eroded by a gradual "embourgeoisement" of the working class. In sum, the convergence theorists see class differences receding as the rich and poor, owners and workers, business and working class have shared the fruit of the continued modernization of America (Blumberg, 1980, pp. 13-28).

The stability theorists acknowledge that things are better for the working class and the poor than they used to be. They acknowledge that working conditions are better, that many of the dangerous and unhealthful jobs have been phased out as blue collar work of today has come to resemble white collar work of the past. However, their primary reference point is not the historical past but an idealistic future. Viewing the same "facts" as the convergence theorists, the stability theorists tend to focus on the continuing gap between the upper and lower strata of American society. It is not so much that things are objectively better for the workers, they argue, as that the workers continue to receive such a small share of the wealth. The workers may work with their minds and fingers rather than their arms and backs, but they still work for someone else.

Trends in the size of the "working class" and the meaning of the historical upgrading of the entire occupational structure are at issue here. Relevant national trends, taken together, amount to what Wattenberg (1978, p. 26) has called "workers lib." Among the trends are the "incredible decline" of farming as an occupation, a drastic reduction in the number of women who work in other women's homes, the decline of "common laborer" as a major job description, a "stunning increase" in professional and technical jobs, massive movement of women into the labor force, and an upgrading of blue collar jobs so that work that once was dangerous, difficult, or dirty is now safer, often power-assisted, and cleaner.

Wattenberg (1978, pp. 40-41, 324) comments that while there is much talk of a "new class," and of "knowledge workers" replacing the old muscle workers, most American men still work with their hands. They are the statistical "old class," but they have acquired "most of the perquisites of the old middle class," "more money, good working conditions, less backbreaking work, more interesting work and . . . leisure time."

The upgrading of the occupational structure as a whole is apparent in the continuing movement of workers into white collar jobs. Between 1960 and 1980, the percentage of all workers in white collar occupations--professional, technical, managerial, clerical, and sales jobs-- increased from 44 to 54% (Table 4), and the "typical" job changed from blue collar to white collar. However, this apparent "embourgeoisement" is less compelling when we see that much of it is accounted for by an increasing percentage of women in the labor force combined with an overrepresentation of women in lower-status white collar jobs. As early as 1930, over half of all working women held business class jobs, and by 1980 the fraction was two-thirds. Most of these women were, and most continue to be, sales workers, clerks and secretaries, teachers and nurses (see the discussion of women's work in Chapter 3.1).

The majority of employed men, a declining majority, to be sure, but still a majority, are working class: in 1970, 60%, in 1980, 56%. They are craftsmen, operatives, laborers and service workers. Grouped according to the Census Bureau's new six-category system, male employment in 1988 in the four categories that may be considered or working class--service, precision production, operator/fabricator, and farming, forestry, and fishing occupations--still accounted for 51% of employed males aged 25 and over (Statistical Abstract 1989, p. 391).

Having noted that a majority of working men still have working class/blue-collar jobs, we should emphasize that the trend is clearly toward the continued reduction in the relative number of such jobs and a corresponding growth in managerial and technical work. If present trends continue, by 1990 persons in working-class occupations will be a minority among both male and female workers.

In a Marxist approach to changes in the U.S. occupational structure, compatible with the stability rather than the convergence perspective, Wright and Singelmann hypothesized that the 1970s would be a time of "proletarianization," when economic stagnation increased the percentage of the labor force in the working class and produced a decline in, or at least an end to the expansion of the managerial and semiautonomous/expert categories of the occupational structure. Using an "exploitation-based" typology that classified workers by their relationship to ownership and control of assets (including capital, organization assets, and skills), they tested the proletarianization hypothesis for the period 1960-1980 (see Table 5) and were forced to reject it. Instead of the expected growth of the working class, they found
> a steady rise in the proportion of the work force in the managerial, supervisory, and expert classes, accompanied by a significant fall in the proportion in each of the self-employed classes (the small employers and the petty bourgeois) in the 1960s and in the proportion in the working class in the 1970s (Wright and Martin, 1987, p. 12).

Occupations vary in the prestige accorded to them, and prestige levels of particular occupations have proved to be extraordinarily persistent both in time and cross-culturally (Hodge, Siegal, and Rossi, 1964; Hodge, Treiman, and Rossi, 1966). In light of the gradual decline in the relative representation of working class occupations in the national occupational structure, we might expect the average level of occupational prestige to be increasing also. In fact, that is what the data seem to reveal, although there are numerous fluctuations and the 1972-1988 period (Table 6) is too brief to establish the trend firmly. Between 1972 and 1982 there seems to be little change in the distribution of occupational prestige, but between 1982 and 1988 the proportion of employed people with low-status jobs (prestige scores of 29 and below) declines from one-fourth to one-fifth, and there is a corresponding increase in workers with high-status jobs (scores of 50 and above).

Concurrent with these changes in labor force composition and occupational status, there has been change in the industrial location of workers. From 1950 to 1987 employment in agriculture continued its long-term decline; the proportion of the labor force engaged in agricultural industries dropped from 14% to 3%. The second most dramatic decline was a sizable shift out of manufacturing: in 1950, manufacturing accounted for 34% of the non-agricultural labor force; by 1987, that figure had dropped to 19%. Employment in transportation and public utilities also showed a relative decline. The only industrial sector showing substantial growth was services--business, health, educational and social services, but not domestic/personal services. The finance sector, including banking, insurance, and real estate, experienced modest growth; so did government, until 1975. Construction and trade, both wholesale and retail, have retained a fairly constant share of the labor force since the 1950s (see Table 7).

Finally, there has been a shift in the auspices of employment, or what the labor force analysts refer to as "class of worker" (Table 8). In the 1950s, 17% of American workers were self-employed, and 42% of the self-employed were agricultural workers. By 1970, only 9 percent were self-employed, and that rate has remained stable ever since. The percentage of the self-employed who are in agriculture has continued to decline, from 30% in 1960 to 26% in 1970 to 15% in 1987. Unpaid work in family enterprises has become increasingly uncommon; in 1987 only .4% of the workforce were unpaid family workers, down from 3.1% percent in 1950. Most American workers--about 92% since 1970--are wage and salary workers (Statistical Abstract 1989, p. 380).

References

Blumberg, Paul. Inequality in an Age of Decline. New York: Oxford University Press, 1980.

Davis, James A. General Social Surveys, 1972-1982: Cumulative Codebook. Chicago: National Opinion Research Center, 1982.

Davis, James A. and Tom W. Smith. General Social Surveys, 1972-1988: Cumulative Codebook. Chicago: National Opinion Research Center, 1988. Annual. Previous years as cited.

Hodge, Robert W., Paul M. Siegal and Peter Rossi. "Occupational Prestige in the United States, 1925-1963." American Journal of Sociology 70 (1964): 286-302.

Hodge, Robert W., Donald J. Treiman, and Petter H. Rossi. "A Comparative Study of Occupational Prestige." In Class, Status, and Power, edited by Reinhard Bendix and Seymour Martin Lipset, pp. 309-321. New York: Free Press, 1966.

Singelmann, Joachim and Marta Tienda. "The Process of Occupational Change in a Service Society: The Case of the United States, 1960-80." In New Approaches to Economic Life, edited by Bryan Roberts, Ruth Finnegan, and Duncan Gallie, pp. 48-67. Manchester, UK: Manchester University Press, 1985.

U.S. Bureau of the Census. Statistical Abstract of the United States, 1989. Washington, D.C., 1989. Annual. Previous years as cited.

Wattenberg, Ben J. In Search of the Real America. New York: G. P. Putnam's Sons, 1978. Berkley Windhover edition.

Wright, Erik Olin and Bill Martin. "The Transformation of the American Class Structure, 1960-1980." American Journal of Sociology 93 (1987): 1-29.

Table 1. SELECTED CHARACTERISTICS OF THE LABOR FORCE,
          1950-1987

Year	Total Labor Force, incl. Armed Forces (millions)	Participation Rates (Percentage of Noninstitutionalized Population Age 16 and Older in the Labor Force)		
		Total	Male	Female
1950	63.4	60%	87%	34%
1955	67.1	60	86	36
1960	71.5	60	84	38
1965	76.4	59	81	39
1970	84.9	61	80	43
1975	95.5	62	78	46
1980	108.5	64	78	52
1985*	117.2	65	76	54
1987*	121.6	66	76	56

* 1985 and 1987 percentages for males and females refer to the
civilian labor force rather than the total.

SOURCE: Based on Statistical Abstract 1989, pp. 376-377; U.S.
    Bureau of Labor Statistics, 1985, pp. 6-7.

Table 2.   PARTICIPATION RATES: PERCENTAGE OF THE NONINSTITU-
TIONAL POPULATION AGED 16 AND OVER IN THE CIVILIAN
LABOR FORCE,* BY SEX AND RACE, 1960-1987

| | | White | | Black** | |
Year	Total	Male	Female	Male	Female
1960	59	83	36	80	47
1970	60	80	43	76	49
1975	61	79	46	71	49
1980	64	78	51	71	53
1985	65	77	54	71	56
1987	66	77	56	71	58

* Figures for 1960 are for the total labor force.
** For 1970 and before, black and other.

SOURCE: Based on Statistical Abstract 1989, pp. 376; 1974, p.
377.

Table 3.   AGE DISTRIBUTION OF THE CIVILIAN LABOR FORCE, 1960-
1987

Year	16-24	25-34	35-44	45-64	65+	Total
1960	17%	21%	23%	35%	5%	101%
1965	19	19	23	35	4	100
1970	22	21	20	34	4	101
1975	24	24	18	30	3	99
1980	24	27	19	27	3	100
1985	20	29	23	25	3	100
1987	19	29	24	25	3	100

SOURCE: Statistical Abstract 1989, p. 379.

Table 4. OCCUPATIONAL STRUCTURE OF U.S. EMPLOYMENT, POPULATION
CENSUSES, 1960-1980, AND CURRENT POPULATION SURVEY,
1975

Occupation	1960	1970	1975	1980
Professional	10%	13%	13%	15%
Technical	2	2	2	3
Manager	9	8	10	11
Clerical	15	18	18	19
Sales	8	7	7	6
Craft	14	14	12	12
Operative	19	18	15	15
Service	12	13	15	13
Laborer	5	5	5	4
Farmer	4	2	2	1
Farm laborer	2	1	1	1
Total	100	101	101	100

SOURCE: Based on Singelmann and Tienda, 1985, p. 55.

Table 5. CHANGES IN THE OCCUPATIONAL CLASS DISTRIBUTION,
WRIGHT/MARTIN "EXPLOITATION-BASED" TYPOLOGY,
CENSUS DATA, 1960-1980

Class	1960	1970	1980
Managers	15%	16%	18%
Supervisors	11	12	13
Experts	6	7	9
Workers	54	54	50
Petty bourgeois	6	4	4
Small employers	8	6	5
Total	100	99	99

SOURCE: Based on Wright and Martin, 1987, p. 13.

Table 6.   CHANGES IN THE DISTRIBUTION OF OCCUPATIONAL PRESTIGE,
           RESPONDENTS IN GENERAL SOCIAL SURVEYS, 1972-1988

Occupational Prestige Score	1972	1974	1976	1978	1980	1982	1984	1986	1988
10-19	12%	10%	11%	10%	8%	11%	11%	7%	7%
20-29	14	17	15	16	17	15	15	14	15
30-39	27	24	28	25	24	30	26	27	28
40-49	27	27	27	27	27	23	23	24	22
50-59	11	10	10	10	15	11	14	16	16
60-69	8	10	8	9	7	8	9	8	8
70-89	1	2	2	2	2	2	2	3	3
Total	100	100	101	99	100	100	100	99	99

SOURCE: Based on Davis, 1982, p. 20; Davis and Smith, 1987, p.
        30; 1988, p. 34.

Table 7. INDUSTRIAL STRUCTURE OF EMPLOYMENT: PERCENTAGE OF
CIVILIAN EMPLOYMENT IN AGRICULTURE INDUSTRIES, AND
DISTRIBUTION OF EMPLOYMENT IN NONAGRICULTURAL
ESTABLISHMENTS* BY INDUSTRY

Industrial Sector	1950	1955	1960	1965	1970	1975	1980	1985	1987
Agriculture	14%	11%	9%	7%	4%	4%	3%	3%	3%
Non-Aricultural Establishments**									
Mining	2	2	1	1	1	1	1	1	1
Construction	5	6	5	5	5	5	5	5	5
Manufacturing	34	33	31	30	27	24	22	20	19
Transportation, public utilities	9	8	7	7	6	6	6	5	5
Trade, wholesale & retail	21	21	21	21	21	22	22	24	24
Finance, insurance & real estate	4	5	5	5	5	5	6	6	6
Services	12	12	14	15	16	18	20	23	24
Government	13	14	15	17	18	19	18	17	17
Total**	100	101	99	101	99	100	98	101	101

* Includes all full- and part-time employees who worked during, or received pay for, any part of the pay period reported. Excludes proprietors, the self-employed, farm workers, unpaid family workers, private household workers, and Armed Forces.
** Note that the percentage base for industrial employment in non-agricultural establishments is <u>not</u> the entire civilian labor force; these categories total to 100% <u>without</u> the inclusion of agriculture.

SOURCE: Based on <u>Statistical Abstract 1989</u>, pp. 391, 397; <u>1974</u>, p. 345. Original source was the U.S. Bureau of Labor Statistics, <u>Employment and Earnings</u>, monthly.

Table 8.   OCCUPATIONAL CLASS OF EMPLOYED PERSONS,* BY SEX,
           1950-1987

Sex and Class of Worker	1950	1955	1960	1965	1970	1975	1980	1985	1987
All Workers									
Wage and salary	80%	82%	84%	86%	90%	90%	91%	91%	91%
Self-employed	17	15	14	12	9	9	9	9	9
Unpaid family	3	3	2	2	1	1	1	--	--
Male Workers									
Wage and salary	77	79	81	84	88	88	89	--	--
Self-employed**	21	19	17	15	12	11	11	--	--
Unpaid family	2	1	1	1	--	--	--	--	--
Female Workers									
Wage and salary	86	87	88	90	93	93	93	--	--
Self-employed**	8	6	7	6	5	5	5	--	--
Unpaid family	6	6	5	4	3	2	1	--	--

* 1965 and before, age 14 and over; 1970 and after, age 16 and over.
** Among both men and women, a sizable but declining percentage of self-employed workers are employed in agriculture. Over the period 1950-1983, that percentage declines for men from 46% to 21%; for women, from 16% to 8%.

SOURCE: Based on <u>Statistical Abstract 1989</u>, p. 380; <u>1985</u>, p. 395; <u>1966</u>, p. 230;

The substantial upward intergenerational mobility throughout most of this century reflects gross change in the occupational structure rather than increased openness of the system. Such structural mobility seems to have slowed in the 1970s and 1980s. Higher education decreases the influence of occupational origin. Since about 1970 circulation mobility has increased (i.e., the association between occupational origin and destination has declined). Career mobility has also increased since 1970. Mobility between generations is generally greater than intragenerational mobility.

Intergenerational Mobility

There is an enormous, highly technical literature on mobility trends in the U.S. (see, for example, Blau and Duncan, 1967; Duncan, Featherman, and Duncan, 1972; Hauser and Featherman, 1977; Featherman and Hauser, 1978; Hout, 1984, 1988). In part, the complexity of treatment is dictated by the topic: the nature of the occupational distribution changes over time, and even if that were not so, an individual worklife may include several different occupations. As some occupations decline and others grow, there may be a great deal of apparent occupational mobility even though the overall openness of a society's occupational system remains unchanged. Occupational mobility which may be explained by changes in the nature, number, and size of occupational categories is called structural mobility; that attributable to other factors, representing real change in the statistical association between parents' and offsprings' occupations, is called circulation mobility.

Analyses of national data and mobility studies in certain cities (cf. Baron, 1980) suggest that although there was substantial occupational mobility in the 1940s and 1950s (and throughout the previous five decades as well), most of that mobility was structural mobility. When changes in occupational structure are taken into account, there seems to have been virtually no change in the association between fathers' occupational origins and sons' occupational destinations. Michael Hout (1988, p. 1359) summarizes:

> The disparity between origin and destination distributions grew out of the decline of farming and other forms of self-employment throughout U.S. history and the concomitant growth of white-collar occupations after World War I. . . . The transition to postindustrial society redistributed occupational positions but did not alter the dependence of occupational destinations on origins.

While most occupational mobility up to about 1960 can be attributed to structural change, there is evidence that since 1960 the statistical association between status of origin and status of destination has decreased more than can be explained by the structural changes. In other words, there has been a slight but significant increase in circulation mobility, and a concomitant decrease in structural mobility, such that an apparently constant rate of mobility masks an increased openness (i.e., universalism) in U.S. society of the 1970s and 1980s.

How much gross mobility occurs depends upon how many occupational categories one applies, and on whether one measures parental occupation against an offspring's first or current job. A five-category system for 1930-1970 produces the finding that over 60% of men moved out of their father's occupational stratum to their own first job, and a 17-category system produces outflow rates of about 80% (Featherman and Hauser, 1978, p. 135). Outflow from father's occupation group and inflow to son's current occupation group are summarized in Table 1 for national samples of U.S. men, 1962-1985. The flows represented are gross mobility, in that they include elements of both circulation and structural mobility. Among the trends apparent in the outflows represented in Table 1 are continuity over the 20-year period in transmission of father's upper nonmanual status (about 60% of sons have the same high status as their fathers); a declining trend in the transmission of lower manual status and farm occupation status; and growing probabilities that the sons of lower manual workers and farmers would achieve upper nonmanual status.

Inspection of the inflow percentages in the second page of Table 1 reveals, among other things, increasing probilities that upper nonmanual workers will be the sons of upper non-manual workers; very high but declining transmission of farmer status (in 1962, 86% of farmers were the sons of farmers; by 1982-85, that had dropped to 75%); and a growing tendency for craft workers (upper manual) to be the sons of craft workers.

Between 1962 and 1973, the circulation mobility in the American occupational structure increased slightly--the system became slightly more "open" (Featherman and Hauser, 1978, p. 137; Hout, 1984; 1988, pp. 1359-1360). The trend continued over the next decade, but the particulars of the increased openness of the system--controlling for structural changes--differed for men and women. Among Hout's (1988, pp. 1358, 1383) other conclusions:

The association between men's and women's socioeconomic origins and destinations decreased by one-third between 1972 and 1985.

. . .

Education is the key factor in occupational placement. . . . Origin status affects destination status among workers who do not have bachelor's degrees, but college graduation cancels the effect of background status. Therefore, the more college graduates in the work force, the weaker the association between origin status and destination status for the population as a whole.

. . .

Overall mobility remains unchanged because a decline in structural mobility offsets the increased openness of the class structure.

. . .

Upward mobility still exceeds downward mobility in the 1980s but by a smaller margin than it did in the 1960s and 1970s.

The measurement of structural mobility presupposes a model of class (or occupational) structure, and the degree of mobility observed is partly a reflection of the way the class structure is conceptualized. Among recent attempts to assess changes in the American class structure is Wright and Martin's (1987) application of a six-category "exploitation-based" typology to the period 1960-80. They find growing numbers of managers, and decline (deproletarianization) in the number of workers, the petty bourgeois, and the small employers.

Another analysis of occupational change in the U.S. for the same period (Singelmann and Tienda, 1985) divides the change in occupational distributions into three components: industry shift effect (change attributable to transformation of the industry structure), mix effect (change attributable to intra-industry variation in occupational composition), and interaction effects from the combined influences of the first two components. Singelmann and Tienda report that the change from goods-producing to service industries continued during the 1970s but slowed somewhat; that the growth of white-collar occupations continued; and that the occupational structure has been gradually tending toward a service economy and an increased division of labor within industrial sectors. They attribute the continued increase in employment in the highest-status occupations during the 1970s largely to intra-industry changes rather than industry shifts. They argue that the upgrading of the occupational structure has been critically important in maintaining relatively high upward mobility rates, and warn that as the transition from a goods-producing to a service economy runs its course, upward mobility will become more difficult to achieve.

Career (Intragenerational) Mobility

In analyses of the association between occupational origins (e.g., fathers' occupations) and destinations (e.g., sons' current occupations), career mobility is a component of intergenerational mobility. That is, the mobility between first and current occupation is part of the total mobility between parent's occupation and one's current occupation. Studies of the components of change in total mobility between fathers' occupations and son's current occupations for cohorts sampled in 1962 and 1970 suggest that career mobility accounts for most of the observed change. In other words, the amount of career mobility in the experience of American men increased slightly between 1962 and 1970 (Hauser and Featherman, 1977: 94-97). However, even though there is evidence of increasing career mobility for this period, it must be remembered that there is more mobility between than within generations. That is, "immobility" or "self-selection" (staying within an occupational category) is more likely in a son's work history than between fathers and sons. There is greater stability of occupational positions within the career than between generations (Featherman and Hauser, 1978, p. 119).

References

Baron, James N. "Indianapolis and Beyond: A Structural Model of Mobility across the Generations." American Journal of Sociology 85 (1980): 815-839.

Blau, Peter M. and Otis Dudley Duncan. The American Occupational Structure. New York: Wiley, 1967.

Duncan, Otis Dudley, David L. Featherman, and Beverly Duncan. Socioeconomic Background and Achievement. New York: Academic Press, 1972.

Featherman, David L. and Robert M. Hauser. Opportunity and Change. New York: Academic Press, 1978.

Hauser, Robert M. and David L. Featherman. The Process of Stratification. New York: Academic Press, 1977.

Hout, Michael. "More Universalism, Less Structural Mobility: The American Occupational Structure in the 1980s." American Journal of Sociology 93 (1988): 1358-1400.

------. "Status, Autonomy, and Training in Occupational Mobility." American Journal of Sociology 89 (1984): 1379-1409.

Singelmann, Joachim and Marta Tienda. "The Process of Occupational Change in a Service Society: The Case of the United States, 1960-80." In New Approaches to Economic Life, edited by Bryan Roberts, Ruth Finnegan, and Duncan Gallie, pp. 48-67. Manchester, UK: Manchester University Press, 1985.

Wright, Erik Olin and Bill Martin. "The Transformation of the American Class Structure, 1960-1980." American Journal of Sociology 93 (1987): 1-29.

Table 1. INTERGENERATIONAL MOBILITY: OUTFLOW PERCENTAGES,
MOBILITY FROM FATHER'S TO SON'S BROAD OCCUPATION
GROUP*; AND INFLOW PERCENTAGES, MOBILITY TO SON'S BROAD
OCCUPATION GROUP FROM FATHER'S OCCUPATION: LABOR FORCE
MALES AGED 21-64 IN MARCH 1962 AND 1973, LABOR FORCE
MALES 1976-1980 AND 1982-1985

Outflow from Father's	Occupation Group to Son's Current	1962	1973	1976-80	1982-85
Upper nonmanual	Upper nonmanual	57%	59%	66%	56%
	Lower nonmanual	17	11	11	16
	Upper manual	11	13	14	14
	Lower manual	14	16	9	14
	Farm	1	1	--	--
	Total	100	100	100	100
Lower nonmanual	Upper nonmanual	43	45	46	38
	Lower nonmanual	24	17	21	24
	Upper manual	15	16	16	15
	Lower manual	17	21	16	21
	Farm	2	1	1	2
	Total	101	100	100	100
Upper manual	Upper nonmanual	25	31	31	29
	Lower nonmanual	17	12	9	10
	Upper manual	28	28	32	33
	Lower manual	29	28	28	26
	Farm	1	1	1	1
	Total	100	100	101	110
Lower manual	Upper nonmanual	18	13	27	26
	Lower nonmanual	15	12	8	12
	Upper manual	22	24	25	24
	Lower manual	43	40	39	37
	Farm	2	1	1	1
	Total	100	100	100	100
Farm	Upper nonmanual	10	16	16	19
	Lower nonmanual	12	9	9	7
	Upper manual	19	23	25	20
	Lower manual	36	37	32	38
	Farm	22	15	18	17
	Total	99	100	100	101
Upper nonmanual	Upper nonmanual	25%	29%	31%	34%
	Lower nonmanual	23	17	16	14
	Upper manual	19	20	23	22
	Lower manual	20	22	21	21
	Farm	13	12	9	9
	Total	100	100	100	100

Table 1.   INTERGENERATIONAL MOBILITY: OUTFLOW PERCENTAGES,
           MOBILITY FROM FATHER'S TO SON'S BROAD OCCUPATION
           GROUP*; AND INFLOW PERCENTAGES, MOBILITY TO SON'S
           BROAD OCCUPATION GROUP FROM FATHER'S OCCUPATION:
           LABOR FORCE MALES AGED 21-64 IN MARCH 1962 AND
           1973, LABOR FORCE MALES 1976-1980 AND 1982-1985
           (continued)

Inflow to Son's Current	Occupation Group from Father's	1962	1973	1976-80	1982-85
Lower nonmanual	Upper nonmanual	12	15	16	25
	Lower nonmanual	20	16	26	23
	Upper manual	20	21	21	19
	Lower manual	26	30	21	25
	Farm	23	18	16	8
	Total	101	100	100	100
Upper manual	Upper nonmanual	6	9	10	12
	Lower nonmanual	10	9	9	9
	Upper manual	26	26	33	37
	Lower manual	30	33	28	29
	Farm	28	24	20	13
	Total	100	101	100	100
Lower manual	Upper nonmanual	5	8	5	10
	Lower nonmanual	7	8	7	9
	Upper manual	17	17	25	24
	Lower manual	38	38	40	36
	Farm	34	28	23	21
	Total	101	100	100	100
Farm	Upper nonmanual	2	3	3	--
	Lower nonmanual	3	3	3	8
	Upper manual	3	6	3	10
	Lower manual	7	7	8	8
	Farm	86	81	84	75
	Total	101	100	100	101

* Broad occupation groups are upper nonmanual: professional and
kindred workers, managers and officials, and non-retail sales
workers; lower nonmanual: proprietors, clerical and kindred
workers, and retail salesworkers; upper manual: craftsmen, foremen
and kindred workers; lower manual: service workers, operatives and
kindred workers, and laborers, except farm; farm: farmers and farm
managers, farm laborers and foremen.

SOURCE: Based on Featherman and Hauser, 1978, p. 89; Hout, 1988,
        pp. 1395-1396. The 1962 and 1973 data are from the national
        "Occupational Changes in a Generation" Current Population
        Surveys; the 1976-80 and 1982-85 data are composite General
        Social Survey samples.

Inequality--the degree to which wealth and earnings are distributed unequally--has remained fairly constant throughout U.S. history. Changes in life style and real earnings have not changed the relative distribution of wealth very much. The richest one percent of the population owns between one-third and one-fourth of the wealth, and the best-paid one-fifth of the population earns between 40 and 50 percent of the income. The inequality of family incomes in the U.S. has been remarkably stable throughout the postwar period, despite innumerable attempts to flatten it directly by progressive educational opportunity and reducing discrimination. The unchanging Gini coefficients mask numerous shifts in family and labor force composition, however, as well as shifts in the income situation of particular social categories, like the elderly, whose incomes have improved and the young, whose economic situation has deteriorated.

Wealth

A high degree of economic inequality has characterized the United States from its beginnings. The detective work of piecing together the historical patterns of wealth holding from such sources as probate records and estate tax records yields the following conclusion, described (Osberg, 1984, p. 47) as having a fair degree of consensus among the experts:

. . . the most likely pattern of change in the United States as a whole over the past two centuries was: (1) some increase in wealth inequality to 1860-1870, (2) possibly continued to a somewhat higher degree of concentration, which may have peaked around 1890 or 1929 or 1940, (3) a mild downdrift in inequality to the 1950's and (4) little change since, at least among top wealthholders.

One depiction of wealth inequality over time compares holdings in 1774 in the Thirteen Colonies with percentage shares of wealth in the U.S. in 1962 and 1973 (Osberg, 1984, p. 44), and reveals that the share of all wealth held by the richest one percent of the population increased from one-six to one-third over the two centuries. The richest tenth (top decile) of the population owned half of all wealth in colonial America, compared to about two-thirds of all wealth in the 1960s and 1970s (Table 1).

Another estimate of historical patterns in wealth (Turner and Starnes, 1976, p. 19) puts the share of wealth held by the richest one percent at about one-fifth in the early nineteenth century, and shows increases to about one-third by the 1930s, followed by a slight decline. Turner and Starnes (1976, pp. 19-20) conclude that

. . . there does appear to have been an increasing concentration of wealth up to the beginning of World War II. Since World War II, there seems to have been a slight decrease in the share of total wealth held by the richest 1 percent of adults. Unfortunately, long-term data are not available for assessing trends throughout the full range of wealthholding.

Contemporary data on wealthholding derive, in the main, from three sources: estimates based on "the estate tax multiplier method" (e.g., Smith, 1973; Smith and Franklin, 1974), infrequent surveys (e.g., Projector and Weiss, 1966), and data from income tax files, sometimes merged with census data (Greenwood, 1983). It appears that estimates derived from all of these methods understate the concentration of wealth, due in part to 1) people's efforts to minimize their apparent incomes and wealth and therefore their taxes, 2) response bias in questionnaire studies, and 3) administrative processes that inadequately reflect the estates of persons with minimal wealth and that give an incomplete picture of wealth dispersed in anticipation of death (David and Menchik, 1988, pp. 317, 331; Kolko, 1962, p. 51).

In the years following World War II, the one-tenth of the nation with the highest incomes owned an average of two-thirds of all liquid assets (Kolko, 1962:48-49). As of 1973, the upper tenth of U.S. families owned about 70% of net wealth, including 93% of corporate stock, while the poorest third of the population had no measurable wealth (Osberg, 1984, p. 43; Greenwood, 1983). Some analysts argue that massive government intervention in the 1930s and early 1940s reduced the inequality of wealth somewhat; most agree that since 1945 the distribution of wealth in the U.S. has remained fairly stable and shown no clear trend.

Estimates of the wealth of "top wealthholders" for the 1953-1976 period, based on the estate tax multiplier method, reveal that the top one percent of wealthholders held about one-fourth of all wealth (Table 2). Between 1953 and 1972 there was little change in the distribution of wealth, but there were changes in the nature of assets held. For instance, the proportion of corporate stock held by the wealthiest one percent of the population declined from 86% to 56%. Between 1972 and 1976, the fraction of total wealth held by the top one percent declined from about one-fourth to less than one-fifth. In other words, during the 1970s there appears to have been a trend toward decreased concentration of wealth.

A change in the way data on wealth are presented in the Statistical Abstract prevents the extension of the trend into the 1980s. The available wealth statistics for the 1980s are presented in terms of number of wealthholders at given levels of wealth, such as number of millionaires, rather than in terms of total wealth held by the top centile of the population (see, for example, Statistical Abstract 1988, p. 438).

Income

Trends in personal income parallel trends in wealth: the distribution of income among the American population is highly unequal and has always been so. The Census Bureau has only collected systematic data on income since 1947, but there are estimates of the national income distribution 1910-1947 which

> . . . reveal enormous income inequality in America during the early years of this century. The upper 20 percent of the income-earning population received close to one-half of all income, with the other 80 percent receiving the other half. The top 10 percent received about one-third of the income in a given year (Turner and Starnes, 1976, p. 50).

Trends since 1947 are more systematically documented. Median family income in constant dollars doubled between 1947 and 1973, from about $15,000 to almost $30,000 (1986 dollars). Since 1973 the net trend in median income has been stability, although there have been some fairly sizable fluctuations, both declines and recoveries. Although real income has almost doubled since 1950, there has been virtual stability in inequality of income.

Throughout the 1950-87 period, families in the lowest fifth received between 4% and 5% of all income, while the fifth of all families having the highest incomes have received between

41% and 44% of all income. In other words, families in the highest-earning quintile have averaged between eight and ten times more income than families in the lowest quintile. This pattern of inequality also fits the black population: the poorest fifth receives less than 5%, while the richest fifth receives well over 40% of all income received by black families. In fact, a tendency to greater concentration of income is even more apparent among blacks than whites. By 1987, over 48% of income earned by blacks was earned by the top fifth of black families.

While patterns of the inequality of income distribution are roughly the same among blacks and whites, the amounts of income to be distributed differ greatly. Analysis of changes in median family income for 1950-1987 (Table 4) show that the median income of blacks runs at just over half that of whites, rising from 54% in 1950 to 62% in 1975 and back to 56% by 1987. In other words, there has been little change in black-white income differentials since 1950, despite the numerous tax and welfare policies that were intended to flatten it. Table 3 shows the almost incredible stability of the family income distribution from 1950 to 1987.

The stability of income inequality conceals several important changes in family structure and in the composition of the labor force. The main changes--especially marked since 1970--have been: an increase in two-earner families, an increase in families headed by someone over aged 65, and an increase in the number of families headed by women. According to Levy, the increase in two-earner families has tended, overall, to favor equality, while the other two changes,on balance, have favored inequality. He concludes that "family income inequality remained roughly constant over the postwar period, even though a declining number of families had earnings, because other income sources grew enough to take up the slack" (Levy, 1987, pp. 162-163, 165). The most important of these other income sources have been government transfers, particularly Social Security and Aid to Families with Dependent Children.

Between 1947 and 1984, government transfer payments to individuals, as a percentage of GNP, rose from 4% to over 11% (Levy, 1987, p. 167). The trend of continued increase in this percentage is built into the Social Security and health insurance programs.

Table 5 shows that the progressive income tax that pays for these programs is not very progressive in its consequences; the reduction of the income shares of the wealthiest families was almost negligible from 1952 to 1981. We do not have comparable figures for the years since 1981 but the tax reforms introduced in that year greatly reduced the nominal tax rates imposed on high-income families and the tax reforms introduced in 1987 reduced them even further. During the same interval, Social Security payroll taxes, which are not progressive at all, and are not reflected in Table 5, increased sharply, making the tax system as a whole clearly regressive.

In 1980, as Table 6 shows, it was the poorest decile of families whose income was most affected by both taxes and transfer payments. Since then the floor for federal income tax obligation has been raised, but payroll and sales taxes, and the loss of transfer benefits because of earned income, combine to impose a higher marginal tax rate on poor families than on rich families.

Table 7 shows the proportion of family heads over 65, of children under 18, and of black families, that fell into the lowest quintile of the family income distribution in 1949 and 1984. The proportion of the elderly in poverty decreased from nearly half in 1949 to fewer than a fifth in 1984, an improvement generally attributed to Social Security pensions. But the proportion of children living in poverty increased significantly during the same period, and the percentage of black families in poverty also increased somewhat. Both of these effects are attributable to the rapid increase in the proportion of black families headed by single women. Black families headed by married couples have done very much better; the representation of black families in the highest quintile tripled between 1949 and 1984.

There has been much discussion recently of the idea that the American middle class has declined, and that America's families in general are polarized into the rich and the poor. Levy's quintile data, discussed above, do not support this notion. But other researchers, using somewhat different measures, have reached different conclusions. For example, Blackburn and Bloom (1985) conclude that the middle class is indeed in decline, "because of the growth in unemployment, the greater number of single-person households, the growing number of two-earner families, the effect of the baby boom on the age composition of the population, and the changing industrial structure of the economy." Recent research by economists of the Bureau of Labor Statistics generally confirms Blackburn and Bloom's findings. Horrigan and Haugen (1988:3) write,

> we find that the proportion of families in the middle class has declined substantially over time [1969-1986] . . . . the majority of the decline in the middle is offset by an increase in the upper class . . . . in terms of its share of aggregate income, there has been a growing disparity between the lower class and the remainder of the distribution.

Economic inequality can be analyzed from the standpoint of poverty as well as wealth. A recent analysis of "earnings poverty" for 1939-1979 concludes that the general trend is

> . . . a long decline in poverty, beginning after the Great Depression and continuing until the early 1970s. Progress against poverty since that time has slowed. However, declines in poverty for the elderly relative to the nonelderly and for nonwhites relative to whites were greater over the 1959-1979 period than during the 1939-1959 period. Households headed by women have been disproportionately poor throughout the 40-year period (Ross, Danziger, and Smolensky, 1987, p. 598).

The proportion of the population in poverty has fluctuated much more than income shares, in part because of periodic adjustments in the definition of poverty. The percent of the population below the poverty line declined from 18.5% in 1959 to a low of 8.8% in 1973, remained below 10% until 1979, and then rose again, reaching 12.4% in 1983, with much higher rates, 32% and 26% respectively, for blacks and hispanics. Table 7 shows the trend.

Other relevant analyses of trends in inequality from the standpoint of poverty and low earnings include Dooley and Gottschalk (1984, 1985) and Chapter 16.4 (Poverty) in this report.

References

Blackburn, McKinley L. and David E. Bloom. "What is Happening to the Middle Class?" American Demographics 7 (1985): 19-25.

David, Martin H. and Paul L. Menchik. "Changes in Cohort Wealth over a Generation." Demography 25 (1988): 317-335.

Dooley, Martin and Peter Gottschalk. "Earnings Inequality among Males in the United States: Trends and the Effect of Labor Force Growth." Journal of Political Economy 92 (1984): 59-89.

------. "The Increasing Proportion of Men with Low Earnings in the United States." Demography 22 (1985): 25-34.

Greenwood, D. "An Estimation of U.S. Family Wealth and Its Distribution from Micro Data, 1973." Review of Income and Wealth 29 (1983): 23-44.

Horrigan, M.W. and S.E. Haugen. "The Declining Middle-class Thesis: A Sensitivity Analysis." Monthly Labor Review 111 (1988): 3-13.

Kolko, Gabriel. Wealth and Power in America: An Analysis of Social Class and Income Distribution. New York: Praeger, 1962.

Levy, Frank. Dollars and Dreams: The Changing American Income Distribution. New York: Russell Sage Foundation, 1987.

Osberg, Lars. Economic Inequality in the United States. Armonk, New York: M.E. Sharpe, Inc., 1984.

Pechman, Joseph A. and Mark J. Mazur. "The Rich, the Poor, and the Taxes They Pay: An Update." The Public Interest 77 (1984): 28-37.

Projector, Dorothy S. and Gertrude S. Weiss. Survey of Financial Characteristics of Consumers. Washington, D.C.: Board of Governors of the Federal Reserve System, 1966.

Ross, Christine, Sheldon Danziger, and Eugene Smolensky. "The Level and Trend of Poverty in the United States, 1939-1979." Demography 24 (1987): 587-600.

Smith, James D. The Concentration of Personal Wealth in America, 1969. Washington, D.C.: Urban Institute Working Paper No.1208-1, August 27, 1973.

Smith, James D. and Stephen D. Franklin. "The Concentration of Personal Wealth--1922-1969." American Economic Review 64 (May, 1974): 162-167.

Turner, Jonathan H. and Charles E. Starnes. Inequality: Privilege & Poverty in America. Pacific Palisades, CA: Goodyear, 1976.

U.S. Bureau of the Census. Statistical Abstract of the United States, 1989. Washington, D.C., 1989. Annual. Previous years as cited.

Williamson, Jeffrey G. and Peter H. Lindert. American Inequality. New York: Academic Press, 1980.

Table 1. SELECTED MEASURES OF WEALTH INEQUALITY, 1774, 1879, AND
          1962

Year	Total Assets		Gini Coefficient
	Percent Held by Top 1%	Percent Held by Top 10%	
1774 Free households	13%	50%	.64
1870 Adult males	27	70	.83
1962 All consumer units ranked by total assets, unadjusted	26	62	.76

SOURCE: Based on Williamson, 1980, pp. 38-39.

Table 2. PERSONAL WEALTH OF THE WEALTHIEST ONE PERCENT OF THE
          POPULATION, AS PERCENT OF NATIONAL AGGREGATE PERSONAL
          ASSETS, 1953-1976

Asset	1953	1958	1962	1969	1972	1976
Total assets	27%	25%	26%	24%	26%	18%
Real estate	15	15	15	14	15	13
Corporate stock	86	75	62	51	63	46
Bonds	53	41	41	53	59	30
Cash	18	15	15	14	15	11
Debt instruments	32	37	42	41	45	37
Life insurance	14	14	11	11	7	7
Trusts	92	92	--	92	95	--
Miscellaneous	9	8	14	11	13	--
Liabilities	21	17	19	18	18	14
Net worth	27	27	27	26	28	19
Number of persons (millions)	1.6	1.7	1.9	2.0	2.1	2.1

SOURCE: Based on Statistical Abstract 1985, p. 463; 1979, p. 470;
        Smith and Franklin, 1974, p. 166.

Table 3. MONEY INCOME OF FAMILIES: PERCENT OF AGGREGATE INCOME
RECEIVED BY EACH FIFTH OF ALL FAMILIES, AND HIGHEST
FIVE PERCENT, 1950-1987

Year	Percent of Aggregate Income, in Fifths					Total	Highest Five Percent
	Lowest	Second	Middle	Fourth	Highest		
All families							
1950	4%	12%	17%	23%	43%	99%	17%
1955	5	12	18	24	41	100	16
1960	5	12	18	24	41	100	16
1965	5	12	18	24	41	100	15
1970	5	12	18	24	41	100	16
1975	5	12	18	24	41	100	15
1980	5	12	17	24	42	101	15
1985	5	11	17	24	43	100	17
1987	5	11	17	24	44	101	17
Black and Other Races							
1950	3	10	18	25	43	99	16
1955	4	10	18	26	42	100	14
1960	4	10	16	25	45	100	16
1965	5	11	17	25	43	101	15
1970	4	11	17	25	43	100	15
1975	5	10	17	25	43	100	15
1985	4	9	16	25	46	100	17
1987	3	8	15	25	48	99	18

SOURCE: Based on <u>Statistical Abstract 1989</u>, p. 446; <u>1987</u>, p. 437; <u>1979</u>, p. 452.

Table 4. MONEY INCOME OF FAMILIES: MEDIAN FAMILY INCOME IN
          CONSTANT (1987) DOLLARS, BY RACE AND HISPANIC ORIGIN OF
          HOUSEHOLDER, 1960-1987 (1000s)

Year	Median Income, in Constant (1987) Dollars			
	All Families	Whites	Blacks*	Hispanics
1950	15.7	16.4	8.8	--
1955	18.7	19.6	10.8	--
1960	21.6	22.4	12.4	--
1965	25.1	26.1	14.4	--
1970	28.9	30.0	18.4	--
1975	29.0	30.1	18.5	20.2
1980	29.0	30.2	17.5	20.3
1985	29.3	30.8	17.7	20.1
1987	30.9	32.3	18.1	20.3

* For 1950-1965, Black and other races.

SOURCE: Based on Statistical Abstract 1989, p. 445; 1984, pp.
        382-383.

Table 5. EFFECTS OF TAXATION ON ANNUAL INCOMES OF TOP EARNERS,
          1952-1981

Year	Income Share of					
	Top 1% of Tax Units		Top 5% of Tax Units		Top 15% of Tax Units	
	Before Taxes	After Taxes	Before Taxes	After Taxes	Before Taxes	After Taxes
1952	9%	7%	19%	16%	33%	30%
1963	8	7	19	17	35	33
1972	8	7	20	17	37	35
1981	8	7	20	17	38	35

SOURCE: Based on Pechman, 1984, p. 31, 33.

Table 6.   TAXES AND TRANSFERS AS PROPORTIONS OF FAMILY INCOME, BY
           INCOME DECILES, 1980

Family Income Percentiles	Taxes	As Percentage of Income Transfers	Taxes less Transfers
0-10	42%	158%	-116%
10-20	23	58	-35
20-30	24	35	-11
30-40	25	24	1
40-50	26	15	11
50-60	26	11	15
60-70	26	8	18
70-80	27	6	21
80-90	28	4	24
90-100	29	3	26

SOURCE: Based on Pechman, 1984, p. 35.

Table 7.   PROPORTION OF CERTAIN SOCIAL CATEGORIES IN THE LOWEST
           INCOME QUINTILE, 1949-1984

Proportion in Lowest Income Quintile	1949	1984
Of All Family Heads Over 65	45%	29%
Of All Children Under Age 18	15	23
Of All Black Families	39	43
Of All White Families	18	17

SOURCE: Based on Levy, 1987, p. 202.

Table 8.   PROPORTION OF FAMILIES BELOW THE POVERTY LEVEL, 1959-
           1987

Year	Proportion Below Poverty Level		
	White	Black	Hispanic
1959	15%	48%	--
1969	8	28	--
1979	7	28	20
1987	11	30	26

SOURCE: Based on Statistical Abstract 1989, p. 455.

The empirical study of American social classes flourished for a generation after the publication of the Lynds' Middletown and then gave way to the statistical investigation of inequalities in occupation, income, and education. If the issue is framed in terms of the simplest possible version of the class structure, recognizing only a business class of white-collar workers and their families and a working class identified with blue-collar occupations, there has been an enormous convergence of education and behavioral patterns between the two classes during the past two generations but no convergence with respect to occupational and income inequality. However, the relative size of the business class has increased sharply since 1970. Self-identification by social class shows no trend at all.

The study of social class has never been a value-neutral exercise, not since Aristotle began it. Every study of class is an essay on social justice. It hardly matters whether a social class scheme is presented as the invention of the analyst or as an objective phenomenon. The distribution of social rewards being the basic political issue, class studies invariably have political implications. Although there was a large literature on American social class in the nineteenth century, including such notable works as Thorstein Veblen's Theory of the Leisure Class (1899), the empirical investigation of social class in the United States dates from the publication of Robert and Helen Lynd's Middletown in 1929. The book's instant fame rested on its exposition of a two-class system--business class and working class--that constituted the framework of private and public life in a moderately typical community. It shocked a public that knew inequality to be ubiquitous in American society but had not supposed it to be so well-organized.

The Lynds were by no means the first observers of the American scene to criticize social inequality, but when they announced their findings, the country took notice and social class became a central theme of social research for several decades thereafter. Class systems were discovered in villages (West, 1945) and great cities (Baltzell, 1941). The place of blacks in the class system was examined with special care (Dollard, 1937; Powdermaker, 1939; Davis, Gardner and Gardner, 1941; Myrdal, 1944; Cayton and Drake, 1945).

The intellectual movement begun by the Lynds was eventually dominated not by them but by Lloyd Warner, the social anthropologist who made the decaying New England seaport of Yankee City as famous as Middletown and inspired the study of social class in a score of other eponymous places (Warner, 1936, 1949; Warner and Lunt, 1941; Warner, Meeker and Kells, 1960; Hollingshead, 1949). Warner and his followers used a six class system: upper-upper, lower-upper, upper-middle, lower-middle, upper-lower, lower-lower, with some local modifications.

The Lynds' position was vaguely Marxist; in their followup study of Middletown in Transition, published in 1937, they became more explicitly so, and attributed the absence of working class solidarity to the machinations of the business class. They protested the class system as they described it.

Warner's position was quite different. The scandal of class, in his version, was that Americans were encouraged by egalitarian myths to seek more rapid social promotion than they could achieve, given the active rejection by each social class of climbers from below.

The Lynds' division of families into business class and working class was based entirely on the reported occupation of the head of household. Warner's assignment of families to one of six classes was based on their patterns of consumption, leisure and social interaction.

Although Warner's work was widely cited in the 1940s and 1950s and his class terminology passed into popular speech, there have been no recent attempts to replicate the elaborate, ethnographic studies of that school. A full-scale replication of the Middletown studies was carried out from 1976 to 1981 (Caplow, Bahr, Chadwick et al., 1982, 1983). Much of the other recent work on American social classes is heavily statistical and relies on occupation as the class identifier, supplemented by education, income, and ethnicity (Form 1983, Bensman and Vidich, 1987). The numerous studies of social class by scholars of Marxist orientation (Braverman, 1974; Wright et al., 1982) rely exclusively on occupational identifiers. There is also an interesting line of studies about "subjective social class" using survey data (Schreiber and Nygren, 1970; Vanneman and Cannon, 1987).

From 1920 to the present, the occupational data show a slow but steady enlargement of the business (or middle or white collar) class after 1920 which accelerated sharply after 1970. Between 1970 and 1986, the proportion of the male labor force in business class occupations increased from 30% to 47%, while the corresponding proportion of the female labor force increased from 46% to 57%. The relative number of men in professional, managerial, technical and clerical occupations increased while the number of operatives and laborers--the core of the factory labor force--declined. Contrary to expectation, the proportion of service workers remained unchanged. Among women, the major increases occurred in clerical and service occupations while the numbers of saleswomen and household workers declined sharply (Caplow, 1990). The net effect is a moderate upgrading of average occupational prestige. But Table 1, using data from Middletown, shows the curious fact that although the occupational prestige of the male labor force measured by Siegel scores rose from 32.8 in 1920 to 37.5 in 1970 and women workers recorded a similar increase, the inequality of occupational prestige increased slightly over the same period.

Occupational income displays a similar trend. Occupational earnings in constant dollars in Middletown grew by about 200% from 1924 to 1984, although most of the improvement occurred before 1960. The inequality of occupational earnings, as measured by Gini coefficients, did not change at all (see Levy, 1987).

The trend was strikingly different for education, where substantial equalization occurred between 1924 and 1978. Fewer than 10% of working class parents in Middletown aspired to a college education for their children in 1924; by 1978, almost 90% reported that aspiration, and actual rates of college attendance were similar for children of working class and business class families.

The equally spectacular equalization of educational opportunity between blacks and whites in the U.S. is shown in Table 2. By 1986, the enormous gap in years of schooling that formerly separated whites and blacks had almost disappeared.

The contrasting trends of occupational income and achieved education--persistent inequality in occupational income, steady equalization of achieved education--are echoed by many other series that show a similar contrast between the economic inequality associated with the occupational stratification of the labor force and the cultural homogenization that has eroded the differences in attitudes, activities, and lifestyles between occupational strata. Tables 3 and 4 illustrate some aspects of this homogenization. The data are from Middletown but similar examples could be supplied by any other American community. The homogenization is particularly striking with respect to leisure activities, media exposure, and organized religion, where interclass differences in participation have been steadily diminishing.

Braverman's 1974 essay on Labor and Monopoly Capital postulated a quite different set of trends for the U.S.: growth of the working class, the inexorable deskilling of labor, systematic exploitation of workers by management, and growing worker alienation. The book stimulated a great deal of empirical research, which, Form (1983) shows, did not support any of Braverman's theses.

The study of self-reported social class has long been a lively branch of stratification research, drawing on the well-known facts that a large proportion of managers and professionals in the U.S. identify themselves as working class and a large proportion of manual workers identify themselves as middle class. These self-identifications are coherently related to parental occupations, age, sex, education, ethnicity, political preferences, and other social attributes as Vanneman and Cannon show in their definitive 1987 study. The problem with this body of research for our present purposes is that self-reported social class shows no recent trend at all (Table 4).

References

Baltzell, Edward Digby. The Protestant Establishment: Aristocracy and Class in America. New York: Random House, 1964.

Bensman, Joseph and Arthur J. Vidich. American Society: The Welfare State and Beyond. South Hadley, MA: Bergin and Garvey, 1987.

Braverman, Harry. Labor and Monopoly Capital: The Degradation of Work in the Twentieth Century. New York: Monthly Review Press, 1974.

Caplow, Theodore. American Social Trends. New York: Harcourt Brace Jovanovich, 1990.

Caplow, Theodore, Howard Bahr, Bruce Chadwick, et al. Middletown Families: Fifty Years of Change and Continuity. Minneapolis: University of Minnesota Press, 1982.

Caplow, Theodore and Bruce Chadwick. "Inequality and Life-styles in Middletown, 1920-1978." Social Science Quarterly 60 (1979): 367-386.

Cayton, Horace and St. Clair Drake. Black Metropolis: A Study of Negro Life in a Northern City. New York: Harper and Row, 1945.

Davis, Allison, Burleigh B. Gardner and Mary R. Gardner. Deep South: A Social Anthropological Study of Caste and Class. Chicago: University of Chicago Press, 1941.

Davis, James Allan. General Social Surveys, 1972-1980: Cumulative Codebook. Chicago: National Opinion Research Center, 1980.

Davis, James Allan and Tom W. Smith. General Social Surveys, 1975-1987: Cumulative Codebook. Chicago: National Opinion Research Center, 1987.

Dollard, John. Caste and Class in a Southern Town. New Haven: Yale University Press, 1937.

Form, William. "Sociological Research and the American Working Class." Sociological Quarterly 24 (1983): 163-184.

Hollingshead, August B. Elmtown's Youth. New York: Wiley and Sons, 1949.

Levy, Frank. Dollars and Dreams. New York, Russell Sage, 1987.

Lynd, Robert S. and Helen Merrell Lynd. Middletown: A Study in American Culture. New York: Harcourt and Brace, 1929.

------. Middletown in Transition. New York: Harcourt and Brace, 1937.

Myrdal, Gunnar, with the assistance of Richard Sterner and Arnold Rose. An American Dilemma: The Negro Problem in Modern Democracy. New York: Harper Brothers. 1944.

Powdermaker, Hortense. After Freedom: A Cultural Study in the Deep South. New York: Viking Press, 1939.

Schreiber, E. M. and G.T. Nygren. "Subjective Class in America: 1945-68." Social Forces 48 (1970): 348-356.

Vanneman, Reeve and Lynn Weber Cannon. The American Perception of Class. Philadelphia: Temple University Press, 1987.

Veblen, Thorstein. The Theory of the Leisure Class. New York, supply publisher, 1899.

Warner, Lloyd. "American Caste and Class." American Journal of Sociology 42 (1936): 234-237.

Warner, Lloyd and Paul S. Lunt. The Social Life of a Modern Community. New Haven: Yale University Press, 1941.

Warner, Lloyd, Marcia Eeker and Kenneth Kells. Social Class In America: A Manual of Procedure for the Measurement of Social Status. New York: Harcourt Torch Books, 1960 (1949).

West, James. Plainville, U.S.A. New York: Columbia University Press, 1945.

Wright, Eric Olin, et al. "The American Class Structure." American Sociological Review 47 (1982): 709-726.

Table 1. DECILE-SLOPE MEASUREMENT OF OCCUPATIONAL INEQUALITY,
MIDDLETOWN, 1920-1970

| Year | Labor Force | | |
	Male	Female	Total
1920	3.30	3.89	3.54
1930	3.54	4.31	3.54
1940	3.44	4.12	3.70
1950	3.58	3.91	3.76
1960	3.62	3.95	3.77
1970	3.77	4.25	3.85

SOURCE: Based on Caplow and Chadwick, 1979, p. 372.

Table 2. MEDIAN SCHOOL YEARS COMPLETED, PERSONS AGED 25 AND
OVER, BY RACE, 1940-1987

| Year | Years of School (Medians) | |
	All Persons	Blacks
1940	8.6	5.7
1950	9.3	6.8
1960	10.6	8.0
1970	12.1	9.8
1980	12.5	12.0
1987	12.7	12.4

SOURCE: Based on Statistical Abstract 1989, p. 130.

Table 3.   CHARACTERISTICS OF WORKING CLASS AND MIDDLE CLASS
           FAMILIES, MIDDLETOWN, 1924-1978

	1924		1978	
Characteristic	Working Class	Business Class	Working Class	Business Class
Family rises by 6 a.m. on a typical day	93%	15%	38%	31%
Wife held a full-time job outside the home during past 5 years	44	3	48	42
Wife's daily housework				
Less than 4 hours	7	23	53	60
4-7 hours	69	55	38	35
Over 7 hours	24	23	10	5
Wife's aspiration for children's education				
High school	57	100	100	100
College	26	93	83	90
Graduate school	--	8	4	7

SOURCE: Based on Caplow and Chadwick, 1979, pp. 374-383; Lynd and
        Lynd, 1929, pp. 186-187.

Table 4.   SELF-REPORTED SOCIAL CLASS OF ADULTS, 1972-1987

Self-Reported Class	1972	1980	1987
Lower Class	6%	5%	5%
Working Class	47	46	43
Middle Class	44	45	46
Upper Class	2	3	4
No Response	1	1	2
Total	100	100	100

SOURCE: Davis, 1980, p. 137; Davis and Smith, 1987, p. 220.

Contrary to expectation, American society is becoming more peaceful.

Since 1970, riots and violent demonstrations have nearly disappeared from the national scene, strikes have declined to the lowest level in a century, and rates of violent crime have leveled off and begun to decline. Political movements that challenge the legal order have dwindled to insignificance.

At the same time, litigation--the principal form of nonviolent conflict--has expanded in all directions, with significant consequences for health care, professional sports, labor relations, urban planning, political campaigning, education, religion, family life, and other institutional patterns.

Several types of rioting are traditional in the United States, including armed clashes between strikers and strikebreakers, lynchings, urban race riots, violent political demonstrations and peaceful political demonstrations violently repressed, student protests and sit-ins, and mass looting. Table 1, based on the report of the National Commission on the Causes and Prevention of Violence (1969) published at the height of the wave on ethnic and political violence that swept the country during the Vietnam War, asserts that 200,000 people participated in the race riots of 1963-68 and 2 million in the political demonstrations of the same era. Riots of these kinds have so completely disappeared from the national scene that no time series can be constructed for recent years. Even prison riots have become quite rare.

Clashes between strikers and strikebreakers, which were a conspicuous feature of American labor relations from the 1880s to the 1960s, are now too mild and infrequent to attract public attention.

Strikes and lockouts fell in 1985 to the lowest level in a hundred years, as may be seen from the unusually complete and reliable data presented in Table 2. The annual number of workers involved in strikes, which averaged 1.8 million in the much smaller labor force of the 1960s, and 1.3 million in the 1970s, fell below 600,000 in 1986 and 1987, while the percent of work time lost to work stoppages dropped to an unprecedented low of .02%.

There has been a parallel, although less dramatic, decline in violent crime, most clearly shown by victimization rates, which declined by 14% from 1973 to 1986 (Table 3; see also Schapiro and Ahlberg, 1986, and Chapter 16.2, Crime and Punishment). Criminologists differ as to the causes of declining rates of violent crime, especially homicide. During the period 1963-1978, which witnessed a sharp increase in violent crime, a variety of causal factors were identified including: unemployment, frustrated aspirations, the disorganization of the family--especially the urban black family--by ill-conceived welfare measures, the spread of the drug culture, the availability of handguns, and the age and race composition of the population. The weight of the evidence favors the composition of the population, since most crimes against persons are committed by males aged 15-29, and a disproportionate share by black males aged

15-29. These groups, having increased in proportion to the total population from 1963 to 1978, are now declining in relative numbers and based upon births recorded through 1987, the relative decline of the high crime population will continue at least through the year 2002. However, this cohort explanation is partial at best and leaves room for many other influences.

The increase of litigiousness in American society is steady, well-documented and, so far, uninterrupted (Koller 1981). Table 4 shows a 200% increase in the number of civil cases brought in federal district courts from 1970 to 1984. Note that the number of criminal cases declined slightly in the same interval. State courts are known to show similar trends. The scope of judicial authority continues to expand in every direction and nearly all sorts of organizations that were formerly autonomous--churches, private schools and colleges, professional associations, sports leagues, social clubs, philanthropic societies--now find their actions subject to judicial review. There is presumably a connection between the new American peaceability and the propensity to go to law at the slightest provocation, but it has not yet been closely analyzed.

References

Cantor, David and Kenneth C. Land. "Unemployment and Crime Rates in the Post-World War II United States: A Theoretical and Empirical Analysis." American Sociological Review 50 (1985): 317-332.

Koller, Jethro. The Litigious Society. New York: Basic Books, 1981.

The National Advisory Committee on Criminal Justice Standards and Goals. Disorders and Terrorism: Report of the Task Force on Disorders and Terrorism. Washington, D.C.: USGPO, 1976.

The National Commission on the Causes and Prevention of Violence. Crimes of Violence: A Staff Report Submitted to the National Commission on the Causes and Prevention of Violence. Washington, D.C.: USGPO, 1969.

The National Commission of the Causes and Prevention of Violence. To Establish Justice, To Ensure Domestic Tranquility. Washington, D.C.: USGPO, 1969.

Schapiro, Morton Owen and Dennis A. Ahlberg. "Why Crime is Down." American Demographics 8 (October, 1986): 56-58.

Smith, M. Dwayne. "The Era of Increased Violence in the United States: Age, Period or Cohort Effect." The Sociological Quarterly 27 (1986): 239-251.

U.S. Bureau of the Census. Historical Statistics of the United States, Colonial Times to 1970. Washington, D.C.: USGPO, 1975.

------. Statistical Abstract of the United States, 1989. Washington, D.C., 1989. Annual. Previous years as cited.

U.S. Bureau of Labor Statistics. United States Department of Labor News (Historical Technical Data, USDL 86-74). Washington, D.C.: USGPO, Feb 26, 1986.

Wright, James D., Peter H. Rossi and Kathleen Daly. Under the Gun: Weapons, Crime and Violence in America. New York: Aldine, 1985.

Table 1.   PARTICIPATION IN, AND CONSEQUENCES OF DEMONSTRATIONS,
           RIOTS, AND INDIVIDUAL VIOLENT CRIME, JUNE 1963-MAY 1968

Forms of Violence	Parti-cipants	Consequences (1000s)		
		Injuries	Deaths	Arrests
Demonstrations and Riots				
Political Demonstrations				
and Protests*	2000.1	1.1	--	21.0
Urban Riots	200.0	8.0	.2	50.0
Individual Violent Crimes				
Homicides	--	--	53.2	39.0
Aggravated Assaults	--	1124.2**	--	457.5

* Including only those demonstrations and protests involving more
than 100 persons.
** This is the number of complaints. Presumably there was at
least psychic injury involved in each instance.

SOURCE: Based on the National Commission on the Causes and
        Prevention of Violence, 1969, p. xx.

Table 2. WORK STOPPAGES, 1960-1987

Year	Work Stoppages	Workers Involved (1000s)	Person-days Idle (millions)	% Total Work Time Lost
1960	222	896	13.3	.1%
1965	268	999	15.1	.1
1967	381	1,192	31.3	.2
1968	392	1,855	36.6	.2
1969	412	1,576	29.4	.2
1970	381	2,468	52.8	.3
1971	298	2,516	35.5	.2
1972	250	975	16.8	.1
1973	317	1,400	16.3	.1
1974	424	1,796	31.8	.2
1975	235	965	17.6	.1
1976	231	1,519	24.0	.1
1977	298	1,212	21.3	.1
1978	219	1,006	23.8	.1
1979	235	1,021	20.4	.1
1980	187	795	20.8	.1
1981	145	729	16.9	.1
1982	96	656	9.1	.0
1983	81	909	17.5	.1
1984	62	376	8.5	.0
1985	54	324	7.1	.0
1986	69	533	11.9	.0
1987	46	174	4.5	.0

SOURCE: Based on <u>Statistical Abstract 1989</u>, p. 413.

Table 3. RATES* OF VICTIMIZATION FOR THREE VIOLENT CRIMES, 1973-
          1986

Year	Rape	Robbery	Assault
1973	1.0	6.7	24.9
1974	1.0	7.2	24.8
1975	.9	6.8	25.2
1976	.8	6.5	25.3
1977	.9	6.2	26.8
1978	1.0	5.9	26.9
1979	1.1	6.3	27.2
1980	.9	6.6	25.8
1981	1.0	7.4	27.0
1982	.8	7.1	26.4
1983	.8	6.0	24.1
1984	.9	5.8	24.3
1985	.7	5.1	24.2
1986	.7	5.1	22.3

* Per 1,000 adult respondents

SOURCE: Based on <u>Statistical Abstract 1989</u>, p. 170; <u>1987</u>, p. 159.

Table 4. CASES COMMENCED IN DISTRICT COURTS, 1960-1987

Year	Civil Cases (1,000s)	Criminal Cases (1,000s)
1960	59.3	28.1
1965	67.7	31.6
1970	87.3	38.1
1975	117.3	41.1
1976	130.6	39.1
1977	130.6	39.8
1978	138.8	34.6
1979	154.7	31.5
1980	168.8	28.0
1981	180.6	30.4
1982	206.2	31.6
1983	241.8	34.9
1984	261.5	35.9
1985	273.7	38.5
1986	254.8	40.4
1987	239.0	42.2

SOURCE: Based on Statistical Abstract 1989, p. 180; 1987, p. 179; 1979, p. 192.

The unionized percentage of the labor force, never high, has been declining since 1935. The effectiveness of collective bargaining has also declined, particularly from 1975-1985, in part because of decreased Federal and public support but mostly because of the economic weakness of the industries that are most unionized, such as transportation. The number of strikes has also declined. Alternatives such as worker participation programs and ESOP firms do not really compensate for these declines.

Labor unionism in the U.S. has never involved more than a minority of the nonagricultural labor force, and that fraction has been declining for many years, from 33% in 1955 to 28% in 1965, 25% in 1975, 22% in 1982, and 17% in 1987 (Table 1). The exact current figure cannot be found; American labor statistics are seldom accurate or up-to-date. In absolute numbers, union membership today is about the same as in 1965--between 17 and 18 million.

The highest proportions of unionized workers as of 1985 were 37% in transportation and public utilities, 36% in government employment, 25% in manufacturing and 22% in construction. Unionization was almost negligible in wholesale and retail trade, agriculture and the service sector. Black workers are more unionized than white workers, and men more than women (Table 2).

The slow decline of union membership from 1975 to 1985 was accompanied by an irregular decline in the coverage and yield of collective bargaining agreements. The average first-year improvement in compensation attributable to major labor-management agreements fell from 11.4% in 1975 to 2.6% in 1987 (Table 3), when a considerable number of new union contracts provided for wage cuts.

The declining effectiveness of collective bargaining from the union standpoint was attributable in part to an unsympathetic Federal administration and lessened public support (Bloom, 1985) but more particularly to the economic weakness of industries that were traditional union strongholds, especially automobiles, steel, rubber, and railroads.

The use of organized labor's primary weapon--the strike--has declined precipitously in recent years. Between 1960 and 1980 there were an average of 226 strikes begun each year. By 1985, the number of strikes was down to 54 and the loss of working time attributable to strikes had become negligible (see Table 2, Chapter 7.1).

To some extent, collective bargaining is being replaced by alternative devices, such as participatory management, employee ownership, and various forms of profit-sharing. But the relative position of labor vis-a-vis management has apparently deteriorated in the past decade.

References

Bloom, Steven M. and David E. Bloom. "American Labor at the Crossroads." American Demographics 7 (September 1985): 30-83.

Borum, Joan, et al. "Collective Bargaining in 1987: Local, Regional Issues to Set Tone." Monthly Labor Review 110 (1987): 23-36.

U.S. Bureau of the Census. Statistical Abstract of the United States, 1989. Washington, D.C., 1989. Annual. Previous years as cited.

7.2 Negotiation

Table 1.   UNION MEMBERSHIP, AS PERCENT OF THE NON-AGRICULTURAL
            LABOR FORCE 1950-1978 AND OF EMPLOYED WAGE AND SALARY
            WORKERS, 1982-1987

Year	Union Members
1950	31%
1955	33
1960	31
1965	28
1970	27
1972	26
1974	26
1976	24
1978	24
1982	22
1983	20
1984	19
1985	18
1986	17
1987	17

SOURCE: Based on Statistical Abstract 1989, p. 416; 1988, p. 402;
    1987, pp. 408, 409; 1980, p. 429.

Table 2.   UNION MEMBERSHIP BY ECONOMIC SECTOR, RACE AND SEX, 1987

Economic Sector	Union Members
Mining	18%
Transportation and Public Utilities	33
Construction	21
Manufacturing	23
Wholesale and Retail Trade	7
Finance, Insurance and Real Estate	2
Services	6
Government	36
Race and Sex	
Male	
White	20
Black	26
Hispanic	20
Total	21
Female	
White	12
Black	19
Hispanic	13
Total	13
Total	
White	16
Black	23
Hispanic	17
U.S. total	17

SOURCE: Based on <u>Statistical Abstract 1989</u>, p. 416.

Table 3. AVERAGE PERCENT ADJUSTMENTS (INCREASES) IN WAGES AND
COMPENSATION NEGOTIATED, COLLECTIVE BARGAINING
AGREEMENTS,* 1974-1987

Year	First Year	Life of Contract
1974	10.7%	7.8%
1975	11.4	8.1
1976	8.5	6.6
1977	9.6	6.2
1978	8.3	6.3
1979	9.0	6.6
1980	10.4	7.1
1981	10.2	8.3
1982	3.2	2.8
1983	3.4	3.0
1984	3.6	2.8
1985	2.6	2.7
1986	1.1	1.6
1987	3.0	2.6

* Data represent private nonfarm industry settlements affecting
production and related workers in manufacturing and nonsupervisory
workers in nonmanufacturing industries.

SOURCE: Based on <u>Statistical Abstract 1989</u>, p. 412; <u>1987</u>, p. 407.

Immoral behavior is traditionally attributed to out-groups. There has been in recent decades a striking decrease in intergroup hostility, which may be indicative of improved intergroup accommodation. Data from six major categories--sexual behaviors, intoxication, common crimes, white-collar crimes, political offenses, and disabilities--reveal a significant decrease in the ethnic connotations of stigmatized behavior which parallels the decrease in intergroup hostility. It should be noted, however, that there are exceptions, like the reaction to the AIDS epidemic.

The United States is a mosaic of religious, ethnic and cultural groups in uneasy adjustment, perpetually trying to modify each other's behavior. The two categories which evoke tolerance and permissiveness (or intolerance and sanctions) are out-groups and immorality. They are linked at all levels by the attribution of every form of immorality to some out-group and of some forms of immorality to every out-group.

The principal intergroup confrontations in this society are white-black, anglo-hispanic, native-immigrant, Protestant-Catholic, Christian-Jew, straight-gay, and radical-reactionary, but there are hundreds of others that are important to those involved.

The continual effort by the American polity to legislate and enforce moral improvement is closely related to intergroup hostility, the disapproved behavior being always attributed to outgroups: nineteenth century drunkenness to Indians and Irishmen; twentieth century drug addiction to blacks and hispanics; insider trading and political radicalism to Jews; abortion to atheists, liberals, and secular humanists; organized crime to Italo-Americans; and so on. Moral crusades in the U.S. are always partly grounded on intergroup hostility.

During recent decades, there has been a striking decrease in the general level of intergroup hostility, following the disestablishment of racial segregation by the Federal courts in the 1950s and the broad prohibition of ethnic discrimination by Federal legislation in the 1960s. Table 1 shows the spectacular decline of overt ethnic and religious intolerance from 1948 to 1987. Table 2 makes the point that substantial intolerance still persists.

Survey evidence also shows increasing tolerance of dissident opinions (Table 3), although Mueller (1988) suggests that the general public's grasp of civil liberty issues may be too minimal to give credibility in survey findings on this topic (See also Weil, 1982).

The decline of overt ethnic and religious bigotry in the U.S. might be expected to have one of two opposed results: (a) a corresponding increase in the tolerance of stigmatized behavior; or (b) intolerance of stigmatized behavior as a way of expressing ethnic and religious hostilities for which other forms of expression are suppressed. On balance, outcome (a) appears to be more prevalent although outcome (b) occurs also.

The tolerance of stigmatized behavior is most appropriately assessed by examining the societal response to each type of behavior in conjunction with data on its incidence.

The important forms of stigmatized behavior seem to fall into six major categories:

1. Sexual behaviors: pre-marital sex (Table 4), adultery, group or public sex, incest, unmarried cohabitation, homosexuality (Table 5), pedophilia, pornography (Table 6), abortion (Table 7) and illegitimacy (Table 8).
2. Intoxication: use (including sale and possession) of heroin, cocaine, marijuana, PCP etc.; nonmedical use of morphine and other prescribable narcotics; addictive use of tranquilizers, antidepressants or analgesics: drinking alcohol (Table 9 and Table 10); smoking tobacco; operating vehicles or machinery when intoxicated; other forms of public intoxication.
3. Common crimes: murder (Table 11), rape, arson, robbery, theft, assault etc. (Table 12 and Table 13).
4. White collar offenses: fraud, embezzlement, forgery, bribery, influence-peddling, industrial pollution, insider trading, usury, abuse of trust, etc.
5. Political offenses: violent advocacy, denial of civil rights, defiance of public authority, rioting, terrorism, espionage, treason.
6. Handicaps and disabilities: Physical handicaps, mental retardation, mental and emotional disorders, disreputable diseases, unemployment, poverty, bankruptcy, homelessness.

Within each of these large and complex categories, there have been some significant changes of incidence in the past 20 years, and some significant changes of response, often in reaction to governmental policies and initiatives. There is no consistent relationship, however, between changes of incidence and changes of response.

In category 1, for example, there has been a vast increase of illegitimacy accompanied by a vast increase of tolerance; a great increase of intolerance towards pedophilia, with no apparent change of incidence; a greatly increased incidence of abortion with an intensification of both tolerant and intolerant responses; a moderate increase in the circulation of pornography and a moderate decline of tolerance; and an increase in overt homosexuality, with fluctuating tolerance.

In category 6, there has been a spectacular increase of tolerance, backed by Federal statutes and regulations, without any significant change of incidence; a spectacular increase of homelessness with little change of response; and a sharp increase in disreputable diseases and declining tolerance.

Although the contemporary U.S. is frequently characterized as a permissive society, it is difficult to demonstrate any consistent movement in that direction. For every form of behavior that used to be sanctioned and is now tolerated--like illegitimacy or pornography--it is easy to find another that used to be tolerated and is now heavily sanctioned--like pedophilia, drunken driving, or insider trading.

There are powerful fashions in the stigmatization of behavior, driven by media and government initiatives. With the decline of intergroup hostility, the forms of behavior selected for public concern and official response are less often associated with disadvantaged minorities than formerly. Among recently fashionable behaviors, pedophilia, influence-peddling, industrial pollution, drunken driving, abortion and homelessness have no ethnic connotations. In the case of drug abuse, the leading subject of popular and official intolerance, concern has shifted in

On the other hand, it must be remembered that intergroup hostility has diminished, not disappeared. As public awareness of the AIDS (or HIV) epidemic developed after 1983, the preponderance of blacks and homosexuals among the victims triggered the traditional connection between intergroup hostility and stigmatized behavior (Shilts, 1987).

References

Lender, Mark Edward and James Kirby Martin. Drinking in America: A History. New York: The Free Press, 1982.

Mueller, John. "Trends in Public Tolerance." Public Opinion Quarterly 52 (1988): 1-25.

"Opinion Roundup." Public Opinion 8 (April/May, 1985): 21-40.

"Opinion Roundup." Public Opinion. 9 (September/October, 1986): 21-40.

"Opinion Roundup. Public Opinion 10 (July/August, 1987): 21-29.

"Opinion roundup". Public Opinion 10 (September/October, 1987): 21-40.

"Premarital Sex." Gallup Report 263 (August, 1987): 20-22.

"Problem Drinking." Gallup Report, 242 (November, 1985): 41-48.

Shilts, Randy. And the Band Played On. New York: St. Martin's Press, 1987.

Smith, Herbert L. and Phillips Cutright. "Thinking about Change in Illegitimacy Ratios: United States, 1963-1983." Demography 25 (1988): 235-247.

"The Death Penalty." Gallup Report 232-33 (January/February, 1985): 3-11.

U.S. Bureau of the Census. Statistical Abstract of the United States, 1989. Washington, D.C., 1989. Annual. Previous years as cited.

Weil, Frederick D. "Tolerance of Free Speech in the United States and West Germany, 1970-79: An Analysis of Public Opinion Survey Data." Social Forces 60 (1982): 973-992.

Table 1.   INTOLERANCE OF NEIGHBORS, 1948 AND 1987

	Residents Overtly Objecting	
	1948	1987
Blacks	63%	13%
Hispanics	41	9
Jews	22	3

SOURCE: "Opinion Roundup," 1987, pp. 22-23.

Table 2.   ATTITUDES TOWARD BLACK FRIENDS AND NEIGHBORS, 1963 AND 1985

	Percentage of Non-blacks Who			
	Support Residential Segregation		Object to Black Dinner Guest in Their Home	
Education of Respondent	1963	1985	1963	1985
Less than high school graduate	64%	45%	40%	19%
High school graduate	49	25	25	12
Some college	46	18	22	8
College graduate	37	12	13	2

SOURCE: Based on "Opinion Roundup," 1987, p. 24.

Table 3. INTOLERANCE OF POLITICAL MINORITIES, 1954-1985

	Percent Agreed		
Item	1954	1972	1985
Someone who is against religion			
. . . should not be allowed to speak	60%	34%	34%
. . . should be fired/not allowed to teach at college/university	84	58	54
. . . their book should be removed from public library	59	37	38
Someone who is a communist			
. . . should not be allowed to speak	68	46	41
. . . should be fired/not allowed to teach at college/university	89	66	53
. . . their book should be removed from public library	66	44	41

SOURCE: Based on "Opinion Roundup," 1987, p. 29.

Table 4. PUBLIC OPINION ON PREMARITAL SEX, 1969-1987

Question: There's a lot of discussion about the way morals and sexual attitudes are changing in this country. What is your opinion about this: Do you think it is wrong for a man and a woman to have sexual relations before marriage, or not?

Year	Wrong	Not wrong	No opinion
1969	68%	21%	11%
1973	48	43	9
1985	39	52	9
1987	46	48	6

SOURCE: Gallup Report, 1987, pp. 20-22.

Table 5. PUBLIC OPINION ON EXTRAMARITAL SEX AND HOMOSEXUALITY,
          1973-1987

Item	Percent Agreed		
	1973	1980	1987
Extramarital sex always/almost always wrong	85%	87%	90%
Homosexual relations always/ almost always wrong	81	79	81

SOURCE: Based on "Opinion Roundup," 1987, p. 26.

Table 6. PUBLIC OPINION ON PORNOGRAPHY LAWS, 1973-1986

Item	Percent Agreed	
	1973	1986
There should be laws against the distribution of pornography to persons under 18	48%	53%
There should be laws against the distribution of pornography whatever the age	43	43
There should be no laws forbidding the distribution of pornography	9	4

SOURCE: Based on "Opinion Roundup," 1986, p. 33.

Table 7. PUBLIC OPINION ON ABORTION, 1975-1985

Item	Percent Agreed 1975	1985
Abortion should be legal under only certain circumstances	56%	57%
Abortion should be legal under all circumstances	22	22
Abortion should be illegal in all circumstances	23	22

SOURCE: Based on "Opinion Roundup," 1985, p. 26.

Table 8. STANDARDIZED AND OBSERVED ILLEGITIMACY RATIOS,* BY COLOR, 1963-1983

Illegitimacy Ratios	1963	1968	1973	1978	1983
Blacks					
1963 standardized ratios					
Marital status	258	292	343	300	277
Marital fertility	258	289	334	426	471
Illegitimacy rates	258	361	491	601	668
Age structure	258	321	431	517	585
Marital status & fertility	258	250	247	227	205
Observed ratios	258	335	449	527	578
Whites					
1963 standardized ratios					
Marital status	31	47	54	58	64
Marital fertility	31	43	39	57	89
Illegitimacy rates	31	45	62	79	92
Age structure	31	52	63	90	137
Marital status & fertility	31	38	33	37	45
Observed ratios	31	53	63	87	125

* The illegitamacy ratio is defined as the number of out-of-wedlock births per 1000 live births.

SOURCE: Based on Smith and Cutright, 1988, p. 242.

Table 9.   APPARENT PER CAPITA CONSUMPTION OF ABSOLUTE ALCOHOL
           (GALLONS PER YEAR, DRINKING AGE POPULATION), 1790-1978

Year	Spirits	Wine	Beer	Total
1790	2.30	0.10	3.40	5.80
1800	3.30	0.10	3.20	6.60
1810	3.90	0.10	3.10	7.10
1820	3.90	0.10	2.80	6.80
1830	4.30	0.10	2.70	7.10
1840	2.50	0.10	0.50	3.10
1850	1.88	0.08	0.14	2.10
1860	2.16	0.10	0.27	2.53
1870	1.53	0.10	0.44	2.07
1871-80	1.02	0.14	0.56	1.72
1881-90	0.95	0.14	0.90	1.99
1891-95	0.95	0.11	1.17	2.23
1896-1900	0.77	0.10	1.19	2.06
1901-05	0.95	0.13	1.31	2.39
1906-10	0.96	0.17	1.47	2.60
1911-15	0.94	0.14	1.48	2.56
1916-19	0.76	0.12	1.08	1.96
1920-30	--	--	--	0.90
1934	0.29	0.07	0.61	0.97
1935	0.43	0.09	0.68	1.20
1936-41	0.63	0.14	0.77	1.54
1942-46	0.83	0.18	1.05	2.06
1947-50	0.73	0.20	1.07	2.00
1951-55	0.76	0.21	1.03	2.00
1956-60	0.82	0.22	0.98	2.02
1961-65	0.92	0.23	1.01	2.16
1966-70	1.09	0.26	1.10	2.45
1971	1.18	0.33	1.17	2.68
1972	1.12	0.31	1.20	2.63
1973	1.12	0.33	1.24	2.69
1974	1.10	0.31	1.25	2.66
1975	1.11	0.32	1.26	2.69
1976	1.09	0.33	1.26	2.68
1977	1.10	0.34	1.31	2.75
1978	1.12	0.36	1.34	2.82

SOURCE: Based on Lender and Martin, 1982, pp. 196-197.

Table 10. PERCENT OF ADULT POPULATION WHO DRINK, BY SEX, 1939-
          1985,

Year	National Total	Men	Women
1939	58%	70%	45%
1945	67	75	60
1946	67	--	--
1947	63	72	54
1949	58	66	49
1950	60	--	--
1951	59	70	46
1952	60	68	53
1956	60	--	--
1957	58	67	50
1958	55	66	45
1960	62	--	--
1964	63	--	--
1966	65	70	61
1969	64	--	--
1974	68	77	61
1976	71	--	--
1977	71	77	65
1978	70	75	64
1979	69	74	64
1981	70	75	66
1982	65	69	61
1983	65	71	58
1984	64	73	57
1985	67	72	62

SOURCE: Based on "Problem Drinking," 1985, p. 41.

Table 11. PUBLIC OPINION ON THE DEATH PENALTY FOR MURDER, 1936-1985

	Attitude about the Death Penalty		
Year	Favor	Oppose	No opinion
1936	61%	39%	--*
1937	65	35	--*
1953	68	25	7
1960	51	36	13
1965	45	43	12
1966	42	47	11
1969	51	40	9
1971	49	40	11
1972	57	32	11
1976	65	28	7
1978	62	27	11
1981	66	25	9
1985	72	20	8

* "No opinion" was not included as an option in these surveys.

SOURCE: Based on "The Death Penalty," 1985, p. 4.

Table 12. CRIME RATES, BY TYPE OF CRIME, 1970-1987

	Rate per 100,000 Persons		
Type of Crime	1970	1980	1987
Murder	8	10	8
Forcible rape	19	37	37
Robbery	172	251	213
Aggravated assault	165	299	351
Burglary	1,085	1,684	1,330
Larceny theft	2,079	3,167	3,081
Motor vehicle theft	457	502	529

SOURCE: Based on Statistical Abstract 1989, p. 166; 1980, p. 182.

Table 13. AVERAGE TIME SERVED BY PRISONERS RELEASED FROM FEDERAL
INSTITUTIONS FOR THE FIRST TIME, 1970-1986

Year	Number Released	Average Time (months) Sentence	Served
1970	8,487	38.6	19.7
1975	11,313	39.8	18.5
1976	10,463	32.3	15.1
1977	10,953	30.7	15.5
1978	12,132	37.2	18.7
1979	10,925	44.1	21.0
1980	9,069	33.9	15.9
1981	9,884	41.0	17.9
1982	11,348	36.6	16.3
1983	11,896	35.4	15.9
1984	15,050	35.5	15.6
1985	14,937	35.5	15.9
1986	16,996	34.0	15.6

SOURCE: Based on Statistical Abstract 1989, p. 186.

Americans have long prided themselves on their independence and nonconformity. Recent experimental studies have challenged the level of Americans' disobedience to unreasonable demands made by those in authority. A strong shift in socialization has decreased parental concern about obedience while increasing children's independence and self-reliance. At the same time there does not appear to be any large scale increase in personal disobedience as measured by dropping out of school, running away, and deserting from the military. There is increased use of the court system to handle disputes between individuals and groups in American society.

Personal

There is a fairly large literature in social psychology on the relationship between authority and obedience or conformity. The assumption has been that Americans are independent non-conformists and do not readily yield obedience to authority. The classic study illustrating conformity to authoritative commands was conducted by Milgram (1963, 1965, 1974). Adult male subjects were asked to participate in an experiment testing the effect of punishment on learning. Each was paired with a trained confederate who was programmed to make a specific number of mistakes on the learning task. After each mistake, the subject was instructed to deliver an electrical shock to the confederate strapped in an electric chair. The subject was instructed to deliver the shock by one of two different authorities. The first was Dr. Milgram, dressed in a white smock, at Yale University, while the second was a Mr. Williams, dressed in a sports shirt, at a temporary "research" center. The intensity of the shock escalated with each mistake to the level of "danger-high voltage." In addition, the confederate acted out increasing pain with each shock. The intent was to determine how strong a shock the subjects would deliver before refusing to continue. Subjects delivered shocks of surprisingly high intensity for both Dr. Milgram and Mr. Williams. Due to ethical concerns, studies such as this have not been replicated and therefore it is difficult to chart trends in level of obedience to authority.

The Middletown III study provides some insight into the traits parents desire their children to have. In 1924 Lynd and Lynd (1929) asked a sample of married women with children to identify the behavior traits their mothers desired of them, and also the traits they desired in their own children. In 1978, Caplow, Bahr and Chadwick (Alwin, 1989) asked a similar sample of women the same questions. The results (Table 1) demonstrate a strong shift away from obedience, loyalty to church and patriotism, and a shift toward independence and tolerance. The differences are substantial. Middletown mothers in 1978 wanted their children to think for themselves, to accept responsibility, to show initiative and to be tolerant of opposing views; Middletown mothers fifty years earlier wanted their children to be obedient, to conform to the rules and to have respect for God, country and family. This trend is not unique to Middletown; national surveys by the National Opinion Research Center reveal a similar shift between 1964 and 1988.

The chapters in this book on norms of conduct, delinquency, crime, conflict, negotiation, dispute settlement, emotional disorders, erotic expression, and mood-altering substances all provide some insight into changes in obedience or conformity to laws, regulations and norms, and also into trends in appeal to government bodies for resolution of disputes.

Dropping out of school is one of the kinds of nonconformity/rejection of authority for which there are excellent records. The rates of dropping out for both black and white students from 1970 to 1986 are presented in Table 2. Interestingly, this form of nonconformity has significantly declined for both black and white youth. This trend is in the opposite direction from that toward independence discovered in Middletown. Perhaps the shift from obedience to independence occurred long before 1970 and thus doesn't show up in the more recent school-leaving data. On the other hand, perhaps young people in the 1980s were more cognizant of the importance of education and were exercising their independence by staying in school.

Data on conflicts between young people and school officials, and also with their parents, are presented in Table 3. As can be seen, the frequency of vandalism of school property, assaults on public school teachers, and arguments with parents remained fairly constant, 1975-1986.

Another form of disobedience to authority by young people is running away from home. The numbers of boys and girls arrested for running away between 1970 and 1986 are presented in Table 4. Although the trend is not consistent, it appears that there has been a slight decline in the number of youth running away from home. At least, it is plain that rates of running away from home did not increase during this 16 year period.

Dishonorable discharges, desertion and absent-without-leave are acts of defiance of authority by persons in the Armed Forces. The incidence of such events for the period 1970-1987 is presented in Table 5. Since 1970 there has been a significant decrease in the desertion and AWOL rates. Nearly 34 men per every 1,000 in the services deserted during 1970 and this fell to only six per 1000 in 1986. The same sharp decline was true for AWOL as well. The military winding down in Viet Nam and the shift to an all volunteer army may have influenced these rates. On the other hand, rates of punitive discharge show the opposite trend: in the 1980s, other-than-honorable discharges increased and seem to have stabilized at about twice the 1979 rate, probabilities of bad conduct discharges doubled between 1970 and 1987, and dishonorable discharges show a consistent increase to over one percent of all discharges.

Institutional

Between 1965 and 1987, the U.S. population increased by one-third. Over the same period, the number of civil cases announced by U.S. district courts quadrupled. In other words, the increase in this form of litigation was 12 times greater than the increase in population. Increases in criminal cases and in trials also outpaced population growth (Table 6), but not so dramatically. It is not clear what the increased litigiousness means, other than a growing tendency to turn to the courts as authoritative mediators of conflict. The same dramatic increase in appeals to court authority appears in the number of cases commenced by the U.S. Courts of Appeals (Table 8). Again, most of the stunning growth is in civil cases (Table 7). So the military data are mixed, partly suggesting increased rejection of authority and normative control, and partly suggesting the opposite.

References

Albrecht, Stan L., Bruce A. Chadwick, and Cardell Jacobson. Social Psychology. 2nd ed. Englewood Cliffs, NJ: Prentice-Hall, 1987.

Alwin, Duane F. "From Obedience to Autonomy: Changes in Traits Desired in Children, 1924-1978." Public Opinion Quarterly 52 (1988): 33-52.

Johnston, Lloyd D. and Jerald G. Bachman. Monitoring the Future 1986. Annual. Previous years as cited.

Jamieson, Katherine M. and Timothy J. Flanagan, eds. Sourcebook of Criminal Justice Statistics-1986. U.S. Department of Justice, Bureau of Justice Statistics, Washington DC: USGPO, 1987.

Milgram, Stanley. "Behavior Study of Obedience." Journal of Abnormal and Social Psychology 76 (1963): 371-378.

Milgram, Stanley. "Some Conditions of Obedience and Disobedience to Authority." Human Relations 18 (1965): 57-76.

Milgram, Stanley. Obedience to Authority. New York: Harper and Row, 1974.

Remley, Anne. "From Obedience to Independence." Psychology Today (October, 1988): 56-59.

U.S. Bureau of the Census. Statistical Abstract of the United States, 1989. Washington, D.C., 1989. Annual. Previous years as cited.

Table 1. TRAITS DESIRED FOR CHILDREN: MOTHERS' PERCEPTIONS OF
WHAT THEIR MOTHERS DESIRED, AND THEIR STATEMENTS ABOUT
WHAT THEY DESIRE FOR THEIR CHILDREN, MIDDLETOWN, 1924
AND 1978

Traits	Their Own Mothers Desired		They Desire in Their Children	
	1924 (N=101)	1978 (N=313)	1924 (N=141)	1978 (N=324)
Strict obedience	64%	44%	45%	17%
Loyalty to church	69	35	50	22
Patriotism	17	8	21	5
Good manners	41	40	31	23
Independence	16	34	25	76
Tolerance	5	22	6	47

SOURCE: Based on Remley, 1988, pp. 56-59; Alwin, 1988, pp. 33-52.

Table 2. HIGH SCHOOL DROPOUTS AGE 14 TO 24, BY AGE AND RACE,
          1970-1986

Age and Race	Percent of Population					
	1968	1970	1975	1980	1985	1986
Total Dropouts*	13%	12%	12%	12%	11%	10%
16-17 years	5	8	9	9	7	6
18-21 years	17	16	16	16	14	14
22-24 years	22	19	16	15	14	14
White*	12	11	11	11	10	10
16-17 years	4	7	8	9	7	6
18-21 years	16	14	14	15	14	13
22-24 years	20	16	14	14	13	14
Black	22	22	20	16	13	12
16-17 years	7	13	11	7	6	5
18-21 years	29	30	32	23	17	16
22-24 years	40	38	23	24	18	17

* Includes persons 14-15 years, not shown separately.

SOURCE: Based on Statistical Abstract 1989, p. 145; 1979, p. 148.

Table 3. CONFLICT WITH SCHOOL OFFICIALS AND PARENTS, REPORTED BY
          HIGH SCHOOL SENIORS, BY SEX, 1975-1986

Frequency and Type of Conflict	1975		1980		1985		1986	
	M*	F*	M	F	M	F	M	F
Once or more during past 12 months:								
Damaged school property	21%	6%	19%	8%	19%	8%	19%	8%
Hit an instructor	5	1	4	1	5	1	4	2
Five or more during past 12 months:								
Argued or had a fight with either parent	42	53	37	45	39	49	39	50

* M=Males, F=Females

SOURCE: Johnston and Bachman, 1975, pp. 65-67; 1980, pp. 100-102;
    1985, pp. 99-101; 1986, pp. 100-102.

Table 4. YOUNG PEOPLE AGE 10-18 ARRESTED FOR RUNNING AWAY FROM
HOME, BY SEX, 1970-1986

Year	Total	Youths Arrested (1000s) Males	Females
1970	167	80	86
1973	169	75	94
1977	189	81	107
1980	141	59	82
1985	129	55	74
1986	139	59	80

SOURCE: Based on <u>Sourcebook of Criminal Justice Statistics</u> -1987;
<u>1986</u>; <u>1983</u>, <u>1978</u>; <u>1976</u>; <u>1974</u>.

Table 5. RATES* OF UNSATISFACTORY AND PUNITIVE DISCHARGES,
DESERTION, AND ABSENT-WITHOUT-AUTHORITY RATES, MILITARY
PERSONNEL, 1970-1987

Type of Separation/ Deviance	1970	1975	1980	1985	1987
Discharges Other than honorable	18.4	39.6	28.7	40.8	39.5
Bad conduct	3.5	5.3	4.1	9.8	6.7
Dishonorable	.3	.4	.5	.6	1.3
Desertion rate***	33.6	26.3	17.9	6.3	6.1
Absent-without- authority rate**	86.3	86.6	46.8	17.1	16.2

* Rate per 1000 average end-of-month strengths
** Absent without authority more than 30 days=desertion; less
than 30 days=absent without authority

SOURCE: <u>Statistical Abstract 1989</u>, p. 338.

Table 6. APPEALS TO AUTHORITY: CIVIL AND CRIMINAL CASES, AND
TRIALS BEFORE U.S. DISTRICT COURTS, 1970-1987

Type of Action	Cases (1000s)						
	1960	1965	1970	1975	1980	1985	1987
Civil cases commenced:	59	68	87	117	169	274	239
Cases terminated	49	63	79	104	155	268	237
No court action	--	29	31	39	69	129	98
Court action total	--	34	48	65	86	139	140
Criminal cases commenced:	28	32	38	41	28	38	45
Defendents disposed of	30	34	36	49	37	47	54
Not convicted	4	5	8	12	8	9	10
Convicted	27	29	28	37	29	38	44
Civil trials	6	8	9	12	13	14	13
Non-jury	3	4	6	8	9	9	8
Jury	3	3	3	4	4	5	6
Criminal trials	3	4	7	8	7	6	7
Non-jury	1	1	2	3	3	3	3
Jury	2	3	4	5	3	4	4
Total trials	9	11	16	19	20	21	20

NOTE: Column subtotals and totals may differ due to rounding.

SOURCE: Statistical Abstract 1989, pp. 179-180; 1979, pp. 192-193.

Table 7. U.S. COURTS OF APPEALS, CASES COMMENCED AND
          DISPOSITIONS, 1950-1987

Type of Action	Cases (1000s)							
	1950	1960	1965	1970	1975	1980	1985	1987
Cases commenced:	3	4	7	12	17	23	33	35
Criminal	--	1	1	3	4	4	5	5
U.S. civil	1	1	1	2	3	5	7	6
Private civil	1	2	3	5	7	10	17	19
Admin. appeals	--	1	1	2	2	3	3	3
Cases terminated:	3	4	6	11	16	21	31	34
Criminal	--	1	1	2	3	4	6	6
U.S. civil	1	1	1	2	3	4	6	6
Private civil	1	2	2	4	6	9	16	18
Admin. appeals	1	1	1	1	2	3	3	3
Cases disposed of:	2	3	4	6	9	11	16	19
Affirmed/granted	2	2	3	5	7	8	12	14
Reversed/denied	1	1	1	1	1	2	3	3
Other	--	--	--	--	1	1	1	2

NOTE: Column subtotals and totals may differ due to rounding.

SOURCE: Statistical Abstract 1989, p. 179; 1979, p. 192.

Governmental growth at the local level has not brought a concomitant growth of electoral control: indeed, the shift from traditional electorally-controlled local governments to functionally-specific, expert-dominated local governments has brought with it something of a dilution of electoral control. This has coicided with a reduction in the proportions of the eligible who vote in elections. On the other hand, social surveys and public opinion polls have become markedly more prevalent, and, apparently, more heavily relied upon both by politicians seeking office and government officials wishing to launch policies requiring public support.

Despite a marked growth in total employment in local government, somewhat fewer local officials stand for election. At most, there has been something of a steady state in the number of opportunities electors have to express their control over local affairs; this represents a definite decline of local voter influence in ratio to the amount of business that local governments do. Within elected officialdom, moreover, there has been a focusing on the more obviously 'political' realms." In the U.S. the number of elections has had no substantial statutory basis for change since World War II, with a single exception, to be discussed later. Thus, we can discern a modest decline in the numbers of elections in which Americans are offered participation. This coincides with a decline in the proportion of eligible Americans who vote. (There have been modest offsets to this tendency in the practical enfranchisement of blacks in the southern states, who, until recent decades, were virtually excluded from the vote, and in the national extension of the franchise to persons 18 to 20 years old, who formerly were disenfranchised in most states).

There has been one major exception to the generalization that Americans have been offered fewer opportunities to vote. This is the "primary" election, the election that serves in lieu of other intra-party mechanisms for nominating its candidates in general elections. These have increased very markedly. The number of states having primary elections for presidential nominations rose from 17 in 1964 and 1968 to 23 in 1972 and then to 33 (Democrats) and 34 (Republicans) in 1980 (Crotty, 1985, p. 126; Aldrich, 1980, p. 57). Many commentators see a paradox here. For one thing, turnouts in primary elections rarely approach those in general elections. For instance, in 1980, when 33 states held Democratic Party primaries and 35 held Republican primaries, 31.8 million people voted in these primaries; for the general election (fifty states), the number voting was 86.5 million (Crotty, 1985, p. 128). Eldersveld (1982, p. 216) examined turnout rates in primary and general elections between 1962 and 1972 in selected states and found that the proportion of eligibles voting in the general election averaged 57.5%, and in the primary elections only 27.5%.

More important, however, is the countervailing impact on voter turnout in the general election that many analysts associate with the rise of primary elections (e.g. Aldrich, 1980). It is argued that as parties have lost control of the nomination mechanism, so professional party politicians and avocational party workers have also lost some of their essential raison d'etre, and so their ability to turn out votes in either the primary or the general election. It is certainly the case, that the best-remarked trend having to do with collective decision-making in the United States since World War II has been the decline in the proportion of eligible voters who vote at all. And this has occurred despite a sustained effort to overcome institutional hindrances to voting in the form of laws that make it either illegal or burdensome to register for voting eligibility. The sustained effort has done a great deal to overcome an earlier structural inequality sustained by low registration rates among black citizens, especially in the South where they were actively discouraged from registering, but in the North as well. (In part, the decline in proportion of eligible voters who actually vote has been a function of enfranchising 18-to-20-year-olds in 1972, for these have persistently been less likely to vote than all other age groups).

Examination of a long series of voter turnout percentages (Austin, 1986, pp. 376-377) suggests that voter engagement with national politics peaked in the 1880s and declined briefly thereafter, attaining a plateau that lasted until the early 1960s. Since then, popular engagement in the voting process has declined once again. It is now a quadrennial concern that voting for president may not attain 50% of the eligible electorate, and in fact this level is rarely attained, nationwide, in elections to Congress. Yet it is the national vote that is the more engaging to the public, by comparision with elections to state and local offices.

Table 1 indicates that, ordinarily, the majority of those eligible by age and not voting in a given election are also those who had never registered to vote: these people were seemingly not disillusioned with the options offered them at a given election, but were non-voters for some more persistent reasons, whether that they found it difficult or impossible to register, or that they did not find it worthwhile to vote at all. These data are based on self-report, rather than on election statistics percentaged to a population base, and do not adequately reflect the actual decline that has occurred in recent years, since voting is socially desirable in the American context, and is a citizen duty more often privately than publicly shirked. The figures do, however, show the approximate differentials between groups in turnout rates, and trends in these. It is apparent that educated people register and vote more often than others; that Hispanic Americans vote relatively rarely; that black Americans vote almost as often as white Americans; and that older people are more likely to vote than younger people. In fact, the decreasing propensity to vote, 1972-1986, does not appear at all among persons 65 and over.

Quantitative evidence on trends in the prevalence of surveys and polls, as a non-official way of registering collective opinion, is hard to come by. The authors of a National Academy of Science investigation into survey research a few years ago commented that "while it is evident to those of us working in survey research that the enterprise has expanded in the last decades, statistical evidence to support these perceptions is meager" (Turner and Martin, 1983, p. 30). It is, however, a relevant commonplace that political parties increasingly rely on surveys in devising platforms and choosing nominees, now regularly commissioning their own, even at the state and local levels. Parties' anticipatory use of polling to a degree preempts the significance of the actual election, and may account in part for voter apathy.

The National Academy reports a credible estimate that between 1971 and 1986, there seem to have been at least 100 million survey interviews conducted; another figure, for 1980, estimates that 28 million survey interviews were conducted by telephone--the most common means for interviewing--for perhaps one interview for each seven adults. The number of organizations conducting surveys has increased, largely because of the establishment of the in-house survey initiated by television stations and newspapers as part of the journalistic enterprise. In addition, uncountable numbers of marketing researchers employ surveys, of varying levels of competence and honesty, to supplant "revealed preference" in the marketplace. According to a 50-year review in Public Opinion Quarterly (Sudman and Bradburn, 1987, p. S75), the number of firms conducting either public opinion polls or market research surveys now numbers in the thousands, with an annual dollar volume of over two billion dollars, of which 90% is market research . . . . The majority of firms are still small.

Fifty academic polling organizations are now in operation, although their number has not grown much in recent years. The Federal government, through the Census Bureau as well as through the Bureau of Labor Statistics, the National Center for Health Statistics, and other agencies, supports a vast survey entrprise. "In the years since 1968 subjective measurements [allowing the expression of people's judgment] have come to play a substantial role in government survey research" (Turner and Martin, 1983, p. 32).

The two trends in collective decision processes, thus, run contrary to one another: people vote less than they formerly did, but they express their wishes and opinions on a diversity of topics in frequent public opinion polls.

References

Aldrich, John H. Before the Convention. Chicago: University of Chicago Press, 1980.

Austin, Erik W. Political Facts of the United States Since 1789. New York: Columbia University Press, 1986.

Crotty, William. The Party Game. New York: W.H. Freeman and Company, 1985.

Eldersveld, Samuel J. Political Parties in American Society. New York: Basic Books, 1982.

Sudman, Seymour and Norman M. Bradburn. "The Organizational Growth of Public Opinion Research in the United States." Public Opinion Quarterly 51 (1987): S67-S78.

Turner, Charles F. and Elizabeth Martin, eds. Surveying Subjective Phenomena. 2 vols. New York: Russell Sage Foundation, 1983.

U.S. Bureau of the Census. Statistical Abstract of the United States, 1989. Washington, D.C., 1989. Annual. Previous years as cited.

Table 1. SELF-REPORTED PARTICIPATION IN NATIONAL ELECTIONS,
BY AGE AND EDUCATION, 1964-1986

			Age			
Year	18-20	21-24	25-34	35-44	45-64	65+
1964	39%	51%	69%*	69%*	76%	64%
1968	33	51	67*	67*	75	66
1972	48	51	60	66	71	63
1974	21	26	37	49	57	51
1976	38	46	55	63	69	62
1978	20	26	38	50	58	56
1980	36	43	55	64	69	65
1982	20	29	40	52	62	60
1984	37	43	54	63	70	68
1986	19	24	35	49	59	61

		Educational Attainment		
	<8 yrs.	H.S.	H.S. Grad.	College	Coll. Grad.
1964	59%	65%	76%	85%**	85%**
1972	47	52	65	75	84
1974	34	36	45	50	61
1976	44	47	60	68	80
1978	35	35	45	51	64
1980	43	46	59	67	80
1982	36	38	47	53	66
1984	43	44	59	67	79
1986	33	34	44	50	62

* Combined in a single category, age 25-44, in the source table.
** Combined in a single category, "more than 12 years."

SOURCE: Based on <u>Statistical Abstract 1989</u>, p. 257; <u>1979</u>, p. 514;
<u>1966</u>, p. 382.

Topic 8:   State and Service Institutions

8.1   EDUCATIONAL SYSTEM

The United States continued to pursue a policy of widening educational opportunity into the first half of the period treated here, bringing the proportion graduating from secondary education to more than four in five and the proportion entering college more than half of that. Enrollment trends for most of the period, however, have been dominated by sharp demographic changes, especially the aging through the school years of the "baby boom" cohort. At the post-secondary level, two long-term trends have been prominent: the addition of numerous institutions offering two-year educational courses ("community colleges") and the shift from predominately male to majority female enrollment. The auspices of education, too, have also shifted somewhat, with increased state education at the post-secondary level, and a decrease in Roman Catholic parochial education at lower levels.

The American educational system includes four levels: 1. Pre-primary, 2. Primary, 3. Secondary, and 4. Post-secondary. As the names denote, the second and third of these are conceptually the cornerstones of the system. Primary education--considered the "basic" intellectual and social tools needed for all citizens--typically runs for six years from about age six. Secondary education, until 1900 or so was understood as a somewhat select and to a degree specialized education for superior students preparing for middle-class occupations. In the early 1900s it increasingly became an element of universal education for Americans. This transformation had been mostly completed by 1945; by 1950, the graduating high school seniors amounted to 59% of the total 17-year-old population.

Pre-primary education includes kindergarten, nursery school, and various compensatory and special educational services. A year of kindergarten had not become universal as early as 1945, but was on its way to becoming so. Nursery school and other pre-primary education is still somewhat uncommon. Post-secondary education in America includes, centrally, college, but also"junior" or "community" college (something of a hybrid of secondary education and college), and a variety of not very well documented proprietary trade training. About one adult in 16 had a college degree in 1950, compared to about one in five in 1986 (Table 1). Graduate and professional training are relatively elite, but have become far more common than they were. In 1986, almost one-fourth of all college degrees awarded were advanced degrees.

The auspices of this complex educational system are also quite complicated. Essentially, there are three providers: the private sector, the not-for-profit sector (including most prominently religious organizations and corporations embracing particular educational institutions, especially colleges and universities), and the government. The latter is particularly complex, for the United States has a federal government system in which several levels of government share authority over particular functions, such as education. The U.S. government conducts no education itself (except through the military, which is in fact an enormous system ponderously articulated to the more usual system of formal education), but offers subsidies both to jurisdictions and organizations that do, and to individuals who are paying for post-secondary education for themselves. All state governments directly sponsor universities, several operating more than one, sometimes through more than one entire university system. All local areas have free schools at the primary and secondary levels, and state governments (and for some purposes, the national government) commonly provide payments to these. In addition, local governments sometimes sponsor institutions of higher education, often with state subvention.

Total expenditures on formal education have been greater at the primary (elementary) and secondary levels than at the post-secondary, but the gap has been declining (Table 2). The post-secondary educational realm has enlarged, as the table indicates, in good part because the contribution of the public sector has increased from not quite parity in the immediate postwar period to a two-to-one advantage over non-public expenditure by 1970, the ratio declining just slightly in the years since then. At the same time, the public commitment to primary and secondary education in terms of proportion of total educational funding, has declined from 67% to 55%. In terms of funding, the national commitment to education has about quadrupled since 1970. In constant (1987) dollars, expenditures for all levels of education rose from $269 per capita to $1187 per capita (see Table 2).

The Roman Catholic Church conducts the largest non-public formal education system, running from pre-primary through graduate and professional school. The Church, of course, is only slightly more monolithic than the government, composed as it is (clearly so in the educational field) of orders that compete for students and contrast somewhat in educational philosophies. Many other religious organizations besides the Roman Catholic also run educational institutions, prominently so at the primary and at the post-secondary levels. Since the mid 1950s, but especially since the 1960s, there has been a trend toward religiously-organized primary education, much of it catering to parents who fear disorder (or race mixing) in the public schools where racial integration has been federally mandated. The private sector is especially prominent on the post-secondary level: many of the most prominent universities in the country are privately sponsored. The private sector also operates many of the schools on the pre-primary area--a growth area--and a number of "private" schools at the primary and secondary level that are famed for their exclusivity and educational excellence.

In the past decade or more, partly on account of the loss of low-wage teaching nuns as the teaching orders have declined in attractiveness, the Catholic schools have been having a hard time "competing" with free public education, even though public distrust for the latter is very apparent. Enrollment in the Catholic schools on the elementary level peaked in 1964 at a level that included approximately 13% of all primary pupils in the country, and fully 90% of all primary-level pupils enrolled in non-public institutions. At the same time, Catholic secondary education (which peaked a few years later) included nearly 9% of all secondary pupils, and 84% of all non-public pupils. By 1985, the Catholic schools enrolled only about 6% of primary and secondary pupils, thereby accounted for only 45% and 63% of all non-public pupils at those levels. The U.S. educational system, while not changing fundamentally, is experiencing considerable alteration through the simultaneous decline of Catholic education and the rise of "white-flight"-inspired private schools.

Because of the simultaneity of rapid population growth and a rapid enlargment of the proportion of young people in attendance at school, the expansion of American schooling was extremely rapid for the first several decades of the twentieth century. In fact, the construction of facilities often could not keep pace with enrollment; in many instances, the number of pupils brought about a temporary redefinition of the school day, so that two sessions were held to accommodate students who could not be housed, or for whom teachers could not be found.

In the first half of the postwar period, both these factors began once again to be felt, and the country saw a period of school building that was even more explosive than that early in the century. Between the end of the 1940s and the end of the 1950s, 7 million more new students were added in the first eight years of public schooling, and an additional 2.5 million more in grades 9-12. At this same time, private schools at the elementary and secondary levels were also growing rapidly. Private schooling, to be sure, amounted to only slightly more than 10% of all schooling at these levels.

The expansion of schooling continued through the next decade. By 1969, another 5.5 million elementary students were added to the public-school population, and another 5 million to the lists of the public high schools. In this period, however, virtually all the growth was in public schooling. And by this time, high schooling was nearly universal, as was, of course, elementary schooling. There was therefore very limited room for subsequent expansion of the educational establishment through increased enrollment rates--except at the upper end of high school, and in pre-schooling. From the end of the 1960s, then, demography dominated; the story from then to the middle of the 1980s was one of slow decline in the number of elementary pupils (of whom, in the face of school integration and a widespread concern of the failure of education, a somewhat increased proportion moved into private schools). At the high-school level, the decline was even sharper, for the parental disenchantment with public schools, already noted, was complemented by a somewhat greater readiness on the part of students themselves--especially boys--to drop out before completing the entire course of study.

Table 3 indicates that in recent years the crescive growth of educational enrollment has nearly finished, except for selective areas. Pre-primary education, at 3 and 4 years, continued to grow through 1985, and still had room to grow thereafter. In the past two decades, the enrollment at the very young age of the school-age spectrum, the most lively of the trends seen in the previous table, occurred most rapidly at the very youngest age included, rising at age 3 from 1-in-20 to over 1-in-4. Attendance has increased far more rapidly on a full-day basis than on a part-day basis: the impact of the massively-increased labor-force participation of mothers is apparent here. Enrollment continued to grow among students age 5 and 6, too, although by 1975 education at these ages was nearly universal. Enrollment rates at the post-secondary ages, however, especially at 18 and 19, stabilized during the 1970s, then increased slightly during the 1980s (Table 3).

A good deal of the continuing growth in post-secondary education has come from the efflorescence of two-year colleges, which offer a mix of college-preparatory education and trades training. The number of two-year institutions, 524 in 1949 (or fewer than one in three of all institutions of higher education) rose to 1240 in 1985-86 (and now were two in five of all institutions). The great bulk of the growth here has been in the public sector, which has taken effective control of this growth area from the often proprietary providers of the early postwar era. By contrast, the non-public sector of higher education that has seen some postwar growth has been in the four-year realm, whose number (but not whose enrollment) has enlarged far more rapidly than the state-sponsored schools, which tend to be fewer but larger.

From the point of view of the institutions themselves, and of the system, total enrollment no longer has been mainly controlled by increasing enrollment rates, but rather by the age-structure of the population. Thus, enrollment in the educational system as a whole declined from its peak in 1975, turning slightly upward again in the last few years (Table 3). It will be seen that primary and secondary schools so far reflect these trends more powerfully than has higher education. Perhaps more interesting, from an interpretive standpoint, is the fact that non-public (here "private") education on the primary level did not decline over the postwar era (despite what we have seen to be the case with the Catholic schools), while public schooling did. This is presumably the result of the reactions of many white people who could afford alternatives to mandated racial integration, and to the substitution of school-busing for neighborhood schools. These have been the issues in which public primary schooling has been at the center of democratic debate in the postwar period--although of late it has spread to issues of the curriculum and to teacher-recruitment and -training procedures. Proposals for the government to stop privileging the public schools economically--as by providing all parents with "chits" so that the government will equally subsidize the education of every child, regardless of the school which his or her parents choose--represent a very important and ongoing arena in which the nation sorts out its social policy priorities.

The number of school teachers at the elementary and secondary levels has increased rapidly since World War II; faster, overall, than the number of pupils. College faculties have grown even more rapidly, especially during the 1960s and then the 1970s, a period of the rapid spread of the idea of the two-year community college, increasing enrollment rates, and large cohorts of youth to instruct.

World War II had seen a massive feminization of the primary-and secondary-school instructional labor force, but immediately after the war, the proportion of males began to climb, considerably exceeding its pre-war level. Increases in the percent of teachers who were men were slower in the 1960s, and stabilized thereafter, reaching a peak slightly exceeding one in three. A much greater masculinization of the faculty can be seen among college teachers. Before the trend reversed in the 1970s and 1980s, three-fourths of teachers at the university level were male.

The educational qualifications required of teachers have periodically been raised, and the tightening of these requirements is commonly viewed as indication of professionalization and a heightening of status. The salaries of classroom teachers were adjudged to be too low after the Sputnik scare in the late 1950s, and they were rapidly raised. In constant dollars, elementary and secondary teachers were earning more in the early 1970s than they were in the mid-1980s, the decline having been gradual. The decline slightly exceeds that for all households over the same period; from this we can probably infer some decline in teachers' social status. Over this same period, college teachers have lost slightly more in relative income. In part, this is a product of the increasing feminization of the college faculty since the early 1970s, and in part a product of the shift toward increased employment of persons in temporary and lower-rank positions, both common in the growing community-college sector of the occupation. Considering teachers in the aggregate, it appears that since World War II their social status has risen and then declined.

References

U.S. Bureau of the Census. <u>Statistical Abstract of the United States, 1989</u>. Washington, D.C., 1989. Annual. Previous years as cited.

U.S. National Center for Educational Statistics. <u>Digest of Educational Statistics 1989</u>. Washington, D.C.: USGPO, 1989. Annual. Previous years as cited.

Table 1. INDICATORS OF EDUCATIONAL ACHIEVEMENT: HIGH SCHOOL
GRADUATES AS PERCENT OF ALL PERSONS AGE 17; HIGH SCHOOL
AND COLLEGE GRADUATES AS PERCENT OF ALL ADULTS AGE 25
AND OVER; AND MASTERS AND DOCTORS DEGREES AS PERCENT OF
ALL COLLEGE DEGREES, 1940-1986

Year	Annual High School Graduates (Percent of persons age 17)	Adult Population Age 25+ High School Graduates		Percent Present Year College Degrees Advanced (MA, PhD)
		Total	With 4+ Yrs. College	
1940	51%	24%	5%	14%
1950	59	34	6	13
1960	65	41	8	18
1965	72	--	--	20
1970	77	52	11	22
1975	74	62	14	25
1980	71	66	16	25
1985	73	74	19	23
1986	73	76	20	23

SOURCE: Based on <u>Statistical Abstract 1989</u>, pp. 130-131, 147;
<u>1979</u>, p. 144; <u>1966</u>, pp. 113, 130, 137.

Table 2.   TOTAL EXPENDITURES ON EDUCATIONAL INSTITUTIONS, IN
           CURRENT AND CONSTANT DOLLARS PER CAPITA NATIONAL
           POPULATION, AND DISTRIBUTION OF EXPENDITURES BY LEVEL
           AND CONTROL, 1950-1987

	Total Expenditures, (Dollars Per Capita)		Distribution of Expenditures Elementary and Secondary		Colleges and Universities	
Year	Current	Constant(1987)	Public	Private	Public	Private
1950	$ 57	$ 269	67%	9%	13%	11%
1960	132	506	65	5	16	14
1970	334	977	59	4	24	13
1975	503	1063	60	4	25	12
1980	727	1004	58	4	25	13
1985	1035	1091	55	5	26	14
1987	1187	1187	55	5	26	14

SOURCE: Based on <u>Statistical Abstract 1989</u>, pp. 7, 125, 462;
        <u>1979</u>, p. 136.

Table 3.   PERCENT OF POPULATION ENROLLED IN SCHOOL, FOR SELECTED
           AGES, 1965-1986

	Age					
Year	3	4	5-6	18-19	20-21	22-24
1965	5%	16%	85%	46%	28%	13%
1970	13	28	89	48	32	15
1975	21	40	95	47	31	16
1980	27	46	96	46	31	16
1985	29	49	96	52	35	17
1986	29	49	95	55	33	18

SOURCES: Based on <u>Digest of Educational Statistics 1988</u>, p. 12;
         <u>Statistical Abstract 1989</u>, p. 129.

Table 4. ENROLLMENT IN EDUCATIONAL INSTITUTIONS, BY LEVEL AND
CONTROL, 1950-1986

	Enrollment (1000s)					
	Kindergarten-Grade 8		Grades 9-12		Higher Education	
	Public	Private	Public	Private	Public	Private
1950	19.4	2.7	5.7	.7	1.4	1.3
1959	26.9	4.6	8.3	1.9	1.8	1.4
1964	39.9	5.0	11.4	1.3	3.5	1.8
1969	32.6	4.2	13.0	1.3	5.9	2.1
1974	30.9	3.7	14.1	1.3	8.0	2.2
1979	27.9	3.7	13.7	1.3	9.0	2.5
1984	26.9	4.3	12.4	1.4	9.5	2.8
1986	27.4	4.3	12.4	1.3	9.5	2.8

SOURCE: Based on <u>Digest of Educational Statistics 1987</u>, p. 8.

The number of physicians, dentists and nurses for each 100,000 individuals in the general population has increased during the past 40 years. The number of hospital beds per 1,000 population has significantly decreased, but at the same time so has the occupancy rate of such beds. It appears that the demand for hospital beds has dropped faster than their decline. At the same time, beds in nursing and related care facilities have increased to accommodate an aging population. The number of visits the average citizen makes to the doctor, dentist, and hospital has increased slightly. Health care costs have risen dramatically and now consume over one-tenth of the gross national product.

Personnel

The number of physicians per 100,000 population remained fairly constant, around 150, until about 1970. Since then it has sharply increased (see Table 1). By 1980, the number of physicians for each 100,000 population in the U.S. had risen to 211, and by 1986, to 246.

The representation of dentists has also increased, but not so sharply. In 1950, there were 50 dentists per 100,000 people. This rate increased to 57 in 1986. Currently there is some concern in American society that there is an over supply of doctors and dentists.

The number of nurses per 100,000 population has increased consistently since 1950. In 1986, there were 661 nurses for every 1000,000 residents in the U.S. Even though the number of nurses is at its highest level in history, there continues to be a serious shortage. The demand for nurses in nursing homes and senior citizen centers has risen dramatically, as the American public has aged. Presently, it is difficult for health care and nursing care facilities to maintain a full nursing staff.

Facilities

The total stock of hospital beds has declined since 1965, and the number of beds per 1,000 population has steadily declined during the past 40 years (see Table 2). In 1960 the rate was 9.6 beds; it dropped to 5.4 by 1986. Although the number of hospital beds per capita has decreased, so has the occupancy rate of the available beds. In 1960, 86% of the available hospital beds were occupied; by 1986, only 69% were. Thus, in spite of fewer hospital beds available, those available are in less demand today than 40 years ago. The number of hospital personnel has steadily risen, even though the number of beds has declined. In 1950, there were 84 hospital personnel for each 100 patients; by 1986, there were 413 (see Table 2).

There are several reasons for the relatively low occupancy rate. Insurance companies have adopted incentives and penalties to encourage clients to seek same-day health care and to reduce time spent in the hospital. Preventive health care programs have corrected many problems before they have become serious enough to require hospitalization. In addition, advances in medical science have reduced the time needed to recover from many surgical procedures. As of the late 1980s, it appears that the U.S. has enough fully staffed, highly equipped hospitals.

The number of beds in nursing homes and related care facilities has not decreased as have hospital beds. Rather, as can be seen in Table 3, there was a significant increase in nursing care beds from 1971 to 1986. It is anticipated that such facilities will continue to increase in number for the foreseeable future.

Patients

The number of patient visits to physicians from 1970 to 1986 is presented in Table 4. Although the number of visits has risen substantially, the number per person each year has increased only slightly. For example, in 1970 the average man made 4.1 visits to the doctor and this rose to only 4.5 visits in 1986. The increase for women was larger as the visits grew from 5.1 to 6.2. As can be seen in the table, women made more visits than men, whites more than blacks, and the young and old more than young adults and the middle-aged.

A similar modest increase occurred in visits to a dentist from 1970 to 1986 (see Table 5). As with physician contacts, women had more dentist visits than men, whites more than blacks, and the young and the older more than the middle-aged.

Table 6 shows the number of patients admitted to hospitals, 1970 to 1986. The number of admissions per 1,000 population rose from 1960-1980, and has since declined. The shift to outpatient visits is readily apparent--they rose almost 50% between 1970 and 1986--as is the movement to deinstitutionalize psychiatric patients.

Costs

In 1986, health care in the United States cost 458 billion dollars! That is more than one-tenth of the gross national product (see Table 7). Medical costs have risen much faster than inflation, and they severely strain the budgets of local, state and federal governments, employers, insurance companies, families and individuals. The effects of serious or prolonged illness can be devastating to family finances, since most medical insurance provides coverage for only specific health problems and limited dollar benefits or periods of coverage. More than half of the personal bankruptcies in America each year are precipitated by medical costs. Real increases, controlling for inflation, may be estimated from the index figures in Table 8. Note that, in 1987, the constant-dollar costs of physician care were six times as high as in 1960; hospital room costs, 14 times; and medical care commodities, three times.

Tables 7, 8, and 9 illustrate how health care costs have risen since 1950. The largest increases in costs have occurred in hospital care, but visits to health care professionals, drugs, medical supplies, and other related costs have also risen. The government's share of the health care bill has significantly increased, the consumer's share has remained fairly constant, while philanthropy's and industry's shares have declined (Table 9).

Conditions

A number of measures of the conditions surrounding the health care system in the United States are presented in Tables 10 through 15. Health status indicators include vital statistics such as death rates (Table 10), infant mortality (Table 11), life expectancy (Table 12), specific death causes (Table 13), immunization rates (Table 14), and selected morbidity rates (Table 15).

Mortality rates, including infant mortality, have gradually declined, and as a consequence life expectancy has increased. Life expectancy at birth was 47 years in 1900, 68 in 1950, and 75 (71 for men, 78 for women) in 1987. Death caused by eleven major infectious diseases declined from 40% of the mortality in the U.S. at the turn of the century to less than 5% in 1980. Immunization efforts certainly have contributed to this decline. Significant progress has been made in both preventing and arresting the effects of the major killers, cancer and heart disease. All of these factors have contributed to the major decrease in infant mortality and the significant increase in life expectancy.

References

National Center for Health Statistics. Health: United States, 1985. DHHS Pub. No. CPHS 86-1232, Public Health Service. Washington, DC: USGPO.

U.S. Bureau of the Census. Statistical Abstract of the United States, 1989. Washington, DC, 1989. Annual. Previous years as cited.

Table 1. NUMBER OF PHYSICIANS, DENTISTS AND NURSES, 1950-1986

Item	Number (1000s, except rate)								
	1950	1955	1960	1965	1970	1975	1980	1985	1986
Physicians	233	255	275	305	348	409	487	577	594
Rate*	149	150	151	153	168	187	211	237	246
Dentists	87	95	105	109	116	127	141	156	158
Rate*	50	48	47	47	47	50	54	57	57
Nurses	375	430	527	613	750	961	1273	1544	1593
Rate*	249	259	293	319	368	446	560	647	661

*Per 100,000 population

SOURCE: Based on <u>Statistical Abstract 1989</u>, p. 97; <u>1979</u>, p. 106.

Table 2. HOSPITAL FACILITIES, 1950-1986

Facility	1950	1955	1960	1965	1970	1975	1980	1985	1986
Number of hospitals									
Total	6788	6956	6876	7123	7123	7156	6965	6872	6841
ShortTerm	5031	5237	5407	5736	5859	5979	5904	5784	5728
Beds (1000s)									
Total	1456	1640	1658	1704	1616	1466	1365	1309	1283
ShortTerm	505	568	639	741	848	947	992	997	977
Beds per 1000 population	10	10	9	9	8	7	6	5	5
Patients admitted									
Total (mil)	18	21	25	29	32	36	39	36	35
Short Term	17	19	23	27	29	34	36	34	32
Average Daily Census(1000s)									
Total	1253	1363	1402	1403	1298	1125	1060	910	883
Short Term	372	407	477	563	662	708	748	650	631
Occup.Rate %									
Total	86	85	85	82	80	77	78	70	69
Short Term	74	71	75	76	78	75	75	65	65
Personnel (1000s)	1058	1301	1598	1952	2537	3023	3492	3625	3647
Rate/100 patients	84	114	95	139	196	269	329	398	413
Total Outpatient Visits (mil)	--	--	--	126	181	255	263	282	295

SOURCE: Based on <u>Statistical Abstract 1989</u>, pp. 101-102; <u>1979</u>, pp. 111-112; <u>1974</u>, p. 79.

Table 3. NURSING AND RELATED CARE FACILITIES, 1963-1987

Item	(1000s) Except Rates)					
	1963	1967	1971	1976	1980	1986
Nursing and related care:						
Facilities	17	19	22	20	23	26
Beds	569	837	1202	1415	1537	1709
Resident patients	491	756	1076	1293	1396	1553
Employees, full-time	242	383	568	653	798	--
Per 1000 patients	491	507	528	505	571	--
Skilled nursing						
facilities	--	4	4277	3922	5052	6897
Beds	--	291	307	309	436	--
Beds Per 1000 Medicare						
enrollees	--	15	15	14	18	--

SOURCE: Based on <u>Statistical Abstract 1989</u>, p. 106; <u>1979</u>, p. 115.

Table 4.   VISITS TO PHYSICIANS BY PATIENT CHARACTERISTICS, 1970-
           1986

Visits	1970	1975	1980	1985	1986
Total Visits (million)					
Sex					
Male	396	435	426	498	515
Female	531	621	610	733	756
Race					
White	832	929	903	1074	1110
Black	87	116	115	132	131
Visits per Person					
Sex					
Male	4.1	4.3	4.0	4.4	4.5
Female	5.1	5.7	5.4	6.1	6.2
Race					
White	4.8	5.1	4.8	5.4	5.5
Black	3.9	4.7	4.5	4.7	4.6
Age					
Under 6	5.9	6.5	6.7	6.3	6.3
6 to 16	2.9	3.2	3.2	3.1	3.3
17 to 24	4.6	4.8	4.0	4.2	4.2
25 to 44	4.6	5.1	4.6	4.9	4.7
45 to 64	5.2	5.6	5.1	6.1	6.6
65 and over	6.3	6.6	6.4	8.3	9.1

SOURCE: Based on Statistical Abstract 1989, p. 99.

Table 5. VISITS TO DENTISTS BY PATIENT CHARACTERISTICS, 1970–
1986

Visits	1970	1975	1980	1986
Total Visits (million)				
Sex				
Male	133	153	158	210
Female	171	188	207	256
Race				
White	283	313	333	416
Black	17	23	26	37
Visits per Person				
Sex				
Male	1.4	1.5	1.5	1.9
Female	1.7	1.7	1.8	2.2
Race				
White	1.6	1.7	1.8	2.1
Black	0.8	1.0	1.0	1.4
Age				
Under 6	0.5	0.6	0.5	0.7
6 to 16	1.9	2.0	2.3	2.4
17 to 24	1.8	1.8	1.6	1.7
25 to 44	1.7	1.7	1.7	2.0
45 to 64	1.5	1.8	1.8	2.2
65 and over	1.1	1.2	1.4	2.1

SOURCE: Based on <u>Statistical Abstract 1989</u>, p. 99.

Table 6.   HOSPITAL USE RATES, BY TYPE OF HOSPITAL, 1960-1986

Type of Hospital	1960	1965	1970	1975	1980	1985	1986
Non-federal short-term							
Admissions per 1000 pop.	128	137	140	156	159	141	136
Admissions per bed	36	36	34	35	36	35	33
Ave. length of stay (days)	7.4	7.7	8.2	7.7	7.6	7.1	7.1
Outpatient visits							
per admission	--	--	4.5	5.9	5.7	6.6	7.2
Outpatient visits							
per 1000 pop.	--	--	641	911	913	935	983
Surgical operations (mil)	--	--	--	16.7	18.8	20.2	20.5
Number per admission	--	--	--	.5	.5	.6	.6
Psychiatric							
Admissions per 1000 pop.	2.3	2.9	3.3	3.2	2.8	2.5	2.6
Days in hospital							
per 1000 pop.	1491	1261	862	490	326	224	219

SOURCE: Based on **Statistical Abstract 1989**, p. 103; **1984**, p. 117.

Table 7. NATIONAL HEALTH EXPENDITURES, 1950-1986

Expenditures	1950	1960	1970	1975	1980	1985	1986
Total (billion $)	13	27	75	133	248	423	458
Per capita	82	146	349	590	1054	1710	1837
Percent of GNP	4	5	7	8	9	11	11
Health Service & Supplies							
Private							
Total (billion $)	9	20	45	73	139	241	263
Direct patient paymts							
Total (billion $)	7	13	27	38	63	105	116
% of total private	80	66	59	52	46	44	44
Insurance premiums							
(billion $)	1.3	6	17	33	73	130	141
Public							
Total (billion $)	3	6	25	51	98	167	180
% total health							
expenditures	22	21	33	39	39	39	39
Medical payments							
Medicare (billion $)	--	--	8	16	37	72	78
Public assistance							
(billion $)	--	1	6	15	28	42	46

SOURCE: Based on <u>Statistical Abstract 1989</u>, p. 90; <u>1984</u>, p. 102.

Table 8.   INDEXES* OF MEDICAL CARE PRICES, 1960-1987

Item	1960	1970	1975	1980	1985	1987
Index total	22.3	34.0	47.5	74.9	113.5	130.1
Medical Care Services	19.5	32.3	46.6	74.8	113.2	130.0
Professional services	--	37.0	50.8	77.9	113.5	128.8
Physicians	21.9	34.5	48.1	76.5	113.3	130.4
Dentists	27.0	39.2	53.2	78.9	114.2	128.8
Hospital rooms	9.3	23.6	38.3	68.0	115.4	131.1
Medical care commodities	46.9	46.5	53.3	75.4	115.2	131.0
Annual percent change	4.1	6.6	12.0	11.0	6.3	6.6

* 1982-1984=100; the indexes of medical care prices are
components of the consumer price index.

SOURCE: Based on **Statistical Abstract 1989**, p. 95; **1984**, p. 106.

Table 9. NATIONAL HEALTH EXPENDITURES, BY OBJECT, 1970-1986

Object of Expenditure	Expenditure (billion of dollars)				
	1970	1975	1980	1985	1986
Total spent	75.0	132.7	248.1	422.6	458.2
Consumers	43.4	71.3	135.6	235.4	256.9
Government	27.8	56.3	105.2	176.0	189.7
Philanthropy & industry	3.9	5.1	7.3	11.2	11.7
Spent for health services and supplies	69.6	124.3	236.2	407.2	442.0
Personal health care exp.	65.4	117.1	219.7	371.3	404.0
Hospital care	28.0	52.4	101.6	167.2	179.6
Physicians' services	14.3	24.9	46.8	82.8	92.0
Dentists' services	4.7	8.2	15.4	27.1	29.6
Other professional serv.	1.6	2.6	5.7	12.4	14.1
Drugs and sundries	8.0	11.9	18.8	28.7	30.6
Eyeglasses & appliances	1.9	3.2	5.1	7.5	8.2
Nursing home care	4.7	10.1	20.4	35.0	38.1
Other health services	2.1	3.8	5.9	10.8	11.9
Net cost of insurance & administration	2.8	4.0	9.2	23.6	24.5
Government public health activities	1.4	3.2	7.3	12.3	13.4
Medical research	2.0	3.3	5.4	7.4	8.2
Medical facilities constr.	3.4	5.1	6.5	8.1	8.0

SOURCE: Based on Statistical Abstract 1989, p. 92.

Table 10. MORTALITY RATES BY SEX AND RACE, 1960-1987

Rates (per 1000*)	1960	1970	1975	1980	1985	1987
Total	9.5	9.5	8.8	8.8	8.7	8.7
Male	11.0	10.9	10.0	9.8	9.5	9.4
Female	8.1	8.1	7.6	7.9	8.1	8.2
White	9.5	9.5	8.9	8.9	9.0	9.0
Male	11.0	10.9	10.0	9.8	9.6	9.5
Female	8.0	8.1	7.8	8.1	8.4	8.5
Black	10.4	10.0	8.8	8.8	8.5	8.4
Male	11.8	11.9	10.6	10.3	9.8	9.7
Female	9.1	8.3	7.3	7.3	7.3	7.3
Age-adjusted rates	7.6	7.1	6.2	5.9	5.5	5.4
Male	9.5	9.3	8.4	7.8	7.2	7.0
Female	5.9	5.3	4.6	4.3	4.1	4.0
White	7.3	6.8	6.0	5.6	5.2	5.1
Male	9.2	8.9	8.0	7.5	6.9	6.7
Female	5.6	5.0	4.4	4.1	3.9	3.9
Black	10.7	10.4	8.9	8.4	7.8	7.7
Male	12.5	13.2	11.6	11.1	10.2	10.1
Female	9.2	8.1	6.7	6.3	5.9	5.8

* Per 1000 population in the specified categories.

SOURCE: Based on <u>Statistical Abstract 1989</u>, p. 74.

Table 11. INFANT, MATERNAL, AND NEONATAL MORTALITY RATES, AND
FETAL MORTALITY RATES BY RACE, 1960-1986

Rates (per 1000 live births)	1960	1970	1975	1980	1985	1986
Infant deaths*	26.0	20.0	16.1	12.6	10.6	10.4
White	22.9	17.8	14.2	11.0	9.3	8.9
Black and others	43.2	30.9	24.2	19.1	15.8	15.7
Black	44.3	32.6	26.2	21.4	18.2	18.0
Maternal deaths**	37.1	21.5	12.8	9.2	7.8	7.2
White	26.0	14.4	9.1	6.7	5.2	4.9
Black and others	97.9	55.9	29.0	19.8	18.1	16.0
Black	103.6	59.8	31.3	21.5	20.4	18.8
Fetal deaths***	16.1	14.2	10.7	9.2	7.9	7.7
White	14.1	12.4	9.5	8.2	7.0	6.8
Black and others	26.8	22.6	16.0	13.4	11.3	11.2
Neonatal deaths#	18.7	15.1	11.6	8.5	7.0	6.7
White	17.2	13.8	10.4	7.5	6.1	5.8
Black and others	26.9	21.4	16.8	12.5	10.3	10.1
Black	27.8	22.8	18.3	14.1	12.1	11.7

* Infants under one year old, exclusive of fetal deaths.
** Per 100,000 live births, infants under 28 days old.
*** Presumed period of gestation 20 weeks or more.
# Represents deaths of infants under 28 days old, exclusive of
fetal deaths.

SOURCE: Based on <u>Statistical Abstract 1989</u>, p. 76.

Table 12. EXPECTATION OF LIFE AT BIRTH, 1950-1987

Population	Expected Years of Life							
	1950	1955	1960	1965	1970	1975	1980	1987
Total	68.2	69.6	69.7	70.2	70.8	72.6	73.7	74.9
Male	65.6	66.7	66.6	66.8	67.1	68.8	70.0	71.5
Female	71.1	72.8	73.1	73.7	74.7	76.6	77.4	78.3
White	69.1	70.5	70.6	71.0	71.7	73.4	74.4	75.5
Male	66.5	67.4	67.4	67.6	68.0	69.5	70.7	72.1
Female	72.2	73.7	74.1	74.7	75.6	77.3	78.1	78.8
Blacks & others	60.8	63.7	63.6	64.1	65.3	68.0	69.5	71.6
Male	59.1	61.4	61.1	61.1	61.3	63.7	65.3	67.6
Female	62.9	66.1	66.3	67.4	69.4	72.4	73.6	75.4
Black	--	--	--	--	64.1	66.8	68.1	69.7
Male	--	--	--	--	60.0	62.4	63.8	65.4
Female	--	--	--	--	68.3	71.3	72.5	73.8

SOURCE: Based on <u>Statistical Abstract 1989</u>, p. 71.

Table 13. DEATHS AND DEATH RATES, BY SELECTED CAUSES, 1960-1986

Cause of Death	1950	Crude Death Rate Per 100,000 Population			
		1960	1970	1980	1986
All causes	964	954	945	878	873
Major cardiovascular diseases	494	515	496	436	402
Diseases of heart	357	369	362	336	317
Cerebrovascular diseases	104	108	102	75	62
Malignancies	140	149	163	184	195
Accidents and adverse effects	61	52	56	47	39
Motor vehicle	23	21	27	23	20
Chronic obstructive pulmonary diseases and allied conditions	--	--	15	25	32
Pneumonia and influenza	31	37	31	24	29
Diabetes mellitus	16	17	19	15	15
Suicide	11	11	12	12	13
Chronic liver dis. & cirrhosis	9	11	15	13	11
Homicide & legal intervention	5	5	8	11	9
Certain conditions originating in the perinatal period	40	37	21	10	8
Congenital anomalies	12	12	8	6	5

SOURCE: Based on Statistical Abstract 1989, p. 78; 1984, p. 78; 1974, p. 62.

Table 14. PERCENT OF CHILDREN 1-4 YEARS OF AGE IMMUNIZED AGAINST
SPECIFIED DISEASES, 1965-1984

Disease	1965	1970	1975	1980	1984
Measles	33%	57%	65%	63%	65%
Rubella	--	37	62	63	61
Diptheria, tetanus, pertusis	74	76	75	66	66
Polio	74	66	65	59	59
Mumps	--	--	44	57	59

SOURCE: Based on National Center for Health Statistics, 1985;
Statistical Abstract 1984, p. 122, 1979, p. 123.

Table 15. SPECIFIED REPORTABLE DISEASES, CASES REPORTED, 1950-1987

Diseases	1950	1960	1970	1980	1987
High Incidence (1000s)					
AIDS	--	--	--	--	21.1
Ambebiasis	4.6	3.4	2.9	5.3	3.1
Aseptic meningitis	--	1.6	6.5	8.0	11.5
Brucellosis	3.5	.8	.2	.2	.1
Chickenpox	--	--	--	190.9	213.2
Diphtheria*	5.8	.9	.4	--	--
Encephalitis:					
Primary infectious	1.1	2.3	1.6	1.4	1.4
Post infectious			.4	--	.1
Hepatitis:					
B (serum)	2.8	41.7	8.3	19.0	25.9
A (infectious)			56.8	29.1	25.3
Unspecified	--	--	--	11.9	3.1
Non-A, Non-B	--	--	--	--	3.0
Legionellosis	--	--	--	--	1.0
Malaria	2.2	.1	3.1	2.1	.9
Measles	319.1	441.7	47.4	13.5	3.7
Meningococcal infections	3.8	2.3	2.5	2.8	2.9
Mumps	--	--	105.0	8.6	12.8
Pertussus	120.7	14.8	4.2	1.7	2.8
Poliomyelitis, acute*	33.3	3.2	--	--	--
Rabies, animal	7.9	3.6	3.2	6.4	4.7
Rheumatic fever, acute	--	9.0	3.2	.4	.1
Rubella	--	--	56.6	3.9	.3
Salmonellosis	1.2	6.9	22.1	33.7	50.9
Shigellosis (1000)	23.4	12.5	13.8	19.0	23.9
Tetanus	.5	.4	.1	.1	--
Toxic-shock syndrome	--	--	--	--	.4
Trichinosis	.3	.3	.1	.1	--
Tuberculosis	--	55.5	37.1	27.7	22.5
Tularemia	.9	.4	.2	.2	.2
Typhoid fever	2.5	.8	.3	.5	.4
Typhus fever (tick-borne)	.5	.2	.4	1.2	.6
Venereal diseases:					
Gonorrhea	287.0	259.0	600.0	1004.0	781.0
Syphilis	218.0	122.0	91.0	69.0	87.0
Other	8.2	2.8	2.2	1.0	5.3
Low Incidence**					
Botulism	20	12	12	89	82
Diphtheria	5796	918	435	3	3
Leprosy	44	54	129	223	238

Table 15. SPECIFIED REPORTABLE DISEASES, CASES REPORTED, 1950-
1987 (continued)

Diseases	1950	1960	1970	1980	1987
Low Incidence					
Leptospirosis	30	53	47	85	43
Plague	--	--	13	18	12
Poliomyelitis, acute	33300	3190	33	9	--
Psittacosis	26	113	35	124	98
Rabies, human	--	--	3	--	1
Tetanus					
Typhus fever (flea-borne)	685	68	27	81	49

* See lower panel of table for more recent "low incidence"
figures.
** The "low incidence" diseases are unit (case) counts, not in
1000s.

NOTE: Blanks (--) for high incidence diseases, 1980 and before,
mean that the disease was not a notifiable disease at that time,
and the data are therefore unavailable. This applies to AIDS,
Aseptic meningitis, chickenpox, hepatitis, Legionellosis, mumps,
rheumatic fever, rubella, toxic-shock syndrome, and tuberculosis.

SOURCE: Based on Statistical Abstract 1989, p. 111; 1979, p. 123.

8.3 WELFARE SYSTEM

The assumption of welfare responsibilities by the Federal government began under the first Roosevelt administration (1933-37) with Social Security and public employment programs; a second wave of welfare legislation, including the Economic Opportunity Act, the Civil Rights Act, Education Acts and others, was enacted in Lyndon Johnson's administration (1964-68). From 1976 to 1984, all of the major programs continued to expand, under Republican as well as Democratic administrations. In-kind programs, such as health and education, grew most quickly, largely by exploitative cost escalation: for example, between 1975 and 1985 the number of Medicaid beneficiaries declined slightly while the amount paid by the government on their behalf increased by 223%. The welfare system is plagued by a lack of coordination.

The American welfare state is unusual in three respects--the lateness of its development, the peculiar division of responsibility between Federal and state agencies, and the frequency with which poorly designed programs have miscarried.

The assumption of welfare responsibilities by the Federal government began in the first Roosevelt administration (1933-1937), with Social Security (pensions), unemployment insurance, the United States Employment Service, financial risk insurance on bank deposits and home mortgages, income support for families with dependent children and the blind, the distribution of surplus food to low-income families, public low-rent housing, the encouragement and supervision of collective bargaining, the establishment of a minimum wage, direct subsidies to farmers--all of which became permanent--as well as programs of price control, industrial planning, and work relief--which were soon discontinued.

The second wave of innovation occurred in 1964-1966 under the administration of Lyndon Johnson and was enacted in a number of major statutes: the Economic Opportunity Act, the Civil Rights Act, the Social Security Amendments of 1965, the Elementary and Secondary Education Act, and the Model Cities Act. More than a hundred new federal programs were established under these statutes, including such goals as work relief for unemployed youth, adult literacy, development loans for minority-owned businesses, social services for migrant workers, health insurance for the population over 65, Federal enforcement of nondiscrimination in employment and public services, subsidized health care for the indigent, legal services for the poor, emergency food and planning services, family planning subsidies, educational facilities for disadvantaged children, special education for the handicapped, and a Community Action Program which established thousands of local community agencies with diverse purposes.

Many of the smaller programs dropped away under subsequent administrations but all of the major ones continued to expand their coverage, increase their benefits, and come more firmly under Federal control as time went on. The process continues to this day as the Bush administration pushes for a vast expansion of subsidized child care.

Table 1 shows the growth of welfare expenditures from 1960 to 1986. The rates of growth have been very steep in most programs, especially social insurance (Social Security), public aid, health and education, but not veterans programs. Aggregate public expenditures for social insurance (Social Security), education, and health assistance rose from $43 billion in 1960 to $749 billion in 1986.

Table 2 shows that in the postwar era, aggregate social welfare expenditures in constant dollars have grown under every administration--Republican as well as Democratic--with the greatest relative increases for health and the least for veterans' benefits.

Table 3 shows the number of Social Security beneficiaries and the total Federal outlay to them, 1970-1987. Table 4 illustrates average amounts of benefits to selected types of beneficiaries in constant dollars, 1970-1987. The number of beneficiaries increased by 58%, partly because of the extension of coverage to previously excluded categories of workers and partly because of growth in the retirement-age population. The average monthly benefits--in constant dollars--increased by 47% during the same interval. The Social Security system, however, does not represent a drain on the resources of the Federal government. It is financed by high and regressive payroll taxes that bring in a large cash surplus every year.

The escalation of in-kind programs, especially those providing health and education benefits, has been much more rapid, partly because of the inclusion of new services, but mostly because these programs involve payments to third parties who, being free of market controls, have been able to raise their fees much more than other providers of goods and services who do not have access to the virtually unlimited resources of the Federal government. Table 5 illustrates this pattern: the number of Medicaid beneficiaries remained almost constant from 1975 to 1987 but the amounts paid by the government on their behalf increased by 275%!

The same problem of exploitative cost escalation afflicts educational programs. Table 6 shows the increase of public expenditures for education at all levels from all sources, from 1960 to 1986. Enrollments during this period showed an overall increase of 29%, while public expenditures increased by 1,025%. The consensus of experts is that there was no commensurate increase in educational quality.

Aside from the tendency of in-kind welfare payments to escalate out of control, American welfare programs suffer from a severe lack of coordination. Browning (1988, p. 15) quotes the 1972 reports of a congressional staff study, which said

It is no longer possible--if indeed, it ever was--to provide a convincing rationale for the programs as they exist in terms of who is covered and who is excluded, benefit amounts, and eligibility conditions. No coherent rationale binds them together as a system. Additionally, the programs are extraordinarily complex, and the eligibility provisions lack uniformity even among programs with similar objectives and structures.

These problems have worsened since that report was written.

References

Browning, Robert X. "Priorities, Programs and Presidents: Assessing Patterns of Growth in U.S. Social Welfare Programs, 1950-1985." In The Distributional Impacts of Public Policy, edited by Sheldon H. Danziger and Kent E. Portnoy. New York: St. Martin's Press, 1988.

U.S. Bureau of the Census. Statistical Abstract of the United States, 1989. Washington, D.C. 1989. Annual. Previous years as cited.

Table 1. PUBLIC SOCIAL WELFARE EXPENDITURES, TOTAL AND SELECTED
          PROGRAMS, 1960-1986

Public Program	1960	1970	1980	1985	1986
Total Outlay (bil.)	$52.3	$145.9	$492.5	$730.4	$770.5
Per capita constant (1986) dollars					
Total*	990	1868	2822	3065	3138
Social insurance	365	698	1313	1561	1587
Public aid	76	210	412	406	421
Health and medical	83	128	160	173	181
Education	333	653	694	700	728
Veterans' programs	104	114	121	112	112

* Includes programs not listed separately.

SOURCE: Based on Statistical Abstract 1989, p. 346.

Table 2. REAL ANNUAL PERCENTAGE CHANGE IN BUDGET OUTLAYS, BY
          PRESIDENTIAL ADMINISTRATIONS, 1950-1985

	Social Welfare Outlays				Education, Manpower, and Social Services
	Total	Income Security	Health	Veterans	
Truman (D)	2%	12%	12%	-8%	23%
Eisenhower (R)	10	15	9	1	8
Eisenhower (R)	11	14	15	1	14
Kennedy-Johnson (D)	4	4	17	-1	18
Johnson (D)	12	7	57	4	38
Nixon (R)	11	13	8	7	10
Nixon-Ford (R)	8	7	11	3	5
Carter (D)	4	4	6	-2	2
Reagan I (R)	2	1	6	-1	-7

SOURCE: Based on Browning, 1988, p. 19

Table 3.   SOCIAL SECURITY (OASDI) BENEFITS, 1970-1987

Year	Number of Beneficiaries (millions)	Benefit Payments During Year (billions)
1970	26	$ 32
1975	32	67
1980	36	120
1981	36	141
1982	36	156
1983	36	167
1984	36	176
1985	37	186
1986	38	197
1987	38	204

SOURCE: Based on Statistical Abstract 1989, p. 354.

Table 4.   AVERAGE MONTHLY BENEFIT, BY TYPE OF BENEFICIARY

Type of Beneficiary	Constant Dollars (1987)		
	1970	1980	1987
Retired workers	342	456	513
Retired worker and wife	577	758	873
Disabled workers	380	496	508
Surviving spouses	171	219	253
Children of deceased workers	238	321	352

SOURCE: Based on Statistical Abstract 1989, p. 354.

Table 5. MEDICAL ASSISTANCE (MEDICAID) RECIPIENTS AND PAYMENTS,
          1975-1987

Year	Recipients (millions)	Payments (millions)
1975	22	$ 12
1980	22	23
1985	22	38
1986	23	41
1987	23	45

SOURCE: Based on <u>Statistical Abstract 1989</u>, p. 363.

Table 6. ENROLLMENT AND EXPENDITURE IN EDUCATION (ALL LEVELS),
          1960-1985

Year	Enrollment (millions)	Expenditures (billions)
1960	45	$ 24
1966	54	45
1970	60	70
1975	61	111
1980	58	166
1985	57	248
1986	58	270*

* preliminary

SOURCE: Based on <u>Statistical Abstract 1989</u>, p. 124, 125, <u>1980</u>, p.
        140, 141, <u>1982-83</u>, p. 135.

The Federal presence in American society has increased considerably in the past 50 years. This intrusion is readily evident in its ever-expanding budget, the growing number of Federal employees and the extension of regulation practiced by various Federal agencies.

Federal Budget

The Federal budget, total receipts and total outlays, from 1945 to 1988 is presented in Table 1. Federal outlays increased from 93 billion dollars in 1945 to over one trillion dollars in 1988. This is a ten-fold increase. The difference would be even greater, but in 1945 World War II was winding down and the U.S. was starting its efforts to help rebuild Europe. Thus Federal outlays were higher than during peacetime. Five years later, in 1950, Federal outlays totaled only 42 billion dollars. In 1950, the Federal government spent $280 for every man, woman, and child in the country. Per capita expenditures rose to $510 in 1960, $954 in 1970, $2,594 in 1980, and $4,290 in 1988.

It can also be seen in Table 1 that the percent of the Gross National Product spent by the various branches of the Federal government has increased modestly, from 16% in 1950 to 22% in 1988.

Table 2 compares Federal budget outlays in current and constant (1982) dollars for the years 1970 to 1988. When inflation is taken into account, the increase in government spending is not so dramatic: the 18-year increase in constant dollars is only 70%, compared to over 400% in current dollars. In 1970, the Federal government and its many agencies spent $2,848 in constant (1982) dollars per capita, compared to $3,069 in 1980 and $3,534 in 1988.

Contrary to the beliefs of many Americans, most of this spending does not go to the poor, and it does not result in any important redistribution of income. The workings of the system are extremely complicated and are not clearly understood by anyone, but their net effect is to subsidize persons at every income level more or less in proportion to their nonsubsidy income. Physicians receive much larger subsidies from the Medicaid program than their indigent patients receive from any of the programs that offer assistance to the poor. Landlords receive much larger dollar payments from the Department of Housing and Urban Development's rent-subsidy program for low-income families than those families obtain from all assistance programs combined. University professors draw larger sums from their Federal research grants than graduate students are paid under their Federal fellowships. The fees of legal-aid lawyers greatly exceed the wages of their clients.

Federal Personnel

Table 3 shows the number of civilians employed by the Federal government for the period 1970-1988. A rather modest increase is evident, from 2.9 to 3.1 million workers. Federal employment has not kept pace with the growth of the labor force as a whole. Over that period, the percentage of the labor force employed by the Federal government dropped from 3.7% to 2.7%. Nevertheless, it remains the nation's largest employer.

Table 4 reports the number of men and women, full-time and part-time, white-collar and blue-collar, employed by the Federal government. The number of male employees dropped slightly, while the number of female workers nearly doubled between 1970 and 1987. Like the national labor force as a whole, the government labor force has shifted from predominantly blue-collar to white-collar workers.

Expansion of Federal Functions

The Federal government greatly expanded its functions during the rather sweeping transformation that took place after 1964 as the executive and judicial branches of the government began to develop far-reaching legislative programs of their own that were only tenuously related to those of the Congress. For example, the Department of Health, Education, and Welfare reached into America's schools to ensure racial integration, to insist on interscholastic competition in girls' basketball, and to forbid the posting of examination grades in the halls. The Department of Transportation told used-car dealers what blandishments they might use in their advertising. The Occupational Safety and Health Administration went through the country's factories and ordered protective installations in settings deemed dangerous. The courts at all levels have broadened their own jurisdictions, so that a woman excluded from a neighborhood tavern or a doctor who wishes to continue treating a reluctant patient now go to court as a matter of course.

The expansion of Federal functions has been largely limited to control and supervision rather than outright ownership. As may be seen in Table 5, there has been a slight decline in Federal land ownership and the number and area of government-owned buildings increased only slightly between 1960 and 1987.

References

Brown-John, Lloyd C., ed. Centralizing and Decentralizing Trends in Federal States. Lanham, MD: University Press of America, 1988.

Caplow, Theodore, Howard M. Bahr and Bruce A. Chadwick. Middletown Families: Fifty Years of Change and Continuity, Minneapolis: University of Minnesota Press, 1982.

Dye, Thomas. American Federalism: Competition Among Governments, Lexington, MA: Lexington Books, 1990.

Greenstein, Fred I. and Nelson W. Polsby, eds. Governmental Institutions and Processes. Reading, MA: Addison-Wesley, 1975.

Griffith, Janice C. Federalism: The Shifting Balance. Chicago: American Bar Association, 1989.

Juster, F. Thomas. The Economic and Political Impact of Revenue Sharing. Ann Arbor: Survey Research Center, University of Michigan, 1977.

Wright, Deil S. and Harvey L. White. Federalism and Intergovernmental Relations. Washington D.C.: American Society for Public Administration, 1984.

Table 1. FEDERAL BUDGET, 1945-1988

| | (billions of dollars) | | |
Year	Total Receipts	Total	% of GNP
1945	45.2	92.7	44%
1950	39.4	42.6	16
1955	65.5	68.4	18
1960	92.5	92.2	18
1965	116.8	118.2	18
1970	192.8	195.6	20
1975	279.1	332.3	22
1980	517.1	590.9	22
1985	734.1	946.3	24
1988 (est.)	909.2	1,055.9	22

SOURCE: Based on **Statististical Abstract 1989**, p. 303.

Table 2. FEDERAL BUDGET OUTLAYS IN CURRENT AND CONSTANT (1982)
         DOLLARS, 1970-1988

Metric	Total Outlays (billions)				
	1970	1975	1980	1985	1988*
Current dollars	195.6	332.3	590.9	946.3	1055.9
Constant (1982) dollars	509.4	586.0	699.1	848.0	869.8

*Estimated.

SOURCE: Based on **Statistical Abstract 1989**, p. 306.

Table 3. FEDERAL CIVILIAN EMPLOYMENT, 1970-1987

Year	Federal Employment Total (millions)	Percent of all Employed Persons
1970	2.9	4%
1975	2.9	3
1980	3.0	3
1985	3.0	3
1987	3.1	3

SOURCE: Based on Statistical Abstract 1989, p. 319.

Table 4. CHARACTERISTICS OF FEDERAL CIVILIAN EMPLOYMENT, 1970-1987

Characteristic	Workers (millions) 1970	1975	1980	1985	1987
Total employees	2.6	2.7	2.8	2.9	3.0
Male	1.9	1.9	1.8	1.8	1.8
Female	.7	.8	1.0	1.1	1.2
Full-time	2.5	2.5	2.5	2.6	2.7
Other	.1	.2	.3	.3	.3
White-collar	2.1	2.3	2.3	2.5	2.6
Blue-collar	.5	.5	.5	.4	.4

SOURCE: Based on Statistical Abstract 1989, p. 319.

Table 5.   FEDERAL LAND AND BUILDINGS OWNED, 1960-1987

Federally Owned	1960	1970	1975	1980	1985	1987
Land (million acres)	772	762	761	720	727	724
Buildings, number (1,000s)	413	418	405	403	454	412
Buildings, floor area (million sq. ft.)	2445	2542	2502	2522	2860	2700
Cost* of lands, bldgs. etc. (billion $)	53	79	91	107	148	165

* Cost as of date of acquisition.

SOURCE: Based on Statistical Abstract 1989, p. 322.

9.1 LABOR UNIONS

The unionized share of the U.S. labor force has been declining for half a century, but more rapidly in the past decade than before. The erosion of membership has been most conspicuous in the manufacturing sector, but has taken place across the board. The loss of public confidence in union leadership appears to be a major factor, but managerial tactics have played a part, as well as the growth of the service industries and the relative decline of mining, railroading, and heavy manufacturing.

Labor union membership is in decline in the United States and has been for some time. Private sector union membership reached its maximum in 1970 with a total of 16,978,000 members. Even this concealed a decline however, for the percentage of unionized private employees had long been declining from its peak of 36% in 1953 (Table 1). An executive order by President Kennedy allowed the recognition of public sector unions in 1962 and they expanded greatly from that time. A membership of 769,800 (11.6% of public sector employees) in 1953 grew to 2,161,000 (24.3%) in 1962 and to 5,980,000 (40.2%) in 1976. After this point, however, the public sector unions began to decline absolutely and relatively, just as private sector unions had done a few years earlier. By 1983, public sector union membership decreased to 5,421,000, 34.4% of public sector employees. In sum, union penetration of the labor market is now less than it was half a century ago (Table 2).

Unions have always had varying degrees of success in the different industrial sectors, as shown in Table 2. At first, construction was the most heavily unionized sector, then mining and transportation gradually began to catch up. In recent decades, union membership in mining and construction has declined precipitously and a number of heavily unionized industries, like steel, rubber and railroads, have been in relative decline.

Perhaps the most important factor in the decline of union membership has been the growth of service industries relative to all others. Service industries have always been resistant to unionization, and they have become more rather than less so in the course of time (Troy, 1986, p. 94).

Another important change has been the increase in the ratio of white collar to blue collar workers. Generally, white collar workers are far less susceptible to unionization, at least in the private sector. Thus, as the proportion of white collar workers in the labor force increases, the percentage of unionized workers tends to decline (Doyle, 1985, p. 17). Corporate managers have sometimes been able to deunionize by moving factories from those (predominantly northern) states which allow the closed shop to those (predominantly southern and southwestern states) which do not (Troy, 1986, pp. 94-97; Doyle, 1985, p. 16). Management has apparently also become more sophisticated in contending by legal means against organizing drives. And since 1980, of course, the executive branch of the federal government has been unsympathetic to organized labor.

The erosion of organizing capability is reflected in the results of representation elections held by the National Labor Relations Board. During the 1950s unions won 65% to 70% of these elections. During the early 1980s they won as few as 45% (Galenson, 1986, p. 68; Doyle, 1985, p. 19).

Another factor contributing to the decline in union membership seems to be a decrease of public support. In 1936, when Gallup first inquired, 72% of the public approved of unions. By 1981 only 56% approved (Table 3). Disapproval was highest among members of non-union families, those whom unions seek to organize. According to Lipset (1986, p. 51) "the public's feelings are a major factor in reduced union strength."

Although a (diminishing) majority of the public remains favorable toward unions, a majority disapprove of union leaders, and their disapproval has become more pronounced over the past 20 years (Table 3). Moreover they rate union leaders as less trustworthy than business leaders (Freeman and Medoff, 1984). It will be difficult to increase union membership as long as these attitudes prevail.

References

Doyle, Philip. "Area Wage Surveys Shed Light on Declines in Unionization." Monthly Labor Review 106 (1985): 13-20.

Freeman, Richard B. and James L. Medoff. What Do Unions Do? New York: Basic Books, 1984.

Galenson, Walter. "The Historical Role of American Trade Unionism."Unions in Transistion: Entering the Second Century, edited by Seymour Martin Lipset, pp. 39-73. San Francisco: Institute for Contemporary Studies, 1986.

Lipset, Seymour Martin. "Unions in Decline." Public Opinion 9 (Sept/Oct, 1986): 52-54.

Troy, Leo. "The Rise and Fall of American Trade Unions: The Labor Movement from FDR to RR. "Unions in Transition: Entering the Second Century, edited by Seymour Martin Lipset, pp. 75-112. San Francisco: Institute for Contemporary Studies, 1986.

Table 1. UNION MEMBERSHIP AND DENSITY, 1953-1983

Year	Membership (millions)		Density (percent)	
	Private Sector	Public Sector	Private Sector	Public Sector
1953	15.5	0.7	36%	12%
1962	14.7	2.2	32	24
1973	16.8	5.1	27	37
1983	13.1	5.4	18	34

SOURCE: Based on Troy, 1986, p. 82.

Table 2. UNION DENSITY BY MAJOR INDUSTRIAL SECTOR, 1940-1985

Industrial Sector	1940	1953	1966	1975	1985
Manufacturing	30%	42%	37%	37%	25%
Mining	72	65	36	32	15
Construction	77	84	41	35	22
Transportation	47	80	--	47	37
Services	6	10	--	14	7
Government	11	12	26	40	33
All Nonfarm	22	32	30	29	19

SOURCE: Based on Troy, 1986, p. 87.

Table 3.   PUBLIC APPROVAL OF UNIONS AND UNION LEADERSHIP, GALLUP
           AND NORC SURVEYS, 1953-1986

| | | Percent Approving of Leadership of | |
| | | Organized | Eight Other |
Year	Unions	Labor	Institutions
1953	75%	16%	33%
1963	67	--	--
1973	60	11	26
1981	55	--	--
1986	--	8	25

SOURCE: Based on Lipset, 1986, p. 53.

Compared to other western nations, the United States has high religious affiliation and activity. About 90% of adults have a religious preference, a slightly lower rate than in the 1950s and 1960s. Rates of church membership have declined slightly, and among Catholics rates of weekly attendance at services are lower than formerly. Church giving and the popularity of the clergy as a vocation have increased for Protestants but decreased for Catholics. There are more religious books being published, but the fraction of all publishing devoted to religious matters is down. The percentage of all philanthropy devoted to religion has been stable for over 30 years, but the percentage of voluntary organizations devoted to religion continues to shrink. Many indicators of religious activity manifest decline in the late 1960s and early 1970s, generally reaching a low point about 1975 followed by a reversal of the downward trend. A superficial interpretation of this recurring pattern is to view it as a concomitant of the anti-war, anti-establishment movement of the sixties and early seventies. These various trends, taken together, support an interpretation of continuity rather than of religious devitalization or secularization.

Membership and Religious Preference

Over 90% of Americans claim a religious preference. In 1986, 59% were Protestants, 27% Catholics, and 2% Jews. These preferences represent a slight increase for Catholics (up from 20% in 1947, 25% by 1952), and a substantial decrease for Protestants and Jews (down from 69% and 5% respectively, in 1947). The percentage claiming no preference shows a fairly consistent increase since the mid-1960s, from 2% to its 1986 level of 8% (Table 1; see also Condran and Tamney, 1985).

About two-thirds of U.S. adults belong to a specific church or synagogue. Membership rates declined gradually for 30 years, 1947-1978, falling from 76% to 68%, then stabilized at about 68% for most of the following decade (Table 2). It is not clear whether the 1988 figure of 65% represents a resumption of the decline or is simply non-meaningful fluctuation about the stabilized membership rates of the 1980s. Women are more apt than men to be church members, and older people are more likely to belong than the young. Education and income seem to have little to do with church membership, but race makes a difference (blacks are more likely than whites to belong) and so does region (westerners are least likely to belong, southerners most likely) ("Religion in America," 1987, pp. 35-36).

Organization and Activities

Attendance to offices. Rates of weekly church attendance have held steady at about 40% since the late 1960s. Attendance rates were somewhat higher during the 1950s, in the 46%-49% range. The decline in church attendance in the late 1950s and 1960s is entirely attributable to decreased attendance among Catholics. Weekly church attendance rates of Protestants have changed very little over the past four decades (Table 3).

Reports of annual donations to churches (Table 4) show that the per capita financial contributions of Protestants have increased substantially over the years. Church members in the late 1980s contributed over twice as much, in constant dollars per capita, as did their counterparts in 1950. In fact, per capita donations in 1986 were the highest on record, and donations in 1987 were only slightly lower. The increase has not been continuous, and there have been long plateaus and some reversals. In fact, most of the increase occurred between 1950 and 1968, and the 1968 peak of over $91 per capita was not surpassed until 1983.

Another source of information on contributions to religion is the Internal Revenue Service, which publishes reports on itemized deductions, corporate profits, and bequests. On the basis of the IRS reports, it appears that about 80% of all private philanthropy comes from individual donors. The total amount of private philanthropy has increased consistently over the years, with 1985 contributions over three times higher than in 1955 (Table 5). The most frequent recipient of private giving is the religious organization. In 1960, half of all private philanthropy went to religion; the proportion declined for 15 years to a low of 43% in 1975, then increased again to 47% by 1985. No other institution approaches the church as an object of individual philanthropy. In 1987, the next most frequent recipients were health organizations, which received 15% percent of all private philanthropy funds.

<u>Clergy and seminarians</u>. One indication of the vitality of religion is the number of people who follow religious vocations. Thus, trends in the number of clergy and in their representation in the labor force are relevant. Census data over the past four decennial censuses, supplemented by annual labor force data on detailed occupation (available since 1978), reveal that the representation of clerics in the labor force has not changed appreciably, and that their representation in the population has increased. As may be seen in Table 6, there were three clerics per 1,000 employed workers in 1950, and the same number in 1988. The number of employed clergy increased from 136,000 to 348,000 over the 38-year period, growing faster than the population generally, such that the number of clergy per 1,000 population rose from .9 in 1950 to 1.4 in 1988. Thus, there are relatively more clergy than there used to be.

Trends apparent in denominational statistics (Table 7), based on compilation of records from the individual churches, roughly parallel the census findings. The denominational figures reveal: (1) A low point in 1970 in representation of pastors in the population, followed by increases until by 1987 the number of pastors per 1,000 population stood at its highest point in over three decades; (2) Ratios of pastors serving parishes to the total population that are remarkably close to those computed from the Department of Labor estimates of employed clergy in Table 6, which range between 1.16 and 1.41 clergy per 1,000 population over the 1978-1988 period, compared to 1.21-1.37 for the same period in the denominational statistics (Table 7).

The general increase in the number of clerics does not apply to all components of the population. Instead, the modest overall increase masks a more substantial increase in the number of Protestant clergy and a sharp decline in the number of Catholic clergy. In 1960, the nation's 42+ million Roman Catholics were served by an ordained clergy of 54,067, or 1.3 clergy for every thousand Catholics. After 1960 the number of Catholics increased while the number of Catholic clergy stabilized and then declined. By 1987 the clergy/member ratio was down to 1.0 per 1,000 members (Table 8).

Clergy/member ratios for Protestants are much higher, and have been increasing since 1970. In 1960 there were 4.4 ordained clergy for every 1,000 Protestants, a ratio over three times higher than the Catholic ratio. By 1987 the gap had widened, and the Protestant ratio of 5.4 clerics per 1,000 church members was 5.4 times higher than the Catholic ratio. There is evidence here of Protestant thriving, of increased Protestant <u>power</u> to support clergy, and an apparent opposite tendency among U.S. Catholics. For additional discussion of the causes and meaning of change in U.S. Catholicism, see Hoge, 1986; in Protestantism, see Hoge and Roozen, 1979; McKinney and Hoge, 1983, and Roof and McKinney, 1987.

Since 1965, Protestant seminaries have increased in number and enrollments. Over 50,000 students enrolled annually in the 1980s, compared to half that many in the 1960s. Over the same period, enrollments in Roman Catholic seminaries plummeted. The total number of Catholic seminarians in 1987 was less than one-fifth the number in 1965. To help interpret the changes in enrollment, consider trends in the ratios of Catholic and Protestant seminarians to the total numbers of Catholic and Protestant clergy and to the national population of 18-24 year-olds for the period 1960 to 1987 (Table 9). Among Catholics, the ratio of seminarians per 1,000 clergy drops from 737 to 158; among Protestants, there are fewer seminarians per cleric, but the trend is in the opposite direction, such that by 1987, the seminarian/cleric ratio has increased from 60 to 107. The same pattern appears in comparing numbers of seminarians with numbers of young adults. Between 1965 and 1987, the ratio of Catholic seminarians per 1,000 adults in the U.S. drops from 2.4 to .4, while among Protestant seminarians the ratio rises from 1.0 to 1.9. In other words, at the same time that attending a Catholic seminary has become increasingly improbable, the likelihood of attending a Protestant seminary has nearly doubled.

The decline in seminarians parallels a drop in numbers of Catholic clergy, with total ordinations down one-third between 1969 and 1980, and total active priests down about the same proportion between 1970 and 1980, from over 37,000 to under 30,000 (see Shoenherr and Sorensen, 1982).

Another measure of religious participation and attendance to offices is support of foreign missionaries. Figures from American Protestant denominations show a marked decline in the number of foreign missionaries supported by "mainline" National Council churches, while the number of foreign missionaries supported by the more fundamentalist conservative Protestants such as Southern Baptists and Assemblies of God almost quadrupled between 1952 and 1976 (Hammond, 1983).

Religious press/publishing. We examined several indicators of the scale and vitality of religious publishing, including the number of new titles published each year which are classified as religious books, industry figures on the dollar value of sales of religious books, consumer expenditures on religious books as estimated by government surveys, changes in the number of book stores that specialize in religious books, and trends in the amount of text that might be considered "religious" which appears in popular magazines.

A uniform pattern appears in all of these indicators, namely a decline from the level characterizing the 1950s and early 1960s to a low point in the early 1970s, and than an increase in whatever trend-line is being followed back toward the previous high levels, such that the 1980s appear as times of a relatively healthy religious press. To illustrate, consider trends in religious books as a percentage of all books published annually (Table 10). Although over four times as many books were published in 1986 as in 1950, the percentage of titles that were religious books differed by only one percent, 5.6% in 1986 compared to 6.6% in 1950. However, over the 36-year period, religious books as percentage of total titles had risen until 1960, declined by more than one-third to a 1975 low of 4.5 percent, then risen again to the 5.6 percent of 1986.

Religious bookstores serve as a second illustration. As may be seen in Table 11, in 1987 there were almost four times as many religious bookstores as in 1955, and 18% of all bookstores were religious bookstores. The percentage religious had been higher in 1960, when almost 20% were religious bookstores, but over the next 15 years it declined to a low of 12% The downward trend reversed in 1975, and by 1986 religious bookstores had almost recovered their previous high representation.

The trends in numbers of religious books sold, titles issued, dollars spent on religious books, firms devoted to selling them, and numbers of religious "mentions" in secular magazines (Perkins, 1984) all point to (1) considerable stability in both production and consumer demand, and (2) modest decline in the late 1960s or early 1970s, at least in relative terms, followed by resurgence.

Paraecclesial organizations. There are at least four types of paraecclesial organizations. Each is considered separately below. First, there are fraternal, recreational, mutual benefit or other organizations that may have historical or contemporary links to specific religious or ethnic traditions but which as formal organizations are independent from any single church body. Examples are the Sons of Norway, the Deseret Mutual Benefit Association, the Knights of Columbus, the Lutheran Brotherhood, and the Aid Association for Lutherans (Bickel and Picard, 1983, pp. 312-313).

Second, there are organizations that are formally secular, but whose organizational activities overlap with those of the churches, or whose efforts represent the combined efforts of many churches or representatives of churches. Such organizations may involve church members or churches themselves in common cause with representatives of secular organizations. Ministerial associations fit this definition, and so do some of the organized charitable activities of communities, such as the United Way, which may reflect denominational involvement both in the stimulation of private philanthropy and in the receipt of portions of the funds collected. Some private foundations, especially those formally designated as religious foundations, also are properly categorized as paraecclesial.

Third, there are organizations that relate to the sacred in non-traditional ways, or that do not fit within the existing and accepted denominational framework, and are therefore labeled "cults." The cults, by definition are "novel, deviant faiths" (Bainbridge and Stark, 1980, p. 199) and the category of parareligious movements includes organizations that use religious rites and symbols in a more-or-less secular context and that "exist as supplements rather than competitors to the organized, denominational patterns of American religion" (Bird and Reimer, 1982, p. 3).

Finally, there are client and audience cults. The former include relationships between "magician and customer," and generally involve short-term exchanges that fit consultant-client or therapist-patient models. The audience cults have even less formal organization, and involvement is usually limited to participation via the mass media (Bainbridge and Stark, 1980, p. 199).

Trends in the growth of cults and new religious movements (numbers 3 and 4 above) are properly covered elsewhere (see the section on innovation in Chapter 11.5, Religious Beliefs). Published trend data covering at least a decade on cults and new religious movements is very rare. It is now possible to apply the methods and benchmarks provided by Bainbridge and Stark

(1980) in their assessment of the publications deriving from client and audience cults, or those provided by Stark, Bainbridge, and Doyle (1979) in their analysis of data from Melton's Encyclopedia of American Religions (1978). However, to create the necessary series using the indicators they introduce, such as listings in spiritualist directories, counts of stories published in Fate magazine, or analyses of Melton's (1985, 1986, 1987) subsequent compilations, will require original research; figures for a 15-year span or more do not appear in the existing research literature.

There is even less published work on the fraternal, mutual benefit and related organizations (number 1 above). Bickel and Picard (1983, p. 312), who urge more attention to the topic, observe that "so-called paradenominational or parareligious organizations have also been largely ignored as a topic for study not only by students of voluntary action but also by the religious research community."

That leaves us with category 2 above, the paraecclesial activity represented in voluntary action, especially in the collection and disbursement of private philanthropy and the activities of private associations. Contributions to community chest or United Way campaigns, converted to constant dollars, show consistent increases between 1950 and 1970, declines to low points in 1975 and 1982, and increases thereafter to the highest level in the entire series in 1985 (Table 12). As for associations, between 1968 and 1987 the number of nonprofit organizations in the U.S. doubled. While the total number of such organizations was growing, between 1970 and 1975 the subcategory of religious organizations declined by about 10 percent. After 1975 the number of religious organizations increased again, but not enough to keep pace with the growing numbers of organizations generally. As a consequence, the percentage of all organizations devoted to religion declined markedly between 1968 and 1985, dropping from 7.7 to 5.0. Between 1985 and 1987 the number of religious organizations increased at about the same rate as the number of all kinds of organizations combined (Table 12).

In summary, trends in parareligious organizations, insofar as we have been able to discern them, are mixed. Although there are more national religious associations than there used to be, they represent a smaller fraction of the total number of nonprofit associations. Contributions to the United Way are high, but not much higher than they were in 1970. The evidence suggests continuing vitality of parareligious organizations as we have defined them, but in a mode of stability or continuity rather than growth.

References

American Book Trade Directory. 33rd ed. New York: R.R. Bowker Company, 1988. Annual.
    Previous years as cited.

Bainbridge, William Sims and Rodney Stark. "Client and Audience Cults in America."
    Sociological Analysis 41 (1980): 199-214.

Bickel, Kenneth and Paul R. Picard. "A Paradenominational Organization Perspective on
    Dialogue Between Voluntary Action and Religious Research Communities." Review of
    Religious Research 24 (1983): 312-317.

Bird, Frederick and Bill Reimer. "Participation Rates in New Religious and Para-Religious
    Movements." Journal for the Scientific Study of Religion 21 (1982): 1-14.

Condran, John G. and Joseph Tamney. "Religious 'Nones': 1957-1982." Sociological Analysis
    46 (1985): 415-423.

Council of National Library Associates. The Bowker Annual of Library and Book Trade
    Information, 1988. New York: R. R. Bowker. 1988. Annual. Previous years as cited.

Hammond, Phillip E. "In Search of a Protestant Twentieth Century: American Religion and
    Power Since 1900." Review of Religious Research 24 (1983): 281-294.

Hoge, Dean R. "Interpreting Change in American Catholicism: The River and the Floodgate."
    Review of Religious Research 27 (1986): 289-299.

Hoge, Dean R. and David A. Roozen, eds. Understanding Church Growth and Decline 1950-
    1978. New York: Pilgrim Press, 1979.

McKinney, William and Dean R. Hoge. "Community and Congregational Factors in the Growth
    and Decline of Protestant Churches." Journal for the Scientific Study of Religion 22
    (1983): 51-66.

Melton, J. Gordon. The Encyclopedia of American Religions. 2 vols. Wilmington, NC:
    McGrath, 1978.

------. The Encyclopedia of American Religions. 1st ed. suppl. Detroit: Gale Research Co.,
    1985.

------. Encyclopedic Handbook of Cults in America. New York: Garland Publishing Inc., 1986.

------. The Encyclopedia of American Religions, 2nd ed. Detroit: Gale Research Co., 1987.

National Council of the Churches of Christ in the U.S.A. Yearbook of American and Canadian
    Churches, 1989. Nashville, Tenn.: Abingdon Press, 1989. Annual. Previous years as
    cited.

Perkins, H. Wesley. "Religious Content in American, British, and Canadian Popular Publications from 1937 to 1979." Sociological Analysis 45 (1984): 159-165.

"Religion in America." Gallup Report 236 (May, 1985); 259 (April, 1987).

Roof, Wade Clark and William McKinney. American Mainline Religion: Its Changing Shape and Future. New Brunswick, NJ: Rutgers University Press. 1987.

Schoenherr, Richard A. and Annemette Sorensen. "Social Change in Religious Organizations: Consequences of Clergy Decline in the U.S Catholic Church." Sociological Analysis 43 (1982): 23-52.

Stark, Rodney, William Sims Bainbridge, and Daniel Doyle. "Cults of America: A Reconnaissance in Space and Time." Sociological Analysis 40 (1979): 347-359.

The Official Catholic Directory, 1989. Wilmette, Ill.: P. J. Kenedy & Sons, 1989. Annual. Earlier years as cited.

U. S. Bureau of the Census. Statistical Abstract of the United States, 1989. Washington, D.C., 1989. Annual. Previous years as cited.

------. Census of Population, 1980: Vol. 2, Subject Reports, Occupation by Industry, 1984; 1970: Vol. 2, Subject Reports, Occupation by Industry, 1972; 1960: Subject Reports, Occupation by Industry, 1963; 1950: Vol. 2, Characteristics of the Population, Part 1, United States Summary, 1953. Washington, D.C., USGPO.

U. S. Bureau of Labor Statistics. Employment and Earnings. Monthly.

Table 1.   RELIGIOUS PREFERENCE, 1947-1986

Year	Religious Preference				
	Protestant	Catholic	Jewish	Other	None
1947	69%	20%	5%	1%	6%
1952	67	25	4	1	2
1957	66	26	2	4	5
1962	70	23	3	2	2
1967	67	25	3	3	2
1972	63	26	2	4	5
1977-78	60	29	2	1	8
1982	57	29	2	4	8
1986	59	27	2	4	8
1987	57	28	2	4	9

SOURCE: Based on "Religion in America," 1987, p. 18; <u>Statistical Abstract 1989</u>, p. 54.

Table 2. CHURCH MEMBERSHIP, 1944-1986

Year	Percent Claiming Church/Synagogue Membership
1944	75%
1947	76
1952	73
1965	73
1975	71
1976	71
1977	70
1978	68
1979	68
1980	69
1981	68
1982	67
1983	69
1984	68
1985	71
1986	69
1987	69
1988	65

SOURCE: Based on "Religion in America," 1987, p. 35; National Council, 1989, p. 277. The question read, "Do you happen to be a member of a church or synagogue?"

Table 3:   CHURCH ATTENDANCE IN THE UNITED STATES, 1950-1987

Year	Attended Church or Synagogue in Past Seven Days Total	Protestants	Catholics
1950	39%	--	--
1954	46	--	--
1955	49	--	--
1957	47	--	--
1958	49	44%	74%
1962	46	--	--
1967	43	--	--
1968	--	38	65
1969	42	--	--
1972	40	--	--
1977	41	--	--
1978	41	40	52
1979	40	40	52
1980	40	39	53
1981	41	40	53
1982	41	41	51
1983	40	39	52
1984	40	39	51
1985	42	--	--
1986	40	41	49
1987	40	--	--

SOURCE: Based on "Religion in America," 1987, p. 38; 1985, p. 42;
Statistical Abstract 1989, p. 54. The item read, "Did you,
yourself, happen to attend church or synagogue in the last
seven days?"

Table 4: FINANCIAL CONTRIBUTIONS TO PROTESTANT DENOMINATIONS,
          1945-1987

Year	Number of Denominations Reporting	Contributions Per Capita Full Member	Contributions Constant 1967 Dollars
1945	15	$18.23	$33.82
1950	15	31.70	43.97
1955	49	48.95	61.04
1960	47	66.76	75.24
1961	46	69.00	77.01
1962	42	68.76	75.89
1963	41	69.87	76.19
1964	41	72.04	77.55
1965	38	77.75	82.38
1968	52	95.31	91.47
1969	48	99.68	90.78
1970	45	96.84	83.27
1971	42	103.94	85.69
1972	39	110.29	88.02
1973	40	118.16	88.77
1974	44	127.16	86.09
1975	43	138.54	85.94
1976	43	149.07	87.43
1977	45	159.33	87.78
1978	42	176.37	90.26
1979	44	197.44	90.82
1980	40	213.41	86.47
1981	45	239.71	88.00
1982	40	261.95	90.60
1983	40	270.67	93.39
1984	39	300.40	96.56
1985	42	321.77	99.87
1986	44	344.42	104.88
1987	42	356.67	104.78

SOURCE: Based on National Council, 1989, p. 260; 1987, p. 262;
1986, p. 261; 1984, p. 259; 1963, p. 273; 1957, p. 277;
1953, p. 281; 1949, p. 162.

Table 5. PERCENTAGE DISTRIBUTION OF PRIVATE PHILANTHROPY FUNDS,
BY SOURCE AND ALLOCATION, 1955-1987

	1955	1960	1965	1970	1975	1980	1985	1987
Total (billions)								
(current $)	6.2	9.4	13.3	20.7	29.7	47.7	79.8	93.7
(1967 $)*	7.7	10.6	14.1	17.8	18.4	19.3	24.7	27.5
Source								
Individuals	82%	81%	78%	77%	82%	83%	83%	82%
Foundations	7	7	8	9	7	6	5	7
Corporations	7	5	6	4	4	6	5	5
Charitable								
bequests	4	6	7	10	7	5	6	6
Total	100	99	99	100	100	100	99	100
Allocation								
Religion	50	51	48	45	43	46	47	46
Health	9	12	11	16	15	14	14	15
Education	11	16	17	16	14	14	14	11
Social								
services	23	15	14	14	10	10	11	10
Arts/								
Humanities	--	2	2	2	3	6	6	7
Civic/Public	7	1	2	2	3	3	3	3
Other	--	3	6	4	9	7	5	7
Total	100	100	100	100	100	100	100	99

* Multipliers for calculation of constant dollars are consumer
price index figures from Statistical Abstract 1989, p. 462; 1987,
p. 454.

SOURCE: Based on Statistical Abstract 1989, p. 371; 1987, p. 368;
1982-83, p. 346; 1972, p. 306.

Table 6. ABSOLUTE AND RELATIVE NUMBERS OF THE CLERGY AMONG
          EMPLOYED PERSONS, RATIO TO TOTAL POPULATION, AND GENDER
          AND RACIAL COMPOSITION, CENSUS DATA, 1950-1980, AND
          LABOR FORCE SURVEY DATA, 1978-1988

Year	Total Employed (thousands)	Clergy Per 1000 Employed Persons	Per 1000 Population	Clergy Who Are: Women	Black*
1950	136	2.98	.90	2.3%	--%
1960	200	3.09	1.10	2.2	--
1970	218	2.85	1.06	2.9	--
1980	281	2.88	1.23	5.8	--

(Annual Averages, Employed Persons Aged 16 and Over)

1978	262	2.78	1.18	3.8	3.1
1979	282	2.91	1.25	4.6	9.2
1980	265	2.72	1.16	4.2	6.8
1981	277	2.82	1.20	5.1	7.6
1982	285	2.86	1.23	5.3	7.0
1983	293	2.91	1.25	5.6	4.9
1984	290	2.76	1.22	6.3	5.3
1985	289	2.70	1.21	6.0	7.3
1986	285	2.60	1.18	7.2	5.5
1987	312	2.77	1.28	6.9	5.7
1988	348	3.03	1.41	8.8	8.6

* Before 1983, includes "Black and other"

SOURCE: Census Data: Based on U.S. Bureau of the Census, <u>Census of Population, 1980: Vol. 2, Subject Reports, Occupation by Industry</u>, 1984, pp. 295-296; <u>1970: Vol. 2, Subject Reports, Occupation by Industry,</u> 1972, pp. 241-242; <u>1960: Subject Reports, Occupation by Industry</u>, 1963, pp. 7-8; <u>1950: Vol. 2, Characteristics of the Population, Part 1, United States Summary</u>, 1953; p. 267. U.S. Bureau of Labor Statistics, <u>Employment and Earnings</u> (monthly); annual averages are published in January of the subsequent year. Annual population figures for the U.S. used in computing clergy per capita are from <u>Statistical Abstract 1989</u>, p. 7.

Table 7.   NUMBER AND RATE PER 1,000 POPULATION OF PASTORS SERVING
           PARISHES AND OF ALL ORDAINED CLERGY, DENOMINATIONAL
           STATISTICS, 1952-1987

Year*	Religious Bodies Reporting	Pastors Serving Parishes		All Ordained Clergy	
		Total	Per 1000**	Total	Per 1000**
1952	196	183899	1.17	323048	2.05
1955	222	222018	1.34	353695	2.13
1960	237	241268	1.34	371258	2.05
1965	251	263199	1.35	402555	2.07
1970	236	235189	1.15	393826	1.92
1975	223	261550	1.21	473188	2.19
1980	218	279366	1.23	498800	2.19
1985	218	325111	1.36	530763	2.22
1987	219	333097	1.37	543152	2.23

* Data from religious bodies summarized here are for the latest
available year if not for the year shown; years shown represent the
"current" or modal year for the figures summarized, and generally
lag one to two years behind the publication date of the annual
Yearbook.

** U.S. annual population figures used in computing these rates are
derived from Statistical Abstract 1989, p. 7.

SOURCE: Based on National Council, 1989, p. 245; 1987, p. 247;
        1982, p. 236; 1977, p. 240; 1972, p. 229; 1967, p. 210; 1962,
        p. 268; 1957, p. 270; and 1953, p. 270.

Table 8. INCLUSIVE CHURCH MEMBERSHIP, NUMBER OF CLERGY, AND
CLERGY PER 1,000 MEMBERS, ROMAN CATHOLICS AND OTHERS
(LARGELY PROTESTANTS*), 1960-1985

	Inclusive Church Membership (millions)		Total Clergy (1000s)		Clergy per 1000 Members**	
Year	Prot.*	Cath.	Prot.*	Cath.	Prot.*	Cath.
1960	72.3	42.1	316	54	4.37	1.28
1965	78.4	46.2	343	59	4.37	1.27
1970	82.8	48.2	335	60	4.05	1.23
1975	82.1	48.9	414	59	5.04	1.21
1980	84.4	50.4	440	59	5.21	1.17
1985	90.3	52.7	474	58	5.25	1.10
1987	90.3	53.5	490	54	5.42	1.01

* "Protestant" inclusive church membership was computed by
subtracting the appropriate entry for "Roman Catholic" from the
national total. In other words, "Protestant" includes all Christian
religious bodies counted in the Yearbook of American and Canadian
Churches' annual tally except for Roman Catholic, and more properly
would be labeled "Other" or "Non-Catholic." Similarly, figures for
"Protestant" clergy were computed by subtracting entries for Roman
Catholic "total clergy" from U.S. totals in the relevant Yearbook.
Figures for Catholic clergy include all cardinals, archbishops,
bishops, abbots, diocesan priests and religious priests listed in
the relevant years of The Official Catholic Directory.

** Computed from precise numbers, not the rounded numbers in the
table.

SOURCE: Based on the annual "General Summary" from Official
Catholic Directory, 1988, 1985, 1980, 1975, 1970; National
Council, 1989, pp. 243, 245; 1987, pp. 245, 247, 270; 1982,
pp. 234, 236; 1977, pp. 238, 240,; 1972, pp. 227, 229; 1967,
pp. 209-210; and 1962, p. 254.

Table 9. SEMINARY ENROLLMENTS, PROTESTANT THEOLOGICAL SCHOOLS
          AND ROMAN CATHOLIC DIOCESAN AND RELIGIOUS SEMINARIES,
          AS COMPARED TO NUMBERS OF CLERGY AND TOTAL POPULATION
          AGED 18-24, 1960-1987

| | | | Protestant Enrollment per 1,000 | | Catholic Enrollment per 1,000 | |
| | Seminary Students | | Age | Prot. | Age | Cath. |
Year	Prot.	Cath.	18-24	Clergy	18-24	Clergy
1960	--	39896	--	--	2.47	737
1965	20716	48992	1.01	60	2.38	834
1970	30022	28906	1.21	90	1.17	486
1975	38930	17802	1.39	94	.64	300
1980	46880	13226	1.55	107	.44	224
1985	52794	11028	1.86	111	.39	191
1987	52194	8556	1.93	107	.32	158

SOURCE: Based on the annual "General Summary," in The Official
Catholic Directory, 1987, 1985, 1980, 1975, and 1970; National
Council, 1989, pp. 243, 245; 1988, p. 270; 1987, pp. 245, 247,
270; 1982, pp. 234, 236; 1977, pp. 238, 240, 265; 1972, pp.
227, 229; 1971, p. 255; 1967, pp. 209-210; and 1962, pp. 267-
268. In computing ratios, population estimates for persons
aged 18-24 are from Statistical Abstract 1989, p. 22; 1987, p.
23; 1982-83, p. 25; and 1968, p. 8, and are, in thousands,
respectively, 16,128, 20,559, 24,711, 28,005, 30,337, 28,492
and 27,107. In computing ratios per 1,000 clergy, figures for
total Protestant clergy were obtained by subtracting entries
for Roman Catholic "total clergy" from U.S. totals in the
relevant National Council Yearbook of American and Canadian
Churches, and were, respectively, 316,313, 343,064, 335,316,
413,954, 439,955, 473,580, and 489,630; figures for Catholic
clergy include all cardinals, archbishops, bishops, abbots,
diocesan priests and religious priests listed in the relevant
volumes of The Official Catholic Directory and were,
respectively, 54,067, 58,730, 59,528, 59,287, 59,059, 57,805,
and 54,030.

Table 10. RELIGIOUS BOOKS IN AMERICAN BOOK PRODUCTION (TITLE
OUTPUT), NEW BOOKS AND NEW EDITIONS, 1950-1986

Year	Total* Titles			New Books		
	All Books	Religion	Percent	Total	Religion	Percent
1950	11022	727	7%	8634	626	7%
1956	12538	909	7	10007	810	8
1960	15012	1104	7	12069	983	8
1965	28595	1855	6	20234	1428	7
1970	36071	1788	5	24288	1315	5
1975	39372	1778	4	30004	1414	5
1980	42377	2055	5	34030	1635	5
1985	46263	2540	5	39753	2211	6
1986	48917	2763	6	41925	2464	6

*Includes new books and new editions.

SOURCE: Council of National Library Associates, 1988, p. 403;
1987, p. 412; 1982, p. 385; 1976, p. 179; 1972, p. 176;
1967, p. 45; 1962, p. 59; 1958, p. 103.

Table 11. NUMBER AND PERCENT OF RELIGIOUS BOOKSTORES AMONG ALL
BOOKSTORES, 1955-1987

Year	Total Bookstores	Religious Bookstores	Percent
1955	7698	1032	13%
1960	8538	1671	20
1965	9881	1820	18
1971	10742	1638	15
1975	11717	1421	12
1980	17218	2487	14
1986	21568	3848	18
1987	21819	3871	18

SOURCE: _American Book Trade Directory_, 1987, p. ix; 1986, p. ix;
1980, p. ix; 1975, p. ix; 1971, p. vii; 1965, p. iii; 1961,
p. v; 1956, p. v.

Table 12. UNITED WAY* CAMPAIGN FUNDS RAISED, 1947-1985

Year	Millions of Dollars		Year	Millions of Dollars	
	Current Dollars	Constant (1967) Dollars		Current Dollars	Constant (1967) Dollars
1947	169	252	1967	680	680
1948	177	245	1968	720	691
1949	188	263	1969	767	699
1950	193	168	1970	817	703
1951	213	274	1971	840	692
1952	241	303	1972	865	691
1953	266	332	1973	915	687
1954	288	329	1974	979	663
1955	302	377	1975	1023	634
1956	340	418	1976	1104	648
1957	378	448	1977	1205	664
1958	415	479	1978	1318	675
1959	427	489	1979	1423	655
1960	458	516	1980	1530	620
1961	478	533	1981	1680	617
1962	502	554	1982	1781	616
1963	525	573	1983	1950	653
1964	547	589	1984	2145	689
1965	594	628	1985	2330	722
1966	636	654			

* Includes "Community Chest," or "United Fund" campaigns

** For annual consumer price index multipliers, see Statistical Abstract 1987, p. 454, and 1979, p. 474.

SOURCE: Based on Statistical Abstract 1987, p. 368; 1982-83, p. 346; 1975, p. 311; 1972, p. 307; 1967, p. 311; 1962, p. 305.

Table 13. NUMBER OF NONPROFIT ASSOCIATIONS,* TOTAL AND RELIGIOUS,
1968-1987

Year	Total	Religious	Percent Religious
1968	10299	794	8%
1970	10734	806	7
1975	12866	736	6
1980	14726	797	5
1985	19121	953	5
1987	20884	1066	5

* Includes non-profit organizations of national scope.

SOURCE: Statistical Abstract 1989, p. 57; 1987, p. 54; 1975, p. 48.

9.3 MILITARY FORCES

Historically, the United States has demobilized rapidly after each major war, but demobilization after World War II left a very large standing force, subsequently expanded for the Vietnam conflict and then reduced to approximately two million persons in the armed forces. There are another million civilian employees in the Department of Defense and at least three million more civilians are employed in defense-related industries, so that upwards of six million persons are presently engaged in active preparation for war. The size of the military establishment has fluctuated in recent years without any clearcut trend.

Since the formation of the federal government in 1789, it has been the American practice to maintain only skeletal military forces in peacetime, augmenting them rapidly with the approach of war. Total forces numbered 12,000 in 1810, increased to 47,000 during the War of 1812 and returned to the previous level during the 1820s. In 1860, the Federal forces numbered only 28,000. By the end of the Civil War their number had grown to 1.1 million, but by 1870, it had shrunk to 50,000 and remained below that figure until the Spanish-American War raised it to 236,000. From that point on, each mobilization had a ratchet effect, the postwar peacetime level being much higher than the prewar level. After 1898, the number of military personnel on active service never dropped below 100,000. It was 166,000 at the outset of World War I, rose to 2.8 million in 1918, and remained above 240,000 in the peacetime years that followed. The greatest expansion of all occurred during World War II, with a total force of 12.1 million in 1945. The ratchet worked again. The lowest postwar total was 1.4 million in 1948. This increased to 3.5 million at the height of the Vietnam War, and has remained above 2 million ever since (Table 1). The ratio of peacetime military personnel to population, which fluctuated in the neighborhood of .003 between World War I and World War II has remained above .009 since 1946; was considerably higher (.014) in 1955-61, and has varied near .009 since 1975.

In addition to the uniformed personnel counted above, the Department of Defense has more than a million civilian employees. The ratio of civilian to uniformed personnel has remained close to .50 since 1950 (Table 1).

The percent of uniformed personnel serving abroad reached a maximum of 34% during the Vietnam War, and then declined to just under 25%, where it has remained ever since.

Although the size and location of U.S. military forces have been fairly stable since 1970, there have been some significant trends in its composition. The proportion of women increased steadily from 3.3% in 1970 to 9.8% in 1985. The proportion of blacks increased from 9.8% in 1970 to 19.0% in 1985. The proportion of black officers has increased from 2.2% in 1970 to 6.4% in 1985, although blacks are still heavily under-represented in the officer corps in proportion to their numbers in the enlisted ranks. The Hispanic component of the armed forces remains very small--appoximately 4% (Table 2).

There was a significant increase in the educational level of active duty military personnel from 1975 to 1986, from 87% of enlisted personnel who had graduated from high school in 1975 to 97% in 1986; and from 92% of officers with two or more years of college in 1975 to 97% in 1986.

Reenlistment rates have varied sharply and without a clear trend in recent years, apparently in reaction to civilian labor market conditions (Table 3).

Desertion rates have shown a dramatic decline in recent years. The army rate which ran as high as 74 per 1000 in the early 1970s has fallen to under 10 per thousand in recent years. The Marine rate, which peaked at 108 in 1975 was down to 11 in 1985. The Navy, which has lower desertion rates, and the Air Force, which has much lower desertion rates than the other services, also show striking declines (Table 4). It is not clear why the interservice differences are so large.

The proportion of officers to enlisted men has remained relatively constant in recent years, but at around 13%, it is very high in relation to historic standards, which suggest 3 to 6 percent as the appropriate ratio for a combat-effective force. Moreover, the officer corps is itself top-heavy, with a disproportionate complement of general officers (Gabriel, 1985, p. 7 ff.). This situation, however, is of long standing and the high ratio of general officers was the same in 1986 as in 1961--5.0 per 10,000 military personnel.

References

Gabriel, Richard. Military Incompetence. New York: Hill and Wang, 1985.

Hart, Gary and William S. Lind. America Can Win. Bethesda, MD: Adler and Adler, 1986.

Luttwak, Edward N. The Pentagon and the Art of War. New York: Simon and Schuster, 1984.

Secretary of Defense. Annual Report to the Congress, Fiscal Year 1987. Washington, D.C.: USGPO.

U.S. Bureau of the Census. Statistical Abstract of the United States, 1989. Washington, D.C., 1989. Annual. Previous years as cited.

Table 1. DEFENSE MANPOWER, 1950-1988

Year	Department of Defense Personnel Military (1000s)	Civilian (1000s)	Defense-related Industrial Personnel (1000s)	Total (1000s)
1950	1459	730	713	2902
1955	2935	1518	2500	6953
1960	2475	1230	2460	6165
1965	2654	1158	2125	5937
1966	3092	1256	2640	6988
1967	3375	1401	3100	7876
1968	3546	1408	3174	8128
1969	3458	1393	2916	7767
1970	3065	1356	2399	6829
1971	2713	1190	2031	5934
1972	2322	1160	1985	5467
1973	2252	1100	1850	5202
1974	2162	1110	1860	5132
1975	2128	1078	1800	5006
1976	2082	1047	1690	4819
1977	2075	1024	1730	4829
1978	2062	1021	1765	4848
1979	2027	996	1860	4883
1980	2051	1013	1990	5054
1981	2083	1037	2085	5205
1982	2109	1049	2310	5468
1983	2123	1104	2530	5757
1984	2138	1131	2785	6054
1985	2151	1182	3050	6383
1986	2169	1176	3275	6620
1987	2174	1193	3325	6692
1988	2247	1123	3350	6720

SOURCE: Based on *Statistical Abstract 1989*, p. 335.

Table 2. ACTIVE DUTY FORCES BY SEX AND ETHNICITY, 1972-1985

Sex/ Ethnicity	Active Duty Forces (1000s)		
	1972	1980	1985
Total	2311.3	2036.7	2137.4
Males	2266.8	1866.4	1928.0
Officers	323.0	256.5	278.8
White	310.2	234.0	251.4
Black	7.4	11.8	16.1
Hispanic	4.0	2.9	4.2
Enlisted	1943.8	1609.0	1649.2
White	1583.8	1124.7	1181.1
Black	244.6	347.0	331.7
Hispanic	77.4	66.0	66.3
Females	44.5	170.2	209.4
Officers	12.6	21.4	30.3
White	--	18.0	24.9
Black	--	2.0	3.7
Hispanic	--	.3	.5
Enlisted	31.9	148.8	179.0
White	--	100.6	113.1
Black	--	38.8	53.1
Hispanic	--	4.5	5.7

SOURCE: Based on Statistical Abstract 1987, p. 327; 1984, p. 353; 1982-83, p. 360.

Table 3. REENLISTMENT RATES, ARMED FORCES, FISCAL YEAR 1979-1986

Year	Reenlistment Rate
1979	53%
1980	55
1981	61
1982	68
1983	68
1984	67
1985	63
1986	64

SOURCE: Based on Secretary of Defense, 1986, pp. 99-100.

Table 4. DESERTION RATES,* BY BRANCH OF SERVICE, ARMED FORCES, 1970-1985

Year	Total	Branch of Service			
		Army	Marine Corps	Navy	Air Force
1965	--	15.7	18.8	6.7	0.4
1968	15.7	29.1	30.7	8.5	0.4
1969	21.1	42.4	40.2	7.3	0.6
1970	33.6	52.3	59.6	9.9	0.8
1971	42.0	73.5	56.2	11.1	1.5
1972	35.1	62.0	65.3	8.8	2.8
1973	29.8	52.1	63.2	13.6	2.2
1974	29.9	41.1	69.2	21.2	2.4
1975	26.3	26.0	105.0	22.4	1.9
1976	20.1	17.7	69.2	24.8	1.2
1977	19.1	16.7	47.0	31.6	0.6
1978	18.0	15.4	39.9	30.4	0.7
1979	18.5	18.1	37.9	29.6	1.1
1980	17.9	19.6	34.2	27.0	1.2
1981	14.7	15.9	28.8	21.8	1.0
1982	10.9	11.0	21.1	18.0	0.6
1983	6.7	7.1	16.2	12.9	0.4
1984	6.5	6.0	11.2	11.6	0.3
1985	6.3	6.5	10.9	10.1	0.3

* Desertions per 1,000 average end-of-month strength.

SOURCE: Based on <u>Statistical Abstract 1979</u>, p. 376; <u>1987</u>, p. 329.

Two powerful trends dominate the era: a decline in the extent of partisan engagement in the electorate at large, together with increased material resources and professionalization on the part of the political parties themselves. Two major parties continued to dominate virtually all elections, as they have through much of U.S. history; neither dominates the other.

Political party activity by Americans, once extremely widespread, declined by stages beginning in the third quarter of the nineteenth century, as a series of reformers and poltical technicians successively removed from the daily activity of local party organizations and the party press the sorts of symbolic functions that compelled the attachment of the rank and file. Well before World War II, most party activity centered about elections to national office, focusing there upon the verbal statements of distant but nevertheless ordinary candidates (McGerr, 1986).

By 1952, when the National Election Survey first asked "did you go to any political meetings, rallies, dinners, or things like that" during the recent national election campaign, the proportion who had was only 7%. The gradual rise in this proportion to 10% in 1978 (it was down to 8% in 1980, however) should probably not be taken as indication of increasing political engagement by the American masses in view of the absence of positive trends in several other indicators from the same survey. Proportions wearing a campaign button or displaying a bumper sticker declined to about one in ten by 1978, while the proportion giving money to support a candidate's campaign grew slightly (Miller, Miller, and Schneider, 1980, pp. 304-305).

For all these activities, presidential election years usually generate higher citizen involvement than non-Presidential years. In the non-presidential years, the participants seemingly represent the real party loyalists. In 1978, this included 10% who said they had gone to a political meeting, 6% who said they had done any other political work, 9% who had a campaign button or bumper sticker, and 13% who gave money to a candidate.

Campaign buttons and bumper stickers convey to beholders exactly one thing: one's partisan affiliation. And they thereby involve the individual in a small but personal declaration of politics. Such declarations, years ago, were something of a staple of American politics. But now, focus has ever more shifted from such things to the transmission of more complex (if not more profound) messages impersonally, via television and other mass communications media.

Campaign-finance laws have been changed so as to make it highly preferable, as campaign methods now make it highly necessary, to extract campaign donations from large numbers of individuals, both through impersonal, automatic check-off methods (e.g., on one's Federal income tax return) and through Political Action Committees (PAC's). These committees do not give out buttons; they transmit donated money to be spent centrally.

PAC's have grown annually since the new campaign expenditures law of 1974 facilitated their formation and increasingly significant impact on electoral campaigning. Their number has expanded enormously, from a total of 608 PAC's in 1974 to 4,165 in 1987 (U. S. Bureau of the Census, 1989, p. 263) and their distribution has moved sharply away from a labor and professional-group basis to a business basis such as employers encouraging their employees to contribute to a common fund. Conversely, however, after 1977 there was a rise in "ideological" PAC's. These are commonly single-issue groupings.

Correspondingly, rank-and-file identification with political parties has declined notably. Table 1, based upon many surveys, gives an overview of this development. The proportion of individuals who, when asked, identified themselves strongly with one or another party declined from about four in ten in 1960 (when campaigning by television really began to overwhelm other methods) to only one in four today. The rise in persons who identify themselves as Independents includes two components: those who said they "lean" toward one party or the other, and all others. Absolutely, the two have risen by about the same amount; relatively, the independent independents have become more than twice as common as they once were. A detailed analysis of the "independent independent" trend concludes that at the core of the rise of this phenomenon are people who "lack integration into the party system and [who are] less involved in politics" than the Independents who nevertheless express a "leaning" toward one party or the other.

The growth in the proportion of those responding "no preference" to the party identification question can most plausibly be interpreted as a function of the declining saliency of political parties in the American political process (Miller and Wattenberg, 1983, p. 120).

Another index, drawn more complexly from repeated open-ended questions on the National Election Survey, asked respondents to name anything they liked and anything they disliked about each of the two major parties. Up to five of these open-ended items were coded, and the measure of "engagement" cumulates the total number of items (up to ten for each party) favorable or unfavorable. Korda and Sigelman's (1987) tabulations suggest that in 1952 each party attracted about one fourth as many mentions as it conceivably might have, suggesting at best a moderate level of political engagement. But even this level declined, at first rapidly, then gradually, settling to a low plateau by about 1972. Always, the Democratic Party seems slightly more interesting (provoking?) than the Republican. Korda and Sigelman (1987) also find that the Democratic Party is not only more interesting, it is slightly more favorably perceived than the Republican. Indeed, overall trend apart, in years when Democrats are perceived particularly favorably, Republicans are perceived particularly unfavorably, and vice-versa. Most relevant to our general argument, however, is a trend: as the parties have become less interesting, in terms of number of positive or negative mentions, they have also become somewhat less favorably perceived overall.

Finally, voting records indicate that the decline in the significance of party, attested above by attitudinal data, is borne out in behavior at the polls. For instance, Tuckel and Tejera (1983) found that where once the right party label in the right year in the right electoral district could bring almost certain victory at the polls to an obscure candidate, this has been decreasingly true since about 1945. The state-to-state variance in proportion of votes for the Democratic candidate that is explained by a common factor in National and Congressional races has declined by close to half since 1916, and mostly since World War II. Correspondingly, the correlation between Senatorial and House races in years where there is no Presidential election, always lower than when there is a Presidential election, has declined to perhaps one-third its initial level. The reduction in the relevance of local parties has focused ever more exclusive attention on Presidential elections.

Political parties themselves are becoming more substantial entities. This is especially measurable in terms of their disbursements (Austin, 1986, Table 3.9). Presidential campaign expenditures have about quadrupled in constant-dollar terms since 1948, with closely-contested elections operating in effect as an upward "ratchet" on presidential campaign costs. Presidential campaign expenditures, of course, do not exhaust the scope of party spending. There are nearly 500 Congressional and Senatorial elections (candidates) each two years, and, at least since 1975, expenditures on these campaigns have grown considerably more rapidly even than expenditures on the Presidential elections. I have found no compilations whatever for expenditures on campaigns for other than federal offices.

There is a distinctive bias in expenditures on elections, and a definite relationship of expenditure to outcome. Tuckel and Tejera, whose studies of trends in the correlates of voting behavior were mentioned above, have been able to add campaign expenditures to their path-analysis model explaining vote outcome in Senatorial elections in 1972-78. They conclude that

> It is apparent that the predominant influence on the Democratic proportion [their example; it is symmetrically true for Republicans] of the vote for Senator is the Democratic proportion of campaign expenditures. Its path coefficient is over three times as large as the coefficients associated with the other two independent variables [state party electoral strength and incumbency status].

They add that incumbency is important mainly because of its indirect effect in enabling the collection of campaign funds, rather than on account of familiarity with or appreciation of the incumbent in his or her constituency (Tuckel and Tejera, 1983, pp. 241-242).

Recent trends in PAC activity in Senate and House campaigns are described in Table 2. The table indicates something of a parity between the two major parties in spending on the legislative level (other parties, taking 1985-86 as an example, spent $325,000 on legislative election campaigns, compared with $449,720,000 by the two major parties--a notable disparity), a signal trend toward increased expenditures by both parties in both arenas, and a conspicuous if uneven trend toward increased PAC commitment to, and involvement in, the campaign expenditure plans of both major parties. Democrats tend to spend more for the House (and more Democrats are active in seeking nomination for House seats), and to have there a PAC commitment that exceeds anything the Republicans muster either in the House or in the Senate. Participation, measured by expenditures, is greater in House than in Senate campaigns.

Much PAC money goes for television advertising, but some of it goes elsewhere. The work of Gibson, et al. (1983) indicates that over the last two decades state party offices have enlarged budgets, hired full-time professional headquarters leaders, increased their staffs, made their headquarters more accessible to candidates, and expanded their publication of newsletters. The PACs have widely and increasingly entered public opinion polling, and have much enlarged the services they offer to candidates. They have, in short, become professional, and indispensable to candidates' successful election to office.

On the local (county) level, parties have also enlarged their activities. A parallel study by the same authors (Gibson, et al., 1985) shows increases in all tabulated activites, although some of these are minor, and few are equal to the expansion of party activity on the state level. More county parties in 1979 than in 1964 distributed campaign literature, arranged campaign activities, raised money, managed publicity, and conducted voter registration drives. The authors point to a relationship between declining partisan political involvement on the part of the rank-and-file and the increasing and increasingly professional activities of political parties:

> A number of important antiparty forces and trends (e.g. the declining partisanship of the electorate, the appearance of amateurism among party activists, the popularization of candidate selection, and the separation of candidate campaign organizations from party) have materialized over the last two decades . . . The implications of these forces and trends must be understood within the context of party organizations that are currently strong and not weakening. Indeed, strong party organizations may have been effective in counteracting adverse public policy and the departisanization of the electorate (Gibson, et al., 1983, p. 217).

References

Austin, Erik W. Political Facts of the United States Since 1789. New York: Columbia University Press.

Barone, Michael and Grant Ujifusa, eds. The Almanac of American Politics. Washington, D.C.: The National Journal, 1988. Previous years as cited.

Gibson, James L., Cornelius P. Cotter, John F. Bibby, and Robert J. Huckshorn. "Assessing Party Organizational Strength." American Journal of Political Science 27 (1983): 193-222.

------. "Whither the Local Parties?: A Cross-Sectional and Longitudinal Analysis of the Strength of Party Organization." American Journal of Political Science 29 (1985): 139-160.

Glenn, Norval D. "Social Trends in the United States. Evidence from Sample Surveys." Public Opinion Quarterly 51 (1987): S109-S126.

Konda, Thomas M. and Lee Sigelman. "Public Evaluations of the American Parties, 1952-1984." The Journal of Politics 49 (1987): 814-829.

McGerr, Michael E. The Decline of Popular Politics. New York: Oxford University Press, 1986.

Miller, Arthur H. and Martin P. Wattenberg. "Measuring Party Identification: Independent or No Partisan Preference." American Journal of Political Science 27 (1983): 105-121.

Miller, Warren E., Arthur H. Miller, and Edward J. Schneider. American National Election Studies Data Sourcebook 1952-1978. Cambridge: Harvard University Press, 1980.

Tuckel, Peter S. and Felipe Tejera. "Changing Patterns in American Voting Behavior, 1914-1980." Public Opinion Quarterly 47 (1983): 230-246.

U.S. Bureau of the Census. Statistical Abstract of the United States, 1989. Washington, DC, 1989. Annual. Previous years as cited.

Table 1.   PERCENTAGE OF RESPONDENTS TO U.S. NATIONAL SURVEYS WHO
           CONSIDERED THEMSELVES TO BE STRONG PARTY IDENTIFIERS,
           1952-1986

Year	Based on National Election Survey	General Social Survey
1952	37%	--
1954	36	--
1956	38	--
1958	40	--
1960	37	--
1962	36	--
1964	38	--
1966	28	--
1968	30	--
1970	29	--
1972	25	29%
1973	--	25
1974	27	25
1975	--	23
1976	24	22
1977	--	25
1978	24	22
1980	--	21
1982	--	25
1983	--	26
1984	--	27
1985	--	29
1986	--	26

SOURCE: Based on Glenn, 1987, p. S113.

Table 2.   EXPENDITURES ON CAMPAIGNS FOR THE HOUSE OF REPRESENTA-
TIVES AND THE SENATE, BY POLITICAL PARTY, AND PERCENT
OF EXPENDITURES CONTRIBUTED BY POLITICAL ACTION
COMMITTEES, 1977-86

| | Total Expenditures | | | |
| | Millions of Dollars | | Percent from PACs | |
	House	Senate	House	Senate
1977-78				
Democrats	61.3	42.1	23%	11%
Republicans	47.5	42.6	21	12
1979-80				
Democrats	67.8	53.6	30	15
Republicans	67.1	48.9	26	18
1981-82				
Democrats	109.1	67.1	33	16
Republicans	104.6	71.8	26	16
1983-84				
Democrats	111.5	83.2	41	17
Republicans	92.7	88.8	31	17
1985-86				
Democrats	128.4	88.9	43	22
Republicans	110.3	122.1	29	20

SOURCE: Based on <u>Statistical Abstract 1989</u>, p. 263; <u>1984</u>, p. 268;
Barone and Ujifusa, various years.

Exposure of the American public to many forms of mass media, including radio, television, movies and videocassettes, has increased markedly since 1950. A few forms, notably newspapers, have managed to maintain a relatively stable level of circulation, but have not shared in the dramatic growth of other forms. The impact of television continues to grow, both with regard to the amount of information and entertainment it offers and its place at the individual or household level. Although television is a major source of news and entertainment, it does not seem likely to replace the more traditional media. Most have continued to expand in numbers of producing/transmitting units (e.g., movie theaters, radio stations), in product units (hours of broadcasting, numbers of tapes or records), and audience size.

Since World War II, in the U.S. as elsewhere, there have been continued improvements in existing media and the invention or expansion of newer forms of communication. As with previous extensions of media from the private/experimental to the public/mass level of use, so the changes of the postwar era were initially viewed as threats to the existing "media order." Thus, many feared that television would destroy the movie industry as well as radio; that paperback books would drive out hardbacks; and more recently, that the combination of television and videocassette recorders will further depress the rates of book-reading in the population.

Some of these fears have proved justified. It now appears that compact disks will replace phonograph records, just as long-playing 33-rpm records replaced the earlier 78s. But fears that television would replace reading have proved unfounded, and the radio industry, although changed by television, continues to thrive, as does the motion picture industry. The role played by the mass media in American society continues to grow, and many of the older forms of media seem to have established fairly secure niches (or particular functions) which permit them to continue successful coexistence with the newer forms.

Radio

The radio had permeated the U.S. before World War II. By 1950, 92% of households had radios, and the direction of industry expansion was in the range of offerings (stations) and in encouraging the ownership of more than one radio. In contrast, at that time only 62% of households had a telephone (Table 1). Over the next 38 years, the role of radio changed, but did not diminish. By 1988, the average household had six radios, and four out of five adults listened to the radio every weekday (Statistical Abstract 1989, p. 523).

There was also a vast expansion in the number and diversity of radio stations. In 1945 there were fewer than 1,000 commercial radio stations, and 95% of these were AM stations. Over the next four decades the number of stations continued to increase, and FM broadcasting became much more popular. By 1987, there were nearly 10,000 stations broadcasting, almost half of them FM (Table 2).

Television

In 1946, there were only six television stations in the U.S.; by 1987, there were 1,290, including almost 1,000 commercial stations and over 300 public (noncommercial) stations (Table 2). Television has become the dominant American communications medium. More households have television sets than have telephones (98% versus 93%), more people watch TV than listen to the radio (in 1987, 91% versus 86%) or read newspapers (also 86%) (Statistical Abstract 1989, p. 544). During prime time viewing hours, as many as three-fourths of the nation's households may be in the audience. Virtually every household (98%) has at least one television set, and by 1988 the average household had two. Hours per day of viewing in those households having television sets increased steadily from 1950 to 1985, rising from 4.6 to 7.1 hours per day, and stabilized at that high level (Table 1).

The television industry's share of the national advertising market, measured by expenditures on advertising, rose from 3% in 1950 to 22% in 1987. During most of this century, the single most important advertising medium in America, in terms of dollars spent on advertising, has been the newpaper. However, the percentage of advertising expenditures going to newspapers has continually decreased, and it appears that television will shortly become the dominant medium in terms of advertising revenue as well as audience coverage. Expenditures on advertising have increased faster than either inflation or population growth would warrant-- between 1950 and 1987, they more than quadrupled, rising from $27 to $110 billion constant (1987) dollars. However, as a percentage of the GNP, advertising expenditures in 1987 were only slightly higher than in 1955-60 (Table 3).

An important development in television programming has been the advent of cable television systems. Table 4 documents the rapid growth in the number of cable systems, from 70 in 1952 to 8,500 in 1988. By then, over half of the nation's households had cable TV, and the number of subcribers was approaching 43 million.

Another important trend in television broadcasting is the growth of public/noncommercial TV (Tables 5 and 6). Broadcast hours of public television have ased even faster than numbers of stations. Between 1961 and 1984, while the number of stations grew six-fold weekly broadcast hours increased 15 times, from 2,186 in 1961 to over 32,293 in 1984. At that time, the typical public television station had over 15 hours per day of programming, and over one-fourth of all programming was instructional.

There have also been significant changes in ownership and support for public television over the years. From the inception of public television, the largest contributors have been local and state governments, followed by the general public. However, the trend is away from government financing (down from 72% to 49% between 1972 and 1987) and toward subscriber and business sponsorship (Table 6).

Newspapers, Periodicals and Books

Newspapers compete with television as a source of news and entertainment and as a medium for advertising. The number of daily newspapers declined slightly between 1950 and 1987, from 1,894 to 1,646, a drop of 13% while the national population was increasing by 60%. The decline was a real decline in newspaper reading, not merely consolidation of many newspapers into fewer with larger circulation. Although total circulation of daily newspapers increased from 54 to 63 million over this 37-year period, that increase did not keep pace with population growth, and represented a decline in per capita circulation from .35 to .26 (Table 7). Sunday newspapers suffered a somewhat smaller decline in per capita circulation, while increasing from 47 to 60 million weekly circulation. The net decline in the total number of newspapers was of comparable scale to that of the dailies, and included a substantial decline in weekly newspaper publication and a solid increase in the number of semiweekly papers.

In contrast, periodicals and books increased both absolutely and relative to the growing population. The number of periodicals increased by 67%, with most notable growth a three-fold increase in bimonthly and quarterly publications, many of them scientific, professional, and trade journals. But the truly stunning growth was in book publication. There were 48,917 new books (including new editions) published in 1986, 4.4 times as many as in 1950 (Table 7). The ratio for new titles (excluding new editions) was even higher, at 4.9 (41,925 new titles, compared to 8,634 in 1950) (Council of National Library Associates, 1988, p. 403; 1958, p. 103).

Motion Pictures

Many people expected the expansion of television to mean the decline of the motion picture industry. That has not happened. Although the motion picture industry's share of the total GNP dropped from about .40% in 1950 to about .25% in 1960, since that time it has generally managed to keep pace with the rest of the national economy. Its 1987 contribution to the GNP was virtually the same as in 1970, and its constant-dollar annual output continues to grow. Rates of attendance at motion pictures have been relatively stable for at least two decades. In 1987, total attendance at U.S. motion picture theaters was 1.1 billion. In terms of number of trips to the movies, that works out to 4.5 attendances per capita (U.S. population), the same rate of attendance as in 1970 and 1980. The number of motion picture theaters (or, more recently, the number of screens, since there is a trend toward multiple screens in single establishments) continues to rise; it more than doubled between 1970 and 1987 (from 10,000 to 21,000). Drive-in theaters are becoming less popular, but as of 1987 there were still about 3,000 of them, bringing the total number of theaters/screens to 24,000 (Table 8). This expansion was more notable because it has happened concurrently with a massive public adoption of videocassette recorders and recorded movies. From 1985 to 1988, the number of households with videocassette recorders increased from 21% to 58% (Table 1), and home showings of rented videos became a major national pastime.

Recording Media: Records, Tapes, Disks

Trends in manufacturers' shipments of phonograph records, pre-recorded tapes, and compact disks reveal a shift in recording technology and consumer tastes along with continued growth in the music/recording industry. There have been some noticeable changes within the industry, but the total value of its output has remained fairly stable, at somewhere between 5.0 and 5.5 billion (constant 1987) dollars. The recording industry has grown along with the population: the number of units (records, tapes, compact disks) shipped was the same in 1987 as in 1973. However, the nature of the units changed over that 14-year period. In 1973, it was primarily a record industry; prerecorded tapes accounted for only about one-sixth of the market, and almost 90% of the tapes sold were eight-track cartridges. By 1980, tapes had almost 30% of the market, and a majority of the tapes sold were cassettes. Five years later, the eight-track cartridge market had virtually disappeared, phonograph records only accounted for 44% of unit sales, and compact disks were at 3.5% and rising. By 1987, three-fourths of unit sales were tapes and disks, and 14% of unit shipments (28% of dollar value) were compact disks (Table 9). It appears that the phonograph record will soon go the way of the eight-track cartridge.

References

Council of National Library Associates. The Bowker Annual of Library and Book Trade Information. New York: R. R. Bowker, 1988. Annual. Previous years as cited.

U.S. Bureau of the Census. Statistical Abstract of the United States, 1989. Washington, D.C., 1989. Annual. Previous years as cited.

Table 1. UTILIZATION OF SELECTED MEDIA, 1950-1988

Item	1950	1960	1965	1970	1975	1980	1985	1988
Percent of Households with								
Telephones	62%	79%	85%	91%	93%	93%	92%	93%
Radios	92	96	99	99	99	99	99	99
Television sets	9	87	93	95	97	98	98	98
Cable TV	--	--	--	--	--	20	45	51
Videocassette								
recorders	--	--	--	--	--	1	21	58
Number per Household								
Radios	2.1	3.7	4.1	5.1	5.6	5.5	5.5	5.6
Television sets	1.0	1.1	1.2	1.4	1.5	1.7	1.8	1.9
Hours television								
viewing/day	4.6	5.1	5.5	5.9	6.1	6.6	7.1	7.1

SOURCE: Based on Statistical Abstract 1989, p. 544; 1988, p. 523; 1985, p. 542.

Table 2.   RADIO AND TELEVISION STATIONS, 1945-1987

	Type of Station			
	Commercial Radio*		Television***	
Year	AM**	FM	Total	Commercial
1945	884	46	--	6
1950	2051	733	--	97
1955	2635	553	--	411
1960	3539	815	--	517
1965	4169	1780	559	515
1970	4323	2196	862	677
1975	4463	2767	953	706
1980	4589	3282	1011	734
1985	4718#	3875#	1182	883
1987	4902	4041	1290	968

* As of December 31. Refers to stations on the air, not merely authorized; original source of data was Federal Communication Commission reports.
** Includes AM and AM-FM stations, but not FM affiliates of AM stations.
*** As of January 1. Refers to stations on the air, not merely authorized.
# As of February, 1986.

SOURCE: Based on <u>Statistical Abstract 1989</u>, p. 544; <u>1985</u>, p. 542; <u>1966</u>, p. 519.

Table 3. ADVERTISING: ESTIMATED EXPENDITURES, BY MEDIUM, 1950-1987

Year	Total Expenditures (Billions of Dollars)		Percent Total GNP
	Current	Constant(1987)	
1950	5.7	26.9	2.0%
1955	9.2	39.0	2.3
1960	11.9	45.7	2.3
1965	15.3	54.9	2.2
1970	19.6	57.2	1.9
1975	27.9	58.9	1.7
1980	53.5	73.9	2.0
1985	94.7	99.9	2.4
1987	109.6	109.6	2.4

	Percent of Total Advertising Expenditures*				
	Newspapers	Radio	Television	Magazines	Business Papers
1950	36%	11%	3%	8%	4%
1955	34	6	11	7	5
1960	31	6	13	8	5
1965	29	6	16	8	4
1970	29	7	18	7	4
1975	29	7	19	5	3
1980	28	7	21	6	3
1985	26	7	22	5	2
1987	27	7	22	5	2

* Percentages for these five categories do not total 100% because other types of advertising not shown separately here are included in the total.

SOURCE: Based on <u>Statistical Abstract 1989</u>, pp. 421, 462, 551; <u>1985</u>, p. 549; <u>1974</u>, p. 772.

Table 4. CABLE TELEVISION: SYSTEMS AND SUBSCRIBERS, 1952-1987

Year*	Systems	Subcribers (millions)
1952	70	.01
1955	400	.15
1960	640	.65
1965	1325	1.27
1970	2490	4.50
1975	3506	9.80
1980	4225	16.00
1985	6600	32.00
1988	8500	42.70

* As of January 1.

SOURCE: Based on Statistical Abstract 1989, p. 547.

Table 5. NUMBER OF PUBLIC TELEVISION STATIONS, AND TOTAL AND
          AVERAGE WEEKLY BROADCAST HOURS, 1961-1984

Item	1961	1964	1968	1972	1976	1980	1984
Stations Broadcasting	56	88	153	220	253	281	303
Total Weekly Broadcast							
Hours (1000s)	2.2	3.7	8.5	15.6	22.1	27.6	32.3
General programs	1.4	2.0	4.7	7.9	14.3	19.5	23.2
Instructional	.8	1.7	3.9	7.7	7.8	8.1	9.1
Average Weekly							
Broadcast Hours							
per Station	39.4	42.3	56.1	70.9	90.9	99.8	106.6
General programs	25.6	22.6	30.7	36.0	59.0	69.4	76.4
Instructional	13.8	19.6	25.4	34.9	31.9	30.4	30.2

SOURCE: Based on Statistical Abstract 1979, p. 587.

Table 6. NUMBER OF STATIONS, AND INCOME BY SOURCE, PUBLIC
          BROADCASTING SYSTEMS, 1972-1987.

Stations/Income Source	1972	1975	1980	1985	1987
Public Radio Stations*	132	169	217	288	299
Public Television Stations	228	260	290	317	323
Total Income, Public Systems (millions $)	234	365	705	1096	1294
Distribution by Source (Percent)					
Federal Government	26%	25%	27%	16%	19%
State and Local Government	46	43	39	33	30
Subscribers, Auction/Marathon	8	12	15	23	23
Business and Industry	--**	7	10	16	15
Foundations	11	8	3	4	4
Other	10	5	6	9	9

* CPB (Corporation for Public Broadcasting) qualified.
** Included in "Other."

SOURCE: Based on Statistical Abstract 1989, p. 547; 1984, p. 563.

Table 7.   PRINT MEDIA: SELECTED CHARACTERISTICS OF BOOK,
           NEWSPAPER, AND PERIODICAL PUBLISHING, 1950-1987

Characteristic	(1000s, except as noted)				
	1950	1960	1970	1980	1987
Newspapers, Total (1000s)*	12.1	11.3	11.4	9.6	9.0
Daily	1.8	1.8	1.7	1.7	1.6
Circulation (millions)	53.8	58.9	62.1	62.2	62.8
Per capita**	.35	.33	.30	.27	.26
Sunday	.5	.6	.6	.7	.8
Circulation	46.6	47.7	49.2	54.7	60.1
Per capita**	.31	.27	.24	.24	.25
Periodicals, Total	7.0	8.4	9.6	10.2	11.6
Books Published					
(new, and new editions)	11.0	15.0	36.1	42.4	48.9#

* Includes semiweekly, weekly, and other newspapers.
** Per capita, U.S. resident population.
# This is the figure for 1986, not 1987.

SOURCE: Based on <u>Statistical Abstract 1989</u>, pp. 7, 549; <u>1979</u>, p.
    589-590; Council of National Library Associates, 1988, p.
    403; 1982, p. 385; 1972, p. 176; 1962, p. 59; 1958, p. 103.

Table 8. CHARACTERISTICS OF THE MOTION PICTURE INDUSTRY, 1970-
1987

Characteristic	1970	1975	1980	1985	1987
Theaters (After 1975,					
Screens) (1000s)	14	15	18	21	24
Drive-ins (1000s)	4	4	4	3	3
Box Office					
Receipts (billions $)	1.2	2.1	2.7	3.7	4.3
Attendance (billions)	.9	1.0	1.0	1.1	1.1
Attendance (per capita)	4.5	4.8	4.5	4.4	4.5
Industry Productivity (constant					
[1982] billions $)	4.8	5.2	5.7	7.5	7.6
Industry Productivity (% of					
Total GNP x 1000)	2.3	1.9	1.8	2.2	2.4

SOURCE: Based on <u>Statistical Abstract 1989</u>, pp. 227, 421, 751.

Table 9. PHONOGRAPH RECORDS AND OTHER RECORDING MEDIA:
          MANUFACTURERS' SHIPMENTS, AND VALUE, 1973-1987

Type of Media	1973	1975	1980	1985	1987
Unit Shipments (millions)					
Total	614	532	684	653	707
Phonograph records	508	421	487	288	189
Pre-recorded tapes	106	111	197	343	415
8-track cartridges	91	95	86	3	--
Cassettes	15	16	110	339	410
Compact disks	--	--	--	23	102
Total units per capita*	2.9	2.5	3.0	2.7	2.9
Value (millions $)					
Total, Constant (1987) $	5118	5024	5332	4627	5567
Total, Current $	2001	2378	3862	4388	5567
Phonograph records	1436	1696	2560	1561	996
Pre-recorded tapes	565	682	1303	2437	2977
8-track cartridges	489	583	526	25	3
Cassettes	76	99	776	2411	2974
Compact disks	--	--	--	389	1594

* Per capita, U.S. resident population.

SOURCE: Based on <u>Statistical Abstract 1989</u>, pp. 7, 225.

Topic 10: Institutionalization of Social Forces

10.1 DISPUTE SETTLEMENT

There has been an extraordinary increase in litigiousness in the United States since 1960, accompanied by a great expansion in the jurisdiction of courts and of some regulatory agencies and of agencies offering alternative modes of dispute resolution.

The increase in litigiousness in American society is steady, well-documented and, so far, inexorable. Jethro Lieberman (1981, p. 5) writes:

By 1980 lawsuits were being filed in the fifty state court systems and the local courts of the District of Columbia and Puerto Rico at the rate of 5 million a year. [In the years 1965 to 1975] the number of lawsuits brought to these courts has increased by 84 percent, and though statistics of state dockets are not nationally maintained, the experience in individual states that do keep statistics suggests a similar rise (for example, California's judicial dockets, in courts of general jurisdiction, had swelled by 90% from 1968 to 1976).

Table 1 illustrates this trend. It shows a 351% increase in the number of civil cases brought in federal District Courts from 1960 to 1987.

As the number of court cases has increased, so the scope of judicial authority has expanded in every direction. Nearly all sorts of organizations that were formerly autonomous--churches, private schools and colleges, professional associations, sports leagues, social clubs, philanthropic societies--now find their actions subject to judicial review. There is surely a connection between the new American peaceability (See Chapter 7.1) and the propensity to go to law at the slightest provocation, but it has not yet been studied in detail.

According to Lieberman, this century has seen a change in the construction of American law, which has evolved from a negative or prohibitory institution ("Thou shalt not . . .") to one that declares positive or affirmative duties ("Thou shalt . . ."). . . . The common legal denominator in this evolution has been the adoption of subjective legal standards . . . . [which energize] the courts, charging them with a far greater governmental burden . . . . [making] the judiciary the ultimate authority that defines legally redressable injury (Lieberman 1981, pp. 24-25).

It is this change, he says, that has led to the vast increase in lawsuits.

While civil lawsuits have risen unambiguously, there has been a mixed trend in public attitudes about the amount of regulation that government should impose on the corporations and institutions that are so frequently sued. There has been great pressure (often conducted through civil lawsuits [Handler, 1978]) for an increase in health and safety, or social regulations, and for a decrease in economic regulation, particularly by government agencies whose activities have seemed to grant or favor monopolies. This has brought pressure to dismantle many of the older government regulatory agencies. Many of the agencies that were established between the 1880s and World War II were organized on a cartel-like industry-by-industry basis to regulate railroads, airlines, banking, telcommunications, etc. However, now they are often accused of promoting unfair and uneconomic monopolies, and some agencies, such as the Civil Aeronautics Board, have actually been abolished. This has also brought pressure for the formation of new regulatory agencies for "social regulation," such as the Environmental Protection Agency. These agencies that are intended to promote health and safety are deliberately organized along functional, rather than industry lines (see Maxey, 1985). Between 1970 and 1980, the personnel of the federal agencies engaged in economic regulation grew from 18 to 23 thousand, while the personnel of social regulatory agencies increased from 10 to 55 thousand. Both sets of agencies suffered minor cutbacks after 1980 (Congressional Quarterly, 1982).

As the use of the state and federal court systems has increased, there has been increasing demand for alternative methods of dispute settlement, methods that are variously intended to be more rapid, less costly, and more oriented to the promotion of social goals than the strict findings of justice required of the courts. The main alternatives now available are the state-run Small Claims and Domestic Relations Courts (in which plaintiffs and defendants may plead their own cases without a lawyer), and a range of different types of mediation and arbitration services. These include federal, state and locally funded mediation and arbitration programs as well as a variety of private professional services (see Pruitt and Kressel, 1985).

References

Congressional Quarterly. Regulation: Process and Politics. Washington, D.C.: Congressional Quarterly, Inc., 1982.

Handler, Joel F. Social Movements and the Legal System: A Theory of Law Reform and Social Change. New York: Academic Press, 1978.

Lieberman, Jethro. The Litigious Society. New York: Basic Books, 1981.

Maxey, Margaret N. "Introduction." In Regulatory Reform: New Vision or Old Curse, edited by Margaret N. Maxey and Robert Lawrence Kuhn, pp. 1-32. New York: Praeger, 1985.

Pruitt, Dean G. and Kenneth Kressel. "The Mediation of Social Conflict: An Introduction." Journal of Social Issues 41 (1985): 1-10.

U.S. Bureau of the Census. Statistical Abstract of the United States, 1989. Washington, D.C., 1989. Annual. Previous years as cited.

Table 1. CIVIL CASES COMMENCED IN DISTRICT COURTS, 1960-1987

Year	Number of Cases (1000s)
1960	59.3
1965	67.7
1970	87.3
1975	117.3
1980	168.8
1987	239.0

SOURCE: Based on Statistical Abstract 1989, p. 180; 1979, p. 192.

With few exceptions, American labor unions have failed to develop the extensive political, educational, religious, leisure, and familistic functions charactertic of trade unions in other industrialized countries. The only important outside relationships of the trade union movement are with the Federal agencies that supervise labor-management relations and workplace conditions. Unions do support political candidates and have secured their election in some cases, but their ability to mobilize votes has been declining.

By and large, trade unions in the United States have not developed the extensive connections to other institutional sectors that are characteristic of trade unions in other industrialized countries. The only American unions that distantly approximate the European model are the International Ladies Garment Workers and the United Mine Workers.

In other American unions, the political, religious, educational, leisure and family functions are relatively undeveloped. The only institutional connection that looms large is with government at various levels. The Federal agencies with which unions are most heavily involved are the Department of Labor and the National Labor Relations Board. The unions are not directly represented in either agency although they have considerable influence in both.

The Department of Labor was made a cabinet department in 1913. Its secretary is appointed by the President and its employees are civil servants. Unions have no say in Department of Labor appointments other than through their lobbyists. The key sections of the Department from the union standpoint are: the Labor-Management Services Administration, the Occupational Safety and Health Administration, the Employment and Training Administration, the Bureau of Labor Statistics and the Employment Standards Administration (see Fossum, 1982, pp. 83-85).

Besides the Department of Labor, there are five executive agencies of special importance for organized labor: the Equal Employment Opportunity Commission, the National Labor Relations Board, the National Mediation Board, the Occupational Safety and Health Review Commission and the Pension Benefit Guarantee Corporation (see Fossum, 1982, pp. 85-87). These agencies are all staffed by presidential appointees and civil servants, and unions have no formal representation in them.

The oldest of these agencies is the National Labor Relations Board, which consists of a chairman and four other members appointed by the president and confirmed by the senate for five year renewable terms. The NLRB determines what group of employees constitutes an appropriate unit for a representation election and it holds such elections to determine which, if any, union is entitled to represent the employees of that unit in collective bargaining. The NLRB may also examine the conduct of employers and unions in order to judge the validity of elections (Fossum 1982, 148). It does not initiate action on its own, but responds to complaints and petitions. Its decisions are enforceable through the Federal courts (Fossum, 1982, p. 73 ff.).

In further contrast to the experience of other countries, American unions have never had a political party of their own. However, union officials frequently attempt to bring out the rank-and-file vote in support of major party candidates, usually but not invariably Democrats, who are deemed more sympathetic to organized labor than their opponents. The nation's largest labor federation, the AFL-CIO, has a political arm called the Committee for Political Education, which lobbies Congress and the White House, attempts to mobilize voters, and plays an active role in presidential campaigns. In some of them, like the Kennedy-Nixon contest of 1960, COPE played a crucial role. On the other hand, labor's support for Mondale in 1984 is considered to have been a major factor in his defeat. It is the consensus of political observers that organized labor's ability to bring out votes for the candidates it endorses declined rather sharply between 1960 and 1984 and shows no sign of reviving.

References

Fossum, John A. Labor Relations: Development, Structure, Process. Plano, Texas: Business Publications, 1982.

10.3 SOCIAL MOVEMENTS

Social movements in the U.S. fall into two broad categories, liberation movements and protest movements. Both types flourished in the 1960s, consolidated their gains in the 1970s, and waned in the 1980s. Both types of movement have become less confrontational and more inclined to work within the legal system.

The purpose of a liberation movement is to raise the status of a disadvantaged social category. Most of the participants in a liberation movement belong to the category whose status is to be raised, although there are always a few outside sympathizers. The major liberation movements of recent decades were organized by blacks, women, Hispanics, Native Americans, homosexuals, students, and the handicapped.

The purpose of a protest movement is to change government or institutional policy regarding some particular activity. In the usual case, the participants in a protest movement strongly oppose an activity that is performed, encouraged, or tolerated by government agencies or other large organizations. There are currently active protest movements regarding abortion, drunken drivers, nuclear weapons, nuclear power, apartheid, gun control, environmental pollution, capital punishment, product labeling, pornography, wife abuse, school prayer, industrial safety, animal experimentation, and some other issues.

Both liberation and protest movements have been conspicuous features of American society since the early part of the nineteenth century, but their influence has been highly variable from one period to another depending upon popular and official moods and the effectiveness in particular circumstances of lobbying, litigation, bloc voting, civil disobedience, terrorism, the mobilization of public opinion, and political alliances.

The measurement of trends in social movements presents a paradoxical problem. On the one hand, the trends are highly conspicuous. On the other hand, it is difficult to describe them numerically, and when we do find a useful series, it is likely to be discontinuous.

It is very difficult to say how many social movements are active at a given time and flatly impossible to count their supporters. Every important social movement includes many competing and overlapping organizations together with a large but unstable constituency.

During the 1960s, both liberation and protest movements burgeoned under the stimulus of the Civil Rights Act of 1964, the Voting Rights Act of 1965, and other initiatives of the Johnson administration and of the social upheaval that accompanied the Vietnam war. Old movements were strengthened and new ones appeared on every hand. Violent and mock-violent forms of protest were very much in vogue. In the 1970s, the tactical emphasis shifted from confrontation to lobbying. The movements consolidated their gains with the help of friendly Federal agencies and favorable court decisions. But they began to lose momentum even before the election of President Reagan in 1980 signaled a decline in official support for the liberation movements and for the predominantly liberal protest movements that had been encouraged by previous administrations. Nevertheless, the programs of the liberation movements had been so far codified into law and regulatory practice that they continued to gain ground. The predominantly liberal protest movements--conservation, gun control, opposition to nuclear weapons--fared less well, while there was a sharp growth in right-wing protest movements concerned with such issues as abortion and pornography.

In general, the liberation movements have been more successful in removing disadvantages with respect to entitlements under government control, such as education and promotional opportunities in the Federal service, than economic disadvantages imposed by the labor market and the distribution of property. Thus, while the educational disadvantage of blacks and hispanics decreased significantly from 1970 to 1985, the income disadvantage did not decrease at all (Table 1).

The recent history of protest movements is not so easily summarized. Some protest movements provide channels of expression for a minority viewpoint that has no immediate chance of winning majority approval (opposition to capital punishment, and animal experimentation, for example). On other issues (abortion, gun control) two opposing protest movements attempt to control public policy. The most effective protest movements are those that enjoy mild majority support and can exert influence on public policy more or less in proportion to the resources they bring to bear (such as opposition to pollution, nuclear power and drunken driving).

To an increasing extent, the issues raised by protest movements are resolved in the courts. Litigation tends to displace other forms of protest, and fund-raising to support legal costs has become the principal activity of many protest organizations.

References

American Council on Education. One Third of a Nation. Washington, D.C., 1988.

U.S. Bureau of the Census. Statistical Abstract of the United States, 1989. Washington, D.C., 1989.

Table 1.   INDICATORS OF THE SUCCESS OF ETHNIC LIBERATION:
            EDUCATION AND FAMILY INCOME, BY ETHNICITY, 1970-1987

Indicator	1970	1975	1980	1985	1987
Percent high school graduates					
Persons age 14-24					
White	81%	84%	83%	84%	--
Black	59	64	66	75	--
Hispanic	--	57	55	62	--
Median Family Income,					
Constant 1987 Dollars (1000s)					
White	30	30	30	31	32
Black	18	19	17	18	18
Hispanic	--	20	20	20	20

SOURCE: Based on American Council on Education, 1988, pp. 8, 14;
        Statistical Abstract 1989, p. 445.

Special interest groups have a long history of influencing American politics. Election laws governing contributions given to candidates running for Federal office have facilitated the study of political action committees (PACs). PACs supported by corporations, labor unions, professional associations, churches, citizen groups, women, and the elderly increased 600% in the 13 years from 1974 to 1987. Contributions to candidates for the House and Senate totaled over 1.3 billion dollars in 1986.

An interest group is an organized association which engages in activities relative to government decisions. Such groups have a long history in the United States (Wilson, 1981 and Wootton, 1985). The New York Chamber of Commerce was organized in 1768 and by the time of the Civil War there were over 30 such groups. The National Chamber of Commerce came into being in 1912. The National Grange was created in 1867, and the American Farm Bureau in 1919.

Business associations, occupational groups, labor organizations, religious bodies, and political parties have organized themselves to increase their influence with government officials and agencies. Examples include the National Association of Manufacturers, the National Federation of Independent Business, the American Political Action Committee, the Business-Industry Political Action Committee, the National Council of Churches, the American Dental Political Action Committee, the American Medical Political Action Committee, the Forest Products Political Action Committee, and the National Organization of Women (Miller, 1983). Proponents of political activity by interest groups argue that as government spending and regulation has increased, so has the need for organized activity to "protect" the interests of specific groups by influencing government policies and practices.

Before World War II, there was little detailed information about the number of special interest groups and the amounts they contributed to political candidates and causes. The Federal Regulation of Lobbying Act, passed in 1946, required lobbists to register and to account for the funds raised and dispersed (Bettelheim, 1975). Table 1 shows the number of lobbyists registered and the amounts they reported spending from 1947 to 1967. The initial registration included more lobbyists than any other year. Over the 20-year period, there was substantial variation in spending and number of lobbyists, and no clear trend in either.

Table 2 reports the spending by different lobby interests for the 18- year period 1949 to 1966. As can been seen,business interest groups made the largest reported contributions to political candidates. The rise of influence of organized labor is obvious; its reported contributions to candidates were five times larger in 1966 than 1949. The only other change as notable was the decline of lobbying by professional associations, 1949-1957. Perhaps the best generalization to be made about the figures in Table 2 is the frequent lack of coherent trend. This raises some doubts about the accuracy of the reporting.

The Federal Election Campaign Act of 1971 required greater disclosure about sources of campaign funds by candidates for federal office. Sweeping changes were made in the Federal Election Campaign Act Amendments enacted in 1974 (Sharp, 1988). These amendments closed many previous legal loopholes in campaign financing and reporting by requiring candidates for Federal offices to establish a single central campaign committee through which all contributions and expenditures were reported. Thus, the contributions of political action committees became much more visible in 1977. Congress strengthened reporting about election campaign funding even more with a series of amendments to the Federal Election Campaign Act.

Political Action Committees

Table 3 presents information about the number of corporate, labor, trade and non-connected political action committees (PACs), 1974-1987. Their growth has been phenomenal, from 608 in 1974 to 4,165 in 1987. The greatest growth was in corporate PACs, which numbered only 89 in 1974, compared to 1,775 in 1987.

Financial support from PACs to candidates for Congress for the period 1979 to 1986 is summarized in Table 4. In 1979-1980, nearly $40 million were contributed to the campaigns of candidates for House seats. Six years later, the amount had more than doubled, to over $87 million. Only about half as much was contributed to Senate campaigns, although PAC funding of Senatorial candidates has increased faster than for House candidates. Corporate-supported PACs contributed the most, but were closely followed by trade associations. Labor organizations were also big spenders. Contributions from "non-connected" PACs were considerably smaller.

Schlozman and Tierney (1986) compared PACs founded in the 1960s with those organized in the 1970s. They reported that PACs supported by citizen groups, civil rights organizations, social welfare groups, women, the elderly and the handicapped appeared more frequently during the later period (Table 5). According to Cigler (1986), as interest groups proliferated during the 1960s, most moved their headquarters to Washington in order to "hunt were the ducks are". Schlozman and Tierney also examined how long PACs remained active in influencing political decisions. They followed the activities of a sample of over 1,000 PACs that were active in Washington D.C. in 1960 to see how many were still involved in politics in 1980 (Table 6). Citizen groups had the lowest rate of survival (33%), a finding attributed to their being frequently organized around a single issue which gets resolved. Civil rights PACs also tended to fade out of existence. A high percentage (around 80%) of PACs sponsored by professional associations, women's organizations, senior citizens' groups and labor unions continued active in 1980.

References

Bettelheim, Judith. Directory of Registered Federal and State Lobbyists. Orange, NJ: Academic Media, 1975.

Cigler, Allan J. and Burdett A. Loomis. Interest Group Politics. 2nd ed. Washington, D.C.: C.O. Press, 1986.

Legislators and the Lobbyists. Washington, D.C.: Congressional Quarterly Service, May, 1968.

Miller, Stephen. Special Interest Groups In American Politics. New Brunswick, NJ: Transaction Books, 1983.

Schlozman, Kay Lehman and John T. Tierney. Organized Interests and American Democracy. New York: Harper and Row, 1986.

Sharp, Michael J. The Directory of Congressional Voting Scores and Interest Groups Rating. New York: Facts on File Publications, 1988.

U.S. Bureau of the Census. Statistical Abstract of the United States, 1989. Washington, D.C., 1989.

Wilson, Graham K. Interest Groups in the United States. New York: Oxford University Press, 1981.

Wootton, Graham. Interest Groups: Policy and Politics in America. Englewood Cliffs: Prentice-Hall, 1985.

Table 1. PERSONS REGISTERING AS LOBBYISTS AND REPORTED SPENDING
UNDER 1946 FEDERAL REGULATION OF LOBBYING ACT

Year	Persons Registered	Spending (millions)
1947	731	$ 5.2
1950	430	10.3
1955	383	4.3
1960	236	3.9
1965	450	5.8
1967	449	4.5

SOURCE: Legislators and the Lobbyists, 1968, pp. 43-44.

Table 2. LOBBY SPENDING BY CATEGORY FOR SELECTED YEARS, 1949-
1966

Category	Spending (1000s)				
	1949*	1957	1959	1963	1966
Business	$3280	$2290	$1762	$1522	$1601
Citizens	1015	616	513	707	801
Labor	257	656	1217	1130	1347
Farm	392	412	315	406	383
Military	106	118	131	140	147
Professional	1672	195	345	319	377

* In addition to those listed in the table, the source reports, for
this year only, spending of $719,000 by foreign policy lobbies,
$374,000 by reclamation lobbies, and $155,000 by tax lobbies.

SOURCE: Legislators and the Lobbyists, 1968, p. 36.

3. POLITICAL ACTION COMMITTEES, BY COMMITTEE TYPE, 1974-1987

Type of Committee	1974	1975	1978	1980	1982	1985	1987
Total	608	722	1653	2551	3371	3992	4165
Corporate	89	139	785	1206	1469	1710	1775
Labor	201	226	217	297	380	388	364
Other	318	357	651	1048	1522	1894	2026
Trade/membership/ health	--	--	453	576	649	695	865
Non-connected	--	--	162	374	723	1003	957
Cooperative	--	--	12	42	47	54	59
Corporation without stock	--	--	24	56	103	142	145

SOURCE: Based on Statistical Abstract 1989, p. 262.

Table 4. CONTRIBUTION TO CONGRESSIONAL CAMPAIGNS BY POLITICAL
ACTION COMMITTEES (PAC) BY TYPE OF COMMITTEE, 1979-1986

Type of Committee	Contributions (millions)		
	1979-1981	1983-1984	1985-1986
House of Representatives			
Total	$37.9	$75.7	$87.4
Corporate	12.1	23.4	26.9
Trade associations	11.7	20.4	23.4
Labor	9.4	19.8	22.6
Non-connected	3.1	9.1	11.1
Senate			
Total	17.3	29.7	45.3
Corporate	6.9	12.0	19.2
Trade association	4.1	6.3	9.5
Labor	3.8	5.0	7.2
Non-connected	1.9	5.4	7.7

SOURCE: Statistical Abstract 1989, p. 263.

Table 5. DATES OF FOUNDING OF INTEREST GROUPS LOCATED IN
          WASHINGTON, D.C., MID-1980s

Type of Organization	Percent of All Organizations of that Type Presently Functioning (mid-1980s) Organized in:		
	1960-1969	1970-1981	Total
Corporations	8%	6%	14%
Trade/business associations	15	23	38
Professional associations	16	14	30
Unions	7	14	21
Citizens' groups	19	57	76
Civil rights	10	46	56
Social welfare	28	51	79
Women/elderly/handicapped	13	43	56
Other/unknown	18	34	52
Total (all organizations)	15	25	40

SOURCE: Based on Schlozman and Tierney, 1986, p. 76.

Table 6.   1980 STATUS OF ORGANIZATIONS ACTIVE IN NATIONAL
           POLITICS (WASHINGTON, D.C. AREA) IN 1960, BY TYPE OF
           ORGANIZATION

Type of Organization	Number in 1960	Still Active	Still Active, Not in Politics	Inactive/ Defunct	No Info
Corporations	84	63%	8%	0%	29%
Trade/ business	216	61	6	10	24
Professional association	28	79	7	0	14
Unions	56	77	7	4	12
Citizens groups	46	33	13	27	27
Civil rights	8	50	12	0	38
Women/ elderly	9	78	11	0	11
Other/ unknown	76	46	18	3	33
Total	523	60	9	7	24

SOURCE: Based on Schlozman and Tierney, 1986, p. 79.

Topic 11: Ideologies

American voters are overwhelmingly centrist, and, within the ambit of the essentially centrist parties, have seemed since the end of World War II to have favored the more conservative candidates for national executive offices, while being on balance more liberal in voting for legislative and local offices. Beyond the vast center, "minor" parties have perilous existences, enlivened by modest and short-lived outbursts of favor for parties of the right and of the left. Within the centrist ambit, the left-right dimension is arrayed as socioeconomic interest might lead one to predict, but this dimension is overlaid by many others.

Since World War II, there has been a tendency for the Republican Party to win the presidential elections, while the Democratic Party holds the House of Representatives and often the Senate. Commonly, it is understood that voters prefer the foreign-policy stands of the Republican Party (tougher on Communism, at least rhetorically) and the domestic-policy stands--or at any rate bread-and-butter performance--of the Democrats; and that the Presidential-Congressional split reflects the relative importance voters place on the differing functions of executive and legislature. Roughly speaking, to be sure, the rise of a given party in each has been paralleled by a rise in the others, in part because in presidential years voters will often vote for a representative or senator of the same party as their presidential choice. Representatives are elected biennially, senators every six years, and presidents every four.

For present purposes, the polarization of the electorate is best analyzed through studying their behavior in presidential elections: here, the issues are less overlaid with strictly local concerns.

The two major parties, between them, almost always carry virtually the entire vote (Table 1). Since World War II, there have been only three exceptions to this generalization: in 1948, when the Democratic Party shed both its right and left wings in the presidential contest, but won nevertheless; in 1980, when an "Independent" Party briefly arose and gained widespread support, its standard-bearer being a liberal Republican alarmed by the rightward swing of the main body of the party (and whose followers included large numbers of Democrats similarly concerned about their own party, as well as many from both parties who were disillusioned with the inability of the major parties to deal with the pressing substantive issues of war and peace and the environment); and especially in 1968, when a vast populist-ethnic coalition, drawn mainly from the Democratic Party, took stands that might be categorized as essentially of the "right," but "right" in the rather American sense of asserting authoritarian positions from a rather moralistic standpoint, a position that at other times (as in the movement to abolish slavery a century before) might have better been considered "left."

The two major parties' ability to control virtually all the vote has contributed to their essential balance. It is also a product of it. Over the past four decades, the balance has moved from Democratic (winners in 1948 of the last of five straight presidential victories) to Republican for two victories, to Democratic for two, to Republican for two, to Democratic for one, and finally, to three Republican victories.

Both major parties are centrist parties, although they occupy different portions of the center of the spectrum, and this changes somewhat over time. The Republican party, nationally, moved from right-center toward the center in 1940s and 1950s, then moved right again in the 1970s and 1980s; the Democratic party, nationally, moved from left-center toward the center in the 1940s and 1950s, then moved further toward the right-center in the 1970s and 1980s. The true parties of the left and of the right have varied in the period since World War II (as before).

The considerable instability in the electorate in support of "left" and "right" is apparent in Table 1, which portrays the proportion of the non-Democrat, non-Republican, "all other" base in presidential elections 1948-1988. The table shows the support within the minor parties for parties of the left and the right and of other parties, which include both single-issue parties (those organized around prohibiting the sale of alcoholic beverages are persistent examples) and parties like the 1980 "Independents" that in some sense are a protest against the way the American political spectrum is ordinarily expressed. 1948, 1968, and 1980 were exceptional. A consideration of distribution of left, right, and "other" parties in "ordinary" years reveals no trend; there is great heterogeneity. The right seems capable of drawing more support than the left, at least since the repression of the early Cold War years. "Other" parties seem to vary markedly, too, but their electoral support has increased slightly in recent years.

The left, arguably, almost became institutionalized within American politics as a relatively large splinter. The 1948 left-Democratic splinter continued on into 1952 and drew enough votes to make 1952 the "golden" year for the left by comparision with the right (within the minor parties); but it was gone by 1956, leaving only the "old left" parties. Relatively, 1964 represented a strong showing for the left, but absolutely it was miserable: these years represented the high-point for the incorporation of the entire spectrum of voters within the two major parties--or their effective suppression or alienation from electoral politics altogether. The right, likewise, continued (with a hiatus in 1952) to be represented in a "States Rights" (anti-national authority) party--representing southern conservatism, especially on racial issues--until the 1960s. Of late, however, the composition of the right wing has been somewhat different, composed of two contrasting elements: populist-racist "fundamentalist" conservatism that is more conservative on "lifestyle" issues than on economic ones; and the Libertarian Party, a purist free-market party that is not necessarily conservative at all on life-style issues, although its opposition to governmental intervention makes it quite conservative in another sense.

What about "other?" In some sense, its marked growth since 1976 is the most significant part of Table 1, since left and right show little trend. What has happened since 1976 seems to be a growth of small parties that either attack the electoral system and the major parties as flawed, or express single issues of one sort or another. The parties (those that achieve any vote at all) have grown in number, and, in toto, in percentage of the "minor-party" vote.

Pollsters regularly ask Americans how they would place themselves along a liberal-conservative continuum. From 1940 through roughly the mid-1960s, the proportions were about equal, with the conservative side gaining somewhat more support than the liberal (Robinson and Fleishman 1984, p. 53). Since the mid-1960s, however, in the public at large there has been a marked increase in the proportions identifying themselves as relatively conservative, a finding replicated in four separate poll series. This shift is part of the political commonplace of the nation, and is surely reflected in the postures of the two major parties, the ardent welfare-statism that defined mainstream liberalism in the U.S. since the 1930s having sustained serious challenges on economic, moralistic ("permissiveness"), and racist grounds.

Robinson and Fleishman go to considerable pains to show that if the words "liberal" and "conservative" have clearcut ideological meanings to some people, they do not to the American public as a whole, and so that the correlates of these expressed leanings are both modest and variable. They note that the General Social Survey, for instance,

> contains over 30 questions relevant to ideological issues, including tolerance of minorities, hard-line domestic and foreign policies, women's rights, traditional religion and family values, and governmental spending priorities. Correlations between each of these items and self-identified ideology [i.e. liberal/conservative] make it clear that liberals and conservatives do differ in their stands on particular issues, and in the predicted [i.e., by persons familiar with the American political spectrum] direction. . . . Nevertheless, while the correlations are statistically significant, they are rather modest . . . in the range of .10 to .24.

Over time, even the advent and re-election of the highly ideological (in the American sense) Ronald Reagan has done nothing to make these positions more crystallized in the public at large.

> Nor is there any tendency for correlations to increase in one issue area at the expense of another; items dealing with government spending and with moral or life-style issues all show gains as well as losses (Robinson and Fleishman 1984: 54-55).

Correlations between liberal/conservative self-placement and political party affiliation are somewhat higher, in the range of .25 to .50, and with no obvious trend. This finding may be interpreted to mean that party choice is determined (if this is the direction of causation) by ideological stance, among perhaps as few as one-tenth and surely no more than one quarter of the electorate (Robinson and Fleishman, 1984, p. 58). This does not appear to be a strong or dominant linkage in American politics.

Since World War II, the liberal/conservative dimension has been strongly and consistently correlated (Miller, Miller, and Schneider, 1980, Table 2.30) with race (blacks are far more liberal), occupation (blue-collar and unskilled workers are more liberal, and farmers more conservative), income (the wealthy are more conservative), religious affiliation (Protestants tend to be conservative, Jews and nonbelievers, liberal), residential location (rural people are conservative, central-city residents relatively liberal), and, more tenuously, with historical period (the most recent birth cohorts [post-1943] seem far more liberal than previous cohorts, among whom there is no consistent trend in liberal-conservatism).

References

Congressional Quarterly Weekly Report 47 (January 21, 1989): 139.

Miller, Warren E., Arthur H. Miller, and Edward J. Schneider. American National Election Studies Data Sourcebook 1952-1978. Cambridge. MA: Harvard University Press, 1980.

Robinson, John P. and John A. Fleishman. "Ideological Trends in American Public Opinion." Annals of the American Academy of Political and Social Science 472 (March, 1984): 50-60.

Scammon, Richard A. and Alice V. McGillivray, comp. and eds. America Votes 17: 1986. Washington, D.C.: Congressional Quarterly, 1987.

Table 1.   PERCENTAGE OF ALL VOTES FOR OTHERS THAN DEMOCRAT OR
           REPUBLICAN AND DISTRIBUTION OF THIS "MINOR PARTY" VOTE,
           PRESIDENTIAL ELECTIONS, 1948-1988

	Non-Major Party	"Minor Party" Vote		
		"Left"	"Right"	Other
1948	5%	46%	45%	9%
1952	0	65	0	35
1956	0	25	53	22
1960	0	41	27	32
1964	0	70	6	24
1968	14	1	98	1
1972	2	11	82	7
1976	2	11	33	56
1980	8	2	14	84
1984	1	10	10	80
1988	1	34	54	12

SOURCE: Based on Scammon and McGillivray, 1986, pp. 20-40;
    Congressional Quarterly Weekly, 1989, p. 139.

Confidence in most institutions, and especially government, declined from the mid-1960s to 1980 or thereabouts, rebounded during the early 1980s, and then declined again. Public confidence is up from the "crisis of confidence" of the late 1970s, but is still lower than formerly. Confidence in organized medicine, and the scientific establishment, religion, and the military is notably high.

Americans place less confidence in their institutions than they did three decades ago. Indeed, the trend of decline in public confidence in the late 1960s and 1970s was such that two of the country's leading social analysts produced a book entitled The Confidence Gap (Lipset and Schneider, 1983:3) in which they drew upon hundreds of public polls in documenting the scope and implications of the decline of public faith in government, business, and labor since the mid-1960s. The deterioration of confidence in public institutions was attributed, in part, to poor performance of the economy:

. . . the analysis indicates that unemployment and inflation have a clear, negative impact upon people's trust in major institutions. Business and government bear the brunt of public disaffection as economic trends take a turn for the worse. They are the core of "the system" and are held most directly accountable for its malfunctions (Lipset and Schneider, 1983, p. 66)

There is some evidence that although government and business are "core," other institutions suffer in the public view along with government and business. That is, the entire institutional system is intertwined and intermeshed and what depresses confidence in one sector also affects others:

. . . the public did not lose confidence in different institutions at different times. Rather, the data reveal a widespread loss of faith in the leadership of business, government, labor, and other private and public institutions at more or less the same time (Lipset and Schneider, 1983, p. 3)

Lipset and Schneider compared the relationships among different institutions in relative confidence rankings over time, and concluded that the relative position of each institution tends to be maintained. In a seven-category system, including the military, the press, the executive branch, congress, big business, major companies, and organized labor, the military consistently ended up on top, organized labor on the bottom, with the executive branch and the press in a middle position and big business, major companies, and congress generating "moderately negative" evaluations. After a lengthy exploration of the antecedents and correlates of the "particular disdain" the public held for business, government, and labor during the 1970s, Lipset and Schneider (1983, pp. 88, 384) concluded:

. . . the decline of confidence has both real and superficial aspects. It is real because the American public is intensely dissatisfied with the performance of their institutions. It is also to some extent superficial because Americans have not yet reached the point of rejecting those institutions.

Lipset and Schneider's book only covered trends up to 1981, and they recognized (pp. 396-397) that an upturn in public confidence might accompany "the renewal of optimism" that appeared with the onset of the Reagan presidency.

Most of the trends charted below (Tables 1-3) support the "decline of confidence" position documented by Lipset and Schneider. However, as predicted, there are some modest increases in public confidence in the mid-1980s, followed again by decline. We present three summary tables, each from a different polling organization, showing changes in levels of confidence expressed in different institutions.

Table 1 summarizes results of Harris Poll surveys of public confidence in 13 institutions for the period 1966-1988. Note that the percentage of people expressing "a great deal of confidence" in specific institutions is generally down quite sharply from the 1966 benchmarks and moderately so from 1971-72. Confidence in doctors and the medical sector is highest, followed by educational institutions, the military, and the Supreme Court. Perhaps the most notable recent decline is the loss of confidence in The White House since 1984, a drop of 25 points. Harris (1988, p. 2) comments:

Taken as a whole, the gains that establishment institutions made back in 1984, when Ronald Reagan led a resurgence of respect for the established leadership of the country, now has [sic] been virtually all wiped out. One of the challenges facing a new president in 1989 will be to find a way to lead the nation back to higher plateaus of regard for leaders both in the public and private sector.

Table 2, from the Gallup Organization, summarizes responses to a question on confidence in eight institutions over the period 1973-1988. As with the Harris data in Table 1, the percentage of people expressing confidence fluctuates from year to year, but the relative position of the various institutions is fairly stable.

Table 3 summarizes responses to questions on confidence in the leaders of national institutions included the National Opinion Research Center's General Social Survey for the years 1973-1987.

Both the Gallup poll (Table 2), which asks how much confidence people have in specific institutions, and the General Social Survey (GSS) (Table 3), with its referring to "the people running these institutions," show relatively high confidence in organized religion, the military, banks and the Supreme Court, and low confidence in organized labor, the Executive Branch of the Federal government, Congress, and television. The highest ratings are for institutions included in the General Social Survey (GSS) but not the Gallup poll, namely medicine and the scientific community.

The numbers in Tables 2 and 3 are not strictly comparable because the Gallup question has a four-category answer--"a great deal, quite a lot, some, or very little," while the GSS question has only three, "a great deal," "only some," or "hardly any." Over the decade covered in the GSS data, medicine retains its preeminent position with about half of the population expressing high confidence in it. Confidence in the scientific community is similarly stable at a somewhat lower level. The most consistent trends, evident in both tables, are declines in the already low stature of organized labor and television, a slight decline in the public's confidence in education, and a slight increase in public confidence in the military. Throughout most of the period Congress and the Executive Branch generated about the same low level of confidence as did organized labor.

Data from a fourth polling organization, the Opinion Research Corporation (ORC), corroborate the patterns evident in the previous tables for the 1975-1981 period. Lipset and Schneider (1983, p. 61) summarize this series by noting that it

. . . suggests a straight decline from 1975 to 1981, with no general revival in the "honeymoon years" 1977 and 1981 beyond those for "the President" himself and other major institutions of government. . . . Overall, what the data suggest is a continuing low level of confidence from the mid-1970s to the early 1980s.

Armed forces. Between 1973 and 1987, support for the military remained constant with about one-third of those sampled expressing "a great deal of confidence" in the leaders of the U.S. military. The Gallup surveys (Table 2) reveal growing confidence in the 1980s, peaking at 63% saying they had "a great deal" or "quite a lot" of confidence in the military in 1986. In that year the military replaced organized religion as the institution in the Gallup list generating the greatest confidence, but military's leading position was made possible by a sharp decline in public confidence in religion. The other surveys (Tables 1 and 3) also reveal relatively high public confidence in the military during the decade of the 1980s. For example, by 1981, only the medical profession, the universities, and the churches had higher rates of confidence in the ORC polls (Lipset and Schneider, 1983, p. 60).

Church. Throughout the 1973-86 period, public confidence in organized religion was higher than in any of the other ten institutions listed by Gallup, including the U.S. Supreme Court, banks, and the military (Table 2). The level of confidence remained relatively stable, with about two-thirds of those questioned expressing "a great deal" or "quite a lot" of confidence in organized religion.

A 1986 Gallup Report (No. 253, p. 2) headlined, "Public Losing Confidence in Organized Religion," but a year later the decline seemed to have reversed: the 1987 Gallup poll showed an increase in confidence in organized religion to the point that it was tied with the military as most esteemed institution. The 1988 figure of 59%, while the highest level of confidence expressed in any of the institutions, was down seven points from peak of 66% three years; the 1989 percentage was lower still, at 52%, by far the lowest rating of religion in the series.

Just how public confidence in religion compares to confidence in other institutions depends on how the confidence is measured. When the indicator is percentage of people claiming "a great deal" of confidence and the question is framed in terms of "the people running these institutions," the relative support for religion declines. The GSS data for 1973-88 (Table 3) and the Harris Polls (Table 1) reveal support for organized religion at about the same level as for education and usually slightly lower than the confidence expressed in banks and financial institutions. These three institutions, along with the U.S. Supreme Court, occupy the second level in the GSS and Harris polls (Tables 1 and 3), clearly less commanding of confidence than the scientific community, medicine, or educational institutions, but ahead of most other institutions mentioned.

School. By 1989, confidence in local public schools was lower than in the early 1970s, only up slightly from a dearth of public confidence in the late 1970s and early 1980s. On a five-point scale ranging from "fail" to a high of "A," in 1974, 18% of those questioned gave the local schools the highest rating, and 48% gave them either A or B ratings. Confidence in local schools dropped sharply between between 1974 and 1979, stabilized briefly, dropped again to a low in 1983 of 6% A ratings, then increased slightly at stabilized at about 10% A and 30% B ratings. In other words, about 60% of the population saw the public schools in their area as just average, or worse. Since 1981 Gallup has also asked respondents to rate "public schools in the nation." Ratings of public schools nationally climbed steadily between 1981 and 1986, rising from 20% A or B scores to a high point of 28%, then declined to 22% by 1989 (Elam and Gallup, 1989, p. 39; Gallup, 1986, pp. 13-14).

Gallup and GSS surveys on confidence in institutions consistently reveal public schools or "education" as generating a fairly high level of confidence, roughly comparable to the confidence in banks. As with the grade-ratings discussed above, the comparative confidence levels in Tables 2 and 3 reveal a modest downward trend in public confidence in education until the mid-1980s, following by a partial recovery.

Nation. Confidence in the nation as a whole, as reflected in statements of satisfaction with "the way things are going in the U.S. at this time," demonstrates a marked rise and fall between 1979 and 1986. The polls reveal generally increasing levels of satisfaction, from a low of 12% in 1979 to a high of 66% in 1986, then a fairly sharp drop over the next two years, to 45% in 1987 and 56% in 1988. Satisfaction with the nation is fairly volatile, sometimes varying by as much as 15 points over a six-month period (Gallup Report, 1988, p. 30; see also Chapter 17.1, Satisfaction).

Another measure of consensus about "the nation" is confidence in government. However, confidence in the institutions of government, as represented in ratings of Congress, the Executive Branch, and the White House is notably low, and even the Supreme Court generates less public confidence than the military, organized religion, the scientific establishment and the medical establishment (Tables 1-3). Other analyses of confidence in government show deteriorating confidence, growing anti-government sentiment, and heightened perceptions of government unresponsiveness in the 1960s and 1970s (Lipset and Schneider, 1983, pp. 17, 25, 33).

"The situation of the country" has also been measured via the Cantril ladder technique, in which respondents estimate the present, past, and future on a 10-step ladder. The trend reveals considerable optimism about the future, even though assessments of the quality of the present show a dip in both the early and the late 1970s. The public has almost always said that the future would be better than the present, the only clear exception being a period in 1978-79 (Lipset and Schneider, 1983, p. 136).

References

Colasanto, Diane and Linda DeStefano. "Public Image of TV Evangelists Deteriorates." Gallup Report 288 (1989): 16-21.

Davis, James Allan and Tom W. Smith. General Social Surveys, 1972-1987: Cumulative Codebook. Chicago: National Opinion Research Center, 1987. Annual. Previous years as cited.

Elam, Stanley M. and Alec M. Gallup. "The 21st Annual Gallup Poll of the Public's Attitudes Toward the Public Schools." Gallup Report 288 (1989): 31-43.

Gallup, Alec M. "The 18th Annual Gallup Poll of the Public's Attitudes Toward the Public Schools." Gallup Report 252 (1986): 11-26.

Gallup Report 279 (1988): 30.

Harris, Louis. "Confidence in Institutions Down, Led by Sharp Decline in Trust in White House." The Harris Poll 37 (1988): 1-2.

Lipset, Seymour Martin and William Schneider. The Confidence Gap: Business, Labor, and Government in the Public Mind. New York: Free Press, 1983.

Table 1. CONFIDENCE IN SELECTED NATIONAL INSTITUTIONS: PERSONS
          EXPRESSING "A GREAT DEAL OF CONFIDENCE" IN "THE PEOPLE
          IN CHARGE OF RUNNING" SPECIFIC INSTITUTIONS, HARRIS
          SURVEYS, 1971-1988

Year	Law Firms	Major Companies	Organ. Relig.	Education	Exec. Branch, Fed. Govt.	Org. Labor
1971	--%	27%	27%	37%	23%	14%
1972	--	27	30	33	27	15
1973	24	29	36	44	19	20
1974	18	21	32	40	28	18
1975	16	19	32	36	13	14
1976	12	16	24	31	11	10
1977	14	10	29	37	23	14
1978	18	22	34	41	14	15
1980	13	16	22	36	17	14
1982	--	18	20	30	--	8
1983	12	18	22	36	--	10
1984	17	19	24	40	--	12
1986	14	16	22	34	18	11
1987	15	21	16	36	19	11
1988	13	19	17	34	16	13

Year	Press	Medicine	TV News	Supreme Court	White House	Congress	Military
1971	18%	61%	--%	23%	--	19%	27%
1972	18	48	--	28	--	21	35
1973	30	57	41	33	18	--	40
1974	25	50	31	40	28	18	33
1975	26	43	35	28	--	13	24
1976	20	42	28	22	11	9	23
1977	18	43	28	29	31	17	27
1978	23	42	35	29	14	10	29
1980	19	34	29	27	18	18	28
1982	14	32	24	25	20	13	31
1983	19	35	24	33	23	20	35
1984	18	43	28	35	42	28	45
1986	16	33	27	32	19	21	36
1987	19	36	29	30	23	20	35
1988	18	40	28	32	15	15	33

SOURCE: Based on Harris, 1988, p. 2.

Table 2. CONFIDENCE IN SELECTED NATIONAL INSTITUTIONS: PERSONS
          EXPRESSING "A GREAT DEAL" OR "QUITE A LOT" OF
          CONFIDENCE IN AMERICAN INSTITUTIONS, GALLUP POLLS,
          1973-1989

Year	Banks	Big Business	Organized Religion	Public Schools	Organized Labor
1973	--%	26%	66%	58%	30%
1975	--	34	68	--	38
1977	--	33	64	54	39
1979	60	32	65	53	36
1981	46	20	64	42	28
1983	51	28	62	39	26
1984	51	29	64	47	30
1985	51	31	66	48	28
1986	49	28	57	49	29
1987	51	--	61	50	26
1988	49	25	59	49	26
1989	42	--	52	43	--

Year	Newspapers	TV	Supreme Court	Congress	Military
1973	39	37	44	42	--
1975	--	--	49	40	58
1977	--	--	46	40	57
1979	51	38	45	34	54
1981	35	25	46	29	50
1983	38	25	42	28	53
1984	34	25	51	29	58
1985	35	29	56	39	61
1986	37	27	54	41	63
1987	31	28	52	--	61
1988	36	27	56	35	58
1989	--	--	46	32	63

SOURCE: Based on Colasanto and DeStefano, 1989, p. 21.

Table 3.   CONFIDENCE IN SELECTED NATIONAL INSTITUTIONS: PERSONS
EXPRESSING "A GREAT DEAL OF CONFIDENCE" IN "THE PEOPLE
RUNNING THESE INSTITUTIONS,"* 1973-87

Year	Sample Size	Banks, Financ. Instit.	Major Companies	Organ. Religion	Education	Exec. Branch, Fed. Govt.	Labor
1973	(1504)	--%	29%	35%	37%	29%	15%
1974	(1484)	--	31	44	49	14	18
1975	(1490)	32	19	24	31	13	10
1976	(1499)	39	22	30	37	13	12
1977	(1530)	42	27	40	41	28	15
1978	(1532)	33	22	31	28	12	11
1980	(1468)	32	27	35	30	12	15
1982	(1506)	27	23	32	33	19	12
1983	(1599)	24	24	28	29	13	8
1984	(989)**	31	30	31	28	18	8
1986	(1470)	21	24	25	28	21	8
1987	(1466)	27	30	29	35	18	10

Year	Press	Medicine	TV	Supreme Court	Scient. Comm.	Congress	Military
1973	23	54	18	31	37	23	32
1974	26	60	23	33	45	17	40
1975	24	50	18	31	38	13	35
1976	28	54	19	35	43	14	39
1977	25	51	17	35	41	19	36
1978	20	46	14	28	36	13	29
1980	22	52	16	25	41	9	28
1982	18	45	14	30	38	13	31
1983	13	51	12	28	41	10	29
1984	17	50	13	33	44	12	36
1986	18	46	15	30	39	16	31
1987	18	52	12	36	45	16	34

* The question read, "I am going to name some institutions in this
country. As far as the <u>people running</u> these institutions are
concerned, would you say that you have a great deal of confidence,
only some confidence, or hardly any confidence at all in them?"

Table 3. CONFIDENCE IN SELECTED NATIONAL INSTITUTIONS: PERSONS
         EXPRESSING "A GREAT DEAL OF CONFIDENCE" IN "THE PEOPLE
         RUNNING THESE INSTITUTIONS,"* 1973-88 (continued)

** A variant 7-point response format was used with one-third of the
sample in 1984, and that third is not included here. All of the
data in the above table derive from the three-point response
format: "A great deal of confidence," "only some confidence," and
"hardly any confidence at all."

SOURCE: Based on Davis and Smith, 1982, pp. 111-114; 1987, pp. 181-
    184.

Some indexes of consumer confidence are leading indicators of national economic trends. Consumer confidence has been high since about 1983, following historic lows in the 1970s. In the late 1980s personal financial optimism was higher than it had been since pollsters began tracking it, but people were much less optimistic about the national economy, although more hopeful than in the gloomy 1970s. Other trends include a continuing decline in the size of the minority who say that poverty can be eradicated and ambivalence about the role of the federal government. While there is continuing support for federal efforts to solve social problems, there is majority agreement that taxes are too high, that the government wastes too much money, that it serves "big interests" rather than all the people, and that it cannot be trusted to "do what is right." In the 1980s, rates of negativism on all of these indicators were lower than during the nation's "crisis of confidence" in the 1970s, but far higher than in the 1960s. Support for the nationalization of essential industries has declined. The public supports the American "free enterprise" system, but is more negative than before about big business. A majority continues to assert that hard work is the most important factor in "getting ahead."

Knowledge and Attitudes about the Economy

Changes in consumer attitudes, most notably variation in expectations for the future and appraisals of current conditions, have been shown to predict changes in the national economy. The oldest summary measure of trends in consumer attitudes, the University of Michigan's Index of Consumer Sentiment, was developed in 1952 as a composite of items on personal finances and business conditions that had been included in periodic consumer surveys since the 1940s. Substantial declines in the Index of Consumer Sentiment have foreshadowed every recessionary period since the mid-1950s, and changes in the Index are closely correlated with such consumer behaviors as total home sales and automobile purchases (Curtin, 1982, pp. 341-348). A similar measure, the Conference Board's Consumer Expectations Index, has since its inception in 1967 demonstrated "an almost uncanny capacity . . . to foretell short-term shifts in the nation's economic growth rate" (Linden, 1982, p. 355).

These indexes highlight change rather than the absolute level of consumer sentiment at any given time (Curtin, 1982, pp. 342-343). Both are reported as summary values and are not directly interpretable except as composite measures of consumer confidence. The trends apparent in the charting of index values over the years--manifest in both indexes after the mid-1960s--are rising consumer optimism in the mid-1950s followed by sharp decline in 1957-58; a recovery nearly to the former level of optimism followed by periodic ups and downs until the late 1960s; and then the historic decline into the 1970s, a decade of "gloom of stunning proportions" (Converse, et al., 1980, p. 285) despite sizable temporary upswings in consumer optimism in 1971 and 1975-76. The downward trend of the 1970s was reversed in the early Reagan years; consumer confidence rose to levels reminiscent of the mid-1950s and early 1960s, and remained high through the decade ("Consumer Confidence," 1988, pp. 38-39).

Among the components of the Index of Consumer Sentiment are items on current personal financial status as compared to last year and next year. Trends in public response to these items are charted in Table 1. For present outlook as compared to last year, at least four distinct periods may be distinguished. In the first, 1947-1952, respondents were almost evenly divided among the three options: better off than a year ago, about the same, and worse off. To the degree that the distribution was unbalanced, it was the "worse off" who predominated. The second period, 1953-1973, was a time of relative success and stability: the percentage who were better off than the previous year rose slightly, and those who experienced stability, being neither better nor worse off than before, increased to almost half of the population. There was a corresponding decline, to about 20%, in the percentage who were worse off than last year.

The third period, roughly 1974-1983, saw an increase in the percentage worse off. For seven of these ten years, decline, rather than stability or improvement, was the most common pattern, and the fraction reporting no change dropped back to between one-fourth and one-third. Finally, there is the 1984-1989 "recovery" period, characterized by the largest proportions ever--consistently over 40% and sometimes approaching 50%--of persons who said they were better off now than they were a year ago. However, unlike the prosperous years of the 1950s and 1960s, in the 1980s there was not much reduction in the number of persons saying they were worse off than last year. While almost half of the population reported economic improvement, another large segment--between one-fourth and one-third--reported financial decline.

Table 1 also shows trends in economic optimism and pessimism as manifest in statements about whether things will be better, the same, or worse in the coming year. Levels of optimism about personal finances were relatively constant, running between 33% and 39%, until the mid-1970s. The typical response, usually accounting for just under half of the population, was to expect no change; there were few pessimists, usually less than 10%. The dramatic change of the mid-1970s was that the number of pessimists sharply increased, reaching a peak of 31% in 1980, and the number expecting no change dropped accordingly. A third pattern emerged in the mid-1980s: optimism reached an historic high, and pessimism declined slightly, such that a majority of respondents looked forward to economic improvement in the coming year, and the expectation of no change became almost as atypical as the expectation of decline. As the United States faced the 1990s, almost 60% of its people anticipated a better financial situation in the coming year.

Trends in the public view of the condition of the U.S. economy are summarized in Table 2. Note the high optimism between 1947 and 1970: only once, in 1958, did the percentage of people expecting "bad times" in the coming year exceed those expecting "good times," and most of the time a majority of the population--sometimes as much as three-fourths--was optimistic. The optimism weakened in the late 1960s; by 1970 those expecting bad times outnumbered the optimists, a condition that continued throughout much of the decade. Not until the mid-1980s did the pessimism dissipate to the degree that those anticipating an improving national economy outnumbered those expecting further deterioration. Even then, the level of public confidence in the national economy did not match that of the 1950s and 1960s.

The economic recession of the late 1970s and the recovery in the 1980s is mirrored in responses to questions on worry about family finances. In 1974, one-fourth of the population said they worried most or all of the time about making enough money to pay the bills. By 1984, over one-third worried that much. After that, things got better and the number of frequent or constant worriers gradually declined to its earlier level of one-fourth, with half that number reporting constant worry about making ends meet. There is also a long-term trend toward greater acceptance of the inevitability of poverty. In 1937, 14% said they thought poverty in the U.S. would be eliminated. In 1989, only 6% thought so (Table 3).

Attitudes about who is ultimately responsible for poverty or achievement have not changed much in the past two decades. About one-third of the people say that the poor are poor because of a lack of effort on their part, another third blame circumstances, and the remainder blame both circumstances and lack of effort. When it comes to explaining success, the public favors individualism: about 67% affirm that hard work is the key to getting ahead, and an additional 20-25% say that both luck and hard work are necessary. These rates have not changed significantly since 1973 (Table 4).

When the issue is framed in terms of who should do something about an economic problem, rather than who is responsible for creating it, a majority favors government action. Although the percentage affirming that the federal government should "do everything possible to improve the standard of living of all poor Americans" dropped 10% between 1975 and 1988, there was no corresponding increase in the percentage who said that poverty was not the government's problem and that it should do nothing. Instead, the percentage who were ambivalent and said they supported both individual responsibility and government action, increased, and with it, overall support for ameliorative action (see Table 5). Support for federal action is even stronger with respect to health care, where the only trend is a slight decrease in the percentage who say that the federal government should stay out of health care. On the other side, since 1975 about half of the people have agreed that the government should help pay for doctor and hospital bills, and another third favor both government action and individual responsibility.

Support for increased federal efforts to solve other social problems shows the same general pattern: a slight decline in those calling explicitly for increased federal efforts and a corresponding increase among those who favor both governmental and private action (Table 5). In summary, it appears that 1) about three-fourths of the population favors increased governmental involvement in combating poverty and other social problems, and 2) support for federal action in these matters held fairly stable over the period 1975-1988.

Turning to what the government is doing, rather than ideas about what it ought to do, reveals a different pattern of popular support (Table 6). Since 1958 there has been a very substantial decline in public respect for government. The low point of public confidence occurred in the now-familiar "trough" of the late 1970s and early 1980s, but the Reagan years did not restore public confidence to its former levels (see Chapter 11.2 above; Lipset and Schneider, 1983; and Lipset, 1985).

In the late 1950s and early 1960s, three-fourths of the public said that most of the time they could "trust the government in Washington to do what is right." By 1980, only 25% were that positive. Although the trajectory reversed during the Reagan years, by 1987 only 40% said that most of the time the government did what was right. Also, citizens used to have confidence in how the government spent their taxes: not until the mid-1960s did a majority agree that "people in the government waste a lot of money we pay in taxes." The percentage who thought that "a lot" of tax money was wasted peaked at 80% in 1980, and most people still define the government that way: in 1987, two-thirds of the people agreed that "when something is run by the government it is usually inefficient and wasteful."

The idea that the government serves special interests rather than the common good has also grown (see Table 6). Until 1970, a majority agreed that the government served everyone.

Ever since, most people have viewed the government as a tool of "big interests," with the most consensus on that point appearing in 1980 (77%). As with many other economy-related attitudes, things improved somewhat over the 1980s, but perception of government for the few has persisted: in 1985, 60% agreed that the government served big interests rather than all the people.

Throughout the 1980s, but especially at the end of the decade, popular opinion was ambivalent: people were highly optimistic about their own financial situation, but cynical about government and not very confident in the national economy. In the late 1970s, during the national "crisis of confidence," Everett Ladd (1979, p. 21) pointed to a sharp disparity between people's satisfaction with their personal lives and their satisfaction with national affairs:

This tension between feelings of public malaise and private well-being remains a most striking feature of U.S. opinion. Should the sense of personal welfare fade, American politics would almost certainly become markedly more angry and contentious, for it is personal optimism which has taken the edge off palpable public sector pessimism.

A decade later, the widespread personal optimism and the sense of public malaise both remained. Although the malaise was not as pervasive as it had been, the ambivalence continued. Ladd now identified it as an "essential property" of American public opinion ("Ten Years of Public Opinion," 1988, p. 21) and characterized "the sharp split between people's perceptions of the record of the economy at large and what they see as their own place in it as the striking feature of contemporary public opinion (Ladd, 1988, p. 28).

Entrepreneurship and Profit

The decline in confidence in American institutions that characterized the late 1970s and early 1980s coincided with substantial changes in the international context of the American economy. Public confidence in personal financial improvement was not matched by high confidence in the American economy as a whole. In 1976, 69% of the population agreed that "the American free enterprise system is the most efficient economically the world has ever known" (Lipset and Schneider, 1983, p. 286). Over the next decade, that confidence dissipated; by 1988, only 35% still thought the U.S. economy was "number one," and most of these agreed that "other nations are catching up with us very quickly" ("Nation's Economic Picture," 1988, p. 27).

A deterioration of the image of American business was also apparent in attitudes about profits. Throughout the 1960s and the early 1970s, most people agreed that American business institutions as a whole made "a reasonable profit." After 1970, that generally positive attitude was replaced by a majority definition that business profits were too high. In 1979, 70% of those questioned agreed that "when the economy goes down, business keeps its profits high and cuts jobs and wages" ("Losses from Profits," 1980, p. 27). The heightened negativism about business continued through the 1980s. In 1987, while agreeing that "good profits" were essential to a strong economy, 64% disagreed that "business profits are distributed fairly," and only 42% said they were optimistic about "the soundness of our economic system over the long run" ("Opinion Roundup," 1988, pp. 22, 24).

Although attitudes about the American economy are more negative than in the 1950s and 1960s, business is held in higher esteem than government. A 1959-1983 Gallup poll series in which three major institutions--business, labor, and government--are compared as to which "will be the biggest threat to the country in the future" shows big government replacing big labor as the chief threat. By 1983, 51% of those questioned identified government as the major threat, compared to 19% for business and 18% for labor (Gallup, 1984, p. 129). Another affirmation of business, as opposed to government, shows up in attitudes about the nationalization of essential industries (Table 7). In the 1930s, about half of the public said they opposed nationalization. There is growing opposition to public ownership over the next half century; in the 1970s, three-fourths of the people opposed nationalization; by the 1980s, opposition rates ran as high as 90%.

References

Colasanto, Diane. "Bush Presidency Tarnished by Growing Public Concern About Poverty." Gallup Report 287 (1989): 2-7.

"Coming Tax Revolt." Public Opinion 1 (1978): 30-31.

"Consumer Confidence." Public Opinion 10 (March/April 1988): 38-39.

Converse, Philip E., Jean D. Dotson, Wendy J. Hoag, and William H. McGee III. American Social Attitudes Data Sourcebook: 1947-1978. Cambridge: Harvard University Press, 1980.

Curtin, Richard T. "Indicators of Consumer Behavior: The University of Michigan Surveys of Consumers." Public Opinion Quarterly 46 (1982): 340-352.

Davis, James Allan. General Social Surveys, 1972-1982: Cumulative Codebook. Chicago: National Opinion Research Center, 1982.

Davis, James Allan and Tom W. Smith. General Social Surveys, 1972-1988: Cumulative Codebook. Chicago: National Opinion Research Center, 1988. Annual. Previous years as cited.

"Dawn of the Ecchh Decade." Public Opinion 3 (February/March 1980): 32-33.

Gallup, George H. The Gallup Poll: Public Opinion 1983. Wilmington, Delaware: Scholarly Resources, 1984.

Gallup Report 276 (1988): 12.

Gallup Report 256-257 (1987): 14.

Ladd, Everett C. "Americans' Split Personality on the Economy." Public Opinion 11 (July/August 1988): 28.

------. "Prospects for '79: Not So Hot." Public Opinion (January/February 1979): 21.

Linden, Fabian. "The Consumer as Forecaster." Public Opinion Quarterly 46 (1982): 353-360.

Lipset, Seymour Martin. "Feeling Better: Measuring the Nation's Confidence." Public Opinion 8 (April/May, 1985): 6-9, 56-58.

Lipset, Seymour Martin and William Schneider. The Confidence Gap: Business, Labor and Government in the Public Mind. New York: Free Press, 1983.

"Losses From Profits." Public Opinion 3 (April/May 1980): 27.

"Nationalization: Unpopular Then and Now." Public Opinion 3 (June/July 1980): 35.

"Nation's Economic Picture: Public Says It's Just So-So." Public Opinion 11 (July/August): 26-30.

"Opinion Roundup." Public Opinion 11 (November/December 1988): 22-24.

------. Public Opinion 8 (August/September 1985): 24-25.

------. Public Opinion 7 (February/March 1984): 26-29.

Shriver, James. "Financial Hardship Affects One-Fourth of American Families." Gallup Report 285 (1989): 19-22.

"Ten Years of Public Opinion." Public Opinion 11 (September/October 1988): 21-30.

Table 1.   PERSONAL FINANCIAL OUTLOOK, NOW VS. PAST YEAR, 1947-
            1989, AND NOW VS. NEXT YEAR, 1953-1989*

	Perceptions of Personal Financial Situation							
	Now. vs. a Year Ago				Now vs. This Time Next Year			
Year	Better Now	Same	Worse Now	Don't Know	Better Next Yr.	Same	Worse Next Yr.	Don't Know
1947	32%	31%	35%	2%	--	--	--	--
1948	30	28	40	2	--	--	--	--
1949	33	35	31	1	--	--	--	--
1950	32	33	34	1	--	--	--	--
1951	33	29	37	1	--	--	--	--
1952	26	41	32	1	--	--	--	--
1953	39	34	27	0	31%	40%	10%	19%
1954	37	32	31	0	31	44	11	14
1955	39	33	28	0	--	--	--	--
1956	33	49	17	1	33	48	6	14
1957	32	43	24	1	33	46	8	13
1958	33	36	31	0	32	47	7	15
1959	38	35	27	0	35	48	5	12
1960	36	38	25	1	41	40	7	12
1961	29	44	26	1	39	41	7	13
1962	34	46	19	1	34	50	5	11
1963	34	44	20	2	33	51	6	10
1964	--	--	--	--	37	46	7	10
1965	37	43	19	1	39	44	7	10
1966	38	44	17	1	38	46	8	8
1967	34	45	19	1	36	46	8	10
1968	34	46	19	1	38	45	8	10
1969	36	44	19	1	38	47	6	9
1970	33	38	27	2	33	43	12	11
1971	31	41	27	1	32	42	10	16
1972	47	34	18	1	38	46	6	10
1973	36	36	27	1	31	46	13	10
1974	29	27	42	1	24	40	24	12
1975	32	33	34	1	32	45	12	11
1976	34	32	33	1	31	47	13	9
1976	33	36	30	1	44	31	12	13
1977	39	28	31	2	47	27	17	9
1978**	34	29	36	1	23	44	26	7
1978	35	31	32	2	38	30	20	12
1979	30	27	41	2	33	27	30	10
1980	30	24	45	1	41	25	31	9

Table 1.   PERSONAL FINANCIAL OUTLOOK, PAST YEAR, 1947-1989, AND
NEXT YEAR, 1953-1989 (Continued)

| | Perceptions of Personal Financial Situation | | | | | | |
| | Now. vs. a Year Ago | | | | Now vs. This Time Next Year | | |
Year	Better Now	Same	Worse Now	Don't Know	Better Next Yr.	Same	Worse Next Yr.	Don't Know
1981	33%	30%	35%	2%	41%	25%	26%	8%
1982	25	26	46	3	37	24	29	10
1983	28	32	39	1	43	28	19	10
1984	40	34	25	1	52	28	12	8
1985	43	26	29	2	52	19	19	10
1986	46	24	30	1	57	17	20	6
1987	43	24	32	1	57	18	17	8
1988	47	28	24	1	63	17	9	11
1989	42	31	25	2	58	20	13	9

* Figures from 1947-1976 (above the solid line) are from the national surveys of the University of Michigan's Survey Research Center; those for 1976-1989 (below the solid line) are from Gallup surveys. The Michigan items are, respectively: "Would you say you people/you and your family are better off or worse off financially now than you were a year ago?" and "(Now looking ahead) do you think that a year from now you people (you and your family) will be better off financially, or worse off, or just about the same as now?" The Gallup items are: "Would you say you are better off now than you were a year ago, or are you financially worse off now?" and "Now looking ahead--do you expect that at this time next year you will be financially better off than now or worse off than now?" Note that on the "next year" item the Gallup polls did not offer "the same" as an alternative, but accepted it when it was volunteered, while the Michigan items offered it as an explicit alternative. This difference in item wording explains the shift from "same" to "better" as the modal response when we shift from the Michigan to the Gallup series for "now vs. this time next year."

** This entry from the Michigan series provides a second point of duplication for comparison between the two series. All other entries below the solid line are from the Gallup series.

SOURCE: Based on Converse, et al., 1980, pp. 235, 248; and Shriver, 1989, p. 20.

Table 2.   PERCEPTIONS OF THE NATION'S ECONOMIC PROSPECTS FOR THE COMING YEAR, 1947-1988: SEGMENTS OF THREE STATISTICAL SERIES

Year	The Coming Year Will Be a Year of						U.S. Economy**		
	Good Times	Bad Times	Other*	Pros-perity	Diffi-culty	Don't Know	Getting Better	Worse	Stay Same
1947	62%	25%	14%	--	--	--	--	--	--
1948	52	28	20	--	--	--	--	--	--
1949	50	26	24	--	--	--	--	--	--
1952	43	16	41	--	--	--	--	--	--
1953	48	19	33	--	--	--	--	--	--
1954	51	31	18	--	--	--	--	--	--
1955	71	14	15	--	--	--	--	--	--
1956	75	5	20	--	--	--	--	--	--
1957	67	11	22	--	--	--	--	--	--
1958	35	45	20	--	--	--	--	--	--
1959	61	19	20	--	--	--	--	--	--
1960	77	8	15	--	--	--	--	--	--
1961	55	19	26	--	--	--	--	--	--
1962	64	10	26	--	--	--	--	--	--
1963	66	9	25	--	--	--	--	--	--
1964	73	10	17	--	--	--	--	--	--
1965	76	7	17	65%	22%	13%	--	--	--
1966	75	10	15	56	33	11	--	--	--
1967	63	16	20	43	45	12	--	--	--
1968	57	18	25	42	47	11	--	--	--
1969	64	13	23	38	48	14	--	--	--
1970	37	39	24	--	--	--	--	--	--
1971	40	30	30	--	--	--	--	--	--
1972	45	27	29	--	--	--	--	--	--
1973	36	37	27	40	47	13	--	--	--
1974	13	68	19	7	85	8	--	--	--
1975	35	41	24	--	--	--	--	--	--
1976	48	27	25	23	70	7	--	--	--
1977	--	--	--	34	54	12	--	--	--
1978	--	--	--	24	52	24	19%	32%	49%
1979	--	--	--	21	69	10	--	--	--
1980	--	--	--	13	79	8	--	--	--
1981	--	--	--	--	--	--	9	55	36
1982	--	--	--	--	--	--	17	51	32
1983	--	--	--	--	--	--	18	46	36
1984	--	--	--	--	--	--	49	19	31
1985	--	--	--	--	--	--	43	12	43
1988	--	--	--	--	--	--	27	22	51

Table 2. NATIONAL ECONOMIC PROSPECTS FOR THE COMING YEAR, 1947-
1988: SEGMENTS OF THREE STATISTICAL SERIES (Continued)

---

* Includes don't know, depends, and pro-con [essentially neutral]
responses.

** For 1978 and 1988, the published source included don't know
responses in the percentage base; they were deleted and the
percentages recalculated to make the figures for these years
directly comparable to the others in this series. See "Nation's
Economic Picture," 1988, p. 27 and "Opinion Roundup," 1985, p. 24.

Note: The items, respectively, are: "Considering the country as a
whole, do you think we will have good times or bad times or what
during the next twelve months?" (Univ. of Michigan); "Which of
these do you think is likely to be true of [named year]: a year of
economic prosperity or a year of economic difficulty?" (Gallup);
"Do you think the nation's economy is: getting better, getting
worse, or staying the same?" (ABC News/Washington Post); and, for
1978 and 1988 in the last series, "A year from now, do you expect
that economic conditions in the country as a whole will be better
than they are at present, or worse, or just about the same as now?"
(Gallup).

SOURCE: Based on Converse, et al., 1980, p. 286; "Nation's Economic
   Picture," 1988, p. 27; "Opinion Roundup," 1985, p. 24; 1984,
   p. 26; "Dawn of the Ecchh Decade," 1980, p. 33.

Table 3. ATTITUDES ABOUT THE ELIMINATION OF POVERTY, 1937-1989,
          AND WORRIES ABOUT MEETING FAMILY FINANCIAL NEEDS, 1974-
          1989

Item	1937	1964	1974	1984	1987	1989
How often do you worry that your total family income will not be enough to meet your family's expenses and bills?						
All of the time	--	--	13%	20%	15%	13%
Most of the time	--	--	12	15	16	13
Some of the time	--	--	36	30	38	35
Almost never	--	--	38	34	30	38
Not sure	--	--	1	1	1	1
Total	--	--	100	100	100	100
Do you think poverty will ever be done away with in this country?"*						
Yes	14%	10%	--	--	--	6
No	86	90	--	--	--	94
Total	100	100	--	--	--	100

* Published percentages have been adjusted to exclude "no
opinion" responses.

SOURCE: Based on <u>Gallup Report</u>, 1987, p. 14; Shriver, 1989, p.
    21; Colasanto, 1989, p. 3.

Table 4. ATTITUDES ABOUT WORK AND SUCCESS: PUBLIC PERCEPTIONS OF
WHETHER LACK OF EFFORT OR CIRCUMSTANCES ARE RESPONSIBLE
FOR POVERTY, AND WHETHER WORK OR LUCK IS MOST IMPORTANT
IN ACHIEVING SUCCESS

Year	More Often to Blame for Poverty*			Most Important in Getting Ahead**		
	Lack of effort	Circum- stances	Both	Hard work	Luck	Both
1964	35%	31%	34%	--	--	--
1967	32	33	34	--	--	--
1973	--	--	--	66%	10%	24%
1974	--	--	--	62	9	29
1976	--	--	--	63	13	24
1977	--	--	--	61	10	28
1980	--	--	--	64	8	28
1982	--	--	--	61	13	26
1984	34	35	32	67	15	18
1985	--	--	--	66	15	19
1987	--	--	--	66	15	19
1988	43	39	18	67	12	21
1989	39	43	18	--	--	--

* Published percentages adjusted to exclude no opinion responses.
The item read, "In your opinion, which is more often to blame if a
person is poor--lack of effort on his part, or circumstances beyond
his control?"

** Percentage base does not include don't know, no answer, or other
neutral responses. The item read, "Some people say that people get
ahead by their own hard work; others say that lucky breaks or help
from other people are more important. Which do you think is most
important?"

SOURCE: Based on Colasanto, 1989, p. 4; <u>Gallup Report</u>, 1988, p.
12; Davis and Smith, 1988, p. 229; 1987, p. 225; 1985, p. 2;
Davis, 1982, p. 152.

Table 5.   AGREEMENT* WITH STATEMENTS ABOUT INDIVIDUAL VS.
GOVERNMENT RESPONSIBILITY FOR POVERTY AND OTHER SOCIAL
PROBLEMS, 1975-1989

Topic	1975	1983	1984	1986	1987	1988
Poverty						
The government in Washington should do everything possible to improve the standard of living of all poor Americans.	39%	32%	28%	31%	29%	30%
It is not the government's responsibility; each person should take care of himself.	23	25	23	22	24	23
Agree with both of the above, or don't know	38	44	49	47	47	47
Total	100	101	100	100	100	100
Health care						
It is the responsibility of the government in Washington to see to it that people have help in paying for doctors and hospital bills.	49	45	43	48	47	48
These matters are not the responsibility of the federal government; people should take care of these things themselves.	21	20	20	18	16	15
Agree with both of the above, or don't know	31	35	38	34	37	37
Total	101	100	101	100	100	100

Table 5.   AGREEMENT* WITH STATEMENTS ABOUT INDIVIDUAL VS.
GOVERNMENT RESPONSIBILITY FOR POVERTY AND OTHER SOCIAL
PROBLEMS, 1975-1989 (Continued)

Topic	1975	1983	1984	1986	1987	1988
Social problems generally						
The government should do even more to solve our country's problems.	36%	23%	27%	25%	28%	28%
The government in Washington is trying to do too many things that should be left to individuals and private businesses.	28	34	31	28	29	27
Agree with both of the above, or don't know	36	43	43	47	43	45
Total	100	100	101	100	100	100

* The opposing statements anchored a five-point scale, with "agree with both" at the mid-point. In computing the above percentages, for each opposing statement persons endorsing the extreme score and the adjoining one--essentially "strongly agree" and "agree"--were combined. Only "no answer" responses are excluded from the percentage base. "Don't know" was offered as an alternative, in the probe: "Where would you place yourself on this scale, or haven't you made up your mind on this?"

SOURCE: Based on Davis and Smith, 1988, pp. 305-306; 1987, pp. 301-302.

Table 6. ATTITUDES ABOUT TAXES AND GOVERNMENT SPENDING*

Year	Government Does Right Always/ Most of the Time	Wastes a Lot of Tax Money	Federal Income Taxes Too High	Government Is Run for the Benefit of — All the People	A Few Big Interests
1957	--	--	61%	--	--
1958	75%	46%	--	82%	18%
1959	--	--	51	--	--
1961	--	--	46	--	--
1962	--	--	47	--	--
1964	77	48	--	69	31
1966	69	--	52	62	38
1967	--	--	58	--	--
1968	63	61	--	56	44
1969	--	--	66	--	--
1970	54	70	--	45	55
1972	54	67	--	42	58
1973	--	--	64	--	--
1974	37	76	69	27	73
1975	--	--	72	--	--
1976	34	76	73	27	73
1977	--	--	69	--	--
1978	30	80	70	26	74
1980	25	--	71	23	77
1982	34	--	73	32	68
1983	46	--	--	38	62
1984	--	--	66	41	59
1985	--	--	65	40	60
1987	40	--	62	--	--
1988	--	66**	58	--	--

* The items are 1) (Government does right): "How much of the time do you think you can trust the government in Washington to do what is right--just about always, most of the time, or only some of the time?"; 2) (Government wastes a lot): "Do you think that people in the government waste a lot of money we pay in taxes, waste some of it, or don't waste very much of it?" 3) (Income tax): 1957-1967, from Gallup: "Do you consider the amount of income tax that you (your husband) have (had) to pay as too high, too low, or about right?"; 1969-1978, from Harris: "From your personal standpoint,

Table 6. ATTITUDES ABOUT TAXES AND GOVERNMENT SPENDING (Continued)

please tell me, for each tax that I read off to you, if you feel it is too high, too low, or about right . . . Federal income tax"; 1980-1988, from General Social Survey (GSS): "Do you consider the amount of federal income tax which you have to pay as too high, about right, or too low?"; 4) (Government run for) "Would you say the government is run by a few big interests looking out for themselves or that it is run for the benefit of all the people?"

** Agreed that "when something is run by the government it is usually inefficient and wasteful."

SOURCE: Based on "Ten Years of Public Opinion," 1988, pp. 22, 30; "Opinion Roundup," 1985, p. 25; 1984, p. 29; "Coming Tax Revolt," 1978, p. 31; Davis, 1982, p. 81; Davis and Smith, 1988, p. 117; 1987, p. 113.

Table 7.   ATTITUDES ABOUT AMERICAN BUSINESS: PRIVATE VS. PUBLIC
           OWNERSHIP OF ESSENTIAL INDUSTRIES, 1936-1985

Opposition to Nationalization of Selected Industries	1936	1953	1974	1979	1985
Railroads*	55%	75%	67%	--	84%
Banks**	50	76	79	--	90
Oil companies	--	--	--	62%	--
Electric power	--	--	70	--	89
Steel producers**	--	--	76	--	90

* 1985, local mass transportation
** 1985, banking and insurance
*** 1985, the steel industry

NOTE: The items differed for each point in this series. The 1936
version was, "Do you favor government ownership of the railroads?
Do you favor government ownership of the banks?" A slight variant
of that wording was used in 1953. The 1974 item read, "Some people
have proposed nationalization . . . Would you favor or oppose
government takeover of any of the following industries?" The 1979
query on oil companies read, "Do you think the oil companies in
this country should be nationalized--that is be taken over and
operated by the government--or do you think that would be a
mistake?" The 1985 item was, "What do you think the government's
role in each of these industries should be?" followed by the name
of the industry and the options "Own it," "control prices and
profits but not own it," and "Neither own it nor control its prices
and profits;" a "can't choose" option was also allowed. The
percentage base in all instances includes "no opinion," "don't
know," and "can't choose."

SOURCE: Based on "Nationalization," 1980, p. 35; Davis and Smith,
        1987, pp. 388-389.

Radicalism was perhaps endemic to the United States political system when substantial proportions of the working class were close to immigrant roots, but during most of the period treated here, such radicalism as there was has been more epidemic (and, at that, relatively low-incidence and transitory) than endemic. The Great Depression left a substantial residue of individuals with a left orientation, both among intellectuals and workers, but these were systematically repressed, especially in the decade following World War II. The "New Left" of the 1960s had some resonance with the intellectual sources of the existing American left, but many other roots as well, leaving the left with essentially no political foothold today.

No extensive documentation is required in order to assert that the U.S. lacks an extensive radical tradition, certainly a Marxian tradition. Indigenous radicalism of the rationalist sort was present and perhaps widespread in the late eighteenth and early nineteenth centuries, but lost ground thereafter in the increasingly corporate society, especially as the gradual decline of the hand trades eroded the occupational basis for such a position. By the late nineteenth century, the main locus for radicalism in the American population was among immigrants and their children; American socialism was exceptionally gradualist by international standards; and even the American Communist Party in the early twentieth century had a cast that was in keeping with the widespread uninterest in truly radical solutions in this country. By the 1920s, aided by a vigorous repression during and especially after the conclusion of World War I, American anarcho-syndicalism and communism were both reduced to small fragments, hardly relevant to the American political system and labor movement as then constituted.

The Great Depression allowed the left to make significant inroads into the intellectual segment of the American population, and to a lesser extent into the popular arts and the labor movement, but the 1939 Hitler-Stalin pact provided an occasion for a powerful revulsion on the American left from international communism, and powerful government repression, common to both Democrats and Republicans although benefiting mainly the latter, had by the 1950s illegalized communism, driven former communists and left sympathizers out of positions of influence in government, the arts, universities, and the professions, and made even a professed interest in Marx or any curiosity about communism anathema.

At the height of the Cold War repression of domestic communism, in 1954, a public opinion poll included an item that asked whether an admitted communist should be permitted to make a public speech in the community, or should be refused (Smith, 1980; Davis and Smith, 1986). So successful was the repression of domestic communism by this time that only slightly in excess of one in four Americans (including those who expressed no opinion) would even permit the speech to be made. The civil libertarian position on this item fared markedly better after the "red scare" period, reaching almost 60% by 1973, but has not more recently continued the trend upward, reflecting instead annual concerns and alarums. Regularly, a small majority would permit the speech; a sizable minority would ban it. One should probably read this as a measure of the extent of popular commitment to civil liberties: a parallel question, introduced in the late 1970s and referring to an avowed militarist who would eliminate free elections, produced approximately the same degree of support for a political deviant's right to make a public speech.

More relevant, perhaps, is a question first asked in 1974, requesting respondents to think "about all the different kinds of governments in the world today," and presenting a rating scale for communism which included "it's a good form of government" and "it's all right for some countries" (Table 1). The modal response was always "it's the worst kind [of government] of all," the first rating presented, and always at least half of the respondents agreed with that position. The remaining choice was "bad, but no worse than some others." Americans very rarely think that communism is a good form of government, to judge from this question (or to judge from radical electoral experience, discussed above). Indeed, only about one in five would even assent to the idea that communism is a good form of government for some countries. Note that the high-point comes in the years following Nixon's opening to China.

Table 2 offers an estimate of the trend in such public interest in Marx and Marxism as is reflected in the numbers of books published on the subject in successive five-year periods that were reviewed in one or more of the periodicals indexed in Book Review Index, an annual publication that provides categorized references (and often brief gists).

At the outset we must note some difficulties with the measure. The Book Review Index is somewhat scholarly, including newspapers, as well as most of the general interest and intellectual journals, and many of the only somewhat specialized academic quarterlies. The number of journals indexed grew over the period, but this definitely did not explain the observed patterns for books published on Marx. Probably the most unfortunate omission in the Index, given the question here, is most of the left and labor press, such as it is. Besides problems of omission, a given book may not be reviewed for two, or even three years after publication. (To prevent double counting of a different kind, while still allowing an efficient procedure, we counted only books on "Marx," but not on "Marxism," a considerably smaller number of entries that typically but not invariably was subsumed under the "Marx" entry).

Despite the crudeness of the indicator of public interest in Marxism, the findings seem unambiguous enough to justify the approximation. It is apparent that mainstream American appetites for information on Marx were extremely limited, indeed almost nonexistent, even before the "official" onset of the Cold War. No book was found in this list for the two years preceding Yalta, for instance. The state of near-zero interest continued through the 1950s, but began to rise steadily in the early 1960s, achieving something of a plateau of substantial interest by the end of that decade that has not abated since. (As chance would have it, an adjacent entry is, charmingly, "Mary, Virgin." we did not conduct a formal count of Mary's entries, but the eye did wander, and noted that for most of the 1946-1965 period, her count exceeded that for "Marx, Karl.") Casual observation, however, would suggest that a large portion of the increased interest in Marxist matters in the 1970s and 1980s is lodged in the academic community, and somewhat removed from the national political scene.

An American city or two, from time to time, has historically (and currently) had socialist administrations, and there have been a few long-term Socialist Congressmen (there is none now [1987]), but in the American context, socialism--especially municipal socialism--has hardly been "radical." The leading argument of municipal socialists in the U.S. has tended to be a kind of public-sector managerial responsibility. This differs from the focus of the national Socialist Party, but there is no basis for denoting the national party "radical," either. So, on the electoral level, as close as we can come to examining the trend of "radical" strength is the proportion of voters selecting the candidates of the Communist Party, the Socialist Workers Party (Trotskyite), or the

Socialist Labor Party (descended from the American Marxist Daniel de Leon). Such votes are exceptionally rare, reaching a peak of two-tenths of one percent in 1972 and 1976, years of remarkable electoral strength for these radical parties. Table 3, below, summarizes trends in the presidential votes for these three parties on a per-million basis.

The trend reflects the broader evolution of Cold War attitudes in the American public as a whole. By 1948, Communists had been purged and essentially forced underground, but there was still a modest residual strength on the left, remaining from the older American tradition. This tradition was further dissipated during the 1950s, partly due to the McCarthy excesses. A modest resurgence can be seen in the 1960 returns. Support for radical candidates increased throughout the 1960s, and especially after 1968, which was, in the U.S. as in Europe, a year of political upheaval. The left took some courage in those years, but the main strength of the 1968 revolt was in the "new Left," and the radical parties are the "old Left" parties. Their "boom," already noted, faded with Jimmy Carter's centrism and redirection of concern to the kind of moral issues not so easily displayed on a European-style Left-Right continuum, so that by 1984--even as various forms of dissent or at any rate non-engagement with the major, centrist, parties grew--electoral radicalism was markedly in retreat. (It is probably fair to say that the "commonsense" reading of the relative strength of the "liberal" wing within the Democratic Party was roughly correlated with the electoral strength of these three radical parties, added together).

There are virtually no radical national labor unions in the U.S., and very few radical locals, and there is no way of attributing any meaningful proportion of labor activism or unrest to the left. This situation was somewhat less true before the purging of Communists from most mainstream labor unions shortly after World War II, but only somewhat. Nor can one discriminate between popular manifestations of the far left and all others--if indeed one can count popular manifestations at all.

References

Congressional Quarterly Weekly Report 47 (January 21, 1989), p. 139.

Davis, James Allan and Tom W. Smith. General Social Surveys, 1972-1986: Cumulative Codebook. Chicago: National Opinion Research Center, 1986.

Scammon, Richard A. and Alice V. McGillvray, comp. and eds., America Votes 17: 1986. Washington, D.C.: Congressional Quarterly, 1987.

Smith, Tom W. A Compendium of Trends on General Social Survey Questions (NORC Report No. 129). Chicago: National Opinion Research Center, 1980.

Table 1. PROPORTION AGREEING THAT COMMUNISM IS A "GOOD" OR "SOMETIMES GOOD" KIND OF GOVERNMENT, 1974-1985

Year	Good	Sometimes good
1974	3%	19%
1976	1	20
1977	1	20
1984	2	11
1985	1	13

SOURCE: Based on Davis and Smith, 1986, p. 122.

Table 2. NUMBER OF DIFFERENT BOOKS ON MARX NOTED IN BOOK REVIEW INDEX, FIVE-YEAR INTERVALS, 1946-85

Years	Books on Marx, Karl
1946-1950	3
1951-1955	2
1956-1960	2
1961-1965	11
1966-1970	27
1971-1975	37
1976-1980	39
1981-1985	44

SOURCE: Based on Book Review Index; see discussion in text.

Table 3.   VOTES FOR "FAR LEFT" CANDIDATES IN PRESIDENTIAL
           ELECTIONS, 1948-1988

| Year | Votes per Million Cast for All Candidates | | |
	Socialist	Socialist Labor	Communist Worker
1948	599	279	--
1952	492	168	--
1956	719	126	--
1960	693	586	--
1964	642	536	--
1968	719	566	15
1972	693	858	329
1976	118	1120	724
1980	--	572	526
1984	--	267	393
1988	--	170	--

SOURCE: Based on Scammon and McGillvray, 1987, pp. 20-40;
          Congressional Quarterly Weekly Report, 1989, p. 139.

Ninety-five percent of Americans say they believe in God, and about three-fourths accept traditional Christian beliefs on the divinity of Jesus, the reality of immortality, and heaven. Most are convinced that religion has practical utility in day-to-day living, and over half affirm that it is very important in their own lives. About one-third are evangelical, or "born again" Christians. None of these rates of belief have changed much over the past three decades. Public perceptions of the influence of religion in American life indicate a decline of religious influence in the late 1960s and 1970s, and a resurgence in the 1980s. A concomitant of that resurgence was an apparent increase in the visibility and political influence of evangelicals and other conservative Christians. American believers seem more committed to a culture of religious individualism, and less to institutional religion, than formerly.

About 95% of Americans say they believe in God, and over three-fourths are literal Christians who say they believe in the divinity of Jesus. About three-fourths of respondents in public polls say they believe in life after death, slightly fewer in "heaven," and just over half in "hell." These rates of reported belief have remained essentially stable for at least four decades (Tables 1 and 2).

Accompanying these relatively high levels of belief is a majority conviction that religion has practical utility in day-to-day living. Almost two-thirds agree that religion "can answer all or most of today's problems," and over half say that religion is very important in their personal life. These rates also manifest stability since the mid-1970s or so (Table 3). Before that, in the 1950s and early 1950s, the personal and social salience attributed to religion was somewhat higher.

Trends in the perceived direction of change in the influence of religion in the nation are much more volatile, and may be indexed by variations in the percent of the population agreeing that religion is gaining (or losing) influence in society. The proportion affirming that its influence was increasing plummeted from 69% to 14% during the 1960s, then rebounded to the 31-38% range during the 1970s, and continued its recovery, albeit with some reversals, in the 1980s. By 1986, almost half of the adult population agreed that the influence of religion in American society was increasing (Table 3). Although we do not know the exact correspondence between public perceptions of the influence of religion and its "objective" influence, it seems appropriate to conclude--partly because there are many other indicators suggesting the same trend--that the influence of religion in the U.S. did decline during the 1960s and the early 1970s, and that much, if not most, of its former influence had been recovered by the mid-1980s.

In the 1970s, a segment of American Protestantism that for some time had been relatively underrepresented in the national political arena--"born again" Christians of various Baptist, Pentecostal, and other Biblical literalist, evangelizing denominations--began to participate successfully in national, interest-group politics. Their ideological conservatism in social and economic matters, their appeals to traditional moral values and family roles, and their emphasis on local rather than central authority, placed them in conflict with many of the goals of the liberal establishment and the left wings of both political parties. By some, the evangelicals' successful entry into national politics and their skillful use of the media were seen as pressing social problems (cf. Hadden and Swann, 1981).

The rather diffuse aggregate of more-or-less conservative Americans whose values were assumed to be congruent with most of the positions of the political right, a disorganized and beleaguered minority during the preceding anti-establishment era--was labeled the "moral majority." At its core were the evangelicals, the born-again Christians who had "committed themselves to Jesus" and believed in a literal interpretation of the Bible. Early in the 1970s, national polls began counting evangelicals, and before the decade was over, one of them was elected President.

About one-third of the population consider themselves "born-again" Christians. A slightly larger percentage say they interpret the Bible literally, and about half say they have tried to teach others to believe in Christ. If an evangelical is one who meets all three criteria, then about one-fifth of the population is evangelical (Table 4). Whichever definition one uses, the representation of evangelicals in the population seems to have remained constant since the mid-1970s (see also Briggs, 1987).

The use of the mass media, especially television, in religious education and evangelizing has vastly increased. Indeed, the evangelical movement is often identified with television evangelism. Over the 1980s the proportion of occasional viewers of religious programming increased slightly, to about half of the total population; about 20% view religious programs at least weekly, and about 5% contribute money to television evangelists (Table 5). Public scandals involving television evangelists eroded their public image during the 1980s (between 1980 and 1989, the percent of the public saying television evangelists were honest dropped from 53% to 23%, and the percent saying they were sincere declined from 56% to 26%). Even so, "the sharp decline in the public's view of television evangelists . . . is not reflected in lower evaluations of organized religion as a whole, nor in any change in the role religion plays in adults' lives" (Colasanto and DeStefano, 1989, p. 17).

A concomitant of the anti-establishment mood of the 1960s was the emergence of new sects ("new organizations reviving an old religion"), renewed vitality among some established sects, and the appearance of numerous cults ("religious movements that represent a new or different religious tradition"). Among the most visible of the cults have been the Hare Krishna movement, the Unification Church, and Scientology, but there have been literally hundreds, many of them small and transitory. The efflorescence of cults and sects in the last quarter century may be viewed as another evidence of the vitality of American religious life, rather than its decline (Stark, 1987, pp. 363-364). Although an established part of the American religious scene, members of cults make up a very small proportion of the total population (see Stark and Bainbridge, 1985).

Quasi-religious beliefs such as astrology still are common in the U.S., and received considerable notoriety during the last years of the Reagan administration when it became known that the President's wife had consulted astrologers. However, belief in astrology has declined significantly since the late 1970s, when about one-fourth of respondents in a national poll (22% in 1976, 29% in 1978) said they believed in astrology. In 1988, only 12% said they did (Gallup Report, 1988, p. 7).

"The religious quests of the countercultural years," say Roof and McKinney (1987, p. 51) in an assessment of change in contemporary American religion, "led to many new spiritual forms, some authoritarian and others more expressive, but all offering moral and religious meaning." The pursuit of self-fulfillment among the youth of the 1960s spread, they suggest, to mainstream America, first to the middle-class and then to "more diverse, more alienated sectors of the society," creating a climate that yielded, in the 1980s, "a more expressive individualism" in religious life (p. 48). This individualism, or "new voluntarism," they suggest, will continue to foster new religious forms and tolerance for increased diversity in religious life:

> The forces of modernity leading to ever-greater pluralism and privatization of religious and moral life show few signs of abating, and those religious traditions most capable of providing an integrated cultural ethic are themselves lacking in the vision and vigor to do so (Roof and McKinney, 1987, p.228).

George Gallup, Jr., summarizing trends in American religion over the past half century, pointed to several major shifts in the "focus" of religious interest:

> In the 1950's there was a tendency to view religion as supportive of the American way of life; in the 1960's, an anti-establishment mood coupled with an emphasis on social activism; in the 1970's, a retreat from activism to individualism and a concentration on personal spirituality; and finally, in the 1980's, a renewed search for spiritual moorings, as well as evidence of "new activism" on the part of the leadership of churches, speaking out on issues such as church and state and abortion (Gallup, 1985, p. 4)

Gallup also enumerated several of the prominent trends presently shaping American religious life, including a proliferation of religious groups, growth in independent (local control) churches, a blurring of boundaries between various faiths and denominations, a continued influence of charismatics and Pentecostals "being felt across denominational lines," a growing interest in interdenominational and interfaith dialogue, a continued decline in the growth of the largest Protestant denominations, continued growth in the evangelical churches, a "rediscovery of the small group as a method for nurturing and multiplying believers," and a "new activism" in the political sphere as various Christian groups react to the "common perception . . . that the civil authorities no longer offer sufficient support for their beliefs and moral standards" (Gallup, 1985, pp. 13-14).

References

Briggs, Kenneth A. "Evangelicals in America." Gallup Report 259 (1987): 3-5.

Colasanto, Diane and Linda DeStefano. "Public Image of TV Evangelists Deteriorates." Gallup Report 288 (1989): 16-21.

Davis, James Allan and Tom W. Smith. General Social Surveys, 1972-1988: Cumulative Codebook. Chicago: National Opinion Research Center, 1988. Annual. Previous years as cited.

Gallup, George, Jr. "50 Years of Gallup Surveys on Religion." Gallup Report 236 (1985): 4-14.

------. Gallup Report 272 (1988).

------. "Religion in America." Gallup Report 259 (1987).

------. "Religion in America: 50 Years: 1935-1985." Gallup Report 236 (1985).

Hadden, Jeffrey K. and Charles E. Swann. Prime Time Preachers: The Rising Power of Tele-Evangelism. Reading, MA: Addison-Wesley, 1981.

Religion in America 1982. Princeton, NJ: Princeton Religion Research Center, 1982.

Roof, Wade Clark and William McKinney. American Mainline Religion: Its Changing Shape and Future. New Brunswick, NJ: Rutgers University Press, 1987.

Stark, Rodney. Sociology, 2nd ed. Belmont, CA: Wadsworth, 1987.

Stark, Rodney and William Sims Bainbridge. The Future of Religion: Secularization, Revival, and Cult Formation. Berkeley: University of California Press, 1985.

The Unchurched American . . . 10 Years Later. Princeton, NJ: Princeton Religion Research Center, 1988.

Table 1.   BELIEFS ABOUT GOD AND JESUS CHRIST,* 1952-1986

	Belief in God or in a	Percent Affirming Jesus Was		
Year	Universal Spirit	God or Son of God	Just a Leader	Other/ Don't Know
1947	94%	--	--	--
1952	99	77%	12%	11%
1959	97	--	--	--
1965	97	75	14	11
1969	98	--	--	--
1975	94	--	--	--
1978	--	78	13	9
1981	95	--	--	--
1983	--	76	11	13
1986	94	--	--	--
1988	--	84	9	7

* The question about Jesus was, "Do you believe that Jesus Christ ever actually lived? Do you think he was God, or just another leader like Mohammed or Buddha?"

SOURCE: Based on "Religion in America," 1987, pp. 51-53; The Unchurched American, 1988, p. 25.

Table 2.   RELIGIOUS BELIEFS: LIFE AFTER DEATH, HEAVEN, AND HELL,
           1944-1988

Year	Percent Affirming Belief* In		
	Life After Death	Heaven	Hell
1944	76%	--	--
1948	68	--	--
1952	77	72%	58%
1957	74	--	--
1960	74	--	--
1961	74	--	--
1965	75	68	54
1968	73	--	--
1975	69	--	--
1978	71	--	--
1980	67	71	53
1981	71	--	--
1983	68	--	--
1984	73	--	--
1986	76	--	--
1987	72	--	--
1988	74	--	--

* The items were, "Do you believe there is life after death?" or,
in 1981, "Which, if any, of the following do you believe in? . . .
life after death?"

SOURCE: Based on "Religion in America," 1987, pp. 54-55; The
    Unchurched American, 1988, p. 28; Davis and Smith, 1988, p.
    138; 1987, p. 134.

Table 3.   INDICATORS OF THE SALIENCE OF RELIGION, 1952-1986

| | Percent Responding That Religion | | |
Year	Can Answer Today's Problems	Is Very Important in My Own Life	Is Increasing Its Influence in American Life
1952	--	75%	--
1957	81%	--	69%
1962	--	--	45
1965	--	70	33
1967	--	--	23
1968	--	--	18
1969	--	--	14
1970	--	--	14
1974	62	--	31
1975	--	--	39
1976	--	--	44
1977	--	--	36
1978	--	52	37
1980	--	55	35
1981	65	56	38
1982	60	56	--
1983	--	56	44
1984	56	56	42
1985	61	55	49
1986	57	55	48

* The items were: At the present time, do you think religion as a whole is increasing its influence on American life or losing its influence? Do you believe that religion can answer all or most of today's problems, or that religion is largely old-fashioned and out of date? How important would you say religion is in your own life-- very important, fairly important, or not very important?

SOURCE: Based on <u>Religion in America</u>, 1987, pp. 7-15.

Table 4. EVANGELICAL BELIEFS, AND EXPERIENCES AMONG ADULTS,
          1976-1989

		Percent Reporting They		
Year	Had a Born-Again Experience*	Hold Literal View of Bible	Encouraged Someone to Come to Christ	"Evangelical" (Agreed to All Three)
1976	34%	38%	47%	18%
1980	38	39	44	19
1981	35	37	53	17
1983	35	39	50	20
1984	40	37	48	22
1985	--	36	--	--
1986	33	--	--	--
1988	--	34	46	--
1989	34	--	--	--

NOTE: The item wording was as follows: Would you say that you have
been born again or have had a born-again experience--that is, a
turning point in your life when you committed yourself to Jesus?
Which of these statements comes closest to describing your feelings
about the Bible?: The Bible is the actual word of God and is to be
taken literally, word for word; The Bible is the inspired word of
God but not everything in it should be taken literally, word for
word; The Bible is an ancient book of fables, legends, history, and
moral precepts recorded by men. Have you ever tried to encourage
someone to believe in Jesus Christ or to accept Him as his or her
Saviour? The 1986 and 1989 items read: Would you describe yourself
as a "born-again" or evangelical Christian, or not?

SOURCE: Based on "Religion in America," 1985, p. 38; "Religion in
    America," 1987, p. 28; Colasanto and DeStefano, 1989, p. 18;
    Davis and Smith, 1985, p. 144; 1988, pp. 159, 379.

Table 5.   PUBLIC VIEWERSHIP OF RELIGIOUS PROGRAMMING ON
           TELEVISION, 1981-1989

Characteristic	1981	1983	1987	1989
Ever watches religious programs on TV	43%	42%	49%	49%
Watched religious programs on TV in the past 7 days	32	18	25	21
Contributed money to television evangelists in the last 12 months	--	--	4	5

SOURCE: Colasanto and DeStefano, 1989, p. 18; "Religion in
     America," 1982, p. 102.

Topic 12: Household Resources

12.1 PERSONAL AND FAMILY INCOME

Personal and family money incomes in the U.S. rose steadily for decade after decade until about 1973 when, for a variety of reasons, income growth leveled off and has not yet resumed. The inequality of the distribution of family incomes has been remarkably stable over time, but the proportion of the population in poverty declined sharply between 1959 and 1973 and then rose to its present intermediate level. Improvement in non-monetary forms of income show a similar pattern--steady growth until the early 1970s, followed by a plateau.

The average value of goods and services consumed by individuals and families is only roughly approximated by estimates of per capita and per family money income. The level of comfort and amenity provided by a given money income depends largely on the natural environment, the available technologies, the quality and value of domestic equipment in place (housing and durable domestic goods), and the nature and value of services and entitlements (like police protection and pension rights).

Distribution of Money Income

Analysis of income trends generally focuses on changes in the distribution of inequalities among subgroups of the population. Thus, for example, Table 1 suggests that the period 1780-1880 was marked by increasing inequality of wealth in those parts of the U.S. for which there are data. Table 1 shows an increase in inequality of assets from 1774 to 1870, followed by a slower decrease from 1870 to 1962. (See also Chapter 6.3, Economic Inequality).

Table 2 shows the distribution of money income for families and for individuals living outside families from 1947 to 1984. The overall distribution of inequality was generally stable during that entire period.

Table 3 shows, however, that median family income increased significantly from 1959 to 1973, as did the tax burden at that income, the ratio of black to white family income and the income share of the lowest quintile of families. The percentage of families in poverty declined by slightly more than half. This progress halted after 1973. Family income ceased to increase, as did the tax burden and the ratio of black to white incomes. The percentage of the population in poverty rose appreciably. The interruption of economic progress is shown more clearly by calculations that trace the path of an average man's income as he passed from age 30 in 1949 to age 40 in 1959, and so on. After 1973, average income ceased to improve with age.

Family incomes vary greatly by family types, as the following estimates of 1984 average incomes suggest (Levy, p. 151): Husband-wife families, aged 45-54, both working, $42,100; Husband-wife families, aged 25-34, only husband working, $23,450; Families headed by a woman age 25 or under, $5,200; Husband-wife families, aged 65 and over, $18,600.

The combined effects of taxes and transfers introduce some uncertainty into estimates of average money income. Table 4 shows how the inequality of family incomes is affected by various adjustments for taxes and transfers. One should note in passing that in 1980, the poorest segment of the population had the highest tax rate--this has now been reformed--and also that the Social Security taxes, which are regressive, are not covered by these tables (Pechman and Mazur, 1986).

The proportion of the population in poverty has fluctuated much more than income shares, in part because of periodic adjustment to the definition of poverty. The percent of the population below the poverty line declined sharply from 1959 to 1973, remained near 11% until 1979, and then rose again, reaching 15% in 1983, with much higher rates, 32% and 26% respectively, for blacks and hispanics.

Non-Monetary Benefits

A steady, although relatively slow, improvement of domestic equipment has occurred in recent decades. Central heating, for example, was extended from barely half of all households in 1950 to 85% in 1983, while coal and wood for domestic heating and cooking were replaced by cleaner and more convenient fuels. There were modest increases from 1960 to 1980 in telephones, public sewers, and piped-in water, and a spectacular increase--from 14% to 88% of U.S. households--in air conditioning.

The case of air-conditioning illustrates an important aspect of rising standards of living which is not captured at all by income statistics--the diffusion of new items of domestic equipment and the improvement of existing equipment.   Entirely new categories of domestic equipment introduced during the past 20 years include telephone answering machines, compact disk players, VCRs, personal computers, motion sensing burglar alarms, microwave ovens, and many other devices which tend to raise the level of comfort and amenity.

With respect to services and entitlements, the long-term trend has been very favorable, but recent trends have been mixed. Some of the important forms of entitlement provided in whole or in part by public authorities are old age pensions, child support, unemployment and disability insurance, education, health care, police and fire protection, and public transportation.

Table 5 shows the sharp rise in government payments to individuals, as a percentage of GNP from 1947 to 1984. The trend of continued increase in this percentage is built into the Social Security and health insurance programs.

Between 1940 and 1987, the median level of educational achievement among all persons aged 25 to 29, most of whom have completed their formal education, rose by 2.5 years, from completion of the junior year of high school, to completion of the first semester of college (Statistical Abstract, 1989, p. 130). Among blacks of the same age, the median rose more than five years, from completion of the seventh grade to partial completion of the first year of college. The educational gap between whites and blacks virtually disappeared. Most of the improvement for both groups, however, occurred before 1970. Progress since then has been disappointing.

The availability of health care is customarily measured either by the per capita supply of physicians and hospital beds, or by changes in life expectancy. These indicators show varying trends. The ratio of physicians per 100,000 population increased from 151 in 1960 to 246 in 1986, of dentists from 47 to 57, of nurses from 293 to 661, while the number of hospital beds per declined from 903 to 540. The costs of health care skyrocketed during the same period; hospital charges per patient day rose from around $50 to $501. Life expectancy at birth rose about five years for both sexes between 1960 and 1987 but this left the U.S. behind other advanced, industrialized countries and American health care is now regarded as substandard in many respects (Statistical Abstract, 1989, pp. 71, 97, 101, 103). Some other types of public service--urban transit, mail delivery, police and fire protection--show similar patterns of deteriorating performance and escalating costs.

References

Levy, Frank. Dollars and Dreams. New York: Russell Sage Foundation, 1987.

Pechman, Joseph A. and Mark J. Mazur. "The Rich, the Poor and the Taxes They Pay: An Update." The Public Interest 77 (1984): 28-37.

U.S. Bureau of the Census. Statistical Abstract of the United States, 1989. Washington, D.C., 1989.

Williamson, Jeffrey G. and Peter H. Lundert. American Inequality. New York: Academic Press, 1980.

Table 1. WEALTH INEQUALITY, 1774-1962

Year	Population	Percentage of Total Assets Held by Top 10%
1774	Adult males	54%
1860	Adult males	75-79%
1870	Adult males	70%
1962	All consumer units ranked by total assets, revised	36%

SOURCE: Based on Williamson and Lindert, 1980, pp. 38-39.

Table 2. SHAPE OF THE INCOME DISTRIBUTION FOR FAMILIES AND FOR UNRELATED INDIVIDUALS, 1949-1984

Year	1st Quintile (Poorest)	2nd Quintile	3rd Quintile	4th Quintile	5th Quintile (Richest)
Percentage of All Family Income Going to					
1949	4%	12%	17%	23%	43%
1969	6	12	18	24	41
1984	5	11	17	24	43
Percentage of All Unrelated Individual Income Going to					
1949	2	8	14	26	50
1969	3	8	14	24	51
1984	4	9	15	24	48

SOURCE: Based on Levy, 1987, pp. 14, 16.

Table 3. LIVING STANDARDS, 1959-1984

Characteristic	1959	1973	1984
Median Family Income (1984 dollars)	$19,300	$28,200	$26,433
Tax Burden at the Median Family Income	13%	21%	22%
Ratio of Black-to-White Median Family Income	.51	.58	.56
Percentage of All Persons in Poverty	22%	11%	14%

SOURCE: Based on Levy, 1987, pp. 56, 66.

Table 4. CORRECTED FAMILY INCOME DISTRIBUTION, 1984

	Share of Income Received by Each Quintile of Families				
Income Definition	1st	2nd	3rd	4th	5th
Current Population Survey Definition (Pretax, Cash Only)	5%	11%	17%	24%	43%
Current Population Survey Definition less Taxes	6	12	18	24	40
Current Population Survey Definition less Taxes plus Medicare, Medicaid, and Food Stamps	7	12	18	24	39
Current Population Survey Definition less Taxes plus Medicare, Medicaid, Food Stamps, and Employer Fringe Benefits	7	12	18	24	39
Line above, Adjusted for Differences in Family Sizes across Quintiles	7	13	18	24	37

SOURCE: Based on Levy, 1987, p. 195.

Table 5.   U.S. GOVERNMENT PAYMENTS TO INDIVIDUALS AS A PERCENTAGE
OF GNP, 1949-1984

Year	Percent of GNP
1949	4%
1959	5
1969	8
1979	9
1984	11

SOURCE: Based on Levy, 1987, p. 167.

The informal economy, by nature clandestine, is difficult to measure but it appears to have increased from 1947 to 1978, the most recent year for which a careful estimate is available, in proportion to inflation. The most important factor enlarging the informal economy since 1970 has been the growth of the drug trade. On the other hand, the computerization of transactions and the increasing proportion of the labor force in bureaucratic employment systems tend to diminish the importance of this sector.

The "informal" or "underground" or "grey" or "shadow" economy in the U.S. has several major components:
1. cash transactions off the books
2. barter of goods and services
3. profitable criminal activities
Moonlighting--which is an important component of the informal economy in some countries--is entirely legal in the U.S.

Since the informal economy deliberately conceals its transactions from public authorities, the delineation of its trends presents formidable problems. Nevertheless the task is occasionally attempted. A semi-official estimate may be generated by comparing adjusted gross personal income--as derived from a national household survey by BEA--with adjusted gross personal income reported to the IRS by taxpayers. Table 1 shows this estimate of the size of the informal economy from 1948 to 1978. The increase was roughly proportional to inflation during that period.

The other leading method of estimating the size of the informal economy is to compare the amount of U.S. currency in circulation with the amount that ought to circulate if all transactions were properly reported. This method produces much higher--and to my mind, implausible--estimates of the size of the informal economy (Table 2) and of its rapid growth after 1960. Tanzi (1982) suggests that most of the excess currency circulates outside the United States in countries where the dollar is an alternative currency.

The principal factor tending to increase the size of the informal economy since 1975 has been the growth in the economic value of the traffic in illegal drugs, especially cocaine. All of the estimates of the value of that trade are unreliable, but they range as high as $200 billion. The principal factors tending to decrease the size of the informal economy are the increasing computerization of economic transactions, an intensified effort by the IRS to identify unreported income, and the increasing proportion of the labor force employed in large-scale, bureaucratic employment systems in which transactions off the books are difficult to arrange.

References

Tanzi, Vito. The Underground Economy in the United States and Abroad. Lexington, MA: Lexington Books, 1982.

Table 1.   ESTIMATED SIZE OF THE INFORMAL ECONOMY, 1948-1978.

Year	(billions of dollars)
1948	$ 23.1
1958	31.6
1968	45.5
1978	100.4

SOURCE: Based on Tanzi, 1982, p. 51.

Table 2.   COMPARISION OF ESTIMATES OF THE UNDERGROUND ECONOMY, 1976 AND 1978.

Analyst/Estimate	(Percent of GNP) 1976	1978
Feige		
Low	13%	25%
High	22	33
Gutmann	10	10
Internal Revenue		
Low	6	--
High	8	--
Tanzi		
(Associated with tax increase)		
Low	3	--
High	5	--
(Associated with tax level)		
Low	8	--
High	12	--

SOURCE: Based on Tanzi, 1982, p. 88.

There appears to have been a slow increase in the inequality of wealth in the U.S. from 1800 to 1870, then a slow decrease to around 1950, and little change since. The very rich hold the lion's share of stocks, bonds, and other financial instruments. The modal family's net worth consists mostly of equity in an occupied home. The rate of home ownership increased rapidly from 1940 to 1960, very slowly from 1960 to 1980, and not at all since then.

Jones (quoted in Osberg 1984, p. 47) summarizes the conclusions of research on the history of trends in the distribution of wealth in the U.S.:

> . . . it would seem that the most likely pattern of change in the United States as a whole over the past two centuries was: (1) some increase in wealth inequality to 1860-1870, (2) possibly continued to a somewhat higher degree of concentration, which peaked around 1890 or 1929 or 1940, (3) a mild downdrift in inequality to the 1950s and (4) little change since, at least among top wealthholders (For more evidence on this topic, see Chapter 6.3).

Although these very general findings are plausible, it is difficult to find detailed data on the current distribution of wealth. Moving up from middle income households through the affluent to the truly rich, "the typical portfolio of assets owned changes rather dramatically--from a portfolio almost exclusively composed of physical assets to a portfolio largely composed of financial assets" (Osberg 1984:39). But no one knows precisely how these are distributed. The surveys are few and far between, the rich are not numerous enough to be captured in survey samples, and both the rich and the poor are secretive about their assets (Ericksen, 1988).

A non-survey method of estimating assets is to analyze estate tax returns, but this method does not take account of the innumerable devices that wealthy people use to minimize inheritance taxes, and it covers only that small fraction (fewer than 5%) of estates that file tax returns. Nonetheless it does give some idea of the distribution of wealth among the very rich. Table 1 shows the percentage of assets owned by the nation's top 0.5% of wealth holders from 1953 to 1972, and shows some fractional shifts in the share of each class of assets held by the very rich during this interval. It also shows that they hold the lion's share of all the wealth represented by corporate stock, bonds, and trusts. The table does not capture the proliferation of new great fortunes that accompanied the leveraged buy-out movement of the mid-1980s.

The most recent national survey on household net worth refers to 1984. Two-thirds of all households, and a much higher proportion of households headed by a married couple, owned the home they occupied, and for the great majority of those, the value of their home equity outweighed the total of their other assets.

The differences in net worth among categories of households are very striking. Households with heads over 60 had a median net worth of $60,266; for those with heads under 35, the figure was $5,754. White households had a median net worth of $39,135; the corresponding figures for black and hispanic households were $3,397 and $4,913, respectively. Households headed by a married couple had a median net worth of $50,116; the corresponding figures for households headed by unmarried men and women were $9,883 and $13,885. The median net worth of households headed by college graduates was twice as high as those of high school graduates. The median net worth of home owners, taken as a group, was 33 times as high as that of renters! (Statistical Abstract 1989, p. 459).

Because equity in a home is the principal form of wealth for the majority of U.S. households, the trend of home ownership tends to be one of the best available indicators of economic welfare. As Table 2 shows, the proportion of housing units occupied by owners increased rapidly from 1940 to 1960, very slowly from 1960 to 1980, and not at all after 1980.

References

Ericksen, Eugene P. "Estimating the Concentration of Wealth in America." Public Opinion 52 (1988): 243-253.

Osberg, Lars. Economic Inequality in the United States. Armonk, New York: M.E. Sharpe, 1984.

U.S. Bureau of the Census. Statistical Abstract of the United States, 1989. Washington, D.C., 1989.

Williamson, Jeffrey G. and Peter H. Lindert. American Inequality. New York: Academic Press, 1980.

Table 1. THE SHARE OF ALL PERSONAL ASSETS HELD BY THE VERY RICH,
          1953-1972

Type of Asset	Share Held By Top 0.5 Percent		
	1953	1962	1972
Total Assets	21%	21%	19%
Real estate	10	10	10
Corporate stock	77	53	49
Bonds	45	35	52
Cash	13	10	8
Debt instruments	24	32	39
Life insurance	10	8	4
Trusts	85	--	81
Miscellaneous	6	10	7
Liabilities	15	15	12
Net Worth	22	22	20

SOURCE: Based on Osberg, 1984, p. 41.

Table 2. PERCENT OF HOUSING UNITS OWNER-OCCUPIED, 1940-1985

Year	Units Owner-occupied
1940	48%
1950	55
1960	62
1970	63
1980	64
1985	63

SOURCE: Based on Statistical Abstract 1989, p. 707.

13.1 MARKET GOODS AND SERVICES

Income, prices and per capita expenditures for goods and services have risen steadily for the past 30 years with a strong burst during the decade of 1975-1985. Prices and associated expenditures for oil products, medical care, and education have led the way. Although families had approximately twice the constant dollar value of expenditures in 1987 as in 1950, the relative proportions of outlay had remained remarkably stable, with the notable exception of medical care (increased), shelter (increased), and food and electricity (decreased). The distribution of expenditures within the category recreation has changed, but not the proportion devoted to recreation. New consumptions patterns are emerging for couples where the wife works, for single individuals and for children.

Prices

Over the four decades since World War II, the U.S., like other nations, has experienced monetary inflation. One useful indicator of the price of market goods and services available in American society is the Consumer Price Index (CPI). The CPI is a measure of the average change in prices over time for a fixed "market basket" of goods and services purchased by either urban wage-earners and clerical workers or by all urban consumers (Bureau of Labor Statistics, 1987). The Index is based on prices of food, clothing, shelter, fuels, transportation fares, charges for doctors' and dentists' services, drugs, etc. purchased for day-to-day living. Prices are collected in 85 areas across the country from over 25,000 tenants, 20,000 home owners and approximately 32,000 establishments. All taxes associated with the purchase or use of these goods and services are included. Formerly change was measured against 1967 prices (1967=100), but recently 1982-1984 or other years have been utilized as base.

If the annual average of consumer prices is used to index inflation, then the purchasing power of the 1987 dollar was only 21% as much as the 1950 dollar, and 26% of the 1960 dollar (Statistical Abstract 1989, p. 462). However, the "size" of a dollar depends upon the product or service one is pricing. Prices in some sectors of the economy have increased much faster than others. Between 1950 and 1986 prices for apparel increased only 2.6 times, while medical care prices increased 8.1 times and the costs of public transportation, 8.7 times.

Table 1 presents the CPIs for seven major categories of goods and services from 1950 to 1986. Price inflation was especially high for the 1975-1985 decade, at 100% (from 161 to 322 for all items). OPEC's oil embargo of the middle 1970s is readily apparent as oil products (fuel oil=501 and gas and electricity=447) led the way in the price increases over the 1967-1986 period. The cost of medical care (433), public transportation (426) and shelter (403) also increased faster than other goods and services. Finally, services as a group experienced a much greater increase in price than did commodities. The CPI for services rose from 59 in 1950 to 401 in 1986, an increase of almost 600%, while the CPI for commodities went from 79 in 1950 to 284 in 1986, an increase of only 259%.

Consumer Expenditures

More interesting than changes in the prices of goods and services are the changing patterns of expenditure. The information on inflation and changing prices is necessary to allow the analyst to distinguish between changes reflecting real alterations in life style and those merely associated with the rising costs of things. In dealing with changing population size, it is also necessary to standardize either with percentages or some measure of per capita expenditure, so that variations associated with increases in the number of consuming units are not confused with those denoting different patterns of consumption.

To begin, consider total national consumption expenditures, by type of product. Table 2 presents the distribution of total expenditure across ten major categories of goods and services. It also includes figures on total per capita consumption, in constant dollars, for the period 1950-1987. Observe that while the total quantity of goods and services consumed almost quadrupled, about half of the increased consumption was due to population growth. Per capita consumption doubled, from $5,031 to $10,500 (constant 1982 dollars). In other words, U.S. citizens in 1987 were living much better than they did in the 1950, each enjoying, on the average, twice the dollar-value of goods and services.

The change in the expenditure patterns over the years are instructive. Almost one-third of 1950 personal consumption expenditures went for food. That percentage declined consistently over the next four decades, and by 1987 just under one-fifth (19%) of total expenditures went for food, beverages, and tobacco. As already noted above, clothing also became relatively cheaper. In 1950, it accounted for 12% of total expenditure; in 1987, 7%.

There were significant changes in housing costs. A cursory inspection of Table 2 may suggest that housing costs Americans less than food. That only appears to be so because housing costs are divided into two parts in the table, namely housing (shelter) and household operations (utilities, repairs and maintenance, furnishings, etc.). The category "housing" refers only to direct rental or purchase costs of the "shell." Essential expenses to furnish it and make it livable come under "household operations." In 1950, total housing costs came to 26% of personal consumption expenditures, with the operations costs accounting for 58% of that total. Over the years, the cost of utilities, maintenance, etc. has, in relative terms, declined, while the direct housing component has increased. By 1987, the relative position of housing and operations had reversed: providing the shell now cost 57% of total housing expenditure. Considering the "housing" component separately, as a fraction of total personal expenditure, housing rental/purchase costs rose by almost half.

The other marked change in the distribution of total consumption expenditure is medical costs. In 1950, they amounted to only 5% of total expenditures, compared to 9% in 1975 and 13% in 1987. In other words, in the case of medical costs, there has been a striking reapportionment of the way Americans spend their money, a change of a scale not reflected in any of the other major categories of personal consumption expenses. In the 1950s and early 1960s, medical costs were not insignificant, but they were of the same relative scale as national outlays for recreation. In contrast, by 1987, medical costs were larger than the household operations component of housing, and were not much smaller than the rental/purchase component. After housing and food, medical care expenses are the next largest category of personal consumption expense.

The other significant thing about the distribution of consumption expenditures over the past 40 years is the remarkable stability of several of the categories of expense (Table 2). Aggregate outlays for recreation, personal care, and transportation all amount to approximately the same proportion of total expenditures as they did 40 years ago, despite a plethora of changes in the fads, fashions and technologies accompanying all three.

Another approach to tracking changes in consumption patterns is the consumer interview survey (U.S. Dept. of Commerce, 1985). Whereas the above discussion is based on aggregates of total expenditures in the economy as a whole, and analysts attempt to generalize to individual consumer behavior from the top down, as it were, consumer interview surveys build upon the individually-reported experience of particular consumer units. They provide a "bottom-up" approach to observing patterns of expenditure and changes in lifestyle.

Table 3 summarizes the annual average expenditures of national samples of households as reported in 1960-61 and at three points in the 1980s. Note that these interview-based data corroborate some of the general patterns noted in the national personal consumption expenditure data, namely a significant decline (from 25% to 15% over the 15-year period) in the fraction of household expenditures for food, and relative stability in housing costs as a whole, with the shelter component becoming larger and the household operations component smaller. However, from the standpoint of the individual household, medical costs do not add up to the large fraction of expenditures that they do for the society as a whole. Here we have an apparent consequence of the American system of third-party payers. From the standpoint of the individual household, medical expenses in the 1980s amounted to about the same fraction of total expenses as they did in 1950 for national aggregate data, namely about five percent.

The grouped data in Table 3 are not very revealing about specific changes in expenditure patterns. More detail is provided in Table 4, which provides current dollar figures (and references the CPI in a note) for more detailed categories for three consumer expenditure surveys.

Housing costs have moved well ahead of inflation, for single-family homes both new and existing (Table 5) and for rental units (Table 6). The 1987 dollar was worth about one-fifth as much as the 1950 dollar, but housing, both rental and owner-occupied, had increased in value not five times, but nine times (Table 6). The lifestyles of millions of Americans in the 1980s have been negatively impacted by their inability to find affordable housing of any kind.

Other lifestyle characteristics indexed by changes in expenditure patterns include the increased tendency to take meals outside the home, the decline of domestic service in the home, and the nation's continued attachment to the automobile. In the 1950s, one-fourth of expenditures for food were for food purchased for consumption outside the home. That level of "eating out" held until the mid-1960s, when the trend toward more meals away from home became noticeable. By 1987, the fraction of food expenditures for "purchased meals" had increased to one-third (Table 7).

Domestic service accounted for almost one-tenth of household operations costs in 1950. It declined rapidly over the next two decades; early in the 1980s, the fraction of home expenditures devoted to domestics was small enough that it no longer merited a separate category. Over the same period, household costs for telephone services doubled; in the 1980s, they amounted to one-eighth of household operations expenses. Finally, distinguished by lack of change, is the continued dominance of transportation expenses by the user-operated vehicle, that is, the personal car. Despite four decades of urban growth, energy shortages, and public concern about mass transit, over 90% of transportation expenditures continue to go to personally-owned vehicles (Table 7).

Some lifestyle changes are apparent in the distribution of personal consumption expenditures for recreation (Table 8), notably the relative decline in expenditures for printed materials (books, magazines, sheet music); the increase in expenditures for "wheel goods" and durable sports equipment (including boats and pleasure aircraft); the great reduction in cash spent for live spectator amusements (from 16% to 5% of recreational expenditures, 1950-1987); the growth of commercial participant amusements, which doubled their share of the entertainment dollar; and the burgeoning "other" category, since 1985 the largest single category, which represents the growing diversity of recreational opportunity and commercial organization of technological advances in recreation.

The movement of women into the labor force has had, and continues to have, a major impact on the consumption of goods and services (Oumlil, 1983; Sethle and Alreck, 1986). A recent study compared the consumption patterns of four types of couples distinguished by the situation of the wife, namely whether she was a working mother, housekeeping mother, working wife of childless couple, or a housekeeping wife with no children (Waldrop, 1989). It turns out that couples have a variety of consumption choices such as to make the bread for their family, to buy the bread and eat it at home, or to eat it in a restaurant. The alternative selected depends to a large degree on whether the wife works and whether the couple have children. Childless couples spend more on new cars, home furnishings, meals in restaurants and alcoholic beverages. Couples with children spend more on food, utilities and apparel. Working mother couples have considerable child care expenditures. The impact of women in the labor force and the decling fertility associated with it will continue to influence consumption patterns.

The growth in the number of single persons in American society has also altered consumption patterns (Shipp, 1988). Most singles are young, and the young have different spending priorities. Sex also impacts consumption. Single women spend more on food consumed at home, housing, apparel, health care and personal care services while single men have larger expenditures on food eaten outside the home, alcohol, transportation, entertainment and retirement.

Children also exert considerable influence on family consumption (McNeal, 1987). Stipp (1988) reviews a national survey of the purchasing habits of 1,200 youth and found that young people spend their money on candy, toys, soft drinks, presents, snacks, books, fast food, clothes, records and tapes, movies and sports equipment. Not only do the young spend their own money, but they also influence the parents' spending. For many families shopping is a leisure time activity and children have a major influence on purchases.

References

Bureau of Labor Statistics. Where to Find CPI Information, Washington D.C., USGPO, 1987.

Geieseman, Raymond and John Rogers. "Consumer Expenditures: Results From The Diary and Interview Surveys." Monthly Labor Review 109 (June, 1986): 14-18.

McNeal, James U. Children as Consumers: Insights and Implications Lexington, MA.: D.C. Heath, 1987.

Oumlil, A. Ben. Economic Change and Consumer Shopping Behavior. New York: Praeger Publisher, 1983.

Sethle, Robert B. and Pamela L. Alreck. Why They Buy: American Consumers Inside and Out. New York: Wiley, 1986.

Shipp, Stephanie "How Singles Spend." American Demographics 10 (April, 1988): 22-27.

Stipp, Horst H. "Children as Consumers." American Demographics 10 (February, 1988): 26-33.

U.S. Department of Commerce. Statistical Abstract of the United States, 1989. Washington D.C. Annual. Previous years as cited.

U.S. Department of Commerce. How is Your Money Spent?: The Quarterly Interview Survey. Washington D.C., USGPO, 1985.

Waldrop, Judith "A Lesson In Home Economics." American Demographics 11 (August, 1989): 26-33.

Table 1. CONSUMER PRICE INDEXES, BY MAJOR CONSUMPTION
          CATEGORIES, 1950-1986

	1950	1955	1960	1965	1970	1975	1980	1985	1986
ALL ITEMS	72	80	89	94	116	161	247	322	328
Food									
Total	74	82	88	94	115	175	255	310	320
Away From Home	--	71	81	91	120	174	267	347	360
Shelter									
Total	--	79	88	94	124	170	282	382	403
Rent	70	84	92	97	110	137	192	265	280
Fuel Oil & Coal	73	82	89	95	110	235	556	619	501
Gas and									
Electricity	81	87	97	99	107	170	302	453	447
Apparel & Upkeep	79	84	90	94	116	142	178	206	208
Transportation									
Private	72	79	91	96	111	150	294	314	299
Public	49	67	81	92	128	159	252	403	426
Medical Care	54	65	79	89	121	169	266	403	433
All Commodities	79	85	91	96	113	158	234	289	284
All Services	59	71	84	92	122	167	270	381	400

NOTE: In all categories, 1967=100. Annual averages of monthly
figures except as indicated. Prior to 1965, excludes Alaska and
Hawaii. Through 1977 represents buying patterns of wage earners and
clerical workers, beginning 1978, reflects buying patterns of all
urban consumers in the 1970's.

SOURCE: Based on Statistical Abstract 1988, p. 450.

Table 2. TOTAL PERSONAL CONSUMPTION EXPENDITURES, BY PRODUCT,
1950-1987

Type of Product	1950	1955	1960	1965	1970
Food, beverages and tobacco	30%	28%	27%	25%	23%
Clothing, access., jewelry	12	11	10	10	10
Personal care	1	1	2	2	2
Housing	11	13	14	15	15
Household operations	15	15	14	14	14
Medical care expenses	5	5	6	7	8
Personal business**	4	4	6	5	6
Transportation	13	14	13	13	13
Recreation	6	5	6	6	7
Other	2	3	3	4	4
Total	99	99	101	101	102
Total (billion $)	191	254	325	433	618
Total (billions, 1982 $)	766	917	1060	1324	1536
Per Capita Consumption*($)	5031	5528	5866	6814	7490

Type of Product	1975	1980	1985	1987
Food, beverages and tobacco	23%	21%	19%	19%
Clothing, access., jewelry	8	8	7	7
Personal care	1	2	1	1
Housing	15	15	15	16
Household operations	15	13	13	12
Medical care expenses	9	11	12	13
Personal business**	5	6	6	7
Transportation	13	14	14	13
Recreation	7	7	7	7
Other	3	4	4	4
Total	99	101	98	99
Total (billion $)	979	1732.6	2629	3012
Total (billions, 1982 $)	1759	2034	2357	2561
Per Capita Consumption	8143	8930	9851	10500

* Constant (1982) dollar total personal expenditures, divided by
total national population.
** Life insurance, legal services, funeral, burial expenses, etc.

SOURCE: Based on Statistical Abstract 1989, pp. 7, 426, 462;
1979, p. 44; 1974, p. 376.

Table 3.   AVERAGE ANNUAL EXPENDITURES OF CONSUMER UNITS,* 1960-1986

Type of Expenditure	1960-61	1982-83	1985	1986
Total Expenditures	$5047	$18892	$22217	$22710
Food	25%	17%	15%	15%
Alcoholic Beverages	2	2	1	1
Housing	29	31	30	30
Shelter	13	17	17	18
Fuel, utilities, furnishings	16	13	13	13
Apparel and Services**	20	5	5	5
Transportation	15	20	21	21
Health Care	--	4	5	5
Recreation, Education, Other***	10	15	15	15
Retirement, Pension, and Social Security	--	7	8	8
Total	101	101	100	100

* 1960-61, families; 1982-83, urban consumer units; 1985 and 1986, all consumer units.
** In 1960-61, includes clothing materials and services, personal care, and medical care.
*** Includes tobacco and smoking supplies, entertainment, personal care (except 1960-61, when personal care is included with clothing), cash contributions, and miscellaneous expenditures.
# Not listed in the 1960-61 data.

SOURCE: Statistical Abstract 1989, p.437 ;1988, p. 420; 1986, p. 443; 1966, p. 340.

Table 4.   AVERAGE ANNUAL EXPENDITURES OF URBAN CONSUMER UNITS,*
INTERVIEW SURVEY, 1972-73, 1982-83, and 1986

Type of Expenditure	1972-73	1982-83	1986
Income before taxes	$12,388	$23,027	$25,481
Total expenditures	9,421	19,128	22,710
Food	1,675	3,175	3,363
Alcoholic beverages	89	286	273
Housing	2,838	5,869	6,888
Shelter	1,507	3,309	3,986
Fuels, utilities, and public services	581	1,512	1,646
Household operations, housefurnishings and equipment	549	1,048	1,256
Apparel and services	732	1,039	1,149
Transportation	1,762	3,766	4,815
Vehicles	709	1,425	2,340
Gasoline and motor oil	404	1,076	916
Other vehicle expenses and transportation costs	650	1,265	1,559
Health care	432	834	1,062
Life and other personal insurance	367	262	293
Retirement, pensions, Social Security	451	1,388	1,836
Other	1,276	2,410	3,031
Entertainment	389	879	--
Personal care services	106	178	--
Reading	50	128	--
Education	126	257	--
Tobacco	131	108	--
Miscellaneous	102	274	--
Cash contributions	372	586	--

* 1986, all consumer units, not just urban.

NOTE: If the Consumer Price Index for 1982-84 is 100, then
1972=2.391, 1973=2.251, and 1986=.913.

SOURCE: Based on <u>Statistical Abstract 1989</u>, p. 437; Geieseman,
1986, p. 17.

Table 5.   TRENDS IN HOUSING COSTS: MEDIAN SALES PRICE OF ONE-FAMILY
HOMES SOLD, AND FOR MOBILE HOMES, 1960-1986

	Median Sales Price (Thousands of Dollars)					
	One-Family Houses					
	New		Existing		New Mobile Homes	
Year	(Cur. $)	(1987 $)	(Cur. $)	(1987 $)	(Cur. $)	(1987 $)
1965	20.0	72.0	--	--	--	--
1970	23.4	68.4	23.0	67.3	--	--
1975	39.3	83.0	35.3	74.6	10.6	22.4
1980	64.6	89.2	62.2	85.9	19.8	27.3
1985	84.3	88.9	75.5	79.6	21.8	23.0
1987	104.5	104.5	85.6	85.6	23.7	23.7

* Privately owned.
** Placed for residential use.

SOURCE: Based on Statistical Abstract 1989, p. 702; 1984, p. 745.

Table 6:   CHARACTERISTICS OF HOUSING UNITS: NUMBER, TENURE, AND
VALUE, 1940-1985

		Occupied Units			
		Owner Occupied			Renter Occupied
	All			$ Median	Median Gross
	Units*	Total		Unit Value	Monthly Rent
Year	(mil.)	(mil.)	Percent	(1000s)	(dollars)
1940**	--	34.9	44%	--	27
1950**	--	42.8	55	7.4	42
1960	58.3	53.0	62	11.9	71
1970	67.7	63.4	63	17.0	89
1980	86.7	80.4	64	47.2	243
1985	96.7	88.4	63	66.3	365

* This total includes all year-round units; seasonal and migratory
units not included.
** Figures for 1940 and 1950 do not include Alaska and Hawaii.

SOURCE: Statistical Abstract 1989, p. 706-707; 1988, p. 688-689;
1974, p. 702; 1966, pp. 752-753, 756.

Table 7. SELECTED TRENDS IN PERSONAL CONSUMPTION EXPENDITURES, 1950-1987

| | Percent of Total Personal Consumption Expenditures on | | |
	All Food Accounted for by Purchased Meals*	Household Operations Accounted for by Domestic Service	Telephone & Telegraph	Transportation Accounted for by User-operated Transportation
1950	24%	9%	7%	89%
1955	24	8	8	91
1960	24	8	10	92
1965	26	7	11	93
1970	27	6	12	93
1975	27	4	12	94
1980	29	--	12	91
1985	30	--	12	92
1987	32	--	12	91

* These percentages are based on expenditures for "food, excl. alcoholic beverages," rather than the category total for "food, beverages, and tobacco."

SOURCE: Based on <u>Statistical Abstract 1989</u>, p. 426; <u>1979</u>, p. 440.

Table 8.   PERCENTAGE DISTRIBUTION OF PERSONAL CONSUMPTION
           EXPENDITURES FOR RECREATION, BY TYPE OF PRODUCT OR
           SERVICE

Product/Service	1950	1955	1960	1965	1970	1975	1980	1985	1987
Total Expenditures (billion $)	11	14	18	26	43	70	115	186	223
Books, maps	6%	6%	7%	8%	7%	5%	5%	4%	4%
Magazines, newspapers, sheet music	13	13	12	11	10	9	9	7	7
Nondurable toys, sport supplies	12	13	13	13	13	13	13	11	12
Wheel goods, durable toys, sports equip.	8	10	12	11	12	15	15	14	15
Radio & TV receivers, records, musical instruments	22	20	19	23	20	19	17	20	18
Radio and TV repair	3	4	4	4	3	3	2	2	2
Flowers, seeds, potted plants	4	4	3	4	4	4	3	3	3
Admissions to spectator amusements	16	13	9	7	8	6	6	5	5
Movie theaters	12	9	5	4	4	3	2	2	2
Legit. theater, opera, etc.*	2	2	2	2	1	1	2	2	2
Spectator sports	2	2	2	1	3	2	2	2	1
Clubs, fraternal orgs.	4	4	4	3	4	3	3	3	2
Commercial participant amusements**	4	4	6	6	6	7	8	8	8
Pari-mutuel net receipts	2	3	3	3	3	2	2	1	1
Other***	6	6	8	8	12	14	17	21	22
Total	100	100	100	101	102	100	100	99	99

* Entertainments of nonprofit institutions, except athletic.
** Consists of billiard parlors; bowling alleys; dancing, riding, shooting, skating, and swimming places; amusement devices and parks; golf courses; sightseeing buses and guides; private flying operations and other commercial participant amusements.
*** Consists of net receipts of lotteries and expenditures for purchase of pets and pet care services, cable TV, film processing, photographic studios, sporting and recreation camps, and recreational services, not elsewhere classified.

SOURCE: Statistical Abstract 1989, p. 221; 1974, p. 210.

The consumption of mass information continues to increase, but the relative contribution of the various individual types of media has changed. The electronic media permeate U.S. society, and the volume of material produced and transmitted continues to increase dramatically. The increases in total consumption are real, but relatively small in contrast to the "explosion" of production. In terms of proportion of total words consumed, the print media have declined in importance and television has become more dominant. A variety of developments already underway, including widespread data communication via home computers, promise continued rapid change.

Among the ways of conceptualizing people's relation to the mass media are incidence, availability, and outlay measures of individual participation. Individual incidence measures reflect time of exposure or number of exposure situations, such as hours spent watching television or number of books read. Availability measures pertain to the presence of particular medium receptors in one's household or social surroundings; an example is the number of television sets per household. Outlay measures refer to the resources, generally money, devoted to a particular medium; examples are the costs of movie tickets or subscription fees for cable television.

Here we shall deal with incidence and availability measures. Outlay measures are readily available for many of the media (e.g., annual expenditures on advertising, consumer expenditures for books, movies, and cable TV, publishing industry financial statistics, producer value of records and tapes shipped) in the annual Statistical Abstract volumes and elsewhere. To combine them in a meaningful way and deal with some of the problems in comparing consumer outlays across media, however, is beyond the scope of this essay. For example, how does one factor in the costs of the radios and television sets, the VCRs and stereo-CD-phonograph systems, along with consumer outlays for books and newspapers and the costs of movie tickets in a meaningful way?

Table 1 presents incidence measures, based in the General Social Survey, for newspapers (1971-88), television (1975-88), and radio (1978-83). There is a distinct trend toward less reading of newspapers: in the early 1970s, two-thirds of U.S. adults read a newspaper daily; by the late 1980s, only half did. There is also a slight trend toward increased television viewing by adults, even though, when this series begins (1975), about three-fourths of adults were already watching two or more hours daily. The figures on radio-listening amply demonstrate that radio continues to be an important medium, but show no trend. During the five-year period in question, only one-tenth of adults did not listen to the radio, and almost one-third reported four or more hours daily.

It is important to distinguish between individual media use (incidence) and reports of household or family participation (availability). The distinction is between living in a household that maintains a subscription to a newspaper and reading the newspaper, or between personal television viewing and the number of hours that a set is on or that someone is watching. Thus, although average hours of television viewing per day per household increased from 4.6 to 7.1 between 1950 and 1985 (see Chapter 9.5, Mass Media), modal individual viewing by adults in the 1975-1988 period was about three hours (Table 1). Another series on personal television viewing for the period 1960-1980 reveals an increase in average time per day from less than three to over four hours. Beginning at 156 minutes per day in 1960, the personal viewing time increases, at five year intervals, to 170, 196, 222 and finally, in 1980, 258 minutes (de Sola Pool, et al., 1984, p. 84).

The hours of reported usage of the different media total to a large proportion of a person's total available time. Analysts caution that the figures for each medium are not truly additive, and that often two or more communications media are in use simultaneously. De Sola Pool and his associates (1984, pp. 11-12) estimate that as much as one-fourth of media use involves concurrent exposure to two media, and that in addition there are biases toward overestimation in most of the major reporting series.

Availability measures of media use for 1960-1987, reported in per capita or per household terms, are given in Table 2. Note the stunning growth in cable TV subscriptions, from 1% to 46% of households; the decline in newspaper circulation per household; the stabilizing of radio sets per household at about 5.5; and the continued increase in number of television sets. Number of books sold per capita continues to increase, but slowly. The number of recording media units sold shows no particular trend over the period 1975-1987--it seems stabilized about about three units per capita per year--but the type of unit changes dramatically: the phonograph record is replaced by the prerecorded tape and annual compact disk sales rise from nothing to .4 per capita.

The interpretation of communications trends is complicated by the differences among the media. An innovative attempt to deal with the noncomparable statistics from media so diverse as computer networks, telephones, books, newspapers, movies, records and tapes, and several others is the work of Ithiel de Sola Pool and his associates (1984) on communications flows. They reduce all of the mass media to a single unit of communication, the word, and then trace trends in words supplied and words consumed. Their data on words consumed come from time budgets and other studies of the behavior of consumers. That on words supplied comes from estimating the number of words broadcast (or printed or pressed into disks). They stress that while there are physiological and psychological limits to the number of words one can consume, there are no such limits to the words a communications technology can produce (de Sola Pool et al., 1984, p. 6). Among their conclusions, based on numerical estimates of words supplied, transmitted, and consumed in all forms of media over the period 1960-1980, are these (pp. 16-27): There has been an explosion of communications supplied, but not in words consumed. Consumption has increased, but slowly. There has been a change in the balance of electronic and print media. In 1960, the print media accounted for almost one-third of all media consumption; by 1980, it had slipped to one-sixth. In words supplied, the electronic media's dominance rose from 92% to 98%. Additional information about trends in the composition of the flow of communications in the U.S., and in patterns of media consumption, are presented in Table 3.

Changes in national media use now underway include the use of interactive cable systems, replacement of conventional by high definition television, growing use of optical fiber systems in place of coaxial cables, expansion of the technology for and use of electronic text, wider distribution of videocassette and videodisc recorders, and increased individual use of satellite receivers, personal videocameras, and home computers (Greenberg, 1985, pp. 63-66). Data communication--the use of the computer for communicating and reducing information overload--promises to be the most significant of the changes in media use now underway (de Sola Pool, et al., pp. 33-34).

References

Davis, James Allan. General Social Surveys, 1972-1982: Cumulative Codebook. Chicago: National Opinion Research Center, 1982.

Davis, James Allan and Tom W. Smith. General Social Surveys, 1972-1988: Cumulative Codebook. Chicago: National Opinion Research Center, 1988. Annual. Previous years as cited.

de Sola Pool, Ithiel, Hiroshi Inose, Nozomu Takasaki, and Roger Hurwitz. Communications Flows: A Census in the United States and Japan. Amsterdam: North-Holland, 1984.

Rogers, Everett M. and Francis Balle, eds. The Media Revolution in America and in Western Europe. Norwood, NJ: Ablex, 1985.

U.S. Bureau of the Census. Statistical Abstract of the United States, 1989. Washington, D.C., 1989. Annual. Previous years as cited.

Table 1.   INDIVIDUAL PARTICIPATION IN THE MASS MEDIA: READING,
           LISTENING, AND VIEWING, 1972-1988

Medium and Frequency	1972	1975	1977	1978	1982	1983	1985	1986	1988
How often reads the newspaper									
Every day	69%	66%	62%	57%	54%	56%	53%	54%	51%
Few times/wk.	15	16	17	20	22	21	21	20	24
Weekly or less	12	14	16	17	18	19	20	20	21
Never	4	4	5	5	6	5	6	6	5
Daily hours watching TV									
None	--	4	4	6	4	6	5	4	3
One	--	17	21	21	21	19	18	18	19
Two	--	27	25	27	25	25	26	27	25
Three	--	20	20	19	19	20	20	20	19
Four	--	15	13	13	14	13	14	13	14
Five	--	8	6	6	6	6	8	7	8
Six and over	--	10	10	8	10	11	9	11	12
Daily hours listening to radio									
None	--	--	--	9	10	11	--	--	--
One	--	--	--	36	33	33	--	--	--
Two	--	--	--	19	19	18	--	--	--
Three	--	--	--	8	10	9	--	--	--
Four	--	--	--	7	7	7	--	--	--
Five	--	--	--	4	5	4	--	--	--
Six and over	--	--	--	17	17	18	--	--	--

Note: The items were: How often do you read the newspaper--every
day, a few times a week, once a week, less often than once a week,
or never? On the average day, about how many hours do you
personally watch television? Do you ever listen to the radio? [If
yes:] On the average, about how many hours a day do you usually
listen to the radio?

SOURCE: Davis and Smith, 1988, pp. 256-257; 1987, pp. 252-253;
        Davis, 1982, pp. 175-176.

Table 2. HOUSEHOLD AND PER CAPITA AVAILABILITY OF SELECTED MEDIA
AND MEDIA RECEIVERS, 1960-1987

Medium	1960	1965	1970	1975	1980	1985	1987
Number per Household							
Radios	3.7	--	5.1	5.6	5.5	5.5	5.4
Television sets	1.1	1.2	1.4	1.5	1.7	1.8	1.9
Cable TV subscriptions							
per 100 households	1.2	2.2	7.1	13.8	19.8	36.9	45.9
Newspapers							
(Daily circulation)	1.1	1.1	1.0	.9	.8	.7	.7
Number per Capita*							
Books sold	--	--	--	7.2	8.2	8.6	8.7
Recorded media, total							
unit shipments	--	--	--	2.5	3.0	2.7	2.9
Phonograph records	--	--	--	2.0	2.1	1.2	.8
Pre-recorded tapes	--	--	--	.5	.9	1.4	1.7
Compact disks	--	--	--	--	--	.1	.4

* U.S. resident population.

SOURCE: Based on <u>Statistical Abstract 1989</u>, pp. 7, 45, 223-225,
544, 547, 549; <u>1979</u>, pp. 44, 587, 589, 593; <u>1966</u>, pp. 523,
525.

Table 3. CHANGES IN THE COMPOSITION OF THE AGGREGATE FLOW OF
          COMMUNICATION, IN WORDS, SELECTED MEDIA, 1960-1980

Medium	Words Supplied		Words Consumed	
	1960	1980	1960	1980
Radio	74.5%	71.8%	17.5%	18.8%
Television	17.6	25.3	38.1	51.7
Cable TV	.0	.5	.0	.8
Records, tapes	--	.0	.1	.1
Movies	.1	.0	1.0	.4
Newspapers	6.2	1.9	20.0	8.5
Magazines	1.0	.3	4.4	3.1
Books	.2	.1	6.2	4.4
Total*	99.6	99.9	87.3	87.8

* Percentages do not sum to 100% because several communications
media are not included here, namely "education in the classroom,"
direct mail, first class mail, telephone, telex, telegraph,
mailgram, facsimile, and data communication.

SOURCE: Based on de Sola Pool, et al., p. 49.

13.3 PERSONAL HEALTH AND BEAUTY PRACTICES

There has been a marked increase of body awareness and of practices designed to conserve or improve health since 1960, together with a dramatic increase of health care expenditures. The results have been less impressive than the effort. Most indicators show improvement, but the overall health status of the population lags behind other advanced industrial countries.

The health of the American population improved significantly from 1960 to 1985 but there was less improvement than in other industrialized countries although the U.S. spends rather more on health care (Table 1).

The essential evidence of improvement is shown in Table 2. From 1960 to 1986, life expectancy at birth increased by more than four years. Much of this improvement was attributable to a sharp decline of infant mortality but even at age 65, life expectancy was up by 1.6 years for men and 2.8 years for women, with corresponding decreases in annual deaths.

Subjective health status, as reported in surveys, is high for all age groups and remained quite level from 1973 to 1982 (National Center for Health Statistics, 1985). About two-thirds of the population 65 and over and much higher percentages of the younger age groups described their own health as good or excellent.

Objective health status, as measured by work-loss days, disability days and bed-disability days, had no clear trend (National Center for Health Statistics, 1985).

Life-threatening conditions show extremely diverse trends. From 1970 to 1985, rates of heart disease, vehicle and industrial accidents, and stroke declined sharply; while rates of cancer, diabetes, suicide and venereal diseases were rising. Hypertension increased sharply; cholesterol levels declined. Some surgical procedures, like lens insertions, were performed much more often, while tonsillectomies and hysterectomies went out of style.

Despite widespread enthusiasm for exercise and dieting, the incidence of obesity in men remained about the same from 1960 to 1980 while obesity in women increased. Cigarette smoking, demonstrated in the 1970s to be a much more lethal habit than had previously been supposed, showed a moderate but not overwhelming decline from 1970 to 1987, from 4000 to 3200 cigarettes per capita (Statistical Abstract 1989, p. 737).

The enthusiasm for exercise was relatively new. As Table 3 shows, the proportion of the population who jogged regularly and the distances they ran increased steadily from 1961 to 1984. Table 3 displays an even more impressive trend with respect to exercise. By 1984, more than half of the general population and of all its major subgroups claimed to engage in some form of daily exercise.

Other signs of body awareness were not lacking. Cosmetic or aesthetic plastic surgery, according to one report (Newsweek, May 27, 1985) increased 61% between 1981 and 1984, when 2,700 surgeons performed 477,000 cosmetic operations to improve the appearance of their patients. There was a simultaneous boom in medical self-care, marked by the development of a large consumer market for medical instruments like stethoscopes and manometers and for sophisticated diagnostic tests (Edmondson, 1985).

Dieting and weight reduction programs flourished in the 1970s and 1980s but it is difficult to establish a clear trend, since nutritional fads and a preoccupation with body weight have been an idiosyncratic feature of American culture since the nineteenth century (Schwartz, 1986; Whelan and Stare, 1983). To an unprecedented extent however, commercial food products and soft drinks have recently been redesigned in accordance with current nutritional fads (as low-calorie, low-fat, low-salt, low-cholesterol, high-fiber etc.) and such "health foods" have captured large market shares.

There are obvious symbolic linkages between the exercise and nutritional cults and a number of trends described elsewhere in these reports: the sexual revolution, the deferral of entry into the labor force, the greater economic independence of women, the growing size of the active elderly population, and the abolition of mandatory retirement. The net effect has been to extend the erotic behaviors and attitudes associated with early adulthood into later stages of the life cycle.

The appearance in rapid succession of two epidemics of venereal disease, herpes in the 1970s and the much more dangerous HIV infections in the 1980s, discouraged some forms of sexual adventure but so far have not perceptibly checked the prolongation into middle age and later of courtship patterns and associated forms of body awareness.

References

Edmonson, Brad. "The Market for Medical Self-Care." American Demographics 6 (1985): 35-37, 51.

National Center for Health Statistics, P. M. Golden. Charting the Nation's Health: Trends Since 1960. Washington, D.C.: USGPO, 1985.

Newsweek. "New Bodies for Sale." Newsweek, May 27, 1985.

"Physical Fitness." Gallup Report 226 (1984): 9-11.

Schwartz, Hillel. Never Satisfied: A Cultural History of Diets, Fantasies and Fat. New York: Free Press, 1986.

U.S. Bureau of the Census. Statistical Abstract of the United States, 1989. Washington, D.C., 1989.

Whelan, Elizabeth M. and Frederick J. Stare. The One-Hundred-Percent Natural, Purely Organic, Cholesterol-Free, Mega-vitamin, Low-Carbohydrate, Nutritional Hoax. New York: Atheneum, 1983.

Table 1.   HEALTH EXPENDITURES AND OUTCOMES IN SELECTED
            COUNTRIES, AROUND 1987

Country	Per Capita Health Expenditures	Life Expectancy at Birth (years)
United States	$ 1,926	75.3
Australia	760	76.1
Austria	996	75.4
Belgium	833	75.4
Canada	1,206	77.1
Denmark	990	75.3
France	1,112	75.7
Greece	157	77.0
Italy	702	76.7
Japan	1,089	77.8
Netherlands	1,003	77.1
Portugal	158	74.1
Spain	358	77.1
Sweden	1,428	77.3
Switzerland	1,649	78.0
United Kingdom	597	75.1
West Germany	1,182	75.8

SOURCE: Based on <u>Statistical Abstract 1989</u>, pp. 817-818, 821.

Table 2.   AVERAGE LIFE EXPECTANCY AT BIRTH, BY SEX, 1950-1987

Year	Years Life Expectancy		
	Total	Male	Female
1950	68.2	65.6	71.1
1955	69.6	66.7	72.8
1960	69.7	66.6	73.1
1970	70.8	67.1	74.7
1975	72.6	68.8	76.6
1980	73.7	70.0	77.4
1985	74.7	71.2	78.2
1987*	75.0	71.5	78.3

* Preliminary

SOURCE: Statistical Abstract 1989, p. 71.

Table 3.   EXERCISE HABITS OF THE ADULT POPULATION, 1961-1984

Year	Report Daily Exercise	Report Frequent Jogging
1961	24%	6%
1977	47	11
1984	59	18

SOURCE: "Physical Fitness," 1984, pp. 9-11.

Patterns of time use vary by age and sex, and so there are exceptions to some of the general trends. People are spending fewer hours in paid work, and have more leisure. Men still have more leisure hours, but not many more, and the trend is toward convergence by sex in time use. Women are spending fewer hours, and men more, in household work and family care, but women still spend about twice as much time as men in these activities.

For most employed people the largest single segment of waking time is time at work. Since 1947, the length of the work week of the average U.S. worker has changed only slightly, declining from an average of 42 hours in the late 1940s to 38 hours in the early 1980s. In 1981, most workers still worked approximately 40 hours a week. However, the weekly figures obscure sizable changes in time use, because they do not reflect changes in paid time off during the year. Weekly hours have remained fairly steady, but annual hours have declined both because of increases in paid time off and in the number of paid hours for time while employees are on plant premises but not actually working.

In 1947, the average 40+ hour workweek in nonfarm industries added up to an average "workyear" of 2,236 hours. By 1978 that figure had dropped by over 12 percent, to 1,955 hours. Only one major industry, mining, did not show a net decrease in annual hours. The decrease in annual hours at work per worker was even greater than these figures suggest, because they represent only full-time workers, and the percentage of part-time workers in nonagricultural industries increased. Rates of part-time participation in the labor force have increased partly because there are more women and students working, and partly because the composition of the labor force has been shifting from the manufacturing to the service sector, and from blue collar to white collar occupations. Part-time employment is more common in the service industries and in white-collar jobs (Greis, 1984, pp. 11-15).

There were earlier local and regional studies, but not until 1954 was there a national survey of individual time-use. About a decade later, in 1965, the Multinational Time Use Study was conducted by the Institute for Social Research at the University of Michigan (Robinson, 1977; see also Szalai, 1972). In 1975, a replication was attempted by researchers at the same institution (1975-76 Study of Americans' Use of Time). Finally, in 1985, John Robinson directed a second national replication (Americans' Use of Time project, University of Maryland). The findings from these four national surveys, plus a follow-up in 1981 of portions of the 1975 sample, are the basis for our generalizations about changes in time use.

For the individual worker, the net consequence of the long-term trend toward fewer work hours is more time for leisure and family activities, and that is what surveys of individual time-use reveal. Between 1954 and 1965, there were relatively few changes in time use, the most notable being an increase in women's hours of employment and a corresponding decline in their hours of free time and family care (Table 1). Between 1965 and 1975, the hours people spent working for pay declined, more so for men than women; hours devoted to leisure activities increased; and hours spent in housework and family care declined for both men and women (Robinson, 1978, p. 217).

It turns out that there are major differences between men and women in time use, and in addition to these sex differences, there are sizable differences by age. Where possible, analysts should control for both age and sex. Tables 2-5 portray patterns of time use for 1965-1975 and 1975-1981, by sex, for two age categories, young (25-44) and middle-aged (45-64). Across the three points, the samples are different enough that direct comparisons are misleading; a more appropriate strategy is to compare the 1965 and 1975 samples, and then the 1981 follow-up of a 1975 subsample with that subsample. Among the patterns revealed in a series of such paired comparisons across Tables 2-5 are these: 1) in work hours: slight decline for young men, increase for young women, and rise-then-fall for middle-aged men and women; 2) in hours of household work: declines for women, rise-then-fall for middle-aged men, and fall-then-rise for young men; 3) in hours of leisure: increase followed by stabilizing for the men, increase followed by slight decline for young women, and consistent increases for the middle-aged women; 4) in hours of passive leisure: up, then down slightly for women and middle-aged men, consistently up for younger men; and 5) in hours of "female-type" housework: no change followed by a slight decline for middle-aged men, down-then-up for young men, and consistently down for women.

Full results of the 1985 replication have not yet been published. Some of the findings now available are summarized in Table 6. The net results of the 20-year trends presented there are a substantial decline in women doing "female" household work; an increase in men's doing "male" or shared-type household work and a very slight increase in their participation in "female" work, such that their total hours in household work have doubled, from a weekly average of five in 1965 to ten in 1985; increases in leisure time for women (men still have more, but women are catching up); and sizable declines in hours at work for the employed of both sexes. Thus, the time-use trends point toward sex-convergence, especially in the availability of leisure.

Among the trends across the 1965-1981 period noted in a summary monograph (Juster and Stafford, 1985, pp. 319, 322) are: 1) Moderate convergence between the sexes in hours of work for pay and hours of work in the home; 2) Sharp increases in television viewing over the 1965-75 period, compared to decreases in the 1975-81 period; 3) Sizable increases in time in conversations, especially in the 1975-81 period, and mostly in telephone conversations; 4) For women, declines in the ratio of household to market work; and 5) For men, declines in the ratio of market to household work.

A reanalysis of the 1965 and 1975 data restricted the 1975 sample to match the 1965 sample and focused on changes in men's time in housework and child care time over the decade. After controlling for demographic changes in the population that could have affected hours of housework and child care, the authors concluded:

> Neither unadjusted nor adjusted means of men's housework or child-care time changed significantly between 1965 and 1975. Further, few systematic changes in the time spent in housework and child care are observed for specific categories of men. . . . Overall, the findings cast doubt on the supposed convergence of men's and women's roles. Clearly, men did little between 1965 and 1975 to offset the household pressures created by women's increased participation in the labor force" (Coverman and Sheley, 1986, p. 413).

It is worth noting that the 30-year trends highlighted in Table 6 show virtually no change in the hours men spend doing female-type housework. Their greater household hours in 1985 come from increased time in male-type or non-sex-typed activity.

Other trend studies showing only non-significant changes in the amount of time husbands spend in family work include 1) research on household work in the Syracuse, New York area, 1967-77, showing that wives' household work decreased slightly (less dishwashing and clothing care, more shopping), children's increased slightly (more shopping), and husbands' remained stable (Sanik, 1981); and 2) a reanalysis of data from the Panel Study of Income Dynamics (Nickols and Metzen, 1978) showing husbands' average weekly hours of housework 1968-73, at 1.9, 1.7, 1.9, 1.9, 2.6, 2.4, respectively, for an average over the six-year period of 2.1 hours per week. While the studies over the 1965-75 decade do not show significant increases in husbands' work in the home, adding the data from the 1980s does indeed suggest a very gradual trend toward convergence (i.e., men do seem to be doing little more of the housework and child care).

Szinovacz (1987) assessed time use and husband-wife equality of workloads as revealed in five studies over the 1965-77 period, including the data from the 1965-66 Multinational Time Use Study. She combined husband's and wife's work hours into a couple total, including both "family work" and market work, and computed the percentage share of the couple's work done by each spouse. She concludes that there is some evidence for "a moderate increase in husband's share of family work since the mid 1960s (Szinovacz, 1987, p. 174), but the clearest pattern in the results seems to be the continued inequity of the family workload in favor of the husband if the wife is employed (his share of family work in the five studies proves to be 46, 44, 49, 49, and 45%, respectively), and in favor of the wife if she is not employed (the husband's share, in that condition, amounting to 53, 52, 60, and 56%; the fifth study--1977--does not produce a percentage because couples in which only the husband worked were not interviewed). Our assessment of Szinovacz's figures is that they show no clear trend over the 12-year period.

References

Coverman, Shelley and Joseph F. Sheley. "Change in Men's Housework and Child-Care Time, 1965-1975." Journal of Marriage and the Family 48 (1986): 413-422.

Greis, Theresa Diss. The Decline of Annual Hours Worked in the United States Since 1947. Philadelphia: The Wharton School, University of Pennsylvania, 1984.

Juster, F. Thomas and Frank P. Stafford, eds. Time, Goods and Well-Being. Ann Arbor: Survey Research Center, University of Michigan, 1985.

Nickols, Sharon Y. and Edward J. Metzen. "Housework Time of Husband and Wife." Home Economics Research Journal 7 (1978): 85-97.

Robinson, John P. "'Massification' and Democratization of the Leisure Class." The Annals of the American Academy of Political and Social Science 435 (1978): 206-225.

------. "Time for Work." American Demographics 11 (No. 4, 1989a): 68.

------. "Time's Up." American Demographics 11 (No. 7, 1989b): 33-35.

------. "Who's Doing the Housework." American Demographics 10 (No. 12, 1988): 24-28, 63.

Sanik, Margaret Mietus. "Division of Household Work: A Decade Comparison--1976-1977." Home Economics Research Journal 10 (1981): 175-180.

Szalai, Alexander, ed. The Use of Time: Daily Activities of Urban and Suburban Populations in Twelve Countries. The Hague: Mouton, 1972.

Szinovacz, Maximiliane E. "Changing Family Roles and Interactions." In Women and the Family: Two Decades of Change, edited by Beth B. Hess and Marvin B. Sussman, pp. 163-201. New York: Haworth Press, 1984.

Table 1. AVERAGE HOURS PER WEEK SPENT IN MAJOR TYPES OF
ACTIVITY, BY SEX, NATIONAL SAMPLES*, 1954-1965

Activity	Men		Women	
	1954	1965	1954	1965
Sleep	54	53	53	54
Work	59	59	52	57
Work for pay	52	51	14	20
Family care	6	5	35	33
Shopping	1	3	3	4
Personal Care	21	21	21	22
Free Time	34	34	41	35
Organizations	2	3	2	3
Television	--	12	--	9
Reading	6	4	6	3
Radio, records	--	1	--	1
Social life	8	7	12	10
Recreation	1	1	1	1
Other leisure	--	6	--	8
Sample Size (N)	4250	521	4250	697

* The samples are not precisely comparable, e.g., the 1965 sample
includes only urban respondents.

SOURCE: Based on Juster and Stafford, 1985, p. 294.

Table 2. HOURS PER WEEK SPENT IN MAJOR TYPES OF ACTIVITY, MEN
          AGED 25-44, 1965-1975 and 1975-1981*

Activity	1965	1975	1975	1981
Total work activities	62.0	58.0	59.6	61.4
Market work	50.3	49.1	48.4	47.4
Direct work hours	41.8	41.2	41.5	40.9
Travel to work	4.4	4.6	3.8	3.6
Other work-related	4.1	3.3	3.1	2.9
Household work	11.8	8.9	11.2	14.0
Male-typed	1.6	2.3	3.2	2.8
Female-typed	1.3	1.0	1.3	2.4
Other	8.8	5.5	6.8	8.9
Personal Care Activities	67.3	65.5	68.5	65.9
Leisure Activities	38.7	44.5	40.0	40.6
Education	1.7	2.5	1.4	0.9
Organizations	2.0	1.3	2.1	2.3
Social entertainment	12.8	14.8	12.8	12.4
Active leisure	3.0	5.1	4.6	5.4
Passive leisure	19.3	20.9	19.0	19.5
Television	12.3	14.5	12.6	12.1
Reading	4.4	3.6	2.8	2.7
Conversations	1.5	1.6	1.6	3.2
Other	1.1	1.2	2.0	1.5
Total time	168.0	168.0	168.0	168.0
Number of cases (N)	(272)	(197)	(191)	(106)

* The 1981 sample (column 4) was only a portion of the 1975 sample,
restudied six years later; it does not entirely match the
characteristics of the 1965 sample or the entire 1975 sample. It
is appropriately compared to the adjusted subsample (column 3)
rather than the unadjusted 1975 subsample (column 2).

SOURCE: Based on Juster and Stafford, 1985, pp. 316-317, 320-321.

Table 3. HOURS PER WEEK SPENT IN MAJOR TYPES OF ACTIVITY, WOMEN
AGED 25-44, 1965-1975 and 1975-1981*

Activity	1965	1975	1975	1981
Total work activities	61.9	54.6	54.2	56.9
Market work	16.0	19.2	21.0	25.1
Direct work hours	13.5	16.5	17.8	21.0
Travel to work	1.3	1.4	1.5	2.2
Other work-related	1.3	1.3	1.6	1.9
Household work	45.9	35.4	33.2	31.8
Male-typed	0.7	1.0	0.9	0.9
Female-typed	19.3	13.4	12.6	11.0
Other	25.9	21.1	19.7	19.9
Personal Care Activities	70.9	72.4	72.0	70.5
Leisure Activities	35.2	41.0	41.9	40.5
Education	0.8	1.7	1.1	0.5
Organizations	3.1	2.5	2.8	2.6
Social entertainment	11.7	11.1	13.9	14.4
Active leisure	2.8	3.5	4.0	4.2
Passive leisure	16.8	22.2	20.1	18.8
Television	8.9	14.3	12.6	11.0
Reading	3.4	2.8	3.2	3.0
Conversations	2.9	2.5	2.5	3.4
Other	1.7	2.5	1.8	1.4
Total time	168.0	168.0	168.0	168.0
Number of cases (N)	(342)	(228)	(222)	(143)

* The 1981 sample (column 4) was only a portion of the 1975 sample,
restudied six years later; it does not entirely match the
characteristics of the 1965 sample or the entire 1975 sample. It
is appropriately compared to the adjusted subsample (column 3)
rather than the unadjusted 1975 subsample (column 2).

SOURCE: Based on Juster and Stafford, 1985, pp. 316-317, 320-321.

Table 4. HOURS PER WEEK SPENT IN MAJOR TYPES OF ACTIVITY, MEN
          AGED 45-64, 1965-1975 and 1975-1981*

Activity	1965	1975	1975	1981
Total work activities	64.5	55.0	48.6	51.9
Market work	53.3	40.9	34.3	38.3
Direct work hours	44.2	34.0	28.9	32.8
Travel to work	5.2	4.0	3.0	3.4
Other work-related	3.8	2.9	2.3	2.1
Household work	11.2	14.0	14.3	13.5
Male-typed	1.6	3.1	4.3	3.7
Female-typed	2.3	2.4	2.9	2.5
Other	7.3	8.5	7.1	7.4
Personal Care Activities	69.4	71.1	74.5	72.2
Leisure Activities	34.0	42.0	45.0	43.9
Education	0.4	0.4	0.2	0.2
Organizations	2.0	2.3	2.9	2.1
Social entertainment	9.6	10.0	11.3	13.0
Active leisure	2.7	3.8	6.1	5.7
Passive leisure	19.3	25.4	24.5	22.8
Television	11.2	18.7	15.9	13.8
Reading	5.2	4.0	4.1	3.7
Conversations	1.6	1.4	1.7	2.0
Other	1.4	1.3	2.8	3.3
Total time	168.0	168.0	168.0	168.0
Number of cases (N)	(197)	(109)	(106)	(63)

* The 1981 sample (column 4) was only a portion of the 1975 sample,
restudied six years later; it does not entirely match the
characteristics of the 1965 sample or the entire 1975 sample. It
is appropriately compared to the adjusted subsample (column 3)
rather than the unadjusted 1975 subsample (column 2).

SOURCE: Based on Juster and Stafford, 1985, pp. 316-317, 320-321.

Table 5. HOURS PER WEEK SPENT IN MAJOR TYPES OF ACTIVITY,
WOMEN AGED 45-64, 1965-1975 and 1975-1981*

Activity	1965	1975	1975	1981
Total work activities	58.9	52.0	49.7	50.3
Market work	23.1	20.9	19.6	22.0
Direct work hours	19.4	17.4	16.7	18.9
Travel to work	1.9	2.0	1.6	1.6
Other work-related	1.7	1.6	1.3	1.5
Household work	35.9	31.0	30.1	28.3
Male-typed	1.0	1.1	1.4	1.2
Female-typed	17.0	13.9	13.6	12.2
Other	17.9	16.0	15.1	14.8
Personal Care Activities	73.3	74.7	75.0	73.4
Leisure Activities	35.7	41.4	43.3	44.3
Education	0.3	0.4	0.3	0.1
Organizations	2.2	2.8	3.3	4.0
Social entertainment	9.9	8.4	11.8	14.5
Active leisure	3.8	5.0	5.2	4.2
Passive leisure	19.5	24.8	22.8	21.4
Television	9.9	15.7	14.2	12.4
Reading	4.6	4.6	4.4	3.5
Conversations	2.4	2.0	2.1	2.8
Other	2.6	2.6	2.0	2.7
Total time	168.0	168.0	168.0	168.0
Number of cases (N)	(236)	(138)	(153)	(86)

* The 1981 sample (column 4) was only a portion of the 1975 sample, restudied six years later; it does not entirely match the characteristics of the 1965 sample or the entire 1975 sample. It is appropriately compared to the adjusted subsample (column 3) rather than the unadjusted 1975 subsample (column 2).

SOURCE: Based on Juster and Stafford, 1985, pp. 316-317, 320-321.

Table 6. HOURS PER WEEK SPENT IN SELECTED ACTIVITIES, BY SEX
          AND EMPLOYMENT STATUS, 1965-1985

Activity	Men			Women		
	1965	1975	1985	1965	1975	1985
Persons employed 10+ hrs./week						
Total work*	53	--	50	57	--	46
Market work	49	--	42	39	--	31
Household work	4	6	8	18	15	15
Female-typed	2	2	3	16	13	12
Male-typed, other	3	4	5	2	3	3
Leisure activities	33	36	36	27	31	34
Unemployed persons (employed less than 10 hrs./week)						
Household work	10	11	15	34	26	24
Female-typed	6	5	6	30	23	20
Male-typed, other	3	6	9	4	4	4
Leisure activities	63	55	56	40	44	47
All persons						
Household work	5	7	10	27	22	20
Female-typed	2	2	4	24	20	16
Male-typed	3	5	6	3	2	3
Leisure activities	40	38	40	34	38	39

* Includes travel to work.

Note: Totals and subtotals may vary due to rounding.

SOURCE: Based on Robinson, 1989a; 1989b; 1988.

Daily life mobility in the United States is heavily dependent upon the automobile, and while one might argue that there are declining, or perhaps even negative returns to increasing automobile concentration, using the automobile as an indicator of people's ability to get around is a convenient shortcut for documentatory purposes here. Trends in the ratio of persons licensed to drive vs. total population, by age cohort, suggest 1) lower mobility among women than men; 2) a slight decline in daily mobility among men, especially younger men, in the 1980s; 3) tendencies to convergence by sex until about 1980, and a stabilization thereafter which continues a relative disadvantage for women, especially at the older ages.

The automobile is a dominant mode of "daily life mobility" in the United States. Comparing two not-strictly-comparable national personal transportation surveys from the 1960s and 1970s (U.S. Department of Transportation, 1984) suggests that the number of miles driven annually varies in proportion to the number of drivers in a given age-sex group. The ability to drive a car is not, of course, the same thing as having a car to drive, but the two are definitely correlated. Presumably these data fairly well track practical ability to drive a car.

Apart from the indirectness of the measure, there are some imperfections owing to the census interpolations and to the fact that in the U.S. automobile licensing is by state rather than by the Federal government, which makes it possible for one to have two or more licenses at the same time. Thus, one may note in Table 1 many instances of higher-than-100% licensing. It is for this reason that the figures in Table 1 are described as ratios rather than percentages. In discussing the trends, we refer to them as percentages, however. In fact, they represent maximum, not minimum proportions of drivers in the various age cohorts.

The worst problem with these materials for our purposes is that a major use of the car is to get to work, or to do nonremunerative but otherwise necessary tasks, like grocery shopping, rather than "daily life mobility." Still, it has been the American experience that even when one acquires a car for practical purposes, one also uses it for other purposes; and therefore having access to a motor vehicle enhances one's daily life mobility. Moreover, there is some suggestion, based on the Nationwide Personal Transportation Surveys, that

> with fewer employment opportunities in the inner city and more rapidly increasing employment in the fringe areas closer to residential zones, commuting distances have been decreasing. . . . After more than a century of slow increases in the average work-trip length followed by a period of sizable increases in the mid-twentieth century, the historical pattern of commuting distances seems to be changing (Monroe and Maziarz, 1985).

By 1963, driving was nearly universal among men. The sole exception was among men over age 65, some of whom never had driven, having been reared in an era when many adults did not drive. In 1963, and consistently down through the 1980s, for young men between age 16 and about age 21, the percent licensed to drive increases consistently until near universality is achieved: everyone knows how to drive. However, the lack of trend since 1963 in the ratio of licenses to population among men aged 16-21 does not hold for men in their twenties. Among these men, as is apparent in the table, the ratios decline 1970-1986, suggesting that young adults in the 1980s are a little less likely to be driving than were their counterparts 10-15 years earlier.

Not until middle age are the license-to-population ratios for the 1980s comparable to those of the earlier years. Indeed, the consistently lower ratios for men under age 45 in 1980 and 1986 suggest a decline in daily mobility among them.

To the degree that these data reflect daily mobility, the figures in Table 1 suggest that women's daily mobility is less than men's, although there has been some convergence, especially over the 1963-80 period. In 1963, the ratio of drivers licences to female population peaked at about .75, and that among women aged 22-29. Among women aged 60 and over, a majority did not drive. By 1980, the peak ratio had increased to about .90, meaning that a maximum of 90 percent of women aged 23-44 had drivers licenses. Between 1980 and 1986 there was virtually no change in the ratios of licenses to female population, except for a slight increase in licenses among older women, a majority of whom (and as many as three-fourths in the age 55-64 cohort) now were licensed to drive.

In sum, the data suggest that virtually all men in U.S. society learn to drive and, by middle age at least, most are licensed to drive. To the degree that the ratio of licenses to population indexes mobility, there is some evidence that the daily mobility of American men is slightly less than it was in the 1960s and 1970s. Women's mobility appears considerably more circumscribed. Allowing for some multiple licenses in the totals shown in Table 1, it appears that well upwards of one-tenth of American women are not licensed to drive. While there was some convergence 1963-1980--women became less disadvantaged than they had been--the ratios for women in the peak licensing years run 5-10 points lower than for men. The most obvious disparity is among the elderly. For men, license-population ratios remain high even after age 70; for women, the increments of decline are sizable from age 45 on, and by age 70, fewer than half are licensed to drive, compared to as many as 85% of the men.

References

Monroe, Charles B. and Thomas Maziarz. "American Work-Trip Distances: A Reversal of the Historical Trend." Geography 70 (1985): 359-362.

U. S. Department of Transportation, Federal Highway Administration. Highway Statistics. Annual. Various years.

U. S Department of Transportation, Urban Mass Transportation Administration. Urban Travel Trends: Historical Observations and Future Forecasts. Washington, D. C.: USGPO, 1984.

Table 1.   RATIO OF DRIVERS' LICENSES TO POPULATION, BY SEX AND
AGE, 1963-1986

	Males					Females			
Age	1963	1970	1980	1986		1963	1970	1980	1986
16	50%	43%	47%	49%		34%	32%	41%	44%
17	87	73	71	68		52	56	61	62
18	70	84	81	81		50	65	70	72
19	77	94	85	84		56	72	75	74
20	85	95	87	86		61	71	78	78
21	101	104	90	89		72	79	83	82
22	116	100	94	93		79	78	85	86
23	113	106	99	96		77	82	89	88
24	107	118	99	94		75	92	89	88
25-29	109	107	102	96		76	85	92	90
30-34	97	105	104	97		69	84	94	95
35-39	98	104	104	98		70	83	93	92
40-44	103	100	102	103		72	78	89	94
45-49	99	100	99	99		69	74	84	89
50-54	99	98	95	97		62	68	78	85
55-59	98	95	95	95		54	61	75	79
60-64	96	91	95	94		45	52	70	76
65-69	88	86	93	93		33	40	61	71
70+	70	63	81	85		17	18	36	45

SOURCE: Based on U.S. Department of Transportation, (various
annual volumes). Populations in various age categories
obtained from U.S. Census Bureau reports.

Most attempts to measure household production have used hours of activity as a substitute for output. National data on more direct output-based indicators are hard to find, but the directions of trends suggested in regional and local studies corroborates the trends apparent in time-use data, namely modest declines in amount of home production and convergence between the sexes in performance of home-based tasks. Even so, household production continues to be defined largely as "woman's work," and most of it is done by women. Although the composite trend in home production seems to be a decline, some types of home production have not declined, and for a few, home production may have increased.

The term, "household production," generally refers to goods and services produced in the home for family use. The products of household work are directly consumed without going through the market. Unpaid household work and household production are distinguished from "work at home," which is market work performed at home rather than elsewhere.

The Federal government did not begin collecting data on the home-based work force until 1985. The results of a baseline survey that year revealed that about 10% of employed Americans did some of their work at home, and 2%--2.2 million workers--did all of their work at home. About two-thirds of home-based workers were women. The largest industry group of home-based workers, accounting for almost half of all home-based work, was in services, including professional (educational, health, and social services such as child care), business and repair, and personal services. Most people in service industries who reported 8+ hours of work at home were private wage and salary workers, who presumably bring work home on a regular basis, but among those who worked 35 or more hours at home, most were self-employed in home-based, unincorporated businesses (Horvath, 1986).

A type of household production for which there are some statistical trend data is unpaid work in family enterprises. However, the products of such work typically are linked to the market and the wider economy. Until about 1970, most unpaid family workers were employed in agriculture, but declining employment in agricultural jobs has changed that. There are many fewer unpaid family workers than there used to be; there were over a million in 1968, compared to about 425,000 in 1986. The sex composition of unpaid family workers has not changed over the years; about 80% are women. Unpaid family workers used to account for a significant portion of the agricultural labor force, but that proportion has consistently declined, from about 15% of persons employed in agriculture in 1969 to about 5% in 1986. (See the relevant monthly issues of the U.S. Bureau of Labor Statistics, Employment and Earnings; see also Chapter 3.4, Women's Employment).

As the term "household production" is usually used, it denotes neither unpaid work in family enterprises nor paid work performed at home. Rather, it refers to productive activity aimed at family consumption which is not mediated by the market. Vanek's (1980, pp. 276-277) description of "household work" is apt:

> Even in modern society a substantial amount of productive activity takes place in the home. Goods must be procured, processed, and maintained for family use. People also need servicing and care. In particular a wide range of tasks is connected with the training of children and with preserving their physical health and safety. Studies show that all these household tasks continue to be time

consuming and that they remain primarily "women's work." . . . a detailed examination of what is done reveals that household tasks are sharply divided by sex. Men's work clusters in only a few activities: yard work, home repairs, shopping, travel on household errands, and to a limited degree child care. The wife is still responsible for routine home and family care, which includes such tasks as meal preparation and clean-up, home care, laundry, mending, and care of children.

The output of household production is generally not measured directly. Instead, most studies estimate the amount of household production via time use studies, and assign value to it by one of two methods, the market alternative cost method and the opportunity cost method. The market alternative cost method usually involves decomposing time spent in household production into various specific tasks and then assigning to each the appropriate wage that would be paid for that service in the market. In contrast, the opportunity cost approach assigns a value to household production time on the basis of the value that might be assigned to the family member's time in alternative, market activity if such employment were not precluded by the household work. In this approach, the human capital characteristics of the family member-- generally the wife--affect the value of the time spent; in the former, only the nature of the home tasks performed influences the value of the time spent (Zick and Bryant, 1983, pp. 133-135).

A third approach, essentially a variation of the market alternative cost method, is "output related evaluation." The researcher begins with household output, assigns a value to that output on the basis of market costs of the same goods and services, deducts the expenses incurred by the household in the process of the production, and arrives at an estimate of "value-added" by the household activity (Goldschmidt-Clermont, 1983, pp. 127-129).

Time use data is an essential component of all three approaches for measuring the economic value of home production. In the absence of national time series data showing changes in the value of home production as estimated by any of the above approaches, we refer to changes in time spent in household work as a rough index of changes in home production. Chapter 13.4 (Time Use) includes estimates of "family care" time for 1954-1965, and of "household work" for 1965-1985. To the degree that changes in time spent in household work correspond to changes in household production, it may be concluded that total household production declined substantially between 1954 and 1975, then stabilized at approximately the 1975 level for the next decade. That aggregate trend reflects countervailing trends by sex: household production by women continually declined over the entire 1954-1985 period, with most of the decline occurring in the first two decades, while household production by men consistently increased, but at a relatively low rate. Most household production continues to be done by women, but the ratio of male-to-female time spent in all types of household work has increased, from about 1-to-6 in 1954 to about 1-to-2 in 1985. See Chapter 13.4 for further details.

One form of household production for which there are national trend data from 1975 on is gardening. Trends in gardening parallel those in household production as estimated by the time studies: gardens are smaller than they were, progressively fewer people are engaged in vegetable gardening, and the estimated dollar-value of yields from gardens is lower than it used to be. There are other aspects of gardening and related forms of household production that do not show declines. At least for the 1975-1987 period, there is no evidence of a decline in the percentage of householders engaged in lawn care, growing fruits and berries, flower gardening, ornamental gardening, or caring for indoor houseplants. Moreover, while the percent of households maintaining vegetable gardens declined significantly between 1975 and 1987 (from 49% to 33%), vegetable gardening in 1975 was more popular than it had been 25 years earlier. In 1951, only 39% of those questioned in a national Gallup poll had vegetable gardens (Gallup, 1972, p. 999).

There are hints of the scale of household production in items in national and, more frequently, local surveys that seem not to have been repeated. There is also trend data on some kinds of household production in particular communities. For example, comparisons of housewives' activities in 1925 and 1977 in the city of Middletown (Caplow, et al., 1982, pp. 105-115 and 365-369), show that sewing and mending and housework generally occupied much less time than formerly, but there were certain activities, such as bread-baking in the home, that were more frequent in 1977, and others, like washing and ironing, that showed no clear trend, being more frequent than before in certain strata and less frequent in others. Most of the available data do not permit a distinction between rate of productivity and time spent. Presumably output-based measures would show increased efficiency in some forms of home production, such that overall output had increased despite declines in time spent.

References

Caplow, Theodore, Howard M. Bahr, Bruce A. Chadwick, Reuben Hill, and Margaret Holmes Williamson. Middletown Families: Fifty Years of Change and Continuity. Minneapolis: University of Minnesota Press, 1982.

Gallup, George H. Gallup Poll: Public Opinion 1935-1971. New York: Random House, 1972.

Goldschmidt-Clermont, Luisella. "Output-Related Evaluations of Unpaid Household Work: A Challenge for Time Use Studies." Home Economics Research Journal 12 (1983):127-132.

Horvath, Francis W. "Work at Home: New Findings from the Current Population Survey." Monthly Labor Review 109 (No. 11, 1986): 31-35.

U.S. Bureau of the Census. Statistical Abstract of the United States, 1989. Washington, D.C., 1989. Annual. Previous years as cited.

Vanek, Joann. "Household Work, Wage Work, and Sexual Equality." In Women and Household Labor, edited by Sarah Fenstermaker Berk, pp. 275-291. Beverly Hills, CA: Sage, 1980.

Zick, Cathleen D. and W. Keith Bryant. "Alternative Strategies for Pricing Home Work Time." Home Economics Research Journal 12 (1983): 133-134.

Table 1. HOUSEHOLDS WITH HOME GARDENS, AND SELECTED
CHARACTERISTICS OF GARDENS, 1975-1987

Characteristic of Gardens	1975	1980	1983	1985	1986	1987
Median Size (sq. ft.)	540	663	505	300	325	--
Median Yield (dollars)	258	460	405	--	278	--
Percent of Households Doing						
Vegetable Gardening	49%	43%	42%	37%	38%	33%
Flower Gardening	39	37	47	41	44	43
Lawn Care	56	52	63	64	58	59
Growing Fruits and Berries	12	21	32	24	30	--
Growing Fruit Trees	--	--	20	17	17	18
Growing Berries	--	--	12	7	8	9
Ornamental Gardening	--	--	7	7	6	8
Indoor Houseplants	40	40	43	42	41	41

SOURCE: Based on <u>Statistical Abstract 1989</u>, p. 229; <u>1988</u>, p. 221;
<u>1985</u>, p. 229; <u>1984</u>, p. 238.

The dominant trend has been liberalization, including 1) increased freedom of sexual expression, both within and outside of marriage; 2) growing public approval of and participation in premarital sex; 3) the emergence of sexuality as a growth industry, both as direct commerce in sex-related behaviors and products, and as part of the advertising and marketing of other products; 4) increased opportunity for vicarious sexual experience via the electronic and print media; and 5) increased public tolerance for sexual diversity and deviation. In the 1980s some trends toward sexual liberalism seem to have peaked, and there were some modest reversals.

The publication of Alfred Kinsey's Sexual Behavior in the Human Male (1948) may be seen as the beginning of the contemporary era in American sexuality. It inaugerated an era of pervasive, highly visible change in sexual attitudes and practices. Analysts characterize the following decades as periods of "sexual revolution," "sexual liberation" (Hunt, 1974, p. 3), and the "Americanization of sex" (Schur, 1988). Within the dominant trend of liberalization are component trends or tendencies, some of which seem to run counter to the manifest thrust of "sexual freedom". Schur identifies three such tendencies--the depersonalization of sex, the commoditization of sex, and the continuity of "coercive sexuality"--as unfortunate "distortions" that have accompanied the modernization of sex.

Premarital Sex

Perhaps the most conspicuous change in sexual expression was the shift toward approval of and participation in premarital sex:
> For all of the changes in sexual mores that occurred in the 1960s and 1970s, the spread of sexual activity among the young marked the sharpest break with the past. . . . Youth engaged not just in occasional experimentation, nor did they have sex only in the context of a marriage-oriented relationship. The erotic became incorporated as a regular, ongoing feature of their maturation (D'Emilio and Freedman, 1988, p. 353).

According to Gallup surveys between 1969 and 1985, public approval of sex relations before marriage more than doubled, from 24% to 57%. General Social Survey (GSS) data for the same period corroborate the growing permissiveness, showing consistent increases until 1982 in agreement with the statement that "it is not at all wrong for a man and woman to have sex relations before marriage." In the 1980s the level of support for premarital permissiveness seems to have plateaued, with about 40% of adults agreeing that premarital sex is "not at all wrong" (see Table 1).

Several national surveys of teenage sexual activity, along with retrospective data from the 1982 National Survey of Family Growth (NSFG), provide fairly reliable estimates of the percent of teenage women who had ever had sexual intercourse, by race and age (Table 2). Taken together, they show: 1) Over the 1970s, young women were becoming sexually active earlier, 15% of 15-year-olds in 1971 having had sexual intercourse, compared to 23% in 1979; 2) Black teenagers were sexually active earlier than whites (e.g., in 1971, almost three times as likely to have had intercourse by age 15) but over the decade the differences declined somewhat, with rates for white teenagers approaching those for blacks, especially in the older teens; 3) By 1982, there is evidence of a leveling or a least a slowing in the trend toward more and earlier sexual experience among teenage women; the percentages having had sexual intercourse are <u>down</u> five points from the high of 1979.

The 1982 NSFG data permit the calculation of rates of premarital sexual intercourse by exact age for teenage women by birth cohort and race, beginning with women born 1938-1940. The general trend, with some minor fluctuations, is of increasing sexual activity for successive cohorts of blacks and whites born after 1943. There are larger absolute increases among whites than blacks because black levels of teenage sexual activity were already high before the "sexual revolution." Thus, the increased permissiveness of the 1960s and 1970s shows up more clearly among whites than blacks, and among the younger black women. Even so, the results of sexual liberation appear in both populations: more sexual activity, and at younger ages (Hofferth, Kahn, and Baldwin, 1987, p. 49).

Longitudinal studies of college-age youth in the 1960s and 1970s also yielded evidence of rising permissiveness: there were fewer college-age virgins of both sexes, more variety in sexual partners, and more liberal attitudes about sex before marriage. Researchers caution that while the overall trend was toward greater permissiveness, it was not unilinear in all segments of society (Clayton and Bokemeier, 1980, pp. 762, 765).

Innovation in Forms of Sexual Expression

The past four decades of "sexual liberation" seem to have extended the range of "normal" sexual behavior as well as increasing rates of sexual intercourse both within and outside marriage. Although much of the research on intimate behavior suffers from sampling problems, generally including low response rates and selection biases from the necessity of relying on volunteers as subjects, the direction of the trends reported manifests quite remarkable reliability. That is, whatever the absolute incidence of the behaviors described--and there is serious question about that inasmuch as the more conservative respondents, sexually speaking, are less likely to participate in sex surveys--the <u>direction</u> of change demonstrated in most of the follow-up studies or replications has been toward increased sexual "liberation" and greater equality between the sexes in sexual experience. The "double standard" between unmarried men and women in rates of "heavy petting," formerly (1965) twice as common among college men as college women, were by 1980 approaching parity, and so were rates of premarital intercourse (Robinson and Jedlicka, 1982, pp. 238-239).

Judging from a comprehensive inquiry into premarital sexual behavior among college-age youth at the University of Wisconsin and in the city of Madison, Wisconsin in the mid-1970s (DeLamater and MacCorquodale, 1979), "heavy petting" meant sexual interaction with one's current "heterosexual partner" which generally included breast fondling (among 75-78% of respondents), genital manipulation (62-74%), and almost half of the time, oral sex (41-51%). A majority (54-70%) of college-age youth, male and female, student and non-student, had experience in heterosexual oral sex. Findings from a national survey of the sexual practices of teenagers in the early 1980s (Coles and Stokes, 1985, pp. 58-59, 73) are congruent with the surveys of college-age youth: by age 18, 46% of boys and 53% of girls have had sexual intercourse; 60% have participated in "vaginal play," and over 40% in heterosexual oral sex.

By the mid-1970s, erotic behavior within marriage had diversified to the extent that Morton Hunt (1974, pp. 197-198), comparing findings from a 1972 survey with Kinsey's from a quarter of a century earlier, concluded that the increased acceptance of oral sex within marriage was a change "of major and historic proportions." Later surveys show the trend continuing: by the 1980s, 90% of couples responding to surveys on marital intimacy had experimented with oral sex, and for many couples it was a continuing part of their erotic life (Tavris and Sadd, 1977, pp. 88, 162-163; Blumstein and Schwartz, 1983, p. 236).

Comparisons between the Kinsey results and a well-designed 1985 survey of the sexual socialization of black and white women in Los Angeles county (Wyatt, Peters and Guthrie, 1988, pp. 227, 315-316) provide further confirmation of the trend toward more liberal sexual mores, both with respect to extra-marital sex among married women and "broadened repertoires of sexual behavior" generally. In 1985, two-thirds of black women and about 90% of white women reported experience with oral sex, up from about 20% and 50%, respectively, in the 1940s. An authoritative review of the relevant research literature concludes that "oral sex has become, over the last 50 years, part of the sexual scripts of many young people and is a common, though not necessarily a frequent, component of sexual relations in contemporary marriage" (Gagnon and Simon, 1987, p. 1).

There are indications that the incidence of homosexual experience as a part of sexual socialization has increased slightly (see, for example, Wyatt, Peters and Guthrie, 1988, p. 223), but such an increase might be explained by the increase in all kinds of sexual experience associated with the "sexual modernization" of U.S. society. In any case, there is no evidence that adult toleration of homosexual sex has increased since the mid-seventies; in fact, the trend 1973-88 is toward less approval of homosexual sex, with the percentage saying that homosexual relations are always wrong increasing at an annual rate of about .4%. However, U.S. adults are more cognizant than formerly of the civil rights of homosexuals. There seems to be no AIDS-related backlash fueling attitudes favorable to the limitation of their civil liberties (Table 3).

Pornography

Sexual liberation has permeated the entire culture, including and perhaps especially the media, both printed and electronic. Indeed, the media have been the primary sources of sexual information and role models. With the exception of the invention of the contraceptive pill, most milestones of the sexual revolution have been media events, including the publishing of the Kinsey reports, Supreme Court decisions permitting the dissemination of sexually explicit material, and the application of contemporary communications technology--telephones, satellites, television, videocassette recorders, and computers--to sex business.

An early milestone was the creation and instant success of Playboy, the first mass-circulation "male sophisticate" magazine. The circulation of Playboy and its imitators is an index of the status of and audience for pornography in the U.S. The allegedly negative personal and social impacts of Playboy and the financial empire it spawned figured heavily in the final report of the Attorney General's Commission on Pornography (U.S. Department of Justice, 1986). Founded in 1953, Playboy had a circulation of 110,000 within a year, and 1.35 million by 1963. Circulation peaked in the early 1970s at about six million. In 1983 its 4.2 million issues per month placed it ahead of Newsweek and not far behind Time (3.0 and 4.7 million circulation, respectively) (Scott and Cuvelier, 1987, p. 283).

Circulation figures for the top-selling sexually explicit magazines reveal a peak distribution of about 16 million issues per month in 1976-80, followed by substantial declines in the following five years (U.S. Department of Justice, 1986, pp. 1409-1411). The declines reflect diversification in the pornography business, most notably the widespread distribution of pornographic videocassettes and the availability of sexually explicit programming on cable television, rather than a general decline in the market for pornography.

Another indicator in the epidemiology of pornography is attendance at X-rated movies. National surveys in the mid-1970s found that about one-third of the public had ever attended an X-rated movie. Attendance trends for 1973-1986 are non-linear, with 25% of those surveyed in 1973 having seen an X-rated movie in the past year, a consistent decline in that percentage to a low of 15% in 1978, and then a return to 25% by 1986 (Table 4). The upturn is attributable to increased home-viewing of X-rated movies on videocassette recorders (Smith, 1987, pp. 259-260).

The best available trend information on pornography is the set of questions in the GSS reflecting public attitudes, 1973-1986 (Table 4). Statistically significant linear trends include an increase in popular belief that pornography leads to the breakdown of morals (from 53% agreement in 1973 to 62% in 1986) and that "sexual materials lead people to commit rape" (from 50% to 57%, respectively).

Among the pornographic materials distributed in the U.S. are motion pictures, videotapes, magazines, satellite and cable television shows, dial-a-porn telephone systems, computer pornography, books, newspapers, photographs, audio tapes, and peep shows. Since the 1950s the pornography industry has grown "from a low yield, covert business" distributing photographs, films and printed materials of poor quality, to "a highly visible multi-billion dollar industry," with sophisticated production, management, and distribution systems. Among the trends documented by the Attorney General's Commission on Pornography (U.S. Department of Justice, 1986, pp. 284-288, 1432) are a dramatic increase in the scale of the industry, a shift from marketing motion pictures to videotapes, proliferation of retail outlets for pornographic videotapes ("as many as half of all the general video retailers in the country include within their offerings at least some material that . . . would commonly be conceded to be pornographic"), and rapid expansion of "dial-a-porn" and similar telephone services.

Much public concern about pornography stems from a belief that it is linked to violence against women. There is also a sense that pornography combining sex and violence is on the increase (Newsweek, 1985). However, history of violence in hard-core films (Slade, 1984) concludes that violence has been much less common in hard-core pornographic films than in the legitimate cinema, and that as the two genres come closer together--as it becomes harder to distinguish the pornographic from the "legitimate" mass circulation film--there may be more violence added because that is what sells in the legitimate film market. Surveys by the Kinsey Institute indicate that in contemporary adult arcades, the number of violent loops runs at about 10% of all loops, and shows no particular trend. In the mid-1970s there was an increase in violence in the films, but "after brief flirtations with such fetishes . . . producers and consumers seemed to agree that brutal force really belonged off to the side of mainstream eroticism . . . where it has been shunted for the present" (Slade, 1984, pp. 161-162).

The finding that violent material makes up a relatively constant proportion of all pornography is not necessarily a finding of "no change" in the availability of such material in the society. If the sheer volume of all kinds of pornographic materials has increased, then the volume of materials linking sex and violence has also grown.

Vicarious Consumption

The viewing of pornography is one form of vicarious consumption. So is participation in the vicarious life of the legimate theater, movies, television programs, novels and stories. Accompanying the sexual revolution was an increased interest in sex in the media. Vicarious sex became a highly visible tool of advertisers, television producers, journalists, publishers, and business generally:

> As the barriers against sensual imagery fell, advertisers could shape their messages around appeals to the erotic and by glamorizing the lifestyle of the unmarried.
> . . . By the 1980s . . . commercials for any number of products projected the message that consumption promised the fulfillment of erotic fantasies and appetites. . . . The visual entertainment media also made sex a staple of their shows (D'Emilio and Freedman, 1988, pp. 327-329).

The growing importance of sex as topic of public discourse shows up in content analyses of mass circulation magazines. Scott (1986) found that from 1950 to 1980, the number of sex references per page of periodical text increased; references classifiable as "conservative" decreased in frequency; and there were more discussions of "perversions" and other controversial sex topics in the 1970s and 1980s than formerly.

A content analysis of best-selling novels for the period 1959-1979 found these trends: a progressive increase in amount of sexual content; a decrease in the amount of time sexual partners knew each other; an increase in the probability that male sexual partners were portrayed as single; and an increase in avoidance of verbal or nonverbal communication after sexual intercourse (Abramson and Mechanic, 1983: 191-193). A similar analysis of major motion pictures produced fewer consistent trends and this conclusion:

> Although sexuality is now exhibited in a more open and explicit manner, highly successful motion pictures are far from being inundated with sexual content.
> . . . sexual content is certainly not essential in attracting viewer interest (Abramson and Mechanic, 1983, pp. 200-201).

Some trends toward sexual liberalism seem to have peaked in the 1980s, as suggested in the title that concludes one history of American sexuality, "the rise and fall of sexual liberalism." Forces directed against continued sexual liberation in the 1980s include the pro-family "purity crusaders" of the New Right, people frightened by the AIDS epidemic, and an anti-pornography movement in which radical feminists and evangelical Protestants make common cause (D'Emilio and Freedman, 1988, pp. 239, 344-360). The impact of these forces on patterns of sexual behavior and on the pervasive eroticism of U.S. culture is unclear, but as of the late 1980s, a plateau in the trend lines--a stabilizing of present modes of behavior and expression--seems more probable than a drastic reversal.

References

Abramson, Paul R. and Mindy B. Mechanic. "Sex and the Media: Three Decades of Best-Selling Books and Major Motion Pictures." Archives of Sexual Behavior 12 (1983): 185-206.

Blumstein, Philip and Pepper Schwartz. American Couples. New York: William Morrow, 1983.

Clayton, Richard R. and Janet L Bokemeier. "Premarital Sex in the Seventies." Journal of Marriage and the Family 42 (1980):759-775.

Coles, Robert and Geoffry Stokes. Sex and the American Teenager. New York: Rolling Stone Press, 1985.

Davis, James Allan. General Social Surveys, 1972-1987: Cumulative Codebook. Chicago: National Opinion Research Center, 1982.

Davis, James Allan and Tom W. Smith. General Social Surveys, 1972-1988: Cumulative Codebook. Chicago: National Opinion Research Center, 1988. Annual. Previous years as cited.

DeLamater, J.D. and P. MacCorquodale. Premarital Sexuality: Attitudes, Relationships, Behavior. Madison: University of Wisconsin Press, 1979.

D'Emilio, John and Estelle B. Freedman. Intimate Matters: A History of Sexuality in America. New York: Harper & Row, 1988.

Gagnon, John. H. and William Simon. "The Sexual Scripting of Oral Genital Contacts." Archives of Sexual Behavior 16 (1987): 1-25.

Glenn, Norval D. "Social Trends in the United States: Evidence from Sample Surveys." Public Opinion Quarterly 51 (1987): S109-S126.

Hofferth, Sandra L., Joan R. Kahn and Wendy Baldwin. "Premarital Sexual Activity Among U.S. Teenage Women Over the Past Three Decades." Family Planning Perspectives 19 (1987): 46-53.

Hunt, Morton. Sexual Behavior in the 1970s. Chicago: Playboy Press, 1974.

Newsweek. "The War Against Pornography." March 18, 1985: 58-67.

Robinson, Ira E. and Davor Jedlicka. "Change in Sexual Attitudes and Behavior of College Students from 1965 to 1980: A Research Note." Journal of Marriage and the Family 44 (1982): 237-240.

Schur, Edwin M. The Americanization of Sex. Philadelphia: Temple University Press, 1988.

Scott, Joseph E. "An Updated Longitudinal Content Analysis of Sex References in Mass Circulation Magazines." Journal of Sex Research 22 (1986): 385-392.

Scott, Joseph E. and Steven J. Cuvelier. "Violence in Playboy Magazine: A Longitudinal Analysis." Archives of Sexual Behavior 16 (1987): 279-288.

Slade, Joseph W. "Violence in the Hard-Core Pornographic Film: A Historical Survey." Journal of Communication (1984): 148-163.

Smith, Tom W. "The Use of Public Opinion Data By the Attorney General's Commission on Pornography." Public Opinion Quarterly 51 (1987): 249-267.

Tavris, Carol and Susan Sadd. The Redbook Report on Female Sexuality. New York: Delacorte Press, 1977.

U.S. Department of Justice. Attorney General's Commission on Pornography: Final Report. Washington, D.C.: USGPO, July 1986.

Wyatt, Gail Elizabeth, Stefanie Doyle Peters, and Donald Guthrie. "Kinsey Revisited, Part I: Comparisons of the Sexual Socialization and Sexual Behavior of White Women Over 33 Years." Archives of Sexual Behavior 17 (1988): 201-239.

------. "Kinsey Revisited, Part II: Comparisons of the Sexual Socialization and Sexual Behavior of Black Women Over 33 Years." Archives of Sexual Behavior 17 (1988): 289-332.

Table 1. PUBLIC ATTITUDES ABOUT PREMARITAL SEX, 1969-1986

	Percent* Who Agreed That	
Year	It is not wrong for a man and woman to have sex relations before marriage. (Gallup)	It is not at all wrong for a man and woman to have sex relations before marriage. (GSS)
1969	24%	--
1972	--	27%
1973	47	--
1974	--	31
1975	--	33
1977	--	37
1978	--	39
1982	--	41
1983	--	39
1985	57	43
1986	--	40
1988	--	41

* Percentage base does not include don't know, no answer or other neutral responses.

SOURCE: Based on Glenn, 1987, p. S121; Davis and Smith, 1988, p. 242.

Table 2.   PERCENTAGE OF METROPOLITAN TEENAGE WOMEN WHO HAD EVER HAD PREMARITAL SEXUAL INTERCOURSE, BY RACE AND AGE; 1971, 1976, AND 1979 NATIONAL SURVEYS OF YOUNG WOMEN AND 1982 NATIONAL SURVEY OF FAMILY GROWTH

Age	1971	1976	1979	1982
Total (N)	(2739)	(1452)	(1717)	(1157)
15-19	30%	43%	50%	45%
15	15	19	23	17
16	22	30	40	29
17	28	46	50	41
18	43	57	63	59
19	48	64	71	72
Whites (N)	(1758)	(881)	(1034)	(767)
15-19	26	38	47	43
15	12	14	18	15
16	18	25	37	27
17	23	40	46	39
18	39	52	60	56
19	44	59	68	70
Blacks (N)	(981)	(571)	(683)	(390)
15-19	54	66	66	54
15	31	39	42	25
16	46	55	51	38
17	58	72	75	49
18	62	78	77	74
19	76	85	89	81

* Percentages are based on weighted data, but N's are unweighted.

SOURCE: Based on Hofferth, Kahn and Baldwin, 1987, p. 47.

Table 3. DISAPPROVAL OF HOMOSEXUALITY AND SUPPORT FOR THE
CIVIL LIBERTIES OF HOMOSEXUALS, 1973-1988

Year	Homosexuality is always wrong	Percent* Who Agreed That Homosexuals shouldn't be allowed to: Make speech	Teach in college	Have book in library
1973	74%	37%	51%	45%
1974	73	35	47	43
1976	70	36	46	43
1977	72	36	49	43
1980	73	32	43	41
1982	73	32	43	42
1984	73	29	39	39
1985	75	31	40	43
1987	77	30	41	41
1988	77	27	40	37

* Percentage base does not include don't know, no answer or other neutral responses.

NOTE: The items read as follows: What about sexual relations between two <u>adults</u> of the same sex--do you think it is always wrong, almost always wrong, wrong only sometimes, or not wrong at all? Suppose this admitted homosexual wanted to make a speech in your community. Should he be allowed to speak, or not? Should such a person be allowed to teach in a college or university, or not? If some people in your community suggested that a book he wrote in favor of homosexuality should be taken out of your public library, would you favor removing this book, or not?

SOURCE: Based on Davis and Smith, 1988, pp. 122-123, 243; Davis and Smith, 1987, pp. 118-119, 239; Davis, 1982, pp. 86-87, 163.

Table 4. TRENDS IN VIEWING SEXUALLY EXPLICIT MOVIES,
          AND PERCEPTIONS OF PORNOGRAPHIC MATERIAL

Year	Viewed X-rated film in past year	Percent* Agreed That Pornographic Materials			
		Provide sexual inform.	Lead to morals breakdown	Lead to rape	Provide outlet for impulses
1973	25%	62%	53%	50%	55%
1975	19	62	51	52	56
1976	18	57	55	53	56
1978	15	61	57	57	59
1980	16	58	60	54	59
1983	20	60	59	55	57
1984	24	58	62	55	61
1986	25	57	62	57	59
1987	28	62	62	54	61
1988	27	58	62	56	56

* Percentage base includes don't know responses.

SOURCE: Based on Davis and Smith, 1988, pp. 243-245; 1987, pp.
        239-241; and Smith, 1987, pp. 259, 264.

The use of mood-changing substances permeates American life. In the 1980s, most Americans drank beverages containing caffeine, two-thirds of adults consumed alcholic beverages, and one-third smoked; over one-fourth of high-school-age children and over half of young adults had smoked marijuana; over one-fourth of young adults had experimented with cocaine. The diversity and availability of mood-altering substances, both legal and illegal, increased enormously, and so, for a time, did usage. In per capita terms, tobacco consumption peaked about 1965, then slowly declined. Alcohol consumption increased until the 1980s, then declined slightly and seems to have stabilized; the use of hallucinogens and narcotics peaked in the mid-1970s and then declined; the use of marijuana and several other drugs peaked about 1980 but remains at a relatively high level, historically speaking. Cocaine use increased during the 1980s, and has not yet stabilized. In addition to the wide exposure to such drugs, the American public consumes vast amounts of mood-changing substances as medicines, both as prescribed by physicians and purchased as over-the-counter drugs.

Between 1950 and 1990, the availability and diversity of mood-altering substances, both legal and illegal, increased enormously in U.S. society. Accompanying the counter-culture movement of the 1960s was an increased public toleration for many forms of drug use, and rates of drug use continued to increase well into the 1970s. By about 1980 usage of most illegal drugs had peaked and there were even some declines in rates of usage in the 1980s. There remained some notable exceptions, however, and during the 1980s public consciousness of the nation's "drug problem" increased to such an extent that by 1989, one-fourth of the adult population identified "drugs" as the single most important problem facing the nation (see Chapter 17.2, Social Problems).

The primary exception to the above generalizations about increasing usage is tobacco. Its use had permeated American society by the decade of the 1940s, and the highest rates of smoking occured in the late 1940s and early 1950s, when almost half of adults smoked. In the late 1950s, the U.S. Surgeon General released the report linking cigarette smoking to cancer, especially lung cancer and emphysema. Subsequent research revealed other pathologies associated with smoking and tobacco use. The tobacco industry has tried to refute these findings, but the weight of evidence is very powerful. Several agencies and interest groups, including the American Cancer Society and the National Institute on Drug Abuse, have sponsored vigorous anti-smoking campaigns in the media and in educational institutions, and in the 1980s they enjoyed a measure of legislative success. Most states have laws forbidding smoking in public buildings and requiring restaurants to maintain non-smoking sections. Many businesses have created smoke-free work environments, and by the end of the 1980s no-smoking policies had been imposed upon airline passengers during flight.

After the mid-1950s, there was a long, slow decline in the percent of adults who smoked, and by the mid-1980s it had dropped to about one-third. Peak prevalence of smoking among men occurred about 1954; among women, about 1971; since then, rates have consistently declined for both sexes (Tables 1 and 2). Tobacco consumption per capita peaked about 1965, and again, at a lower level, in 1975, and has declined ever since (Table 3).

The most widely-used mood-inducing drug in American society is caffeine, generally consumed in beverages. Caffeine is a stimulant that reduces hunger, fatigue, and boredom and improves alertness and motor activity. It is readily available in three major forms: coffee, soft drinks, and tea. Most Americans drink at least one of these beverages daily.

Per capita coffee consumption declined by 37% between 1950 and 1984, then stabilized at about 10 lbs. of green coffee beans (or 26 gallons per capita). Tea consumption was also stable in the 1980s, at a level slightly higher than previous decades. The most remarkable change in non-alcoholic beverage consumption is the increase in soft drink consumption, much of it cola drinks. Between 1960 and 1985, per capita annual consumption almost quadrupled, rising from 14 to 46 gallons. In the 1950s and 1960s coffee was the most popular beverage, accounting for more consumption than soft drinks and tea combined. By 1980, soft drinks had replaced coffee as the number one beverage, and by 1984, annual consumption of soft drinks exceeded coffee and tea combined by more than 10 gallons per capita (Table 4). Many soft drinks do not contain caffeine, but the colas account for more than half of soft drink consumption.

Alcohol is the most widely abused drug in American society. Drinking is socially acceptable in most circles, it is expected at many ceremonial occasions and leisure activities, and alcohol use, per se, is not defined as a social problem. Alcohol consumption may be seen as an overall index of the nation's drug problems: consumption increased in the 1960s and 1970s, peaked at about 1980, and seems to have stabilized in the 1980s at a level only slightly lower than peak consumption. In 1980, Americans consumed an average of 35 gallons of beer and almost three gallons each of wine and distilled spirits for each adult in the population. Levels of consumption during the 1980s were not much lower (Table 4).

Self-reported alcohol use does not show much decline in the 1980s, but rather stabilization at near-peak historical usage. Gallup polls in 1983 and 1987 found that 65% of the adult population were drinkers; the highest rate on record was 69% in 1979 (Table 5). Or consider lifetime prevalence--the percentage of persons who have ever consumed alcohol--by age. For each of the age groups--persons 12-17, 18-25, and 26 or more at the time of survey--the highest prevalence rates occur in the 1980s. Current usage shows either the same pattern, or an alternative in which high levels of usage in the 1970s continue in the 1980s (Tables 6-8).

National statistics on prevalence of illegal drugs are not very good before the mid-1970s, but the scale of increase is apparent from numerous outcroppings. For example, from 1965 to 1972, the number of new narcotics addicts added to the files of the Drug Enforcement Administration quadrupled, going from 6,012 to 24,692; between 1971 and 1977, the percent of 12-17 year-olds currently using marijuana almost tripled, rising from 6% to 16% (Statistical Abstract 1974, p. 87; 1979, p. 125).

Trends in current (past 30 days) and lifetime prevalence of the most common illegal drugs, for the period 1972-1985, are summarized in Tables 6-8. Table 9 presents trends in the same drugs for national samples of high school seniors for 1975-1985. Among the notable patterns apparent in these tables are the following. Marijuana use among young people increased until the early 1980s, and then declined slightly. By 1985, over one-fourth of the entire adult population had used marijuana at some time, and one-fourth of young adults and high school seniors were current users. That rate of current use was down from the 1977-1983 era, when about 30% of the young adult and high school senior population were current users.

Hallucinogen use is also down among high school seniors and young adults. Other drugs show mixed patterns of prevalence, but generally, even when the trend in the 1980s is toward lower prevalence, rates remain very high by comparison to decades prior to the 1970s.

The most dramatic increase in drug use in the 1980s is the growing prevalence of cocaine. Cocaine is a very powerful stimulant and anti-fatigue agent. A potent form of cocaine called "crack" is relatively inexpensive and produces a rapid and intense high. Formerly, cocaine was known as a "rich man's drug," but in the 1980s it became widely available in many forms, and usage increased rapidly despite official government efforts to suppress it. By 1985, 9% of the population 26 and over and 25% of young adults had tried cocaine, and 8% of young adults were current users (Tables 7, 8). Throughout the decade of the 1980s, about one-sixth of high school seniors used cocaine at least once, and about 6% were current users (Table 9).

Non-medical usage/abuse of other drugs is also epidemic. In the 1980s, high school seniors and young adults had lifetime rates of nonmedical stimulant, sedative, and tranquilizer abuse ranging from 12% to 27% (Tables 7, 9). For most of the less prevalent forms of abuse, the dominant trend is continuity rather than decline.

We have not collected statistics on legal consumption of drugs under medical supervision or as obtained in over-the-counter transactions. However, it seems likely that the sheer volume of mood-altering drugs distributed legally and semi-legally dwarfs the illegitimate distribution, except in unusual situations such as the cocaine traffic in the 1980s.

References

Gallup Report 276 (1988): 33-40.

Johnston, Lloyd D., Patrick M. O'Malley, and Jerald G. Bachman. Drug Use Among American High School Students, College Students, and Other Young Adults. Washington, D.C.: National Institute on Drug Abuse, 1986.

Miller, Judith Droitcour. National Survey on Drug Abuse: Main Findings, 1982. Washington, D.C.: National Institute on Drug Abuse, 1983.

U.S. Bureau of the Census. Statistical Abstract of the United States, 1989. Washington, D.C., 1989. Annual. Previous years as cited.

Table 1.   PERCENT WHO SMOKE CIGARETTES, 1944-1988

Year	Total	Men	Women
1944	41%	48%	36%
1949	44	54	33
1954	45	57	32
1957	42	52	34
1969	40	55	36
1971	42	47	37
1974	40	45	36
1978	36	39	34
1981	35	38	33
1985	35	37	32
1988	32	34	30

* The question was, Have you, yourself, smoked any cigarettes in the past week?

SOURCE: Gallup Report, 1988, p. 40.

Table 2. CURRENT AND LIFETIME PREVALENCE OF CIGARETTE SMOKING,
BY SEX, NATIONAL HEALTH INTERVIEW SURVEYS, 1970-1985

Year	Never Smoked			Current Smokers		
	Total	Men	Women	Total	Men	Women
1970	45%	31%	57%	37%	43%	31%
1980	46	35	56	33	37	29
1983	46	37	55	32	35	29
1985	44	34	52	30	32	27

SOURCE: Based on <u>Statistical Abstract 1989</u>, p. 119.

Table 3. PRODUCTION AND CONSUMPTION OF TOBACCO PRODUCTS, 1950-
1987

Year	Production (billions)		Consumption per Capita		
	Cigarettes	Cigars	Cigarettes	Cigars	Other*
1950	392	5	3522	53	1.50
1955	412	6	3597	55	1.22
1960	506	7	4171	61	.99
1965	562	9	4258	70	.88
1970	562	8	3971	60	.83
1975	627	8	4100	39	.72
1980	702	5	3800	25	.69
1985	665	4	3400	18	.61
1987	678	3	3200	15	.67

* Smoking and chewing tobaccos and snuff.

SOURCE: Based on <u>Statistical Abstract 1989</u>, p. 737; <u>1974</u>, p. 733.

Table 4. PER CAPITA CONSUMPTION OF BEVERAGES, BY TYPE,
          1950-1987

	Alcoholic (Gallons per Adult Age 18+)			Non-Alcoholic (Gallons or Pounds)				Soft Drinks
			Distilled	Tea		Coffee		
Year	Beer	Wine	Spirits	lbs.	gals.	lbs.*	gals.	gals.
1950	25.0	1.3	1.5	.6	--	16.1	--	--
1955	23.9	1.3	1.6	.6	--	15.3	--	--
1960	24.0	1.4	1.9	.6	--	15.8	--	13.6
1965	25.5	1.5	2.1	.7	--	14.8	--	19.2
1970	28.6	1.8	2.6	.7	6.8	13.7	33.4	23.7
1975	32.8	2.3	2.5	.8	7.5	12.2	31.4	27.3
1980	34.9	2.8	2.9	.8	7.3	10.3	26.8	37.8
1984	32.8	3.0	2.8	--	7.0	10.1	26.5	44.2
1984**	35.0	3.4	2.6	--	--	--	--	--
1985**	34.5	3.5	2.5	--	7.1	10.2	26.7	45.6
1987**	34.4	3.4	2.3	--	7.0	10.2	26.5	--

* Green beans.
** Except for these last three rows, the figures on alcohol
consumption are from the U.S. Dept. of Commerce. However, per
capita consumption figures past 1984 are not available for that
series. Another series on alcohol consumption derives from the U.S.
Dept. of Agriculture's Food Consumption survey. The levels of
reported consumption in the latter run higher than in the Dept. of
Commerce series (see Statistical Abstract 1989, pp. 121, 736) and
therefore we have reported 1984 twice, once to terminate the Dept.
of Commerce series and once to begin, at a somewhat higher level,
the Dept. of Agriculture series.

SOURCE: Based on Statistical Abstract 1989, pp. 22, 120-121, 736;
    1988, pp. 114-115, 718; 1985, pp. 121, 765; 1974, pp. 33,
    90, 732; 1967, p. 88; 1958, p. 84.

Table 5.   PREVALENCE OF DRINKING*, 1939-1987

	Percent of Adult Population		
Year	Total	Men	Women
1939	58%	70%	45%
1945	67	75	60
1951	59	70	46
1957	58	67	50
1966	65	70	61
1974	68	77	61
1979	69	74	64
1983	65	71	58
1987	65	72	57
1988	63	72	55

* The question was, Do you have occasion to use alcoholic
beverages such as liquor, wine, or beer or are you a total
abstainer?

SOURCE: Gallup Report, 1988, p. 34.

Table 6. CURRENT (PAST 30 DAYS) AND LIFETIME PREVALENCE OF
SELECTED DRUGS, PERSONS AGE 12-17, 1972-1985

Type of Drug	1972	1974	1977	1982	1985
Percent Who Ever Used					
Marijuana	14%	23%	28%	27%	24%
Inhalants	6	8	9	--	9
Hallucinogens	5	6	5	5	3
Cocaine	1	4	4	6	5
Heroin	1	1	1	0	0
Analgesics*	--	--	--	4	6
Stimulants*	4	5	5	7	5
Sedatives*	3	5	3	6	4
Tranquilizers*	3	3	4	5	5
Alcohol	--	54	53	65	56
Cigarettes	--	52	47	49	45
Percent Current Users					
Marijuana	7	12	16	11	12
Inhalants	1	1	1	--	3
Hallucinogens	1	1	2	1	1
Cocaine	1	1	1	2	2
Heroin	0	0	0	0	0
Analgesics*	--	--	--	3	2
Stimulants*	--	1	1	1	2
Sedatives*	--	1	1	1	1
Tranquilizers*	--	1	1	1	1
Alcohol	24	34	31	27	31
Cigarettes	17	25	22	15	16

* Nonmedical use.

SOURCE: Based on Statistical Abstract 1989, p. 118; 1985, p. 118;
1984, p. 126; 1979, p. 125.

Table 7. CURRENT (PAST 30 DAYS) AND LIFETIME PREVALENCE OF
SELECTED DRUGS, PERSONS AGE 18-25, 1972-1985

Type of Drug	1972	1974	1977	1982	1985
Percent Who Ever Used					
Marijuana	48%	53%	60%	64%	60%
Inhalants	--	9	11	--	13
Hallucinogens	--	17	20	21	11
Cocaine	9	13	19	28	25
Heroin	5	4	4	1	1
Analgesics*	--	--	--	12	11
Stimulants*	12	17	21	18	17
Sedatives*	10	15	18	19	11
Tranquilizers*	7	10	13	15	12
Alcohol	--	82	84	95	93
Cigarettes	--	69	66	77	76
Percent Current Users					
Marijuana	--	25	28	27	22
Inhalants	--	0	0	--	1
Hallucinogens	--	2	2	2	2
Cocaine	--	3	4	7	8
Heroin	--	0	0	0	0
Analgesics*	--	--	--	5	2
Stimulants*	--	4	2	3	4
Sedatives*	--	2	3	2	2
Tranquilizers*	--	1	2	1	2
Alcohol	--	69	70	68	71
Cigarettes	--	49	47	39	37

* Nonmedical use.

SOURCE: Based on Statistical Abstract 1989, p. 118; 1985, p. 118;
1984, p. 126; 1979, p. 125; Miller, 1983, p. 17.

Table 8.   CURRENT (PAST 30 DAYS) AND LIFETIME PREVALENCE OF
           SELECTED DRUGS, PERSONS AGE 26 AND OVER, 1972-1985

Type of Drug	1972	1974	1977	1982	1985
Percent Who Ever Used					
Marijuana	7%	10%	15%	23%	27%
Inhalants	--	1	2	--	5
Hallucinogens	--	1	3	6	6
Cocaine	2	1	3	8	9
Heroin	0	1	1	1	1
Analgesics*	--	--	--	3	6
Stimulants*	3	3	5	6	8
Sedatives*	2	2	3	5	5
Tranquilizers*	5	2	3	4	7
Alcohol	--	73	78	88	89
Cigarettes	--	65	67	79	80
Percent Current Users					
Marijuana	--	2	3	7	6
Inhalants	--	0	0	--	1
Hallucinogens	--	0	0	1	0
Cocaine	--	0	0	--	2
Heroin	--	0	0	1	0
Analgesics*	--	--	--	--	1
Stimulants*	--	0	1	--	1
Sedatives*	--	0	0	--	1
Tranquilizers*	--	0	0	1	1
Alcohol	--	54	55	57	61
Cigarettes	--	39	39	35	33

* Nonmedical use.

SOURCE: Based on <u>Statistical Abstract 1989</u>, p. 118; <u>1985</u>, p. 118;
       <u>1984</u>, p. 126; <u>1979</u>, p. 125; Miller, 1983, p. 18.

Table 9. CURRENT (PAST 30 DAYS) AND LIFETIME PREVALENCE OF
SELECTED DRUGS, HIGH SCHOOL SENIORS, 1975-1985

Type of Drug	Senior Class of					
	1975	1977	1979	1981	1983	1985
Percent Who Ever Used						
Marijuana	47%	56%	60%	59%	57%	54%
Inhalants	--	11	13	12	14	15
Hallucinogens	16	14	14	13	12	10
Cocaine	9	11	15	16	16	17
Heroin	2	2	1	1	1	1
Other opiates*	9	10	10	10	9	10
Stimulants*	22	23	24	32	35	--
Stimulants, adj.*,**	--	--	--	--	27	26
Sedatives*	18	17	15	16	14	12
Tranquilizers*	17	18	16	15	13	12
Alcohol	90	92	93	93	93	92
Cigarettes	74	76	74	71	71	69
Percent Current Users						
Marijuana	27	35	36	32	27	26
Inhalants	--	1	2	1	2	2
Hallucinogens	5	4	4	4	3	2
Cocaine	2	3	6	6	5	7
Heroin	0	0	0	0	0	0
Other opiates*	2	3	2	2	2	2
Stimulants*	8	9	10	16	12	--
Stimulants, adj.*,**	--	--	--	--	9	7
Sedatives*	5	5	4	5	3	2
Tranquilizers*	4	5	4	3	2	2
Alcohol	68	71	72	71	69	66
Cigarettes	37	38	34	29	30	30

* Nonmedical use.
** Adjusted to allow for the inappropriate reporting of non-
prescription stimulants.

SOURCE: Based on Johnston, O'Malley, and Bachman, 1986, pp. 42,
44.

Topic 14: Leisure

14.1 AMOUNT AND USE OF FREE TIME

Between 1890 and 1935, the standard industrial work week declined from more than 60 hours to 40 hours or less; since then there has been no appreciable change. Nevertheless, the amount of leisure time available to the adult population has greatly increased, largely because of three factors--the diminishing length of the work year, the diminishing time required for household chores, and an increase in the lifetime ratio of leisure time to work time because of later entry into the labor force, increased life expectancy, and earlier retirement.

Leisure time is generally regarded as a function of working time, on the assumption that the time required for sleep, personal care, and commuting to work is approximately constant. Working time includes paid working time for an employer, time devoted to gainful work by the self-employed, and unpaid time devoted to obligatory household chores.

Patterns of time use change very slowly and changes are difficult to measure because the variation among occupations, industries, and population groups is so much greater than the secular variation. The gross trends, however, are quite clear. (See also Chapter 13.4, "Time Use").

Between 1885 and 1935, the industrial work week in the United States declined dramatically from more than 60 hours to less than 40 hours. Between 1935 and 1985, there was no trend at all--the average industrial work week has oscillated between 36 and 40 hours, and remains in that range today. The work week for white-collar workers has followed a similar trend--a sharp reduction from 1885 to 1935, followed by long-term stability.

Despite the stability of the scheduled work week, the aggregate amount of available leisure time has increased steadily in recent decades. The incremental free time comes mainly from three sources.
1. While the work week has been stable, the work year has been declining. Greis (1985) shows that the work year declined in nearly every branch of industry between 1947 and 1978. Various estimates on the decline in the work-year between 1960 and 1989 converge around 10%. The decline is accounted for by increases in the length of paid vacations, the number of paid holidays, the amount of paid nonworking time at the workplace (lunch hours, rest periods, union duties), paid sick leave, and paid leave for family obligations, civic duties and military service.
2. The working time required for obligatory household chores has declined steadily, especially for women, because of smaller households, improvements in domestic materials and machinery, and the availability of substitute services like fast-food restaurants and daycare centers, as Table 1 shows rather vividly.
3. The joint effect of later entry into the labor force, earlier retirement, an increase in elective unemployment, and the extension of life expectancy, is to raise the lifetime ratio of leisure time to working time. This effect is only partly offset by the increasing employment of women.

References

Caplow, Theodore, Howard M. Bahr, Bruce A. Chadwick, Reuben Hill, and Margaret Holmes Williamson. <u>Middletown Families: Fifty Years of Change and Continuity</u>. Minneapolis, University of Minnesota Press, 1982.

Greis, Theresa Diss. <u>The Decline of Annual Hours Worked in the United States Since 1947</u>. Philadelphia: The Wharton School, University of Pennsylvania, 1984.

Table 1. HOURS OF HOUSEWORK REPORTED BY MIDDLETOWN
          HOUSEWIVES, BY SOCIAL CLASS, 1890, 1924 AND 1978

Social Class, Year	Percent Distribution by Hours Spent			
Daily hrs., housework		<4	4-7	7+
Working class, 1924		7%	69%	24%
Business class, 1924		23	54	23
Working class, 1978		52	38	10
Business class, 1978		60	35	5
Weekly hrs., washing & ironing	<2	2-4	5-8	9+
Working class, 1890	6%	3%	30%	61%
Business class, 1890	52	10	15	23
Working class, 1924	2	20	54	24
Business class, 1924	60	15	20	5
Working class, 1978	1	21	41	37
Business class, 1978	2	31	41	26
Weekly hrs., sewing & mending		<3	3-6	6+
Working class, 1890		6%	94%	
Business class, 1890		31	69%	
Working class, 1924		22	42	36
Business class, 1924		51	23	26
Working class, 1978		78	14	8
Business class, 1978		80	10	9

SOURCE: Based on Caplow, Bahr, Chadwick *et al.*, 1982, pp. 365-
    366.

Between 1929 and 1979, Americans traveled much more than the residents of other countries and the volume of automobile and air travel grew steadily from year to year. Since then, volume of travel has leveled off. The average American takes about four long trips a year, most of them for pleasure or family visits. Americans still go abroad in great numbers but comparable numbers of foreign tourists come here.

The 50 years between 1929 and 1979 witnessed an enormous growth in every form of long-distance travel, made possible by the increase of discretionary income, the diffusion of the automobile, and the expansion of air travel. The U.S. began this period with half of the discretionary purchasing power, one-third of the hotel rooms, two-thirds of the automobiles, and two-thirds of the air passenger miles of the world. By 1979, the U.S. population still had half of the discretionary purchasing power, but only one-fourth of the hotel rooms, half the automobiles, and less than half of the air passenger miles (Murphy, 1965). The relative decline was completely masked, however, by the rapid growth of automobiles (448%), auto-miles (700%), and air passenger miles (2,249 times larger in 1979 than 1929). Hotel rooms, however, did not participate in this spectacular growth, increasing only 42% during this half-century (Table 1).

U.S. residents in the 1980s took more trips than their counterparts in the 1960s and 1970s. In the 1980s, the average American man, woman and child took more than four trips a year (Table 2). About two-thirds of these trips were defined as--or taken during--the travelers' vacation time. About one-sixth of all trips were for business purposes, and over one-third were for visiting relatives or friends. The mode of transportation has changed. Auto travel is down from 89% in 1963 to 75% in 1987. One-fifth of personal trips are now by air.

The cost of travel--especially air travel--escalated sharply between 1980 and 1985, which may partly account for the leveling off of growth. A rather sharp decline in the American share of automobiles, auto-miles, and air passenger miles is thought to have occurred, but the number of trips, if not the distance, continues to grow.

The U.S. Department of Commerce (1988) reports some growth in travel in 1986 and 1987, noting that travel accounted for 6.4% of GNP in 1986, that Americans took a total of 1.1 billion trips for all purposes in 1987, and spent approximately 5.7 billion nights in both years in lodgings away from home. More than two-thirds of all travel was for pleasure or family visiting, and the remainder for business or schooling.

The frequency of travel is not much affected by gender, age (among those below 65), or family income (above the poverty level), but nonwhites and the poor travel much less than others.

Historically, tourism has been a movement of recreational travelers from rich countries to poorer countries, where the travelers were doubly favored by their higher incomes and favorable exchange rates for their currencies. Tourists expected either to live more cheaply or to enjoy more luxurious conditions abroad than at home. If the economic gap was very large, as in the case of Americans traveling in Spain in the 1950s, they were able to do both at the same time.

During the 1970s, as the economic advantage of the United States over Europe and Asia dwindled, the one-way character of tourism was transformed. Americans still go abroad in great numbers--more than 13 million in 1987--but more than 10 million foreign tourists came to the U.S. in the same year, and in some recent years (1980-1982), the number of foreign visitors has exceeded the number of Americans visiting abroad (Table 3).

U.S. statistics do not provide reliable figures on second and seasonal homes. The proportion of the population having second homes appears to be relatively stable, and the use of mobile homes appears to have somewhat declined in recent years.

References

Murphy, Peter E. Tourism: A Community Approach. New York: Methuen, 1985.

U.S. Bureau of the Census. Statistical Abstract of the United States, 1989. Washington, D.C., 1989. Annual. Previous years as cited.

U.S. Department of Commerce. 1988 U.S. Industrial Outlook. Washington, D.C.: USGPO, 1988.

Table 1.   GROWTH TRENDS IN U.S. AND WORLD TRAVEL, 1929-1979

	1929		1979	
	U.S.	World	U.S.	World
Population (billions)	.12	2.0	.22	4.3
Hotel Rooms (millions)	1.43	4.2	2.03	8.0
Automobiles (millions)	21	30	115	230
Auto Miles (billions)	150	210	1200	2300
Air Passenger Miles (trillions)	.08	.13	180	400

SOURCE: Based on Murphy, 1985, p. 28.

Table 2.   NUMBER AND CHARACTERISTICS OF PERSON-TRIPS,* U.S.
           RESIDENTS, 1963-1987

	Trips#			Purpose of Trip**		Mode of Transport**	
Year	Total (millions)	Per Capita	Vacation	Conven- tion or Business	Visit Kin, Friends	Auto,RV, Truck	Air
1963	487	2.6	--	14%	45%	89%	4%
1972	458	2.2	--	20	38	85	12
1977	539	2.5	--	20	37	82	12
1982	1069	4.6	62%	14	38	82	14
1983	1058	4.5	61	14	36	79	16
1984	1012	4.3	68	15	38	78	17
1985	1078	4.5	68	17	40	74	20
1986	1121	4.7	67	17	39	74	21
1987	1191	4.9	65	17	37	75	20

* Person-trips are defined as the number of individuals who
traveled 100 miles or more away from home. Each traveler on a trip
generates a person-trip.
** Categories do not sum to 100%; not all categories are included
under either mode of transport or purpose of trip. Moreover, trips
considered "vacation" may also have other purposes; in the tables
from which these figures derive, "vacation" is not an alternative
to "convention or business" or to "visit kin, friends," but rather
belongs to a separate category system.
Units in the total are millions of person-trips; the per capita
refers to person-trips per resident population.

SOURCE: Based on Statistical Abstract 1989, pp. 7, 237; 1979, p.
    247; 1966, p. 212.

Table 3.   INTERNATIONAL (OVERSEAS) TRAVEL TO AND FROM THE U.S.,*
1970-1987

Year	U.S. Travelers Abroad (1000s)	Foreign Travelers in the U.S. (1000s)	Ratio, U.S. Travelers Abroad to Foreign Travelers in U.S. (1000s)
1970	5260	2288	2.30
1974	6467	3700	1.75
1975	6354	3674	1.73
1976	6897	4456	1.55
1977	7390	4509	1.64
1978	7790	5764	1.35
1979	7835	7230	1.08
1980	8163	8200	1.00
1981	8040	9069	0.89
1982	8510	8761	0.97
1983	9628	7873	1.22
1984	11252	7527	1.49
1985	12309	7538	1.63
1986	11706	8860	1.32
1987**	13248	10434	1.27

* Excludes travel to and from Canada and Mexico by U.S. travelers,
and travelers from Canada and Mexico to the U.S.
** Preliminary

SOURCE: Based on Statistical Abstract 1989, pp. 234-235; 1984, pp.
244-245.

There has been a steady and continuing expansion of outdoor recreational activities in the United States during the past three decades. The increase has been particularly marked among middle-aged and elderly adults, and for activities that are strenuous and require skill.

This category includes both active and passive (spectator) participation in athletic games and many other forms of outdoor recreation.

The principal data sources are the five National Recreation Surveys conducted by the Department of the Interior in 1960, 1965, 1972, 1977, 1982 (Tables 1 and 2). These surveys are adequate for comparing the sporting activities of population subgroups at a given point of time, but defective for delineating trends. The number of activities, the definition of activities, and the method of sampling varied from each survey to the next.

Both active and passive sporting activities are influenced by age, gender, location, education and income.

Both forms of participation decline with age. For example, swimming engaged 80% of adolescents but only 11% of persons over 65, in the 1982 survey. But adolescents were somewhat less athletic, and the elderly were much more athletic, in 1982 than they had been in 1965.

Male participation in active and passive sports is significantly higher than female participation. There is some evidence that the gap has been decreasing, particularly with respect to the activities favored by the affluent and educated: walking and jogging, tennis, golf, skiing.

Active participation is higher in suburban than in urban or rural places. Both active and passive participation are somewhat higher in the Sun Belt than in northern locations, but no definite trends are ascertainable.

Education is a powerful stimulant of sporting activity. College graduates report more participation in every form of sport than high school graduates. Tennis, riding, sailing and skiing are virtually monopolized by the college-educated but even traditional blue collar activities like fishing, hunting and swimming are much more extensively practiced by the more educated sector of the population. Thus, it appears that from 1945 to around 1970, as the educational level of the population rose sharply, active and passive participation in sports climbed to unprecedented levels. Since that time, the rise in educational levels has been more moderate and the increase in outdoor recreation now shows signs of subsiding.

Sports participation is also correlated with real family income which, like educational level, rose spectacularly from 1945 to about 1975 but then leveled off.

The trend data for spectator sports are much more reliable than the trend data for participant sports. Table 3 shows the leveling off of attendance at football, horseracing, and hockey, and continued increases in attendance at basketball, baseball, and greyhound racing. The major change in spectator sports--televised viewing--does not show up in these figures.

Contrary to popular assumption, spectator participation does not tend to reduce active participation; frequent attenders at sports events show much higher rates of participation across the whole range of active sports, and vice versa. Active and passive trends run parallel, and the recent plateau in spectatorship is matched by a plateau in participation, although the popularity of particular sports continues to oscillate.

References

Robinson, John P. "Where's the Boom?" American Demographics 9 (March 19, 1987): 34-37.

U.S. Bureau of the Census. Statistical Abstract of the United States, 1989. Washington, D.C. 1989. Annual. Previous years as cited.

U.S. Department of the Interior. The Third Nationwide Outdoor Recreation Plan. Washington, D.C., 1979.

------. 1982-1983 Nationwide Recreation Survey. Washington, D.C.: USGPO, 1986.

Table 1.   PARTICIPATION OF ADULTS IN OUTDOOR ACTIVITIES, 1960-
1977

Activity	1960	1977
Picnicking	53%	72%
Driving for pleasure	52	69
Sightseeing	42	62
Walking and jogging	33	68
Playing outdoor games	30	56
Fishing	29	53
Attending outdoor sports events	24	61
Bicycling	9	47
Nature walks	14	50
Attending putdoor concerts, plays	9	41
Horseback riding	6	15
Hiking or backpacking	6	28
Waterskiing	6	16
Canoeing	2	16
Sailing	2	11

SOURCE: Based on <u>The Third Nationwide Outdoor Recreation Plan</u>,
1979, p. 41.

Table 2. PERCENT OF ADULTS PARTICIPATING IN OUTDOOR RECREATIONAL
ACTIVITIES, BY AGE, 1965 AND 1982

	Age					
	18 − 24		25 − 44		45 − 64	
Activity	1965	1982	1965	1982	1965	1982
Bicycling	26%	43%	15%	35%	3%	35%
Horseback riding	18	15	8	9	2	3
Golfing	15	14	10	11	6	9
Tennis	14	33	5	15	1	7
Canoeing	8	13	3	9	1	4
Sailing	6	9	3	7	2	4
Boating	38	29	28	26	20	15
Waterskiing	17	16	7	10	1	2
Swimming	75	67	56	55	27	33
Fishing	38	39	35	37	30	27
Hunting	20	14	15	13	9	11
Camping	16	34	15	27	6	15
Hiking	14	20	7	18	4	9
Walking	61	61	52	57	42	50
Birdwatching	4	9	6	11	7	11
Picnicking	71	52	71	58	47	40
Pleasure driving	76	58	66	56	53	45
Sightseeing	62	49	60	54	49	43
Attending outdoor sports	59	50	44	44	29	30
Attending outdoor concerts	18	37	14	28	10	19
Ice skating	18	9	7	6	2	1
Skiing	8	15	3	9	1	3
Sledding	20	16	13	11	2	2

SOURCE: Based on Robinson, 1987, p. 36.

Table 3. ATTENDANCE AT SELECTED SPECTATOR SPORTS, 1960-1987

Sport	Attendance (millions)			
	1960	1970	1980	1987
Baseball, major leagues	20	29	44	53
Basketball, college	--	--	31	38*
Basketball, professional	2	7	11	13
Football, college	20	29	36	36
Football, professional	4	10	14	15
Hockey	3	6	12	13
Horseracing	47	70	75	70
Greyhound racing	8	13	21	26

*Including women's basketball.

SOURCE: Based on Statistical Abstract 1989, p. 226; 1980, p. 248.

14.4 CULTURAL ACTIVITIES

We include under this heading the non-athletic forms of organized leisure, such as reading, music-listening and television-viewing. Contrary to general belief, the rise of the electronic media has encouraged the expansion of other cultural activities, although there has been some leveling off since 1975.

National time series on the two most important cultural activities--reading and television-radio--are sparse and unsatisfactory. Local studies reveal the pattern more fully, as in the following excerpt from Middletown Families (Caplow, et al.,1982, pp. 23-25).

The amount of time Middletown's residents devoted to viewing television staggers the imagination. According to one estimate, the median for the entire population was 28 hours per week in 1976. Elderly women (35 hours), elderly men and middle-aged women (32 hours) and preschool children (29 hours) had the highest viewing rates. Adolescents, at 21 hours, had the lowest rate, a mere 3 hours per day! The phenomenon is unprecedented in human history. No large population anywhere had ever spent so much their time being entertained. We could try to explain away these staggering statistics by supposing that people keep their sets turned on without actually watching them, but viewers in Middletown, at any rate, are able to recall the programs they claim to have watched, even though most of them have developed the trick of doing housework or homework at the same time and intermittent family conversation accompanies television viewing more often than not.

The whole commonplace phenomenon is steeped in mystery, and the mystery deepens as we investigate some of the obvious questions. Where did all the time come from? What other activities were replaced? What are the moral and cultural effects of incessant exposure to other people's fantasies?

It is hard to believe, but the older mass media have not been displaced at all. Middletown had a single morning newspaper in 1925. It was still being published in 1975 under the same name and with much the same editorial tone, and its circulation increased in exact proportion to the increase of Middletown's population during the interim. The Sunday edition of the same paper and Middletown's evening newspaper did considerably better; the growth of their circulation between 1925 and 1975 outpaced the growth of the population. The circulation of out-of-town newspapers increased enormously more. All these newspapers contained many more pages in 1975 than in 1925, the division of space between editorial and advertising matter remained about the same, and there was no evidence that readership was more thinly spaced.

Radio broadcasting did equally well . . . from 1925 to 1975 the radio audience never ceased to grow.

Motion picture theatres were at first hard hit by the advent of television [but later recovered] . . . By 1977, Middletown had a larger array of movie theaters than ever before. . . .

We might expect that reading would have been swamped by this audiovisual deluge, but the reverse seems to have occurred . . . . There is much more recreational reading in Middletown today than in 1925, and its content is not noticeably less serious.

Similar patterns may be discerned for the U.S. as a whole. After 1975, the overall growth of cultural activities seems to have leveled off, but as Table 1 shows, the number of new books and editions published has continued to grow at a spectacular rate.

Daily television viewing has leveled off since 1985, and that change is at least partly explained by the introduction of video recorders and home computers. Table 2 describes the consumer electronic market as of 1987; more than half of the products listed were developed after 1975.

The recent fortunes of the various performing arts have been uneven, as Table 3 suggests. The legitimate theatre gained, then lost audience as the number of houses declined and ticket prices skyrocketed. Opera flourished as never before on this side of the ocean; the number of performances more than doubled between 1970 and 1980, and continued to rise thereafter. The number of symphony concerts and aggregate attendance increased sharply in the early 1970s as government support became available for the first time, and then leveled off. For reasons not entirely clear, the rising cost of all cultural activities greatly outpaced the rate of inflation after 1970. For example, while aggregate attendance at symphony concerts increased by 98% between 1970 and 1987, the gross expenses increased by 588%.

References

Caplow, Theodore, Howard M. Bahr, Bruce A. Chadwick, Reuben Hill, and Margaret Holmes Williamson. Middletown Families: Fifty Years of Change and Continuity. Minneapolis: University of Minnesota Press, 1982.

U.S. Bureau of the Census. Statistical Abstract of the United States, 1989. Washington, D.C., 1989. Annual. Previous years as cited.

Table 1. NEW BOOKS AND EDITIONS PUBLISHED, 1960-1985

Year	Number (1000s)
1960	15.0
1965	28.6
1970	36.1
1975	39.4
1980	42.4
1985	50.1

SOURCE: Based on <u>Statistical Abstract 1989</u>, p. 224; <u>1987</u>, p. 214; <u>1979</u>, p. 593.

Table 2. THE CONSUMER ELECTRONIC MARKET, 1987

Product	Units Shipped (millions)
Audio components	11.3
Portable tape equipment	30.8
Radios	30.7
Automobile sound systems	23.0
Radar detectors	1.8
CB radios	2.0
Cellular telephones	.3
Calculators	33.8
Personal computers	3.6
Satellite earth stations	.3
Specialty radios	8.4
Audio recordings	327.6
Blank videotape	280.6
Prerecorded videotape	69.2
Blank floppy discs	545.4
Home computer software	20.7
Color televisions	19.8
Projection televisions	.3
Video cassette recorders	12.3
Video cameras	.1

SOURCE: Based on Statistical Abstract 1989, p. 225.

Table 3. TRENDS IN THE PERFORMING ARTS, 1960-1987

Activity	1960	1970	1980	1987
Legitimate Theater				
Playing weeks (1000s)	1.9	2.1	2.9	1.9
Attendance (millions)	--	--	9.4	7.0
Opera				
Performance (1000s)	4.2	4.8	9.4	11.8
Attendance (millions)	--	4.6	10.7	16.4
Symphony Concerts				
Number (1000s)	--	6.6	22.2	20.1
Attendance (millions)	--	12.7	22.6	25.1

SOURCE: Based on <u>Statistical Abstract 1989</u>, p. 232; <u>1979</u>, p. 246.

Topic 15: Educational Attainment

15.1 GENERAL EDUCATION

A dramatic "universalization" of secondary education in the U.S. was largely accomplished in the years 1910-1940, although peak high school graduation rates, at about 75% of the eligible population, were not attained until the mid-1960s. A growing "credentialism," in which the high school diploma became a minimal requirement for entry into most occupations, explains part of this trend. On the average, there is a direct return in increased personal income for each additional increment of formal education. Post-secondary education expanded at the same time, and by the 1980s one-fifth of the adult public had graduated from college. Along with increases in school enrollment has come more diversity in the subjects studied. There is some reason to suspect that the cognitive content of American secondary education declined in the 1970s and 1980s. Blacks and Hispanics, while sharing in the general increase in years of schooling, remain disadvantaged because of higher drop out rates and much lower enrollments in post-secondary education.

At the beginning of this century Americans were not well-educated. Among the population at the mid-teen years, 90% had already ended their formal schooling. High school graduation was a privilege for an elite few: in 1900, graduates amounted to 6% of the 17-year-old population. The performance of the first decade of the 20th century did not seem to foreshadow the massive changes about to take place; school enrollment and high school gradation rates improved only slightly. But the next three decades saw an enormous expansion of education; at least some high school education was extended to a majority of the nation's young people.

In relative terms, the decade of 1910-1920 experienced the greatest change. Enrollments of persons aged 14-17 more than doubled, to 31%, and the percentage of high school graduates among 17-year-olds grew from 9% to 17%. In absolute terms, the 1920s had more dramatic growth: the increased enrollment of high-school-age people amounted to 20% of the entire eligible population (from 31% to 51%). The expansion continued at a slightly slower rate through the 1930s. By 1940, almost three-fourths of the mid-teenaged population were in school, and over half of 17-year-olds were graduating.

After that, improvement continued at a much slower rate; the massification of secondary education had been largely accomplished, although it would be three decades before peak proportionate enrollment (77% of 14-17-year-olds) would be attained in 1968-69 (National Center for Education Statistics, 1989, pp. 62, 103). For secondary education, the expansion ended in the 1960s. Since then, enrollment and graduation rates have stabilized, and even declined slightly (see Table 1).

The growth in collegiate education, too, has been marked--even more marked than in high-school education, because it started from a far more modest base--and its period of most rapid expansion was later than for secondary education. Measured by the percent of recent high school graduates attending college, the expansion of university education peaked in 1968, declined slightly in the mid-1970s, then increased to peak in 1985 (Table 2).

The years of the Vietnam war saw the rapid extension of college education. Male enrollment reached a peak in 1975, two years after military conscription ended; female enrollment continued to rise even into the 1980s. Over the entire period only about half of all students who entered college actually received a degree, the closer (and by no means declining) connection of such completion to parental socioeconomic background offsetting the mitigating impact on educational stratification of the now high rate of high-school completion (Mare, 1981).

The capacity of American colleges to turn out students with degrees, large initially by international standards, was strained enormously in the late 1940s by the effects of World War II manpower policy, which made government financing available for demobilized veterans who wished to extend their educations after the war. The added capacity reflected in the huge crop of Bachelor's degrees in 1949-50 led to policy changes by the colleges which facilitated enrollments, and bridged the period until the fertility upturn of the mid-1930s began to impact enrollments. Not only was this demand accommodated by American colleges when it arrived, but in addition enrollment rates and completion rates increased, fueled both by increased demand for college-trained employees and by greatly increased governmental financial commitments to higher education. By the mid-1960s, military deferment also played a role on the demand side. By the early 1970s, these dynamics had seemingly played themselves out, and the number of bachelor's degrees leveled off.

The impact of the near-universalization of high school education and the growing availability of college education is summarized in Table 3. By 1950, the median level of education for young adults (ages 25-29) was the high school degree, and two decades later, the median educational attainment of the entire adult population was just beyond the 12 years represented in high school graduation. Median education has continued to increase; by 1987, it was 12.7 years, or almost a full year beyond high school graduation.

The proportion of the adult population having a college education continues to rise. Between 1940 and 1970 the percent of adults with four or more years of college doubled, from 5% to 11%; since 1970, it has doubled again; by 1987, one adult in five was a college graduate. Post-secondary education has been much less available to the nation's black minority, but their rates of college education have increased faster than among whites, such that inter-racial convergence in educational attainment has taken place (Table 3). By the mid-1980s, blacks were almost as likely as whites to graduate from high school, and their disadvantage in college education had declined from about five-to-one to roughly two-to-one (that is, in 1940, only 1% of blacks and 5% of whites had completed college; by 1985, those rates had increased to about 22% and 11%, respectively).

Over the 1970s and 1980s, increasingly higher proportions of college students were women. Likewise, considerably higher proportions were older students. The percent of all students in the modal age-sex category for college attendance--male, 18-24 years of age--actually declined from 30% in 1972 to 27% in 1982. At the same time female representation among students of these ages increased from 21% to 26%, attaining near-parity with men. The only male age group to increase its representation among college students was men over 40, who were a miniscule proportion of all students. Proportionately, the greatest additional commitment to college was found in women above 30. In 1972, 43% of college students were women; in 1982, 52% were. In 1972, 14% of college students were age 30 or over; in 1982, 20% were.

The utility of formal education in facilitating access to higher-status occupations and higher incomes is shown in Table 4, which presents figures on median annual income for persons at various levels of education, 1970-1987. Without exception, for every year shown, attainment of the next higher level of education generates a higher income. Moreover, the relative size of the differentials in income by education seems to be increasing. In 1970, male high school graduates earned 1.6 times as men who had not finished the 8th grade, and men with post-graduate university education earned 1.5 times as much as the high school graduates. In 1987, the corresponding ratios were slightly higher, 1.7 and 1.6, respectively. The same trend of increasing scale of economic reward for educational attainment applies to women.

The other notable thing about the statistical series summarized in Table 4 is the disadvantage of women in economic return for education. The proportionate advantage granted by education is comparable; that is, male college graduates in 1987 made about 1.4 times as much as male high school graduates, and women college graduates also made about 1.4 times as much as high school graduates. But whatever their level of education, women earn only about two-thirds what men with the same education earn, and over the past two decades that pattern has not changed much (see also Chapter 3.4, Women's Employment).

Given the demonstrated direct association between education and earning power, the persistence of ethnic differentials in school enrollment guarantees the continuation of economically-grounded ethnic differences in consumption patterns, lifestyle, and life changes in general. Ethnic differences in rates of dropping out of school for 1970-1986 are shown in Table 5. Note that dropout rates at the earliest ages--before age 16--are roughly the same for blacks and whites, and higher for Hispanics. Moreover, since about 1975, dropout rates at ages 16-17 have been comparable for whites and blacks. Among persons aged 18 and over, however, blacks are distinctly disadvantaged, and Hispanics even more so: dropout rates of blacks are twice those of whites; and Hispanics three times higher.

Although quantitative measures of educational attainment receive the most attention--both at the personal and bureaucratic level, people are usually more concerned with how many years of schooling one has completed than with the quality of that education--there has been considerable national furor in the past several decades about what students do, or don't, learn in school. The "why Johnny can't read" concern of the 1960s and 1970's was supplanted in the 1980s by a "back to basics" movement, sustained in part by evidence that the quality of education was declining. Among the indicators of decline were scores on national college-aptitude tests.

Several national examinations of scholastic aptitude yield trend-data on student learning. Of these, by far the longer series is from the Scholastic Aptitude Test, a test administered in the senior year of high school to students who aspire to enter universities that require the tests for admission. SAT tests were administed earlier than 1966, when our series begins (Table 6), but until then, there was a steadily-expanding clientele for the examination, providing an ambiguous base for an observed statistical decline in average scores.

By 1966, the proportion of high school seniors seeking to go to college had stabilized, as had the proportion of colleges demanding the SAT exam. From 1966-67 to 1980-81, the trajectory in test scores was one of steady decline in both verbal and mathematical skills. The verbal decline was worse than the mathematical; women's declines were more marked than men's; and these two differentials were additive. Over this period, women's propensity to attend college increased a bit, while that of men declined slightly. Proponents of educational reform, who rely upon these and similar figures in making their case, pronounced early signs of victory when the decline in scores seemed to have ended, and the trajectory plateaued, about 1980. However, it has been pointed out that aptitudes measured at age 17 could hardly have been affected by educational reforms made in the year or two preceding.

The National Assessment of Educational Progress is a periodically-administered examination given to members of particular age groups who are in school. The results do not suffer from whatever college-planners-only bias that the SAT's suffer. Reading levels, stable between 1974-75 and 1979-80, had marginally improved by 1983-84. These findings are consistent with those for the SAT. The gains are greater for females than males, more pronounced among blacks than whites, and more pronounced among students from educationally disadvantaged backgrounds. That is, a relatively good proportion of whatever gain was achieved in recent years was achieved among those most in need of improvement. These results are, however, very tenuous. Similar NAEP tests in science and mathematics showed no gain and perhaps a small overall decline.

References

Mare, Robert D. "Change and Stability in Educational Stratifiction," American Sociological Review 46 (1981): 72-87.

U.S. Bureau of the Census. Statistical Abstract of the United States, 1989. Washington, D.C., 1989.

U.S. National Center for Educational Statistics. Digest of Educational Statistics 1987. Washington, D.C.: USGPO, 1988.

Table 1.   INDICATORS OF THE UNIVERSALITY OF HIGH SCHOOL
            EDUCATION: ENROLLMENT IN GRADES 9-12 AS PERCENT OF THE
            POPULATION AGE 14-17, AND GRADUATES* AS A PERCENT OF
            THE 17-YEAR-OLD POPULATION, 1929-1988

School Year	Enrollment as Percent of Population Age 14-17	Graduates as Percent of 17-Year-Old Population
1929-30	51%	29%
1939-40	73	51
1949-50	76	59
1953-54	79	60
1959-60	83	69
1965-66	92	76
1970-71	92	76
1975-76	91	74
1980-81	91	72
1985-86	93	73
1987-88	92	74

* Includes graduates from public and private schools in regular
day school programs; does not include graduates of other programs
or recipients of high school equivalency certificates.

SOURCE: Based on National Center for Education Statistics, 1989,
         pp. 62, 103.

Table 2. COLLEGE ENROLLMENT RATES OF HIGH SCHOOL GRADUATES,* BY
RACE, 1960-1987

| Year | Percent of Preceding Year's High School Graduates Enrolled in College | | | |
	All Students	Whites	Blacks**	Hispanics**
1960	45%	46%	--	--
1962	49	51	--	--
1964	48	49	--	--
1965	51	52	--	--
1966	50	52	--	--
1968	55	57	--	--
1969	53	55	--	--
1970	52	52	--	--
1972	49	49	--	--
1973	47	48	--	--
1974	47	47	--	--
1975	51	51	--	--
1976	49	49	42%	53%
1977	51	51	50	51
1978	50	50	46	43
1979	49	50	45	45
1980	49	50	42	53
1981	54	55	43	52
1982	51	52	36	43
1983	53	55	38	54
1984	55	58	40	44
1985	58	59	42	51
1986	54	56	36	44
1987	57	57	52	33

* The percentage of individuals age 16-24 enrolled in college who
graduated from high school during the preceding 12 months.
** Due to small sample size, the data are subject to relatively
large amounts of sampling error. Note also that Hispanics may be of
any race, and therefore the black and white categories include some
people of Hispanic origin.

SOURCE: Based on National Center for Education Statistics, 1989, p.
369.

Table 3. HIGH SCHOOL AND COLLEGE GRADUATES, AND MEDIAN YEARS OF
SCHOOLING, BY AGE AND RACE, 1940-1987

	All Persons			Blacks		
	Graduates of		Median	Graduates of		Median
	High		Years of	High		Years of
Year	School	College	School	School	College	School
Persons Age 25 and Over						
1940	24%	5%	8.6	7%	1%	5.7
1950	34	6	9.3	13	2	6.8
1960	41	8	10.6	20	3	8.0
1970	52	11	12.1	31	4	9.8
1980	66	16	12.5	51	8	12.0
1985	74	19	12.6	60	11	12.3
1987	75	20	12.7	63	11	12.4
Persons Age 25-29						
1940	38	6	10.3	12	2	7.0
1950	53	8	12.0	22	3	8.6
1960	61	11	12.3	38	5	9.9
1970	74	16	12.6	55	6	12.1
1980	84	22	12.9	75	11	12.6
1985	86	22	12.9	81	11	12.7
1987	86	22	12.8	83	11	12.7

SOURCE: Based on Statistical Abstract 1989, p. 130.

TABLE 4. OUTCOMES OF EDUCATION: MEDIAN ANNUAL INCOME OF YEAR-ROUND, FULL-TIME WORKERS AGE 25 AND OVER, BY EDUCATION AND SEX, 1970-1987

| | Median Annual Income, in Current Dollars (1000s) Among Persons Having Completed the Following Years of School | | | | | | |
| | Elementary | | High School | | | College | |
Year	<8	8	9-11	12	13-15	16	17+
Men							
1970	$ 6.0	$ 7.5	$ 8.5	$ 9.6	$11.2	$13.3	$14.7
1972	7.0	8.6	9.5	11.1	12.4	14.9	16.9
1974	7.9	9.9	11.2	12.6	13.7	16.2	18.2
1976	9.0	11.3	12.3	14.3	15.5	18.2	20.6
1978	10.5	13.0	14.2	16.4	17.4	20.9	23.6
1980	11.8	14.7	16.1	19.5	20.9	24.3	27.7
1982	12.4	16.4	17.5	21.3	23.6	28.0	32.3
1984	14.6	16.8	19.1	23.3	25.8	31.5	38.8
1986	14.5	18.5	20.0	24.7	28.0	34.4	39.6
1987	14.9	18.9	21.3	25.4	29.5	35.2	41.7
Women							
1970	3.8	4.2	4.7	5.6	6.6	8.2	9.6
1972	4.2	4.8	5.3	6.2	7.0	8.7	11.0
1974	5.0	5.6	5.9	7.1	8.1	9.5	11.8
1976	5.6	6.4	6.8	8.4	9.5	11.0	13.6
1978	6.6	7.5	8.0	9.8	10.6	12.3	15.3
1980	7.7	8.9	9.7	11.5	13.0	15.1	18.1
1982	8.4	10.1	10.7	13.2	15.6	17.4	21.4
1984	9.8	10.8	11.8	14.6	17.0	20.3	25.1
1986	10.2	11.2	12.3	15.9	18.5	22.4	27.3
1987	9.9	12.2	12.9	16.5	19.8	23.4	29.7

SOURCE: National Center for Education Statistics, 1989, p. 367.

Table 5.   PERCENT OF HIGH SCHOOL DROPOUTS, SELECTED AGES, BY RACE
AND SEX, 1970-1986

Age/Race	1970 Male	1970 Female	1975 Male	1975 Female	1980 Male	1980 Female	1986 Male	1986 Female
All Races, 14-34	16%	18%	13%	15%	13%	13%	12%	11%
14-15	2	2	2	2	1	2	2	2
16-17	7	9	8	10	9	9	6	6
18-19	16	16	15	16	17	15	13	11
20-21	16	17	16	17	18	14	16	13
22-24	18	19	14	15	16	14	15	13
25-29	21	24	14	16	14	14	14	13
30-34	26	27	19	22	14	15	13	12
Whites, 14-34	14	16	12	13	12	12	12	11
14-15	2	2	1	2	1	2	2	2
16-17	6	8	7	10	9	9	7	6
18-19	13	15	14	16	16	14	13	11
20-21	14	15	14	15	16	13	16	13
22-24	15	17	13	13	15	13	15	13
25-29	19	21	13	15	13	13	14	12
30-34	24	25	17	20	13	14	12	11
Blacks, 14-34	30	29	22	25	19	19	15	15
14-15	2	3	2	3	1	2	3	4
16-17	13	12	10	11	7	7	5	5
18-19	36	27	28	23	23	20	15	15
20-21	30	30	30	27	31	20	20	17
22-24	39	36	26	29	25	23	19	16
25-29	43	46	25	30	22	23	17	19
30-34	46	41	33	40	22	25	22	20
Hispanics,* 14-34	--	--	30	36	36	35	34	30
14-15	--	--	2	6	3	8	4	4
16-17	--	--	11	15	18	15	14	15
18-19	--	--	26	33	43	35	29	24
20-21	--	--	30	33	41	42	39	31
22-24	--	--	40	43	43	39	41	35
25-29	--	--	41	45	40	42	40	37
30-34	--	--	45	52	44	47	40	41

* Persons of Hispanic origin may be of any race.

SOURCE: Based on National Center for Education Statistics, 1989,
p. 106.

Table 6. SCHOLASTIC APTITUDE TEST SCORE AVERAGES FOR VERBAL AND
MATHEMATICAL APTITUDES, 1967-1987

School Year	Test Score	
Ending	Verbal	Mathematical
1967	466	492
1968	466	492
1969	463	493
1970	460	488
1971	455	488
1972	453	484
1973	445	481
1974	444	480
1975	434	472
1976	431	472
1977	429	470
1978	429	468
1979	427	467
1980	424	466
1981	424	466
1982	426	467
1983	425	468
1984	426	471
1985	431	475
1986	431	475
1987	430	476

SOURCE: Based on National Center for Educational Statistics,
1988, p. 94; <u>Statistical Abstract, 1989</u>, p. 144.

Professional education has shown marked phases of growth and stasis since World War II, representing an uneven and sometimes uncomfortably generous supply side for the trends toward professionalization seen in the occupational structure. These spurts are only partly explained by technogical change. Redefinitions of what constitutes a "profession" explain others. In any case, even the pronounced aggregate trends conceal markedly different histories for different professions.

The concept of the "profession" has been considerably expanded as practitioners of numerous skills--some old, some new--have worked to gain the prestige and occupational autonomy characteristic of the professional form. It is post-collegiate education more than anything else--more than state certification, for example--that marks out a realm of professional practice, and accordingly, the education industry has played a powerful role in the enormous proliferation of the professions since World War II. The largest part of this discussion will concern itself with post-baccalaureate education, although certain commonly-recognized professions, such as architecture, often have as their typical qualification the bachelor's degree (for example, B. Arch., in the case of architecture).

In a more international sense, "professional education" includes a wider range of instruction than for the high-prestige occupations Americans understand as the professions, and trends here may be indicated (Table 1) by examination of patterns in the awarding of "Associate" degrees. This degree, ordinarily requiring two years of full-time study (and often achieved by part-time study), is awarded by "community colleges" and other two-year institutions. It, and such institutions, have become considerably more common in recent decades. As can be seen in Table 1, the AA degree increasingly signifies having received training in one of the occupations in the service sector of the economy, the exact field being determined largely by labor-market demand. All of these programs have grown at the cost of general "arts and sciences" training.

Trends in number of degrees conferred are summarized in Table 2. Several patterns deserve notice. In 1950, 82% of all degrees granted were bachelor's degrees, and most other degrees granted were master's degrees. Doctor's degrees accounted for only one percent of the total. Over the next 25 years the production of advanced degrees, as a proportion of all degrees, almost doubled. By 1975, almost 3% of all degrees were doctor's degrees, and more than 22% were master's degrees. The increase in absolute terms was even more impressive, because much more of the population was attending college at all levels. The production of doctor's degrees increased almost five times, from 7,000 to 34,000, and the rate of increase was almost as high for master's degrees (from 58,000 to 293,000).

This expansion of educational attainment at all levels 1950-1975 was followed by an equally universal plateau and, for master's and doctor's degrees, an absolute, if slight, decline. Since 1975, the production of master's degrees has been stabilized at about 290,000 annually (just over 20% of all degrees), and doctor's degrees have been similarly stabilized at about 33,000 annually (just over 2%).

Table 3 illustrates changes in the composition of the annual production of advanced degrees, by type of training, for the period 1950-1986. Among the readily observable patterns are the incredible growth of professional education in business and management (their output of master's degrees increased 16 times, and by 1986 they were approaching education as the most common master's degree); the decline of interest in professional education after 1975; the striking growth in master's level education in computer science, health sciences, and psychology; the decline, after 1975, in the popularity of social science degrees at the master's level; the surprising lack of growth in advanced study in foreign languages (which increased until 1970 and then declined almost as rapidly) and physical sciences (which have not kept pace with the overall increase of advanced education at either the master's or the doctor's level); and the relative stability of output of doctoral level specialists in business and management.

Certain professions have successfully limited entry, medicine being the most striking example. That limitation is particularly evident in comparisons of degree trends with law; the number of law school graduates has risen sharply. Physicians and lawyers--professions that Americans often mention in the same breath--represent two distinct patterns with regard to professional preparation, and in regard to control of entry into the profession. In the 1970s, the legal profession as a whole evidently lost control of entry to the profession to the legal educators, for most of the gains in numbers being graduated were achieved by the enlargment of existing law schools rather than the creation of new schools. Physicians, on the other hand, were able to control medical schools' inclinations to produce more physicians, the output of new M.D.'s merely doubling between 1960 and 1980, and output continuing to grow just marginally since then. This is to be contrasted to a production of new lawyers that quadrupled between 1960 and 1980 (Table 3). Apparent, too, in Table 2, is the growth of professionally-qualified allied health professions, including a good portion of the enlargment in degrees awarded in psychology, many of which prepare their holders to offer psychological counseling in professional competition with M.D. psychiatrists.

It is worth emphasizing that professional education has declined quantitatively in a rather dramatic way in at least one formerly major field, namely education. Nowadays, one hears of a revival of demand in this field; whether this will call back into life many of the Schools of Education eliminated in the past two decades is a question that remains to be answered.

References

U.S. Bureau of the Census. Statistical Abstract of the United States, 1989. Washington, D.C., 1989. Annual. Previous years as cited.

U.S. National Center for Educational Statistics, Digest of Educational Statistics 1988. Washington, D. C.: USGPO, 1989.

Table 1.   ASSOCIATE'S DEGREES CONFERRED, BY TYPE, 1974-1986

	Total AA's (1000s)	Field of Study		
		Data Processing	Health Services	Mechanical Engineering
1974	344	2%	13%	9%
1975	360	2	15	9
1976	391	2	14	9
1977	406	2	15	9
1978	412	2	15	10
1979	401	2	15	10
1980	401	3	15	11
1981	416	3	14	12
1982	435	5	14	13
1983	456	--	--	--
1984	452	--	--	--
1985	455	--	--	--
1986	446	--	--	--

	Business	Other	Arts & Sciences
1974	17%	10%	48%
1975	17	11	46
1976	19	12	45
1977	20	12	42
1978	21	12	40
1979	22	11	39
1980	23	10	38
1981	23	10	38
1982	22	9	36
1983	--	--	--
1984	--	--	--
1985	--	--	--
1986	--	--	--

SOURCE: Based on U.S. National Center for Educational Statistics, 1989, p. 191.

Table 2. EARNED DEGREES CONFERRED, BY LEVEL OF DEGREE, 1950-1986

		Degrees Conferred (1000s)			
Year	Total Degrees	Bachelor's	Master's	First Professional	Doctor's
1950	499	411	58	23*	7
1955	354	270	58	18*	9
1960	477	372	75	20*	10
1965	664	502	118	28	17
1970	1065	792	209	35	30
1975	1305	923	293	56	34
1980	1330	930	298	70	33
1985	1374	980	286	75	33
1986	1384	988	289	74	34

* First professional degrees include medicine (M.D.), dentistry (D.D.S.), law (LL.B), divinity (B.D) and others. They are included with bachelor's degrees for 1950-1960 in the sources for this table. To more accurately reflect trends in both bachelor's and first professional degrees, we have removed the medical, dentistry, and law degrees listed separately for these years from the total for bachelor's degrees (column 2) and listed them here. Because other first professional degrees were not itemized in the source tables, the total for first professional degree for 1950-1960 given here is lower than, in fact, it was and some of the 1960-1965 increase is artifactual.

SOURCE: Statistical Abstract 1989, p. 156; 1979, p. 168.

Table 3.   NUMBERS OF EARNED PROFESSIONAL AND ADVANCED DEGREES IN
SELECTED FIELDS, 1950-1986

Field and Degree	Earned Degrees Conferred (1000s)						
	1950	1960	1965	1970	1975	1980	1986
Master's Degrees							
All fields	58.2	74.5	112.2	209.4	292.4	298.1	288.6
Agriculture, natural res.	1.5	1.2	1.4	1.8	3.1	4.0	3.8
Biological, life sci.	3.0	2.2	3.6	5.8	6.5	6.5	5.0
Business, management	4.3	4.6	7.6	21.4	36.2	55.0	67.1
Computer, infor. sci.	--	--	.1	1.5	2.3	3.6	8.1
Education	18.3	33.5	43.7	79.8	120.2	104.0	76.4
Engineering	4.5	7.2	12.1	15.6	15.3	16.2	21.7
English, letters	2.6	3.2	5.5	9.4	10.1	6.8	6.3
Foreign languages	.9	1.1	4.2	5.2	3.8	2.2	1.7
Health sciences	.5	1.9	2.5	4.6	9.9	15.1	18.6
Mathematics	1.0	1.8	4.1	5.6	4.3	2.9	3.2
Philosophy, religion	1.4	1.7	2.0	3.9	4.6	5.1	5.6
Physical sciences	3.0	3.4	4.9	5.9	5.8	5.2	5.9
Psychology	1.3	1.4	2.2	4.1	7.1	7.8	8.3
Social sciences	4.4	6.2	11.0	24.2	32.7	31.4	27.7
Visual, performing arts	2.7	2.9	4.2	7.8	8.4	8.7	8.4
Doctor's Degrees							
All fields	6.6	9.8	16.5	29.9	34.1	32.6	33.7
Agriculture, natural res.	.4	.4	.5	.8	1.0	1.0	1.2
Biological, life sci.	.2	1.2	1.9	3.3	3.4	3.6	3.4
Business, management	.1	.1	.3	.6	1.0	.8	1.0
Computer, infor. sci.	--	--	--	.1	.2	.2	.3
Education	.9	1.6	2.7	5.9	7.4	7.9	7.1
Engineering	.4	.8	2.1	3.7	3.1	2.5	3.4
English, letters	.2	.4	.7	1.2	2.0	1.5	1.2
Foreign languages	.2	.2	.4	.9	.9	.5	.4
Health sciences	.1	.1	.2	.4	.6	.8	1.2
Mathematics	.2	.3	.7	1.2	1.0	.7	.7
Philosophy, religion	.3	.4	.5	.8	1.4	1.7	1.7
Physical sciences	1.2	1.8	2.9	4.3	3.6	3.1	3.6
Psychology	.3	.6	.8	1.7	2.4	2.8	3.1
Social sciences**	.7	1.3	2.1	3.9	4.6	3.7	3.5
Visual, performing arts	.1	.3	.4	.7	.6	.7	.7
Law (LL.B., J.D.)	14.3	9.2	12.0	14.9	29.3	35.6	35.8
Medicine (M.D.)	5.6	7.0	7.3	8.3	12.4	14.9	15.9
Dentistry (D.D.S.,D.M.D.)	2.6	3.2	3.1	3.7	4.8	5.3	5.0

* Includes forestry.
** Includes geography, public affairs, area and ethnic studies.

SOURCE: Based on <u>Statistical Abstract 1989</u>, pp. 157-158; <u>1972</u>, p.
133; <u>1967</u>, p. 140; <u>1962</u>, p. 137; <u>1951</u>, p. 124.

Adult education, while growing to involve 2.5 million people by 1984, nevertheless represents little of a force in American life. For the most part, the people who study are already relatively well-educated, and are studying to improve their occupational prospects in their current occupations. These tendencies, so far as can be discovered from scant data, are, if anything, intensifying.

In most available data we are not able to distinguish between adults who are participating in special programs for adults alone, and those who are participating in educational programs more generally. For the purposes of this series, then, the best we can do is to present the series on the overall proportion of adults at given ages who are enrolled in educational programs of any kind.

Taking ages 25-29 and 30-34 as our adult categories (as shown in Table 1) the first undoubtedly contains larger proportions than the second of persons who are still completing their professional or graduate educations and thus in "regular" programs (although other data indicate that graduate education is rapidly becoming more and more accomplished by part-time programs). We see that, as with college education generally, the percent at these ages who were in school increased markedly into the mid-1970s, then reversed and stabilized, more or less, at a plateau considerably higher than at the opening of the period. The dominant point in this table, for our purposes, would seem to be that it is these adults rather than younger, conventional-age college students, whose attendance has become less common in recent years.

Nevertheless, as Table 2 shows, the number of students who are enrolled in courses definitively characterized as "adult education" has increased markedly and steadily. Only a few short data series give any continuing view of the characteristics of students in adult education and the trends in the diversity of adult education programs. Covering only periods since 1969, these nevertheless point to a widening of sponsorship of programs that corresponds well to what one would expect might happen, once educators recognized the "market" that was rapidly opening before them.

We find that as participants increased by around 5% per year during this period, "traditional" four-year college educators, the majority "vendors" at the 1969 survey, enlarged their numbers of adult students considerably, but then failed to hold them; during these periods, other sponsors captured larger proportions of students. The same pattern was true for secondary schools, and even for the trade and vocational schools, employers, and community organizations.

Other sponsors of adult education achieved relative as well as absolute gains: two-year colleges (community colleges), always highly accepting of new programs, were the largest gainers. Gaining, too, however, were such relatively small contributors as labor organizations and professional associations, private instructors, and, especially, the composite category of government agency, correspondence school, and "other." In 1984, job-related reasons explained almost two-thirds of the enrollment in adult education, most prominently (48% of all courses taken) the wish for promotion (U. S. National Center for Educational Statistics, 1988, p. 286). On the other hand, "personal or social" reasons accounted for one-quarter of the adult study, and "general education" another eight percent.

   Students in adult education programs are overwhelmingly part-time; the programs have more appeal to the middle-aged than to the elderly; to those already the most educated rather than those lacking in education, and to the employed rather than to those out of work or not in the labor force (Statistical Abstract 1989, p. 161; U.S. National Center for Educational Statistics, 1988, p. 284). The proportion of students in adult educational programs who were already college graduates increased between 1978 and 1984, exceeding one in three at the latter date, and fewer than one in twelve at this time had not attained at least a high school diploma. Adult education seems to be becoming a relatively more conventional phenomenon, and hence a relatively more elite phenomenon, rather than the contrary, as it grows. And as it grows, it seems to attract students who are increasingly younger.

References

U.S. Bureau of the Census, Social Indicators III. Washington, D.C.: USGPO, 1980.

------. Statistical Abstract of the United States, 1989. Washington, D.C., 1989. Annual. Previous years as cited.

U.S. National Center for Educational Statistics. The Condition of Education 1989. Washington, D.C.: USGPO, 1989. Annual. Previous years as cited.

Table 1. PERCENT OF THE YOUNG ADULT POPULATION ENROLLED IN
          SCHOOL, 1965-1986

Year	Age	
	25-29	30-34
1965	6.1%	3.2%
1970	7.5	4.2
1975	10.1	6.6
1980	9.3	6.4
1985	9.2	6.1
1986	8.8	6.0

SOURCE: Based on U.S. National Center for Educational Statistics,
        1989, p. 14.

Table 2. PARTICIPANTS IN ADULT EDUCATION PROGRAMS, 1972-1984

Year	Enrollment in Adult Education (1000s)	Percent Eligible Population*
1959	3421	--
1969	13041	10
1972	15734	11
1981	21252	13
1984	23303	13

* Persons 17 and over regardless of their enrollment status in
high school or college.

SOURCE: Based on <u>Statistical Abstract 1989</u>, p. 161; <u>1984</u>, p. 172;
        <u>1979</u>, p. 172; <u>1962</u>, p. 139.

TOPIC 16: INTEGRATION
AND MARGINALIZATION

16.1 IMMIGRANTS AND ETHNIC MINORITIES

The U.S. population is highly diverse ethnically. The sharpest divisions are between a white majority and so-called "racial" minorities. The sharpest cleavage is between whites and blacks, but there are also notable differences in identity and economic status between whites and the Hispanic and Native American minorities. The most common ancestries of white Americans are English, German, Irish, and Italian, but there are also notable numbers of Scandinavian, Eastern European, and Central European origins. Recently there has been substantial immigration from Asia, Mexico and Latin America. Most of the ethnic populations, even those of fairly recent immigration, are well along the way to functional assimilation, although ethnic identities persist. The racial minorities, blacks in particular, are a partial exception to this generalization.

The major ethnic division in the U.S. is the division between black and white, a division often termed racial rather than ethnic. In 1987, 12% of the population was black, up from 10% in 1950. The second largest ethnic minority, the Hispanic, accounts for at least 8% of the population (it is often estimated as much more; many Hispanics are not readily identifiable, and recently as many as a million per year have entered the country illegally from Mexico).

Other so-called "racial" minorities include the American Indians (1.4 million in 1980, or about .6% of the total population, and Asian and Pacific Islander Americans (3.7 million, or about 1.6%), of whom the Chinese, Filipinos, and Japanese are the most numerous at about 800,000 each, followed by Asian Indians, Koreans, and Vietnamese, in that order (Table 1). The Asian-origin population increased ten-fold between 1950 and 1980, and the increase continued during the 1980s.

The ancestors of most white Americans originally migrated from Europe. The peak migration flows were the "old" migration, largely from northern Europe, in the 1840s and 1850s, and the "new" migration, largely from southern and eastern Europe, between 1880 and 1915. Most Americans are of mixed ancestry, and most identify with only one or two "dominant" strains of their European origin. Persons of English and German origin are most numerous, followed by the Irish, Hispanics, Italians, and Poles, in that order. In 1980, almost one-fourth of Americans claimed English origins, about the same proportion claimed German ancestry, and almost one-fifth were of Irish descent (Table 2).

After absorbing a small proportion of the Europeans dislocated by World War II, the U.S. settled into a period in which immigration was exceptionally low, relative to its resident population, by comparison with most of the previous 150 years. Assimilative trends--the movement out from relatively dense ethnic enclaves in central cities and the acquisition of increasing amounts of formal education--continued apace, operating as they had in the past. What was new in the system was the extent to which blacks were incorporated in the same trends, for the black migration from southern rural places to northern urban places was easily the largest migration (apart from suburbanization) in the half-century ending around 1970. At this point, immigration reasserted itself in American life, with large numbers arriving from Asia and Latin America. For these groups, too, the residential and educational patterns characteristic of the American assimilative process seem to be present.

That immigration to the U.S. has risen markedly, and its composition shifted remarkably, is apparent from Table 3. Europe, historically the source of most of the nation's population, has fallen far behind both Asia and Latin America. In the late 1980s, annual immigration from Asia ran at over 250,000 a year and accounted for almost half of all immigration.

The redistribution of population from rural to urban areas has included all nativity categories of the population: native whites of native parentage, native whites of foreign or mixed parentage, foreign-born whites, and blacks, regardless of nativity (almost all of whom are native-born). But this has been true in varying degrees: the urban/rural location of the foreign-born and foreign-stock nativity groups have converged (from an initially far higher proportion) upon the native white of native parentage. Blacks, on the other hand, not especially highly urbanized at first, have been moving to urban areas somewhat more rapidly than the white population (although reflecting roughly the same urban/rural fertility differentials). For the most part, differential urbanization has declined in the 1980s. Foreign-born people became marginally more urban as native-whites, but not native-born blacks, became less so, as a result of the surburbanization trend.

We can derive some picture of the process of ghettoization of the foreign-born, and of the counter-trends, by using data in the 1980 Census that presents residence by year of immigration, for the foreign-born. When we look at the 1980 residence of pre-1950 immigrants, we find that close to nine in ten live within Standard Metropolitan Statistical Areas, and of these nearly half are in central cities. Of the rural dwellers in this group of immigrants, 11% were living in rural places in 1980. Roughly similar proportions of immigrants who arrived in the 1950s and in 1960-64 had like dwelling patterns, although the more recent their arrival the less rural they are. Among progressively more recent immigrants, the proportion living in central cities increases markedly, at the expense of all other residential categories. It is probable that as immigrants are longer in the country, more of them choose to and are able to move away from the center cities that are still the primary places of reception for new immigrants.

In this sense, Asian immigrants are typically "ghettoized" immigrants, but Hispanics are not, in that (as one would anticipate), they are quite unlikely to be urban if not in the center city, and, by comparison with other groups of recent immigrants, are relatively likely to live in rural places.

Just as the immigrant and second-generation residential patterns are generally converging upon those of native whites of native parentage, so also their educational experience gives evidence of a gradual assimilation into the American body social. It is eloquent testimony to how successful Americans believe their educational system has been in providing ample educational (and other) opportunities for the children of immigrants that, after 1970, the Census Bureau ceased to publish education data tabulated by nativity and parentage.

At least between 1950 and 1970, the story was not a very diverse one: however one cuts it, the American-born children of immigrants received about as much education as did native-born Americans of native-born parents. This is true at all levels of educational attainment, although probably more so at the college level. Too, if there is a trend, it is toward an increasing advantage in educational attainment on the part of the native-born children of immigrants. Why should there be an advantage, and why a growth in this advantage? Urban location is a part of the explanation, and non-Southern location is another part. The decades during which these cohorts completed their education were still within that period in which urban populations were increasingly outpacing the rural in educational attainment, and the second generation were, as the figures indicate, quite readily able to take advantage of their location to get an above-average education.

References

U.S. Bureau of the Census. 1980 Census of Population, General Social and Economic Characteristics: U.S. Summary. Washington, D.C.: USGPO, 1983.

------. Statistical Abstract of the United States, 1989. Washington, D.C., 1989. Annual. Previous years as cited.

U.S. Immigration and Naturalization Service, 1986 Statistical Yearbook of the Immigration and Naturalization Service. Washington, D.C.: USGPO, 1987.

Table 1. RACIAL COMPOSITION OF THE POPULATION, 1930-1980

Racial Group	1930	1940	1950	1960	1970	1980	1987
Major Racial Groups							
(in millions)							
All Races	123	132	151	179	203	227	244
White	110	118	135	159	178	195	206
Black	12	13	15	19	23	27	30
Other	1	1	1	2	3	5	8
Hispanic*	--	--	--	--	9	15	19
"Other" Racial Groups							
(1000s)							
Total	597	589	713	1619	2883	5150	7845
Indian (American)	332	334	343	524	793	1420	--
Japanese	139	127	142	464	591	701	--
Chinese	75	77	118	237	435	806	--
Filipino	45	46	62	176	343	775	--
Other**	6	5	49	218	721	1448	--

* Hispanics may be of any race, and are included in the three categories above.
** Aleuts, Asian Indians, Eskimos, Hawaiians, Indonesians, Koreans, Polynesians, and others not shown separately.

SOURCE: Based on <u>Statistical Abstract 1989</u>, pp. 16, 38-39; <u>1985</u>, p. 31; <u>1974</u>, pp. 30, 34; <u>1966</u>, p. 22, 26.

Table 2. COMPOSITION OF THE POPULATION BY ETHNIC ORIGIN,
          1969-1980

Ethnic Origin*	1969	1973	1980
Total (millions)	198	206	227
English	10%	13%	22%
French	3**	2	6
German	10	10	22
Irish	7	6	18
Italian	4	3	5
Polish	2	2	4
Russian	1	1	1
Spanish	5	5	6
Mexican	3	3	3
Puerto Rican	1	1	1
Other	50	47	3
Scotch	--	--	4
Dutch	--	--	3
Swedish	--	--	2
Norwegian	--	--	2
Czech	--	--	1
Hungarian	--	--	1
Welsh	--	--	1
Danish	--	--	1
Canadian (incl. French Can.)	--	--	1
Afro-American	--	--	9
American Indian	--	--	3
Not reported	9	11	--
Total	101	100	119

* In 1980, "Ancestry Group;" persons were permitted to name
multiple ancestry groups and therefore the total sums to more than
100%. Permitting identification with multiple ancestry groups is a
much more accurate way of classifying ethnic origin than requiring
persons to list only one, as in previous years. Of course, as a
result the 1980 figures are only roughly comparable, in relative
terms, to those for 1973 and 1969.
** Estimated from figures for 1971; persons of French origin were
included in "other" in 1969; the percent in the "other" category
here has been adjusted accordingly. See Statistical Abstract 1974,
p. 34.

SOURCE: Based on Statistical Abstract 1989, p. 41; 1974, p. 34.

Table 3. QUANTITY OF IMMIGRATION, SELECTED COUNTRIES OF ORIGIN, AND PROPORTION OF TOTAL IMMIGRATION FROM SELECTED REGIONS, 1951-1986

Country/Region of Origin	Immigrants (1000s)					
	1951-60	1961-70	1971-80	1982	1984	1986
France	51	45	25	2	3	4
Germany	478	191	74	7	7	10
Greece	48	86	92	3	3	3
Ireland	48	33	11	1	1	2
Italy	185	214	129	4	6	6
Poland	10	54	37	6	7	7
Portugal	20	76	102	4	4	4
U.K.	204	215	137	15	17	16
China	10	35	124	37	29	32
Hong Kong	16	75	113	5	12	10
India	2	27	164	22	24	25
Japan	46	40	50	4	5	44
Korea	6	35	26	32	33	35
Philippines	19	98	355	45	47	61
Vietnam	--	4	173	73	26	15
Canada	378	413	170	11	16	16
Mexico	300	454	640	56	58	67
Cuba	79	209	265	8	6	31
Dominion Republic	10	93	148	17	23	26
Jamaica	9	75	136	19	19	19
Colombia	18	72	77	9	11	11
Total	2515	3322	4493	594	544	602
Europe	53%	34%	18%	12%	13%	11%
Asia	6	13	35	53	46	43
Latin America	17	31	30	21	24	28
Other America	19	21	14	12	14	14

SOURCE: Based on U.S. Immigration and Naturalization Service, 1987, pp. 3-4.

Rates of both violent and property crime increased dramatically in the 1960s and 1970s. There are indications that in the 1980s, crime rates have stabilized or are declining, but rates remain very high in historical terms. Arrest and incarceration rates have not increased as rapidly as crime rates; in effect, law enforcement has become less "efficient." Per capita expenditures for crime control have risen substantially, and so have the numbers of inmates in federal and state prisons. Capital punishment, common in the 1930s and 1940s, virtually disappeared during the late 1960s and early 1970s. Since 1977 there have been a few executions, but the most dramatic trend regarding capital punishment is the growing number of condemned inmates who are living out their lives on "death row."

There are two main sources of crime statistics: the official records of law enforcement agencies, and sample surveys in which individuals report on their own experience, either as victims of crime (victimization surveys) or as perpetrators (self-report surveys). The main source of statistics on punishment--arrests, trials and convictions, sentences and incarcerations--is the institutional records of the judicial and corrections agencies themselves.

Crime

The longest series of national crime statistics in the U.S. is the Federal Bureau of Investigation's Uniform Crime Reports (UCR), which aggregate reports of crimes known to the police (and arrests made) from local police jurisdictions. From 1973 on, there are annual victimization surveys as well. These surveys, sponsored by the Justice Department, were undertaken because there is reason to doubt the accuracy of the UCR. For one thing, it reflects only those crimes known to the police; for another, changes in the absolute level of criminality it reveals are greatly affected by the number of law enforcement personnel and by variations in enforcement policy.

Of course, the victimization surveys also suffer from methodological problems. However, analysts are much more comfortable making generalizations from two different series on the incidence of crime, even if both are flawed, than with just one. No one was surprised that the victimization surveys revealed much more crime than did the UCR. For example, even allowing for the different base (victimization survey rates are based on 1,000 persons age 12 and over, or, in 1985, about 80% of the population; or, for certain property crimes, they are based on 1,000 households), robbery rates computed from the victimization surveys run two or three times higher than those in the UCR, burglary rates twice as high, and assault rates five times higher (Tables 1 and 2).

As for trends in criminal behavior, generalizations must be based on only the UCR data until 1973; after that, there are some generalizations supported by both types of data. Note that the UCR does not report all types of crime, but seven "index crimes," or "street crimes," namely murder, forcible rape, robbery, aggravated assault, burglary, larceny-theft, and motor vehicle theft. In 1979 an eighth "index crime," arson, was added to the standard list.

On the basis of the available series (Tables 1 and 2), we may conclude that crime rates increased rapidly between 1960 and 1980 (or perhaps, judging from the victimization data in Table 2, until 1975). Over that period, murder rates doubled; burglary, larceny and motor vehicle theft rates tripled; forcible rape and robbery rates quadrupled. After 1980 or so, crime rates in every category (victimization data), or at least in every category except rape and assault (UCR data) declined, often substantially. However, for some crimes, judging from the UCR data, the declines were shortlived; assaults and motor vehicle theft rates were higher in 1987 than ever before (Table 1).

Judging from the victimization data in Table 2 in the 1980s U.S. society was becoming less violent. However, the declines in violent crime are slight, and on the basis of the UCR trends for the period 1960-1975 (Table 1), it must be assumed that the levels of personal violence discovered in the first victimization surveys in the mid-1970s are relatively high. Presumably victimization data, if it existed for the 1960-1975 period, would show the same rapid increases in crimes of violence that the UCR data reveal.

In part, the increases in crime generally, and in violent crime in particular, are related to increases in the proportion of the national population that resides in metropolitan areas. There is a direct, very strong relationship between rates of violent crime and city size. However, the increase in crime rates 1960-1980 was a society-wide phenomenon. For example, note that violent crime rates increased faster in cities under 250,000 population than in the largest cities; while they quadrupled in the latter, they increased sixfold in smaller cities. In 1980, the violent crime rate in the smallest cities (under 10,000 population) was higher than it had been in the largest cities (250,000+) in 1960 (Table 3).

There are also age, sex, and ethnic differentials in criminal behavior. As may be seen in Table 1, in the general population murder rates were about five in 100,000 in 1960 and eight in 100,000 in 1987. But for black men, the corresponding rates were 37 and 55, and for black women, 10 and 12. In 1987, the probabilities of becoming a murder victim were six times higher for black than white men, and four times higher for white than black women (Statistical Abstract 1989, p. 168). According to U.S. Bureau of Justice statistics, in the mid-1980s three percent of Americans were victims of violent crimes each year, and being young, male, and black greatly increased the likelihood that one would be victimized (Langan, 1985).

White collar crime. The definition of white collar crime has long been a matter of dispute among criminologists and criminal justice practitioners. A major point of contention was whether white collar crime was defined by the nature of the offense or by the status, profession, and skills of the perpetrator. In practice, the matter was resolved in favor of characteristics of the offense rather than the offender. The definition of white collar crime used by the national Bureau of Justice Statistics is "nonviolent crime for financial gain committed by deception" (Balog, 1987). As thus defined, white collar crime includes counterfeiting, embezzlement, forgery, fraud, and white collar regulatory offenses. The latter is a residual category containing all violations of Federal regulations or laws not categorized as counterfeiting, embezzlement, forgery or fraud.

One indication of the magnitude of white collar crime is the enormous amount of money involved. For example, among the white collar cases filed by Federal attorneys in the year ending Sept. 30, 1985, there were more than 140 defendants charged with offenses estimated to involve over a million dollars each, and 64 were charged with offenses valued at over $10 million each (Balog, 1987). In contrast, losses from all bank robberies reported to the police in 1985 were under $19 million, and from all robberies, only $313 million.

Table 4 shows trends in arrest rates for forgery and counterfeiting, fraud, and embezzlement. Note that from 1960 to 1987, arrests for embezzlement remained fairly stable, while arrests for forgery/counterfeiting almost doubled, and fraud arrests increased four times.

In 1985, the Bureau of Justic Statistics started to track electronic fund transfer fraud, which includes automatic teller machine fraud, use of lost or stolen credit cards, and wire transfer fraud. It was estimated that these kinds of white collar crime would increase by 70% between 1985 and 1990 (Tien, Rick, and Cahn, 1985).

One of the major issues about white collar crime is an alleged leniency toward white collar offenders in the criminal justice system. It is often argued that few white collar offenders are prosecuted, even fewer are convicted, and that those who are convicted receive relatively light sentences. In fact, over the period 1980-1985, convicted white collar offenders were significantly less likely to be incarcerated (about 40%, vs. 49-54% for other offenders), and their sentences were only about half as long (15 months, versus 24 months for other offenders) (Statistical Abstract 1989, p. 181).

Punishment and Corrections

Although arrest rates are sometimes interpreted as indicators of crime, they are actually reflections of enforcement policies. To be arrested and charged with violating the law represents the first level of formal negative sanctioning of criminal behavior. Arrest rates for selected offenses for 1960-1987 are shown in Table 4. That the arrest rates do not accurately index the incidence of criminal behavior is apparent in the sharp declines in arrests for drunkenness (in 1960, it accounted for over one-third of all arrests, compared to 6% in 1987), vagrancy, and gambling. There were not, in fact, such drastic declines in drunkenness, vagrancy, and gambling, but law enforcement guidelines and arrest policies changed.

Trends in total arrest rates parallel the increases in crime rates documented in Tables 1 and 2, but the increases in rates of arrest are smaller than the increase in crime rates. Rates of violent crime increased 3.8 times, and property crimes, 2.8 times. Between 1960 and 1987, over the same period, arrest rates increased about 1.5 times. In 1960, two percent of Americans were arrested; in 1987, four percent were.

Notable trends in arrest rates apparent in Table 4 include continuing increases in arrests for forcible rape (the doubling of arrest rates is less impressive when it is remembered that rapes known to the police quadrupled over the same period); very large increases in arrests for drug violations (16 times higher), dealing in stolen property (5 times), driving while intoxicated and fraud (4 times), and aggravated assault and larceny-theft (3 times higher). Observe also the declines in arrests for crimes against family and children, and the relative stability in rates of arrest for embezzlement, sex offenses, and auto theft, despite rapidly rising rates of arrest for most other offenses.

Comparisons of arrest and crime rates for particular years and offenses is instructive. Judging from the UCR data (Table 1), the ratio of motor vehicle thefts to arrests for that offense was 3.1 in 1960 and 7.2 in 1987; for forcible rapes, the ratio of offenses to arrests was 1.3 in 1960 and 2.5 in 1987; for burglary, the corresponding ratios are 4.0 and 7.2. In other words, the efficiency of law enforcement has declined. In the 1980s, for most offenses, the number of arrests per offense was substantially lower than it had been in the 1960s.

This decline in efficiency is not due to lack of funding. Over the same period, in constant dollars per capita, the funding the nation's criminal justice system tripled. Another trend apparent in the distribution of expenditures for law enforcement and corrections is a significant decline in the proportion of total expenditures controlled at the local level (from 68% to 55% of all funding), and corresponding increases in the concentration of financial resources at the state (23% to 32%) and federal (9% to 12%) levels (Table 5).

Most arrests do not result in court action. Of defendants charged in criminal cases commenced in federal courts, a majority are convicted, and about half of those convicted (53% in 1987) are sentenced to imprisonment. Some sense of the scale of decline (statistical mortality) between numbers of persons arrested and numbers imprisoned may be gained by comparing arrest rates with incarceration rates. Table 6 lists numbers of inmates in federal and state prisons, and numbers of new inmates added annually, for selected years 1960-1986. Comparing the rates per 100,000 population of new inmates with aggregate arrest rates (Table 4) for the preceding year yields ratios of arrest to incarceration in the range of 77 to 1 (1965) or 60 to 1 (1985).

The number of inmates in U.S. prisons increased by about one-fourth in the 1950s, declined slightly in the 1960s, and has steadily increased since 1970. In 1987, there were three times as many prison inmates as in 1970, and rates of imprisonment had increased 2.4 times. Moreover, the nation's prisons are processing record numbers of new inmates. The 219,000 inmates added to the nation's prison system in 1986 was a larger population than the total number occupying all state and federal prisons at any one time in the 1950s and 1960s (Table 6).

Table 7 summarizes the application of capital punishment in the U.S., 1930-1987. In the early decades of the century the nation executed thousands of people, including almost 1,700 in the 1930s and almost 1,300 in the 1940s. The number of executions dropped sharply, to just over 700 in the 1950s and fewer than 200 in the 1960s, as it was established that the death penalty was being applied in ways that discriminated against blacks (note, for example, that almost as many blacks as whites were executed for murder, despite their being only about 10% of the population, and that blacks are approximately eight times as likely as whites to have been executed for rape). In the 1960s, the Supreme Court placed forceful restrictions on capital punishment, making it unconstitutional as long as it was administered unfairly, and consequently there was a moratorium on executions between 1968 and 1976. Eventually, the states revised their capital punishment laws in ways that met the conditions imposed by the Supreme Court, and beginning in 1977, prisoners condemned to capital punishment began to be executed once more. Since then, relatively few executions have been carried out, the peak number being 25 in 1987. But the inmate population on "death row" has continued to grow, with 200-300 newly condemned persons added each year to the population of inmates awaiting execution (Table 8). By 1987, the condemned population amounted to 1,800, and there had been only 93 people executed since the practice began again in 1977.

Public opinion polls on people's attitudes about whether crime rates are increasing or decreasing generally parallel changes in the rates themselves: the percent saying crime was increasing peaked about 1975-1980 at 70%, then declined to 40% in 1985. The public is uniformly convinced that the courts are too lenient on criminals. Between 80% and 90% of respondents questioned 1975-1985 said that the courts were not harsh enough in their punishment of criminals (Jameson and Flanagan, 1987).

References

Balog, Frank D., ed. Special Report: White Collar Crime. Washington, D.C.: U.S. Department of Justice, Bureau of Justice Statistics, 1987.

Jamieson, Katherine M. and Timothy J. Flanagan, eds. Sourcebook of Criminal Justice Statistics: 1986. Washington, D.C.: U.S. Department of Justice, Bureau of Justice Statistics, 1987.

Langan, Patrick A., ed. Special Report: The Risk of Violent Crime. Washington, D.C.: U.S. Department of Justice, Bureau of Justice Statistics, 1985.

Tien, James M., Thomas F. Rich, and Michael F. Cahn, eds. Special Report: Electronic Fund Transfer Fraud. Washington, D.C.: U.S. Department of Justice, Bureau of Justice Statistics, 1985.

U.S. Bureau of the Census. Statistical Abstract of the United States, 1989. Washington, D.C., 1989. Annual. Previous years as cited.

Table 1.   CRIME RATES (OFFENSES KNOWN TO THE POLICE PER 100,000 POPULATION), BY TYPE OF CRIME, 1959-1987

			Violent Crime		
Year	Total	Murder	Forcible Rape	Robbery	Aggravated Assault
1960	160	5	9	60	85
1965	198	5	12	71	110
1970	364	8	19	172	165
1975	482	10	26	218	227
1980	597	10	37	251	299
1985	557	8	37	209	303
1987	610	8	37	213	351

		Property Crime			Total Crime
Year	Total	Burglary	Larceny-Theft	Motor Vehicle Theft	(Viol.+ Prop.)
1960	1710	504	1024	182	1870
1965	2224	655	1314	255	2423
1970	3621	1085	2079	457	3985
1975	4800	1526	2805	469	5282
1980	5353	1684	3167	502	5950
1985	4651	1287	2901	462	5207
1987	4940	1330	3081	529	5550

SOURCE: Based on <u>Statistical Abstract 1989</u>, p. 166; <u>1979</u>, p. 177; <u>1974</u>, p. 147.

Table 2. CRIME RATES* (OFFENSES TO VICTIMS, PER 1,000 PERSONS
          12 YEARS OLD AND OVER), BY TYPE OF CRIME, 1973-1986

	Personal Sector				
	Violent Crime				
Year	Total	Rape	Robbery	Assault	Larceny/ Theft
1973	33	1	7	25	91
1975	33	1	7	25	96
1980	33	1	7	26	83
1985	30	1	5	24	69
1986	28	1	5	22	67

	Personal Sector (All Crimes)	Household Sector**			
Year	Total	Total	Burglary	Larceny	Motor Vehicle Theft
1973	124	218	92	107	19
1975	129	236	92	125	19
1980	116	227	84	126	17
1985	99	174	63	97	14
1986	96	170	61	93	15

* These are victimization rates.
** Rates are per 1,000 households.

SOURCE: Based on **Statistical Abstract 1989**, p. 170.

Table 3. CRIME RATES FOR VIOLENT CRIMES* IN CITIES, BY CITY
SIZE, 1960-1985

	Violent Crimes per 100,000 Population in Cities of					
Year	250,000+	100,000 to 249,999	50,000 to 99,999	25,000 to 49,999	10,000 to 24,999	Under 10,000
1960	294	154	104	70	57	48
1965	410	242	145	113	93	81
1970	980	450	273	214	159	141
1975	1159	632	451	343	268	232
1980	1414	812	602	455	352	298
1983	1294	736	511	403	297	260
1985	1345	802	536	420	307	272

* Rates of violent crimes per 100,000 population; crimes classed as
violent include four of the UCR index crimes, namely murder,
forcible rape, robbery, and aggravated assault.

SOURCE: Based on Statistical Abstract 1987, p. 157; 1979, p. 179;
1974, p. 149.

Table 4.   NUMBER OF ARRESTS AND ARREST RATES,* BY OFFENSE
CHARGED, 1960-1987

Offense Charged	Arrests Per 100,000 Population							
	1960	1964	1968	1972	1976	1980	1984	1987
Total arrested (millions)	4.0	4.6	5.6	7.0	7.9	9.7	8.9	10.8
Total arrest rate	3640	3460	3866	4372	4521	4665	4957	5345
Criminal homicide	7	7	9	11	10	9	8	8
Forcible rape	7	7	9	12	13	14	16	15
Robbery	30	29	48	68	63	67	61	61
Aggravated assault	55	60	73	97	110	125	129	150
Burglary	127	141	176	196	233	231	186	186
Larceny--theft	218	271	319	423	530	540	561	622
Auto theft	58	73	86	76	63	62	52	73
Other assaults	141	145	165	192	202	220	227	333
Arson	--	4	6	7	9	9	8	7
Forgery, counterfeiting	23	23	24	27	32	35	35	39
Fraud	39**	35	39	60	92	126	113	139
Embezzlement	--	6	4	4	5	4	3	5
Stolen property	11	14	26	45	53	56	53	59
Vandalism	--	58	76	81	100	112	106	114
Weapons (carrying, etc.)	35	36	58	75	70	75	77	82
Prostitution, vice***	24	21	29	28	34	41	49	50
Sex offenses	46	44	33	32	30	30	42	43
Drug abuse violations	25	28	112	269	286	256	312	401
Gambling	113	78	53	44	37	23	15	11
Offenses vs. fam.,children	46	43	35	33	33	24	18	24
Driving while intox.	169	170	211	377	479	627	748	698
Liquor laws	98	116	148	130	173	206	213	250
Drunkenness	1298	1101	974	863	612	505	492	347
Disorderly conduct	437	359	408	363	312	348	286	297
Vagrancy	141	100	68	35	19	14	13	16
Curfew, loitering (juv.)	--	49	68	72	50	32	37	38
Runaways (juv.)	--	53	103	124	95	69	63	67
Suspicion	--	--	62	26	18	8	9	6
Other offenses, except traffic	490	386	443	603	761	798	1025	1203

* Arrest rates per 100,000 population. Population figures for
computing rates are <u>not</u> the entire population of the U.S., but
rather the aggregate population of the jurisdictions served by the
agencies reporting arrests. Those populations, respectively, in
millions, were 1960, 109; 1964, 132; 1968, 145; 1972, 160; 1976,
175; 1980, 208; 1984, 180; 1987, 202.
** For 1960 only, fraud and embezzlement are combined.
*** Commercial vice.

SOURCE: <u>Statistical Abstract 1989</u>, p. 173; <u>1986</u>, p. 173; <u>1981</u>, p.
180; <u>1974</u>, p. 153; <u>1970</u>, p. 147; <u>1966</u>, p. 151; <u>1962</u>, p. 152.

Table 5.   CRIMINAL JUSTICE SYSTEM: PUBLIC EXPENDITURES, BY
           LEVEL OF GOVERNMENT, 1960-1985

Year	Total Expenditures Billions of Dollars Current	Total Expenditures Billions of Dollars Constant*	Per Capita**	Distribution of Expenditures by Level of Government Federal	Distribution of Expenditures by Level of Government State	Distribution of Expenditures by Level of Government Local
1960	3.3	12.2	68	9%	23%	68%
1965	4.6	15.6	81	8	25	67
1970	8.6	23.8	117	11	25	64
1975	17.2	34.6	160	13	27	61
1980	22.1	28.9	127	10	28	62
1985	45.6	45.6	191	12	32	55

* 1985 dollars, based on the Consumer Price Index.
** 1985 dollars per person, resident national population.

SOURCE: Based on <u>Statistical Abstract 1989</u>, pp. 7, 176, 462;
        <u>1979</u>, p. 187; <u>1974</u>, p. 156.

Table 6.   INMATES* IN FEDERAL AND STATE PRISONS, AND NEW INMATES
           ADDED ANNUALLY: NUMBERS AND RATES PER 100,000
           POPULATION, 1950-1987

Year	Inmates Present at End of Year		New Inmates Received from Courts	
	Number (1000s)	Rate	Number (1000s)	Rate
1950	166	110	69	46
1955	186	112	78	47
1960	213	119	89	49
1965	211	109	88	45
1970	196	97	79	39
1975	241	113	130	61
1980	316	139	142	63
1985	481	201	198	83
1986	524	216	219	91
1987	557	228	--	--

* Inmates sentenced to a maximum term of more than one year.

SOURCE: Based on Statistical Abstract 1989, p. 183; 1970, p. 158.

Table 7. PRISONERS EXECUTED UNDER CIVIL AUTHORITY, 1930-1987

Year or Period	Total*	White	Black	Executed for Murder Total*	White	Black
Total, 1930-1987	3952	1808	2102	3427	1721	1666
1930-1939	1667	627	816	1154	803	687
1940-1949	1284	490	781	1064	458	595
1950-1959	717	336	376	601	316	280
1960-1964	181	90	91	145	79	66
1965-1967	10	8	2	10	8	2
1968-1976	--	--	--	--	--	--
1977-1980	3	3	--	3	3	--
1981	1	1	--	1	1	--
1982	2	1	1	2	1	1
1983	5	4	1	5	4	1
1984	21	13	8	21	13	8
1985	18	11	7	18	11	7
1986	18	11	7	18	11	7
1987	25	13	12	25	13	12

Year or Period	Executed for Rape			Other Offenses**		
Total, 1930-1987	455	48	405	70	39	31
1930-1939	125	10	115	28	14	14
1940-1949	200	19	179	20	13	7
1950-1959	102	13	89	14	7	7
1960-1964	28	6	22	8	5	3
1965-1967	--	--	--	--	--	--
1968-1976	--	--	--	--	--	--
1977-1980	--	--	--	--	--	--
1981	--	--	--	--	--	--
1982	--	--	--	--	--	--
1983	--	--	--	--	--	--
1984	--	--	--	--	--	--
1985	--	--	--	--	--	--
1986	--	--	--	--	--	--

* Includes races other than white or black.
** 25 armed robbery, 20 kidnapping, 11 burglary, 8 espionage (6 in 1942 and 2 in 1953), and 6 aggravated assault.

SOURCE: Based on Statistical Abstract 1989, p. 187.

Table 8.   MOVEMENT OF PRISONERS UNDER SENTENCE OF DEATH, 1963-
1987

Status	1963	1965	1970	1975	1980	1985	1987
Under sentence of death, Jan. 1	275	333	575	244	595	1420	1800
Received death sentence*	91	67	133	322	203	281	299
White	--	--	66	145	125	165	190
Black	--	--	66	174	77	114	106
Dispositions other than executions	48	62	77	78	101	106	90
Executions	21	7	--	--	--	18	25
Under sentence of death, Dec. 31*	297	331	631	488	697	1575	1984
White	--	--	293	218	425	896	1138
Black	--	--	335	262	268	664	821

* This total includes races other than white or black.

SOURCE: Based on <u>Statistical Abstract 1989</u>, p. 187; <u>1984</u>, p. 197;
<u>1966</u>, p. 166.

Trends in the various emotional and self-destructive disorders show little congruence. Substance abuse increased until the 1980s and then, with the marked exception of cocaine use, stabilized and declined slightly in most age groups. Trends in emotional problems and mental illness are subject to fluctuations on the basis of changing definitions of what constitutes disorder, what kinds of ameliorative efforts are appropriate, and the number of diagnosticians and care-givers. Trends in the incidence in mental illness are divergent, depending on the indicator and disorder: the incidence of children's disorders is generally up, hospitalization rates for psychiatric illness are down, outpatient episodes for adults appear to have stabilized, and reported child abuse tripled between 1976 and 1986. Suicide rates rose from the late 1940s until the mid-1970s, peaked in 1977, declined slightly and seem to have stabilized. The apparent stability in suicide rates masks substantial variation by subgroup, including increases among teenagers and young adults, relative stability among adult males, and declines since the mid-1970s among women.

Mental Illness and Nervous Breakdowns

One measure of the availability of mental health services is the number of organizations that provide care. Between 1970 and 1987 the number of organizations providing care grew from 3,005 to 4,747, an increase of 58%. Over the same period, the number of state and county mental hospitals declined by 8%, while the number of private psychiatric hospitals and general hospitals with psychiatric services more than doubled, from 947 to 2,102. An increase in facilities for emotionally disturbed children--up 30% between 1970 and 1982--is also noteworthy (Taube and Barrett, 1985, p. 26; Statistical Abstract 1989, p. 109). There have been substantial increases in services and organizations, with a shift away from public care in state and county residential facilities and toward general hospital and private care.

Another indicator of the status of mental illness in society is the financial outlay for mental health care. Total expenditures by mental health organizations in 1969 amounted to 3.3 billion dollars. In constant (1969, based on the medical care component of the consumer price index) dollars, the series of annual expenditures over the following 18 years looks like this:

1969, $3.3 billion
1975, 4.4 billion
1979, 4.1 billion
1983, 4.7 billion
1987, 4.5 billion

Observe that the level of total funding has remained relatively stable since the mid-1970s. Taking into account the growing U.S. population and considering per capita expenditures, the evidence for stability is even stronger. Per capita costs in constant (1969) dollars for the six points noted above are, respectively, 17, 21, 19, 20, 20, and 19 dollars. The fraction of total costs spent by state and county mental hospitals has dropped sharply. In 1969, such places accounted for over 55% of all costs; by 1987, their share was only 33% (Taube and Barrett, 1985, p. 69; Statistical Abstract 1989, p. 109; 1987, p. 100).

Estimating the prevalence of mental illness in the population has been attempted hundreds of times, with disparate, often unreliable results. For example, specialists impaneled by a Presidential Commission on Mental Health to estimate the "true" prevalence of "the problem" reviewed three decades of epidemiological literature in an attempt to establish average rates for each type of psychopathology. Their findings illustrate the shortcomings of diagnostic procedures generally employed: the "true" prevalence of all types of psychopathology in the U.S. was estimated at somewhere between 13% and 56% of the population (Dohrenwend, et al., 1980, pp. 72-73). Given the difficulty of obtaining reliable estimates of the prevalence of mental disorder in the general population, here we shall simply trace trends in the number of patients served by mental health facilities. However, it must be remembered that reports of the number or characteristics of patients bear no necessary relation to the prevalence of disorders in the population, and are subject to fluctuations reflecting organizational changes that may have nothing to do with epidemiological trends.

Number and rates of "patient care episodes" in U.S. mental health facilities for the period 1955-1987 are presented in Table 1. The total number of patient care episodes increases markedly between 1955 and 1975, then stabilizes. The rapid increase--a quadrupling of total episodes between 1955 and 1975--is almost entirely accounted for by the expansion of outpatient services. Rates of inpatient care peaked in 1969 and decline thereafter, with occasional reversals. By 1983, there were 13% fewer inpatients per 100,000 population than there had been 14 years earlier. We lack statistics on numbers of outpatients for the 1980s, but rates of inpatient care seem to manifest the same pattern over the 1980s as in the previous decades, namely relative stability or modest decline. The exception is the last year in the series, 1987, when the rate of inpatient episodes makes a sharp reversal, increasing almost to the 1969 peak. It is unclear whether this change represents a reversal of trend, an atypical annual fluctuation, or a change in reporting procedures.

The decline in the absolute number of inpatients reflects the policy of "deinstitutionalization" of mental patients that began in the mid-1950s. Prior to that time, the number of institutionalized mental patients had been steadily increasing for several decades. In part, deinstitutionalization was a response by the states to the rising costs of inpatient care in state mental hospitals. The process was facilitated by other factors, including the introduction of psychotropic drugs into mental hospitals, which made it possible to treat patients outside hospital settings; expanding federal health and welfare programs that changed the norms about appropriate mental health care; and growing public support for protecting the rights of the mentally ill (Gronfein, 1985).

Partially counterbalancing the consistent decline in rates of hospitalization in state and county mental hospitals (from 502 patient care episodes per 100,000 population in 1955 to 183 in 1987) was an increase in hospitalization rates in private psychiatric hospitals (from 76 episodes per 100,000 population in 1955 to 126 in 1987) (Statistical Abstract 1989, p. 109; 1982-83, p. 117). Hospitalization rates for emotionally disturbed children also increased, from 11 inpatient episodes per 100,000 population in 1969 to 15 in 1981 (Taube and Barrett, 1985, p. 32).

Admission rates to inpatient psychiatric services vary by sex and race. Men are much more likely to be admitted to state and county hospitals, women are more likely to be served in private hospitals. Inpatient admission rates in state and county hospitals for nonwhites run about twice as high as for whites, and the difference seems to be increasing. In fact, while inpatient admission rates at state and county mental hospitals decreased for all other race/sex categories, rates for nonwhite males increased, from 420 per 100,000 in 1970 to 458 in 1980 (Taube and Barrett, 1985, pp. 51-52).

Child Neglect and Abuse

Rates of reported child neglect and abuse are sharply up since the mid-1970s, with reports of maltreatment doubling and the number of affected children tripling between 1976 and 1985 (Table 2). Most of the apparent increase is due to improved reporting systems and expanded facilities and personnel devoted to this problem. There is no clear evidence that the actual incidence of child maltreatment has increased. Expert analysts disagree on this point, but many argue that the true incidence has, in fact, decreased, and that it is only the visibility of child neglect and maltreatment that has increased. The following statement about the incidence of sexual abuse of children applies as well to other forms of child abuse:

> It is impossible to tell whether the current awareness of sexual abuse of children has developed because the problem has been getting worse or because it is simply getting more serious attention from the public. Efforts by women's groups to get women to report rape and spouse abuse may be having similar effects on the reporting of child abuse of all types. Whatever the reason for the increased attention, it has become clear that various forms of child abuse are probably much more widespread than was realized until recently (Farley, 1987, p. 209).

Suicide

Mortality from suicide has been relatively stable since the early 1970s, with annual age-adjusted rates running at about 12 deaths per 100,000 population (11.9 in 1986). The 40-year peak was 12.8 in 1977. The stabilized rates of the 1970s and 1980s represent a considerable increase over the the early 1950s, when there were fewer than 10 suicides per 100,000 population (Table 3).

The total suicide rate masks widely diverse rates among population subgroups, with annual rates in the 1980s varying around 2.5 for black women, compared to 6.0 for white women, 11.0 for black males and 19.0 for white males (Taube and Barrett, 1985, p. 149; Metropolitan Life, 1986, pp. 16-17). There are also significant age differentials. Although men of all ages are more apt than women to commit suicide, the general trend apparent over the years is a decline in the male-to-female ratio for persons over age 35; relative stability, with some increase after the mid-1970s, for adults aged 25-34; and a sizable increase in the male-to-female ratio in suicides for persons aged 15-24 (McIntosh and Jewell, 1986, p. 21).

While suicide rates for persons aged 15-24 rose from 4.8 in 1958 to a peak of 13.3 in 1977 (13.1 in 1986), the rates for older persons declined. For example, among 75-84 year-olds, the suicide rate dropped from 27.7 in 1958 to a low of 18.6 in 1981 and then increased again, to 25.2 in 1986. Thus, there are concomitant patterns of increasing suicide among the young and decreasing suicide among the older adults (Taube and Barrett, 1985, p. 149; Statistical Abstract 1989, p. 80).

Factors mentioned by researchers as affecting the increase in suicide rates among young people include the assertion that adolescence has become more difficult, as well as "increased competition associated with the baby boom cohort, increased drug and alcohol use, changing marriage patterns, parental marriage difficulties and divorce, and high youth unemployment rates" (McIntosh, 1986, p. 25; Maris, 1985). The problematic nature of such post hoc explanations is apparent when one addresses sex differences in youth suicide. Among white females, such factors seem to have had only modest effects, pushing up suicide rates by only 2.5 suicides per 100,000. Stabilized during the 1980s at about 5.0, the suicide rate for women aged 15-24 is about twice as high as for young women in the 1950s, but lower than the rates for young men have ever been. In contrast, while rates for young white women were increasing from about 2.5 to about 5.0, those for young men almost tripled, from about 7.5 in the 1950s to over 21.0 by 1982. To complicate the picture still further, rates for young black males and females show significant declines since the 1970s, for young black women a decline of about 50%, and yet the factors cited as producing teenage suicides and complicating modern adolescence are far more common among young blacks than whites (Taube and Barrett, 1985, pp. 150-154; Metropolitan Life, 1986, pp. 16-17).

Addictions

Slowly, very slowly, the consumption of mood-changing substances seems to be declining in the United States. Since 1980, the regular use of marijuana, stimulants, tranquilizers, sedatives, barbiturates, hallucinogens, alcohol, and tobacco has declined, particularly among young adults. The only important exceptions are cocaine, the users of which have more than doubled since 1980 but are still only a small fraction of the population, and heroin, the users of which constitute a smaller fraction, which remains unchanged.

What has caused the decline nobody can say. It is certainly not government enforcement, which is directed primarily at the two kinds of usage--cocaine and heroin--that have not diminished. Indeed, there is some reason to suppose that enforcement efforts do more to advertise and promote these products than to suppress them.

The decline of marijuana smoking is largely attributable to the loss of its symbolic significance. The shared joint no longer makes an intelligible statement. The declining popularity of tranquilizers is simple to explain; they are no longer so actively promoted by prescribing physicians.

As to the reduced consumption of hard liquor, it has something to do with the aging of the population, the campaign against drunken driving, the craze for physical fitness, the eclipse of the neighborhood tavern, the promotion of mildly alcoholic soft drinks, and changes of public mood. Intoxicants, like other consumer goods, are subject to fashions that are partly cyclical, partly capricious, and reliably unpredictable (Caplow, 1988, p. 3).

National data on drug use among youth have been collected in the "Monitoring the Future" project of the University of Michigan's Institute for Social Research. Available trend studies, drawing upon annual surveys of high school seniors begun in 1975, and surveys of college students and post-high-school youth begun later, reveal increasing marijuana use until about 1980 and a decline thereafter, with usage in 1985 higher than at the beginning of the decade. Frequency of daily usage has declined more than prevalence of lifetime use.

Usage of any illicit drugs increased steadily until 1978 and has declined since then. The proportion of students who have ever used an illicit drug other than marijuana increased gradually until 1982 and declined slightly thereafter. Cocaine usage increased in the late 1970s, plateaued until 1984, and has since risen again. Use of heroin and other opiates exhibits a fairly level pattern throughout the decade. High school seniors' use of both alcohol and tobacco has declined slowly but steadily, with the decline in alcohol use beginning about 1980 and that in tabacco about 1977. Sex contrasts reveal higher usage of marijuana and alcohol by male seniors; higher use of tobacco by females; and declines in usage by both males and females since 1978-80 in marijuana and cigarette use, and alcohol use for males. Alcohol use by females remained relatively stable throughout the 1975-1985 decade (see Johnston, et al., 1986, pp. 42-45, 54-61).

Figures on lifetime prevalence of drug use from a different source (Miller, 1983) for the period 1972-82 show increased usage across the entire spectrum of drugs for adults aged 26 and over, similar increases for young adults except for a decline in heroin use, and increased usage among youth except for cigarettes (stability) and heroin (a decline).

Usage figures for youth and adults collected in 1985 show current cocaine use to be highest in the western U.S.; slightly more frequent among whites than blacks, except among persons over age 35; and most common among young adults aged 18-34, with 9% of males and about 5% of females of that age current users (Statistical Abstract 1988, p. 112). Additional information on drugs and addictions appears in Chapter 13.8 (Mood-Altering Substances).

References

Caplow, Theodore. "The Market for Intoxicants." Social Change Report (Center for Middletown Studies) 2 (No. 1, 1988): 3.

Dohrenwend, Bruce P., Barbara Snell Dohrenwend, Madelyn Schwartz Gould, Bruce Link, Richard Neugebauer, and Robin Wunsch-Hitzig. Mental Illness in the United States: Epidemiological Estimates. New York: Praeger, 1980.

Farley, John E. American Social Problems: An Institutional Analysis. Englewood Cliffs, N.J.: Prentice-Hall, 1987.

Gronfein, W. "Psychotropic Drugs and the Origins of Deinstitutionalization." Social Problems 32 (1985): 437-454.

Johnston, Lloyd D., Patrick M. O'Malley, and Jerald G. Bachman. Drug Use Among American High School Students, College Students, and Other Young Adults. Washington, D.C.: National Institute on Drug Abuse, U.S. Department of Health and Human Services, 1986.

McIntosh, John L. and Barbara L. Jewell. "Sex Difference Trends in Completed Suicide." Suicide and Life-Threatening Behavior 16 (1986): 16-27.

Maris, R. "The Adolescent Suicide Problem." Suicide and Life-Threatening Behavior 15 (1985): 91-109.

Metropolitan Life Insurance Company. "Suicide: An Update." Statistical Bulletin 67 (April-June, 1986): 16-23.

Miller, Judith Droitcour. National Survey on Drug Abuse: Main Findings, 1982. Washington, D.C.: National Institute on Drug Abuse, U.S. Department of Health and Human Services, 1983.

Taube, Carl A. and Sally A. Barrett, eds. Mental Health, United States 1985. Washington, D.C.: U.S. Department of Health and Human Services, National Institute of Mental Health, 1985.

U.S. Bureau of the Census. Statistical Abstract of the United States, 1989. Washington, D.C., 1989. Annual. Previous years as cited.

U.S. Department of Justice. Sourcebook of Criminal Justice Statistics: 1988. Washington, D.C., 1988.

Table 1. PATIENT CARE EPISODES IN MENTAL HEALTH FACILITIES, BY
TYPE OF TREATMENT FACILITY, 1955-1987, AND NUMBER OF
INPATIENTS, 1970-1987

	Patient Care Episodes*						Number
	Number (1,000s)			Per 100,000 Population			of In-
		In-	Out-		In-	Out-	patients
Year	Total	patient	patient	Total	patient	patient	(1,000s)
1955	1675	1296	379	1032	799	234	--
1965	2637	1566	1071	1374	816	558	--
1967	3140	1659	1480	1604	848	756	--
1969	3573	1678	1894	1798	850	948	--
1971	4038	1721	2317	1982	847	1134	--
1973	4749	1680	3070	2282	807	1475	--
1975	6409	1791	4618	3033	847	2185	284
1977	6393	1817	4577	2964	842	2122	--
1979	6405	1803	4602	2863	806	2058	230
1981	--	1720	--	--	755	--	214
1983	--	1711	--	--	742	--	221
1987	--	2052	--	--	849	--	238

* Patient care episodes are defined as the number of residents in
inpatient facilities at the beginning of the year (or the number of
persons on the rolls of noninpatient facilities) plus the total
additions to these facilities during the year.

SOURCE: Based on **Statistical Abstract 1989**, p. 109; **1987**, p. 100;
1982-83, p. 117; **1975**, p. 83.

Table 2.   CHILD NEGLECT AND ABUSE: MALTREATMENT CASES, 1976-1986,
           AND MALTREATMENT REPORTS,* 1978-1985

Year	Child Maltreatment Cases		Child Maltreatment Reports*	
	Number (1,000s)	Rate/10,000 Children	Number (1,000s)	Rate/10,000 Children
1976	669	101	--	--
1977	838	128	--	--
1978	836	129	607	94
1979	988	154	707	110
1980	1154	181	785	123
1981	1225	194	846	134
1982	1262	201	924	147
1983	1477	236	1001	160
1984	1727	273	1156	183
1985	1928	306	1299	206
1986	2086	--	--	--

* Maltreatment reports may involve more than one child; maltreatment cases refer to individual children, but the totals
include children counted twice or more if maltreatment involving
those children was reported twice or more in the same year. The
Statistical Abstract lists maltreatment report rates per 1,000
population rather than 10,000 children. However, even though some
reports involve several children, it seems more appropriate to base
the index on numbers of children (the population at risk) than on
general population.

SOURCE: Based on Statistical Abstract 1989, p. 172; U.S. Dept. of
   Justice, 1989, p. 324.

Table 3. AGE-ADJUSTED SUICIDE RATES, BY SEX, 1950-1986

Year	Deaths per 100,000 Population		
	Total	Male	Female
1950	11.0	--	--
1951	10.0	--	--
1952	9.7	--	--
1953	9.8	--	--
1954	9.9	--	--
1955	9.9	--	--
1956	9.7	--	--
1957	9.6	--	--
1958	10.5	16.8	4.7
1959	10.5	16.6	4.7
1960	10.6	16.6	5.0
1961	10.5	16.4	5.0
1962	11.0	16.9	5.6
1963	11.2	17.0	6.0
1964	11.0	16.6	5.8
1965	11.4	16.9	6.3
1966	11.1	16.6	6.1
1967	11.1	16.4	6.3
1968	10.9	16.4	6.1
1969	11.3	16.7	6.5
1970	11.8	17.3	6.8
1971	11.8	17.2	7.0
1972	12.1	17.8	6.9
1973	11.9	17.8	6.6
1974	12.1	18.1	6.6
1975	12.5	18.8	6.8
1976	12.1	18.3	6.6
1977	12.8	19.4	6.7
1978	11.9	18.2	6.1
1979	11.7	17.9	5.9
1980	11.4	18.0	5.5
1981	11.5	18.0	5.7
1982	11.6	18.3	5.4
1983	11.4	18.2	5.2
1984	11.6	18.7	5.2
1985	11.5	18.8	4.9
1986	11.9	19.3	5.1

SOURCE: Based on Taube and Barrett, 1985, pp. 146, 149; <u>Statistical Abstract 1989</u>, p. 80; <u>1987</u>, pp. 76, 78.

Public social welfare programs increased dramatically during the 1960s, and made significant inroads on poverty. Total public expenditures for social welfare, in constant dollars per capita, increased through the mid-1970s and then leveled off. Since about 1970, the percent of the population in poverty has stabilized at about 12%; it rose slightly during the 1980s. In absolute numbers, in the 1980s there were fewer poor people than in the 1950s, but since 1969 the absolute number of the poor has been increasing. Blacks and Hispanics are about three times as likely to be poor as whites, but a majority of the poor are white, and as of 1985, over half were members of female-headed, husband-absent households.

Poverty, always present in the U.S. as elsewhere, was "rediscovered" in the late 1950s and became the focus of much public attention and political action during the 1960s. A highly visible, heavily politicized "war on poverty," launched under President Lyndon Johnson, made significant inroads on some forms of poverty (see Caplow, 1975, pp. 161-168, for a critical assessment of the achievements and failures of the Johnson Administration's anti-poverty programs; see also Haveman, 1987). Eventually some of its programs were terminated or cut back and the "war" itself concluded, although many of its objectives, under different labels, have continued to occupy subsequent administrations. Helping the poor and dealing with the concomitants of poverty continue to be major justifications for domestic spending by the government.

In fact, public expenditures for social welfare programs, in constant dollars per capita, increased by 51% in the decade of the 1970s, and another 9% between 1980 and 1985 (Table 1). The category of expenditures most directly focused on the poor, public aid, increased faster than social welfare spending as a whole. It doubled between 1970 and 1980, then stabilized at the 1980 level, increasing only slightly in constant dollar outlay per capita between 1980 and 1986.

Another way to assess trends in government outlay for social welfare it to compare expenditures for social welfare to the Gross National Product, and to the total outlay of federal, state and local funds for all purposes. Judged in these terms, the trends in governmental funding for social welfare are as follows: 1) As a percentage of the GNP, social welfare spending by all levels of government increased consistently from 1955 to 1975, then stabilized at the 1975 level for the next decade, at about 18% of the GNP; 2) In 1950, social welfare outlays amounted to only about one-fourth of total federal expenses; by 1975, they accounted for more than half, and during the 1980s they remained at about that level; 3) The proportion of state and local public expenditure devoted to social welfare programs has been stable at about 60% for almost four decades (Table 2).

In 1964 the Social Security Administration devised a poverty index based on money income that took into account the different consumption requirements of families of various size and composition. The index is adjusted annually to reflect changes in the Consumer Price Index, and thus represents a "sliding scale" for measuring relative poverty. As measured by this official poverty index, 22% of the American people, and 55% of all black Americans, were living below the poverty level in 1959. Over the next decade, the absolute number of the poor dropped from 40 million to a low of 24 million, then began to increase slowly. Although the numbers of the poor were growing, so was the total population, and the percentage of the population below the poverty level hovered around 12% for the next decade, reaching the lowest point in the entire 30-year series in 1978, at 11%. It then rose, averaging about a point increase per year, until 1983, peaked at just over 15%, and has declined slowly every since (Table 3).

For the population as a whole, and for many of the major components of the population--children, families, blacks, the families of female householders--the trends in poverty rates are the same, namely a sharp decline between 1959 and 1969, and then little change over the next two decades, with perhaps a slight increase in the percent below the poverty level in the mid- or late-1980s. Among blacks, for example, the percent in poverty drops from 56% to 32%, and then remains at the latter level; among whites, it drops from 18% to 9% and then stabilizes. Most of the declines had run their course by 1975; after that, government programs may have been able to hold the line, or "lose" only a little, but they did not make further inroads on poverty. In 1987, the poor included one-eighth of the total population, one-fifth of all children, one-third of blacks and 45% of black children, one-third of female households with no husband present and 55% of the children in such households (Table 4).

Having considered the probabilities of poverty in various segments of the general population, let us turn to the composition of the population in poverty (Table 5). In 1959, about three-fourths of the poor were white, one-fourth were black, almost half were under age 18, and one-fourth were members of families headed by women without husbands present. Over the years, these rates changed but little, and what change there was had generally run its course by 1970. In other words, while the numbers of poor people declined, both relatively and absolutely, during the 1960s, the characteristics of those who remained, or later became poor did not. The dominant pattern shown in Table 5 is stability: the composition of America's poor in 1987 was about the same as in 1977, and in 1967. The primary exception to that statement is that the proportion of poor people belonging to female-headed, husband-absent families consistently increased until by 1987, a majority of the poor were in such families. As of that date, the poor people in America were mostly white (66%), relatively young (38% were children under 18), and living in female-headed, no-husband present families (52%). The odds of being poor are three times as high for blacks and Hispanics as for whites, but there are many more whites in the population, and so the typical poor person is white.

Many factors combine to create and perpetuate poverty in America. Among those identified as most important are these:

1. Unemployment, some of it due to the displacement of workers that has accompanied changes in the industrial structure of the national economy as a whole (see Chapter 4.1, Unemployment; see also Steidlmeier, 1987).

2. Discrimination in the labor market against subordinate groups, especially ethnic minorities (racism), women (sexism), and older people (ageism) (see Chapter 3.4, "Women's Employment").

3. Family instability, namely the combination of high rates of divorce and prevailing norms about alimony, child support, and day care which leave many women largely responsible for the economic support of their children and at the same time unable to work outside the home (cf. Weitzman, 1985).

4. Exploitation of the poor, because it is in the interests of the more powerful segments of society to continue a dual labor market situation whereby one segment of the labor force works for minimum or near minimum wage levels that, in themselves, are not sufficient

to keep a family out of poverty even when a parent is employed. See, for example, Gans' (1972) discussion of the positive functions of poverty.

5. A "culture of poverty" that fosters attitudes about education, work, saving and spending that are not compatible with successful employment in bureaucratic settings (cf. Gutkind, 1986; Banfield, 1974; Lewis, 1968).

6. Physical, mental, or social disadvantage, which place a person at least temporarily in a situation where self-support is impossible.

These last are the "deserving poor," and systems of public and private welfare for their support continue to be inadequate. George Ritzer (1986, p. 349) is talking of these variously "handicapped" persons when he writes that

the vast majority of poor people are the victims of adverse circumstances that are far beyond their control. The vast majority of the poor among children, old people, the handicapped, and female heads of households did not create their situation and are virtually powerless, on their own, to change it.

The poor benefit from private philanthropy as well as from public programs. However, as presently organized, private efforts are dwarfed by the public programs. In 1986, just one category of public social welfare expenses--the public aid segment--spent more ($103 billion) than the entire volume of private philanthropy as indicated in individual, corporate, and foundation tax returns ($88 billion). The total outlay for social welfare programs from all levels of government in 1986 was $771 billion dollars, almost nine times greater than the combined private donations to all causes (Statistical Abstract 1989, pp. 346, 371).

References

Banfield, Edward. The Unheavenly City Revisited. Boston: Little, Brown, 1974.

Caplow, Theodore. Toward Social Hope. New York: Basic Books, 1975.

Gans, Herbert J. "The Positive Functions of Poverty." American Journal of Sociology 78 (1972): 275-289.

Gutkind, Efraim. Patterns of Economic Behavior Among the American Poor. Basingstoke, NH: Macmillan Press, 1986.

Haveman, Robert H. Poverty Policy and Poverty Research: The Great Society and the Social Sciences. Madison: University of Wisconsin Press, 1987.

Lewis, Oscar. The Study of Slum Cultures--Backgrounds for La Vida. New York: Random House, 1968.

Ritzer, George. Social Problems. 2nd ed. New York: Random House, 1986.

Steidlmeier, Paul. The Paradox of Poverty: A Reappraisal of Economic Development Policy. Cambridge, MA: Ballinger, 1987.

U.S. Bureau of the Census. Statistical Abstract of the United States, 1989. Washington, D.C., 1989. Annual. Previous years as cited.

Weitzman, Lenore J. The Divorce Revolution. New York: Free Press, 1985.

Table 1.   SOCIAL WELFARE EXPENDITURES UNDER PUBLIC PROGRAMS, IN
           CONSTANT (1985) DOLLARS PER CAPITA NATIONAL POPULATION,
           BY TYPE OF PROGRAM, 1950-1986

| | | Expenditures, Constant (1985) Dollars per Capita | | | | | | |
| | | Social | Public | Health | | | | |
Year	Total	Insur.	Aid	& Med.	Vets.	Educ.	Housing	Other
1950	648	136	69	55	187	185	--	--
1955	732	221	67	72	105	251	--	--
1960	969	357	75	82	102	326	7	20
1965	1226	445	100	100	94	447	--	--
1970	1828	683	206	125	112	639	10	52
1975	2506	1060	357	155	146	699	28	60
1980	2763	1286	403	156	119	680	43	76
1985	3001	1528	398	169	110	685	52	57
1986	3072	1554	412	177	110	713	48	59

SOURCE: Based on <u>Statistical Abstract 1989</u>, p. 346; <u>1988</u>, p. 334;
        <u>1984</u>, p. 370.

Table 2. SOCIAL WELFARE EXPENDITURES UNDER PUBLIC PROGRAMS AS
PERCENT OF GNP AND TOTAL GOVERNMENT OUTLAYS, 1950-1986

	Social Welfare Expenditures (billion $, except percent)								
	Total Government			Federal			State and Local		
			Percent of			Percent of			Percent of
			Total			Total			Total St.
			Govt.			Federal			& Local
Year	Total	GNP	Outlays	Total	GNP	Outlays	Total	GNP	Outlays
1950	23	8%	37%	10	4%	26%	13	4%	59%
1955	33	8	33	15	4	22	18	4	55
1960	52	10	38	25	5	28	27	5	60
1965	77	11	42	38	5	33	39	6	60
1970	146	15	48	77	8	40	68	7	64
1975	290	19	57	167	11	54	123	8	63
1980	492	18	56	303	11	54	190	7	61
1985	730	18	51	453	11	48	277	7	59
1986	770	18	48	472	11	48	298	7	58

SOURCE: Based on <u>Statistical Abstract 1989</u>, p. 348; <u>1984</u>, p. 370.

Table 3. PERSONS BELOW POVERTY* LEVEL, BY RACE, 1959-1987

Year	Number Below Poverty Level				Percent Below Poverty Level			
	All Races	White	Black	Spanish Origin	All Races	White	Black	Spanish Origin**
1959	39.5	28.5	9.9	--	22%	18%	55%	--
1960	39.9	28.3	--	--	22	18	--	--
1966	28.5	20.6	8.9	--	15%	12	42	--
1969	24.1	16.7	7.1	--	12	9	32	--
1970	25.4	17.5	7.5	--	13	10	33	--
1975	25.9	17.8	7.5	3.0	12	10	31	27
1976	25.0	16.7	7.6	2.8	12	9	31	25
1977	24.7	16.4	7.7	2.7	12	10	31	22
1978	24.5	16.3	7.6	2.6	11	9	31	22
1979	25.3	16.6	7.8	2.9	12	9	31	22
1979	26.1	17.2	8.1	2.9	12	9	31	22
1980	29.3	19.7	8.6	3.5	13	10	32	26
1981	31.8	21.6	9.2	3.7	14	11	34	26
1982	34.4	23.5	9.7	4.3	15	12	36	30
1983	35.3	24.0	9.9	4.6	15	12	36	28
1984	33.7	23.0	9.5	4.8	14	11	34	28
1985	33.1	22.0	8.9	5.2	14	11	31	29
1986	32.4	22.2	9.0	5.1	14	11	31	27
1987	32.5	21.4	9.7	5.5	13	10	33	28

* Poverty is defined by the poverty index originated at the Social Security Administration in 1964 and revised by Federal Interagency Committees in 1969 and 1980. The poverty index is based solely on money income and does not reflect the fact that many low-income persons receive noncash benefits such as food stamps, medicaid, and public housing. The index is based on the Dept. of Agriculture's 1961 economy food plan and reflects the different consumption requirements of families based on their size and composition. The poverty thresholds are updated every year to reflect changes in the Consumer Price Index.
** Hispanic persons may be of any race. Some Hispanics are represented among the whites and blacks in this table, and therefore the three columns showing race sum to more than the total "all races" column.

SOURCE: Based on Statistical Abstract 1989, p. 452.

Table 4. THE DISTRIBUTION OF POVERTY* IN THE GENERAL POPULATION,
BY RACE AND FAMILY STATUS, 1959-1987

Race/Family Status of Householder	1959	1966	1969	1975	1979	1985	1987
Number (millions)							
Below Poverty Level							
All persons	39.5	28.5	24.1	25.9	26.1	33.1	32.5
In families	34.6	23.8	19.2	20.8	20.0	25.7	25.0
Children < 18	17.2	12.1	9.5	10.9	10.0	12.5	12.4
Whites	28.5	19.3	16.7	17.8	17.2	22.9	21.4
In families	24.4	15.4	12.6	13.8	12.5	17.1	15.8
Children < 18	11.4	7.2	5.7	6.7	5.9	7.8	7.6
Blacks**	11.0	9.2	7.1	8.1	8.1	8.9	9.7
In families	10.1	8.4	6.2	7.0	6.8	7.5	8.0
Children < 18	5.8	4.9	3.7	4.1	3.7	4.1	4.3
Female householder, no husband present	10.4	10.3	10.4	12.3	13.5	16.4	16.9
In families	7.0	6.9	6.9	8.8	9.4	11.6	12.1
Children < 18	4.1	4.3	4.2	5.6	5.6	6.7	7.1
All other families	29.1	18.3	13.7	13.6	12.6	16.7	15.6
In families	27.5	16.9	12.3	11.9	10.6	14.1	12.9
Children < 18	13.1	7.9	5.3	5.3	4.4	5.8	5.4
Percent of Population							
Below Poverty Level							
All persons	22%	15%	12%	12%	12%	14%	13%
In families	21	13	10	11	10	13	12
Children < 18	27	17	14	17	16	20	20
Whites	18	11	9	10	9	11	10
In families	16	10	8	8	7	10	9
Children < 18	21	12	10	12	11	16	15
Blacks**	56	40	32	29	31	31	33
In families	56	39	31	28	30	30	32
Children < 18	67	48	40	39	41	43	45
Female householder, no husband present	50	41	38	35	32	33	34
In families	40	40	38	37	35	38	38
Children < 18	72	58	54	53	49	54	55
All other families	19	11	8	8	7	9	8
In families	18	10	7	7	6	8	7
Children < 18	22	13	9	10	8	12	11

* See note, Table 3.
** For 1959, 1966, and 1975, Blacks and other races.

SOURCE: Based on <u>Statistical Abstract 1989</u>, p. 453; <u>1984</u>, p. 473; <u>1979</u>, p. 463.

Table 5.   CHARACTERISTICS OF THE POOR: SELECTED ETHNIC, FAMILY
           STATUS, AND AGE ATTRIBUTES OF THE POPULATION BELOW
           POVERTY LEVEL, 1959-1987

		Population Below the Poverty Level					
		Percent of the Poor That Are					
		Ethnic Status			Age		In Female-head, No-husband-present
Year	Total (millions)	White	Black*	His-panic	<18	65+	Families
1959	39.5	72%	25%	--	44%	14%	26%
1966	28.5	68	32	--	42	--	36
1969	24.1	69	29	--	39	20**	43
1975	25.9	69	31	12%	42	13	47
1979	26.1	66	31	11	38	14	52
1981	31.8	68	29	12	38	11	49
1985	33.1	69	27	16	38	10	50
1987	32.5	66	30	17	38	11	52

* For 1959, 1966, and 1975, black and other races.
** For 1970, not 1969.

SOURCE: Based on Statistical Abstract 1989, pp. 452-455; 1984,
        pp. 473- 474; 1979, pp. 463-464

Topic 17: Attitudes and Values

17.1 SATISFACTION IN LIFE DOMAINS AND IN GENERAL

Satisfaction with various aspects of personal life shows marked stability, while satisfaction with the nation and its institutions shows considerable short-term fluctuation and long-term change. Family life generates very high satisfaction rates, followed by friendships, health, residential location, and present financial situation. Job satisfaction has been stable for over 40 years, with about 80% of workers expressing satisfaction with their work. Since 1974, rates of satisfaction with the nation have varied from 19% to 74%, with the low points in 1979-1980 and the peaks in the mid-1980s.

The general finding in studies of trends in public satisfaction over the past three decades is that the varieties of personal satisfaction are fairly stable, while satisfaction with the nation and its institutions, especially those associated with the vagaries of politics, shows more fluctuation. As two distinguished trend analysts put it, "The distinction between people's personal well-being and their assessment of the situation in the country as a whole comes across dramatically in many surveys" (Lipset and Schneider, 1983, p. 126).

Job Satisfaction

Lipset and Schneider's exhaustive assessment of trends associated with confidence in business and government included a review of trends in job satisfaction, 1950-1980. Their conclusion for that 30-year period:

whenever the question has been asked, an overwhelming majority of Americans--usually 80 to 90 percent--have said they are satisfied with the work they do there is no evidence of any decline in job satisfaction over the years (Lipset and Schneider, 1983, p. 114).

That conclusion is corroborated by the figures in Table 1, which extend the trend for another nine years, to 1989, and reveal no hint of change in the high levels of job satisfaction described by Lipset and Schneider. Note that the data in Table 1 derive from three different polling organizations--Gallup, the University of Michigan's Survey Research Center, and the University of Chicago's National Opinion Research Center. All yield the same general findings, that most Americans--usually between 80% and 90%--say they are satisfied with their work, and that this high level of job satisfaction has continued for a long time. Job satisfaction is lower among blacks than whites, and there is considerably more variability: the percentage satisfied over the period 1949-1988 ranges 51%-82%. The variability does not seem directional; there are "lows"--satisfaction rates of 55% or below--in 1949, 1963, 1973, and 1984. Despite such exceptions, job satisfaction among blacks is typically high, though not as high as among whites. In 10 of the 14 instances charted in Table 2, at least 67% of blacks questioned said they were satisfied with their work.

Sex and educational attainment of the worker do not seem to make much difference in rates of satisfaction, but age makes a big difference. In the 1970s rates of dissatisfaction among young adult workers (ages 18-24) were about twice as high as among older workers (Converse, et al., 1980, pp. 160-163).

The apparent stability in the aggregate level of reported job satisfaction masks other differentials, and the global satisfaction item does not get at changes in satisfaction with certain aspects of work. A 1955-1980 comparison designed to explore some of these issues (Glenn and Weaver, 1982) found substantially lower rates of enjoyment of work in 1980 than in 1955, and the declines appear consistently across age, occupation, and religion categories. The researchers lack the data to fully explain the decline, but judging from an unexpected absence of change in enjoyment of work among the single cohort of workers aged 25-39 in 1955 and aged 50 and over in 1980, it is suggested that the downward trend is largely a result of "cohort succession", i.e.,

> . . . the dying off and retirement of workers from the cohorts with high mean work orientation and their replacement with members of less work-oriented younger cohorts. . . . the decline grew out of changes in the orientations and attitudes workers brought to their jobs rather than out of changes in job conditions and in the nature of work (Glenn and Weaver, 1982, p. 468).

Marital and Family Satisfaction

Analysis of the relationship between marital status and happiness for the 13 General Social Surveys conducted over the period 1972-86 (Glenn and Weaver, 1988) suggests that the advantage in happiness formerly held by married people over single people is declining. The findings indicate that the oft-reported positive association between marital status and reported happiness has declined for the population generally, but especially for males and for younger adults. Year-by-year changes in the regression of reported happiness on marital status "reflect primarily changes in the reported happiness of never-married and married persons. All of the indicated trends are significantly downward." The researchers conclude that if marriage ever typically had strong positive effects on people's personal happiness, "those effects apparently have waned considerably in the last few years" (Glenn and Weaver, 1988, pp. 320, 322).

The correlation between measures of happiness and marital status is an indirect measure of family satisfaction, and it may be argued that direct questions about family satisfaction are more appropriate. For 1972-88, there is no clear direction in reports of personal happiness in the population as a whole, and the safest conclusion is that rates of personal happiness have not changed. There is a very slight drop in the percentage of married people saying they are "very happy" in their marriages--from a three-year average of 68% in 1973-75 to 64% in 1986-88--but it is too soon to say whether this tendency represents a real change or random variation (Table 3).

Personal Satisfaction, Global and Particular

Lipset and Schneider (1983, pp. 130-133) traced two decades of personal satisfaction ratings on the self-anchoring ladder scale, and concluded that Americans' ratings of their own lives remained fairly stable from the mid-1960s until the 1980s. Generally stable trajectories also characterize specific components of life satisfaction, as may be seen in the pattern of satisfaction with particular life domains shown in Table 4. Note that the table shows percentages reporting "high" satisfaction. The levels of satisfaction with family life--consistently between 70% and 80%--are higher than satisfaction rates for any of the other life domains, and there is no evidence of decline. Satisfaction with friendships is only a few points behind satisfaction with family, running at about 70% high satisfaction, compared to about 57% for leisure activities and about 60% for health and physical condition.

Rates of satisfaction with the life domains represented in Table 4 are surprisingly stable. Just under half of the population express high satisfaction with their place of residence; just over half are highly satisfied with their non-work activities; three-fourths are highly satisfied with their families, slightly fewer than that are highly satisfied with their friends, and about three out of five express high satisfaction with their health. Family financial situation generates the least favorable ratings; just under one-third say they are highly satisfied with that. These rates of expressed satisfaction seldom vary from year to year by more than three or four points, and often shift only a point or two.

Some other measures of personal satisfaction show more variation. For instance, responses to a Gallup poll item on "the way things are going in your personal life" asked in 1979 and thereafter reveal an slight upward trend in the 1980s, ranging from 79% satisfied in 1979 to 87% in 1988. Satisfaction with housing shows an upward trend, from 71% satisfied in 1963-65 to 87% in 1988, while satisfaction with household income remains stable over the same period ("Public More Upbeat," 1989, pp. 6-7; Gallup Political Index, 1966, p. 16).

Satisfaction with the Nation

Unlike the various forms of personal satisfaction, satisfaction with the nation fluctuates sharply from year to year and often from month to month. For instance, positive responses ("fairly well" or "very well") to the question, "How do you feel that things are going in the country these days?", rise from a low of 23% in 1975 to a peak of 65% in 1977, decline to a new low of 21% in 1980, then rise, albeit with sizable fluctuations in both directions along the way, to a high of 74% in 1984. Trends in agreement with the statement, "the problems we face are no worse than at any other time in recent years," show a similar pattern. The item, "In general, are you satisfied or dissatisfied with the way things are going in the U.S. at this time?" yields levels of satisfaction ranging from 19% in 1979 to 58% in 1986, and a pattern of rising satisfaction in the early 1980s, stabilizing in the late 1980s--temporarily, one would assume--at about 50% satisfied (Table 5).

Most Americans are dissatisfied with the levels of public morality they see about them, but the size of the dissatisfied majority varies considerably. In 1963, 34% said they were satisfied with "the honesty and standards of behavior of people in this country today," and 58% were dissatisfied. Events of the following decade further eroded that relatively low level of confidence. By 1973, only 22% were satisfied and 72% said they were dissatisfied. The Gallup organization asked the question again in 1986, and found satisfaction levels roughly equivalent to those of 1963: 33% satisfied, 63% dissatisfied (Gallup Report, 1986, p. 12).

References

Converse, Philip E., Jean D. Dotson, Wendy J. Hoag, and William H. McGee III. American Social Attitudes Data Sourcebook: 1947-1978. Cambridge, Mass.: Harvard University Press, 1980.

Davis, James Allan. General Social Surveys, 1972-1980: Cumulative Codebook. Chicago: National Opinion Research Center, 1982. Annual. Previous years as cited.

Davis, James Allan. and Tom W. Smith. General Social Surveys, 1972-1988: Cumulative Codebook. Chicago: National Opinion Research Center, 1988. Annual. Previous years as cited.

Gallup, George H. Gallup Poll: Public Opinion 1985. Wilmington, Delaware: Scholarly Resources, 1986.

------. Gallup Poll: Public Opinion 1972-1977. Wilmington, Delaware: Scholarly Resources, 1978.

Gallup Opinion Index 47 (May, 1969): 7-13.

Gallup Political Index 18 (November/December, 1966): 15-18.

Gallup Report 248 (May, 1986): 12-13.

Glenn, Norval D. and Charles N. Weaver. "Enjoyment of Work by Full-Time Workers in the U.S., 1955 and 1980," Public Opinion Quarterly 46 (1982): 459-470.

------. "The Changing Relationship of Marital Status to Reported Happiness." Journal of Marriage and the Family 50 (1988): 317-324.

Kohut, Andrew and Linda DeStefano. "Modern Employees Expect More from Their Careers; Job Dissatisfaction Particularly High Among the Young." Gallup Report 288 (September, 1989): 22-30.

Lipset, Seymour Martin and William Schneider. The Confidence Gap: Business, Labor, and Government in the Public Mind. New York: Free Press, 1983.

"Public More Upbeat About State of Nation." Gallup Report 280 (January, 1989): 4-8.

"State of the Nation." Public Opinion 8 (August/September, 1985): 21.

Table 1.   JOB SATISFACTION: PERCENT EXPRESSING SATISFACTION,
           AMBIVALENCE, AND DISSATISFACTION WITH THEIR EMPLOYMENT,
           VARIOUS SURVEYS, 1953-1989

| | How Satisfied Are You with the Job/the Work You Do?* | | | | | |
| | Gallup and SRC Surveys | | | General Social Survey | | |
Year	Satis-fied	Dissatis-fied	No Opinion**	Satis-fied	Dissatis-fied	No Opinion
1953	80%	7%	13%	--	--	--
1957	78	8	14	--	--	--
1963	84	11	5	--	--	--
1966	86	8	6	--	--	--
1969	87	7	6	--	--	--
1971	79	8	12	--	--	--
1972	--	--	--	85%	15%	--
1973a	77	11	12	87	12	--
1973b	81	7	12	--	--	--
1974	80	8	12	85	15	--
1975	78	13	9	87	13	--
1976	74	12	13	86	14	--
1977	--	--	--	87	13	--
1978	--	--	--	87	13	--
1980	--	--	--	82	17	--
1982	--	--	--	85	15	--
1983	--	--	--	87	13	--
1984	70	20	10	81	19	--
1985	--	--	--	86	14	--
1986	--	--	--	88	12	--
1987	--	--	--	82	18	--
1988	76	8	16	86	14	--
1989	89	11	--	--	--	--

* For the Michigan (SRC) surveys (1953, 1957, 1971, 1973b, 1974-
1976), the item read, "All things considered, how satisfied are you
with your job?" Persons selecting the mid-point on the five-point
response scale ("neutral or ambivalent") are included along with
"don't know" in the "no opinion" category above. For the Gallup
surveys, the item read, "On the whole, would you say you are
satisfied or dissatisfied with the work you do?" The 1988 wording
was, "Overall, how satisfied are you with your job? Are you
completely satisfied, mostly satisfied, mostly dissatisfied or
completely dissatisfied?" Persons who said they were completely or
mostly satisfied are included in the percentages in the "satisfied"
column above. The 1984 item was the Gallup "satisfaction index,"
which asks for a rating on a 10-point scale, with 6-10 representing
satisfied. In the General Social Surveys, the item read, "On the
whole, how satisfied are you with the work you do--would you say
you are very satisfied, moderately satisfied, a little
dissatisfied, or very dissatisfied?" Persons who said they were

Table 1.   JOB SATISFACTION: PERCENT EXPRESSING SATISFACTION,
            AMBIVALENCE, AND DISSATISFACTION WITH THEIR EMPLOYMENT,
            VARIOUS SURVEYS, 1953-1989 (continued)

---

very or moderately satisfied appear in the "satisfied" column
above.

SOURCE: Based on Kohut and DeStefano, 1989, p. 25; "Public More
    Upbeat," 1989, p. 8; Gallup Opinion Index No. 47, 1969, p. 7;
    Gallup Political Index No. 18, 1966, p. 15; Gallup, 1986, pp.
    39-40; 1978, p. 108; Converse, et al., 1980, pp. 160-163;
    Davis, 1982, p. 141; Davis and Smith, 1988, p. 217; 1987, p.
    213.

Table 2. JOB SATISFACTION: PERCENT EXPRESSING SATISFACTION,
AMBIVALENCE, AND DISSATISFACTION WITH THEIR EMPLOYMENT,
BY RACE, VARIOUS SURVEYS, 1949-1988

| | How Satisfied With Job/the Work You Do?* | | | | | |
| | Whites | | | Blacks | | |
Year	Satis-fied	Dissatis-fied	No Opinion	Satis-fied	Dissatis-fied	No Opinion
1949g	69	19	12	55	33	12
1953m	83	7	10	82	11	7
1957m	78	8	15	74	15	11
1963g	90	7	3	54	33	13
1966g	87	8	5	69	18	13
1969g	88	6	6	76	18	6
1971m	81	8	11	69	9	22
1973g	80	10	10	53	22	25
1973m	83	7	11	68	7	26
1974m	81	7	12	79	9	12
1975m	78	9	12	76	9	16
1976m	74	13	13	71	13	16
1984g**	72	18	10	51	39	10
1988g	76	7	17	71	11	18

* See Table 1 for the wording of the items.
** 10-point scale, with 6-10 = satisfied.

Note: The 1973 figures apply to "nonwhite" rather than "black" respondents. All the others specify blacks. The 1953, 1957, 1971, 1973b, 1974, 1975 and 1976 responses are from surveys conducted by the University of Michigan (Converse, et al); the response options included the midpoint on a five-point scale, which was labeled "neutral or ambivalent," and was included along with "don't know" in the "no opinion" category above. The Michigan surveys are identified in the table by an "m" following the year of the survey, and the Gallup surveys by a following "g".

SOURCE: Based on Gallup Opinion Index, 1969, p. 8; "Public More Upbeat," 1989, p. 8; Gallup, 1986, pp. 39-40; 1978, p. 108.

Table 3. PERSONAL HAPPINESS AND MARITAL SATISFACTION, 1972-1988

Year	Personal Happiness			Marital Happiness		
	Very Happy	Pretty Happy	Not Too Happy	Very Happy	Pretty Happy	Not Too Happy
1972	30%	53%	17%	--	--	--
1973	36	51	13	68%	30%	3%
1974	38	49	13	69	27	3
1975	33	54	13	67	30	3
1976	34	53	13	67	31	2
1977	35	53	12	65	31	4
1978	34	56	10	65	32	3
1980	34	53	13	68	29	3
1982	33	54	13	66	31	3
1983	31	56	13	62	34	3
1984	35	52	13	66	31	3
1985	29	60	11	57	40	3
1986	32	56	11	63	33	3
1987	32	56	12	65	32	2
1988	34	57	9	63	34	3

Note: Percentage bases (N's) do not include don't know and no
answer responses. The base for the marital happiness items includes
only married persons. Percentages may not sum to 100 due to
rounding. The items read: "Taken all together, how would you say
things are these days--would you say that you are very happy,
pretty happy, or not too happy?" and "Taking all things together,
how would you describe your marriage? Would you say that your
marriage is very happy, pretty happy, or not to happy?"

SOURCE: Based on Davis and Smith, 1988, p. 182; 1987, p. 178;
     Davis, 1980, p. 102.

Table 4. PERCENT EXPRESSING HIGH* SATISFACTION WITH PLACE OF
RESIDENCE, LEISURE ACTIVITIES, FAMILY LIFE,
FRIENDSHIPS, HEALTH, AND INCOME, 1973-1988

Life Domain	19 73	19 74	19 75	19 76	19 77	19 78	19 80	19 82	19 83	19 84	19 86	19 87	19 88
City/place you live in	47	47	51	49	47	47	55	41	47	52	43	50	49
Non-working activities-- hobbies and so on	55	55	57	57	55	58	62	52	53	61	53	60	58
Your family life	74	77	77	76	75	75	78	76	74	77	71	74	77
Your friendships	70	72	71	69	70	68	76	66	67	75	66	71	70
Your health and physical condition	60	61	61	60	61	59	64	63	57	63	55	60	59
Your present financial situation**	31	31	31	31	34	34	29	26	29	28	30	30	31

* "High" satisfaction as shown in these percentages includes the
top two--"a very great deal" and "a great deal"--of the seven
possible responses ranging from "a very great deal" to "none." The
item read: "For each area of life I am going to name, tell me the
number that shows how much satisfaction you get from that area."
The numbers corresponded to the seven categories, including "quite
a bit," "a fair amount", "some," and "a little" in addition to the
three mentioned above.
** This item read: "So far as you and your family are concerned,
would you say that you are pretty well satisfied with your present
financial situation, more or less satisfied, or not satisfied at
all?" Percentages above refer to the first of the three possible
responses, "pretty well satisfied."

Note: Numbers of cases, by year, were: 73, 1504; 74, 1484; 75,
1490; 76, 1499; 77, 1530; 78, 1532; 80, 1468; 82, 1506; 83, 1599;
84, 1473; 85, 1534; 86, 1470; 87, 1466; and 88, 997. Percentages
above are based on these N's, minus a very few (generally somewhere
between 5 and 20 cases in all) instances of don't know and no
answer responses for each item.

SOURCE: Based on Davis, 1982, pp. 110-111, 149; Davis and Smith,
1987, pp. 180-181, 221; 1988, pp. 184-185.

Table 5.   OUTLOOK TOWARD THE NATION: PERCENT EXPRESSING
           SATISFACTION/APPROVAL, SELECTED INDICATORS, 1974-1988

| Year* | In the Country as a Whole | | Satisfied with "the way things are going in the U.S. at this time" |
	Things are going very/ fairly well (Agreed)**	"Problems are no worse than at other times" (Agreed)**	
1974	29%	32%	--
1975	23	29	--
1976	46	41	--
1977	65	56	--
1978	53	56	--
1979	36	33	19%
1980	21	16	--
1981	27	31	27
1982	38	39	24
1983	45	39	35
1984	74	65	52
1985	68	55	51
1986	--	--	58
1987	--	--	45
1988	--	--	56

* Most years, these items appeared in several polls, and there is
substantial variation within years. The percentages in this table
were chosen to represent the range of variation--the highs and the
lows that appear in the trend lines--rather than representing the
average for a given year or a consistent month or quarter.
** Respondents for 1977-1985 are registered voters rather than all
adults.

SOURCE: Based on "State of the Nation," 1985, p. 21; "Public More
        Upbeat," 1989, p. 5.

Public perceptions of national problems reveal something about the populace as well as the historical experience of the nation. Foreign affairs dominated public concern from shortly after World War II until the early 1960s, when attention was briefly shifted to the domestic concern of civil rights. From 1965 to the early 1970s, international tensions and conflicts were again defined by most people as the country's most serious problems. Since then, domestic issues have taken the forefront, with economic matters almost completely dominating public definitions of the nation's most pressing problems.

Social problems are conditions identified by the people of a nation, or by significant interest groups, as conditions which threaten their well-being or their values, and which, in principle at least, can be altered by remedial action of some kind (Kornblum and Julian, 1989, pp. 2-3). Many societal conditions that have negative effects are not social problems, strictly speaking, because the public does not define them as problems or marshall resources to attempt to alter them. Social problems, by definition, involve relatively large numbers of people who are aware of the condition, who believe it can be changed or its adverse effects ameliorated, and who define collective action to those ends as appropriate (Ritzer, 1986, pp. 5-8).

Inasmuch as public awareness of and agitation toward changing adverse conditions are essential to their designation as social problems, it follows that public opinion polls are ideal for identifying social problems and tracing changes in their salience and priority. Items on social problems were included in some of the earliest national surveys, and have been regularly repeated. George Gallup began asking about "the most important problem facing this country today" in 1935, and by 1984 that item had been included in at least 178 Gallup surveys. Tom Smith, a contemporary analyst of national trends, argues that among the many trends Gallup collected, the "most important problem" series is unique because of the span of data available, the fact that the question was asked so often (only the item on presidential popularity appears more frequently in Gallup polls over the years), and because of the inherent significance of the item.

Perhaps no other single item gives us as deep an understanding of American history over the last five decades. The most important problem question provides a grand overview of social change, describes history from the perspective of the participants, and helps to define distinct historical periods and turning points. . . . The frame of reference is the country as a whole and elicits mentions of national and international problems rather than of local or personal problems (Smith, 1985, p. 264).

Shifts in public concerns over the past four decades--representing only 15 points in a series that by 1989 included some 200 separate surveys--are summarized in Table 1. Because the item is not forced-choice but rather allows respondents to specify a problem and, if they choose, to name more than one, the nature of responses as well as their distribution changes over time, making it difficult to construct reliable standardized categories for a lengthy period. We have tried to reflect the historical changes in the nature of problems perceived by listing many of the individual categories from the periodic Gallup reports, even if these categories of response appear only briefly as matters of public concern and then disappear. Accordingly, Table 1 includes 18 response categories, including such entries as "strikes, labor unrest," which only shows up in the 1948-1954 period, and "farmer's plight," which first appears in 1986.

Table 1 is based on the Gallup organization's published reports of poll results. For an entry to appear there, it had to receive enough mentions to be listed separately as a category in the report published shortly after the poll was completed. A more satisfactory approach to tracing trends in most important problem over the years is secondary analysis of the Gallup data files. Table 2 illustrates the findings produced in Tom Smith's (1980, 1985) effort to represent the entire series in a uniform, manageable category system. In both tables, the percentages are based on total number of problems mentioned rather than number of respondents.

Smith's analysis uses an eleven-category coding scheme. He has two substantive categories--foreign affairs and domestic--along with "not classified" and "don't know." Foreign affairs is subdivided into Vietnam and other. Domestic affairs is divided into six categories: economics, social control, civil rights, government, energy, miscellaneous, and unspecified. All responses are classified in one of the eleven categories. In Table 2 we illustrate the application of Smith's system to the period 1948-1984. The summary of key trends below draws upon Smith's (1980, 1985) essays as well as the illustrative material shown in Tables 1 and 2.

By the late 1940s, when that segment of the series charted in Table 1 begins, concerns about the Cold War, the spread of communism, and the potential for international conflict combined to make international tensions the single most important problem facing the nation. There was consensus about the priority of international affairs that the nation would not see again. If concern about communism, especially communist subversion, is included, we find almost three-fourths of Americans identifying international tensions/communism as the nation's chief problem. Over the next six years attention to confronting communism within the U.S. pushed that topic to third priority, after international tensions and cost of living. Thereafter, except for a brief resurgence during the Vietnam war, it disappears from the charts as a significant "most important problem."

The relative importance of problems in the domestic economy increases until, in 1958, they replace international concerns as most important. Their priority is short-lived. By the early 1960s the U.S. involvement in Vietnam is underway, and Vietnam itself becomes a significant national problem. There are times in the mid-1960s when Vietnam is the single most frequently-mentioned problem, and even when it is not, it and other foreign policy matters are consistently identified as the nation's most important concern. Vietnam remains a major, often dominant problem until 1973, when it's position drops from 30% to 3%. By the end of 1974 it disappears as a separate category, never to reappear.

During the period that Vietnam was often cited as the nation's most important problem, the civil rights movement pushed domestic concerns ahead of foreign tensions for a time. Smith (1985, p. 265) summarizes the position of civil rights/race issues this way:

In 1963 the hegemony of foreign affairs was interrupted by the emergence of the civil rights movement. Civil rights ranked as the most important problem for most of the next two years until foreign affairs, boosted by the Vietnam War, regained the top position in 1965. From 1965 to 1970 Vietnam and other international issues dominated public concern. The only exception occurred in August 1967, when race riots pushed social control to the forefront.

After Vietnam, the dominance of foreign affairs as the nation's top problem is over. Instead, domestic concerns, especially the economy, take top priority. There is a resurgence of concern with international problems in the mid-1980s (Table 1), but even then--with one-fourth of all mentions pertaining to foreign affairs--public concern with domestic matters predominates.

Problems of national economy occupy center stage between the mid-1970s and the late 1980s. Inflation, the high cost of living, and related issues are the key concerns, but unemployment is typically the second most cited problem, accounting for between one-sixth and one-third of all problems mentioned for much of the 1976-1986 era. Government overspending, in various terminology, shows up now and then, but not until the 1980s does it become a top-ranked problem.

Since about 1970, crime and delinquency have occupied a consistent position, accounting for 2-7% of all problems mentioned. Another "most important" problem, cited since the mid-1960s at about the same frequency as crime and delinquency, is national moral/religious decline. Smith lists both topics, along with riots, violence, and drugs, as "social control" issues, and demonstrates that public worry over social control issues rose dramatically in the mid-1960s, peaked in 1967, continued at a high level until the mid-1970s, and then declined to a low level. From then until the late 1980s, when doing something about drugs became a high priority, the most social control-related concern was fear of crime (Smith, 1980, p. 171; 1985, p. 267). By the late 1980s, drug abuse had become a major concern, and in May, 1989, it was identified as the nation's top problem (Table 1).

Dissatisfaction with the federal government, sometimes expressed as lack of trust or confidence, was a central problem in the 1970s. In 1974, it accounted for as many as one-eighth of all problems mentioned. It reappears in the 1980s, but at a much lower level. A related issue, government corruption, receives an occasional mention but does not show up as a consistent major concern except in the Watergate era, 1974-76. The "government" category in Table 2 includes corruption and lack of trust as well as inefficiency, red tape, and the perception that "big government" is a critical problem. Smith (1985, p. 267) concludes that government has never ranked as a top problem, was rarely mentioned prior to Watergate, and that following Nixon's departure it "declined once again into the background as a minor issue."

Other problems identified as most important by enough people to receive occasional explicit listings in Gallup reports include energy, which briefly topped the list in 1974; poverty and hunger, cited by many respondents in 1966-70 and again 1986-89; housing, an issue in the late 1940s that reappears as homelessness in the late 1980s; and the economic plight of the American farmer, briefly surfacing in 1986.

References

Gallup, George H. Gallup Poll: Public Opinion 1935-1971. 3 vols. New York: Random House, 1972.

Gallup Opinion Index 177 (1980): 25; 157 (1978): 8; 131 (1976): 18-25; 104 (1974): 1-3; 56 (1970): 4-5.

Gallup Report 252 (1986): 27-31; 226 (1984): 16-21.

Kohut, Andrew and Larry Hugick. "Colombians Question Worth of Drug War; Americans Skeptical It Can Be Won." Gallup Report 288 (1989): 2-11.

Kornblum, William and Joseph Jullian. Social Problems. 6th ed. Englewood Cliffs, NJ: Prentice-Hall, 1989.

Ritzer, George. Social Problems. 2nd ed. New York: Random House, 1986.

Smith, Tom W. "America's Most Important Problem--A Trend Analysis, 1946-1976." Public Opinion Quarterly 44 (1980): 164-180.

------. "The Polls: America's Most Important Problems Part I: National and International." Public Opinion Quarterly 49 (1985): 264-274.

Table 1. PUBLIC PERCEPTIONS OF THE MOST IMPORTANT PROBLEM FACING THE UNITED STATES,* 1948-1989

Problem	Percent of Total Problems Mentioned**							
	Mar. 1948	Mar. 1950	Mar. 1954	Mar. 1958	Apr. 1962	May 1966	Jan. 1970	Jan. 1974
International tensions, foreign policy, preventing war, helping other nations, defense, foreign policy	66%	46%	34%	27%	58%	9%	6%	5%
Vietnam crisis/war	--	--	--	--	--	42	31	--
High prices, cost of living, inflation, depression, recession	8	15	17	40	9	15	16	21
Unemployment	--	10	14	--	7	2	--	4
Communism	7	8	15	--	--	5	--	--
Civil rights, race relations & conflict	--	--	--	4	6	8	12	--
Dissatisfaction with govt., lack of trust, domestic politics	9	--	2	--	--	--	--	12
Strikes, labor unrest	2	4	2	--	--	--	--	--
Religious, moral decline	--	--	--	--	--	5	4	3
Government corruption	--	3	--	--	--	--	--	6
Cost of govt., spending, budget deficit	--	--	3	--	--	--	--	--
Poverty, hunger, housing	2	3	--	--	--	2	5	--
Crime, delinquency	--	--	2	--	3	--	7	2
Drugs	--	--	--	--	--	--	5	--
Ecology, pollution	--	--	--	--	--	--	4	--
Energy	--	--	--	--	--	--	--	38
Miscellaneous	2	11	8	20	9	10	10	6
Don't know, no opinion	4	--	4	9	8	2	2	2
Total	100	100	101	100	100	100	102	99
International tensions, foreign policy, preventing war, helping other nations, defense, foreign policy		4%	7%	15%	9%	20%	25%	5%
High prices, cost of living, inflation, depression, recession		29	46	66	28	13	10	19
Unemployment		18	15	4	34	25	15	5
Civil rights, race relations & conflict		2	--	--	--	--	--	--

Table 1.   PUBLIC PERCEPTIONS OF THE MOST IMPORTANT PROBLEM FACING
THE UNITED STATES,* 1948-1989 (continued)

Problem	Percent of Total Problems Mentioned**						
	Apr. 1976	Apr. 1978	Mar. 1980	Apr. 1982	Feb. 1984	Jan. 1986	May 1989
Dissatisfaction with govt., lack of trust	10	3	4	--	2	--	2
Religious & moral decline	3	3	2	2	6	3	4
Government corruption	3	--	--	--	--	--	--
Cost of government, spending, budget deficit	--	--	--	3	11	9	6
Government budget cuts	--	--	--	6	6	--	--
Poverty, hunger, housing	--	--	--	--	--	6	9
Crime, delinquency	6	3	2	2	4	2	5
Drugs	2	--	--	--	--	2	24
Ecology, pollution	--	--	--	--	--	--	4
Energy	--	7	7	--	--	--	--
Farmers' plight	--	--	--	--	--	3	--
Quality of education	--	--	--	--	--	--	3
Miscellaneous	20	15	--	13	10	20	8
Don't know, no opinion	2	3	1	2	4	3	6
Total	99	102	101	99	101	98	100

* The standard wording for the item was "What do you think is the
most important problem facing this country today?"
** Multiple responses permitted; these percentages are based on the
total number of problems mentioned, not respondents.

SOURCE: Based on Gallup, 1972, pp. 726-727, 907, 1125-1126, 1545-
1546, 1764, 2009; Gallup Opinion Index, 1970, p. 5; 1974. 2;
1976, p. 25; 1978, p. 8; 1980, p. 25; Gallup Report, 1984, p.
17; 1986, 28-29; Kohut and Hugick, 1989, pp. 4-5.

Table 2. PUBLIC PERCEPTIONS OF THE MOST IMPORTANT PROBLEM FACING
THE UNITED STATES,* SUMMARY CATEGORIES, 1948-1984

	Percent of Total Problems Mentioned**							
Problem	Mar. 1948	Mar. 1950	Mar. 1954	Mar. 1958	Apr. 1962	Mar. 1964	May 1966	Jan. 1968
Foreign affairs	68%	45%	35%	25%	45%	28%	57%	52%
Vietnam	--	--	--	--	0	2	42	47
Domestic	23	53	60	63	34	54	39	47
Economic	10	29	36	47	18	13	16	12
Social control	--	11	18	4	5	1	8	16
Civil rights	--	1	0	4	6	30	8	11
Government	--	3	2	0	1	--	3	2
Misc., named	2	6	1	2	2	6	4	5
Unspecified	12	3	3	5	2	4	1	1
Not classified	6	--	--	3	13	10	--	--
Don't know	3	3	5	9	8	8	4	1
Total	100	101	100	100	100	100	100	100

Problem	Jan. 1970	Feb. 1972	Jan. 1974	Apr. 1976	Apr. 1978	Mar. 1980	Jan. 1982	Feb. 1984
Foreign affairs	33%	25%	4%	4%	7%	14%	10%	24%
Vietnam	28	20	0	--	--	--	--	--
Domestic	66	74	90	94	90	85	88	73
Economic	16	27	24	51	62	67	70	50
Social control	22	25	7	16	9	4	7	10
Civil rights	11	4	1	3	1	0	--	--
Government	1	3	18	14	3	4	2	2
Energy	--	--	34	2	7	7	1	1
Misc., named	15	12	3	6	6	2	6	7
Unspecified	1	2	3	2	2	0	2	4
Don't know	1	2	6	2	2	1	2	3
Total	100	101	100	100	99	100	100	100

* The standard wording for the item was "What do you think is the
most important problem facing this country today?"
** Multiple responses permitted; these percentages are based on the
total number of problems mentioned, not respondents.

SOURCE: Based on Smith, 1985, pp. 267-274.

The usual American orientation to the future is one of optimism, both about the nation as a whole and self and family. Levels of satisfaction with the present vary considerably, but a majority consistently affirms that the future will be better than the present. This optimism is maintained despite general belief that international discord and war will continue. Other stable aspects of personal outlook include a commitment to work and an affirmation of life as exciting or at least not dull. In the late 1980s, the outlook for the next generation seemed less favorable than that for the near future.

For almost three decades, persons who expect the next year to be better than the present one have outnumbered those who think it will be worse, the only exceptions occurring in the late 1970s (see Table 1; cf. Chapter 11.3). Typically, a majority defines the future as better than the present, while one-fifth to one-third of respondents take the opposing view.

Specific elements of the general orientation to the future are illustrated in Table 2. There is a solid commitment to work, such that about 70% of the people say that even if they were financially secure, they would continue to work. About half say they find life "pretty routine," and almost all of the remainder--between 43% and 48%--say life is exciting. Those persons with a "life is exciting" outlook outnumber persons who find it dull by about eight to one. Both the commitment to work and the affirmation of life as exciting are stable characteristics. Neither shows much evidence of trend since 1973.

There is more variation in responses to two items from Leo Srole's Anomia Index. Both reveal sagging national self-confidence at the close of the 1970s (Table 2). Over the entire period, a majority agree that "the lot of the average man is getting worse, not better," but the peak pessimism about the situation of the average man--not the respondent--is in 1980-1982, when almost 70% agree. National confidence is regained by the mid-1980s, when only half agree, but then the trend toward greater pessimism reasserts itself. The dip in optimism at the end of the 1970s also shows up in reactions to the statement, "it's hardly fair to bring a child into the world with the way things look for the future," but on this item there is no evidence of declining confidence at the end of the 1980s. Excepting the atypical "high anomia" point of 1980, about 60% of Americans consistently disagree with this statement.

Although they tend to view both personal and national welfare optimistically, Americans assess their own situation better than that of the country (see Table 3). Comparing the present and the future five years hence on a 10-point "ladder-scale" rating system, persons interviewed between 1959 and 1985 consistently scored their own present personal situation in the 6-7 range, while the nation rated scores in the 4-6 range. Looking forward, they anticipated roughly the same degree of improvement in their own situations as in the nation generally--an average of about one point on the ladder scale--such that average personal scores for five years later run above 7 on the 10-point scale, while those for the entire country are in the 5-7 range. Considering personal situation, the public is chronically optimistic: over the entire period, there is never a time when the average ladder-ranking score for the future is lower than the average score for the present.

The chronic optimism also shows up in assessments of the nation's future. Judging from variations in average ladder-scale ratings, it appears that Americans' optimism about their nation was highest in the late 1950s and early 1960s, declined in the national crisis of confidence of the 1970s, then made a partial recovery in the 1980s. Only once, in 1979, did the average rating for the future situation of the nation drop below the rating of the present (Table 3).

Responses to other kinds of questions about the future of the U.S. corroborate the ladder-scale ratings. Numerous public opinion polls conducted between 1962 and 1988 yield a two-thirds majority in the "high confidence" or "high optimism" categories (Table 4).

Another aspect of the public view of the future is the expectation of international conflict, and here an ambivalence surfaces. People's general optimism about the future is counterbalanced by the expectation of international discord and war. Asked to predict whether the coming year will have international peace or discord, a majority--two-thirds in the mid-1970s and 80% in 1980--predict discord. Only at the beginning and the end of the series represented in Table 5--in 1960 and in 1987--is there relatively low expectation of discord.

The ambivalence, or even incongruity, of the public view of the future is highlighted by contrasting their overall optimism with the expectation of the majority that another war looms in the near future (Table 6). Across the entire period--from 1950 through 1988--an astonishingly high percent expect war soon. In the 1950s, about half said they expected another U.S. war within five years; in the 1970s and 1980s, about two-thirds expected war in the next decade. Even more chilling is the high expectation that World War III is just around the corner. In the 1950s, there was considerable variation: from 19% to 53% said they expected a world war in the next five years. In the 1980s, there was more consistency, but at a higher level: 40% to 47% expected another world war in the coming decade.

Another aspect of the public's view of the future is that the overriding, persistent optimism about personal futures occurs in a context of unfulfilled aspirations. Surveys in the late 1980s of desired changes in personal lifestyle and of people's "major hopes"--topics for which we do not have long-term trend data--reveal an attitudinal atmosphere of pragmatic resignation and at least nominal dissatisfaction:

> If they could do it, 91 percent of the American people would opt for a radical
> change in their lifestyle. Most would like to break loose from the confines of their
> current pressures and obligations. . . . Of course, while these lifestyle alternatives
> might be the subject of many millions of daydreams, most of them will remain
> in the realm of fantasies, just beyond realization (Harris, 1987, pp. 1-2).

The most frequent "possible changes in lifestyle" mentioned were "a move to the wide open spaces in the country" (25%), a shift in personal orientation toward being "less concerned with material possessions and more concerned with caring for people" (18%), a desire to "quit work and see the world" (16%), and a wish to "find a way to get away from the steady diet of stress and tension" (16%).

In addition to their personal aspirations, Americans have "major hopes" that pertain to the larger issues of peace and human equity. In these matters, they aspire for improvement, but do not really expect it. In December, 1987, the Harris Survey offered a list of possible "hopes for the future," asking whether people would like to see each hope realized in their lifetimes, and then whether they realistically thought it might be. Almost everyone desired an end to poverty and ethnic discrimination in America, and an end to war, terrorism, violence, and starvation. But the percent who thought that any of these hopes might be realized in their lifetime ranged from only 13% (elimination of starvation in the world) to 34% (an end to war between nuclear powers). It may be that to find 13-34% of a national population who say they think such "major hopes" can be achieved in their lifetimes represents high optimism. Lacking trend data in these matters, Harris (1988, pp. 1-2) reached a different conclusion:

> Big majorities of the American people deeply desire a whole host of developments, ranging from elimination of starvation in the world to an end to war. . . . However, only relatively small minorities expect to see the fulfillment of those hopes. . . . Taken together, these unfulfilled aspirations for America and the world can be taken as a mark of the frustration of living in the current era. . . . These results add up to a kind of sadness and pessimism about the seeming inability of humankind to solve the major problems confronting the human race. . . . Yet, it must be emphasized that rather than giving up on reaching society's goals, most people settle each year for some movement toward the goals.

There is short-term trend data suggesting that the pervasive personal optimism of the 1980s does not extend beyond the near future. Over the period 1984-1988, several national samples responded to this question: "If things continue the way they are going now, do you think the future of the next generation of Americans will be a good one, or will it be bogged down by too many problems left behind for them?" The number choosing "bogged down" was always larger than the number choosing "a good one," and usually amounted to a majority. Commenting on these and other findings from the 1980s, Samuel Popkin concluded that while a superficial optimism still existed, it was now alloyed with fears and apprehensions about America's place in the future.

> You can still go from poor to rich, most Americans say, but they no longer believe that everyone is going to be better off in the future than he is today. . . if the American Dream is the belief that everyone will live better than his parents did, that the United States possesses endless frontiers with gains for all who work hard, then the dream is fading. . . . [Americans] have also lost confidence that they are the best in the world, that they are world leaders in science and technology or manufacturing. Americans' attitudes about their work ethic and their moral standards also reflect this lack of self-confidence.

> Part of the uneasiness seems to come from a growing sense of inferiority to Japan (Popkin, 1988, p. 51).

References

"American Journey: Malaise and Back." Public Opinion 7 (February/March 1984): 24-25.

"Americans Assess Opportunity." Public Opinion 5 (June/July 1982): 22-27.

Davis, James Allan. General Social Surveys, 1972-1980; Cumulative Codebook. Chicago: National Opinion Research Center, 1980.

Davis, James Allen and Tom W. Smith. General Social Surveys, 1972-1988; Cumulative Codebook. Chicago: National Opinion Research Center, 1988. Annual. Previous years as cited.

"Dawn of the Ecchh Decade." Public Opinion 3 (February/March, 1960): 32.

Gallup, George, Jr. Gallup Poll: Public Opinion 1987. Wilmington, DE: Scholarly Resources, 1988.

Gallup, George H. Gallup Poll: Public Opinion 1935-1971. 3 vols. New York: Random House, 1972.

------. Gallup Poll: Public Opinion 1972-1977. 2 vols. Wilmington, DE: Scholarly Resources, 1978.

Harris, Louis. "Major Hopes of People Not Expected to Be Fulfilled." The Harris Poll (January 4, 1988): 1-2.

------. "Over Nine in Ten Would Opt for Radical Lifestyle Change." The Harris Poll (June 29, 1987): 1-3.

Lipset, Seymour Martin and William Schneider. The Confidence Gap: Business, Labor, and Government in the Public Mind. New York: Free Press, 1983.

"Opinion Roundup." Public Opinion 8 (August/September 1985): 25.

"Outlook." Public Opinion 11 (November/December 1988): 22-26.

Popkin, Samuel. "Optimism, Pessimism, and Policy." Public Opinion 11 (November/December 1988): 51-55.

"Questions of Confidence." Public Opinion 11 (September/October 1988): 30.

Table 1.   GENERAL OUTLOOK TO THE COMING YEAR: WILL IT BE
           BETTER OR WORSE THAN THE PRESENT YEAR?, 1959-1986

Present Year	Will Coming Yr. Be Better Or Worse Than Present Yr.			
	Better	Worse	Same	Don't Know
1959	56	7	28	9
1971	57	22	*	21
1977	45	30	18	7
1978	33	55	*	12
1979	31	56	*	13
1980	49	26	19	6
1981	41	44	11	4
1982	50	32	10	8
1983	70	15	7	8
1984	61	20	12	6
1985	65	20	9	6
1986	53	25	11	11

Note: The question was, "So far as you are concerned, do you think
19__ (coming year) will be better or worse than 19__ (present
year)?"

SOURCE: Based on Gallup, 1988, p. 1.; Gallup, 1972, p. 1649.

Table 2. FUTURE ORIENTATION, AS REVEALED IN RESPONSES TO
SELECTED ATTITUDE STATEMENTS, GENERAL SOCIAL
SURVEYS, 1973-1988

Item	Year									
	19 73	19 74	19 76	19 77	19 80	19 82	19 84	19 85	19 87	19 88
If you were to get enough money to live as comfortably as you would like for the rest of your life, would you continue to work or would you stop working? [continue working]	69%	65%	69%	70%	77%	73%	76%	70%	75%	71%
In spite of what some people say, the lot (situation/condition) of the average man is getting worse, not better. [agree]	56	61	61	56	69	68	57	50	64	62
It's hardly fair to bring a child into the world with the way things look for the future. [agree]	37	37	43	39	48	35	41	33	40	39
In general, do you find life exciting, pretty routine, or dull? [exciting]	45	43	45	44	46	45	47	48	46	45
[dull]	5	5	4	7	6	6	5	6	4	5

Note: In computing these percentages, don't know and no answer responses were deleted from the percentage bases.

SOURCE: Based on Davis and Smith, 1988, pp. 182, 215, 217; 1987, pp. 178, 211, 213; 1985, pp. 163, 198, 200, Davis, 1980, pp. 103, 133, 135.

Table 3.   FUTURE ORIENTATION, AS SHOWN IN MEAN LADDER-SCALE
RATINGS OF "YOUR LIFE" AND "THE SITUATION OF THE
COUNTRY," AT THE PRESENT TIME AND FIVE YEARS FROM
NOW, AND MEAN IMPROVEMENT EXPECTED, 1959-1985

	Your Life			The Country		
Year*	Now	Five Yrs. From Now	Expected Improve- ment	Now	Five Yrs. From Now	Expected Improve- ment
1959	6.6	7.8	1.2	6.7	7.4	.7
1964	6.9	7.9	1.0	6.5	7.7	1.2
1971	6.6	7.5	.9	5.4	6.2	.8
1972	6.4	7.6	1.2	5.5	6.2	.7
1974	6.1	7.0	.9	4.5	5.7	1.2
1975	6.3	7.0	.7	4.3	5.4	1.1
1976	6.4	7.4	1.0	4.8	5.8	1.0
1977	6.1	7.2	1.1	5.0	6.3	1.3
1978	6.2	6.9	.7	4.9	5.4	.5
1979	6.4	6.7	.3	4.7	4.6	-.1
1980	6.6	7.3	.7	4.3	5.0	.7
1981	6.3	7.1	.8	4.6	5.7	1.1
1983	--	--	--	5.5	6.0	.5
1985	6.4	7.6	1.2	--	--	--

* For 1975-1981, ratings in the sources are available by quarter;
entries above are scores for the first quarter.

Note: The items read: "Here is a ladder representing the 'ladder of
life.' Let's suppose the top of the ladder represents the best
possible life for you; and the bottom, the worst possible life for
you. On which step of the ladder do you feel you personally stand
at the present time? . . . on which step do you think you will
stand in the future, say about five years from now?" and "Looking
at the ladder again, suppose the top represents the best possible
situation for our country; the bottom the worst possible situation.
Please show me on which step of the ladder you think the United
States is at the present time . . . five years from now."

SOURCE: Based on Lipset and Schneider, 1983, pp. 142-143; "The
American Journey," 1984, p. 24; "Opinion Roundup," 1985, p.
25.

Table 4. OPTIMISM ABOUT THE FUTURE OF THE UNITED STATES:
          ITEMS FROM OPINION POLLS, 1962-1988

Year	Confidence in U.S. Future				Life in the Future Will Be			
	Quite a Lot	Some	Little /None	No Opin.	Better	Same	Worse	No Opin.
1962	--	--	--	--	55%	12%	23%	10%
1972	--	--	--	--	64	15	15	6
1974	68%	19%	12%	1%	--	--	--	--
1975	68	30	--	2	--	--	--	--
1982*	--	--	--	--	64	--	36	--
1986	76	19	4	1	--	--	--	--
1988**	64	17	17	1	--	--	--	--

* The percentage in the "better" column applies to those who disagreed that "America's best days are behind it."

** Response categories differed somewhat; these percentages correspond, respectively, to optimistic, uncertain, pessimistic, and don't know.

Note: The above entries derive from the following questions: 1962: "As you look to the future, do you think life for people generally will get better--or will it get worse?"; 1972: "Will life generally be better for the mass of people in your nation in the year 2000 than it is at present--will it be better or worse?"; 1974-1975, 1986: "How much confidence do you have in the future of the United States--quite a lot, some, very little or none at all?"; 1982: "[do you] agree or disagree . . . America's best days are behind it?"; 1988: "We'd like to know about the things on this list whether you feel generally optimistic about them as far as the future is concerned, or generally pessimistic about them, or uncertain . . . Quality of life in this country?"

SOURCE: Based on "Outlook," 1988, p. 22; "Americans Assess Opportunity," 1982, p. 24; "Questions of Confidence," 1988, 0; Gallup, 1972, pp. 1781-1782; 1978, pp. 75-76, 268, 527-528.

Table 5.   EXPECTATIONS* REGARDING INTERNATIONAL PEACE/DISCORD
           IN THE COMING YEAR, 1960-1987

Named Year	(Coming Year) Will Be A Year Of		
	Trouble	Peace	Same/Don't Know
1960	27%	48%	25%
1974	65	24	11
1975	61	29	10
1978	45	35	20
1979	53	38	9
1980	80	14	6
1987	35	9	56**

* For 1960-1980, the item read, "Which of these do you think is
likely to be true of (named year), a peaceful year, more or less
free of international disputes, or a troubled year with much
international discord?" The question for 1987 read, "Do you think
that 1987 will be a peaceful year more or less free of international dispute, a troubled year with much international discord,
or remain the same?"
** Includes 48% who said "remain the same."

Source: Based on Gallup, 1988, p. 2.; 1972, p. 1650; "Dawn of the
        Ecchh Decade," 1980, p. 32;

Table 6. EXPECTATIONS ABOUT U.S. INVOLVEMENT IN FUTURE WARS,
NEXT FIVE/TEN YEARS, 1950-1988

Year	Within Five Yrs., Will U.S. Be Involved In Another			World War?		
	Yes	No	No Opinion	Yes	No	No Opinion
1950 (Feb)	41%	42%	17%	--	--	--
1950 (Oct)	60	10	30	--	--	--
1952	--	--	--	53%	17%	30%
1953	42	19	38	--	--	--
1955	--	--	--	48	30	22
1956*	--	--	--	19	49	32
1957	--	--	--	32	49	19
1958	--	--	--	24	76	--
1960	--	--	--	34	66	--
1961	--	--	--	53	47	--
Within Ten Yrs. . . .						
1973	57	38	6	--	--	--
1975	70	26	4	--	--	--
1976	57	35	7	44	50	6
1978	54	40	6	--	--	--
1981**	--	--	--	47	49	4
1982**	69	27	4	47	45	8
1983**	64	32	4	40	53	7
1985	56	41	2	43	51	6
1986	--	--	--	46	51	3
1988	--	--	--	40	56	4

* The question referred to "the next four years," and "another
major war," rather than "a war," or "a world war."
** Entries in the "world war" column are responses to Gallup
questions about "nuclear war."

Note: Several variations in item wording are represented in the
above series. The General Social Survey items (1973-1988, except
for the "nuclear war" items of 1981 and 1983) were: "Do you expect
the United States to fight in another war within the next ten
years?" and "Do you expect the United States to fight in another
world war within the next ten years?" There are minor variations
in the wording of the Gallup items (1950-1961 and 1981-1983). For
example, the 1950-1953 questions follow a similar question about
the next one year, thereby making it possible to divide persons
expecting war into those who expect it next year and those who
expect it in the next five, but not the coming year) and the 1956
item refers ahead four, rather than five years. The more-or-less
basic versions of the items read: "Do you think we are likely to

Table 6. EXPECTATIONS ABOUT U.S. INVOLVEMENT IN FUTURE WARS,
          NEXT FIVE/TEN YEARS, 1950-1988 (Continued)

get into another world war in the next five years?" and "Do you
think the United States will find itself in another war within,
say, the next five years?"

SOURCE: Based on Gallup, 1972, pp. 899, 947-948, 1113, 1142,
          1304, 1444, 1488, 1554, 1673, 1738; Gallup, 1984, p. 266;
          Davis, 1982, p. 89; Davis and Smith, 1988, p. 129; 1987, p.
          125; 1985, p. 117.

Early nineteen century observers of American values noted an emphasis on family life, strong Christian religious beliefs and a commitment to participate in local politics. More recently, Robin Williams identified 15 core values, including achievement via hard work and applied science and reason. He also found strong values supporting human rights. Rokeach developed a model of terminal and instrumental values which he tested on a national sample of adults. He discovered that Americans are "peace loving, freedom loving, family oriented, honest, hardworking and responsible." The pollster Daniel Yankelovich is convinced that the U.S is experiencing a cultural revolution that is drastically altering values. He sees Americans struggling to find the middle ground between the old ethic of sacrifice for others and new set of values supporting self-fulfillment. Other observers contend that although the means of expression may have changed, basic values in the U.S. have remained constant.

Values are ideas shared by members of a society about what is worthwhile and important. Dominant values define the national character of a society. When the U.S. was founded, observers were intrigued by its experiment with democracy, and social analysts watched to identify America's dominant values and how they nurtured the political system (Crevecoeur, 1782/1981). In 1830 Alexis de Tocqueville (1961) toured the U.S and recorded his view of American values, which he called "habits of the heart," in Democracy in America. Tocqueville identified attachment to family life, Christian religious values, and a commitment to participate in local politics as the values that sustained American democracy. He also warned that individualism, another highly regarded value, could pose a serious threat to American democracy at some future time by isolating Americans from each other.

After World War II, Robin Williams (1970) described the dominant values or "statements of preference" that characterized American society. Drawing upon a diverse body of historical, economic, political and sociological data, Williams identified fifteen core values that had long been salient in American society (Table 1). These fifteen values clustered around two or three themes, and there were some apparent incompatibilities among them. A common theme manifest in several of the values is an emphasis on achievement or "progress," including concern with material comforts, appropriately achieved via efficient hard work, applied science, and reason. A second theme is the protection of human rights through democratic principles including equality, freedom, and humanitarian concern for others.

The achievement value observed by Williams may actually have been less important in his time than earlier. A content analysis of editorials from National 4-H Club News, 1924-1958, suggests a long-term erosion in the value of achievement (Straus and Houghton, 1960). A similar finding surfaced in an analysis of Ladies Home Journal advertisements for the period 1890-1956 (Dornbusch and Hickman, 1959).

A generation later, Williams (1979) attempted to discern which of the fifteen values had changed between 1945 and 1976. He concluded that six had increased in importance, four had remained the same, and nine had decreased in salience. The changes tended to be modest and were more a shift in emphasis than the disappearance of obsolete values and the emergence of new ones. Williams noted an increase in expressive values like humanitarianism, democracy, equality, and individual personality development and a weakening of norms stressing rigid adherence to value-based rules. Williams also reported a shift away from blind obedience to set rules in favor of evaluations or personal judgments about the relevance of the rules in particular circumstances and the likely consequences of adherence versus rule-breaking.

Later analysts have modified Williams' list. For example, Henslin (1975) replaced some of the statements of preference identified by Williams with values supporting education, religiosity, male supremacy, romantic love, monogamy, and heterosexuality.

Milton Rokeach (1973, 1979) argues that most American values fit into one of two different conceptual categories: terminal values and instrumental values. In other words, there are two families of values: those related to the goals and those relevant to the process of goal attainment. Rokeach says that these particular values are present in all societies, but that societies differ in their hierarchy of value priorities or the relative order of the values.

In 1968, a national sample of adults were surveyed about their basic values as suggested by the Rokeach model. The respondents' terminal and instrumental values are presented in Table 2. World peace, family security and freedom plainly were the top terminal values in the late 1960s. Social acclaim and pleasure ranked at the bottom. The major sex differences were in men's desire for a comfortable life (4th among men's values and 13th among women's) and women's religious values (salvation ranked 4th for women, 12th for men).

The important instrumental values for both men and women were being honest, ambitious and responsible. Given the individuality Americans proclaim, it was a little surprising that being imaginative, intellectual and logical were at the bottom of the hierarchy. Differences between men and women in instrumental values were insignificant.

Rokeach (1979) replicated the study three years later with another national sample. Given America's continued entanglement in Viet Nam, a growing awareness of institutional racism and sexism and increasing attention to pollution, Rokeach anticipated some shift in the salience of both terminal and instrumental values. Although there were some modest differences, he found the value hierarchies to be "remarkably stable" between 1968 and 1971. In his words (p. 132):

> More than anything else, adult Americans perceived themselves as peace loving, freedom loving, family oriented, honest, hardworking and responsible; they perceived themselves as neither hedonistically, aesthetically, nor intellectually oriented; nor at least consciously, as status oriented.

The pollster, Daniel Yankelovich (1981a, 1981b) is convinced that the U.S is experiencing a cultural revolution that is drastically altering people's ideas about the meaning of life. He describes the revolution in terms of four outstanding characteristics. First, there is a shift in values from the orderly, work-centered life style of earlier decades to a search for the "full, rich life, ripe with leisure, new experience and enjoyment." The breadth of this change is impressive, he argues, has invaded our personal inner lives as well as our public lives. The second characteristic of the revolution is a conflict between the goal of self-fulfillment and the means people use to pursue it. Self-fulfillment seekers focus so intently on their own needs that they fail to achieve the more intimate interpersonal relationships they desire. Third is the conflict created as the affluence that originally supported the search for self-fulfillment diminishes, yet the seekers refuse to return to the outlook that prevailed during less prosperous times. In Yankelovich's words, "we have moved from an uptight culture set in a dynamic economy to a dynamic culture set in an uptight economy." The final feature of the cultural revolution is that the stakes are high. Yankelovich is convinced that the revolution is on the verge of leading America either to a "higher stage of civilization" or to national disaster.

Yankelovich perceives that Americans are struggling to find a middle ground between the old ethic of sacrifice for others and a new set of values supporting self-fulfillment. He is optimistic that something healthy and vital will be emerge from the cultural revolution (Yankelovich, 1981b, p. 44).

The Gallup organization has lately documented the change in certain values held by the American public. They collected information about people's rankings of eight different aspects of their lives, including family life, self-image, physical health, having a sense of accomplishment, working for a better America, personal morality, excitement in life, and material possessions. As can be seen in Table 3, Americans in the 1980s considered the intangible aspects of their lives to be most important. Family life, self-respect, sense of accomplishment and health topped the list in both 1981 and again in 1989. Relationships with others followed: working to better America and following a strict moral code were important to over half of all Americans, and living a stimulating life and possessing material things ranked at the bottom of the list. Levels of support for family values, self respect and health were about the same, while concern about improving America and being a moral person, were identified as important by 13% to 15% more people in 1989 than in 1981. Support for pleasurable experiences and seeing material possessions as important received similar rankings in both surveys.

In conclusion, it should be noted that not all observers find that America's dominant values have changed. For example, Gray (1989) argues that if we look beyond "the externals to the essentials," and carefully examine the basic values, it turns out that America's "national virtues remain constant." Based on his own observations and interpretation of history, Gray concludes that America has achieved greatness because these unchanging, basic values are ingrained in her citizens' character.

References

De Crevecoeur, J. Hector St. John, Letters from an American Farmer. New York: Penguin Books, 1981; original edition, 1782.

De Tocqueville, Alexis, Democracy in America, 2 Vols. New York: Schocken Books, 1961; original edition, 1835.

Dornbusch, Sanford M. and Hickman, L. C. "Other-Directedness in Consumer-Goods Advertising: A test of Riesman's Historical Theory." Social Forces 38 (1959): 99-102.

"Social Values." Gallup Report 282-283 (1989): 35-44.

Gray, Harry J. "America's Basic Values have Not Changed." In American Values: Opposing Viewpoints, edited by David L. Bender, pp. 67-72. San Diego: Greenhaven Press, 1989.

Henslin, James M. Introductory Sociology. New York: Free Press, 1975.

Rokeach, Milton. The Nature of Human Values. New York: Free Press, 1973.

-----. Understanding Values. New York: Free Press, 1979.

Straus, Murray A. and L. J. Houghton. "Achievement, Affiliation and Cooperation Values as Clues to Trends in American Rural Society: 1924-1958." Rural Sociology 25 (1960): 394-403.

Williams, Robin M., Jr. American Society: A Sociological Interpretation. 3rd ed. New York: Alfred Knopf, 1970.

Yankelovich, Daniel. New Rules: Searching For Self-Fulfillment In a World Turned Upside Down. New York: Random House, 1981a.

-----."New Rules in American Life: Searching for Self-Fulfillment in a World Turned Upside Down." Psychology Today 15 (4, 1981b): 35-91.

Table 1. AMERICAN VALUES, 1950s

1. Achievement & Success	Great value is placed on personal achievement, especially occupational success.
2. External Conformity	Tend to be conformists and are suspicious of nonconformists.
3. Democracy	Advocacy of majority rule and representative institutions.
4. Activity & Work	Regular, hard work is valued.
5. Moral Orientation	See the world in terms of what is right or wrong, good or bad.
6. Humanitarian Mores	An emphasis on being kind and charitable to those less fortunate.
7. Efficiency & Practicality	Stress of innovation, expediency and getting things done.
8. Progress	Looking to the future, to improve conditions of life. Optimistic.
9. Material Comfort	A strong desire for the "good life," including material things.
10. Equality	An emphasis on equality of opportunity, not outcome.
11. Freedom	People should be allowed to run their own lives.
12. Science & Rationality	Master the environment by solving problems with rational science.
13. Nationalism-Patriotism	Pride in the United States and its accomplishments.
14. Individualism	A high value on individual responsibility and independence.
15. Racism	Privilege on basis of race.

SOURCE: Based on Williams, 1970.

Table 2.   TERMINAL AND INSTRUMENTAL VALUES OF AMERICAN ADULTS

Value	Men* Rank	Men* Mean	Women* Rank	Women* Mean
Terminal values				
A World at Peace	(1)	3.8	(1)	3.0
Family Security	(2)	3.8	(2)	3.8
Freedom	(3)	4.9	(3)	6.1
A Comfortable Life	(4)	7.8	(13)	10.0
Happiness	(5)	7.9	(5)	7.4
Self-Respect	(6)	8.2	(6)	7.4
A Sense of Accomplishment	(7)	8.3	(10)	9.4
Wisdom	(8)	8.5	(7)	7.7
Equality	(9)	9.2	(8)	8.3
National Security	(10)	9.2	(11)	9.8
True Friendship	(11)	9.6	(9)	9.1
Salvation	(12)	9.9	(4)	7.3
Inner Harmony	(13)	11.1	(12)	9.8
Mature Love	(14)	12.6	(14)	12.3
A World of Beauty	(15)	13.6	(15)	13.5
Social Recognition	(16)	13.8	(17)	15.0
Pleasure	(17)	14.1	(17)	15.0
An Exciting Life	(18)	14.6	(18)	15.8
Instrumental values				
Honest	(1)	3.4	(1)	3.2
Ambitious	(2)	5.6	(4)	7.4
Responsible	(3)	6.6	(3)	6.8
Broadminded	(4)	7.2	(5)	7.7
Courageous	(5)	7.5	(6)	8.1
Forgiving	(6)	8.2	(2)	6.4
Helpful	(7)	8.4	(7)	8.1
Capable	(8)	8.9	(12)	10.1
Clean	(9)	9.4	(8)	8.1
Self-Controlled	(10)	9.7	(11)	9.5
Independent	(11)	10.2	(14)	10.7
Cheerful	(12)	10.4	(10)	9.4
Polite	(13)	10.8	(13)	10.7
Loving	(14)	10.9	(9)	8.6
Intellectual	(15)	12.8	(16)	13.2
Logical	(16)	13.5	(17)	14.7
Obedient	(17)	13.5	(15)	13.1
Imaginative	(18)	14.3	(18)	16.1

* Sample size = 665 men, 744 women.

SOURCE: Based on Rokeach, 1973, pp. 57-58.

Table 3. CHANGES IN VALUES OF AMERICAN ADULTS, 1981-1989

Value	Percent Affirming	
	1981	1989
Having a good family life	82%	89%
Having a good self-image	79	85
Being in good physical health	81	84
Having a sense of accomplishment	63	69
Working to better America	51	67
Following a strict moral code	47	60
Having an exciting, stimulating life	46	48
Having a nice home, car and other things	39	41

SOURCE: "Social Values," 1989, pp. 35-44.

American national identity has two strands, one drawn from a set of political values, the other based on ethnic stratification. The developments of recent years have weakened the ethnic aspect of that identity but the political values seem to have remained intact.

From the very beginning, American national identity has had two distinct strands, one drawn from a loosely joined but powerful set of political values, the other from an ethnic hierarchy defined for whites by priority of arrival and for nonwhites by group ascription. The political values are often put under the heading of "American exceptionalism," which is a claim to superiority over other nations based in part on divine favor, in part on material achievements, and most particularly on moral excellence.

Under this rubric, American history was—and is—taught in the public schools as a periodically renewed struggle for freedom at home and abroad, beginning with the first settlers and running without interruption through the Cold War. Freedom has referred on occasion not only to free speech, free elections, religious freedom and freedom of movement, but also to private property, representative government, the rule of law, ethnic equality. Educational opportunity, access to careers, family solidarity, thrift, economic independence, and the dignity of manual labor. The concept is so flexible that it can accommodate without strain any value shared by a large number of citizens.

American exceptionalism has been remarkably resistant to the disillusioning experiences of the past three decades—the Vietnam War; the Watergate scandals; the national humiliations sustained in Iran, Lebanon and Central America; the loss of industrial supremacy to Japan; and the plunge towards national insolvency. In a survey of Middletown high school students in 1977, we found that 78% agreed that "the United States is unquestionably the best country in the world"—a decline from the 92% recorded in 1924, but still a solid majority (Caplow, 1981, p. 53). Nor are such attitudes unaccompanied by a sense of patriotic duty. In a 1984 national survey, 83% of respondents rated the obligation of young men to serve in the military as "very important," and barely 2% denied the obligation (Davis and Smith, 1987, p. 300).

Fervid public displays of patriotism have been customary in the United States since the early 1800s. There is no evidence of any recent decline; the celebrations marking the successive bicentennials of the Declaration of Independence and the Constitution, and the centennial of the Statue of Liberty, were extraordinarily enthusiastic.

There is always some degree of tension, however, between the abstract ideals of American exceptionalism and the realities of a stratification system largely based on color, national origin, and religious affiliation. The descendants of the white Anglo-Saxon Protestants who were most of the original settlers have always held a near-monopoly on political office and on high rank in the private and institutional sectors. Table 1 shows the proportion of Cabinet officers in the presidential cabinets of the past 70 years with Anglo-Saxon names. The proportion has diminished in recent administrations but it is still strikingly high, since the number of citizens who described themselves as predominantly British by descent plus those whites who gave their ancestry as "American" amounted to fewer than a fourth of the U.S. population in 1980 (Lieberson and Waters, 1989). In addition to the benefits of office, white Anglo-Saxon

Protestants hold a disproportionate share of the national wealth. These advantages carry over into intellectual and artistic fields, as the table shows.

The tension between exceptionalism and ethnic stratification arises not only from a perceived contradiction between the equality of opportunity promised by exceptionalism and the hereditary advantages conferred on some ethnic groups, but also from the fact that the favored ethnic groups have a closer and more personal claim on the icons of exceptionalism; the founding fathers were their real, as well as their spiritual, ancestors. The tension is especially acute for black citizens whose recalled past is more a denial than an affirmation of exceptionalism.

During the first century of independence, unrestricted freedom of immigration was an intrinsic part of the pattern. But as the arrival of non-Protestant and non-white immigrants began to change the ethnic configuration of the country, this freedom was gradually restricted, beginning with the Chinese Exclusion Act of 1882 and the selection policies introduced in the same year and culminating in the Immigration Acts of 1917, 1921, 1924, and 1929. The last of these limited the annual number of immigrants to 150,000 and assigned immigration quotas in proportion to the national origins of the existing population, with the explicit purpose of preventing future immigration from changing the ethnic configuration.

This policy was abandoned in the 1950s, since when the ground rules for immigration have been changed in nearly every congressional session. Current immigration policy has no explicit rationale, but it encourages a high rate of legal immigration (Table 2), including many Asians and West Indians, and it permits an even higher rate of illegal immigration, mostly from Mexico and Central America. The effect of this recent immigration has been, on the one hand, a considerable increase in ethnic diversity, especially in the larger American cities, and on the other, a startling increase in the high-fertility population of Hispanic origin which, according to some projections, will outnumber the population of Anglo-Saxon origin before the middle of the next century. Curiously enough, these momentous shifts have not generated much political resistance. For the time being, the majority of Americans seem to consent uneasily to the further displacement of ethnicity by exceptionalism as the basis for national identity.

References

Caplow, Theodore. "Evaluation des Changements Sociaux a Middletown." Science et Theorie de l'Opinion Publique, Paris, Retz, 1981.

Carrier, Achsah. Unpublished data, 1988.

Davis, James Allen and Tom W. Smith. General Social Surveys, 1972-1987: Cumulative Codebook. Chicago: National Opinion Research Center, 1987.

Lieberson, Stanley and Mary C. Waters. "The Rise of a New Ethnic Group: The Unhyphenated American." Social Science Research Council, Items 43 (1989): 7-10.

U.S. Bureau of the Census. Statistical Abstract of the United States, 1989. Washington, D.C., 1989.

Table 1.   ANGLO-SAXON SURNAMES IN POLITICS AND LITERATURE:
           CABINET MEMBERS, 1929-1980 AND PULITZER PRIZE WINNERS,
           1940-1988

Cabinet Members Administration	Percent Anglo-Saxon	Pulitzer Prize Winners	
		Year	Percent Anglo-Saxon
Hoover	100%	--	--
Roosevelt	82	1940	44%
Truman	88	1950	85
Eisenhower	94	--	--
Kennedy	62	1960	63
Johnson	85	--	--
Nixon	65	1970	71
Ford	59	--	--
Carter	45	1980	66
Reagan	--	1988	48

SOURCE: Based on Carrier, 1988.

Table 2. LEGAL IMMIGRANTS TO THE U.S., BY PLACE OF BIRTH, 1961–
1987

	Immigrants (1000s)		
Place of Birth	1961–1970	1971–1980	1981–1987
All Countries	3322	4493	4068
Europe	1239	801	445
Asia	445	1634	1902
North America*	1351	1645	1310
Canada	287	115	78
Caribbean	520	760	576
Mexico and Central America	541	770	655
South America	228	284	270
Africa	39	91	112
Australia, New Zealand and other countries	13	37	27

* Includes countries not shown separately.

SOURCE: Based on Statistical Abstract 1989, p. 10.

APPENDIX A

INTERNATIONAL RESEARCH GROUP
ON THE COMPARATIVE CHARTING OF SOCIAL CHANGE

BAHR, Howard
Dept. of Sociology
842 SWKT
Brigham Young University
PROVO UTAH 84602
USA
Tel.: (801) 378-6275

BAILLARGEON, Jean-Paul
IQRC
14, rue Haldimand
QUEBEC (Québec)
CANADA GIR 4N4
Tel.: (418) 643-4695

CALDWELL, Gary
IQRC
14, rue Haldimand
QUEBEC (Québec)
CANADA GIR 4N4
Tel.: (418) 643-4695

CAPLOW, Theodore
University of Virginia
Dept. of Sociology
CHARLOTTESVILLE VA 22903
USA
Tel.: (804) 973-3453

CHADWICK, Bruce
Dept. of Sociology
938 SWKT
Brigham Young University
PROVO UTAH 84602
USA
Tel.: (801) 378-6026

DECHAUX, Jean-Hugues
OFCE
69, Quai d'Orsay
75007 PARIS FRANCE
Tel.: 45-55-95-12

DEL CAMPO, Salustiano
La Masô 27
Colonia Mirasierra
MADRID 28034
ESPAGNE
Tel.: 734-8503

DRAUS, Renata
Fritz-Tenter-STR 10-12
D-5000 KÖLN 51
FRG W-GERMANY
Tel.: 221-3736 11 (home)

FORSÉ, Michel
OFCE
69, Quai d'Orsay
75007 PARIS FRANCE
Tel.: 45-55-95-12

FRÉCHET, Guy
IQRC
14, rue Haldimand
QUEBEC (Québec)
CANADA GIR 4N4
Tel.: (418) 643-4695

GAUTHIER, Madeleine
IQRC
14, rue Haldimand
QUEBEC (Québec)
CANADA GIR 4N4
Tel.: (418) 643-4695

GLATZER, Wolfgang
Goethe Universtät
Fachbereich
Gesellschaftswissenschaften
Robert Mayer - Straße 5
Postfach 11 19 32
6000 FRANKFURT/MAIN
FRG W-GERMANY
Tel.: (069) 798-3584

HONDRICH, Karl-Otto
Goethe Universtät
Fachbereich
Gesellschaftswissenschaften
Robert Mayer - Straße 5
Postfach 11 19 32
6000 FRANKFURT/MAIN
FRG W-GERMANY
Tel.: (069) 798-3584

JASLIN, J.-Pierre
OFCE
69, Quai d'Orsay
75007 PARIS FRANCE
Tel.: 45-55-95-12

LANGLOIS, Simon
IQRC
14, rue Haldimand
QUEBEC (Québec)
CANADA G1R 4N4
Tel.: (418) 643-4695

LEMEL, Yannick
Observatoire Economique de Paris
195, rue de Bercy
Tour Gamma A
75582 PARIS Cédex 12
FRANCE
Tel.: 43-45-73-74

MENDRAS, Henri
OFCE
69, Quai d'Orsay
75007 PARIS FRANCE
Tel.: 45-55-95-12

MODELL, John
History Department
Carnegie Mellon University
PITTSBURGH PA 15213
USA
Tel.: (412) 268-3280

NOLL, Herbert Heinz
ZUMA
B2, 1
D-6800 MANHEIM
FRG W-GERMANY
Tel.: (062) 292-5335

SIMARD, Jean-Pierre
IQRC
14, rue Haldimand
QUEBEC (Québec)
CANADA G1R 4N4
Tel.: (418) 643-4695

STIEHR, Karin
Goethe Universtät
Fachbereich
Gesellschaftswissenschaften
Robert Mayer - Straße 5
Postfach 11 19 32
6000 FRANKFURT/MAIN
FRG W-GERMANY
Tel.: (069) 798-3584

STOCLET, Denis
OFCE
69, Quai d'Orsay
75007 PARIS FRANCE
Tel.: 45-55-95-12

TSOUKALAS, Constantin
Centre national de recherche sociale
Sophocleos, #1, 122
ATHENS
GREECE
Tel.: 32-48-281

WORNDL, Barbara
Goethe Universtät
Arbeitsgruppe Soziale Infrastruktur
Bettinastraße 64
6000 FRANKFURT/MAIN
FRG W-GERMANY
Tel.: (069) 798-3966

APPENDIX B

LIST OF TRENDS, TOPICS, AND AUTHORS*

0. Context

    0.1   Demographic Trends   (JM)
           Population size
           Natality
           Migration
           Life expectancy at birth
           Sex ratio
           Age distribution
           Linguistic distribution

    0.2   Macro-economic Trends   (TC)
           Growth of the economy
           Wholesale and retail prices
           Savings and investments
           Public sector expenditures
           Public and private debt
           Foreign trade and trade balances
           Productive capital

    0.3   Macro-technological Trends   (TC)
           Energy consumption
           Inventions
           Publications
           Research and Development
           Productivity

1. Age Groups

    1.1   Youth   (JM)
           Duration of studies
           Denesting
           Precarious employment
           Age at first marriage
           Age at first childbirth

    1.2   Elders   (JM)
           Life expectancy at older ages
           Retirement pattern
           Health
           Income and wealth

2. Microsocial

    2.1   Self Identification   (JM)
           By social class
           By religion, locality, status group and ethnicity

2.2 Kinship Networks (HB)
   Size
   Spatial distribution
   Frequency of contacts and rituals
   Network support

2.3 Community and Neighborhood Types (JM)
   Types of communities by size and function
   Ex-urbanization, re-urbanization and suburbanization
   Multiple and single dwellings
   Second homes
   Local ecology
   Types of neighborhood

2.4 Local Autonomy (JM)
   Number of elected officials
   Number of local civil servants
   Local and regional budgets
   Local and central responsibilities

2.5 Voluntary Associations (HB)
   Number, size and type
   Participation and leadership
   Changed in objectives and activities

2.6 Sociability Networks (HB)
   Spatial distribution and interaction
   Frequency of contacts and rituals
   Network support

3. Women

3.1 Female Roles (HB)
   Maternal roles and child care
   Housework
   Educational differentials
   Occupational differentials
   Earnings and power differences
   Differentiating attitudes and practices, consumption styles

3.2 Childbearing (JM)
   Numbers and timing of births
   Family size
   Illegitimacy

3.3 Matrimonial Models (JM)
   Marriages
   Other types of cohabitation
   One-parent families
   Divorce
   Celibacy

3.4 Women's Employment (HB)
   Labor force participation
   Work at home (paid and unpaid)
   Part and full-time employment

3.5   Reproductive Technologies   (JM)
       Contraception, abortion, and sterilization
       New reproductive technologies
       Ethical and legal problems

4.   Labor Market

4.1   Unemployment   (TC)
       Unemployment differentials
       Duration of unemployment
       Experience and attitudes of unemployed

4.2   Skills and Occupational Levels   (TC)
       Qualifications, skills and responsibilities through
           major occupational categories

4.3   Types of Employment   (AC)
       Steady employment
       Precarious employment
       Part-time employment

4.4   Sectors of the Labor Force   (TC)
       Distribution of labor force by primary, secondary and tertiary sectors
       Relationships between goods and services
       Intangible commodities

4.5   Computerization of Work   (TC)
       Computer applications
       Words and pictures processing
       Data storage and dissemination
       Robotics

5.   Labor and Management

5.1   Structuring of Jobs   (AC)
       Time and motion studies
       Self-management and worker participation
       Job enlargement
       Job sharing
       Immaterial investment
       Flexible schedules
       Other innovations

5.2   Personnel Administration   (TC)
       Job classification
       Wage and salary determination
       On-the-job training
       Counseling
       Career development
       Fringe benefits
       Grievance procedures

5.3   Size and Types of Enterprises   (AC)
       Variations in structure and organizational structure

6. Social Stratification

    6.1   Occupational Status   (HB/JM)
            Occupational prestige
            Occupational hierarchy

    6.2   Social Mobility   (HB)
            Inter-generational mobility
            Career mobility

    6.3   Economic Inequality   (HB)
            Income
            Wealth

    6.4   Social Inequality   (TC/HB)
            Social class
            Status groups

7. Social Relations

    7.1   Conflict   (TC)
            Industrial
            Political
            Moral and cultural
            Conflict and violence

    7.2   Negotiation   (TC)
            Labor relations policies and collective bargaining
            Labor contracts and agreements

    7.3   Norms of Conduct   (TC)
            Permissiveness and constraint in various contexts

    7.4   Authority   (BC)
            Institutional in various contexts
            Personal in various contexts

    7.5   Public Opinion   (JM)
            Number of elections
            Number of polls

8. State and Service Institutions

    8.1   Educational System   (JM)
            Enrollment
            Graduates
            Teaching personnel
            Curricula
            Costs

    8.2   Health System   (BC)
            Patients
            Conditions
            Personnel
            Facilities
            Costs

8.3   Welfare System   (TC)
       Programs and welfare system
       Personnel
       Costs
       Private social agencies

8.4   Presence of State in Society   (BC)
       State budgets
       Personnel
       Expansion of functions

9. Mobilizing Institutions

9.1   Labor Unions   (TC)
       Membership
       Organizations
       Activities

9.2   Religious Institutions   (HB)
       Membership
       Organizations
       Activities

9.3   Military Forces   (TC)
       Membership
       Organizations
       Activities

9.4   Political Parties   (JM)
       Membership
       Organizations
       Activities

9.5   Mass Media   (BC)
       Membership
       Organizations
       Activities

10. Institutionalization of Social Forces

10.1   Dispute Settlement   (AC)
       Litigation
       Regulation and deregulation
       Arbitration and mediation

10.2   Institutionalization of Labor Unions   (TC)
       Expanded and auxiliary functions
       Professionalization of leadership

10.3   Social Movements   (TC)
       Feminism
       Consumerism
       Ecological movements
       Pacifism
       Regional movements

10.4   Interest Groups   (BC)

11. <u>Ideologies</u>

   11.1   Political Differentiation   (JM)
            Election results
            Extremist and marginal parties
            Self location on the left-right axis

   11.2   Confidence in Institutions   (HB)
            Armed forces
            Church
            School
            The political system

   11.3   Economic Orientations   (HB)
            Knowledge of and attitudes about economy
            Viewpoints on entrepreneurship and profit

   11.4   Radicalism   (JM)
            Manifestations of the extreme left and right

   11.5   Religious Beliefs   (BC)
            Mainline and sectarian practices
            Innovations in practices
            Quasi-religious rituals and celebrations
            Anti-religious manifestations
            Combination of religious and secular activity

12. <u>Household Resources</u>

   12.1   Personal and Family Income   (TC)
            Individual and family income
            Purchasing power
            Origin of income (wages, transfers, etc.)
            Non-monetary benefits

   12.2   Informal Economy   (TC)
            Black economy
            Non-monetarized economic activities

   12.3   Personal and Family Wealth   (TC)
            Securities, entitlements and real property
            Savings
            Other forms of wealth

13. <u>Lifestyle</u>

   13.1   Market Goods and Services   (BC)
            Consumer patterns of expenditures and consumption (including routine
              and exceptional expenditures)
            Standard and alternative consumer choices

   13.2   Mass Information   (BC)
            Consumer exposure to T.V., radio, newspapers, magazines, cinema,
              audio and video systems and other media

13.3   Personal Health and Beauty Practices   (TC)
        Exercises
        Cosmetics
        Dieting and abstinence
        Sun bathing
        Changing health beliefs
        Use of health services

13.4   Time Use   (HB)

13.5   Daily Mobility   (JM)
        Commuting and local travel
        Transportation and communication expenses

13.6   Household Production   (BC)
        Masculine and feminine activities
        Hobbies, gardening
        Other forms of home production

13.7   Forms of Erotic Expression   (HB)
        Pornography
        Innovations in sexual practices
        Vicarious involvement
        Sex in publicity

13.8   Mood-Altering Substances   (BC)
        Tobacco
        Caffeine
        Tranquilizers
        Narcotics
        Alcohol
        Cocaine
        Other mood-altering substances

14. Leisure

14.1   Amount and Use of Free Time   (TC)

14.2   Vacation Patterns   (TC)
        Tourist and recreational travel, domestic and foreign

14.3   Athletics and Sports   (TC)
        Participation sports
        Spectator sports
        Para-sporting activities (jogging, etc.)
        Non-athletic contests

14.4   Cultural Activities   (TC)
        Music, dance, art and drama
        Literature
        Parades, carnivals, concerts, museum visits
        Records produced, attendances at spectacles, tickets sold, books bought
        Number of people whose occupation is in cultural activities

15. Educational Attainment

    15.1   General Education   (JM)
                Level of schooling
                Diplomas and job qualifications
                Level of general qualification required
                Selection and orientation of students

    15.2   Professional Education   (JM)
                Level of schooling
                Diplomas and job qualifications
                Level of professional qualification required
                Selection and orientation of students

    15.3   Continuing Education   (JM)
                Activities, diversity and role
                Enrollment of adults to regular school programs

16. Integration and Marginalization

    16.1   Immigrants and Ethnic Minorities   (JM)
                By place of birth, ethnic origin and language
                Residential segregation
                Minorities in school
                Second generation identification

    16.2   Crime and Punishment   (BC)
                Property crime
                Violent crime
                White-collar crime
                Operation of criminal justice administration

    16.3   Emotional Disorders and Self-destructive Behaviors   (BC)
                Mental illness
                Suicides
                Addictions

    16.4   Poverty   (BC)
                Extent and composition
                Causative factors
                Anti-poverty programs
                Hidden poverty, homelessness

17. Attitudes and Values

    17.1   Satisfaction in Life Domains and in General   (HB)

    17.2   Perceptions of Social Problems   (HB)
                Most important problem?

    17.3   Orientations to the Future   (HB)
                Aspirations and expectations

    17.4   Values   (BC)

17.5   National Identity   (TC)

*Authors are identified by the initials following the trend titles ( ).

    AC = Achsah Carrier
    HB = Howard Bahr
    BC = Bruce Chadwick
    TC = Ted Caplow
    JM = John Modell

Series
COMPARATIVE CHARTING OF SOCIAL CHANGE

Editor: Simon Langlois
Laval University and IQRC, Canada

Recent Social Trends in the United States 1960-1990.
Theodore Caplow, Howard M. Bahr, John Modell, Bruce A. Chadwick

Recent Social Trends in The Federal Republic of Germany 1960-1990.
Wolfang Glatzer, Karl-Otto Hondrich, Herbert Heinz Noll, Karin Stiehr, Barbara Worndl

Recent Social Trends in France 1965-1985.
Louis Dirn, Jean-Hugues Dechaux, Michel Forsé, Jean-Pierre Jaslin, Yannick Lemel

Recent Social Trends in Québec 1960-1990.
Simon Langlois, Jean-Paul Baillargeon, Gary Caldwell, Guy Fréchet, Madeleine Gauthier, Jean-Pierre Simard

(In preparation)

Recent Social Trends in Greece 1960-1990.

Recent Social Trends in Spain 1960-1990.

Recent Social Trends in USSR 1960-1990.